The Unnatural History of Man-Eating Plants

The Unnatural History of Man-Eating Plants

By

Kevin J. Guhl

Table of Contents

PART II: SHORT STORIES

AN INTRODUCTION TO CARNIVOROUS AND MAN-KILLING PLANTS

"When an animal bites a plant, that is hardly news. Animals are doing that all the time: Cows and caterpillars, mice and men; they'd die very soon if they didn't. But when a plant bites an animal there may be an interesting story in it."—Dr. Frank Thone

The plant kingdom finds itself situated at the very bottom of the planetary food chain. Silently, Earth's flora subsists, providing sweet nectar for butterflies and bees, filling the air with the oxygen that life requires, and resigned to consumption by everything from nibbling bunnies to humans taking full advantage of an open salad bar. But what if plants turned the tables, and decided to make a meal out of us?

If you happen to be a common housefly, carnivorous plants are a going concern. A number of plant species have developed into stealthy predators, blending into the unassuming greenery and utilizing their charms to lure in hapless victims.

The Venus Flytrap clamps down on prey attracted to the sweet nectar within its traps. When a victim grazes trigger hairs on the inner surface, the trap closes around them, looking very much like a savage mouth lined with sharp teeth (interlocking cilia). Digestive liquid then fills the trap, drowning the occupant as they become lunch. Venus Flytraps are endemic only to humid, boggy areas along a small coastal region of the Carolinas within a 75-mile radius of Wilmington, North Carolina. The Venus Flytrap (*Dionaea muscipula*) resides within the Carolina Bays—shallow, rounded depressions that were once hypothesized to have been created by meteorite or comet impacts. This connection led some to imagine an extraterrestrial origin for this carnivorous plant, much like the "Mean Green Mother from Outer Space" from "Little Shop of Horrors."

Venus Fly Trap (Dionaea muscipula). By Mokkie, CC BY-SA 4.0, via Wikimedia Commons.

The mostly aquatic species of Bladderwort (*Utricularia*) possesses a very different sort of trap resembling an airtight balloon. When prey touches the feather-like trigger on the trap's outer wall, a secret hatch swings open, creating a vacuum that pulls in the victim and bathes them in digestive enzymes.

The leaves of the Sundew (*Drosera*) are coated with sticky, aromatic goo that insects cannot resist. They land, become mired and face the horror of tentacles that wind around their bodies to dissolve and ingest them.

Byblis, suggested author and carnivorous plant enthusiast Randall Schwartz, "might have given rise to those rumors about man-eating plants." Native to western Australia, this relative of the Sundew resembles a leafless shrub that stands about two feet tall and has been known to trap and absorb insects, lizards and frogs—possibly even rabbits and squirrels—that become stuck on its sticky branches.

Introduction

Drosophyllum, meanwhile, functions like living fly paper, continually squirting sticky ooze onto insects until they become bogged down and sucked dry by sessile glands lining each leaf.

Butterwort (*Pinguicula*), wrote Schwartz, contains an antibiotic in its digestive fluid that has been used as a traditional healing ointment for humans and animals. It is not so beneficial for the tiny bugs it captures, though, rolling up its leaves to form a shallow cup in which to digest them in the same fluid.

Nepenthes bellii upper pitcher. By Thomas Gronemeyer, CC BY-SA 3.0, via Wikimedia Commons.

Pitcher plants (Nepenthaceae and Sarraceniaceae) are found throughout the world and in various sizes and shapes. (One California variety, the Cobra Plant, resembles the hooded serpent, complete with leaves that evoke fangs or a forked tongue). Pitcher Plants capture prey from insects up to, reportedly, giant rats.

The Unnatural History of Man-Eating Plants

Pitcher traps look exactly like their namesake, vessels filled not with iced tea but prey-dissolving fluid. It's a diabolical design, each pitcher structured like a maze with no exit, spikes and slippery surfaces forcing prey further and further downward to their doom.

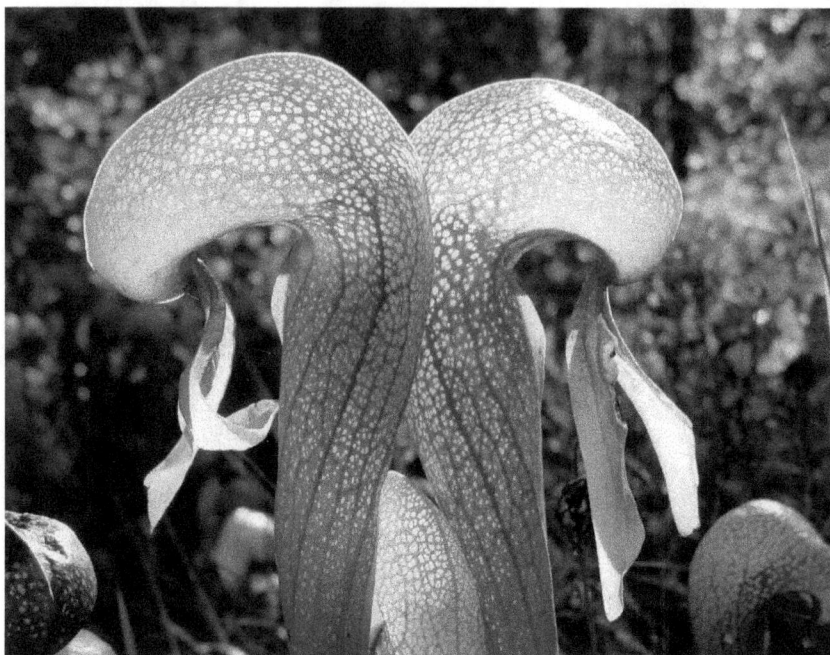

California "Cobra" Pitcher Plant (Darlingtonia californica). By NoahElhardt, CC BY-SA 3.0, via Wikimedia Commons.

Charles Darwin published "Insectivorous Plants" in 1875, drawing attention to species such as the Sundew and Venus Flytrap, and describing his attempts to understand their natural mechanisms. Darwin, who conducted experiments on the plants over a 16-year period, would later remark, "The fact that a plant should secrete, when properly excited, a fluid containing an acid and ferment, closely analogous to the digestive fluid of an animal, was certainly a remarkable discovery."

As fearsome as this all sounds, these are but tiny monsters. However, nature did allow these plants to develop adaptations for supplementing their diet with living creatures. Fossil evidence of extinct, prehistoric carnivorous plants is scarce, and any potential specimens likely were comparable in size to today's

Introduction

species. It's only natural to wonder, though, in the deep recesses of our imaginations, if the same evolutionary twist could have allowed for a much larger predatory plant capable of devouring more sizeable prey...

Public fascination with the possibility of carnivorous plants able to consume a human being emerged around the same time as Darwin's efforts to describe their insect-eating cousins, as evidenced by the first known newspaper report of a Man-Eating Plant in 1874. (The Venus Flytrap, arguably the most "animalistic" of the insectivorous plants, was first recorded by North Carolina Colonial Governor Arthur Dobbs in 1759.)

Man-Eating (and Killing) Plants are mostly recognized today from popular fiction. Moviegoers in 1963 were thrilled by the plant-monster invasion film, "The Day of the Triffids," based on the 1951 novel by John Wyndham. Audrey II, the star of "Little Shop of Horrors" (originally Roger Corman's 1960 B-movie but most pertinently the 1986 musical film) was a giant, singing Venus Flytrap who represented the perils of greed and fame. The Piranha Plant from Super Mario Bros. taught gamers to exercise caution around suspicious sewer pipes. Harry Potter's Whomping Willow instinctively twisted its branches to attack all interlopers in its territory. But there was a time when deadly plants capable of aggressively capturing, consuming and/or strangling a person were a prominent danger featured not just in popular adventure and horror fiction but in news articles contending to present true horrors in unexplored realms.

I've presented the following catalogue of Man-Eating Plants as a travelogue, examining the strange flora once thought to reside within the uncultivated frontiers of the globe. We will focus on the tales presented in newspapers and other sources as fact, however unbelievable they might seem to modern (or even contemporary) eyes. There was also no shortage of fiction during this era centered on carnivorous or otherwise aggressively deadly plants. (And by fiction, I mean published without any haze of being anything other than entertainment.) I've included a curated selection of 20 short stories about these dastardly and mysterious vegetables that were published between 1883 and 1933.

According to One Report, Which Scientists Haven't Been Able to Verify, Native Girls Were Fed to a Man-eating Tree in Madagascar.

Madagascar Man-Eating Tree. American Weekly, May 28, 1939. Image included here on a Fair Use, educational basis.

Keep in mind, as you read this book, that we're dealing with lurid newspaper accounts, fiction and even scientific publications from the 18th, 19th and early 20 centuries. There are ample examples of racial and cultural insensitivity, especially as it comes to the native inhabitants of less developed nations. I will present the original texts unvarnished, so please keep the historical context in mind as you read these stories. They are a product of their time. I have also (mostly) retained the authentic text of the

Introduction

articles, including outdated or slightly misspelled scientific names and such.

Now, let's put on our pith helmets, khakis and hiking boots as we set off on a journey to the locale where news accounts of Man-Eating Trees first emerged, the dense and humid rainforests of Madagascar off the eastern African coast...

SOURCES:

"*Archaeamphora.*" *Wikipedia*, https://en.wikipedia.org/wiki/Archaeamphora. Accessed 22 Jul. 2025.

"Carolina Bays." *Wikipedia*, https://en.wikipedia.org/wiki/Carolina_bays. Accessed 22 Jul. 2025.

Darwin, Charles. *Insectivorous Plants*. New York, D. Appleton and Company, 1875.

"Insectivorous Plants." *Wikipedia*, https://en.wikipedia.org/wiki/Insectivorous_Plants. Accessed 22 Jul. 2025.

The Life and Letters of Charles Darwin, Including an Autobiographical Chapter, Vol. I. Edited by Francis Darwin, London, John Murray, Albemarle Street, 1888.

O'Dale, Charles. "Carolina Bays Structure." *Crater Explorer*, https://craterexplorer.ca/carolina-bays-structure/. Accessed 22 Jul. 2025.

Pain, Stephanie. "How Carnivorous Plants Evolved." *Smithsonian Magazine*, 9 Mar. 2022, https://www.smithsonianmag.com/science-nature/how-carnivorous-plants-evolved-180979697/. Accessed 22 Jul. 2025.

"*Palaeoaldrovanda.*" *Wikipedia*, https://en.wikipedia.org/wiki/Palaeoaldrovanda. Accessed 22 Jul. 2025.

Prior, Sophia. *Carnivorous Plants and "The Man-Eating Tree."* Botany Leaflet 23, Field Museum of Natural History, 1939.

Schwartz, Randall. *Carnivorous Plants*. Edited by Deborah Leavy, Avon, 1974.

Stinson, Craig M. "Venus Flytrap." *NCpedia*, 2006, https://www.ncpedia.org/venus-flytrap. Accessed 22 Jul. 2025.

Thone, Dr. Frank. "Plants that Kill Animals and Devour their Flesh." *Sunday Star Magazine* [Washington, D.C.], 16 Jul. 1933, p. 11.

"Venus Flytrap." *Wikipedia*, https://en.wikipedia.org/wiki/Venus_flytrap. Accessed 22 Jul. 2025.

Wahab, Phoebe. *Plants that Bite Back. Carolina Beach State Park: An Environmental Education Learning Experience Designed for the Middle Grades*. North Carolina State Department of Environment, Health, and Natural Resources, Raleigh Division of Parks and Recreation, 1993.

"Was the Venus Flytrap Brought to Earth by a Meteor?" *Straight Dope*, 3 Dec. 2002, https://www.straightdope.com/21343185/was-the-venus-flytrap-brought-to-earth-by-a-meteor. Accessed 22 Jul. 2025.d 1 Jun. 2025.

"VAMPIRE VINE" OF NICARAGUA.

"Vampire Vine" of Nicaragua, Sacramento Bee, Apr. 29, 1893.

PART I: TRAVELOGUE

AFRICA

CRINOIDA DAJEEANA

In the strange realm of Cryptobotany (the investigation of plants reported to exist but as of yet unacknowledged by science), there is no greater star than the Man-Eating Tree of Madagascar. First reported widely by the press in 1874, many explorers have tried and failed to find this carnivorous plant deep in the jungles of the sprawling African island nation, despite tales of natives who worship the tree with human sacrifice. There is even a claim that one adventurer not only found the Man-Eating Tree of Madagascar and escaped with his life, but brought home photographs to prove its existence. Let's untangle these odd, compelling claims to see where the truth may lie...

As first reported by the New York World newspaper on April 28, 1874 (and oft-told ever since), botanist Karl Leche first encountered the Man-Eating Tree (Crinoida Dajeeana) in the company of a pygmy tribe called the Mkodos.

Leche described the trunk as resembling a pineapple eight feet in height, with eight 12-foot-long leaves that hung to the ground, "like doors swung back on their hinges." Plate-shaped receptacles in the tree oozed a sweet, violently intoxicating liquid. The tree possessed long, hairy, green tendrils and palpi that reached toward the sky, constantly twitching. As Leche watched in horror, the Mkodos forced one of their women up onto the tree and made her drink its noxious sap. As the tribe fervently chanted, the tree sprang to life, its tendrils coiling tightly around the victim and its giant leaves closing around her. As Crinoida Dajeeana squeezed

Madagascar's Man-Eating Tree. Published in the Nov. 13, 1932 American Weekly. Included here on a Fair Use, educational basis.

the life out of the woman, "streams of the viscid, honey-like fluid, mingled horridly with the blood and oozing viscera of the victim" trickled down its trunk. Leche fled the terrible scene but later returned to find the tree prone once again and the victim's skull resting quietly at its base, a haunting reminder of a meal well-digested.

For your reading pleasure and horror, here is the full version of the Madagascar Man-Eating Tree article as it first appeared in the April 28, 1874 New York World:

CRINOIDA DAJEEANA.

The Man-Eating Tree of Madagascar.

In the last number of Graefe and Walther's *Magazine*, published at Carlsruhe, there is a letter in regard to the newly-discovered *Crinoida Dajeeana*, from the discoverer, Karl Leche, the eminent botanist, prefaced by some notes from Dr. Omelius Friedlowsky, whose deep research in vegetable physiology has had so many important results. Leche's letter, it appears, was originally addressed to Friedlowsky, and they seem to have been pursuing together for some time a subject of novel and startling interest, which is likely to give some remarkable discoveries to science.

Dr. Friedlowsky says: "My motive for publishing prematurely the history of my friend Leche's half-developed discovery is similar to that which influenced Darwin to bring out his book on the origin of species. His theory was not near developed, but his title to priority in discovery was imperilled by the announcement of Mr. Wallace's researches in the Malayan Archipelago. Darwin himself, as well as several American botanists, have lately come so perilously near to the discovery of the problem Leche set himself to investigate, in their studies of the habits of drosera and sarracenia, that I think it is due to my friend's credit to make some preliminary announcement of the great progress he has already made towards establishing a point of contact of our organic systems with those of the universe at large through analysis of the constitution of some abnormal plants which have always hitherto puzzled the botanists.

"The point to which Karl Leche (at my suggestion) has been giving his attention latterly is briefly this: Certain plants, such as drosera (with its outlying species, dionea muscicapa), sarracenia, and some others, departing from the general law, instead of supplying food to animals turn the tables, capture them, and are themselves carnivorous. It has often occurred to me in connection with these insectivorous plants, so abnormal in their constitution, that they might have a widely different origin (or at least an origin widely different in point of time) from the common orders of plants inhabiting our globe, and that if I could establish the nature of this different origin upon reasonable grounds I might at the same time afford a reasonable explanation at once of the origin and the primordial variations of life. In 1869 I had made a journey to the sandy regions of the territory of North Carolina (U.S.A.), with the express object of critically examining the exceedingly limited territory in which alone the entirely anomalous dionea is to be found. I confess it was my hope—I will not go so far as to say my expectation—to find somewhere about the centre of this sandy and desolate region near the coast, evidences either of the fall of a meteoric shower, or the actual presence of a fallen aerolite. For it is my theory—which I hold in common with my esteemed correspondent Nordenskiold—that the germs of life not only may have been, but may still be brought to this earth from some other point in space, by means of aerolites, meteoric dust, or some such kindred agency. Had I found dionea spreading in growth from a centre and that centre occupied by an aerolite, it would have gone very far to confirm my theory. That I did not find such a nucleus is on the other hand no proof of its non-existence.

"When Leche went to Bombay in response to the liberal call extended to him by the Grant Medical College of that prosperous city, he went full of my ideas upon this vastly important subject, and prepared, as I advised him, to make

special investigations into the habitats of all such
abnormal plants as seem to depart from the characteristic
traits of the flora of their respective countries, and
also particularly to examine the topography of the places
where such plants exist most numerously. This I state
here, because, while the theory is by no means far

**Wooden Idol of the Man-Eating Tree
Which Is Hung in Their Huts and
Secretly Worshipped by the
Natives of Madagascar.**

*"Moreover, these savages are firm believers in the evil eye, and
fear the attacks of evil spirits who live in the trunks of trees and in
queer-shaped stones. To protect themselves from these baleful
influences the Mkodos wear charms about their necks. And there is
not a hut or cave in which they dwell where their religious fervor is
not excited by the presence of a wooden idol shaped very much like
the man-eating tree, which they reverence by smearing with blood
and fat." - Published in the Oct. 19, 1924 American Weekly.*

advanced, it was while in search of facts to countenance this theory that Leche discovered the remarkable and terrible Crinoida Dajeeana, of which his letter gives such a graphic and forcible description.

"After quite a long sojourn in India Leche was induced to go to Madagascar by Dr. Bhawoo Dajee, the liberal-minded, intelligent Parsee physician of Bombay, who, indeed, supplied the means for the expedition, and made so many thoughtful provisions for my colleague's comfort as to win his gratitude and love. Dr. Dajee, it seems, represented to Leche that it was impossible to glean much in a field so carefully worked over by many botanists, and indeed almost exhausted by Hooker. When quite a young man Dr. Dajee had made a voyage to Madagascar in one of Sir Jamsetjee Jeejeebhoy's trading ships, and had been deeply impressed with the remarkably various and beautiful flora of that almost untravelled region. An excellent opportunity offered for going out in one of Cursetjee Jeejeebhoy's traders, which was to stop at Tametave on her way to the Cape, so Leche embarked, attended by a Madagasy sailor for servant, Dr. Dajee having hired the fellow, thinking he would be useful to Leche as guide and interpreter.

"That was more than two years ago. Since then I have received three letters from Leche—two by way of Bombay, one by way of the Cape—and now last week, a fourth, which he had the luck to send by an Arabian trader to Zanzibar, whence it reached me via Aden. After writing of many other things Leche proceeded to say:

But I do not know how soon Seid ben Yalhamah may take a notion to sail, and I want to tell you about the remarkable tree which I have discovered, and which I have named, in honor of my benefactor, Crinoida Dajeeana. About two weeks after my last letter to you I went from Tananarivou to a point in the mountains over against

"Mystery of the Man-Eating Tree of Madagascar." - Published in the Oct. 19, 1924 American Weekly. Slightly restored by author.

Mananzari, to visit a Christianized chief there who had sent me a great many messages. On the way thither my Madaagasy servant deserted me, saying he did not want to be killed and eaten by Mkodos, a tribe of inhospitable savages of whom little was known, but who were supposed to dwell in the mountains further to the south, and to be cannibals. In Telliyimat's place I hired (when I reached the chieftain's village), a perfect treasure who in the shape of a Namaqua Caffre, named Henrick, who had fled Graham Town on account of some scrape, and after many wanderings found himself in the chief's retinue. Henrick—he is with me now—is a fearless and intelligent fellow, full of enterprise and spirit, a good hunter, and a most devoted, untiring, and unquestioning follower. I had taken him with me on several botanizing excursions, when he asked me why I did not go to visit the land of the Mkodos, where I would find a great number of curious plants, such as he had never seen elsewhere. I answered that they had the reputation of being inhospitable, cannibals, and all that, but he pooh-poohed the idea. He had been among them twice, he said, and had been well received, and he would guarantee me kind treatment amongst them. They got their bad name from being continually at war with the other tribes, and from successfully barring their country against all invaders. He then gave me an account of the country and particularly of the strange plant I have spoken of above, and so excited my curiosity that I resolved to go thither at once, and accordingly, as we were tolerably well equipped, we set out over the mountains without returning to take leave of the chief, my entertainer.

The country of the Mkodos began about five days' journey from the point whence we started, and was a long valley sloping and descending towards the East and ingirt on three sides by rough, inaccessible mountains, on the fourth separated from the coast by jungles and morass. The approach to it was most arduous, over the crests of several sharp mountain ridges, frowning with basaltic precipices. No sooner had we come into the valley, however, than I felt the warm breath of the Indian Ocean and saw its influence in the vegetation, which grew rapidly more and more tropical, majestic, and colossal as we descended. The valley had an average breadth of about thirty miles, and was about 175 miles long, in the course of which it descended over 3,000 feet.

The Mkodos are a very primitive race, going entirely naked, having only faint vestiges of tribal relations, and no religion beyond that of the awful reverence which they pay to the sacred tree. They carry a javelin about six feet long, with which they conquer the chetah and do not hesitate to encounter the formidable buffalo (bos caffer) that ranges the woody slopes and savannahs of their country. They are also armed with a short bow and a quiver of poisoned arrows. They dwell entirely in caves hollowed out of the limestone rocks in their hills, and are one of the smallest of races, the men seldom exceeding fifty-six inches in height.

Their country must be a very productive one, if I may judge from the abundance of animal and vegetable life it contains. At different elevations in the valley, during my short sojourn in it, I noticed droves of antelopes (the klip-dos of the Cape), the chetah (felis jubata), hyrax, manis pentadactyla, histrix cristala, and many other animals, while the lower forests were full of new species of gigantic pteropi, which at night flew about as if the land belonged to them. The variety and richness of the flora of this valley (the Mkodos have no name for their country, calling it simply Mzemp, *the* land), may be inferred when I tell you that I saw and examined species of all the palms (including umbraculifera, or talipot, and sagus rhumphii), and that among the plants growing commonly I found acaciae, numerous equisetaceae, mimosae, goseypia, areca, ricinus, rhamnus lotus, and nymphaea coerulea, eupatoriae, diosmata, salices, cassiae, juncus, solandra, aloes spicata, balsamodendun myrrha, croton tiglii, cucumis colcocynthis, & c., & c. I attribute this richness and variety to several causes—the latitude half tropical half temperate, the variety of altitude, and the warm, sultry, vapor-laden winds from the Indian Ocean, which cause a vast rain fall.

At the bottom of the valley (I had no barometer, but should think it not over 400 feet above the level of the sea) and near its eastern extremity, we came to a deep tarn-like lake, about a mile in diameter, the sluggish oily waters of which overflowed into a tortuous reedy canal that went unwillingly into the recesses of a black forest, jungle below, palm above. This lake was filled with alligators, and its jungled borders were the home of the chetah and a variety of venomous serpents. Great ferns bent over its margin, and its surface was spotted with leaves and flowers of the lotus. A path, diverging from its Southern side, struck boldly for the heart of the forbidding and seemingly impenetrable forest. Henrick led the way along this path, I following closely, and behind me a curious rabble of Mkodos, men, women, and children. After we were fairly in the forest, the shade overhead was so dense that the jungle and undergrowth almost disappeared and instead there was a damp, boggy turf, cold, spongy, and yielding to the tread. The stalks of the tall trees rose like columns, the vines hanging down from them in festoons, and their roots running over the ground in every direction made walking difficult.

Suddenly all the natives began to cry "Tepe! Tepe!" and Henrick, stopping short, said, "Look!" The sluggish, canal-like stream here wound slowly by, and in a bare spot in its bend was the most singular of trees. I have called it Crinoida, because when its leaves are in action it bears a striking resemblance to that well-known fossil the crinoid lilystone, or St. Cuthbert's beads. It was now at rest, however, and I will try to describe it to you. If you can imagine a pineapple eight feet high and thick in proportion resting upon its base and denuded of leaves, you will have a good idea of the trunk of the tree, which, however, was not the color of an anana, but a dark, dingy brown, and apparently hard as iron. From the apex of this truncated cone (at least two feet in diameter) eight leaves hung sheer to the ground, like doors swung back on

Believe It or Not

—By Ripley

THE MAN-EATING TREE FOLDED UP AROUND ITS HUMAN VICTIM

THE MAN-EATING TREE of Madagascar.

ENTICES ITS HUMAN VICTIM WITH AN INTOXICATING FLUID AND THEN COILS UP AROUND HIM WITH SAVAGE TENACITY

CAPT. JOSHUA SLOCUM
MADE A VOYAGE AROUND THE WORLD IN A 25 FOOT BOAT

BOB WHITE
PLAYED 72 HOLES
— 25 miles —
IN 306 STROKES IN ONE DAY

Olympus Field Chicago

Ripley's "Believe It or Not" comic about the Madagascar Man-Eating Tree. Published in the Aug. 8, 1924 Arizona Republican.

their hinges. These leaves, which were joined to the top of the tree at regular intervals, were about eleven or twelve feet long and shaped very much like the leaves of the American aguave, or century plant. They were two feet through in their thickest part and three feet wide, tapering to a sharp point, that looked like a cow's horn, very convex on the outer (but now under) surface, and on

26

the inner (now upper) surface slightly concave. This concave face was thickly set with very strong thorny hooks, like those upon the head of the teazle. These leaves, hanging thus limp and lifeless, dead green in color had in appearance the massive strength of oak fibre.

The apex of the cone was a round, white, concave figure, like a smaller plate set within a larger one. This was not a flower but a receptacle, and there exuded into it a clear, treacly liquid, honey-sweet, and possessed of violent intoxicating and soporific properties. From underneath the rim (so to speak) of the undermost plate a series of long, hairy, green tendrils stretched out in every direction towards the horizon. These were seven or eight feet long each, and tapered from four inches to half inch in diameter, yet they stretched out stiffly as iron rods. Above these (from between the upper and under cup) six white, almost transparent, palpi reared themselves towards the sky, twirling and twisting with a marvellous incessant motion, yet constantly reaching upwards. Thin as reeds, and frail as quills apparently, they were yet five or six feet tall, and were so constantly and vigorously in motion, with such a subtle, sinuous, silent throbbing against the air, that they made me shudder in spite of myself with their suggestion of serpents flayed yet dancing on their tails.

Here were not corolla, pistils, stamens, a flower, mind you, nor nothing like it. For Crinoida, unknown, new species as it is, is nighest akin to the cycadaceae, and perhaps its exact prototype may be found among the fossil cycadae, though I confess I do not remember any one that presents all its peculiar features. The description I am giving you now is partly made up from subsequent careful inspection of the plant. My observations on this occasion were suddenly interrupted by the natives, who had been shrieking around the tree in their shrill voices, and chanting what Henrick told me were propitiatory hymns to the great tree devil.

The Unnatural History of Man-Eating Plants

With still wilder shrieks and chants they now surrounded
one of the women, and urged her with the points of their
javelins until slowly, and with despairing face, she
climbed up the rough stalk of the tree and stood on the
summit of the cone, the palpi twirling all about her.
"Tsik! tsik!" ("drink! drink!") cried the men, and,
stooping, she drank of the viscid fluid in the cup, rising
instantly again with wild frenzy in her face and
convulsive chores in her limbs. But she did not jump down,
as she seemed to intend to do. O no! The atrocious
cannibal tree that had been so inert and dead came to
sudden savage life. The slender, delicate palpi, with the
fury of starved serpents, quivered a moment over her head,
then, as if instinct with demoniac intelligence, fastened
upon her in sudden coils round and round her neck and
arms; then, while her awful screams and yet more awful
laughter rose wilder to be instantly strangled down again
into a gurgled moan, the tendrils, one after another, like
great green serpents, with brutal energy and infernal
rapidity rose, retracted themselves, and wrapped her about
in fold after fold, ever tightening, with the cruel
swiftness and savage tenacity of anacondas fastening upon
their prey. It was the barbarity of the Laocoon without
its beauty—this strange, horrible murder. And now the
great leaves rose slowly and stiffly like the arms of a
derrick, erected themselves in the air, approached one
another, and closed about the dead and hampered victim
with the silent force of a hydraulic press and the
ruthless purpose of a thumb-screw. A moment more, and,
while I could see the bases of these great levers pressing
more tightly towards each other, from their interstices
there trickled down the stalk of the tree great streams of
the viscid, honey-like fluid, mingled horridly with the
blood and oozing viscera of the victim. At sight of this
the savage hordes around me, yelling madly, bounded
forward, crowded to the tree, clasped it, and with cups,
leaves, hands and tongues, got each one enough of the
liquor to send him mad and frantic. Then ensued a
grotesque and indescribably hideous orgie, from which,
even while its convulsive madness was turning rapidly into

delirium and insensibility, Henrick dragged me hurriedly away into the recesses of the forest, hiding me from the dangerous brutes and the brutes from me. May I never see such a sight again!

Comic strip panel from "Le Tépé-Tépé, par Asy," published in the Nov. 3, 1929 issue of La Jeunesse Illustrée.

Seid ben Yalhamah says he will go aboard his ship in half an hour and sail, so I must be brief. In the course of my stay in the valley of twenty-one days, I saw six other specimens of the Crinoida Dajeeana, but none so large as this which the Mkodos worshipped. I discovered that they are unquestionably carnivorous, in the same sense that dionea and drosera are insectivorous. The retracted leaves of the great tree kept their upright position during ten days, then, when I came again one morning, they were prone again, the tendrils stretched, the palpi floating, and nothing but a white skull at the foot of the tree to remind me of the sacrifice that had taken place there. I climbed into a neighboring tree and saw that all trace of the victim had disappeared and the cup was again supplied with the viscid fluid.

The Unnatural History of Man-Eating Plants

The indescribable rapidity and energy of its movements may be inferred from the fact that I saw a smaller one seize, capture, and destroy an active little lemur which, dropping by accident upon it while watching and grinning at me, in vain endeavored to escape from the fatal toils.

With Henrick's assistance and the consent of some of the head men of the Mkodos (who, however, did not dare stay to witness the act of sacrilege), I cut down one of the minor trees and dissected it carefully. Seid, however, is waiting for me, and I must defer to my next the details of this most interesting examination.

***

KARL LECHE.

"In this tantalizing fashion, after some private matters and messages, does Leche's letter end. I have been expecting his next with the utmost impatience, and will communicate its contents to you as soon as received.

"DR. OMELIUS FRIEDLOWSKY."

***

In explaining how he chose the fearsome tree's name, Leche compared its form to Crinoidea. This class of marine invertebrates are commonly known as sea lilies when attached to the sea floor and feather stars in their unstalked forms. Crinoids are structured with a mouth on their upper surface, surrounded by waving feeding arms that grab onto food, very much like the literary description of the Man-Eating Tree of Madagascar.

Crinoidea was named by John Samuel Miller of the Linnean Society in 1821, in his scientific paper on the class, so it was well-established when the original New York World article about the jungle predator of Madagascar was written in 1874. Crinoids belong to the phylum Echinodermata, which includes fellow echinoderms such as starfish, brittle stars, sea urchins and sea cucumbers. Dajeeana, chosen to honor Bhawoo Dajee, should have been lowercase if following standard genus/species binomial nomenclature.

Crinoid on the reef of Batu Moncho Island (near Komodo, Indonesia). Photo by Alexander Vasenin, CC BY-SA 3.0, via Wikimedia Commons.

Bhawoo Dajee, the namesake of Crinoida Dajeeana, is most certainly Dr. Bhau Daji Lad, the renowned physician who is still honored today for his contributions to the making of modern Mumbai. Daji sometimes spelled his name Bhawoo Dajee, such as in his prize-winning 1844 paper written while a student teacher at Elphinstone Institution (College). "An Essay on Female Infanticide," penned for a Bombay Government contest, decried the practice among the Rajputs of Kattiawar (Kathiawar) and Kutch. (He won 600 rupees for the essay.) Daji joined Grant Medical College in 1845, going on to become a lauded doctor. Dajee took an interest in assessing the medical value of plants that the ancient Hindus assigned marvelous powers. In doing so, he discovered the efficacy of the oil of Hydnocarpus inebrians, known locally as Kauti, to treat leprosy.

Simultaneously, Daji became an expert on Sanskrit, studying antiquarian artifacts. A social activist, he worked with the Bombay Association to secure the needs of the Indian people via the British Government. Daji promoted libraries, founded a girl's school, and helped establish both the University of Bombay and Mumbai's Victoria and Albert Museum and gardens; the museum was renamed in his honor in 1975. He also served two terms as

Sheriff of Bombay. Daji passed away on May 31, 1874, mere weeks after the publication of the Crinoida Dajeeana story in the New York World. (I'm not suggesting a connection.)

Dr. Bhau Daji Lad

But it is interesting that Dajee had an interest in how plants long used as natural remedies by native peoples could be utilized in modern medical applications... Could he have enlisted Karl Leche to seek such specimens in Madagascar?

Africa

Sir Jamsetjee Jejeebhoy was indeed a real person, as well. The 1874 article was likely referring to Sir Jamsetjee Jejeebhoy, 2nd Baronet, born Cursetjee, who lived from 1811-1877. He inherited the title from his father, Sir Jamsetjee Jejeebhoy, 1st Baronet (1783-1859), the famous Parsi merchant and philanthropist. The 1st Baronet achieved his wealth via avenues such as trading in cotton and illegally exporting opium from India to China. Queen Victoria knighted him in 1842 and bestowed his hereditary baronetcy in 1857, making him the first Indian subject to receive these honors.

The New-York Daily Tribune published a widely circulated article by Bayard Taylor in 1853 called "Life in Bombay," detailing the author's meetings with "Dr. Bhawoo Dajee" and the Jamsetjee family. It's not impossible that an old copy of this article in the New York World morgue might have provided some background inspiration for the Man-Eating Tree piece.

Queen Ranavalona I, sometimes called the "Mad Monarch" of Madagascar, was the subject of a World Word II-era addition to the saga of the Man-Eating Tree. According to the Oct. 11, 1942 American Weekly, Ranavalona "is said to have had a man-eating tree planted in the garden of her palace at Antananarivo. It served as a sort of vegetable guillotine, being reserved exclusively for her Christian subjects, whom she loathed and persecuted with the enthusiasm of a Nero. Lesser offenders, such as cutthroats, thieves and ambitious relatives, were merely boiled in oil."

Ranavalona was an isolationist sovereign who, during her 1828-1861 reign, severed ties with Europe in an effort to preserve Madagascar's self-sufficiency and independence. She expelled the London Missionary Society and persecuted indigenous Christians. The Catholic Mission reported in 1860 that Madagascar's population was falling due to imperial military campaigns and the state-sanctioned Tangena poison ordeal—to which many Christians were subjected during Ranavalona's rule, accused of undermining the Queen and promoting foreign interests. Tangena, the product of another deadly plant, is clearly the inspiration for the apparently exaggerated legend conveyed in the pages of American Weekly.

Africa

Thought to have been introduced by the Sakalava of Madagascar in the late 1700s, Tangena was the method by which the island's ruling elite meted out justice and eliminated their political rivals. George L. Robb wrote for Harvard University's Botanical Leaflets in 1957 that poison ordeals on Madagascar, Tangena being the most common, were employed in judging all personal and social crimes, but mainly the accusation of sorcery, viewed as a plague upon society. Demonic forces could inhabit people consciously or unconsciously and were deemed responsible for every unfortunate occurrence. During times of societal stress, all groups were viewed as possible contributors to evil.

Accused were forced to drink poison derived from the highly toxic nut of the *Cerbera manghas* (formerly *Cerbera tanghin*) tree, which grew primarily on Madagascar's eastern coast, and then consume three small pieces of chicken skin. If they regurgitated all three pieces of skin, they were innocent. If they failed to vomit or only threw up some of the pieces, they were judged guilty. This is because evil spirits were thought to survive on the flesh of human victims, and retention signified demonic possession. "They believed that there was a good spirit present who would strike the hearts of the guilty, and pass by those of the innocent," wrote Robb. Those who failed the test were usually attacked and killed before the toxin could complete its work.

Over time, exceptions emerged in the Tangena ritual. By the 1840s, dogs or chickens would occasionally be substituted for lesser offenses, with losers levied a fine. Medicine men who administered the trials were subject to bribery by those who could afford it, and could adjust the potency of the poison accordingly. "However, in spite of these corrupt practices, the people usually had an unswerving faith in the ordeal's inherent justice, and drank the poison with willingness and assurance," wrote Robb. Tangena ultimately became almost exclusive to the lower classes and slaves who could not afford a reprieve; non-royal slaves were often given a non-toxic dose and resold, while royal slaves often died.

During Ranavalona's 1828-1861 rule, it is estimated that 3,000 Malagasy were killed annually in the Tangena trials. But there were spikes, such as in 1838 when as estimated 20% of the population, as many as 10,000 people, were massacred, per Gwyn Campbell's "An Economic History of Imperial Madagascar, 1750-1895: The Rise and Fall of an Island Empire." Ordeal trials were officially outlawed on Madagascar in 1865, although they continued in less populous areas into the early 20th century.

"Huge Spiders, Native Legends Say, Infest the Jungle Fastnesses of the Mysterious Island. And a German Artist Named Voh Fed the Berlin Populace With This Fantastic Drawing." - Published in the Oct. 11, 1942 American Weekly. Included here on a Fair Use, educational basis.

Another interesting tidbit from American Weekly's "3 Weird Mysteries of Madagascar":

Local legends about the equally murderous Malagasy spiders are abundant. These nightmarish creatures, horned, beclawed and carrying enough venom to kill a regiment, are supposed to live in inland caves, from which they pounce on man and beast alike. Color is lent their possible existence by pretty well authenticated accounts of a similar giant species, native to the Amazon regions. Some of the latter drop upon their unsuspecting victims from the skies, using huge webs as parachutes. They don't carry

tommy-guns and the rest of the modern parachutists'
equipment, but are said to manage well enough with what
nature gave them. Others, concealing themselves in the
treetops, employ a different technique. They drop their
webs first, on the heads of men, horses, or other likely
subjects, and then, when the prey is enmeshed, make a
leisurely descent and polish it off.

Harvard botanist Asa Gray was one of Charles Darwin's greatest
supporters in America, publicizing Darwin's multi-year study on
insectivorous plants in articles for the publications The Nation
and Gardeners' Chronicle. Gray read the 1874 "Crinoida
Dajeeana" article in the New York World and promptly mailed a
copy to the eminent scientist.

"Do hurry up the book about Drosera &c," wrote Gray, sensing
competition for the discoveries, both real and fictitious. Gray
referenced two articles written for The Nation to reclaim Darwin's
work on insectivorous plants from Alfred William Bennett, who
reported similar findings on Drosera at the 1873 meeting of the
British Association for the Advancement of Science. And then you
have the (possibly fictitious) Dr. Omelius Friedlowsky stating that
his motive for prematurely publishing Leche's findings was to
beat Darwin and others to the punch.

"I began reading the Madagascan squib quite gravely," Darwin
replied to Gray on June 3, 1874, "and when I found it stated that
Felis & Bos inhabited Madagascar, I thought it was a false story,
and did not perceive it was a hoax till I came to the woman."

It's rather amusing that "Crinoida Dajeeana" managed to make
Charles Darwin himself sweat, even momentarily. Nevertheless,
he would publish his book "Insectivorous Plants" on July 2, 1875,
so perhaps the New York World provided some motivation, after
all!

Robert L. Ripley of "Believe It or Not" fame claimed to have come
across the Man-Eating Tree on a journey to Madagascar but kept
a safe distance. At a time when world travel was financially out of
reach for most people, Ripley scoured the planet collecting
astounding facts from exotic locations, which he presented to the
public via newspaper and radio. He reportedly backed up his

Robert L. "Believe It or Not" Ripley with his drawing of the Madagascar Man-Eating Tree. Published in the Sep. 15, 1932 Toronto Daily Star. Included here on a Fair Use, educational basis.

facts with careful research. Ripley featured the Madagascar Man-Eating Tree in his popular "Believe It or Not" newspaper cartoon in 1924. He also showcased the tree in the second of his "Ripley's Believe It or Not!" Vitaphone short films, released in 1930. In the short, Ripley summarized the legend and even presented a short, animated sequence depicting the sacrifice of a female victim to the tree.

Flip through this book and glance at the many illustrations of the Madagascar Man-Eating Tree (and other carnivorous plants) that were published in the press throughout the early 20th century.

A still from Ripley's animated cartoon about the Madagascar Man-Eating Tree, as seen in his 1930 Vitaphone "Believe It or Not" short film. Included here on a Fair Use, educational basis.

You might notice a trend—many depict scantily-clad ladies in distress caught up in the plant's deadly grip. There is undoubtedly a strange sexual element to the story, not just in the visual representations but in the original 1874 New York World article. The naked Mkodos woman is forcibly prodded forward by the men with "the points of their javelins," climbing the cone with the palpi twitching frantically. She drinks from its fluid, the narcotic causing a "wild frenzy in her face and convulsive chores in her limbs." The tree's serpentine tentacles coil around the woman, tightening her in a fatal embrace, the tribesmen shrieking and chanting. As the leaves press in and crush the victim, the crowd frantically rushes in to drink the viscid fluid that streams down the tree. "Then ensued a grotesque and indescribably hideous orgie... its convulsive madness... turning rapidly into delirium and insensibility," Leche wrote. By Victorian standards, it's near pornographic.

The Unnatural History of Man-Eating Plants

Cheryl Blake Price commented on the carnal nature of the article's presentation of the Mkodos ceremony in the 2013 paper, "Vegetable Monsters: Man-Eating Trees in Fin-de-Siècle Fiction," writing, "The sexual undertone of the woman's sacrifice is typical of colonial narratives that emphasized native abuse of women and the necessity of protective empirical rule. In not partaking in the orgy, the European scientist is carefully distinguished from both native inhabitants and the predatory plant."

SKEPTICAL VIEWPOINTS

There is no shortage of doubt, obviously, about there being a Man-Eating Tree in Madagascar.

Many investigators have pored over the story with a magnifying glass, trying and failing to find factual evidence for the account...

An early detractor was the London Missionary Society, who first established a presence on Madagascar in 1814 (despite a false start and a 26-year repression during the reign of Queen Ranavalona). The organization took notice of the ongoing, worldwide press attention given to the carnivorous tree supposedly hiding on the island, and provided comment in its annual publication, Antananarivo Annual and Madagascar Magazine. Reprinting the Crinoida Dajeeana story in 1881, the magazine stated, "It is needless to say that such a phenomenon as the one described below is *non est*." In the 1884 issue, writer L. Dahle called the Man-Eating Tree of Madagascar a "cock-and-bull story."

George A. Shaw of the London Missionary Society spent nearly 14 years on Madagascar, stationed at Tamatave. During this tenure, he developed a great knowledge and deep respect for the Malagasy people. Shaw reflected on his experiences in his 1885 book, "Madagascar and France with Some Account of the Island, Its People, Its Resources and Development." In its pages, he wrote, "Many of the curiosities of vegetable life are found in the island, and the romance of the early travelers has added many extraordinary forms unknown, except in the imagination of the writers. Such is the *man-eating tree*, which was said to be able to entangle in its fibrous, tendril-like leaves human beings, whom it crushed to death and devoured. No such plant exists, but it is doubtless the romancers' magnified description of the insectivorous plants, which are not uncommon."

Chase Salmon Osborn, ex-governor of Michigan, published a 1924 travelogue called "Madagascar: Land of the Man-Eating Tree." Osborn admitted up front that he headlined the Man-Eating Tree to grab reader interest and sell books. "In travelling from one end of Madagascar to the other a thousand miles and across the great island, many times traversing the nearly four hundred miles of breadth, I did not see a man-eating tree," the author revealed. "But from all the peoples I met, including Hovas, Sakalavas, Sihanakas, Betsileos and others, I heard stories and myths about it. To be sure the missionaries say it does not exist, but they are not united in this opinion, despite the fact that it is properly their affair and responsibility to discredit and destroy anything and everything that fosters demonism and idolatry. No missionary told me that he had seen the devil tree, but several told me that they could not understand how all the tribes could believe so earnestly in it, and over hundreds of miles where intercourse has been both difficult and dangerous, unless there were some foundation for the belief. Again, it may be emphasized that while a man-eating tree is an unlikely thing it is not an impossibility."

Dr. Ralph Linton of Philadelphia spent two years in Madagascar on an ethnological survey for the Field Museum of Natural History in Chicago. Upon his return to London in December 1927, he told the Associated Press that the tale of the Man-Eating Tree is ridiculous and always was. He suggested that the fellow who told the story had instead heard about the man-eating *fleas* of Madagascar. "If so, he was at least a little nearer right," joked Linton. During his stint in Madagascar, Linton said he encountered several persons who believed that such a thing existed but the tree was always in some other part of the country. He therefore arrived at the conclusion that the story was a myth.

"The man-eating tree is a myth," George W. Stimpson unequivocally stated after examining the subject for his 1930 book, "Popular Questions Answered." Stimpson reached this conclusion in part on the testimony of Charles F. Swingle of the U.S. Bureau of Plant Industry, who investigated the story. "After traveling through much of Madagascar and asking on many occasions about the man-eating tree, I concluded that this fable has no more basis on fact than any ordinary fairy tale," wrote Swingle to the author in 1929. "I did hear of the fable on several occasions in Madagascar, but, like the end of the rainbow, the plant always grew in some other part of the island. It is, of course, always difficult to disprove stories such as this, but it seems to me that there is no basis of truth for the story of the man-eating tree."

Science writer Willie Ley probed the myth of the Madagascar Man-Eating Tree in his 1955 book, "Salamanders and Other Wonders: Still More Adventures of a Romantic Naturalist." Ley consulted the Library of Congress and other libraries for Graefe and Walther's Magazine of Carlsruhe (or the modern spelling of Karlsruhe), supposed to be the original source of Leche's letter, and found no record of such a publication. Neither did he find any information about Leche or Friedlowsky. Ley referenced several pre-1874 books about Madagascar written by naturalists and missionaries, but located zero mention of the Mkodos or Man-Eating Tree. "Of course the man-eating tree does not exist," concluded Ley. "There is no such tribe. The actual natives of Madagascar do not have such a legend."

Lawrence G. Green, who described himself as "an author in search of the grain of truth in Africa's strangest tales," delved into the Man-Eating Tree story in his 1959 book, "These Wonders to Behold." Green wrote, "One theory which I mention only because of its romantic interest is that the man-eating tree was invented by the old Indian Ocean pirates, Kidd and the rest, at the time when they declared a republic in Madagascar. They did not want anyone exploring their haunts, and possibly finding their treasures, and they relied on the tree to keep unwelcome visitors away."

Roy P. Mackal, a biochemist and zoologist, researched the Man-Eating Tree of Madagascar for his 1980 book, "Searching for Hidden Animals." He couldn't find the Mkodos anywhere, not in lists of Madagascan words or lists of tribal groups. Mackal realized that the Mkodos were described as not exceeding 56 inches in height, and that Madagascar did not have such diminutive groups of people. In a two-volume set entitled "Madagascar," written by Captain Samuel Pasfield Oliver and published in 1886, Mackal did find an ethnology entry for a pigmy race called the Quimos or Kimos. Circumstantial accounts from M.M. Commerson and De Maudeave (governor of Fort Dauphin from 1768-1770) placed this tribe in the southern center of Madagascar, about 180 miles northwest of Fort Dauphin. The Quimos or Kimos were stated to be lighter in color than the majority of the Malagasy, with woolly hair and very long arms. They were very bold in defending their own territory, excelled in handicraft, and had "an ingenious and active disposition" and pastoral habits. Mackal couldn't locate any other corroboration for this group's existence. He did learn that "m" is a common prefix for many African words, and considered that Kimos could be a variation of Kodos. They were the only native people of small stature ever described in Madagascar, and lived in about the correct area in the southeastern region of the island. "However, they were hardly described as primitive, as Liche had painted the Kodos," wrote Mackal.

Ley pointed out the inefficiency of the Man-Eating Tree needing prey to climb atop its trunk and touch the palpi in order to trigger its trap. "This arrangement would leave the tree in a badly undernourished condition because it would virtually depend on natives feeding it, with or without ceremony," wrote Ley. The only other regular victims would be tree-climbing lemurs, who would quickly learn to avoid the tree, said Ley.

Pavlovič, et al. demonstrated in 2010 that it is energetically expensive for the Venus Flytrap to repeatedly close and open its traps, reducing photosynthesis and spiking respiration. Individual traps can only be triggered a handful of times before they die. Larger traps capable of catching more sizeable prey would therefore require upscaled energy penalties, an unfavorable adaptation without reliably substantial nutritional payoffs. Prey as large as man, smart enough to avoid the grasp of a hungry plant, likely (hopefully) makes this an untenable scenario.

Mackal wrote, "We note that Liche's tree incorporated not one, but five or six of the special adaptations found singly in carnivorous plants [such as honey-excreting Pitcher Plants,

The Unnatural History of Man-Eating Plants

Sundew tentacles and the spring-loaded leaves of the Venus Flytrap-Ed.]. Clearly such a set of redundancies are a never-never-land combination that could not reasonably be the result of effective evolutionary adaptation. Nor could the adaptation to humans as a food source be possible, since even primitive man, including man's closest relatives, the apes, are far too intelligent to permit themselves to be trapped regularly for plant food."

Zoologist and Cryptozoologist Dr. Karl Shuker doubted that such a tree as Liche described could have ever evolved to possess such a fantastic combination of specialized traits from unrelated plant species. "Moreover," he wrote, "its ever-animate, writhing palpi are unlike any structure ever reported from *any* known species of plant.

Concluding a far-reaching investigation into the Man-Eating Tree of Madagascar, the website Museum of Hoaxes wrote, "Almost every detail in the story was fictitious... The tree itself, most significantly, was pure fantasy—a gothic horror of the colonial era."

The Museum of Hoaxes did discover that there was a publication called Journal der Chirurgie und Augenheilkunde (The Surgical and Ophthalmic Journal), founded by German surgeons Karl Ferdinand von Graefe and Philipp Franz von Walther. However, it was published in Berlin, not Carlsruhe, and from 1820-1850, 24 years before the publication of Leche's letter in the New York World.

AUTHORSHIP

Charles Spencer Sarel, a career British journalist, issued the bold claim in 1924 that the Man-Eating Tree was his creation. Sarel worked in editorial roles for The South Wales Daily News, The Times of India, The Daily Express, The Midland Express, The Tribune, and The Electrical Engineer, before retiring from The Daily Express after 35 years of service in 1936. Sarel also wrote fiction under the pseudonym of Arthur R. Amory. Notably, he published the following article in the Feb. 7, 1924 Daily Express using his pseudonym, after reading the account of the New Orleans "Plant-Animal," which is covered in our North America chapter:

Africa

The Undying Tale.

By Arthur R. Amory

A news agency has just circulated the story of a thrilling fight for life with a man-eating plant. Two men, it is declared, were collecting specimens in a swamp forty miles from New Orleans when one of them was seized by "snake-like creepers with enormous muscular power," and both men were engaged for two hours in cutting and slashing these creepers with their axes in order to escape a horrible death.

In the light-hearted irresponsibility of youth, I wrote that story as a jest thirty years ago, and it has pursued me ever since. I was in India, imprisoned in my bungalow by an unusually severe monsoon, when the rain came down almost in a solid mass. We had been talking about a new variety of "pitcher plant," the harmless-looking piece of vegetation that catches insects, which had recently been received for the gardens of the old Government House beyond Byculla, and, by way of relieving the monotony of the dreary afternoon. I speculated on what might happen if that pitcher-plant grew up into a giant.

I pictured a member of a party of orchid hunters in the Upper Amazon separating himself from his companions to go in search of his dog, whose cries indicated that it had met with a misadventure. I showed him crashing through the jungle in the direction of the cries, and eventually finding his terrier in the grip of that giant pitcher plant, the gummy tendrils of which were squeezing the life out of the poor beast.

Vegetable Octopus.

Warming to my task, I described the man's valiant efforts to rescue the dog by cutting away the tendrils with his sheath knife, and how for every one he cut, a dozen other arms of this vegetable octopus shot out and gripped the man in their deadly embrace; and how in the end he was slowly and remorselessly crushed to death.

The Unnatural History of Man-Eating Plants

Then in this fantasy of mine I sketched the agonized search made for the missing man by the other members of the party, and how a week later they came upon his skeleton lying beside that of his dog.

It was pure fiction, and did not even pretend to be fact, but after it had been published in a Bombay newspaper it was quoted as fact all over India, and with each reproduction numerous small details were added to give it verisimilitude. It reached the Straits and China, penetrated Australia and New Zealand, found its way to San Francisco and all over the United States and Canada, always growing longer and more circumstantial.

It came in due course to England, with the names of the whole orchid-hunting party filled in, and biographical details of most of them, and then it went again on its travels. It has been touring the world ever since, and yesterday it came back to London again.

Don't talk to me about the monster that Frankenstein created. Frankenstein was a mere amateur.

***

A search of the Times of India, presumably where Sarel was working when he composed his Man-Eating Pitcher Plant story, did not turn up the article. However, his statement of the publication being three decades before his admission would place it in the 1890s, well after Crinoida Dajeeana first appeared in the New York World. It is possible that Sarel wrote one of the many Man-Eating Plant tales in circulation during this era and presumed they were all based upon his idea.

What Sarel, and most of the world, missed was a much earlier, low-key reveal in the second-ever issue of Current Literature. Published and edited in New York City by Frederick Maxwell Somers, Current Literature ran from 1888-1925. In August 1888, Somers reprinted the infamous "Crinoida Dajeeana" article and, in the process, revealed the name of its formerly anonymous author:

46

Africa

Each number we propose to give at least one of the famous stories that have drifted back into the past—and generally into oblivion. Thousands of readers want a copy of the Man-eating Tree. Mr. Edmund Spencer, the author of this story, was for some years a member of the staff of the New York World...

It will be worth the while of those who read this gossip to turn to page 154 and run over the wonderful story of The Man-Eating Tree. It was written years ago by Mr. Edmund Spencer for the N. Y. World. While Mr. Spencer was connected with that paper he wrote a number of stories, all being remarkable for their appearance of truth, the extraordinary imagination displayed, and for their somber tone. Mr. Spencer was a master of the horrible, some of his stories approaching closely to those of Poe in this regard. Like many clever men his best work is hidden in the files of the daily press. This particular story of the Crinoida Dajeeana, the Devil Tree of Madagascar, was copied far and wide, and caused many a hunt for the works of Dr. Friedlowsky. It was written as the result of a talk with some friends, during which Mr. Spencer maintained that all that was necessary to produce a sensation of horror in the reader was to greatly exaggerate some well-known and perhaps beautiful thing. He then stated that he would show what could be done with the sensitive plant when this method of treatment was applied to it. The devil-tree is, after all, only a monstrous variety of the "Venus fly trap," so common in North Carolina. Mr. Spencer died about two years ago in Baltimore, Md.

Museum of Hoaxes couldn't locate any further details regarding the existence of an Edmund Spencer of the New York World (and neither could I). However, wrote the website, "Somers was highly knowledgeable about the New York literary scene, so there's no reason his information shouldn't be accepted as credible." Prior to launching Current Literature in New York City, Somers co-founded The Argonaut, a weekly politics and society newspaper, in San Francisco.

The Unnatural History of Man-Eating Plants

However, I suspect that Somers accidentally conflated the name of Edmund Spenser, the great Elizabethan poet, with Edward Spencer, a well-known writer and dramatist from Maryland who was the true author of "Crinoida Dajeeana."

The Baltimore Weekly Sun ran Phillip Robinson's story "The Man-Eating Tree: A Tale of Nubia" during the third week of October 1888. (More on that story below.) This prompted the daily Baltimore Sun, on Oct. 18, to publish the following note giving credit to where it was due:

THE WEEKLY SUN this week contains a story called "The Man-Eating Tree," which, in addition to the graphic power with which it is told, has a special interest for Baltimoreans and Marylanders generally from the fact that the idea on which it is based is derived from a clever literary hoax, of which Mr. Edward Spencer, a native of this State, and formerly of THE SUN'S editorial staff, was the author. His story of the "Crinoida Dajeeana, the Devil Tree of Madagascar," was copied far and wide, and caused many inquiries for the works of Dr. Omelius Friedlowsky, an imaginary German scientist, whom Mr. Spencer created for the purpose of his scientific romance. In Mr. Spencer's article Dr. Friedlowsky was represented as having recently published in a German magazine a letter from a brother scientist in Madagascar who had just discovered this terrible tree, and both the learned German doctor's preface and his friend's letter were quoted at length. The whole story was told with such detail and such solemn, scientific gravity as to give it a wonderful air of probability, and there are no doubt many people who read his grave but powerful account of the man-eating tree who yet labor under the impression that it was a genuine discovery. The paper was written as the result of a talk with some friends, in which Mr. Spencer maintained that all that was necessary to produce a sensation of horror in the reader was greatly to exaggerate some well-known and perhaps beautiful natural phenomenon, and he declared that he would show what could be done with the sensitive plant when this method of treatment was applied to it, the devil-tree, in his view, being after all only a monstrous

variety of the "Venus fly-trap" so common in North
Carolina. Mr. Phil Robinson, an English writer and
traveler, has taken Mr. Spencer's idea, and developed it
into the story which is published in the WEEKLY SUN. It
loses nothing in horror or realism in Mr. Robinson's
hands, but it seems quite certain that he owes his
inspiration to Mr. Spencer's article.

***

Spencer was raised in Baltimore, part of the influential Spencer
family from the Eastern Shore and Talbot County. Spencer Hall,
the family homestead on the Miles River, was established in and
occupied continuously since 1670. Spencer distinguished himself
with rare promise in literary studies at Princeton College. He
quickly became noted as "a writer of versatility and many quaint
conceits," producing essays, tales, newspaper articles and poems.
His work appeared in Putnam's Magazine, Galaxy, Southern
Magazine, Harper's, the Richmond Examiner and Washington
Capitol. Spencer was a regular editorial contributor to the New
York World for several years under the management of Manton
Marble, "and furnished it with many brilliant articles," per the
Baltimore Sun. Spencer also wrote for the New York Sun, New
York Herald, Philadelphia Times, Baltimore Sunday Telegram and
Baltimore Bulletin, and joined the editorial staff of the Baltimore
Sun in 1878. He left the newspaper world behind in 1881, outside
of occasional articles, and focused on his efforts as a playwright.
His most famous work was the play "Kit, the Arkansas Traveler,"
which elevated actor and producer F. S. Chanfrau to great
success.

"Mr. Spencer's chief characteristic as a writer was his astonishing
versatility. From the preparation of a paper dealing in the dryest
of facts and statistics he would pass with ease to the lightest and
airiest composition. He was a man of retiring habits and had few
intimate friends. He shrank from contact with the world, and
rather avoided social intercourse, preferring to lead a quiet life
with his books and his work," wrote the Baltimore Sun.

Spencer did maintain a friendship and correspondence with
William Hand Browne, an English professor and the second-ever
librarian at Johns Hopkins University. Like Spencer, he was a

longtime resident of the Baltimore area. (Browne was also a Confederate sympathizer who helped to promote the racist "Lost Cause" mythology following the U.S. Civil War, according to Johns Hopkins University, although that aspect of his life doesn't factor into this discussion.) The Johns Hopkins Libraries hold papers in their collection from both men, including their letters to each other. Much of their communication was focused on encouragement of each other's literary pursuits and interests.

"I have no correspondent but you—as for my friends, I could count them on my fingers, keep one hand in my pocket, and have fingers to spare," Spencer told Browne. "You have influenced me—always on my best side—far more than you are aware. Being only half baked I am mouldable. There are a good many of the most shapely plants in my garden that the weeds would have strangled but for you."

In a letter dated April 28, 1874—the very day that "Crinoida Dajeeana" debuted in the New York World—Spencer wrote to Browne, sending him a copy of the article—*and admitting that it was a hoax.*

"I send you Crinoida—you will notice that the 'scientific notes' below it are also mine," Spencer wrote. Referencing *Dionaea* (the Venus Flytrap), Spencer explained, "A couple of papers in the Nation (from which I got the notion) insist that those plants digest the insects & so fertilize themselves."

Spencer was most likely referring to the April 2 and April 9 issues of The Nation, which featured a two-part series called "Insectivorous Plants," written by Harvard botanist Asa Gray to defend his friend Charles Darwin's discoveries on the subject. As previously noted, Gray would later see Spencer's article and mail it out of concern to Darwin, who momentarily fretted before realizing it was a hoax. The prank had come full circle!

Spencer mused on the New York World's desire for stories such as "Crinoida Dajeeana," referencing Managing Editor Jerome B. Stillson. "If these hoax papers injure the World, why should Stillson ask to have them come weekly not monthly? As for people being provoked, fol de rol—each one broaches a new theme—each one is separately credible in its own merits—and it don't hurt overmuch unless you puncture the cicatrice of an unhealed wound."

Spencer and Browne conspired to continue the hoax, with Browne submitting his own article about a mysterious plant to the World. His creation was called Apocynacea, which is puzzling, since *Apocynaceae* is a real family of flowering trees, shrubs, herbs, stem succulents and vines found throughout much of the world. Notable members of Apocynaceae include dogbanes (also a name for the family), oleander, milkweeds and periwinkles. Many Apocynaceae are toxic, with the poison from some species once used on arrow tips in parts of Africa. While we don't know the details of what Browne had planned for his exotic plant, Spencer described it as a "carnal plant" and joked that "a decoration made from those flowers would be useful as an aphrodisiac."

"By all means send your letter as proposed to the World," Spencer encouraged Browne. "If you would make your paper a complementary one to mine it would puzzle some of the 'scientists,' as they call 'em."

"Odds boddikins! caro compagno mio, if anyone else but you had done it I should have fancied you sent me your Apocynacea to put me out of conceit with Crinoida, and show me how to do it," Spencer wrote to Browne on May 3. "If the <u>World</u> should not publish it, it will be because you have so ingeniously disguised the wonder that Stillson may not see it." Spencer gently recommended "an advantage in painting on large canvas with broad brushes" when penning a hoax, meaning "more people are struck by our daubs."

"And yet it does its work with the very experts whom one does not even expect, much less lay out to deceive," wrote Spencer. He referenced the infamous Great Moon Hoax of 1835, in which New York City newspaper The Sun ran a series of six articles claiming that an alien civilization had been spotted by telescope on Earth's Moon. Some readers were fooled, and Spencer couldn't have asked for a finer pedigree of hoax to inspire his Man-Eating Plant story.

Spencer bragged that the previous week, Stillson had forwarded him a card "all the way from Frisco" from "Gustaf Eisen," a zoologist from the University of Upsala, "respectfully asking the author of 'Discoveries in the Sargasso Sea described by A. B. Ankarswärd,' to do him the favor to give him—'the address of Mr. Lisle.'" It's unclear if this note refers to a separate hoax Spencer wrote for the World about a discovery in the Sargasso Sea [I can't find it.] or if this was a garbled reference to the Madagascar story, with "Lisle" being kind of close to "Leche."

This writer was very likely Gustav Eisen, a polymath who worked in the fields of zoology and horticulture. He graduated from the University of Uppsala in 1873 and relocated to the U.S. in 1874 to work for the California Academy of Sciences in San Francisco. Eisen is best known for his studies of worms, and he was a correspondent of Darwin.

"Papae! my boy—what do you think of that?" Spencer asked Browne of Eisen's message. "When your paper is printed (you must by all means send it) you must expect to be overrun with applications for seeds of your carnal plant."

"Read the Nation of last Thursday," Spencer wrote on May 17. "It also lauds Crinoida Dajeeana right agreeably."

Indeed, The Nation was impressed! "The story of the Insectivorous Plants which we lately published appears to have excited no little attention," the paper noted on May 14. "The *World* has followed it up with a capital account of the man-eating tree of Madagascar, *Crinoida Dajeeana*, just discovered by Karl Leche, and most ingeniously and elaborately described. Perhaps the best point in it is its taking-off of Sir William Thomson's famous suggestion, viz., that the gorms of life not only may have been, but still may be, brought to this earth from some other part of space, by means of aerolites, meteoric dust, or some such kindred agency. The story of the visit to the sandy and desolate region where alone the entirely anomalous Dionæa is to be found, in the expectation or hope of finding evidences of a meteoric shower or a fallen aerolite, is very well told."

Browne confirmed on May 20 that he had submitted his article to the World but had not as yet heard back. It's unclear if the hoax was ever published [Again, I haven't found it.] or just ended up buried in the slush pile.

Africa

Spencer died on July 17, 1883, at only 49. His cause of death was described as "nervous prostration," which he suffered from for 10 days, deteriorating to the point of no return despite his doctor's best efforts. Spencer's wife, the former Miss A. C. Braddie Harrison, predeceased him in 1882. The couple had married young, and one might infer that Spencer was absolutely heartbroken after her death. They were survived by two daughters and two sons, the oldest, a boy, being 17 when Spencer died. In a letter enclosed with his will, Spencer referred to his eventual death "as not too soon for my own comfort."

***

I have written numerous times, in my various investigations of American and world strangeness, about how the late 19th century and early 20th century press had a tendency to stray into the fanciful. The New York World, in fact, infamously pioneered "Yellow Journalism" in 1898, when publisher Joseph Pulitzer engaged in a press war with Randolph Hearst's New York Journal over who could print the most sensational (and often unsubstantiated) news about the explosion of the USS Maine in Havana Harbor, helping to incite the Spanish-American War.

It was exceptionally common to find tales of monsters, ghosts, anachronistic archeological finds and such wonders amongst sober reporting on politics, crime, social events in American newspapers. Its purpose appears to have been to entertain and sell papers, with many readers in on the joke. However, weird newspaper tales also generated debate and complaints, the latter often coming from rival editors chiding competitors for their poor journalistic ethos. The plethora of Man-Eating Plant stories during this era did not go unnoticed:

"It would seem, however, that there is a regular 'boom' in carnivorous plants at the present date. I do not mean that the well-known insect-eating habits of the sundew, or Venus' flytrap, are being exploited. The plants which are coming to the front (in the newspapers) are trees big enough to catch and devour chickens, at least. As a biologist, I am interested in these flesh-eating trees: only one will naturally require a good deal more than the mere *ipse dixit* of a newspaper paragraph to convince him of the real existence of the vegetable wonders thus described," wrote

The Unnatural History of Man-Eating Plants

Dr. Andrew Wilson in the Sep. 24, 1892 edition of "Science Jottings," his regular column in the Illustrated London News. "Are they simply treated as substitutes for the sea-serpent or the big gooseberry of the dull season in journalism? Or are we to believe in the flesh-eating trees at all?"

American Botanist, naturally one to be offended by bogus plant stories, wrote in July 1905, "The realms of Nature have always furnished the monger of sensations with a free field for the play of his imagination. From excursions into these regions he has returned with the sea-serpent, the unicorn, the roc, the barnacle-goose that grows on trees, the man-eating tree, the upas tree and a vast number of other equally entertaining and untruthful creations. One after another science has killed these off, but 'newspaper science,' the product of fledgling reporters who would not know true science if they met it squarely in the way, is ever ready with new and equally wonderful stories to tickle our credulity. Nature is full of wonders, but the wonders of the reporter's imagination so far outstrip the wonders of nature, that as a people, we still prefer the reporter's version. The best selling popular science is that in which animals think, act and often talk, exactly like human beings, and in which plants are endowed with instincts that properly belong to animals alone. Instances are so abundant in the lay press that scientific publications no longer take notice of them, but when a publication devoted to science publishes such stories for the truth, it is time someone pointed out their falsity." American Botanist made this impassioned statement in reference to an article in the February 1905 edition of Floral Life, which described such fantastic plants as the "coughing bean," a vine which coughed and sneezed when covered in dust, and a South American orchid capable of locating and slurping up water via a prehensile, straw-like tube.

"Among the most important and horrendous botanical discoveries are those recently made by 'American Weekly Inc.' and broadcasted, through the agency of the press, to the furthermost parts of our country. These discoveries relate to nothing less than certain horrible man-eating trees which lie in wait for their victims in the tropical forests and when they have secured their prey, suck their blood with great gusto," wrote Willard M. Clute in the April 1925 edition of American Botanist. "To be sure no botanist of note has ever seen such marvels. They are always discovered by some ignorant native or some credulous traveller. The scientist is likely to spoil the whole affair by demanding the facts." American Weekly was a Sunday magazine supplement of wide circulation, published by the Hearst Corporation and syndicated to a large number of American newspapers from 1896-1966.

SEARCH FOR THE MAN-EATING TREE

Despite all these declarations that the Madagascar Man-Eating Tree is a myth, people continue to search for it, sensing some fascinating truth at the core of this sordid account. One of those searchers was the late Czech Cryptozoologist and adventurer Ivan Mackerle.

In 1998, Mackerle set out for Madagascar in search of the Man-Eating Tree. He cited as one of his inspirations a doomed explorer who had tried to collect a $10,000 bounty offered by the journal American Botanist for a living specimen of the notorious tree.

Translated from Czech, Mackerle wrote, "It is difficult to say whether it was the prospect of this reward or just a desire for adventure that led former British army officer L. Hearst to search for the man-eating tree in the jungles of Madagascar in 1935." According to Mackerle, Hearst couldn't locate the Mkodos but did meet a hunter who confirmed the existence of the Man-Eating Tree, and that natives were still secretly offering it human sacrifices. "Hearst spent four months searching the island and finally came across the giant carnivorous plants," wrote Mackerle.

"Although the natives had kept the revered man-eating Tepe tree a secret from him, Hearst brought back photographs of large pitchers swallowing small rodents and pictures of some unknown trees under which lay the skeletons of larger animals," wrote Mackerle.

Unfortunately for Hearst, the tree was too large to cart out of the jungle, and scientists disregarded his photos as evidence, considering them a forgery. "Therefore, Hearst went into the jungles again, but this time he did not return. He died under mysterious circumstances somewhere in the growths of succulent harpagophytes in the southeastern region of the island," wrote Mackerle. "That is where our search began."

Fellow Cryptozoologist Karl Shuker wrote that Mackerle elaborated on the Hearst story in a personal letter to him, stating that the 1935 photos of the mysterious, possibly man-eating trees had been published in print. Mackerle was unable to determine where the photos had been published, and this remains an open question, as he passed away in 2013, before Shuker could ask him further about it.

The possibility of there being lost photographs of the Madagascar Man-Eating Tree is compelling, just like the Missing Thunderbird Photo mystery. However, I wonder if Mackerle's story about British army officer L. Hearst's 1935 expedition isn't a garbled recollection of *Captain Victor de la Motte Hurst*, who in 1932 announced his intention to search for the Man-Eating Tree in Madagascar.

Hurst and his wife (her first name unrevealed in the press) planned to search for the Roc ("that mythical monster bird which may not be mythical at all but a survival of something from the prehistoric past") but was especially focused on locating a specimen of the Man-Eating Tree. On two previous trips to Madagascar, Hurst collected testimony from natives and missionaries that convinced him of the tree's existence. These testimonies corresponded with each other as well as the description provided by Leche. According to American Weekly, early missionaries to the island were horrified by the tree and the human sacrifice connected to it, and ordered the natives to cut every specimen down. But the inhabitants, viewing the tree as sacred, refused to comply. In these accounts, it was the Malagasy who worshipped the tree (not the Mkodos specifically). Hurst hoped to obtain their permission to let him film moving pictures of the ceremony, "not with a human sacrifice, but with some other animal." One reporter worried that the French government would be unable to protect the explorers once they began hacking their way into the jungle, and that the journey put Mrs. Hurst in danger of being sacrificed, herself. The group was said to include a botanist, biologist, geologist and naval officer. They were to begin their exploration within a few months at the small village of

Africa

Morondava on the Madagascar coast before passing through the
territories of half a dozen tribes, some said to be hostile.
According to one account, the team would be armed with tear-gas
bombs.

"Madagascar, a great island in the Indian Ocean off the coast of
Africa, has been constructed by Nature so that it has always been
burglar-proof to the conquerors of the past and still resists the
white man of today," commented American Weekly on Nov. 13,
1932 in reporting the planned Hurst expedition. "It is as if Nature
had deliberately constructed a game-sanctuary here where
anything may have survived from before the ice ages, before man
started his exterminating career."

Hurst, described as "a fascinating fellow who talks about strange
places like a travel-book come to life," was soliciting volunteers for
the expedition, particularly "eight husky, adventurous youth with
perfect health" who could front $3,000 cash or £525 each for
their spots on the team. He promised applicants "a list of
menaces to life, limb and health, forbidding enough to most
persons, but alluring to the type of man he wants." Hurst was
stated to had lived for some years at various addresses in the
Brighton district and was then at Braemore Road, Hove.

John Bull magazine, perhaps taking the piss out of Hurst,
claimed that he had been a "commercial traveler selling soap
powder" until losing his job a few weeks earlier and turning to
advertising for adventurers. The magazine similarly expressed
skepticism that an experienced traveler like Hurst would refer to
Madagascar as "unexplored."

Perhaps continuing this jocular tone, John Bull also described
the expedition as containing "a great fleet of canoes and a
hundred or so porters and guides," said Hurst was bringing
actors to play the natives should the Malagasy decline to re-enact
the ceremony, and that Hurst ultimately planned to blow up the
Man-Eating Tree with dynamite in order to take fragments back
to Britain for dissection.

Some of the news coverage qualified Hurst as a fellow of the Royal
Geographical Society, although I couldn't find anything about him
or his Madagascar venture in their publications. Hurst did serve

the Royal Air Force, with a March 1941 RAF directory listing him as a pilot officer in the RAF Reserve, attached to the Administrative and Special Duties Branch.

Captain de la Motte Hurst and His Wife Who Are Setting Out to Find the Cannibal Plant.

"Captain de la Motte Hurst and His Wife Who Are Setting Out to Find the Cannibal Plant." Published in the Nov. 12, 1931 American Weekly. Included here on a Fair Use, educational basis.

Africa

Hurst's planned adventure was covered widely in the press. American Weekly, the magazine supplement in Hearst (no relation) newspapers, included a vivid, now classic, illustration of a woman being sacrificed to the Man-Eating Tree. It also displayed a photo captioned as a "remarkable photograph of a giant Venus flytrap in which a rat has been caught," although it looks more like a rat with its head stuck in a pitcher plant. (See next page.) This is confirmed by the inclusion of the same photo in a 1924 American Weekly article about former Michigan Governor Chase Salmon Osborn's search for the tree in Madagascar, with the pitcher plant correctly captioned.

However, the fact that the American Weekly article about Hurst's proposed expedition includes the memorable photo of a rat in a pitcher plant, just like Mackerle recalled in photos that Hearst supposedly took *in* Madagascar, suggests that perhaps the eminent Cryptozoologist misremembered the 1932 article as recounting an adventure that had already happened, complete with photos.

I hope my hypothesis is not truly the case, and that photos of a real Man-Eating Tree in Madagascar are buried in the pages of a dusty old magazine or science journal. Time and research will tell.

On the bright side, it appears untrue that Hurst met his demise trying to secure proof of the tree. There was no follow-up news regarding his journey, so it's possible that it never even got off the ground. Also, on Aug. 8, 1947, Hurst and his wife celebrated the wedding of their only son, Roger, to Isabelle Evan Smith, so it seems unlikely that anyone was gobbled up by a hungry plant. The adventurous Hursts were reported at that time to be living in Durban, South Africa (formerly residing in East Grinstead, U.K.).

In any case, Mackerle had an exciting time trying to track down the Man-Eating Tree himself. He described encountering *Harpagophytum grandidieri* (*Uncarina grandidieri*), also known as the Clawed Tree, Mouse Trap Tree, Succulent Sesame and, per Mackerle, as Andrindritra locally. As Mackerle explained, the tree's long, flexible branches and hooked seed pods can wrap around and ensnare passing people and animals to aid in seed dispersal. He pointed out that the wind might sway the branches and cause such entanglement (as opposed to purposeful movement by the plant) and that they do not suck blood like the legendary Vampire Vine of Nicaragua. (See our Central America chapter.)

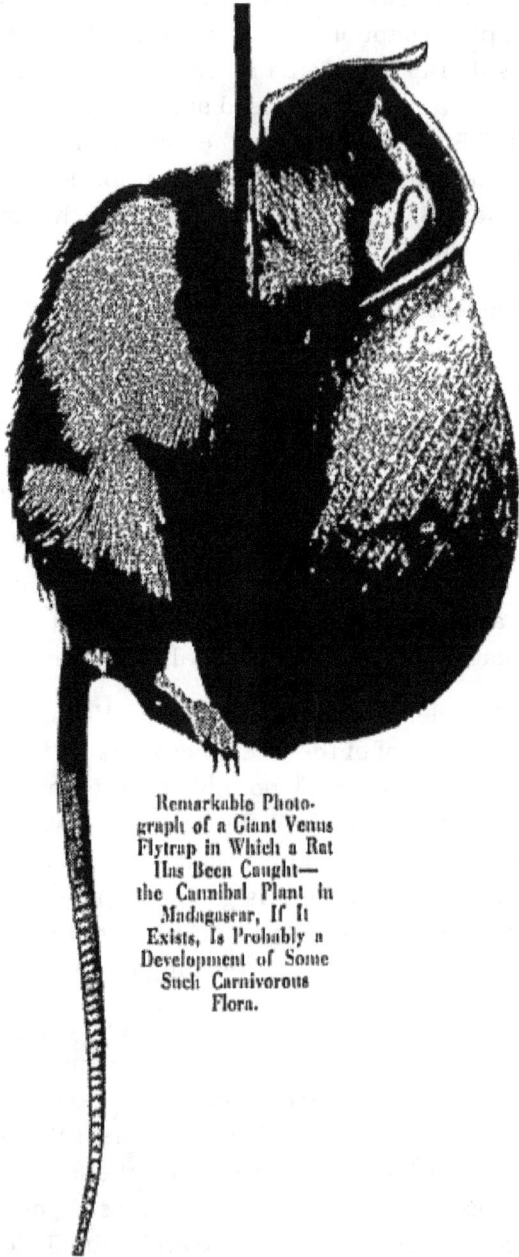

Remarkable Photograph of a Giant Venus Flytrap in Which a Rat Has Been Caught—the Cannibal Plant in Madagascar, If It Exists, Is Probably a Development of Some Such Carnivorous Flora.

To Solve the Mystery of Madagascar's Man-Eating Tree?

An English Explorer and His Wife Prepare to Hunt Down a Legendary Plant-Monster Which is Said to Furnish Its Worshipers Intoxicating Juices in Return for Human Sacrifices Fed to It

A Typical Madagascar Village in the Country Where the Stories Locate the "Man-Eating Tree."

According to One Explorer's Description of the Man-Eating Tree, the Sacrifice, a Girl, Was Forced to the Top of the Monstrous Plant and Then the Thick Tendrils Wound Around Her Like Ropes, Then the Leaves from an Their Long Stalks and Closed in on Her, the Claws Inside Them Tearing Into Her Flesh and Pulling Her Down to the Cup That Was the Mouth of the Thing, While the Medicine-Man and Warriors Watched.

Captain Victor de la Motte Hurst and His Wife Who Are Setting Out to Find the Cannibal Plant

American Weekly story about the Hurst expedition to Madagascar, as published in the Nov. 13, 1932 edition of the Washington Herald. Image included here on a Fair Use, educational basis.

The Unnatural History of Man-Eating Plants

The Missouri Botanical Garden, which has been exploring Madagascar and conserving its local flora since establishing an office for that purpose in 1987, said it is important to learn the specific *fady*, or taboos, from each area in which they plan to examine or collect specimens. They present themselves to village elders in order to learn the local fady, which can include "things to avoid like foods, times and places to walk or bathe, or wearing particular articles of clothing or colors. Hunting certain animals and disturbing the environment around sacred places are common fady in many locations."

Mackerle and his team "did not miss a single opportunity" to ask natives about "Devil Trees," but the subject was fady, especially for white visitors. Their Malagasy guide, however, was able to glean details about where the sacred tree was located. Without permission from tribal elders, Mackerle and his group decided to sneak off under the cover of night, roaring down the potholed roadway in their jeep. According to Mackerle, they were accosted by members of the Antandroy tribe wearing white robes and carrying spears. The screaming figures ran next to the jeep and jumped onto the bumper, but the driver accelerated, forcing the scary hitchhikers to leap off.

Mackerle finally located the Devil's Tree in the middle of a moonlit plain. According to local lore, it was inhabited by the spirit of a local king and demanded human sacrifice. But Mackerle soon realized that the spooky, twisted tree was not a Man-Eating Tree at all, but an ordinary, harmless Baobab (aka the Upside-Down Tree).

Later, an old villager directed the adventurers to Lake Kinkony, where they supposedly could find a sacred tree able to kill a person, sometimes from afar. The group followed a rough road to another village called Ananalava [Analalava?-Ed.], where the locals warned them about dangerous trees called Kumangas.

"Although they don't eat people or animals, they are so poisonous that they can kill even from a distance. Especially when they are in bloom," Mackerle learned. "The layer of poisoned air from the flowers is said to reach quite a distance when there is no wind. Birds that sit among their leaves fall dead to the ground, and animals that try to hide in their shade die immediately." (This is very similar to legends surrounding the Upas tree of Java, *Antiaris toxicaria*. See our Asia chapter.) Mackerle imagined a scenario in which a careless person laid down in the shade of such a poison tree and perished; a discoverer might assume the tree consumed the victim and spat out their skeleton.

After bribing a young native man with gifts, he led the search party to the tree. Though armed with gas masks, the explorers saw the tree wasn't in bloom and approached without them. "I expected that we would be risking our lives here. I was a little disappointed," boasted Mackerle. The air smelled clean, although he did note a couple dead birds and a skeletal turtle beneath the tree. Mackerle learned that natives had burned many of the Kumanga trees after domestic cattle grazed on its juicy leaves and died, leaving him to worry that the "Devil Tree" could soon go extinct.

Erythrophleum couminga (also known as Komanga, Kiminga, Kimanga, Koumanga, Koumango, Kimango and Couminga) is a leguminous tree endemic to the Western coast of Madagascar. It has highly toxic bark that was once used as a poison in ordeal trials (an alternative to the Tangena) throughout Madagascar and the Seychelles.

"So greatly did its toxicity impress the natives, that they attributed great power to all parts of the tree. The mere odor of its blossoms, the rain water that washed its leaves, and the smoke from burning parts of the plant were all supposed to be fatal," George L. Robb wrote for Harvard University's Botanical Leaflets in 1957. "Native folklore abounds with tales of people and cattle dying from the slightest contact with any of these elements." However, scientific investigation has revealed that although the active poison (erythrophlein and coumingine) is present in varying concentrations throughout the tree, it is unlikely that anything but ingesting the bark would be deadly.

Botanist Édouard Heckel wrote in 1903 (translated from French) that, "The superstitious beliefs current about this plant among the Malagasy are all imbued with the great fact that its toxicity is said to be limitless." He wrote that the Sakalava people (of western Madagascar) were said to cut down Komanga trees that grew around their villages. Heckel also described receiving

Komanga fruit and flower specimens that a correspondent had collected from trees growing along Lake Kinkony, where Mackerle also encountered it.

Erythrophleum couminga Baill branch, from the collection of botanist Édouard Heckel, 1903.

"Erythrophleum couminga, due to its extremely toxic properties, is also seen as highly mystical, and is generally feared, revered and rumours abound concerning the location of individuals," David Du Puy wrote for Curtis's Botanical Magazine in 1997. "Only the local 'ombyasy' (priest-doctors) dare to approach the tree, which is often said to be surrounded by the skeletons of small birds which have been killed, especially during the flowering season when the smell of the flowers is reputed to be poisonous. It is often difficult to find someone who is willing to point out the 'Komanga.'"

According to Journal d'Agriculture Tropicale, eradication campaigns were carried out against *Cerbera venenifera* and *Erythrophleum couminga*, both ordeal trees in Madagascar, during the 19th century but that practice had been abandoned by the time of the 1965 report. This information reflects Mackerle's observation about locals burning the Komanga trees, so perhaps it was still happening in the late 1990s.

Mackerle's expedition reinforced the fact that, while the Man-Eating Tree remains elusive, Madagascar does indeed have deadly vegetation tied to fatal ceremonial tradition. If the New York World completely dreamed up the original story, they managed to land not too far off from the truth of real species like the Komanga tree.

Is it possible that Hearst/Hurst made it to Madagascar and, like Mackerle, found and photographed *Erythrophleum couminga*, complete with animal skeletons beneath its threatening branches? Or did he truly find the actual Crinoida Dajeeana, bringing home photographs of this rare and much sought-out carnivorous tree?

Just like how there are continual searches for the Man-Eating Tree despite evidence against it, I can't help wanting to delve into historical records, hoping to uncover long-lost photographs that prove a myth to be reality.

By the way, it's true that American Botanist offered a $10,000 reward, in 1925, for a living specimen of the Man-Eating Tree. Do you think it's too late to collect?

***

There is a strange bit of serendipity regarding the Man-Eating Tree of Madagascar—the trunk, described by Leche as a dingy brown, iron-hard "pineapple eight feet high and thick in proportion resting upon its base and denuded of leaves." Why in

The Unnatural History of Man-Eating Plants

the world would Crinoida Dajeeana resemble a giant pineapple? What an odd detail. Well, as it turns out, the pineapple belongs to the large family of monocot flowering plants known as Bromeliaceae, and a few of its cousins have developed carnivorous tendencies. *Brocchinia reducta*, in particular, is native to northern Brazil, Guyana and Venezuela, where it grows in nutrient-poor soil and can root itself in rocky areas. Like the Venus Flytrap, it evolved a way to acquire nutrients missing from the soil in which it grew, such as nitrogen, from captured insects. The plant forms a tight rosette of bright, yellow-green leaves that hold rainwater like a pitfall trap. The surrounding vertical leaves are coated with a fine wax that reflects UV light and makes them dangerously slippery. Insects attracted to the rosette often tumble inside, where they drown in the acidic fluid. As the prey decays, specialized leaf trichomes absorb the released nutrients.

Brocchinia reducta on Roraima-Tepui, Venezuela. Photo by Christian Hummert, CC BY-SA 2.0 DE, via Wikimedia Commons.

The pineapple itself is not carnivorous, but the entire plant, including its fruit and stem, contain bromelain, a protein-digesting enzyme mixture. While bromelain's natural role is primarily defense against pathogens and pests, humans have found it useful as a meat tenderizer, anti-inflammatory, and skin exfoliant. Prolonged contact can damage skin, which is why commercial pineapple handlers often wear gloves. So, the next time you bite into a zesty slice of pineapple, remember—it just might be nibbling you back!

Puya chilensis, the "Sheep-Eating Plant." Photo by penarc, Public Domain, via Wikimedia Commons.

There IS a potentially protocarnivorous (able to trap but not directly digest prey) bromeliad, *Puya chilensis*, known ominously as the "Sheep-Eating Plant." It is endemic to hillsides in the Andes of central Chile. Standing over six feet tall with green/yellow flowers that grow on spikes, the plant has been said to resemble a medieval mace. It also grows dense rosettes of strap-like leaves edged with hooked, outward-pointing spines.

Birds and sheep are said to become stuck on the plant and die, their decaying bodies supplying the plant with nutrients. Although unconfirmed, this would make *Puya chilensis* the truest real-world analogue to the many fantastical plants detailed in this book.

As described in print and depicted in early artwork, Crinoida Dajeeana bears a resemblance to *Pachypodium lamerei*, aka the Madagascar Palm (even though it is not a palm at all). *Pachypodium lamerei* is a stem succulent from western Madagascar which is sold globally as a house plant. It can grow six feet in height indoors, but reaches 20 feet outdoors. It has a silvery-gray trunk covered in spines and long, narrow leaves that grow only at the top of the trunk.

Pachypodium lamerei in flowerpot. Photo by Beko, CC BY-SA 4.0, via Wikimedia Commons.

Pachypodium lamerei can look pineapple-eque, especially when young and squat, before the trunk elongates and branches. It would seem feasible that Spencer could have based the odd and specific appearance of Crinoida Dajeeana on the Madagascar Palm, exaggerating it to man-eating proportions and habits. Though *Pachypodium* as a genus was first described from the Cape of Good Hope in 1830, it wasn't identified in Madagascar until 1882, so the jury is out on whether this is just a coincidence.

Special thanks to Redditor VampiricDemon, who has done solid work researching Ivan Mackerle's 1998 expedition to Madagascar in search of Crinoida Dajeeana. Credit is also due to Pattock, a reader of ShukerNature, for posting several links that clued me in to the background of Komanga (and its many spellings).

MAN-SUCKING TREE OF NUBIA

In January 1883, some American papers published an article called "The Man-Eating Tree: A Tale of Nubia," an excerpt from "Under the Sun" by Phillip Robinson. In the story, the writer shares a tale of "a man-sucking tree... more terrible than the Upas." This version appeared in the Jan. 4, 1883 Peabody [Kansas] Gazette:

THE MAN-EATING TREE.

A Tale of Nubia.

Peregrine Oriel, my maternal uncle, was a great traveler, as his prophetical sponsors at the font seemed to have guessed he would be. Indeed he had rummaged in the garrets and cellars of the earth with something more than ordinary diligence. But in the narrative of his travels he did not, unfortunately, preserve the judicious caution of Xenophon between the things seen and the things heard, and thus it came about that the town-councilors of Brunsbüttel (to whom he had shown a duckbilled platypus, caught alive by him in Australia) had him posted for an importer of artificial vermin.

Thus, for instance, who could hear and believe the tale of the man-sucking tree from which he had barely escaped with life? He called it himself more terrible than the Upas. "This awful plant, that rears its splendid death-shade in the central solitude of a Nubian fern forest, sickens by its unwholesome humors all vegetation from its immediate vicinity, and feeds upon the wild beasts that, in the terror of the chase or the heat of noon, seek the thick shelter of its boughs; upon the birds that, flitting across the open space, come within the charmed circle of its power, or innocently refresh themselves from the cups of its great waxen flowers; upon even man himself when, an infrequent prey, the savage seeks its asylum in the storm, or turns from the harsh foot-wounding sword-grass of the glade to pluck the wondrous fruit that hang plumb down among the wondrous foliage." And such fruit!— "glorious golden ovals, great honey drops, swelling by their own weight into pear-shaped translucencies. The foliage glistens with a strange dew, that all day long drips on to the ground below, nurturing a rank growth of grasses, which shoot up in places so high that their spikes of fierce blood-fed green show far up among the deep-tinted foliage of the terrible tree, and, like a jealous body-guard, keep concealed the fearful secret of the charnel-house within, and draw round the bleak roots of the murderous plant a decent screen of living green."

Such was his description of the plant; and the other day, looking it up in a botanical dictionary, I find that there is really known to naturalists a family of carnivorous plants; but I see that they are most of them very small, and prey upon little insects only. My maternal uncle, however, knew nothing of this, for he died before the discovery of the sundew and pitcher plants; and, grounding his knowledge of the man-sucking tree simply on his own terrible experience of it, explained its existence by theories of his own.

"How," he would ask, "can we claim for man the consequence of perceptions, and yet deny to beasts, that hear, see, feel and taste, a percipient principle coexistent with their senses? And if in the whole range of the animate world there is this gift of self-defense against extirpation and offense against weakness, why is the inanimate world, holding as fierce a struggle for existence as the other, to be left defenseless and unarmed? And I deny that it is. The Brazilian epiphyte strangles the tree and sucks out its juices. The tree, again, to starve off its vampire parasite, withdraws its juices into its roots, and, piercing the ground in some new place, turns the current of its sap into other growths. The epiphyte then drops off the dead boughs on to the fresh, green sprouts springing from the ground beneath it, and so the fight goes on. Again, look at the Indian peepul tree, and the fierce yearning of its roots toward the distant well.

"Is the sensitive plant unconscious? I have walked for miles through plains of it, and watched, till the watching almost made me afraid lest the plant should pluck up courage and turn upon me, the green carpet paling into silver gray beneath my feet, and fainting away all round me as I walked. So strangely did I feel the influence of this universal aversion that I would have argued with the plant; but what was the use? If only I stretched out my hands the mere shadow of the limb terrified the vegetable to sickness; shrubs crumbled up at every commencement of my speech, and at my periods great sturdy looking bushes, to whose robustness I had foolishly appealed, sank in pallid supplication. Not a leaf would keep me company. A breath went forth from me that sickened life. My mere presence paralyzed life, and I was glad at last to come out among a less-timid vegetation, and to feel the resentful spear-grass retaliating on the heedlessness that would have crushed it. The vegetable world, however, has its revenges. You may keep the guineapig in a hutch, but how will you pet the basilisk? The little sensitive plant in your garden amuses your children (who will find pleasure also in seeing cockchafers spin round on a pin), but how could you transplant a vegetable that seizes the running deer, strikes down the passing bird, and, once taking hold of him, sucks the carcass of man himself, till his matter becomes as vague as his mind, and all his animate capabilities cannot snatch him from the terrible embrace of an inanimate tree?

The Unnatural History of Man-Eating Plants

"Many years ago," said my uncle, "I turned my restless steps toward Central Africa, made the journey from where the Senegal empties itself into the Atlantic to the Nile, skirting the Great desert, and reaching Nubia on my way to the eastern coast. I had with me then three native attendants—two of them brothers, the third, Otona, a young savage from the gaboon uplands, a mere lad in his teens; and, one day, leaving my mule with the two men, who were pitching my tent for the night, I went on with my gun, the boy accompanying me, toward a fern forest, which I saw in the near distance. As I approached it I found the forest was cut into two by a wide glade; and, seeing a small herd of the common antelope, an excellent beast in the pot, browsing their way along the shaded side, I crept after them. Though ignorant of their real danger the herd was suspicious, and, slowly trotting along before me, enticed me for a mile or more along the verge of the fern growths. Turning a corner I suddenly became aware of a solitary tree growing in the middle of the glade—one tree alone. It struck me at once that I had never seen a tree exactly like it before; but, being intent upon venison for my supper, I looked at it only long enough to satisfy my first surprise at seeing a single plant of such rich growth flourishing luxuriantly in a spot where only the harsh fern-canes seemed to thrive.

"The deer, meanwhile, were midway between me and the tree, and looking at them I saw they were going to cross the glade. Exactly opposite them was an opening in the forest, in which I should certainly have lost my supper; so I fired into the middle of the family as they were filing before me. I hit a young fawn, and the rest of the herd, wheeling round in their sudden terror, made off in the direction of the tree, leaving the fawn struggling on the ground. Otona, the boy, ran forward at my order to secure it, but the little creature, seeing him coming, attempted to follow its comrades, and at a fair pace held on their course. The herd had meanwhile reached the tree, but suddenly, instead of passing under it, swerved in their career, and swept round it at some yards distance.

Africa

"Was I mad, or did the plant really try to catch the deer? On a sudden I saw, or thought I saw, the tree violently agitated, and, while the ferns all round were standing motionless in the dead evening air, its boughs were swayed by some sudden gust toward the herd, and swept, in the force of their impulse, almost to the ground. I drew my hand across my eyes, closed them for a moment, and looked again. The tree was as motionless as myself!

"Toward it, and now close to it, the boy was running in excited pursuit of the fawn. He stretched out his hands to catch it. It bounded from his eager grasp. Again he reached forward, and again it escaped him. There was another rush forward, and the next instant boy and deer were beneath the tree.

"And now there is no mistaking what I saw.

"The tree was convulsed with motion, leaned forward, swept its thick-foliaged boughs to the ground, and enveloped from my sight the pursuer and the pursued; I was within 100 yards, and the cry of Otona from the midst of the tree came to me in all the clearness of its agony. There was then one stifled, strangling scream, and except for the agitation of the leaves where the tree had closed upon the boy, there was not a sign of life.

"I called out, 'Otona!' No answer came. I tried to call out again, but my utterance was like some wild beast smitten at once with sudden terror and its death-wound. I stood there changed from all semblance of a human being. Not all the terrors of earth together could have made me take my eye from the awful plant, or my foot off the ground. I must have stood thus for at least an hour, for the shadows had crept out from the forest half across the glade before that hideous paroxysm of fear left me. My first impulse then was to creep stealthily away, lest the tree should perceive me, but my returning reason bade me approach it. The boy might have fallen into the lair of some beast of prey, or it might be the terrible life in the tree was that of some great serpent among its

Illustration of the Madagascar Man-Eating Tree from the Ripley-like, one-panel comic strip "Wrong Again!" Published in the Mar. 28, 1930 Boston Globe. Included here on a Fair Use, educational basis.

branches. Preparing to defend myself, I approached the
silent tree, the harsh grass crisping under my feet with a
strange loudness, the cicadas in the forest shrilling till
the air seemed throbbing round me with waves of sound. The
terrible truth was soon before me in all its awful
novelty.

"The vegetable first discovered my presence at about fifty
yards' distance. I then became aware of a stealthy motion
among the thick-lipped leaves, reminding me of some wild
beast slowly gathering itself up from long sleep, a vast
coil of snakes in restless motion. Have you ever seen bees
hanging from a bough—a great cluster of bodies, bee
clinging to bee—and by striking the bough or agitating the
air caused that massed life to begin sulkily to
disintegrate, each insect asserting its individual right
to move? And do you remember how, without one bee leaving
the pensile cluster, the whole became gradually instinct
with sullen life and horrid with multitudinous motion?

"I came within twenty yards of it. The tree was quivering
through every branch, muttering for blood, and, helpless
with rooted feet, yearning with every branch toward me. It
was that terror of the deep sea which the men of the
northern fiords dread, and which, anchored upon some
sunken rock, stretches into vain space its longing arms,
pellucid as the sea itself and as relentless—maimed
Polypheme groping for his victims.

"Each separate leaf was agitated and hungry. Like hands,
they fumbled together, their fleshy palms curling upon
themselves and again unfolding, closing on each other and
falling apart again—thick, helpless fingerless hands
(rather lips or tongues than hands), dimpled closely with
little cup-like hollows. I approached nearer and nearer,
step by step, till I saw that these soft horrors were all
of them in motion, opening and closing incessantly.

"I was now within ten yards of the farthest reaching
bough. Every part of it was hysterical with excitement.
The agitation of its members was awful—sickening, yet
fascinating. In an ecstasy of eagerness for the food so

near them, the leaves turned upon each other. Two, meeting, would suck together, face to face, with a force that compressed their joint thickness to a half, thinning the two leaves into one; now grappling in a volute like a double shell, writhing like some green worm; and at last, faint with the violence of the paroxysm, would slowly separate, falling apart as leeches gorged drop off the limbs. A sticky dew glistened in the dimples, welled over and trickled down the leaf. The sound of it, dripping from leaf to leaf, made it seem as if the tree were muttering to itself. The beautiful golden fruit, as they swung here and there, were clutched now by one leaf and now by another, held for a moment close enfolded from the sight, and then as suddenly released. Here a large leaf, vampire-like, had sucked out the juices of a smaller one. It hung limp and bloodless, like a carcass of which the weasel has tired.

"I watched the terrible struggle till my starting eyes, strained by intense attention, refused their office, and I can hardly say what I saw. But the tree before me seemed to have become a live beast. Above me I felt conscious was a great limb, and each of its thousand clammy hands reached downward toward me, fumbling. It strained, shivered, rocked and heaved. It flung itself about in despair. The boughs, tantalized to madness with the presence of flesh, were tossed to this side and to that, in the agony of a frantic desire. The leaves were wrung together as the hands of one driven to madness by sudden misery. I felt the vile dew spurting from the tense veins fall upon me. My clothes began to give out a strange odor. The ground I stood on glistened with animal juices.

"Was I bewildered by terror? Had my senses abandoned me in my need? I know not—but the tree seemed to me to be alive. Leaning over toward me, it seemed to be pulling up its roots from the softened ground, and to be moving toward me. A mountainous monster, with myriad lips, mumbling together for life, was upon me!

Africa

"Like one who desperately defends himself from imminent
death, I made an effort for life, and fired my gun at the
approaching horror. To my dizzied senses the sound seemed
far off, but the shock of the recoil partially recalled me
to myself, and, starting back, I reloaded. The shot had
torn their way into the soft body of the great thing. The
trunk, as it received the wound, shuddered, and the whole
tree was struck with a sudden quiver. A fruit fell down—
slipping from the leaves, now rigid with swollen veins, as
from carven foliage. Then I saw a large arm slowly droop,
and without a sound it was severed from the juice-fattened
bole, and sank down softly, noiselessly, through the
glittering leaves. I fired again, and another vile
fragment was powerless—dead. At each discharge the
terrible vegetable yielded a life. Piecemeal I attacked
it, killing here a leaf and there a branch. My fury
increased with the slaughter till, when my ammunition was
exhausted, the splendid giant was left a wreck—as if some
hurricane had torn through it. On the ground lay heaped
together the fragments, struggling, rising and falling,
gasping. Over them drooped in dying languor a few stricken
boughs, while upright in the midst stood, dripping at
every joint, the glistening trunk.

"My continued firing had brought up one of my men on my
mule. He dared not (so he told me) come near me, thinking
me mad. I had now drawn my hunting-knife, and with this
was fighting—with the leaves. Yes but each leaf was
instinct with a horrid life; and more than once I felt my
hand entangled for a moment, and seized as if by sharp
lips. Ignorant of the presence of my companion, I made a
rush forward over the fallen foliage, and, with a last
paroxysm of frenzy, drove my knife up to the handle into
the soft bole, and, slipping on the fast-congealing sap,
fell exhausted and unconscious among the still panting
leaves.

"My companions carried me back to the camp, and, after
vainly searching for Otona, awaited my return to
consciousness. Two or three hours elapsed before I could
speak, and several days before I could approach the

terrible thing. My men would not go near it. It was quite dead; for, as we came up, a great-billed bird, with gaudy plumage, that had been securely feasting on the decaying fruit, flew up from the wreck. We removed the rotting foliage, and there among the dead leaves, still limp, with juices, and piled round the roots, we found the ghastly relics of many former meals, and—its last nourishment—the corpse of little Otona. To have removed the leaves would have taken too long, so we buried the body as it was, with a hundred vampire leaves still clinging to it."—*Philip Robinson's "Under the Sun."*

Philip Stewart Robinson was an Indian-born British naturalist, journalist and popular author, who the Boston Globe once called "The Prince of Humorists." Robinson's 1882 book "Under the Sun" contains loving sketches of Eastern animals, the places, people and customs of India, and a potpourri of other subjects. The Globe glowingly praised "Under the Sun" as a "rich treasury of culture, literary art and humor." The book contains the same "Man-Eating Tree" story that was published later in newspapers, with the addition of a footnote by Robinson acknowledging that many readers would regard the story as incredible and deserving of ridicule. However, he points out that credulity is not of itself shameful or contemptible, and invites readers to measure their own wisdom or unwisdom in believing the story as they please. Robinson also included the story in his 1888 book, "Under the Punkah," and his 1902 book, "Tales By Three Brothers."

CARNIVOROUS CACTUS

Another fearsome African vegetable predator was revealed in the May 24, 1904 Freeport [Illinois] Daily Bulletin. It sounds like a cross between Joe Mulhatton's Magnetic Cactus and the Devil's Snare of Nicaragua. [See the North America and Central America chapters, respectively.]:

A TREE THAT FEEDS ON FLESH.

Man Eating Cactus Used to Execute Criminals in West Africa.

"THE LEAVES CLOSE ABOUT THE VICTIM."

The Unnatural History of Man-Eating Plants

A remarkable flesh eating or cannibal tree has been found on the west coast of Africa. The tree is shaped like a giant cactus, and the natives in the region where it is found use it for the purpose of executing criminals and prisoners of war.

The method of execution is unique. A stage is built close to the tree, and then the prisoner is led to the platform and thrown among the branches. The moment the flesh touches the leaves of the tree they close about him like so many snakes and begin slowly to assimilate his flesh. Not a fragment of the body remains after a few days.

AL-MUSANĀ & WĀQ-WĀQ

"The Book of Curiosities" was written in Arabic by an anonymous author in 11th Century Fatimid Egypt (North Africa and West Asia). It is an educational, entertaining treatise containing beautifully illustrated maps of the Earth and heavens, along with several chapters focused on bizarre animals and plants found in foreign lands. Oxford University's Bodleian Library purchased one of the only surviving copies in 2002 and has since published it digitally alongside English annotations.

Among the oddities of the vegetable kingdom catalogued in "The Book of Curiosities" is Al-musanā, said to grow in the lands of the Sudan in the environs of Kawkaw (presumably the modern city of Gao). It functioned as an instrument of divine justice. The branches of the tree were said to hang down loosely. If anyone sat down in the tree's midst and undertook a false oath before "the Master of the Heavens," the branches intertwined around the person until they died. But if the person swore truthfully, the branches did not coil around them.

There are numerous shockingly strange flora and fauna described in "The Book of Curiosities," including a tree that cuts directly to the undercurrent of aberrant sexuality present in many Man-Eating Tree accounts, dispensing of the "middle man" of a female human sacrifice. Wāq Wāq Trees are said to reside on Wāq-Wāq Island, which borders on "Sofalah, one of the Islands of the Zanj" (coastal Southeast Africa). The Wāq Wāq Tree bears fruit that resemble women, suspended by their hair as if by green cords.

Illustration of the Wāq Wāq Tree from the Kitāb al-Bulhān (Book of Wonders), a 14th-15th Century, illustrated Arabic manuscript covering subjects such as astronomy, astrology, geomancy and folklore. Image scan courtesy of Oxford University's Bodleian Library.

The Unnatural History of Man-Eating Plants

According to the book, "They have breasts, female sexual organs, and curvaceous bodies, and they scream 'wāq wāq'. When one of them is cut off the tree, it falls down dead and does not talk any more. Their insides and outsides, their faces and their limbs, are entirely made of something resembling the down of a feather. When a person advances further into the island, he finds a tree with more attractive fruits with plumper posteriors, bosoms, genitalia, and faces, which scream louder than the ones described above. If this fruit is cut off, it survives for a day or part of a day before it stops talking and screaming. The person who cuts down this second type of fruit may sometimes have sexual intercourse with it and derive pleasure from it."

Wāq-Wāq Island appears throughout medieval Arabic geographical and imaginative literature. Like Themiscyra, Wāq-Wāq Island was said to be ruled by a queen and populated exclusively by women. In this context, the Wāq Wāq Tree explains how the residents of Wāq-Wāq Island asexually perpetuated themselves. Scholars have identified the people of this island, the Waqwaq or Wakwak, as possibly being, in reality, the Javanese or the Malay of the Srivijaya empire (who were based on Sumatra but began migrating to Madagascar in the 9th Century). One of these groups is thought to have invaded the coast of Tanganyika and Mozambique in 945–946 AD, inspiring myths about the Wāq-Wāq Island nation. The tale of a mysterious tree growing in that location fittingly dovetails with Java and Madagascar being home to the most legendary Cryptobotanical trees of all time, the Poison Upas and Crinoida Dajeeana, respectively.

***

Though considered a myth by many, Crinoida Dajeeana— Cryptobotany's most infamous plant— and its carnivorous relatives continue to fascinate 150-plus years on. Of course, there are tales of Man-Eating Plants the world over... Let's go meet them!

SOURCES:

"3 Weird Mysteries of Madagascar." *American Weekly*, 11 Oct. 1942, p. 4.

"1930 Believe It or Not #2 Vitaphone Short." *YouTube*, uploaded by BetaGems Lost Media, 5 Sep. 2021, https://youtu.be/ZfbZJP8lHkQ?si=rilmvP-wgKAEA0l1.

"*Adansonia*." *Wikipedia*, https://en.wikipedia.org/wiki/Adansonia. Accessed 22 Jun. 2025.

The Air Force List, London, His Majesty's Stationery Office, March 1941.

"al-Wakwak." *Wikipedia*, https://en.wikipedia.org/wiki/Al-Wakwak. Accessed 28 Aug. 2025.

"The American Weekly." *Wikipedia*, https://en.wikipedia.org/wiki/The_American_Weekly. Accessed 24 Aug. 2025.

Amory, Arthur R. "The Undying Tale." *Daily Express* [London], 7 Feb. 1924, p. 6.

"Apocynaceae." *Wikipedia*, https://en.wikipedia.org/wiki/Apocynaceae. Accessed 18 Sep. 2025.

"Asa Gray." *University of Cambridge Darwin Correspondence Project*, https://www.darwinproject.ac.uk/asa-gray.

Bedekar, V. M. "Reviewed Work: Writing and Speeches of Dr. Bhau Daji by T. G. Mainkar." *Annals of the Bhandarkar Oriental Research Institute*, vol. 56, no. 1/4, 1975, pp. 252-254.

"Bhau Daji." *Wikipedia*, https://en.wikipedia.org/wiki/Bhau_Daji. Accessed 30 Aug. 2025.

Blake Price, Cheryl. "Vegetable Monsters: Man-Eating Trees in Fin-de-Siècle Fiction." *Victorian Literature and Culture*, vol. 41, no. 2, 2013, pp. 311-327.

"Book of Curiosities." *Wikipedia*, https://en.wikipedia.org/wiki/Book_of_Curiosities. Accessed 26 Aug. 2025.

"Book of Wonders." *Wikipedia,* https://en.wikipedia.org/wiki/Book_of_Wonders. Accessed 26 Aug. 2025.

Boyd, Stanley. "The Bhau Daji Treatment of Leprosy." *British Journal of Dermatology,* vol. 5, July 1893, pp. 203-209.

"*Brocchinia reducta.*" *Royal Botanical Gardens Kew: Plants of the World Online.* https://powo.science.kew.org/taxon/urn:lsid:ipni.org:names:122255-1. Accessed 24 Aug. 2025.

"*Brocchinia reducta.*" *Wikipedia,* https://en.wikipedia.org/wiki/Brocchinia_reducta. Accessed 24 Aug. 2025.

"Bromelain." *Wikipedia,* https://en.wikipedia.org/wiki/Bromelain. Accessed 24 Aug. 2025.

"Bromeliaceae." *Wikipedia,* https://en.wikipedia.org/wiki/Bromeliaceae. Accessed 24 Aug. 2025

Browne, William Hand. Letter to Edward Spencer. 20 May 1874. *William Hand Browne Papers,* Johns Hopkins Libraries, MS-0011.

Campbell, Gwyn. *An Economic History of Imperial Madagascar, 1750-1895: The Rise and Fall of an Island Empire.* Cambridge University Press, 2005.

"*Cerbera manghas.*" *Wikipedia,* https://en.wikipedia.org/wiki/Cerbera_manghas. Accessed 17 Aug. 2025.

"Chronological List of the Publications of Asa Gray." *Harvard University Herbaria & Libraries,* https://www.huh.harvard.edu/book/publications.

Clute, Willard M. "Man-Eating Trees." *American Botanist,* vol. 31, no. 2, April 1925, pp. 70-73.

"Crinoid." *Wikipedia,* https://en.wikipedia.org/wiki/Crinoid. Accessed 17 Aug. 2025.

"Crinoida Dajeeana." *Daily Chronicle & Sentinel* [Augusta, GA], 10 May 1874, p. 1.

"Crinoida Dajeeana." *World* [New York], 28 Apr. 1874, p. 7.

"Current Literature." *Wikipedia,* https://en.wikipedia.org/wiki/Current_Literature. Accessed 24 Aug. 2025.

Dahle, L. "Geographical Fictions with Regard to Madagascar." *Antananarivo Annual and Madagascar Magazine,* no. 8, 1884.

Dajee, Bhawoo. *An Essay on Female Infanticide.* Bombay, Government Press, 1847.

Darwin Correspondence Project, "Letter no. 9455," accessed on 24 August 2025, https://www.darwinproject.ac.uk/letter/?docId=letters/DCP-LETT-9455.xml.

Darwin Correspondence Project, "Letter no. 9480," accessed on 11 June 2025, https://www.darwinproject.ac.uk/letter/?docId=letters/DCP-LETT-9480.xml.

Darwin Correspondence Project, "Letter no. 9492," accessed on 24 August 2025, https://www.darwinproject.ac.uk/letter/?docId=letters/DCP-LETT-9492.xml.

"Darwin in Letters, 1874: A Turbulent Year." *University of Cambridge Darwin Correspondence Project,* https://www.darwinproject.ac.uk/letters/darwins-life-letters/darwin-letters-1874-turbulent-year. Accessed 14 Jun. 2025.

"Death of Edward Spencer." *Sun* [Baltimore], 18 Jul. 1883, p. 1.

Decary, R. "Some spreading or noxious plants of Madagascar." *Journal d'Agriculture Tropicale,* vol. 12, no. 6/7/8, 1965, pp. 343-350. Abstract: https://www.cabidigitallibrary.org/doi/full/10.5555/19672301738. Accessed 23 Jun. 2025.

"Dr. Bhau Daji Lad Museum." *Wikipedia*, https://en.wikipedia.org/wiki/Dr._Bhau_Daji_Lad_Museum. Accessed 30 Aug. 2025.

Du Puy, David. "The Leguminosae of Madagascar." *Curtis's Botanical Magazine*, vol. 14, no. 4, Nov. 1997, pp. 231-241.

"Elphinstone College." *Wikipedia*, https://en.wikipedia.org/wiki/Elphinstone_College. Accessed 30 Aug. 2025.

"*Erythrophleum couminga*." *Wikipedia*, https://en.wikipedia.org/wiki/Erythrophleum_couminga. Accessed 23 Jun. 2025.

Fathman, Liz. The Missouri Botanical Garden in Madagascar. *Missouri Botanical Garden*, 2013.

"Fighting for a Fortune." *Kansas City Star* [Kansas City, MO], 13 Apr. 1896, p. 6.

"Forthcoming Marriages." *Daily Telegraph & Morning Post* [London], 8 Aug. 1947, p. 4.

"Frederick M. Somers Dead." *Kansas City Star* [Kansas City, MO], 3 Feb. 1894, p. 1.

"Girl-Eating Tree." *Witness* [Belfast, Ireland], 12 Aug. 1932, p. 3.

"Gao." *Wikipedia*, https://en.wikipedia.org/wiki/Gao. Accessed 26 Aug. 2025.

Gray, Asa. "Insectivorous Plants, I." *Nation*, no. 457, 2 Apr. 1874, pp. 216-217.

Gray, Asa. "Insectivorous Plants, II." *Nation*, no. 458, 9 Apr. 1874, pp. 232-234.

"Great Moon Hoax." *Wikipedia*, https://en.wikipedia.org/wiki/Great_Moon_Hoax. Accessed 18 Sep. 2025.

Green, Lawrence G. *These Wonders to Behold*. Cape Town, South Africa, The Standard Press Ltd., 1959.

Africa

Guhl, Kevin J. "An Exploration of Shoddy & Sensational 19th Century Journalism." *American Strangeness*, 6 Apr. 2025, https://thunderbirdphoto.com/f/an-exploration-of-shoddy-sensational-19th-century-journalism. Accessed 21 Aug. 2025.

"Gustav Eisen." *Wikipedia*, https://en.wikipedia.org/wiki/Gustav_Eisen. Accessed 18 Sep. 2025.

Heckel, Dr. Édouard. *Les Plantes Médicinales et Toxiques de Madagascar: Avec Leurs Noms et Leurs Emplois Indigènes (Catalogue Alphabétique et Raisonné)*. Marseille, France, Institut Colonial, 1903.

"History of *Pachypodium*." *Wikipedia*, https://en.wikipedia.org/wiki/History_of_Pachypodium. Accessed 5 Sep. 2025.

"Huge Flea Lives in Madagascar." *Los Angeles Times*, 8 Dec. 1927, p. 6.

"Ivan Mackerle." *Wikipedia*, https://en.wikipedia.org/wiki/Ivan_Mackerle. Accessed 23 Jun. 2025.

"Jamsetjee Jejeebhoy." *Wikipedia*, https://en.wikipedia.org/wiki/Jamsetjee_Jejeebhoy. Accessed 30 Aug. 2025.

"Jejeebhoy Baronets." *Wikipedia*, https://en.wikipedia.org/wiki/Jejeebhoy_baronets. Accessed 30 Aug. 2025.

"John Samuel Miller." *Wikipedia*, https://en.wikipedia.org/wiki/John_Samuel_Miller. Accessed 17 Aug. 2025.

Kelly, Kate. "Robert Ripley Brought an Expanded World to Audiences." *America Comes Alive!*, https://americacomesalive.com/robert-ripley-brought-an-expanded-world-to-audiences/. Accessed 23 Jul. 2025.

Kitāb Gharā'ib al-funūn wa-mulaḥ al-'uyūn (The Book of Curiosities). Oxford, Bodleian Library MS. Arab. c. 90:

https://digital.bodleian.ox.ac.uk/objects/748a9d50-5a3a-440e-ab9d-567dd68b6abb/.

Ley, Willy. *Salamanders and Other Wonders, Still More Adventures of a Romantic Naturalist.* Viking Press, 1955.

Lindley, John. "Pachypódium tuberósum." *Edwards's Botanical Register*, vol. 16, 1830.

"Literature of the Week." *Boston Daily Globe*, 17 Sep. 1882. p. 3.

Mabberley, D. J. *The Plant-Book.* Cambridge University Press, 1997.

Mackal, Roy P. *Searching for Hidden Animals.* Doubleday & Company, Inc. 1980.

Mackerle, Ivan. "Lidožrout, Nebo Jenom Zabiják?" *MACKERLE – expedice*, https://mackerle-expedice.cz/lidozrout-nebo-jenom-zabijak/, 11 Apr. 2021, Archived: https://web.archive.org/web/20240616035243/https://mackerle-expedice.cz/lidozrout-nebo-jenom-zabijak/. Accessed 22 Jun. 2025.

"Madagascar & Mauritius." *Jisc Archives Hub*, https://archiveshub.jisc.ac.uk/search/archives/938794da-7729-319a-86bd-a827477c176b?component=5199c191-3d77-32eb-a928-4adc7a7a469b. Accessed 22 Aug. 2025.

"Madagascar's Man-Eating Tree." *Montgomery Advertiser* [Montgomery, AL], 16 May 1924, p. 4.

McCord, Garrett. "The Curious Flesh Eating Enzymes in Pineapple and Papaya." *The Spruce Eats*, 21 Sep. 2019, https://www.thespruceeats.com/flesh-eating-enzymes-of-pineapple-and-papaya-4047013. Accessed 24 Aug. 2025.

"Man-Eating Tree of Madagascar." *Antananarivo Annual and Madagascar Magazine*, no. 5, 1881.

"The Man-Eating Tree of Madagascar." *Daily Inter-Ocean* [Chicago], 2 May 1874, p. 8.

Africa

"The Man-Eating Tree of Madagascar." *Museum of Hoaxes,* https://hoaxes.org/archive/permalink/man_eating_tree_of_mada gascar. Accessed 14 Jun. 2025.

"Mystery of the Man Eating Tree of Madagascar." *Pittsburgh Press,* 19 Oct. 1924, American Weekly supplement, p. 7.

"Mystery of the Man-Eating Tree." *John Bull* [London], 17 Sep. 1932, p. 19.

"Mystery of the Man Eating Tree of Madagascar." *Pittsburgh Press* [Pittsburgh, PA], 19 Oct. 1924, American Weekly supplement, p. 7.

Nadler, Georgia. "Madagascar---Land of Fantastic Tales." *Plain Dealer* [Cleveland], 5 Nov. 1942, p. 8.

"No Man-Eating Tree." *Punxsutawney Spirit* [Punxsutawney, PA], 29 Nov. 1930, p. 2.

"Notes." *Nation,* no. 463, 14 May 1874, pp. 314-316.

"Obituary: Edward Spencer." *New York Times,* 18 Jul. 1883, p. 4.

Osborn, Chase Salmon. *Madagascar: Land of the Man-Eating Tree.* Republic Publishing Company, 1924.

"*Pachypodium.*" *Wikipedia,* https://en.wikipedia.org/wiki/Pachypodium. Accessed 5 Sep. 2025.

"*Pachypodium lamerei.*" *Wikipedia,* https://en.wikipedia.org/wiki/Pachypodium_lamerei. Accessed 5 Sep. 2025.

Pavlovič, Andrej and Michaela Saganová. "A Novel Insight into the Cost–Benefit Model for the Evolution of Botanical Carnivory." *Annals of Botany,* no. 115, 2015, pp. 1075-1092. https://pmc.ncbi.nlm.nih.gov/articles/PMC4648460/.

Pavlovic˘, Andrej, et al. "Trap Closure and Prey Retention in Venus Flytrap (Dionaea muscipula) Temporarily Reduces Photosynthesis and Stimulates Respiration." *Annals of Botany,* no. 105, 2010, pp. 37-44.

"Philip Stewart Robinson." *Wikipedia,* https://en.wikipedia.org/wiki/Philip_Stewart_Robinson. Accessed 17 May 2025.

"Pineapple." *Wikipedia,* https://en.wikipedia.org/wiki/Pineapple. Accessed 24 Aug. 2025.

"Plant 160: Pachypodium lamerei Drake (Apocynaceae)." *Oxford Plants 400,* https://herbaria.plants.ox.ac.uk/bol/plants400/Profiles/OP/Pachypodium. Accessed 5 Sep. 2025.

"Protocarnivorous Plant." *Wikipedia,* https://en.wikipedia.org/wiki/Protocarnivorous_plant. Accessed 5 Oct. 2025.

"*Puya chilensis.*" *Wikipedia,* https://en.wikipedia.org/wiki/Puya_chilensis. Accessed 5 Sep. 2025.

Quisenberry, W. G. "British Scientific Party to Seek Man-Eating Tree." *Washington Herald* [Washington, D.C.], 18 Aug. 1932, p. 5.

Ripley. "Believe It or Not." *Arizona Republican* [Phoenix], 8 Aug. 1924, p. 13.

"Ripley Is Coming Here, Believe It or Not!" *Toronto Daily Star,* 15 Sep. 1932, p. 2.

"Ripley's Believe It or Not! (Vitaphone Shorts)." *Wikipedia,* https://en.wikipedia.org/wiki/Ripley%27s_Believe_It_or_Not!_(Vitaphone_shorts). Accessed 23 Jul. 2025.

Robb, George L. "The Ordeal Poisons of Madagascar and Africa." *Botanical Museum Leaflets,* Harvard University, vol. 17, no. 10, 18 Mar. 1957, pp. 265-316.

Robinson, Phillip. "The Man-Eating Tree." *Citizen* [Battle Creek, MI], 13 Jan. 1883, p. 6.

Robinson, Phillip. "The Man-Eating Tree." *Peabody Gazette* [Peabody, KS], 4 Jan. 1883, p. 2.

Robinson, Phil, et al. *Tales By Three Brothers.* Isbister and Company Limited, 1902.

Robinson, Phil. *Under the Punkah.* London, Sampson Low, Marston, Searle, & Rivington Limited, 1888.

Robinson, Phil. *Under the Sun.* Boston, Roberts Brothers, 1882.

"San Francisco Brevities." *Oakland Evening Tribune* [Oakland, CA], 14 Mar. 1877, p. 4.

Shaw, George A. *Madagascar and France with Some Account of the Island, Its People, Its Resources and Development.* London, William Clowes and Sons, Limited, 1885.

Shuker, Karl P.N., Ph.D. *The Beasts That Hide from Man.* Paraview Press, 2003.

Shuker, Dr. Karl. "The Madagascan Man-Eating Tree - More than Just a Monstrous Myth?" *ShukerNature*, 8 Nov. 2012, https://karlshuker.blogspot.com/2012/11/the-madagascan-man-eating-tree-more.html. Accessed 23 Jun. 2025.

Shuker, Dr. Karl. Personal correspondence, 12 Jun. 2025.

"Sir Jamsetjee Jeejeebhoy." *Royal Collection Trust*, https://www.rct.uk/collection/618774/sir-jamsetjee-jeejeebhoy. Accessed 30 Aug. 2025.

"Sofala." *Wikipedia*, https://en.wikipedia.org/wiki/Sofala. Accessed 26 Aug. 2025.

"Some Plant Myths." *American Botanist*, vol. 9, no. 1, Jul. 1905, pp. 11-12.

Spencer, Edward. Letters to William Hand Browne. 28 Apr., 3 & 17 May 1874. *Edward Spencer Papers*, Johns Hopkins Libraries, MS-0149.

"Srivijaya." *Wikipedia*, https://en.wikipedia.org/wiki/Srivijaya. Accessed 26 Aug. 2025.

Stimpson, George W. *Popular Questions Answered.* George Sully & Company, Inc., 1930.

Stradling, Jan. *Bad Girls.* Pier 9, 2008.

Sun [Baltimore], 18 Oct. 1888, p. 2.

"Taxon: *Pachypodium rosulatum* Baker." *USDA, Agricultural Research Service, National Plant Germplasm System.* Germplasm Resources Information Network (GRIN Taxonomy). National Germplasm Resources Laboratory, Beltsville, Maryland, https://npgsweb.ars-grin.gov/gringlobal/taxon/taxonomydetail?id=410790. Accessed 5 Sep. 2025.

Taylor, Bayard. "Life in Bombay." *New-York Daily Tribune*, 19 Apr. 1853, p. 6.

Thone, Dr. Frank. "Plants that Kill Animals and Devour their Flesh." *Sunday Star Magazine* [Washington, D.C.], 16 Jul. 1933, p. 11.

"To Solve the Mystery of Madagascar's Man-Eating Tree?" *American Weekly*, 13 Nov. 1932, p. 9.

"A Tree that Feeds on Flesh." *Freeport Daily Bulletin* [Freeport, IL], 24 May, 1904, p. 7.

Twain, Mark. Letter to Jerome B. Stillson, 23 Mar. 1874. *Mark Twain Project: The Letters of Mark Twain*, https://www.marktwainproject.org/letters/uccl02469/. Accessed 18 Sep. 2025.

"*Uncarina grandidieri.*" *Exotic Plants*, https://www.exotic-plants.de/seeds/caudiciforms/Uncarina-grandidieri.php. Accessed 23 Jun. 2025.

"*Uncarina grandidieri* (Mouse Trap Tree)" *Tropical Plant Encyclopedia*, https://toptropicals.com/catalog/uid/uncarina_grandidieri.htm. Accessed 22 Jun. 2025.

VampiricDemon. "Should the Tepe Tree, the Kumanga and Andrindritra Still Be Considered Cryptids?" *Reddit*, 28 May, 2023, https://www.reddit.com/r/Cryptozoology/comments/13v1swk/should_the_tepe_tree_the_kumanga_and_andrindritra/.

"Venus Flytrap." *National Wildlife Federation.* https://www.nwf.org/Educational-Resources/Wildlife-Guide/Plants-and-Fungi/Venus-Flytrap, Accessed 5 Sep. 2025.

"Venus Flytrap." *Wikipedia*, https://en.wikipedia.org/wiki/Venus_flytrap. Accessed 24 Aug. 2025.

Wheeler, Edward J., editor. *Current Literature*, vol. LIII, July-December 1912, Current Literature Publishing Company.

Who Was Who 1929-1940. London, Adam & Charles Black, 1967.

"William Hand Browne papers." *John Hopkins Libraries*, https://aspace.library.jhu.edu/repositories/3/resources/16. Accessed 18 Sep. 2025

Wilson, Dr. Andrew. "Science Jottings." *Illustrated London News*, 24 Sep. 1892, vol. 101, no. 2788, p. 403.

"Wonderful Stories—The Man-Eating Tree" (and Editorial Notes). *Current Literature*, vol. 1, no. 2, Aug. 1888, pp. 109, 154-155.

"Yellow Journalism: The 'Fake News' of the 19th Century." *Public Domain Review*, 21 Feb. 2017, https://publicdomainreview.org/collection/yellow-journalism-the-fake-news-of-the-19th-century/. Accessed 8 Feb. 2025.

"Zanj." *Wikipedia*, https://en.wikipedia.org/wiki/Zanj. Accessed 26 Aug. 2025.

ASIA

UPAS, THE POISON TREE OF JAVA

The island of Java in Indonesia is the setting for a story that is, in many ways, the grand-daddy of Man-Eating Plant legends. Nearly a century before the New York World announced the voracious presence of Crinoida Dajeeana in Madagascar, London Magazine stunned readers with a detailed report on the poisonous Upas Tree of Java. Unlike the Man-Eating Tree of Madagascar, the Vampire Vine and other rapacious floral predators of later centuries, the Upas neither ate its victims nor actively killed them. But it was no less powerful, deadly, feared and revered. And unlike any of those other botanical monsters, the Upas Tree was undoubtedly real. (More or less.)

The reason we will delve so deeply into the tangled branches of the Upas tale is that it was deeply influential in world culture and clearly inspired the later stories explored in this book. All the building blocks are there—courageous European explorers, the untamed jungles of a distant land, and a fearsome vegetable monster worshipped by native inhabitants.

As described by surgeon N. P. Foersch (translated from Dutch) in the December 1783 London Magazine, the Bohon-Upas or Poison Tree of Java was said to stand at the center of a barren, lifeless zone up to 18 miles wide, its lethal vapors killing all surrounding plants and any animals that ventured near. The tree's gum, extracted from beneath the bark, was so deadly that it was used to coat the blades of weapons and poison water supplies in times of war, providing a lucrative revenue for the Emperor. Only condemned criminals, given protective leather hoods and gloves, were sent to collect it—most never returned. Foersch claimed to have seen catalogues of hundreds so sent, witnessed executions where lancets tipped with Upas gum killed in minutes, and conducted animal experiments confirming its rapid, violent effects. Local legend held that the tree sprang from divine punishment for ancient sins, and that the Malayans regarded death by its poison as honorable. Though some details strained credulity, Foersch insisted he had seen the barren wasteland, heard accounts of a community devastated after settling too near, and concluded the Upas held the most dangerous vegetable poison known to man.

I've pieced together the saga of the Upas Tree from numerous sources, many of them obscure and some unavailable in English. We shall start with the full article in London Magazine, all the way back in December 1783...

NATURAL HISTORY.

THE following description of the BOHON UPAS, or POISON-TREE, which grows in the island of Java, and renders it unwholesome by its noxious vapours, has been procured for the London Magazine, from Mr. Heydinger*, who was employed to translate it from the original Dutch, by the author, Mr. Foersch, who, we are informed, is at present abroad, in the capacity of surgeon on board an English vessel.

This account, we must allow, appears so *marvellous*, that even the Credulous might be flaggered. The readers of this narrative will probably think of the celebrated Psalmanazar, and his equally famous History of the Island of Formosa. But this narrative certainly merits attention and belief. The degree of credibility which is due to the several circumstances rests with Mr. Foersch. With regard to the principal parts of the relation, there can be no doubt. The existence of the tree, and the noxious powers of its gums and vapours, are certain. For the story of the *thirteen* concubines, however, we should not choose to be responsible.

Travellers and naturalists have mentioned trees of the same destructive nature in other places, and particularly, if we are not mistaken, in some parts of South America. This very Bohon-Upas is mentioned by the learned Kemptfer [Engelbert Kaempfer-Ed.], but its situation, its nature, and its destructive qualities, have never been so clearly, so fully, or so philosophically described, as by the author of the following description.

It may probably be asked, why no efforts have been made to destroy so dreadful a tree?—more dreadful, indeed, in its effects, than the union of plague, pestilence, and famine. The reasons are obvious. No man could venture to remain near it for so long a space of time as would be requisite to cut down a tree of such magnitude; nor could materials to set it on fire be carried to the place without almost certain destruction. But of all the arguments, the most forcible probably is, that the Emperor derives a very considerable revenue from the sale of the gum which is distilled from the Bohon-Upas. The *auri sacra fames!* the rage for possessing riches, is too powerful to be withstood, even in the most cultivated ages, and among the most polished nations! What then can be expected from an inhabitant of Java, and that man an Emperor! Who, like Achilles,

"Jura neget sibi nata, nihil non arroget [armis]!"

*Formerly a German bookseller near Temple-Bar.

DESCRIPTION OF THE POISON-TREE, IN THE ISLAND OF JAVA.

BY N. P. FOERSCH

TRANSLATED FROM THE ORIGINAL DUTCH, BY MR. HEYDINGER.

THIS destructive tree is called in the Malayan language, BOHON-UPAS, and has been described by naturalists. But their accounts have been so tinctured with the *marvellous*, that the whole narration has been supposed to be an ingenious fiction by the generality of readers. Nor is this in the least degree surprising, when the circumstances which we shall faithfully relate in this description are considered.

Illustration of the Poison Tree, or Upas, of Java, with Rafflesia flower in the foreground, by Auguste Faguet, published in J. W. Buel's "Sea and Land," 1887.

The Unnatural History of Man-Eating Plants

I must acknowledge, that I long doubted the existence of this tree, until a stricter enquiry convinced me of my error. I shall now only relate simple, unadorned facts, of which I have been an eye-witness. My readers may depend upon the fidelity of this account. In the year 1774, I was stationed at Batavia, as a surgeon in the service of the Dutch East-India Company. During my residence there I received several different accounts of the Bohon-Upas, and the violent effects of its poison. They all then seemed uncredible to me, but raised my curiosity in so high a degree, that I resolved to investigate this subject thoroughly, and to trust only to *my own observations*. In consequence of this resolution, I applied to the Governor-General, Mr. Petrus Albertos can der Parra, for a pass to travel through the country. My request was granted, and having procured every information, I set out on my expedition. I had procured a recommendation from an old Malayan priest to another priest, who lives on the nearest inhabitable spot to the tree, which is about fifteen or sixteen miles distant. The letter proved of great service to me in my undertaking, as that priest is appointed by the Emperor to reside there, in order to prepare for eternity the souls of those who for different crimes are sentenced to approach the tree, and to procure the potion.

The *Bohan-Upas* is situated in the island of *Java*, about twenty-seven leagues from *Batavia*, fourteen from *Soura-Charta*, the seat of the Emperor, and between eighteen and twenty leagues from *Tiukjoe*, the present residence of the Sultan of Java. It is surrounded on all sides by a circle of high hills and mountains, and the country round it, to the distance of ten or twelve miles from the tree, is entirely barren. Not a tree, not a shrub, nor even the least plant or grass is to be seen. I have made the tour all around this dangerous spot, at about eighteen miles distant from the center, and I found the aspect of the country on all sides equally dreary. The easiest ascent of the hills, is from that part where the old ecclesiastic dwells. From his house the criminals are sent for the poison, into which the points of all warlike instruments are shipped. It is of high value, and produces a considerable revenue to the Emperor.

ACCOUNT OF THE MANNER IN WHICH THE POISON IS PROCURED.

THE POISON which is procured from this tree, is a gum that issues out between the bark and the tree itself, like the *camphor*. Malefactors, who for their crimes are sentenced to die, are the only persons who fetch the poison; and this is the only chance they have of saving their lives. After sentence is pronounced upon them by the judge, they are asked in court, whether they will die by the hands of the executioner, or whether they will go to the Upas tree for a box of poison. They commonly prefer the latter proposal, as there is not only some chance of preserving their lives, but also a certainty, in case of their safe return, that a provision will be made for them in future, by the Emperor. They are also permitted to ask a favour from the Emperor, which is generally of a trifling nature, and commonly granted. They are then provided with a silver or tortoiseshell box, in which they are to put the poisonous gum, and are properly instructed how to proceed while they are upon their dangerous expedition. Among other particulars, they are always told to attend to the direction of the winds; as they are to go towards the tree before the wind, so that the effluvia from the tree are always blown from them. They are told, likewise, to travel with the utmost dispatch, as that is the only method of insuring a safe return. They are afterwards sent to the house of the old priest, to which place they are commonly attended by their friends and relations. Here they generally remain some days, in expectation of a favourable breeze. During that time, the ecclesiastic prepares them for their future fate by prayers and admonitions.

When the hour of their departure arrives, the priest puts them on a long leather cap with two glasses before their eyes, which comes down as far as their breast, and also provides them with a pair of leather gloves. They are then conducted by the priest, and their friends and relations, about two miles on their journey. Here the priest repeats his instructions, and tells them where they are to look for the tree. He shews them a hill, which they are told to ascend; and that on the other side they will find a rivulet, which they are to follow, and which will conduct them directly to the Upas. They now take leave of each other, and amidst prayers for their success, the delinquents hasten away.

The worthy old ecclesiastic has assured me, that during his residence there, for upwards of thirty years, he had dismissed above seven hundred criminals in the manner which I have described; and that scarcely two out of twenty have returned. He shewed me a catalogue of all the unhappy sufferers, with the date of their departure from his house annexed, and a list of the offences for which they had been condemned. To which was added the names of those who had returned in safety. I afterwards saw another list of these culprits, at the gaol-keeper's at *Soura Charta*, and found that they perfectly corresponded with each other, and with the different informations which I afterwards obtained.

I was present at some of those melancholy ceremonies, and desired different delinquents to bring with them some pieces of the wood, or a small branch, or some leaves of this wonderful tree. I have also given them silk cords, desiring them to measure its thickness. I never could procure more than two dry leaves, that were picked up by one of them on his return; and all I could learn from him concerning the tree itself, was, that it stood on the border of a rivulet, as described by the old priest, that it was of a middling size, that five or six young trees of the same kind stood close by it; but that no other shrub or plant could be seen near it; and that the ground was of a brownish sand, full of stones, almost impracticable for travelling, and covered with dead bodies. After many conversations with the old Malayan priest, I questioned him about the first discovery, and asked his opinion of this dangerous tree, upon which he gave me the following answer in his own language:

*"Ditalm kita ponjoe Alcoran Baron Suda tulis touloe
Seratus an Soeda jlang orang Soeda Dengal disenna orang
jabat di Soeda main Same Die punje pinatang pigidoe kita
pegi Sam prambuange."*

Which may be thus translated:

"We are told in our New Alcoran, that, above an hundred
years ago, the country around the tree was inhabited by a
people strongly addicted to the sins of Sodom and
Gomorrhà. When the great prophet Mahomet determined not to
suffer them to lead such detestable lives any longer, he
applied to God to punish them; upon which God caused this
tree to grow out of the earth, which destroyed them all,
and rendered the country for ever uninhabitable."

Such was the Malayan's opinion. I shall not attempt a
comment, but must observe, that all the Malayans consider
this tree as an holy instrument of the great prophet to
punish the sins of mankind, and, therefore, to die of the
poison of the Upas is generally considered among them as
an honourable death. For that reason I also observed, that
the delinquents, who were going to the tree, were
generally dressed in their best apparel.

This, however, is certain, though it may appear
incredible, that from fifteen to eighteen miles round this
tree, not only no human creature can exist; but that, in
that space of ground, no living animal of any kind has
ever been discovered. I have also been assured by several
persons of veracity, that there are no fish in the waters,
not has any rat, mouse, or any other vermin been seen
there; and when any birds fly so near this tree, that the
effluvia reaches them, they fall a sacrifice to the
effects of the poison. This circumstance has been
ascertained by different delinquents, who, in their
return, have seen the birds drop down, and have picked
them up *dead*, and brought them to the old ecclesiastic.

I will here mention an instance which proves this is a
fact beyond all doubt, and which during my stay
at Java.

The Unnatural History of Man-Eating Plants

In the year 1775 a rebellion broke out among the subjects of the Massay, a sovereign prince, whose dignity is nearly equal to that of the Emperor. They refused to pay a duty imposed upon them by their sovereign, whom they openly opposed. The Massay sent a body of a thousand troops to disperse the rebels, and to drive them, with their families, out of his dominions. Thus four hundred families, consisting of above sixteen hundred souls, were obliged to leave their native country. Neither the Emperor nor the Sultan would give them protection, not only because they were rebels, but also through fear of displeasing their neighbor, the Massay. In this distressful situation, they had no other resource than to repair to the uncultivated parts round the Upas, and requested permission of the Emperor to settle there. Their request was granted, on condition of their fixing their abode not more than twelve or fourteen miles from the tree, in order not to deprive the inhabitants already settled there at a greater distance of their cultivated lands. With this they were obliged to comply: but the consequence was, that in less than two months their number was reduced to about three hundred. The chiefs of those who remained returned to the Massay, informed him of their losses, and intreated his pardon, which induced him to receive them again as his subjects, thinking them sufficiently punished for their misconduct. I have seen and conversed with several of those who survived, soon after their return. They all had the appearance of persons tainted with an infectious disorder; they looked pale and weak, and from the account which they gave of the loss of their comrades, of the symptoms and circumstances which attended their dissolution, such as convulsions, and other signs of a violent death, I was fully convinced that they fell victims to the poison.

The violent effect of the poison, at so great a distance from the tree, certainly appears surprising, and almost incredible; and especially when we consider, that it is possible for delinquents who approach the tree, to return

Antiaris toxicaria. Photo by Dinesh Valke from Thane, India, CC BY-SA 2.0, via Wikimedia Commons.

alive. My wonder, however, in a great measure, ceased, after I had made the following observations:

I have said before, that malefactors are instructed to go to the tree with the wind, and to return against the wind. When the wind continues to blow from the same quarter while the delinquent travels thirty, or six and thirty miles, if he be of a good constitution he certainly survives. But what proves the most destructive is, that there is no dependance on the wind in that part of the world for any length of time. There are no regular land winds; and the sea wind is not perceived there at all, the situation of the tree being at too great a distance, and surrounded by high mountains and uncultivated forests. Besides, the wind there never blows a fresh regular gale, but is commonly merely a current of light, soft breezes, which pass through the different openings of the adjoining mountains. It is also frequently difficult to determine from what part of the globe the wind really comes, as it is divided by various obstructions in its passage, which easily change the direction of the wind, and often totally destroy its effects.

I, therefore, impute the distant effects of the poison, in a great measure, to the constant gentle winds in those parts, which have not power enough to disperse the poisonous particles. If high winds were more frequent and durable there, they would certainly weaken very much, and even destroy the obnoxious effluvia of the poison; but without them, the air remains infected and pregnant with these poisonous vapours.

I am the more convinced of this, as the worthy ecclesiastic assured me that a dead calm is always attended with the greatest danger, as there is a continual perspiration issuing from the tree, which is seen to rise and spread in the air, like the putrid steam of a marshy cavern.

EXPERIMENTS MADE WITH THE GUM OF THE UPAS-TREE.

IN the year 1776, in the month of February, I was present at the execution of thirteen of the Emperor's concubines, at *Soura-Charta*, who were convicted of infidelity to the Emperor's bed. It was in the forenoon, about eleven o'clock, when the fair criminals were led into an open space within the walls of the Emperor's palace. There the judge passed sentence upon them, by which they were doomed to suffer death by a lancet poisoned with Upas. After this, the Alcoran was presented to them, and they were, according to the law of their great prophet Mahomet, to acknowledge and to affirm by oath, that the charges brought against them, together with the sentence, and their punishment, were fair and equitable. This they did, by laying their right hand upon the Alcoran, their left hands upon their breast, and their eyes lifted towards heaven; the Judge then held the Alcoran to their lips, and they kissed it.

These ceremonies over, the executioner proceeded on his business in the following manner: — Thirteen posts, each about five feet high, had been previously erected. To these the delinquents were fastened, and their breasts stripped naked. In this situation they remained a short time in continual prayers, attended by several priests, until a signal was given by the judge to the executioner; on which the latter produced an instrument, much like the spring lancet used by farriers for bleeding horses. With this instrument, it being poisoned with the gum of the Upas, the unhappy wretches were lanced in the middle of their breasts, and the operation was performed upon them all in less than two minutes.

My astonishment was raised to the highest degree, when I beheld the sudden effects of the poison, for in about five minutes after they were lanced, they were taken with a *tremor*, attended with a *subsultus tentinum*, after which they died in the greatest agonies, crying out to God and Mahomet for mercy. In fifteen minutes by my watch, which I held in my hand, all the criminals were no more. Some hours after their death I observed their bodies full of livid spots, much like those of the *Petechiae*, their faces swelled, their colour changed to a kind of blue, their eyes looked yellow, &c. &c.

About a fortnight after this, I had an opportunity of seeing such another execution at Samarang. Seven Malayans were executed there with the same instrument, and in the same manner, and I found the operation of the poison, and the spots in their bodies exactly the same.

[WARNING: The next two paragraphs contain detailed, horrible descriptions of animal experimentation.-Ed.]

These circumstances made me desirous to try an experiment with some animals, in order to be convinced of the real effects of this poison; and as I had then two young puppies, I thought them the fittest objects for my purpose. I accordingly procured with great difficulty some grains of Upas. I dissolved half a grain of that gum in a small quantity of arrack, and dipped a lancet into it. With this poisoned instrument, I made an incision in the lower muscular part of the belly of one of these puppies. Three minutes after it received the wound, the animal began to cry out most piteously, and ran as fast as possible from one corner of the room to the other. So it continued during six minutes, when all its strength being exhausted, it fell upon the ground, was taken with convulsions, and died in the eleventh minute. I repeated this experiment with two other puppies, with a cat and a fowl, and found the operation of the poison in all of them the same, none of these animals survived above thirteen minutes.

I thought it necessary to try also the effect of the poison given inwardly, which I did in the following manner. I dissolved a quarter of a grain of the gum in half an ounce of arrack, and made a dog of seven months old drink it. In seven minutes a reaching [retching?-Ed.] ensued, and I observed, at the same time, that the animal was delirious, as it ran up and down the room, fell on the ground, and tumbled about; then it rose again, cried out very loud, and in about half an hour after was seized with convulsions, and died. I opened the body, and found the stomach very much inflamed, as the intestines were in some parts, but not so much as the stomach. There was a small quantity of coagulated blood in the stomach, but I could discover no orifice from which it could have issued, and therefore, supposed it to have been squeezed out of the lungs, by the animal's straining while it was vomiting.

From these experiments I have been convinced, that the gum of the Upas is the most dangerous and most violent of all vegetable poisons; and I am apt to believe that it greatly contributes to the unhealthiness of that island. Nor is this the only evil attending it, hundreds of the natives of Java, as well as Europeans, are yearly destroyed and treacherously murdered by that poison, either internally or externally. Every man of quality or fashion has his dagger or other arms poisoned with it; and in times of war the Malayans poison the springs and other waters with it; by this treacherous practice, the Dutch suffered greatly during the last war, as it occasioned the loss of half their army. For this reason, they have ever since kept fish in the springs of which they drink the water; and centinels are placed near them, who inspect the waters every hour, to see whether the fish are alive. If they march with an army or body of troops into an enemy's country, they always carry live fish with them, which they throw into the water, some hours before they venture to drink it, by which means they have been able to prevent their total destruction.

This account, I flatter myself, will satisfy the curiosity of my readers, and the few facts which I have related will be considered as a certain proof of the existence of this pernicious tree, and its penetrating effects.

If it be asked why we have not yet any more satisfactory accounts of this tree, I can only answer, that the object of most travelers to that part of the world consists more in commercial pursuits than in the study of Natural History and the advancement of sciences. Besides, Java is so universally reputed an unhealthy island, that rich travelers seldom make any long stay in it, and others want money, and generally are too ignorant of the language to travel, in order to make inquiries. In future, those who visit this island will probably now be induced to make it an object of their researches, and will furnish us with a fuller description of this tree.

I will, therefore, only add, that there exists also a sort of Cajoe-Upas on the coast of Macassar, the poison of which operates nearly in the same manner; but is not half so violent and malignant as that of Java, and of which I shall likewise give a more circumstantial account in a description of that island.

J. N. FOERSCH.

[We shall be happy to communicate any authentic papers of Mr. Foersch to the public, through the channel of the London Magazine.]

***

British poet and naturalist Erasmus Darwin helped to perpetuate the lore of the Upas when he included and treated the Foersch account seriously in his 1791 book, "The Botanic Garden, Part II: The Loves of the Plants." His grandson, naturalist and evolutionary theory pioneer Charles Darwin, would later help fuel public fascination with carnivorous flora via the publication of his 1875 book, "Insectivorous Plants."

American naturalist Thomas Horsfield, who conducted extensive research in Indonesia, including the island of Java, during the early 19th century, took great issue with the story of the Upas Tree that had been circulating widely in print since the London Magazine article in 1783. In 1814, he wrote an essay addressed to Sir Thomas Stamford Raffles, his friend and then the British lieutenant governor of Java, dispelling the wilder myths about the Upas tree and expounding on its true nature based on his first-hand investigation. Horsfield used the alternative spelling of "Oopas" for the tree.

"The literary and scientific world has in few instances been more grossly and impudently imposed upon than by the account of the *Pohon Oopas*, published in Holland about the year 1780. The history and origin of this celebrated forgery still remains a mystery. *Foersch*, who put his name to the Publication, certainly was (according to information I have received from creditable persons who have long resided on the Island) a Surgeon in the Dutch East India Company's service, about the time the account of the Oopas appeared. It would be in some degree interesting to become acquainted with his character. I have been led to suppose that his literary abilities were as mean as his contempt of truth was consummate," Horsfield wrote witheringly. "Having hastily picked up some vague information concerning the Oopas, he carried it to Europe, where his notes were arranged, doubtless by a different hand, in such a form, as by their plausibility and appearance of truth, to be generally credited."

Horsfield noted that, "*Foersch* was a Surgeon of the third class at Samarang in the year 1773. His account of the Oopas Tree appeared in 1783."

Along with misrepresentations of the island's geography and leaders, Horsfield wrote that Foersch presented the Upas Tree as a much greater danger than it actually is in its natural state. Horsfield wrote that the Antshar or Oopas Tree, as he called it [*Antiaris toxicaria*-Ed.], grows on the Eastern extremity of Java. It is one of the largest trees in the forest, its cylindrical trunk rising "completely naked" to a height of between 60-80 feet into a hemispherical crown of branches and leaves. Native inhabitants indeed tapped the bark of the Upas for its milky white sap, which they compounded with additional spices into a deadly poison that they used on spear tips which delivered the toxin into a victim's bloodstream. However, Horsfield said that the tree spreading its deadly poison into the air was a myth, as was a barren field around it filled with dead bodies. Horsfield said that the bark of the tree, when wet, and the ejection of effluvia into the air when an Upas was felled caused no more than mild skin and eye irritation.

In addition, Horsfield suggested that Foersch consulted an earlier account of the Upas in the fabrication of his story, that being "Herbarium Amboinense," a catalogue of Indonesian flora published in 1741. The author was Georg Eberhard Rumphius, a German-born botanist employed by the Dutch East India

Company. Rumphius studied plant life in what is now eastern Indonesia during the 17th Century. Horsfield noted that this scientific work was itself "mixed with many assertions and remarks of a fabulous nature."

Writing about "Arbor Toxicaria. Ipo." in the second volume of "Herbarium Amboinense," Rumphius stated [translated from Latin], "I have not yet found a more horrible and detestable poison produced by any vegetable than that which is collected from this milky tree." Rumphius wrote that the toxin wasn't a serious threat to humans unless mixed with the juice of the Lampoejang, aka bitter ginger, and introduced to the bloodstream. But he pointed out that, "Nature... has separated this noxious tree far from the habitations of men."

Rumphius added that, in order for the Upas poison to be more harmful, natives immediately cut down the tree with long axes after extracting its sap. The indigenous belief was that if the tree itself died, all opponents wounded with poison-tipped weapons would also perish. If the tree was allowed to live, the poison would gradually lose its strength [as it naturally would over time-Ed.]. Rumphius suspected that this practice would have been carried out with few established trees, as it would have greatly diminished their population.

In his account of the Upas, Rumphius falls somewhere between the sensationalism of Foersch and the grounded description of Horsfield, possibly because Rumphius wasn't relaying first-hand information. He owned samples of the branches, but apparently did not collect them himself.

"Under this tree also no plants, shrubs or grass grow its entire circumference, nay, not even within a stone's throw, and the ground is barren, barren, and as if it were exhausted. The most pernicious species of this tree bear as an indication of its malignancy, that the feathers and plumes of birds are found under it, for the air around this tree is so infectious and poisonous, that birds, sitting on its branches, become dizzy and fall dead; its branches, transmitted to me in a large bamboo reed, were so effective and caustic that if hands were placed on the reed, they would immediately tingle, almost in the same way as frozen limbs are warmed. Everything also perishes that is touched by its breath, so that even all animals avoid the tree, nor do they pass it, and indeed birds avoid flying over it," Rumphius wrote. "No man dares to approach it unless he has his arms, feet, and head wrapped in linen, otherwise it soon causes a severe tingling of the joints, from which they become stiff and lose their strength. Its drops falling on someone's body make it swollen, and no one can stand with his head exposed to this tree without suffering a loss of hair."

It is clear how Foersch might have simply read Rumphius' work and amplified the traits of the Upas. Rumphius makes short mention of condemned persons being administered Upas poison via a nick on the thumb or foot on the orders of Makassarian kings, unlike the elaborate rituals Foersch presents regarding executions and condemned men being sent to gather the tree's noxious sap.

It should be noted that the 18th Century references to the Javanese as Makassarian appears to be a broad use of the term, as the Makassar people are in actuality concentrated in the Indonesian province of South Sulawesi.

In writing his book, Rumphius himself might have consulted an earlier source, "Amoenitatum Exoticarum," a natural science work published in 1712 by German physician and world traveler Engelbert Kaempfer. It appears likely to have been a source for Foersch, as well.

"The scorching heat of the sun among the tropics, not only intensifies and sharpens the salutary virtues of natural things, but also the deleterious quality of poisons, more than under the colder zones of the sky. For who, to omit other things, is not astonished at the rapid malignancy of the sap of the Maccassarian tree, with which, infected by a weapon, at the slightest contact with blood, they suddenly extinguish life like a lamp?" wrote Kaempfer, who spent time on Java in the 1690s.

Translated from Latin, Kaempfer wrote of the Upas:

For in order to search for a tree, places infested with bushes and wild animals must be penetrated; but once found, unless it is wounded from a distance, it will suddenly suffocate the attackers with a burst of breath from that side from which the wind is blowing or the breeze is blowing. Birds are also said to experience this fate when they fly over a recently wounded tree. The collection of the deadly liquid is committed to those condemned to death for the evil they have done, on the condition that the punishment be remitted if they bring back the liquid. Therefore, returning from Scylla to Charybdis, they undertake this work with great caution and circumspection. Namely, they enter the forest equipped with a long reed, of that large and robust kind with which they build their homes, which they sharpen at the other end... with an ax, so that it is able to pierce the bark of the tree. They attack the tree, seen from afar, with the wound that we have warned about. Then, standing as far away from the tree as they can, they forcefully insert the edge of the reed into the tree, and extract as much of the liquid, flowing from the wound, as far as it can reach through the hollow of the reed up to the nearest internode. Loaded with this spoil, they retreat against the wind, and soon, standing in a shallow place beyond the exhalation of the wound, they pour the liquid into a glass vessel, but with equal caution, and close it. They bring it back... and offer it to the King [for their lives]. Thus told me the people of Celebani, now called Macassar. But who can relate anything true from the mouth of Asiatics that is not mixed with fiction? It is certain that the King of Macassar, and the rest of his princes... used to infect their lances and tainted their lances and daggers (with which alone they were armed) with that deadly juice, but which from the surrounding air, unless the weapons were well covered, softens with time; not so easily if it sticks to the crevices of the weapons (more densely packed).

The July 31, 1858 edition of Scientific American offered an alternative explanation for the nightmarish Upas tree known from Foersch's account:

An exchange says the story that the Upas tree of Java exhales a poisonous aroma, the breathing of which causes death, is now known to be false. The tree itself secretes a juice which is deadly poison, but its aroma or odor is harmless. Strychnine is made from the seeds of a specie of Upas tree. Such is the name of a district the atmosphere of which produces death. This effect is not occasioned by the Upas tree, but by an extinct volcano near Batar, called Guava Upas. From the old crater and the adjoining valley is exhaled carbonic gas, such as often extinguishes life in this country in old wells and foul places. This deadly atmosphere kills everything that comes within its range—birds, beasts and even men—and the valley is covered with skeletons. By a confusion of names, the poisonous effects of this deadly valley have been ascribed to the Upas tree, the juice of which is poisonous, and hence the fable in regard to the deadly Bohun Upas tree.

Indonesia has approximately 150 volcanoes, with 127 of them considered active. Java itself has a high concentration of volcanic activity, with 45 active volcanoes noted on the island. There is a Mount Batar on Bali (to the immediate east of Java), an active volcano whose first recorded eruption was in 1804.

"There are very few popular beliefs of any duration, however extravagant or incredible, that cannot be traced to some foundation in truth, however much distorted by ignorance, superstition or folly; and we have a remarkable instance of this in the celebrated Upas, or Poison Tree of Java, whose shade was believed to extinguish life in the unhappy beings who sought refuge under it," Lieut. Col. W. H. Sykes read to the Royal Asiatic Society of Great Britain and Ireland on March 4, 1837. He shared a letter from an Englishman and landholder in Java, Loudon, who claimed to have visited the Guwo-Upas, or Poisoned Valley, near Batur. Loudon was well-known to Horsfield and considered reliable.

"A perusal of it will, I presume, afford satisfactory reasons to conclude, that in this deadly spot originated the belief in the Poison Tree, the mistake of the mephitic vapour escaping from vegetation, rather than from the soil, being natural and probable," said Sykes. He added, "Dr. Horsfield informs me that he was at

Batur in 1815 and 1816, and aware of the vicinity of the poisonous valley, but the natives refused to conduct him to it."

Loudon wrote, in his letter to Horsfield, that he learned the existence of the "Valley of Death," located only three miles from Batur on the road from the Djung, from a Javanese chief. On July 4, 1830, Loudon and companions made an excursion to the location. They arrived at the foot of a mountain and scrambled up the side of a hill for a quarter mile, holding on to extended tree roots and branches as they navigated the steep path made slippery by heavy rains. Within a few yards of the valley, the fatigued adventurers experienced a strong, sickening, and suffocating smell. It abated as they reached the edge.

"We were now lost in astonishment at the awful scene below us," wrote Loudon. "The valley appeared to be about half a mile in circumference, oval; the depth from thirty to thirty-five feet, the bottom quite flat, and the whole covered with the skeletons of human beings, tigers, pigs, deer, peacocks, and all sorts of beasts and birds; we could not perceive any vapour, or opening in the ground, which last appeared to be of a hard sandy substance. The sides of the valley, from the top to the bottom, are covered with vegetation, trees, shrubs, &c."

Utilizing a bamboo stalk, the party descended within 18 feet of the bottom. They experienced no difficulty in breathing but were accosted by a strong odor that made them nauseous. The group then conducted experiments, sending down dogs and chickens, who died within minutes.

"On the opposite side of the valley is a large stone, near which is the skeleton of a human being, who must have perished on his back with his right arm under his head; from being exposed to the weather, the bones were bleached, and as white as ivory. I was anxious to get this skeleton, but any attempt to get at it would have been madness," wrote Loudon. "The human skeletons are supposed to have been rebels, who may have been pursued from the main road, and taken refuge in the different valleys, and a wanderer cannot know his danger, till he is in the valley, and when once there, he has not the power or presence of mind to return." Loudon's party clambered out of the valley following a two-hour stay.

Loudon did not detect the scent of sulfur in the Valley of Death, nor any appearance of an eruption ever having taken place near it. However, he knew the whole range there was volcanic, "as there are two craters at not great distance from the side of the road, at the foot of the Djring, and they constantly emit smoke."

Though admittedly having not visited the Poisoned Valley himself, Sykes felt certain that it was a volcanic crater in which the igneous action was latent and the noxious vapor was carbonic acid gas. Sykes said that there were many such volcanic craters in Italy, one called Grotta del Crane near Naples producing deadly fumes in even more toxic concentrations. The layer of nearly pure carbon dioxide accumulates only a couple feet from the ground in Grotta del Crane, mainly a threat to small animals, according to science writer Willie Ley.

"The ground of this awesome valley is littered with whitening bones." Illustration from "Java's Mysterious Valley of Death" by Charles Low, published in the May 30, 1942 Vancouver Sun. Included here on a Fair Use, educational basis.

Ley deeply researched the history of "The Tree of Death" for his 1955 book, "Salamanders and Other Wonders: Still More Adventures of a Romantic Naturalist." He felt that Sykes made a convincing argument for the mechanism of the Poison Valley, as carbon dioxide issuing from a fissure in the floor of a dead volcano is a well-known occurrence. The ringwall of a crater, such as Loudon described, would permit the gas to build up to a high and deadly concentration. Ley could find no other mention of the Poisoned Valley in Java, so he presumed it might no longer exist, as an open-air valley would clear up quickly if the source of carbon dioxide ceased. Dangerous accumulations of CO_2 in a volcanic area, opined Ley, "may well have contributed its share to the story of the Tree of Death which is so poisonous that it cannot even be approached."

The Djung in Sykes' letter is likely the Dieng Plateau, with the Javanese pronunciation of Dieng being "dijéng." It is the highest plateau on Java, and part of the Dieng Volcanic Complex at the center of the island. There are more than 20 small volcanic craters, with toxic gas being a continual hazard. In 2001, a villager named Sahmad, 40, died from inhaling poisonous gas in the Dieng mountain range. A. Djumarma Wirakusumah, director of the Vulcanology office in Bandung, blamed the tragedy on a "lack of danger zone signs put up by the local administration around the mountain." Increased levels of poisonous gas were detected at the time around three fumaroles (openings in or near a volcano, through which hot sulfurous gases emerge) in the Dieng mountain plateau, at Timbang I, Sigludug and Sinila. The carbon dioxide concentration at those fumaroles was between 40 to 70%. In the deadliest incident on record, poisonous gas from the Sinila fumarole killed 149 people on Feb. 29, 1979. The Dieng Plateau is partially within the Banjarnegara Regency in the southwestern section of Central Java, which includes the Batur district. Whether it still exists or not at the precise location, this seems to be the likely location of Loudon's "Valley of Death."

There is one fantastic ethnographic detail described by Rumphius that did not make it into later accounts—a dragon-like cryptid said to live among the Upas Trees. Doing my best to translate the passage from Latin, Rumphius wrote:

Under this tree lives a horned snake, like a rooster, running, whose eyes flash like fire at night, called in Macassar Ular Balu, which sometimes also gathers around human habitations or villages, where its roaring is often heard. Other inhabitants of Celebes describe to me the form and appearance of this snake, which lives under the Toxicaria tree, like a Basilisk, namely that it is a small animal, standing on two short legs on the front part of its body, from which it proceeds with an erect head, on which it bears a crest or horn, infecting men and birds with its breath as if with poison, from which it is killed from afar by arrows. King Lubo or Tolubo, (which is a region situated on the northern coast of Celebes at the great southern gulf) had a stone or mestica of the first described roaring snake, which was red and as if fiery; Of another animal, or Basilisk, I have a single specimen of a double scale, above of a semi-spherical shape, below flat, like a dissected ball, of an opaque crystalline color, which bore a whitish spot on one side, and in another place was described by me under the name Dracontias.

Based on this description, Ular Batu sounds rather like a mythological creature, whose fiery appearance, poisonous breath and loud roar might be a representation of volcanic activity. This could support the assertion that at some point the Upas tree became entangled with the description of a volcano and merged into one legend. (Rumphius' claim to have a scale of a similar creature is, however, rather nebulous in the text.)

The real Upas Tree, *Antiaris toxicaria*, is a member of the mulberry and fig family. It is widely distributed in tropical regions of Australia, Asia, Africa, Indonesia, the Philippines, Tonga, and various islands. "It happens to be a beautiful tall tree with a whitish bark and very 'normal'-looking foliage, without any vestige of the threatening appearance the white men indubitably expected," wrote Ley. Its red fruit is very attractive to birds, and edible. Its sap, however, is indeed toxic, and was traditionally applied to arrows, darts, and blow-darts in Southeast Asian island cultures.

The Poison Tree appealed to "philosophically minded bookworms," said Ley, because they believed that everything in nature must have its opposite. "A Tree of Death, reported to exist in the vast distance, almost seemed a philosophical necessity after the statement in the Bible that the Tree of Life had grown in Paradise and presumably still grew there, even though nobody could tell to which place Paradise had been removed by the Lord," wrote Ley.

"So nobody doubted the stories of the deathly tree, whether they came from the East or from the West."

And it was just the beginning. As Cheryl Blake Price states in "Vegetable Monsters: Man-Eating Trees in Fin-de-Siècle Fiction," "The passive upas tree was the pattern for Victorian depictions of deadly plants until the twilight of the century, when authors refigured the upas legend to create much more actively sinister plants."

MAN-KILLING TREE OF CEYLON

Despite laying claim to the infamous Poison Tree, Asia was no slouch when it came to vegetation of the man-eating variety. This 1893 American Press Association news report from Ceylon (today Sri Lanka) is a grand adventure much in the Man-Eating Tree of Madagascar style:

SOME ODD STORIES.

INTERESTING TALES OF ADVENTURE ON SEA AND LAND.

The Search For the Man Eating Tree of Ceylon and Its Fatal Termination—The Deadly Valley and Its Mystery—An English Army Officer's Story.

"It was something more than the love of sport and adventure that took me back to Ceylon for a second visit," said Major Carter of her majesty's service. "I had resolved to solve the mystery of Lieutenant Gordan's most unaccountable disappearance on that wild island five years before. Gordan was a fine fellow, young, daring and enthusiastic, with a promising future before him, and the uncertainty of his fate preyed upon my mind.

"I had often heard weird stories of the man killing tree of Ceylon, but I did not believe there was the least foundation for them. To my mind the story was a myth, for I had found a man might rest in security beneath the so called deadly upas, and yet the story of the upas was never so improbable as that of the fiendish tree said to live on flesh and blood.

"Lieutenant Gordan had shared my skepticism to a certain extent, and yet he was inclined to search for the demon tree in dark depths of the wildest jungles. He had a daring and dangerous way of rambling far into the forests, his only companions being a native guide and his dark skinned servant. More than once I told him he would provide a square meal for a tiger or some other wild animal, but he only laughed at my fears.

"One night he did not return. The guide and the servant came back, both frightened nearly to death, and they told a story that aroused our party to a high pitch of excitement. They declared Lieutenant Gordan had fallen a victim to the man eating tree, saying it was near midafternoon when they came to the mouth of a deep and dark valley, into which the venturesome young man insisted on penetrating. At the mouth of the valley the natives found a small stone idol, before which were scattered human skulls and bones. This served to warn them against entering the forbidding place, and they refused to accompany the lieutenant.

"Gordan was not daunted, and he bade them await his return, after which he boldly went down into the gloom of the place, leaving the natives mumbling and prostrating themselves before the idol.

"In about 20 minutes the guide and the servant heard a terrible shriek of fear and agony that came up from the mysterious and dismal valley. The cry was that of a human being in greatest agony, and so frightened were the natives that they instantly took to their heels and fled from the spot.

"We rebuked them for their cowardice, and all of us believed Gordan had been attacked by a wild animal or a serpent. We even entertained hope that he might put in an appearance, but the night passed and morning came without any sign of him. Then nearly the entire party set out to find the dismal valley and solve the mystery of our comrade's fate.

The Unnatural History of Man-Eating Plants

"The guide was very reluctant about leading us, but we forced him to do so. For hours we tramped about in the jungle without finding the valley, and the guide finally declared he did not know how to lead us to it. This made us very angry, and we nearly scared the fellow to death, asserting we would flay him alive if he did not take us to the place. He started on again, and we followed, but night found us unrewarded for our pains. In returning to the camp, both the guide and Gordan's servant slipped away and disappeared in the forest, and neither was seen afterward.

"This mysterious affair threw a damper on our spirits, and the hunt was far from a success. The most of the party were inclined to believe the lieutenant had been murdered by the two natives, and I thought it not improbable.

"During the five years that elapsed before I again visited Ceylon, I often thought of Jack Gordan and longed to know the truth concerning his fate. When I found myself once more in the vicinity of our former adventures, I resolved to search for the fatal valley. Captain Starbuck, a loyal friend and man with plenty of courage, agreed to accompany me, poor fellow! I was glad to have a white man as a companion, although I protested against taking him from his elephant shooting, but he professed some faith in the story of the man eating tree and expressed a desire to look upon the monster of the vegetable kingdom.

"Taking our servants along, we made a party of four, although we knew we could not depend on the blackskins in case of emergency. It was near midday of our first and final search that we came to the mouth of a valley that seemed to me like the one described by the native guide and Gordan's servant. All at once both our dusky aids flung themselves face downward on the ground and began chanting something in the most doleful tones, and then we saw they were bowed before a hideous stone image, around which were scattered bones and human skulls!

"'We have found the fatal valley!' I cried.

"It was useless to attempt to persuade the blackskins to accompany us into the gloom of the place, and they entreated us not to go there, saying we would never come forth if we ventured. Telling them to await our return and looking to make sure our weapons were ready for instant use, we entered the valley.

"A deep gloom hung over the place, which was disturbed by no sound save our footfalls and they did not seem to make an echo. As we moved slowly onward a feeling of horror gradually and surely crept over me, although I tried to throw it off. It seemed that there was something uncanny about the valley—something weird and deadly. I looked at the captain and saw his face was pale, although his jaws were set and determination was written on his features.

"In vain we looked about for sign of living creature in that dismal vale. No bird nor animal greeted our vision: not even a snake squirmed across our path. For all of the gloom, the vegetation was luxurious and rank, but the air seemed laden with perfumes that were sweet to the point of nauseation.

"In a short time we came to a wall of barren stone. A cry broke from my lips, and stooping I picked up a rusty rifle that lay at the foot of the wall. After a minute examination I asserted:

"'This was Lieutenant Gordan's gun. His initials are carved on the stock.'

"My voice sounded hollow and strange. I looked up at the rugged wall and made a motion to ascend. Captain Starbuck nodded, and we were soon climbing side by side.

"As we mounted upward a singular sound came to our ears. It was a sort of swishing or hissing, like the sound of a strong wind in rank reeds, and yet unlike it. This grew more distinct as we neared the top of the wall, and there was something blood chilling in the sound.

"The top was soon reached, and we looked over into a circular basin, in the very center of which rose a tree

IN THE DEADLY MESHES.

that was of a vividly green hue from its roots to its
highest point. And such a tree! There were no leaves upon
it, and its bare branches were round and supple, like so
many serpents. From its body to its upper limit the tree
was in motion. The slender limbs were whipping and cutting
through the air like things of life, making the hissing
sound we heard.

122

"A cry of amazement broke from Starbuck's lips. In an instant the tree was still, and every branch pointed straight at us. At that moment I lost my footing and slipped back a bit, falling below the level of the wall's highest point. I felt something knock my hat from my head, and then I heard a terrible shriek from my companion. My horrified eyes beheld a hundred twining, twisting things encircle him and snatch him from view in a twinkling. For a moment others played and squirmed over the wall as if feeling for me, and then they vanished.

"A short time I clung there, paralyzed with such horror as never possessed me before, and then I drew myself up to the top of the wall again. I can never forget the horrible sight that greeted my eyes. Captain Starbuck was in the grasp of that demon tree, the limbs of which were twined about him like serpents. Some had twisted themselves about his neck, and I saw he was already dead, having been strangled. And over the body the snaky arms of the accursed tree fought and squirmed.

"Sick and fainting with terror, I slid down to the foot of the wall and ran from that infernal spot as fast as my legs could carry me. I did not stop when I reached the mouth of the deadly valley, and the two natives, reading the truth on my face, kept me company.

"When I told the story at camp, it was received with mingled doubt and credulity. Some of the men could not bring themselves to believe such a thing possible, while others, knowing me better, did not doubt my word.

"We spent three days searching for that valley, and, singular as it may seem, it could not be found again. I do not know that it has been found to this day. But were I able to go direct to it," concluded Major Carter, "the wealth of England would not tempt me into its horrid confines!"

THE TWISTED TEMPLE TREE

The Unnatural History of Man-Eating Plants

In the 1901 volume "The Garden of Kama and Other Love Lyrics from India," poet Laurence Hope included a story attributed to Lalla-ji, the Priest. It told of a man, assisted by a child, who tended day and night to a twisted tree growing at a temple:

Story by Lalla-ji, the Priest

He loved the Plant with a keen delight,

A passionate fervour, strange to see,

Tended it ardently, day and night,

Yet never a flower lit up the tree.

The leaves were succulent, thick, and green,

And, sessile, out of the snakelike stem

Rose spine-like fingers, alert and keen,

To catch at aught that molested them.

But though they nurtured it day and night,

With love and labour, the child and he

Were never granted the longed-for sight

Of a flower crowning the twisted tree.

Until one evening a wayworn Priest

Stopped for the night in the Temple shade

And shared the fare of their simple feast

Under the vines and the jasmin laid.

He, later, wandering round the flowers

Asia

Paused awhile by the blossomless tree.

The man said: "May it be fault of ours,

That never its buds my eyes may see?

"A slip it came from the further East

Many a sunlit summer ago."

"It grows in our Jungles," said the Priest,

"Men see it rarely; but this I know

"The Jungle people worship it; say

They bury a child around its roots—

Bury it living:—the only way

To crimson glory of flowers and fruits."

He spoke in whispers; his furtive glance

Probing the depths of the garden shade.

The man came closer, with eyes askance,

The child beside them shivered, afraid.

A cold wind drifted about the three,

Jarring the spines with a hungry sound,

The spines that grew on the snakelike tree

And guarded its roots beneath the ground.

* * * *

The Unnatural History of Man-Eating Plants

After the fall of the summer rain

The plant was glorious, redly gay

Blood-red with blossom. Never again

Men saw the child in the Temple play.

Laurence Hope was the pen name of British poet Adela Florence Cory, who spent several years of her teen and young adult life in India, first as part of her family's newspaper business, then with her husband, a Bombay Army officer.

"The Garden of Kama" was Cory's first collection of verse and attained widespread popularity. Although the book was presented as a translation and arrangement of genuine and exotic Indian tales steeped in Sufi symbolism, it was later questioned if the content was not just a product of the poet's imagination.

"Just how much Laurence Hope borrowed from India, just how much she added herself from that side of her which remained English, we cannot decide, nor is it useful to pursue the question," The Saturday Review reflected in 1914 (10 years after the poet's tragic death at age 39). "With her verses... we are tempted to think of transformation of the writer rather than of translation of the written word. It is at least evident that the poet tried to delve deep into native feeling, and, with marvelous appearance of truth, gave us much more than appears on the surface."

While it is unclear if Hope based the grim tale of the tree that flowers only with the sacrifice of a child on a traditional Indian story she gleaned during her residency, there is a more recent Indian account of a carnivorous tree.

TIGER TREE

On Oct. 23, 2007, NewIndPress.com reported on the "Cow-Eating" trees of Padrame (or Padrane), near Kokkoda in the Uppinangady forest range. (Uppinangady is a town in the southwestern Indian state of Karnataka, located at the foothills of the Western Ghats mountain range and surrounded by forests.)

"Carnivorous trees grabbing humans and cattle and gobbling them up is not just village folklore," began the dispatch from Mangalore (the city today called Mangaluru). On Thursday, Oct. 18, a cow belonging to Anand Gowda was left to graze in the forests when the bovine was suddenly grabbed by the branches of a tree and pulled to the ground. Witnessing this violence, the terrified cowherd raced back to the village and enlisted Gowda and a group of townsfolk to accompany him back to the forest. Before the tree could consume its rare beef, the crowd struck numerous mortal blows upon its branches until they went limp and released the cow. Subramanya Rao, an Uppinangady range forest officer (RFO) said that the tree was called a "Pili Mara" (Tiger Tree) in native lingo. The RFO said he had personally received many complaints about cattle returning home from grazing in the evenings without tails. The following day, his field staff confirmed that they had come across a Tiger Tree in Padrane, partially felled.

SUMATRAN DEATH FLOWER

A 1905 article titled "Ferocious Cannibal Plants" (quoted here from the Dec. 17 Commercial Appeal of Memphis, Tennessee) introduced a fatal flower of Sumatra:

The subject of carnivorous and death dealing plants has enlisted the pens of imaginative writers time out of mind. Of such was the story of the upas tree of Java, published in the letter of "a Dutch physician" in the London Magazine in 1783, which hoaxed Erasmus Darwin and the world and proved to be nothing but an invention. What was long considered a myth is now proved a substantiated fact, for a plant has been discovered in Sumatra that gives out poisonous exhalations.

An intrepid Frenchman had been told by the natives of a giant lily to be found in the pathless forests of the interior that gave out death dealing fumes and after a long search he found several. The largest discovered covered an area of some sixty feet with its evil smelling growth. The spadix was over six feet high and the spiked leaves from ten to twelve feet long.

The Unnatural History of Man-Eating Plants

At sundown and about an hour before sunrise the poisonous fumes were found to be most virulent. A dog, a goat and other small animals tethered in the vicinity were found dead and cold in the morning. The discoverer himself was taken violently ill while examining this vulture among lilies. In the depths of the bell shaped flowers were found the bodies of numerous small animals and birds. So the old legend of the upas tree has in measure become verified.

This article is likely an exaggerated report on Titan arum (*Amorphophallus titanum*), also known as the Corpse Flower. Endemic to Sumatran rainforests, Titan arum was discovered in 1878 by Italian botanist Odoardo Beccari. Titan arum grows a single leaf that can span 15 feet in length. Every few years or so it will instead produce an inflorescence that can stand 10 feet tall, consisting of a spadix of flowers wrapped by a spathe that is shaped like an inverted bell. When in bloom, Titan arum produces a nauseating aroma (hence its nickname) that is detectable up to half a mile away. The scent is strongest from late evening until the middle of the night, attracting pollinators active at that time, like carrion beetles and fresh flies.

The account also bears some resemblance to *Rafflesia*, the Stinking Corpse Lily, another smelly plant which grows on Sumatra and produces flowers that have been known to reach four feet in diameter. An 1895 news feature on *Rafflesia* stated that, "The odor was not poisonous, but was well calculated to keep both man and beast at a distance."

Large Pitcher Plants such as *Nepenthes sumatrana* also grow on Sumatra. Rats and other small animals have been found drowned in *Nepenthes rajah*, which grows on Borneo, so this might help explain that gruesome element of the dangerous "giant lily."

DEATH BOWL OF INDIA

The St. Louis Globe-Democrat provided another rip-roaring jungle adventure starring a Carnivorous Tree in its Oct. 27, 1907 edition:

WOMAN EXPLORER TELLS OF "CARNIVOROUS" TREE

Asia

MLLE. LECOMTE RELATES AMAZING TALE OF CRIMINALITY PRACTICED IN INDIA.

WAS SAVED BY SOLDIERS.

Tree Squeezed Woman Like Cider Press, and Fanatics Drank Liquid.

FROM A GLOBE-DEMOCRAT STAFF CORRESPONDENT

PARIS, October 16.—Writing from Marseilles, a correspondent of the Weekly Nos Loisirs sends to his journal the following amazing story of a "carnivorous tree" in the depths of the Indian jungle which, he states, was related to him by Mlle. Marguerite Lecomte. This woman has reached France, after a lengthy journey through India and other Asiatic countries, and if her other adventures are on a par with this one, Nos Loisirs probably is correct in describing her as one of the most remarkable heroines that exist. It is stated, by the way, that a previous reference to the "carnivorous tree" described by Mlle. Lecomte was made recently by an English major in a report to his government.

According to her story, Mlle. Lecomte, who was traveling with her cousin, a war correspondent, was asleep one night in a tent on the outskirts of a forest. They had lit huge fires in a circle around the camp to keep off wild beasts, and two natives were set to keep watch and to give the alarm if anything untoward happened.

Captured by Natives.

In spite of these precautions, however, whether for want of proper watching or on account of a complicity on the part of the natives, Mlle. Lecomte awoke in the middle of the night to find on her face a wet mask which stifled her cries and caused her to faint. When she came to herself she found herself in the midst of a group of fanatic Indians, who were yelling and brandishing their arms around her. She was stretched on her back, her limbs bound with cords, and she distinguished near her another white girl, similarly bound and unconscious.

129

The Edges of the Bowl Went Together.

The dawn broke. The Indians ranged themselves in a group, seized the two girls and carried them, chanting the while a monotonous sort of funeral chant, to the foot of a giant tree without leaves and whose forbidding aspect struck terror into the heart of Mlle. Lecomte. It had only two branches, stiff like outstretched arms, and its summit was finished in the form of a large bowl, from which dripped a white sap like milk.

Mlle. Lecomte says that she saw them seize her companion and plunge her into this bowl up to her neck, and suddenly, just as the first rays of the sun fell on the tree, a horrible thing happened.

Girl's Horrible Death.

The water seemed endowed with sudden life. The edges of the bowl drew together, strangling the girl, whose face reflected the agonies of a frightful death. There were some terrible crackling noises, the whole body seemed pounded up under the effort of the sides of the tree, and a pinkish liquid, made of blood and sap, commenced to glide down the carnivorous tree.

Then, with maniacal cries, the Indians approached and, catching this horrible liquid in wooden cups, commenced to drink it, their eyes shining with ecstasy.

Mlle. Lecomte, perceiving the fate which awaited her, thought she would go mad every moment. Fortunately, the arrival of her cousin and a troop of Englishmen, well armed, dispersed the criminal fanatics. Many were killed on the spot, the tree was cut down and it threw up a spout of pinkish water with the force of a water spout. The wretched victim had lost all human form. This horrible adventure decided Mlle. Lecomte to leave India, and she has just arrived at Marseilles. She says she will marry the cousin who saved her life.

MINDANAO CANNIBAL TREE

After reading about the Man-Eating Tree of Madagascar in the pages of American Weekly in late 1924, W. C. Bryant, a well-regarded citizen and plantation owner from Bryant, Mississippi, contacted the magazine to share his own experience with a "Cannibal Tree" (cannibal in this case just meaning the consumption of human flesh) in the Philippines:

Escaped from the Embrace of the Man-Eating Tree

Mr. W. C. Bryant, Exploring in the Island Jungle of the Philippines, Tells of the Hungry Grasping Arms and Hissing Leaves of the Cannibal Tree Which Strained to Reach Him

READERS of this page will remember an extremely interesting article printed in these columns a few weeks ago about the mysterious man-eating tree of Madagascar, the big island lying off the African coast in the Indian Ocean. Former Governor Chase Salmon Osborn, of Michigan, made a journey into the island jungle to find one of these cannibal trees, but was disappointed in his search. The Governor, however, in his recent book of travels, "Madagascar," gives a fascinating description of the tree and its human sacrifices, as described in detail by a German explorer, Dr. Carl Liche.

The story of the Madagascar man-eating tree recently printed in these columns attracted the attention of Mr. W. C. Bryant, a distinguished citizen of Bryant, Miss., who had an experience with a cannibal tree in the Philippine Islands. Mr. Bryant came suddenly upon this vegetable monster in the trackless jungle of the interior of Mindanao Island, and he narrowly escaped with his life.

In September, 1906, when this Mississippi planter landed in the city of Surigao, on the northern tip of the big Philippine island of Mindanao, he had never heard of the carnivorous tree and would not have been interested if he had. The visitor was there on business, in a hurry and exasperated at the delays and obstructiveness of the natives in Manila. Every American in the hot countries feels that way at first, but he gets over it or dies.

With him were three other white men, including C. W. King, farm manager of the Scuna Valley plantation back home, a powerfully muscled man who stood six feet, two inches and loomed like a giant beside the spindly Moros. The business of the Americans was to explore certain lands between Lake Mainit and the west coast with a view to planting on a large scale.

The Tree Seemed Horribly Alive and Alert, and from All Directions the Tentacled Branches Reached for Him and He Saw in the Deadly Circle Around the Trunk the Skulls and Bones of Its Unfortunate Victims.

The Tree Seemed Horribly Alive and Alert, and from All Directions the Tentacled Branches Reached for Him and He Saw in the Deadly Circle Around the Trunk the Skulls and Bones of Its Unfortunate Victims.

In Manila old-timers, both American and Spanish, had advised against the trip, but their reasons seemed vague and would not stand analysis. What did Bryant care if the ignorant Moros shunned that area? He would get Chinese to work it, and just because the only expedition on record had never returned was no reason why the place should be taboo forever. It did not make sense to these middle-west "go-getters"—they were going through.

When prowling around the fringes of the world it is well to go armed with letters from important people to important people, and Bryant had such a one from Governor-General Luke E. Wright to Captain Frederick E. Johnston, of the local constabulary, who proved to be a hard-bitten adventurous type after the Mississippian's own heart. Captain Johnston was invaluable in getting them five carabaos, the native draft animal, with drivers and sleds and two guides. These guides, while the best on the island, were not exactly perfect. One of them, Leon, was an aged, bow-legged bag of bones, who looked like a small black ant and was ridden by every superstition known to the Pacific Ocean, but he was experienced, faithful and not immoderately dishonest. Pedro was young and strong, but a drug-addict, which apparently did not interfere with his business as long as he had plenty of the drug. Johnston also gave them the following advice:

"It is my duty to warn not to enter that country, but I hope you will disregard my advice, because I have been looking for an excuse to get in there myself."

"You mean we are going to get into trouble?" asked Bryant.

"Probably, and I'll have to send back a report together with your bones. Washington always wants bones and reports. I wonder what they do with them all."

"You don't really believe those black liars," protested Bryant.

"No," admitted the constabulary chief, "you can't believe them, and yet once in a while they are just mean enough to hand you a piece of truth, and that's where they fool you. I've been told of devils and monsters and nonsense that would make a kid laugh, but there is something out there— maybe it's only a little dinky volcano or a bit of quicksand. Don't forget to leave a trail I can follow."

The party started off cheerfully enough because the natives had been deceived as to its destination. At the headwaters of the Surigao River it became necessary to change their course, but it was done gradually, veering more and more to the westward as they approached Lake Mainit.

Old Leon became uneasy and was seen in anxious conversation with the younger guide who, serene in his drug, seemed to pay no attention until one day it was discovered that his entire supply of the stuff had been lost or stolen. No reward on earth would make him stay another hour, and home he went at a dog-trot.

Next day Leon transferred his complaints to the leader of the expedition: "No, Poidra," he protested, "no can do." All that night there was much jabbering among the natives and bright prospects of mutiny. Partly to give the impression that they were not going much further, the carabao and the more cowardly of the natives were left in camp with two white men, while Bryant, King, Leon and five pack boys went on.

Mountains began to rise, and with them mounted the old guide's warnings about diaboles, demonios, kotras and other inventions of a superstitious mind lurking just ahead. The following day he began hugging Bryant's knees and weeping on them, and repeated this gesture so often that it impeded progress until King picked up the old fellow like a child and carried him half a mile. Then the mutiny came to a head and the white men won because, scared as the natives were to go on where the diaboles were thicker, they were even less willing to go back alone without the protection of the white men and their guns.

Like men counting themselves already dead, the Moros plodded along into the foot-hills of the mountains. Noon of the next day found the party preparing its meal in the midst of a small plateau covered with tall, wiry grass, high as a man's head.

The Unnatural History of Man-Eating Plants

While the meal was cooking, Bryant decided to push forward a short distance to a knoll from which he might hope to see what was ahead, for the guide in this strange country was of little use save to cut a path with his naked bolo through the grass and ferns.

Leon went with him, his blade rhythmically mowing right and left two paces in advance. It was a windless day, without even a breath to ripple the surface of the sea of grass in which there was a notable absence of animal tracks. Not even birds were in evidence. The old man paused, listened and cocked a watery eye, full of fear and rebellion at the white man. Bryant listened and realized that he had never been in such complete silence. There was not even a rustle in the grass nor the whirr of an insect.

It was uncomfortable, and he motioned for Leon to proceed, but the old man burst into a pitiful plea to go back and fell at Bryant's knees, but the white man gave him a shove and again the swish-swish went on until a lone tree rose in their path.

The tree was perhaps 35 or 40 feet high, a compact sort of a tree with heavy, dull-green leaves lying close together with a shingly look and concealing the boughs and upper trunk. Approaching nearer, the American was impressed with several things at once. The foliage stopped all around at a beautifully even distance from the ground as if carefully trimmed by human hands, and the thick trunk stood in the centre of a perfect circle of barren ground about thirty feet in diameter.

All about this park-like opening the cogonale grass stood like a wall, but in the clearing itself not a wisp of any sort of vegetation was visible, nothing but what appeared to be a sort of volcanic ash. The air was heavy with an odor that struck an unpleasant chord in Bryant's memory, and yet to this day he cannot place it. It was an animal smell, something between that of carrion and the circus, and yet neither.

At the base of the trunk, shiny with some sort of sticky exudation, was a pile of white bones too dry to taint the atmosphere. Instead of saving himself thirty feet of unnecessary mowing, as any sensible person would, Leon started to carve himself a path around the edge. Bryant looked upon this as one more example of the stupidity and perversity which all white men have remarked in the Moro. Lazy as a dog, nevertheless when the Philippine aborigine does do anything he chooses for himself the hardest and most inefficient way.

The American did not mind. He was glad of the extra time to examine that tree. His guess was that the big, thick leaves, like a shingle roof, had made the ground barren and dead within the circle. Still some rain should have blown in. Why was the boundary so sharp?

Among the bones Bryant saw what might be a human skull and started across the open to pick it up. As he moved he noted half-consciously that a breeze must be springing up, for the leaves just above his head were beginning to undulate. A faint hissing made him look again to see if it could be a snake.

The thought was knocked out of his mind by the sudden impact of the guide's body on his back. The Moro landed with a yell, pinioned both his master's arms and tried to pull him over backward, all the time shrieking like a fiend. Bryant, certain that the man was insane, wondered gratefully why the old fool had not struck with his bolo. The American was helpless until he could free his arms, which should have been easy with this rather frail old man, but was not, because the guide fought with the strength of a maniac.

Bryant set himself to break that grip and finally loosened it enough to get one hand on his pistol and to look into his assailant's face. Leon's complexion was the dirty grey of utter terror and his bulging eyes were not looking at Bryant at all. Bryant was impelled to twist his head in the direction of that gaze and became paralyzed at what he saw. The tree was reaching for him.

The Unnatural History of Man-Eating Plants

The whole thing had changed shape and was horribly alive and alert. The dull, heavy leaves had sprung from their compact formation and were coming at him from all directions, advancing on the ends of long, vine-like stems which stretched down like the necks of innumerable geese and, now that the old man had stopped his screaming, the air was full of hissing sounds.

The leaves did not move straight at their target, but with a graceful, side-to-side sway, like a cobra about to strike. From the far side, the distant leaves were peeping and swaying on their journey around the trunk and even the treetop was bending down to join in the attack. The bending of the trunk was spasmodic and accompanied by sharp cracks.

The effect of this advancing and swaying mass of green objects was hypnotic, like the charm movements of a snake.

Bryant could not move, though the nearest leaf was within an inch of his face. He could see that it was armed with sharp spines on which a liquid was forming. He saw the heavy leaf curve like a green-mittened hand, and as it brushed his eyebrows in passing, he got the smell of it—the same animal smell that hung in the surrounding air. Another instant and the thing would have had his eyes in its sticky, prickly grasp, but either his weakness or the brown man's strength threw them both on their backs.

The charm was broken. They crawled out of the circle of death and lay panting in the grass while the malignant plant, cracking and hissing, yearned and stretched and thrashed to get at them.

The paroxysm worked up to a climax and then gradually began to subside, and Bryant, having overcome a faintness and nausea, walked with Leon to the opposite side. Immediately the commotion was set up anew and the huge organism bent its energies to grasping them from the new direction. After a more careful survey, Bryant estimated the leaves at about three inches across, roughly three times that in length and thick like a cactus. Each was on a vine-like tendril the thickness of a man's thumb and appeared to have the property of extension in length as well as uncoiling like a spring.

The bones, on second thought, he considered hardly large enough for a man, perhaps not even for a full-sized ape. There were many feathers and he was not certain that he did not see hair and fur.

The distant report of King's rifle reminding them of dinner, brought to an end the study the deadly tree. His last backward look showed it with leaves still slightly ruffled like the feathers of an angry parrot.

On the way back, Leon explained as well as he could that this was a devil-tree, a cannibal tree. Its sticky spine-covered leaves caught and smothered birds, small animals and even quite large children. The leaves sucked the juices of the body and dropped the rest to fertilize the earth for its roots.

Bryant wished to know why the natives, knowing all this, did not make a business of exterminating these murderous growths. The Philippino replied that a naked man with a bolo "no can do." This was probably not the truth. A band of Moros could easily destroy any tree if they really tried. They let them live from superstitious fear.

When Bryant reported this to Captain Johnston, he replied that he had heard of the tree and understood that it stupefied as well as held its victims by force but heretofore had always been inclined to doubt the yarns.

In one sense it is not remarkable that vegetables should eat men. It is the natural fate of humans, like all other animals, to be eaten by vegetables in the form of microbes. With a few exceptions, the microbes that sicken and kill us, as well as the putrefactive bacteria that afterward consume all but our bones, are not little animals but plants, vegetables, just as much as a tree. Only embalming and mummifying will thwart this destiny. As all animals live on vegetables or on other vegetarian animals, the microbe thus completes nature's cycle and evens up the score.

There is some evidence that such carnivorous trees may have been numerous at one time, perhaps in the carboniferous age. If so, these vegetable monsters should have come down to us in the form of myth and religion just as the great lizards have as dragons. Such is the case. Tree worship seems to have been prevalent in most parts of the world.

***

Unlike the several apparently made-up names in the Madagascar ree account, William Clarence Bryant was actually a merchant, banker and plantation owner who managed several farms in Mississippi. One of his businesses was a general store at the station in Bryant, which by 1928 was a shell of what had previously been a good-sized town. A resident of Coffeeville, Bryant was a local historian who created a dozen concrete tablets that told the area's history. Throughout his life and upon his death at age 75 in 1939, Bryant was often described as one of Mississippi and Yalobusha County's most well-liked, big-hearted and valuable citizens, a community leader who was active in state affairs.

Bryant wasn't the only adventurer to report a near-deadly encounter with the Man-Eating Tree of Mindanao. Just two years later in 1927, the Christmas Day edition of the syndicated Western Weekly Magazine regaled readers with the story of Mrs. Leona Eddison, "the only woman explorer living who has successfully met and combated the awful clutches of the man-eating cannibal tree of Mindanao Island." Eddison's late husband was stated to be one of the most intrepid explorers of his day, although we sadly do not learn his name or the manner of his demise in the following article about his wife's frightful adventure while following in his footsteps:

Trapped in Devil-Tree Tentacles

Woman Narrowly Escapes Death

Asia

Intrepid Jungle Guide Averts Horrible Fate With Sheer Heroism

By Muriel E. Eddy

TO Mrs. Leoda Eddison of San Francisco, Cal., belongs the unique distinction of being the only woman explorer living who has successfully met and combated the awful clutches of the man-eating cannibal tree of Mindanao Island, and escaped death with scarcely a scratch as a relic of her hair-raising experience.

Mrs. Eddison, whose late husband well earned the reputation of being one of the most intrepid explorers of his time, felt the urge, upon his demise, to follow in her husband's footsteps and continue explorations where he had left off. Her children were grown and she no longer had any family ties to bind her to the filial fireside.

Thus it happened that one day last spring the plucky little widow, who tips the scales at exactly 100 pounds, packed her trekking outfit and started off to begin her adventure on the long and somewhat dubious trail into the jungle lands of Mindanao Island.

Outside of having taken frequent excursions with her late husband, Mrs. Eddison knew little or nothing about the land which she was about to explore. Once he had ventured into the interior intent on discovering [illegible] and vegetable world in the confines of the Mindanao jungle, but owing to an exceptionally severe electrical storm he had been forced to turn back. It was Mrs. Eddison's firm intention to finish her husband's investigations as nearly as possible.

Auspicious Start

The plucky little woman pursued the journey alone until she reached the head waters of the Surigao River, where it became suddenly necessary for her to engage a native, or Moro, guide, as here the river changes its whole course abruptly, and to the uninitiated it is a discouraging

141

prospect to attempt to follow those swift, extremely treacherous green waters.

Sambino, the guide, experienced no difficulty in passing over the turbulent rapids until Lake Mainit was reached. Here camp was pitched in the midst of a dry plateau covered with tall, wiry grass, and Mrs. Eddison slept that night under the blood-red tropical moon undisturbed by any qualms as to the future. So far, in the vernacular of the day, everything had been "peaches."

The next day dawned blazing hot, and the Moro pleaded with his demure "boss" to abandon her explorations into the heart of the steaming jungle for at least another day. The air was unspeakably close and fetid, which foretold all too plainly to one accustomed to that climate an oncoming storm. But Mrs. Eddison was obdurate in her plans, and soon persuaded him, despite his protests, that no harm would come while he guided her on her expedition into the semi-everglades of the island.

A Strange Tree

There was not even a rustle of grass or the sound of an insect as the pair plodded along, finally reaching a junglelike growth of oddly clinging vines covered with bright scarlet blossoms and stiff, prickly, green, heart-shaped leaves. Through a labyrinth of tropical wilderness Sambino led his unfaltering companion, past the clustering flowers into a veritable forest of peculiarly shaped, moss-hung trees that stood huddled together as if in deadly fear of intruders into their hitherto un-[illegible] the jungle.

As Mrs. Eddison pondered over the unusual scene she stopped short in her tracks, as if deliberating whether or not to follow the trail further. For there, standing directly in her path, stood the queerest looking tree it had ever been her good fortune—or misfortune—to witness!

This tree stood about forty feet high, and had an amazingly mottled, or shingled, appearance. Its trunk was

swollen and distended, and the bark was ashen-colored,
covered in white, leprous patches, over which a dense
canopy of heavy, dull-green leaves clung closely together
as if hiding something extremely repellent.

Caught in the tentacles of a devil-tree, a strange jungle
growth which crushes human life, Mrs. Leoda Eddison was
snatched from the jaws of a horrible death by her brave
native guide.

The Unnatural History of Man-Eating Plants

Native Fear

Down near the foot of the tree trunk was a shiny, sticky exudation. Beneath this moisture could be seen a pile of dry, white bones, the sun-bleached bones of jungle animals, Mrs. Eddison thought, little dreaming of the near-tragedy lurking at that very moment so near herself and the Moro guide at her side.

"We go 'round dis way," came from the dry lips of the now shaking native, clutching at Mrs. Eddison's khaki skirt, while the nervous perspiration streamed down his dusky face. "Me no want you get keel. Tree eat up peoples, mebbeso."

"Why, Sam, you funny fellow. Of course, a mere tree, no matter how interesting or peculiar it may look, cannot harm us. If you're afraid, I'LL lead YOU! Come on!"

So saying, the fearless little widow swished dauntlessly through the unnaturally thick growth of congonal grass into the very heart of the ground on which stood the unknown tree. At that precise moment, a sudden and unexplainable breeze sprang up, dispelling the torrid heat of the day and causing the branches of the tree to sweep suddenly down and treat Mrs. Eddison to an unexpected, none too gentle caress. As she reached out a slender hand to grasp one of those peculiar dull green leaves to take back home as a souvenir, she perceived with horror that the foliage was undulating with increasing rapidity.

A FAINT, HISSING NOISE MADE HER START IN TERROR AS SHE RECALLED TALES OF JUNGLE REPTILES RELATED TO HER BY HER LATE HUSBAND. THEN LIKE A FLASH OF LIGHTNING THE TRUTH STRUCK HOME TO HER—THIS MYSTERIOUS TREE, WITH ITS STRANGLING TENDRILS, WAS NONE OTHER THAN THE DEATH-DEALING CANNIBAL TREE, ABOUT WHICH HER EXPLORER HUSBAND HAD OFTEN TOLD HER AND WARNED HER AGAINST! IN A TWINKLING SHE RECALLED THE DESCRIPTION OF IT WHICH HE HAD GIVEN HER, AND, TO HER INCREASED HORROR, IT TALLIED EXACTLY WITH THE TREE WHICH NOW HELD HER A PRISONER!

Asia

In vain the terrified woman sought to break away from the grasp of those slimy, talon-like tentacles which were the branches of the tree. With doubled fists she tried to fight off those living, pulsating boughs. The branches were literally reaching out for her from every direction, stretching down on their snaky stems with uncanny speed and sense of accuracy. The air was full of horrible hissing sounds, and the woman, plucky and brave though she was, felt herself involuntarily growing weak and giddy, unable to withstand the terrific strain on her nerves and body.

A Close Call

Had not Sambino, the Moro guide, had the rare presence of mind, not unusual in an aborigine of the islands, to throw his body quickly upon that of Mrs. Eddison, bearing her swiftly to the earth and out of the clutches of the tree monster, it is not at all doubtful as to what might have been her fate. No doubt her bones would now be bleaching beside those others under what is now left of that frightful man-eating cannibal tree!

Now, to add to his native superstition and dread of the "devils" supposed to be confined within that tree, the leaves commenced an attack upon Sambino, but by this time the wily Moro's anger was aroused and, not to be outwitted by a mere devil tree, he reached forth his sinewy brown hands and grasped each slippery tentacle violently and firmly, and placing them between his sharp white teeth quickly severed the leaves from their stems. As he did so a slimy, putrid, oily substance slowly trickled from each severed tentacle of the tree.

Finally Sambino, by dint of much biting and backward crawling, dragging the body of Mrs. Eddison along with him as gently as possible, managed to evade the clutches of the dripping, broken tendrils and reach the sheltering border of congonal grass, where he crouched and bathed his unconscious mistress' face with cool water from the skin pouch he carried in the emergency kit.

As soon as Mrs. Eddison had recovered consciousness she gave one look at the tree and urged her guide to aid her in retracing her steps as quickly as possible.

EVEN AS SHE LOOKED, THE HEAVENS DARKENED OMINOUSLY AND THUNDER PEALED AND ROARED THROUGH THE IMPENDING GLOOM. SUDDENLY A VIVID FLASH OF LIGHTNING RENT THE HEAVENS, AND WITH INCREDIBLE SPEED THE DAZZLING BOLT OF "HELL-FIRE," AS THE NATIVES CALL IT, STRUCK THE TREE WITH A RESOUNDING CRASH THAT ECHOED WEIRDLY THROUGH THE JUNGLE, SPELLING THE DOOM OF THAT DEATH-DEALING TREE AND CLEARING THE JUNGLE FOREVER, IT IS TO BE HOPED, OF THAT ABHORRENT GROWTH. THEN, AS IF BY MAGIC, THE HEAVENS CLEARED, LEAVING MRS. EDDISON GASPING AND PRAYING, BOTH IN THE SAME BREATH.

***

Although this fantastic tale isn't presented outright as fiction, the author was Muriel E. Eddy, who in the following decades would build a successful career as a writer in several genres, including romance, occult, biography and poetry. She was married to C. M. Eddy Jr., who was known for his horror, mystery and supernatural short stories.

The Eddys were close friends and collaborators of Cthulhu Mythos creator H. P. Lovecraft throughout the 1920s. C. M. and Lovecraft edited each other's works, and Muriel typed Lovecraft's manuscripts. The couple ultimately wrote a biography of Lovecraft, "The Gentleman from Angell Street," following his 1937 death.

Intrepid explorers Leona Eddison and her unnamed husband appear absent from the historical record, but the unusual spelling of "Eddison" offers a suggestion as to where Muriel Eddy sourced the name (aside from being similar to her own, and the plucky adventurer possibly an author-insert character). It might be an homage to E. R. Eddison, author of the 1922 high fantasy novel, "The Worm Ouroboros."

Lovecraft was a fan of Eddison's book, urging fellow writer Donald Wandrei to read the novel in a 1927 letter. "Art? Phantasy? Prose-poetry? Look & see! Man, what a style!" Lovecraft wrote. In a separate letter after Wandrei read Eddison's book, Lovecraft gushed, "Didn't you find it magnificently poetic?"

In fact, as I type this, Lovecraft's own copy of Eddison's "The Worm Ouroboros" sits on eBay with a Buy It Now price of a mere $5,500. It seems likely that Lovecraft would have recommended "The Worm Ouroboros" to the Eddys, and that Muriel might have slipped a sly reference into her story about the Man-Eating Tree of Mindanao, inspired by Bryant's earlier account.

RAUK YAS

The March 1958 edition of Man's Life magazine included an article by Robert Moore titled "Trapped by a Man-Eating Tree." Moore presented a tale told to him by Lt. Ret. RDN Oscar Schnee that took place in March 1943.

Schnee recounted how he and two fellow Royal Dutch Navy officers, Johnny Krumann and Paul Doers, escaped in a small boat after 13 months in a Japanese prison on Sumbawa in the Dutch East Indies. They nearly wiped out in the wake of a typhoon, the boat springing leaks and losing its rudder. But they made it to Laut Island, capsizing on the outer sandbar. Dragging themselves onto the beach, the hopeful trio began carving out a new life on the island, subsisting on fish and coconuts.

On the morning of the third day, the group traversed a rough series of coral beaches and ascended a volcanic hump that rose 600 feet above sea level. Hacking through waist-high sedge with a knife, they saw trees that possessed wide, tobacco-like leaves they were optimistic could be smoked.

Krumann and Doers went over to investigate. Each of the trees was shaped like a deformed tulip, a halo of poinsettias waving and gyrating sensuously as the men approached. Suddenly, a net of undulating, vinelike tendrils flung out from one of the trees, ensnaring Krumann and Doers. The tendrils coiled around Krumann's legs and stomach, peeling back his shirt and reaching for his mouth. They stung him with purple, hairy nettles, searing purple welts on whatever flesh they grazed. A tentacle as thick as a bullwhip swung out from the red-flowered halo and whipped around Doers' throat. He gurgled and sobbed, dropping his knife as he fruitlessly pulled at the tightening vines. The tendrils surged over his thighs and bare feet. Krumann chopped frantically with his knife but the fastening vines formed a green shroud over his body. They pulled him toward the trunk, a giant polyp that was now open. The captives' eyes bulged as they were totally engulfed.

Schnee instinctively raced forward to assist them, but stopped at 20 yards, knowing there was nothing he could do to save his friends. As the tendrils strained to reach him, sensing more flesh, Schnee fell backward and held his ears, trying fruitlessly to drown out the screams. Doers' purple-streaked right ankle remained momentarily visible until both men were completely engulfed by the deep green folds.

Schnee raced back down the path they had cut, but tripped and choked as he tried to catch his breath. In sheer frustration at failing to rescue his friends, he plunged his knife into the earth. Then Schnee felt a sting on his ankle, and looked up to see another tree above him, red poinsettias undulating. The vine that had whipped around his ankle shot hot, electric shocks up into his hip. He even felt oscillating under his tongue.

Schnee snatched his knife from the sand and chopped the tendril in two. Then, he raced back to the beach and hurriedly lit a fire. Without hesitation, he cut away the inflamed welt that had formed on his ankle and bled the wound to drain the toxin.

Schnee fell into a comatose state for days before finally being rescued by Celeb fishermen. Even so, blood poisoning resulted in the amputation of his leg. While Schnee referred to the killer plant as Crinoida Dajeeana, the proper name of the Madagascar Man-Eating Tree, the fishermen called the devil tree *Rauk Yas.*

"It grows in terrible profusion along the south coast of Makassar," Schnee learned. "On the Postilion Islands, especially, [the] cannibal or devil tree is taboo. No islander will approach within a mile of it. I shouldn't wonder why."

Men's Adventure Magazines (MAMs) like Man's Life were enormously popular in the decades following World War 2. They presented "true" pulpy and exotic tales of square-jawed heroes, scantily-clad women, fiendish Nazis, fearsome wild animals, etc. They also at times delved into the weird, presenting supposedly factual tales of UFOs, Bigfoot, voodoo cults, and the like.

"Never mind that MAMs played fast and loose with facts and definitions of 'true,' or that most of the time writers were making it up as they went," cautioned Robert Deis and Wyatt Doyle, who have written several excellent books collecting these classic MAM adventure tales.

JUBOKKO & OTHER BOTANICAL YOKAI

Vegetation dangerous to human beings appears among the Japanese Yokai, a parade of shape-shifting, supernatural creatures inherent to the nation's folklore. Hiroko Yoda and Matt Alt, in their 2015 translation of Toriyama Sekien's seminal late-18th century "Demon Horde" encyclopedias, described the Yokai as "superstitions with personalities, the things that go bump in Japan's night."

Some of Sekien's botanical Yokai were harmless, such as **Bashō-no-sei**, the spirit of a plantain tree, originating in China, that takes human form and tells stories; and **Kodama**, the souls of ancient trees that can manifest as people, similar to the dryads of Greek mythology. However, a couple entries were less benign:

Nozuchi (or Field-Hammer) is a floral and greenery spirit that is large but lacks eyes, a nose, hands or feet. But it does have a mouth, which it uses to feed on human beings. Nozuchi is said to be the reincarnation of a monk who studied Buddhism but only for honor and profit. As translated by Yoda and Alt from "Shasekishū" (Sand and Pebbles), a 1283 collection of Buddhist parables, "His mouth was clever, but he did not have the eyes of wisdom, the hands of faith, nor the legs of righteous behavior. And so he was reborn as this fearsome thing."

Furutsubaki-no-rei is a spirit, like a sprite or fairy, that resides in aged camelia trees and manifests as an apparition to fool people. Sekien used the Chinese characters for the camelia tree, possibly referencing an older text. The dull dropping of the tree's heavy red flowers was said to evoke the falling of a human head removed by a sword, creating an association with death.

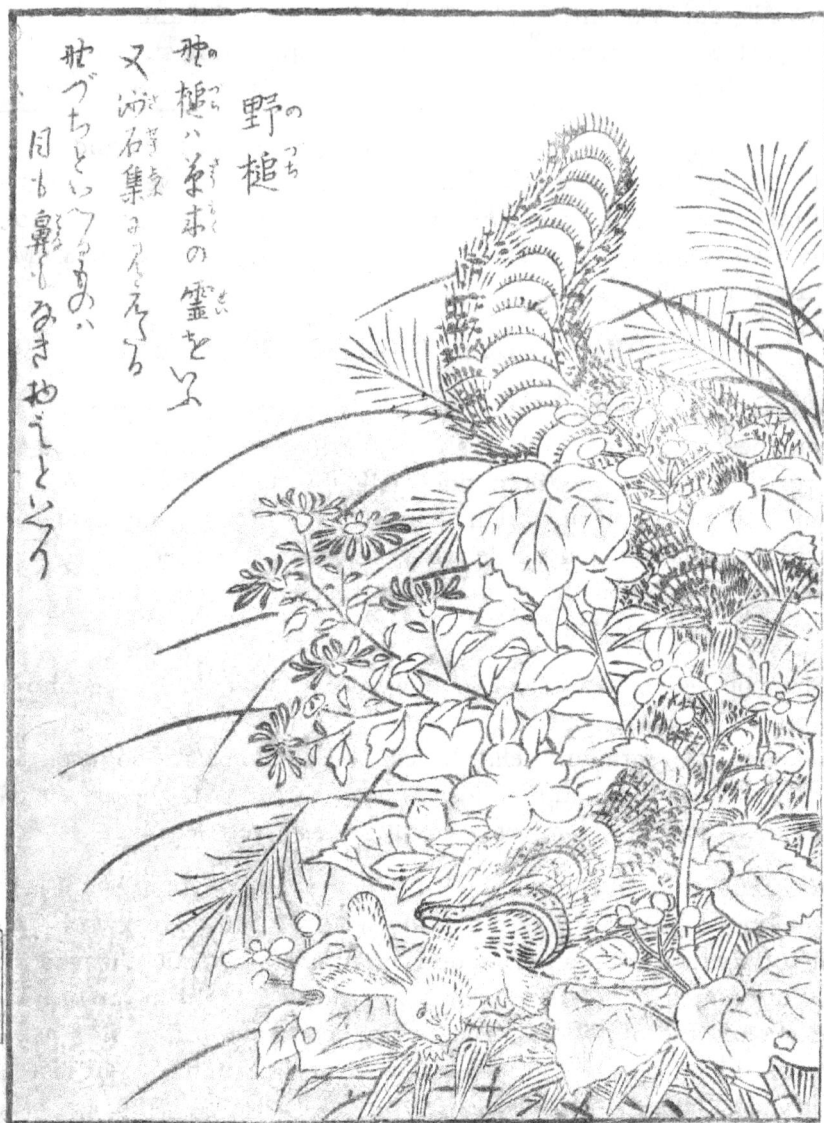

野槌

野槌ハ草木の霊をよ
又渕石集みえたる
牡づちといへるもの
同も鼻もなきものと云う

Nozuchi by Toriyama Sekien, from "Konjaku Gazu Zoku Hyakki"
(The Illustrated Demon Horde from Past and Present, Continued),
1779. Note the Audrey II-like mouth eating a rabbit!

In some traditions, Furutsubaki-no-rei appears as a young,
beautiful woman wearing a kimono. Sometimes she draws
attention with her cries, garnering a victim's sympathy or
signaling a future tragedy; other times she frightens anyone who

approaches; and on rare occasions she mysteriously vanishes with her victim.

British writer Lord Redesdale, best known for his 1871 book, "Tales of Old Japan," wrote that some camellias, "like spectres, walk about at night, the terror of mankind." He related, "There was one in the garden of a Matsné Samurai which did this so much that it had to be cut down. Then it writhed its arms and groaned, and blood spurted at every stroke of the axe."

There are several instances throughout world folklore of trees inhabited by spirits that bleed when cut down, with the person who destroyed it often incurring great punishment. Roman poet Ovid wrote of how Erysichthon, king of Thessaly, with "impious axe" and ignoring all warnings, felled the ancient Dryads' Oak in the sacred grove of Ceres:

The trembling tree sent forth an audible groan!

From its pale leaves and acorns died the green,

Dark oozing sweat from every branch distilled,

And as the scoffer smote it, crimson-red

Gushed from the wounded bark the sap, as streams

When at the altar falls some mighty bull

The life-blood from his neck.

                                    Then from its heart

Issued a voice, "Thou strikest in this trunk

A nymph whom Ceres loves, and for the deed

Dearly shalt pay. With my last voice thy doom

I prophesy, and in thy imminent fate

Find solace for my own."

Ceres punished Erysichthon with Fames, the spirit of unrelenting and insatiable hunger, resulting in the king ultimately eating *himself,* with nothing remaining. That's a different, roundabout twist on a "Man-Eating Tree" story!

Indeed, the eager lumberjack risks their life when chopping down any supernatural trees. A German legend recounts how an old woman uprooted an ancient fir tree, accidentally injuring the elf who lived within. She was immediately struck with overpowering weakness and was scarcely able to walk. A mysterious stranger informed the woman that her fate was now tied to the elf's; if the elf recovered, so would she. The old woman died later that night, suggesting the elf had also perished.

A similar tale recounts how a young man felling a tree in India suddenly broke out in a profuse sweat and was overcome with sudden weakness. He fainted and died on the spot, having mortally wounded the indwelling tree spirit.

Wrote Seiken, "Old trees do many strange things."

***

Renowned manga artist Shigeru Mizuki featured many Yokai in his popular series "GeGeGe no Kitarō," which he launched in the 1960s. His profiles of these spirits have been collected in similar form to Sekien's volumes from centuries earlier. Mizuki spotlighted a few arboreal menaces in his work:

Jubokko is a vampire tree that grows on the sites of former battlefields. Having nourished itself on human blood since first sprouting, the adult tree has developed an unquenchable thirst. When a person unwittingly walks beneath its shade, the Jubokko stretches out its branches like arms and snatches up the hapless victim. Greedily, the vampire tree begins sucking out its victim's blood until not one drop remains in the limp body.

Mannentake resemble normal groves of bamboo but hide a terrible secret—they are dangerous monsters that reach out their branch-like hands to suck out the life-force of anyone who wanders across their path. Considering that Japanese citizens were once advised to run into bamboo groves for safety during earthquakes due to the assumed sturdiness of the root system, this made the Mannentake an especially insidious threat.

However, if the Mannentake's branches are broken, they are powerless to harm anyone.

Jubokko, the Vampire Tree. -KJG.

The Unnatural History of Man-Eating Plants

Mizuki's version of **Kodama** also looks like an ordinary tree but is inhabited by a spirit. But if one cuts down the tree, they bring a curse upon themselves. Misfortune will befall not only the woodchopper but everyone around them. It is said that an incredibly ancient Kodama stands tall in the mountains of Hachijō-jima Island.

Mizuki is on record stating that about 30 of the Yokai he featured in "GeGeGe no Kitaro" were his original creations, but he did not specify which ones. According to blogger Dr. Yokai, several years ago a group of Yokai experts held an academic conference and thoroughly discussed the history of the Jubokko. They were unable to find any evidence of the story prior to its appearance in Mizuki's Yokai encyclopedia and concluded it was likely one of his inventions.

However, even the influential Sekien pulled some of the Yokai he catalogued from his imagination. While most were drawn on Japanese oral tradition and text sources, he presented his personal interpretations and even admitted to extracting the "Haunted Housewares" featured in the fourth volume from his own dreams. So, adding to the legend is just part of the Yokai tradition!

***

From the formative legends of the poisonous Upas Tree to modern accounts of bovine-chomping flora, Asia has long been a fruitful source for tales of exotic arboreal terrors.

SOURCES:

Abe, Namiko. "Bamboo and Japanese Culture." *ThoughtCo.*, 13 Feb. 2019, https://www.thoughtco.com/bamboo-in-japanese-culture-2028043. Accessed 26 Aug. 2025.

"*Antiaris.*" *Wikipedia*, https://en.wikipedia.org/wiki/Antiaris. Accessed 31 May 2025.

"Banjarnegara Regency." *Wikipedia*, https://en.wikipedia.org/wiki/Banjarnegara_Regency. Accessed 30 Aug. 2025.

Asia

"Bertram Freeman-Mitford, 1st Baron Redesdale." *Wikipedia,* https://en.wikipedia.org/wiki/Bertram_Freeman-Mitford,_1st_Baron_Redesdale. Accessed 15 Sep. 2025.

Blake Price, Cheryl. "Vegetable Monsters: Man-Eating Trees in Fin-de-Siècle Fiction." *Victorian Literature and Culture,* vol. 41, no. 2, 2013, pp. 311-327.

"The Botanic Garden." *Wikipedia,* https://en.wikipedia.org/wiki/The_Botanic_Garden. Accessed 31 May 2025.

Breland, Rev. R. L. "Baptist Church News." *Coffeeville Courier* [Coffeeville, MS], 21 Sep. 1934, p. 2.

"C. M. Eddy Jr." *Wikipedia,* https://en.wikipedia.org/wiki/C._M._Eddy_Jr. Accessed 14 May 2025.

"'Cow-Eating' Trees of Padrame." *NewIndPress,* 23 Oct. 2007, http://www.newindpress.com/NewsItems.asp?ID=IEK200710230 40252&Page=K&Headline=%27Cow-eating%27+trees+of+Padrame&Title=Southern+News+-+Karnataka&Topic=0. Archived: https://web.archive.org/web/20071121023043/http://www.new indpress.com/NewsItems.asp?ID=IEK20071023040252&Page=K& Headline=%27Cow-eating%27+trees+of+Padrame&Title=Southern+News+-+Karnataka&Topic=0. Accessed 13 May 2025.

Dalrymple, Donald Gordon. "William Clarence Bryant." *Find a Grave,* 22 Mar. 2009, https://www.findagrave.com/memorial/35086099/william-clarence-bryant. Accessed 12 Apr. 2025.

Darwin, Erasmus. *The Botanic Garden, Part II: The Loves of the Plants. A Poem. with Philosophical Notes.* London, J. Johnson, 1791.

Deis, Robert, and Wyatt Doyle, editors. "Atomic Werewolves and Man-Eating Plants." *New Texture,* 2023.

"Dieng Plateau." *Wikipedia*, https://en.wikipedia.org/wiki/Dieng_Plateau. Accessed 30 Aug. 2025.

"Dieng Volcanic Complex." *Wikipedia*, https://en.wikipedia.org/wiki/Dieng_Volcanic_Complex. Accessed 30 Aug. 2025.

Dr. Yokai. "Jubokko, the Japanese Vampire Yōkai." *Dr. Yokai Blog*, 24 Oct. 2012, https://dr-yokai.blogspot.com/2012/10/jubokko-japanese-vampire-yokai.html. Accessed 25 Aug. 2025.

Eddy, Muriel E. "Trapped in Devil-Tee Tentacles Woman Narrowly Escapes Death." *San Angelo Daily Standard* [San Angelo, Texas], 25 Dec. 1927, Western Weekly Magazine Section, p. 5.

"Engelbert Kaempfer." *Wikipedia*, https://en.wikipedia.org/wiki/Engelbert_Kaempfer. Accessed 6 Aug. 2025.

"Erysichthon of Thessaly." *Wikipedia*, https://en.wikipedia.org/wiki/Erysichthon_of_Thessaly. Accessed 18 Sep. 2025.

"Escaped from the Embrace of the Man-Eating Tree." *San Francisco Examiner*, 11 Jan. 1925, American Weekly supplement, p. 6.

"Ferocious Cannibal Plants." *Commercial Appeal* [Memphis, TN], 17 Dec. 1905, Part 2, p. 4.

Foerch, N. P., "Description of the Poison Tree, in the Island of Java." *Translated by Mr. Heydinger. Appendix to the Hibernian Magazine or Compendium of Entertaining Knowledge for the Year 1783*, Dec. 1783.

Foersch, N.P. "Description of the Poison-Tree, In the Island of Java." Translated by Mr. Heydinger, *London Magazine*, Dec. 1783, pp. 511-517.

"Fumarole Death Blamed on Poor Signs." *Jakarta Post*, 6 Feb. 2001, Archived: https://web.archive.org/web/20160304232410/http://www.thej

akartapost.com/news/2001/02/06/fumarole-death-blamed-poor-signs.html.

"Furutsubaki-no-rei." *Wikipedia,* https://en.wikipedia.org/wiki/Furutsubaki-no-rei. Accessed 25 Aug. 2025.

"Furutsubaki no rei." *Yokai.com,* https://yokai.com/furutsubakinorei/. Accessed 25 Aug. 2025.

"Georg Eberhard Rumphius." *Wikipedia,* https://en.wikipedia.org/wiki/Georg_Eberhard_Rumphius. Accessed 31 May 2025.

"A Giant Flower." *Cincinnati Enquirer,* 13 Jan. 1895, p. 17.

"Girl Squeezed to Death in a Tree." *Olathe Register* [Olathe, KS], 26 Mar. 1908, p. 8.

Hope, Laurence. *The Garden of Kama and Other Love Lyrics from India.* William Heinemann, 1901.

Horsfield, Thomas, M. D. "An Essay on the Oopas or Poison Tree of Java: Addressed to the Honorable Thomas Stamford Raffles, Lieutenant Governor." *Batavian Society of Arts and Sciences,* 1814.

"The Indian Eros." *Saturday Review,* vol. 118, no. 3,082, 21 Nov. 1914, pp. 537-538, 540.

"Insectivorous Plants." *Wikipedia,* https://en.wikipedia.org/wiki/Insectivorous_Plants. Accessed 6 Aug. 2025.

"Jubokko." *Wikipedia,* https://en.wikipedia.org/wiki/Jubokko. Accessed 25 Aug. 2025.

Kaempfero, Engelberto, D. *Amoenitatum Exoticarum Politico-Physico-Medicarum Fasciculi V, Quibus Continentur Variae Relationes, Observationes & Descriptiones, Rerum Persicarum & Ulterioris Asiae, Multa Attentione, in Peregrinationibus Per Universum Orientem, Collectae.* Lemgoviae, Henrici Wilhelmi Meyeri, Aulae Lippiacae Typographi, 1712.

Lampton, E. C., "In the Heart of the Old South." *Mississippi Sun* [Charleston, MS], 13 Dec. 1928, p. 4.

"Laurence Hope." *Poetry Foundation,* https://www.poetryfoundation.org/poets/laurence-hope. Accessed 13 May 2025.

Ley, Willy. *Salamanders and Other Wonders, Still More Adventures of a Romantic Naturalist.* Viking Press, 1955.

"List of Volcanoes in Indonesia." *Wikipedia,* https://en.wikipedia.org/wiki/List_of_volcanoes_in_Indonesia. Accessed 31 May 2025.

"Makassar people." *Wikipedia,* https://en.wikipedia.org/wiki/Makassar_people. Accessed 30 Aug. 2025.

"Mangaluru." *Wikipedia,* https://en.wikipedia.org/wiki/Mangaluru. Accessed 13 May 2025.

Mizuki, Shigeru. *Yokai Picture Book.* Tokyo, Kodansha Co., Ltd., 2024.

"Muriel E. Eddy." *H. P. Lovecraft Wiki,* https://lovecraft.fandom.com/wiki/Muriel_E._Eddy. Accessed 14 May 2025.

"*Nepenthes rajah.*" *Wikipedia,* https://en.wikipedia.org/wiki/Nepenthes_rajah. Accessed 30 Jul. 2025.

"*Nepenthes sumatrana.*" *Wikipedia,* https://en.wikipedia.org/wiki/Nepenthes_sumatrana. Accessed 30 Jul. 2025.

Nurhayati, Desy. "Mt. Batur Alert Raised to `Caution'." *Jakara Post,* 11 Nov. 2009, https://www.thejakartapost.com/news/2009/11/11/mt-batur-alert-raised-caution039.html. Accessed 1 Jun. 2025.

"Of Local Interest." *North Mississippi Herald* [Water Valley, MS], 13 Feb. 1920, p. 6.

Philpot, J. H. *The Sacred Tree or The Tree in Religion and Myth.* London, MacMillan and Co., Limited, 1897.

"*Rafflesia.*" *Wikipedia,* https://en.wikipedia.org/wiki/Rafflesia. Accessed 30 Jul. 2025.

"Railroad Boys Hold Fortyfifth Annual Picnic." *North Mississippi Herald* [Water Valley, MS], 13 Jun. 1919, p. 1.

Redesdale, Lord. *Further Memories.* London, Hutchinson & Co., 1917.

Rumphius, Georg. Everhard. *Herbarium Amboinense, Part II.* Amsterdam, François Changuion, Jan Catuffe, Hermanus Uytwerf, 1741.

"Shigeru Mizuki." *Wikipedia,* https://en.wikipedia.org/wiki/Shigeru_Mizuki. Accessed 25 Aug. 2025.

Skullsinthestars. "E.R. Eddison's The Worm Ouroboros." *Skulls in the Stars,* 6 Nov. 2012, https://skullsinthestars.com/2012/11/06/e-r-eddisons-the-worm-ouroboros/. Accessed 14 May 2025.

"Some Odd Stories." *Newark Daily Advocate* [Newark, OH], 4 Oct. 1893, p. 3.

"Stamford Raffles." *Wikipedia,* https://en.wikipedia.org/wiki/Stamford_Raffles. Accessed 31 May 2025.

Steen, Rev. Moses D. A., D.D. *The Steen Family in Europe and America.* Library of Princeton Theological Seminary, 1917.

Sykes, Lieut. Col. W. H. "Remarks on the Origin of the Popular Belief in the Upas, or Poison Tree of Java." *Journal of the Royal Asiatic Society of Great Britain and Ireland,* vol. 4, 1837, pp. 194-199.

"Thomas Horsfield." *Wikipedia,* https://en.wikipedia.org/wiki/Thomas_Horsfield. Accessed 31 May 2025.

"Titan arum." *Wikipedia,* https://en.wikipedia.org/wiki/Titan_arum. Accessed 30 Jul. 2025.

"The Upas Tree." *Scientific American*, vol. 13, no. 47, 31 July 1858, p. 374.

"Uppinangady." *Wikipedia,* https://en.wikipedia.org/wiki/Uppinangady. Accessed 13 May 2025.

"Violet (Adela Florence) Nicolson." (Excerpted and adapted from An Encyclopedia of British Women Writers, edited by Paul Schlueter and June Schlueter.)" *Laurence Hope,* http://www.h.ehime-u.ac.jp/~marx/LH/em/bio.htm. Archived: https://web.archive.org/web/20120729073134/http://www.h.ehime-u.ac.jp/~marx/LH/em/bio.htm. Accessed 13 May 2025.

"Woman Explorer Tells of 'Carnivorous' Tree." *St. Louis Daily Globe-Democrat*, 27 Oct. 1907, Editorial Section p. 6.

Wood, Walker. "A Good Friend Has Gone." *Winona Times* [Winona, MS], 10 Mar. 1939, p. 1.

Worm Of Ouroboros by Eddison--Lovecraft's Copy with His Signature and Bookplate. eBay auction by greymatterbooks, https://www.ebay.com/itm/146036403597. Accessed 14 May 2025.

Yoda, Hiroko and Matt Alt, translators and annotators. *Japandemonium Illustrated: The Yokai Encyclopedias of Toriyama Sekien.* Dover Publications, 2016.

EUROPE

As a rule, Man-Eating Plants are found in the wilds of unexplored realms. Like sea monsters that sailors feared inhabited far-off-waters, and the isolated Realm of Prester John that medieval Christians expected would save them from the heathen hordes, these voracious vegetables were an exotic enigma, hidden in jungles yet untouched by the western world. Emerging in the back half of the 19th century, these stories were in a way the last vestige of imaginative horrors to take hold before the planet became more extensively explored, connected and arguably less interesting.

It is unsurprising that there aren't many Man-Eating Plant tales based in well-trod continental Europe. There are, however, plenty of stories about European explorers who stumbled upon this deadly flora in "uncivilized" corners of the world. As observed by Cheryl Blake Price in the paper, "Vegetable Monsters: Man-Eating Trees in Fin-de-Siècle Fiction," published in 2013, "The obvious imperialist agenda of the Liche letter [from 1874, describing the Man-Eating Tree of Madagascar-Ed.] is also common to late-century 'colonial hunting narratives' that glorified the imperial enterprise of expansion and domination." Blake Price places Man-Eating Plant stories from this era in the sub-genre of Imperial Gothic fiction, the prose displaying cultural anxiety about Darwinian evolution, a process in which a plant might develop mammalian characteristics. These "hybrid monstrosities," wrote Blake Price, reflected "fears that were particularly directed towards the unknowable natural world and the dangerous, still-undiscovered species lurking within the colonial jungles."

The Unnatural History of Man-Eating Plants

Elizabeth Chang, in the 2017 essay, "Killer Plants of the Late Nineteenth Century," wrote that "the expansion of the British empire was inextricably combined with environmental change, and the final years of the nineteenth century marked the strongest alignment yet between imperial expansion and ecological alteration." One reading of Victorian fiction about carnivorous plants, wrote Chang, is that they are "allegories of the bad effects of British colonial rapaciousness in which the landscape, for once, can actually fight back against resource extraction and exploitation." Chang also pointed out that the emergence of Man-Eating Plant fiction followed a growing understanding and appreciation for global plant life among the British populace. The founding of the (Royal) Horticultural Society and the debut of gardening periodicals reflected a burgeoning public interest in studying, collecting and raising a variety of plants.

Orchids, in particular, became big business in the western world. "Very few realize the amount of money invested in the orchids, the aristocrats of the flowery world, and though they have been attracting widespread interest for the past dozen years, the general public may not be acquainted with the fact that millions of dollars are involved in the magnificent collections of these plants. Cargoes of bulbs and roots are annually imported, which are readily disposed to the flower-loving public for sums ranging from $1 up to the thousands," read an 1892 American dispatch. "One rare bulb from the forests of Mexico, Brazil or India will frequently sell for the price of a grand diamond ring, and occasionally a small fortune is represented by half a dozen poor-looking bulbs that a street boy would kick aside with his foot if found in his way. The great floriculturists of this country and Europe employ orchid hunters to explore the woods and jungles of every known country for some rare specimen of these plants, and thousands of dollars go annually to pay the expenses of these trips into unknown lands. Danger, death and sickness of every conceivable kind threaten the hunters, but despite these they penetrate to the most dangerous wilds to find their plants."

In this light, Man-Eating Plant accounts appear to have capitalized on a fad for exotic plants and the adventure inherent in seeking them out in the darkest corners of the planet. Sci-Fi luminary H. G. Wells even wrote a short story about an exotic killer orchid, contained later in this volume.

STRANGLING OAK OF NANNAU WOODS

Not every Man-Killing Plant falls into the category of undiscovered vegetable life, a "Floral Cryptid," though. An old legend in Merionethshire, North Wales, England attributes supernatural means to a deadly tree that was said to stand in woodlands around Nannau Mansion, the ancient seat of the Vaughan family. Elliott O'Donnell, "The Ghost Man," recounted the tale vividly in a 1924 article published in American Weekly:

The Strangling Oak of Nannau Woods

Peculiar Exploits of a "Demon Tree" in Whose Hollow Trunk Old Owen Glendower of British History Stuck the Body of the Treacherous Welsh Chieftain He Had Slain

READERS of this magazine will remember the interesting series of ghost stories written by Mr. Elliott O'Donnell, known in England as "The Ghost Man" because of his tireless researches in the world of "spooks" and his experiences there.

Mr. O'Donnell has made similar careful investigation into the legends and whispered stories of certain "cursed" houses and families abroad, and one of his articles on this subject appears on this page. Others will follow from time to time.

By Elliot O'Donnell

(The Ghost Man)

ABOUT six and a half miles from Dolgelly, the county town of Merionethshire, North Wales, in a beautifully wooded park, lies Nannau Mansion, the ancient seat of the Vaughan family.

About the end of the fourteenth century or beginning of the fifteenth there lived at Nannau a Welsh chieftain called Howel Sele. Now, Howel had many relatives, and among them was his cousin, the famous Owen Glendower,

Historic Nannau Hall, in Whose Forests the Old Tragedy Happened That "Cursed" the Oak.

who lived not very far away. Unfortunately, however, between the two there was a very bitter animosity; some said owing to rivalry in the field of sport, i.e., archery, quarterstaff and other of the pastimes then in vogue; and others to a love affair, Howel being jealous of his cousin, toward whom he thought, either rightly or wrongly, his wife showed too friendly a spirit.

Their mutual dislike was well known, and it grieved no one more than the Abbot of Kymmer, who was fond of them both. The Abbot had often planned how he could effect a reconciliation between them, and at last one day he made a bold attempt at it.

Without giving either a hint as to what was in his mind, he invited them to dine with him. Neither suspecting, of course, his enemy was coming, they both appeared, and for a short while the worthy Abbot had a very anxious time of it.

In the end, however, he managed to pacify them, and before they left his presence the hatchet was apparently buried, and they seemed to be on the best of terms. A few days later Howel invited Owen to the chase, as a day's deer hunting was then termed, and the two, accompanied by several of their respective retainers, went off together to the woods round Nannau. Pursuing quarry hour after hour, through sunny glade and cool and shadowy dell, the two cousins suddenly found themselves side by side in a small clearing.

"Hush!" Owen whispered, touching his kinsman lightly on the arm, "do you see that doe over there. Prove your prowess by shooting it."

The Woods of Nannau, in Which Lived the "Demon Oak" of Dark Legend.

He pointed, as he spoke, with his disengaged hand to a brown object, half hidden by bushes and high waving grass, a dozen or so yards ahead of them. Howel at once fitting an arrow to his bow and was apparently taking aim in the direction indicated, when suddenly, and without the slightest warning, he swung round and discharged the missile full at Owen's breast!

Walter Thornbury, in his "Demon Oak," has alluded to the incident thus:

"Then cursed Howel's cruel shaft

The Unnatural History of Man-Eating Plants

His royal brother's blood had quaffed,

Alas, for Cambria's weal!

But the false arrow glanced aside,

For 'neath the robe of royal pride

Lay plate of Milan steel."

Owen, luckily, had under his shirt a coat of mail, probably ringed mail, for that was the lightest kind of armor then in use, so, consequently, the arrow glanced merely off it without penetrating any further. Roused to a fury by this abominable act of treachery, Glendower at once drew his sword. Howel fell, mortally wounded. Before dying he cursed Owen, telling him he would never enjoy a moment's peace again and that he would haunt him and his heirs forever. Glendower realized that to make the matter public would mean the beginning of a feud between the Seles and Glendowers which might easily lead to a civil war in Wales and thus engender a national catastrophe.

Yet, to keep it dark was something out of keeping with Glendower's character. In a land where all men at that period were deemed valiant, he was rightly regarded as being a great warrior, a most perfect gentleman, and all great warriors and perfect gentlemen hate doing anything that is any degree underhand and cowardly.

It was, indeed, a dilemma. It was solved, however, by the sudden arrival of one Madog, Glendower's bosom friend, who, perceiving the danger in which Owen stood, at once suggested hiding the dead body in the hollow trunk of a great oak that stood near by.

This oak had a very sinister appearance. It was not only all black and scorched, where it had been once struck by lightening, but its widespreading, knotted and gnarled branches bore a peculiar resemblance to the malshaped arms of a human being. It was known and shunned for this reason, though hitherto there were no substantial grounds for associating it with the supernatural. Yielding to the persuasions of his friend, Glendower caught hold of the bleeding corpse and between them both they carried it to the oak and dropped it in the hollow.

On the morrow, as Howel had not yet returned home, a great search was made for him.

All Nannau and the surrounding country was scoured, but, odd to relate, although caves, bushes and ditches were examined, no one thought of looking in the hollow of the notorious oak. Some thought he had fallen down some well or into some obscure pit, others that he had been drowned while attempting to ford the swift and treacherous river Mawddach; others, again, that he had been seized and carried off, either by brigands or by a band of marauding English soldiers.

Time passed, and his fate became one of those mysteries that the whole countryside loved to discuss in the chimney corner round an old-fashioned roaring fire.

In the meanwhile, however, strange stories got afloat. Close to Nannau there is a hill called Moel Offrwn, and more than one person crossing it after dusk testified to seeing the shadowy form of Howel Sele standing by the wayside, his corpse-like face scowling. One peasant declared that he was pursued for more than a mile by the figure, which followed him persistently through briars, brushwood and water, only leaving him when he came within sight of a church.

Phenomena were encountered, too, on the rugged slopes of Cader Idris. One stalwart farmer stated that when he went to look for his cattle one night on the sides of the mountain he saw pale lights of a nasty bluish-green hue flitting in and out of the boulders.

Thinking they must be Canhywllam Cyrth, or what in Wales are known as Corpse Candles, that is to say spirits in the shape of candle flames that appear to some Welsh people before the death of some relative, he stood still, rooted to the ground with fear, and stared, open mouthed, at them.

Then, quite suddenly, they came together, taking at first the form of a huge flame, and almost immediately afterward that of a man, gigantic and shadowy. The farmer was terrified, for he recognized in the shape that towered above him the features and figure of the missing Lord of Nannau, Howel Sele.

The expression on the apparition's face was dreadful, the eyebrows scowled diabolically, the mouth was contracted into a savage snarl, while the eyes blazed with a hate that the wretched farmer felt could only owe its origin to Hell.

Raising one hand, the figure was in the act of striking the farmer, when the latter instinctively crossed himself and muttered a prayer. The moment he did this the whole expression and attitude of the apparition changed. Fear and dread, a dread that was really terrible to see, seemed to sweep through it, and turning on its heels with a gesture of despair, it glided away.

As it went, winding its way in and out the huge black boulders that lay scattered in all directions on the mountain side, a dull and melancholy wind rose suddenly, and tossing the branches of the naked trees against the starlit sky, flew after it like one lost soul following another. An owl hooted dismally and a hare screamed, and the farmer, now having at length recovered his faculties, slunk fearfully home.

Among others of the people who witnessed strange phenomena were Howel's aged nurse, who had always been most devoted to him, and his venerable steward. Tradition says that both these two frequently used to see a tall, spectral figure, which they recognized as their lost master, in the grounds of Nannau, though never once, in their experience, did it actually enter the house. Sometimes, when they were sitting in one of the rooms on the ground floor, they saw a white, haggard face appear at a window and look in at them, angrily, until they prayed or uttered some pious exclamation, when it at once became sorrowful and withdrew with a groan or sigh.

At other times, when they were looking out of their windows at night they would see it peering up at the house from among the trees, and, perhaps, wringing its hands and going through all the antics and gesticulations of a lost soul. Indeed, the idea conveyed to them both by its appearance and behavior was that it was damned, damned and laboring under some dreadful curse.

But it was the actual oak itself, the spot where the body of Howel was hidden, that was the worst haunted. No horse ever passed it, either in the day time or at night, without shying, while all kinds of phenomena were seen and heard in its immediate vicinity. Sometimes uncanny lights were observed hovering in its branches, while at others awful moans and groans were heard to proceed from it. More than that, a party of haymakers passing the tree on their way home one night are alleged to have heard a voice cry out, apparently from its trunk:

"I'm cursed! I'm cursed! So are ye all!"

Knowing the tree and its evil reputation only too well they did not dally to investigate the seeming phenomenon, but fled panic stricken.

To return to Owen Glendower. Though he knew there was ample justification for his having fought with Howel, and even excuse for his having killed him, he couldn't get the vision of his cousin's bleeding corpse from his mind. It haunted him day and night, wherever he went, whatever he was doing.

Often at night he awoke with a start to hear, or fancy he heard, a voice whisper from the darkness, "Accursed!" and he recognized that voice as Howel's. The feeling that he actually was cursed grew on him, and he became seized with a deep melancholy. Still, something always held him back when he felt impelled to disclose his dread secret.

The Unnatural History of Man-Eating Plants

At last, after ten years of torment, he finally succumbed to an illness. Just before he died he sent for the faithful Madog and bade him hie away to Howel's widow and tell her the entire truth.

In the words of the poet again:

"To Sele's sad widow bear the tale,

Nor let our horrid secret rest:

Give but his corse to sacred earth,

Then may my parting soul be blest."

Promising to do as requested, Madog set off at once to Nannau, and Glendower, feeling that the curse had been removed from him, breathed his last.

True to his trust, Madog sought Howel's widow and gave her a detailed account of her husband's death. A party of retainers was at once sent with him to the oak and the truth of his story was speedily established by the discovery of the armor-clad skeleton.

But though it was true the skeleton was taken to the chapel of Nannau, where prayers were said over it, most other recorders of the grim tragedy maintain the priestly efforts were in vain. There is a saying that curses not infrequently have a habit of recoiling on the heads of those who utter them, and this would appear to have been so in the case of Howel Sele.

The spirit of Glendower troubled no one, though Sele had declared it should know no rest, but with Sele's own spirit it was otherwise. The blasted oak still continued to moan and groan and yield other phenomena that seemed unquestionably to be associated with the Lord of Nannau.

One of the most extraordinary stories, vouched for by the local peasantry, concerns the evil power of the oak to kill those straying into its grip. Half a dozen men have been found dead at its base with marks around their throats as though they had been strangled. But in the story referred to there was an eyewitness of what is alleged to have occurred.

Two travellers were making their way through the Nannau Woods and were overtaken by darkness. They decided to spend the night at the base of a great oak which, although they did not much like its appearance, promised the best shelter about. After preparing their supper they stretched themselves out and went to sleep.

One of the travellers awakened from a dreadful nightmare. He had dreamed that from the trunk of the tree under which he slept long knotted arms had begun to drop. At their ends were smaller branches that looked like grotesque hands. And these uncanny arms and hands crept slowly down and down toward him while he lay helpless in terror. Just as they were about to touch him he managed to awaken and with a scream rolled away, leaping to his feet and fled.

He ran perhaps fifty paces, and then this terror of what had seemed a too vivid dream dropped from him. He stopped, shamefacedly, and looked back wondering if he had awakened his companion.

To his amazement he saw that his companion was apparently climbing up the trunk of the oak. Then, as he looked closer, he saw that his comrade seemed to be enmeshed in branches.

At this moment fleecing clouds which had half-veiled the moon drifted away, leaving it shining in its full splendor.

He then saw that a branch of the tree was actually wound around his comrade's neck, while stronger branches held him firmly clasped to the bole itself. And in the weird light of the moon a huge, evil, grotesque and demure face seemed to gleam out from that trunk, staring with malevolent eyes upon the contorted face of the strangling man!

The sight was too much for the traveller. He fled in earnest now. He stumbled at dawn into the village, told his story and when the sun was up led a party back to where he had slept.

"The second traveler saw, as he first thought, his friend climbing the tree. And then he realized that he was entangled in the branches which seemed to be clutching his throat in a strangling grip, while under the weird light of the moon a hideous face was outlined on the great trunk."

There, at the base of the tree, lay the body of his comrade. He had been strangled to death. The neck was bruised and on his body were cuts as though great claws had torn him.

So sinister became the tree's reputation that it was at last ordered cut down and burned.

If there is any truth in rumor, however, its site is still haunted and all who venture within its cursed radiance at nightfall meet with some dire catastrophe.

The Strangling Oak of Nannau Woods isn't an isolated case. There is a similar Bengal folk tale about a banyan tree haunted by several ghosts, who wrung the necks of all who were rash enough to approach the tree during the night.

OTESANEK

A Bohemian (today Czech) fairy tale called "The Long-Desired Child" revolves around Otesanek, a sentient tree stump with an insatiable appetite. This is the story as collected by John T. Naaké in his 1874 anthology, "Slavonic Fairy Tales":

THE LONG-DESIRED CHILD.

(FROM THE BOHEMIAN.)

IN a hut at the farther end of a village, close to the forest, there once lived a man with his wife. Although they were very poor—the man was a daily labourer and the woman spun for sale—yet they were continually wishing for children, and saying, "Would we had a child."

"Be thankful that heaven has not granted you one," said the neighbours: "you yourselves have not enough to eat."

But the man and the woman said,—

"When we eat and are satisfied there would be always something left for our child. Would we had one."

One morning, as the man was digging out stumps of trees in the forest, he came across a small root which looked exactly like a little child—it had a head, body, arms, and legs,—he had only to smooth its forehead a little with his axe to make it round, and to cut off the roots from its little arms and legs to give them shape, and then the child was perfect, and wanted only voice to scream. The man took this root home, and said to his wife,—

"Here you have what you wished for—an Otesanek [a hewn-out child]. If you like, you can bring him up."

The woman put the child into swaddling clothes, then took it up, nursed it in her arms and sang to it:

"Bye, bye, my little Otesanek! When you awake, my little boy, I will boil you some food. Bye, bye!"

Suddenly the child began to kick about, raised up its head and cried,—

"Mother, I want something to eat!"

The woman was overjoyed. She put the child quickly in bed and hastened to prepare its food. When the food was ready Otesanek ate it all up, and then screamed again,—

"Mother, I want something to eat."

"Wait a moment, my dear child, wait a moment," said the woman, "and I will bring you something to eat."

She then ran to a neighbour's and brought in a basin of milk. Otesanek drank the milk, and then screamed again that he wanted something more to eat. The woman was greatly surprised at this, and said,—

"What, my child, have you not yet had enough?"

She then went out and borrowed in the village a loaf of bread, put it on the table, and again left the room to boil some water and make soup. As soon as she was gone, Otesanek, seeing the bread on the table, scrambled out of the swaddling clothes, jumped upon a bench, and in an instant swallowed up the bread, and then screamed again,—

"Mother, I want something to eat!"

The woman came in to cut the bread for the soup,— she looked about for it everywhere, but it was gone! In a corner stood Otesanek looking like a small barrel and staring at her.

"Heaven have mercy upon us!" cried the woman; "Otesanek, surely you have not eaten the loaf of bread?"

"Yes, mother," answered Otesanek; "I have eaten it, and now will eat you too."

He opened his mouth, and before the woman could recover from her astonishment, swallowed her up.

In a short time the man returned home. As soon as he had entered in, Otesanek screamed,—

"Father, I want something to eat!"

The man was greatly alarmed at the sight of a child with open mouth and rolling eyes, and looking as big as an oven. Having, however, recognised Otesanek, he said,—

"O-ho! is it you? Where is your mother?"

"I have eaten her," answered Otesanek; "and now it is your turn."

He opened his mouth and in an instant swallowed up the man. But the more Otesanek ate the more he wanted. There being nothing now in the hut that he could swallow up, he went into the village to look about him. He met a girl wheeling from the field a wheelbarrow full of clover.

"What have you eaten," cried the girl full of wonder, "that you look so big?"

Otesanek answered: "I am an eater, and have eaten some grits from a saucepan, a basinful of milk, a loaf of bread, my mother and father, and now will eat you too."

He rushed up to her, and the girl with the wheelbarrow disappeared. Afterwards Otesanek met a peasant who was driving a cart loaded with hay from the meadow. He advanced into the middle of the road and the horses stopped.

Otesánek by Samuele Madini, Public domain, via Wikimedia Commons.

Europe

"Can't you get out of the way, you monster? I shall drive over you," cried the peasant angrily, and began to urge the horses forward. Otesanek, however, did not pay the least attention to him, but began to say,—

"I am an eater, and have eaten some grits from a saucepan, a basinful of milk, a loaf of bread, my mother and father, a girl with the wheelbarrow, and now will eat you too."

Before the peasant recovered from his surprise he himself, with the horses and cart, was swallowed up by Otesanek. Then Otesanek went farther on. In the field there was a man watching pigs. Otesanek took a fancy to them and swallowed them all up, together with the man—there was not a sign left of them. Afterwards he perceived on a hill not far off a shepherd with a flock of sheep.

"Having already eaten so much," said Otesanek to himself, "I will eat these too."

He came nearer and swallowed them all up—the sheep, the shepherd, and his dog Vorish. Then he staggered forward and at last came to a field where an old woman was attending to cabbages. Otesanek did not reflect long, he went into the field, began to break off cabbages from the stumps and eat them up.

"Why are you destroying my property, Otesanek?" cried the old woman. "Surely you have eaten enough to be satisfied."

Otesanek looked at her with a grin and said: "I am an eater, and have eaten some grits from a saucepan, a basinful of milk, a loaf of bread, my father and mother, a girl with a wheelbarrow, a peasant and a cart loaded with hay, a swineherd and pigs, a shepherd and his sheep, and now will eat you too." And he wanted to swallow her up. But the old woman was too sharp for Otesanek—she struck him with her mattock and cut him in half. Otesanek fell down dead. Then there was a sight to see! First jumped out of the body the dog Vorish, after him came out the shepherd, and after the shepherd jumped out the sheep. Vorish collected the sheep together, the shepherd whistled and drove them home. Afterwards the herd of pigs rushed out, after them jumped out the swineherd, who cracked his whip and drove them after the shepherd. Then came out the horses drawing the cart loaded with hay; the peasant shook the reins angrily, and drove after the swineherd also to the village. After the cart came out the girl with the wheelbarrow, and after the girl jumped out the man and his wife, and carried home, alternately, under their arms the borrowed loaf of bread. From that moment neither of them ever said, "Would we had a child."

Mandrake the female.

A female Mandrake, pictured in the 1526 medicinal encyclopedia, "The Great Herbal."

"The Long-Desired Child" offers a nebulous moral for a fairy tale, other than perhaps to be careful for what you wish. However, it does bear resemblance to medieval European myths about the mandrake root. The mandrake, a relative of the nightshade, is a toxic plant that has throughout the centuries been used in small doses as an aphrodisiac, pain-killer, sleep-aid and something of a cure-all. Its fork-shaped root has been interpreted as human-shaped (with both male and female variations), leading to sinister superstitions about its nature in medieval Europe. The mandrake root was said to shriek when uprooted, causing anyone within earshot to go mad. Dogs would be tricked into pulling the root from the ground. Wrapped in silk and kept in a chest, the root was said to bring its owner perpetual wealth. Bryony roots were sold as mandrake in England, as true mandrake did not thrive in the country's soil. In the 16th and 17th centuries, Britons trimmed down bryony roots to emphasize the human shape, adding "hair" by inserting sprouting millet or barley seeds; this tradition persisted in later centuries, per the Oxford Dictionary of English Folklore.

"LE TÈPÉ-TÉPÉ"

The story of the Madagascar Man-Eating Tree inspired a French opera, which did not go down in history as a classic. I doubt we'll see a Broadway revival. A Montpellier theater critic described the experience in the April 28, 1902 La Vie Montpelliéraine et Régionale [translated from French]:

I returned to the theater eight days later to attend the first performance of Le Tèpé-Tépé, a new operetta in three acts and four scenes by Mr. Joseph Lacroix, with music by Mr. Lavello.

Despite the official recognition given to this play by the Commission of Local Authors and the laudatory articles generously bestowed upon it by the press throughout the run, the house was no better filled than at the last performance of Lohengrin.

This shared misfortune with Wagner would be in no way humiliating for Messrs. Lavello and Lacroix, if they could still hope for revenge: but it is likely that the premiere of Le Tèpé-Tépé will also be their last, and no one would dare claim that this would be a serious detriment to art.

Mr. Lavello's score is a suite of monotonous waltzes, without any character, and from which no truly original motif stands out.

As for the libretto, it's... astounding. Let's try to explain it in a few words:

The Tèpé-Tépé is a mechanical tree invented by King Mikakou to renew his harem at little cost. The king has persuaded his subjects that this carnivorous tree must absorb all the young widowed women; in reality, they descend into the Sapphire Cave, where the king finds them.

"The day after the opening, the red moon having finished, the flower was seen to open equally and Klipopette, volume XXVIII in hand, cried out: 'I know it, our plant.' Since that time, two friends have been traveling across the new continent, showing the phenomenal plant and the man it could not digest." -Panel from the comic strip "La Fleur Mystérieuse [The Mysterious Flower]" by Benoni, published in the Jun. 8, 1907 issue of La Jeunesse Moderne.

Europe

A European ship wrecks near Mikakou's island, and he wants to seize one of the passengers, a French diva; but the queen foils her fickle husband's scheme, and the Europeans are released.

On this basis, renewed from the Grand-Mogul, Mr. Joseph Lacroix has rhymed couplets that are mostly bawdy, and sown with handfuls of words, puns and approximations that do not exactly shine with good taste, finesse and novelty.

**

Damn, those French theater critics can lay down a sizzling burn!

MOUSE-EATING PITCHER PLANT

The same year that The Ghost Man wrote about "The Strangling Oak of Nannau Woods," an intriguing tale about a carnivorous plant housed in London appeared widely in press reports. The 1924 article stated:

Tropical Plant Eats Mice.

A most unusual plant, that reverses the natural order of things by eating animals, has recently been put on display at the London horticultural hall in England.

This extraordinary meat-eating plant is a native of the tropical East Indies. Its principal prey is mice, which are attracted to it by a very pungent odor emanating from the mouth of the blossom, formed into almost a perfect hole. The mice crawl into this opening and natural bristles on the petals close about the victim as it makes an attempt to escape. Digestive juices similar to those secreted in the stomachs of animals are given off and the victim is slowly consumed.

It has long been known that plants breathe and sleep, eat and drink much the same as animals; but this is the only plant known that eats meat.

**

The Unnatural History of Man-Eating Plants

Dr. Karl Shuker, zoologist and Cryptozoology expert, wrote in "The Beasts That Hide from Man" that this mouse-eating plant was the most feasible of the anomalous carnivorous plants he documented in his book. Shuker said it resembled familiar pitcher plants, with the addition of retaining spines inside its traps that were reminiscent in function to the external tentacles of sundews.

Larger species of *Nepenthes*, or tropical pitcher plants, have been documented to capture small vertebrates such as frogs, birds and smaller mammals. During a drought in 1987, two juvenile rats were found dead inside two separate *Nepenthes rajah* pitchers inside Borneo's Kinabalu Park. According to researcher and discoverer A. Phillips, the thirsty rats (possibly also sick and weakened) made the fatal mistake of climbing into the *N. rajah* pitchers seeking water and were unable to escape "the very slippery rim of the pitchers and strong, sharply pointed peristome."

Pitcher plants, though, are passive predators. Prey needs to enter the trap and is then caught inside by its one-way structure. As described, the East Indies specimen sounds rather like an active predator, similar to the Venus Flytrap, with a trigger mechanism causing the trap to move, closing around its rodent prey. That aspect makes the meat-eating plant of the East Indies a truly puzzling, intriguing mystery. Though not a "man-eating" monster, could this specimen have been a truly undiscovered species, never recognized officially by science during its London showcase and now possibly extinct or thus far un-rediscovered?

SOURCES:

Blake Price, Cheryl. "Vegetable Monsters: Man-Eating Trees in Fin-de-Siècle Fiction." *Victorian Literature and Culture*, vol. 41, no. 2, 2013, pp. 311-327.

Chang, Elizabeth. "Killer Plants of the Late Nineteenth Century." *Strange Science: Investigating the Limits of Knowledge in the Victorian Age*, edited by Lara Karpenko and Shalyn Claggett, University of Michigan Press, 2017.

Europe

Folkard, Richard. *Plant Lore, Legends, and Lyrics*. London, Sampson Low, Marston, Searle, and Rivington, 1884.

"Mandrake." *Wikipedia*, https://en.wikipedia.org/wiki/Mandrake. Accessed 17 Aug. 2025.

Naaké, John T. *Slavonic Fairy Tales*. London, Henry S. King & Co., 1874.

"*Nepenthes*." *Wikipedia*, https://en.wikipedia.org/wiki/Nepenthes. Accessed 14 Jun. 2025.

O'Donnell, Elliot. "The Strangling Oak of Nannau Woods." *San Francisco Examiner*, 19 Oct. 1924, American Weekly supplement, p. 2.

Phillips, A. "A Second Record of Rats as Prey in Nepenthes Rajah." *Carnivorous Plant Newsletter*, vol. 17, no. 2, Jun. 1988, p. 55.

Shuker, Karl P.N., Ph.D. *The Beasts That Hide from Man*. Paraview Press, 2003.

Simpson, Charles A., and Jacqueline, and Steve Roud, editors. *A Dictionary of English Folklore*. Oxford University Press, 2003.

"Théatre." *La Vie Montpelliéraine et Régionale* [Montpellier, France], 28 Apr. 1901, p. 8.

"Tropical Plant Eats Mice." *Washington County News* [Chatom, AL], 27 Mar. 1924, p. 1.

"Wealth in Orchids." *Maryville Daily Democrat* [Maryville, MO], 2 Jan. 1892, p. 3.

The Unnatural History of Man-Eating Plants

NEXT PAGE: "It is said that the little pitcher plant of our own country, which satisfies its flesh-craving appetite with insects, grows to enormous proportions in some tropical climates and feeds upon men. Travelers have told strange and affrighting stories of this freak of flowers; stories in which some wanderer groping his way at night, perchance, is caught on the thorns of the hungry plant and devoured, the shreds of clothes still clinging to the thorns, being the only clue to the man's unhappy end."

—Artwork from "Man-Eaters" newspaper advertisement for "Dr. Pierce's Common Sense Medical Adviser." The ad warned, "The man-eating plant may be a myth, but even if it be a reality its perils are rare and insignificant compared with the dangers to which we are exposed in our own country from an insatiable man-eating microbe." For just the cost of shipping (31¢ for hardbound or 21¢ for cloth-bound), Dr. R. V. Pierce of Buffalo, New York would send you his 1,000-plus-page tome outlining his "Golden Medical Discovery" to cure lung ailments and consumption, or tuberculosis, at its early stages.

Published in the Nov. 27, 1901 Evening Star of Washington, D.C.

The Unnatural History of Man-Eating Plants

MEANWHILE, AT SEA...

PORTIONS of the South Pacific ocean produce a wonderful species of the sea weed called the "vegetable boa constrictor." According to recent published accounts they are likely to be met with at any point of Southern California and the Sandwich Islands on the one side and between Chile and Australia on the other. These vine-like stranglers are frequently found tightly entwined about the body of a dead whale, shark or porpoise, but whether they had fastened upon the bodies of these dead sea animals before life had become extinct, or had only ventured to attack the remains after the vital spark had fled, are conundrums which, of course, cannot be answered. Experiments made with this curious vine and the carcass of a porpoise washed ashore in the harbor at Apia tend to prove that the vine, like that of our common bean, will not entwine itself around anything dead, whether that thing be of vegetable or animal creation. Dr. Chadbourne, in his "Annals of the Caroline Islands," says: "I have often seen monster specimens of macrocystis (the giant seaweed) with every vestige of life squeezed out of them by that ocean demon, the 'constrictor' vine, which is itself a species of seaweed. Macrocystis often grows to be from 20 to 30 inches in diameter and 1,500 to 2,000 feet in length, while the constrictor vine seldom exceeds 100 feet in length, and is never larger in diameter than a pound and half salmon can. It is the 'squeeze snake' of the ocean, however, and woe to the unlucky man, animal or plant that comes within its reach." At Apia the piles driven in the harbor all show marks like those you have seen made by ivy on the forest trees—marks which the natives gravely inform you were made by the constrictor vine. Cases wherein human beings are said to have lost their lives as a result of coming in contact with the vegetable boa constrictor are like the cases of death attributed to centipedes and tarantulas—often reported but seldom conclusively proven.

—*Savannah Morning News, 12/23/1892*

AUSTRALIA

AUSSIE CANNIBAL TREE

William Jennings Bryan, the famous orator, provided a lengthy description of Australia's Man-Eating Tree during his first full speech in U.S. Congress on March 16, 1892. Bryan, serving Nebraska's 1st district in the U.S. House of Representatives and a member of the Ways and Means Committee, cited the tree as a metaphor in his stance against the protective McKinley tariff on the wool industry. Bryan argued that the tariff enriched companies and placed undue financial burden on farmers and consumers. He stated:

Out in the West the people have been taught to worship this protection. It has been a god to many of them. But I believe, Mr. Chairman, that the time for worship has passed. It is said that there is in Australia what is known as the cannibal tree. It grows not very high, and spreads out its leaves like great arms until they touch the ground. In the top is a little cup, and in that cup a mysterious kind of honey. Some of the natives worship the tree, and on their festive days they gather around it, singing and dancing, and then, as a part of their ceremony, they select one from their number, and, at the point of spears, drive him up over the leaves onto the tree; he drinks of the honey, he becomes intoxicated as it were, and then those arms, as if instinct with life, rise up; they encircle him in their folds, and, as they crush him to death, his companions stand around shouting and singing for joy.

Protection has been our cannibal tree, and as one after another of our farmers has been driven by the force of circumstances upon that tree and has been crushed within its folds his companions have stood around and shouted, "Great is protection!"

Perhaps it was a tad melodramatic, but Bryan appears to have read and enjoyed the accounts of an Australian Man-Eating Tree that first appeared in print a few years before his speech.

However, this particular plant does not seem to have been an Australian original, but a plagiarism of the more famous Madagascar story, "Crinoida Dajeeana," which was first published by the New York World newspaper on April 28, 1874.

The Australia version appeared in various forms in publications across the world over the course of at least three decades. The earliest and lengthiest copy I can find was published in the Nov. 23, 1889 edition of The Cincinnati Enquirer. Titled "Wonderful Trees," this survey of "Some of the Living Wonders of the World's Forests" was attributed to the St. Louis Republic, a newspaper whose 1889 output is absent from online archives.

The following copy of the story, focused on two mysterious trees from Australia, was printed in the Jan. 3, 1890 Wichita Daily Eagle:

TWO WONDERFUL TREES.

THEY ARE THE LIVING WONDERS OF THE WORLD'S FORESTS.

The Stinging Tree of Australia, Which Causes Great Suffering to All Who Touch It—"The Devil of Trees," Which Is a Veritable Cannibal.

One of the most remarkable—not the most remarkable—trees known to the botanist is the stinging tree of Queensland, Australia. It hardly attains to the dignity of a tree, seldom growing to be more than 10 or 12 feet in height, which, even in this country of less luxuriant vegetation, would rank it with the shrubs and bushes. Whether the tree is a foot or 12 feet in height, it always grows in a cone shape, with whitish, birch colored limbs and trunk, with saucer shaped dark colored leaves and flaming red berries. The edge of the peculiarly shaped leaf is deeply notched, each point being provided with a thorn like that of the thistle. This thorn is the famous "sting" about which travelers tell wonderful stories.

A puncture from one of these thorns leaves no mark, but the pain is said to be maddening in the extreme. If one is stung on the right hand, the pain extends all over that side of the body, causing excruciating agony for hours or even days afterwards, having, in fact, been known to cause loss of the senses and even partial or total paralysis. An Australian hunter tells of how he was reminded during every damp spell for a period of nine years of a slight wound on the wrist, caused by one of the withered leaves of this tree blowing from one of the bushes and touching him in its flight. If a horse, while grazing, accidentally touches his nose to one of these leaves, he exhibits every symptom of an animal suffering from hydrophobia. He rushes open mouthed at every moving thing—tree, man, weed or anything that attracts his attention—and almost invariably must be disposed of in the same manner as if suffering from the terrible malady above mentioned. Dogs that have been stung on the legs by the poisonous spikes of the stinging tree chew off the limb above the wound and seem to think the pain caused by the amputation slight compared to that caused by the sting.

THE CANNIBAL TREE.

The cannibal tree, which I am strongly tempted to call the most wonderful of God's many wonders in vegetable life, contests for space to spread its horrid leaves with the stinging monster above mentioned in many parts of the South Australian jungles. If the stinging tree could be appropriately styled the demon of the antipodean wilds, the cannibal tree is surely "a thousand devils painted brown," as Wilson says of the feelers of the devil fish. It grows up in the shape of a huge pineapple and seldom attains a height of over 8 feet, in rare instances 9 to 11. Its height has no control of its diameter, as the reader may imagine when told that one of 8 feet is frequently 3 to 5 feet through at the ground. The leaves, which resemble wide boards of a dark olive green more than anything else, are frequently 10 to 12 feet long and 20 inches through in the pulpy part, next to the trunk. These thick, board like leaves all put out from the top of the tree and hang down to the ground, forming a kind of umbrella around the stem.

Upon the apex of the cone, around which all these mammoth leaves center, and looking much like the pistils of a huge flower, are two concave figures, resembling dinner plates, strung one above the other on a stick. These are constantly filled with a sickening, intoxicating honey distilled by the tree.

The natives of South Australia worship the cannibal tree in the name of "The Devil of Trees," and perform many uncanny rites about its death dealing leaves, not infrequently going so far as to sacrifice one of their number to the blood-thirsty monster.

AN AWFUL SCENE.

A description of a scene of this kind, written by Cherrie, the Scotch traveler, and printed in The South Australian Register, March 11, 1875, I give below:

"* * * My observations on this occasion were suddenly interrupted by the natives chanting what Hendricks told me were propitiatory hymns to the great tree devil. With still wilder shrieks and chants they now surrounded one of the women and urged her with the points of their javelins until, slowly and with despairing face, she climbed up the huge leaves of the tree and stood upon the concaved honey receptacle in the center. 'Tisk! tisk!' (drink! drink!) cried the men. Stooping, she drank of the viscid fluid in the cup. Rising instantly, with wild frenzy in her face and convulsive cords in her limbs, she made an effort to spring from the fatal spot. But, oh, no! The atrocious cannibal tree, that demon that had stood so inert and dead, came to sudden and savage life. The delicate but long palpi, like the threads in the center of a flower, danced above her head with the fury of starved serpents; then, as if they had instincts of demoniac intelligence, they fastened upon her in sudden coils around and around her neck and arms, and while her awful screams and yet more awful drunken laughter rose wildly, to be instantly strangled down again into a gurgling moan, the tendrils, one after another, like great green serpents, with brutal energy and infernal rapidity, rose, protracted themselves and wrapped her about in fold after fold, ever tightening with the cruel swiftness and savage tenacity of anacondas fastening upon their prey.

Sacrificed to a Man-Eating Tree. San Francisco Examiner, Oct. 3, 1920.

"It was the barbarity of the Laocoon without its beauty—this strange, horrible murder. And now the giant leaves, which had hung so limp and lifeless to the ground, rose slowly and stiffly like the arms of a derrick, and erected themselves like a huge pointed church spire high in the air, approaching each other and locking their bony fingers over the dead and hampered woman with the silent force of an hydraulic press and the ruthless purpose of a thumb screw. A moment more, and while I could see the bases of these great levers pressing more tightly toward each other from their interstices, there trickled down the trunk of the tree great streams of viscid, honey-like fluid, mingled horribly with the blood of the poor victim. At sight of this the savage hordes around me, yelling madly, bounded forward, crowded to the tree, clasped it, and with cups, leaves, hands and tongues, each one obtained enough of the liquid to send him mad and frantic."—John W. Wright in St. Louis Republic.

***

The March 11, 1875 edition of the South Australian Register did not include any stories about Man-Eating Trees (the closest match being a feature on the Adelaide Botanic Gardens). However, such an article did appear in the Oct. 27, 1874 issue—the oft-published and nearly identical article about the Man-Eating Tree of Madagascar.

Some reprints of the "Wonderful Trees" article that shifted the Man-Eating Tree to Australia attributed the story to John W. Wright of the St. Louis Republic. Wright was a prolific writer throughout the 1880s and 1890s, penning stories that appealed to popular interest and were carried in newspapers across the United States. Among his output were articles cataloguing examples of the world's tallest people, the world's shortest people, people with horns, Moon myths, the history of the Bible, "Marvelous Wells... Wells That Roar and Wells That Boil. Some Are Hot and Others Are Cold. Electric Wells Are Very Common—A Few of the Most Noteworthy," and the Red Spectre, a ghost dressed in red who thrice warned Napoleon (futilely) to cease his attempts to conquer Europe or lose supernatural protection.

As pointed out by "VampiricDemon," mod of the Cryptobotany Subreddit, The Stinging Tree appears to be a description of

Australia

Dendrocnide moroides (aka the Stinging Bush or Gympie-Gympie), a shrub found in Australian and Malaysian rainforests. The entire plant is covered with fine and brittle, toxin-coated hairs that can become embedded in the skin at the slightest touch. Victims experience an immediate and intense burning and stinging pain that gets worse over the next half hour and can persist for hours or days, even weeks or months. Gympie-Gympie is the most urticant plant in Australia, possibly the world. *Dendrocnide moroides* was first collected in 1819 and described in 1857 by Hugh Algernon Weddell.

I can't help wondering if one factual basis for grabbing, man-devouring trees in Australia is *Calamus australis*, a climbing plant with a long, flexible stem that grows in the rainforests of northeast Queensland. Its fronds and tendrils are lined with sharp, sturdy hooks that enable the plant to scale tall trees. It also has a habit of snagging clothing and ensnaring passersby, leading to its nickname, "Wait-a-While."

ANGRY TREE

Another curiosity: "There is a species of acacia which grows in Australia, called the angry tree, writes a botanist and traveler. The shoots when handled move restlessly, making the leaves rustle. If the plant is moved from one place to another it seems angry, and its leaves stand out in all directions like the quills of a porcupine, and do not quiet down for an hour or two; the plant giving out when thus disturbed a very sickening odor," wrote the St. Louis Post-Dispatch in 1892. "When the sun sets the leaves fold together and the little twigs curl tightly. This closing of the leaves is not, however, a peculiarity of the angry acacia, for other varieties do this, and the locust-tree, which is allied."

PINK-FLOWERED CARNIVORE

The press was not totally lacking in originality when it came to Australia and carnivorous trees. A French newspaper, Le Petit Parisien, published this slightly tongue-in-cheek account [translated from French] of a fearsome, blood-sucking tree on May 10, 1879. It is therefore one of the earliest reports of a Man-Eating Tree outside of Madagascar, and an original creation:

The Unnatural History of Man-Eating Plants

THE CARNIVOROUS TREE

We absolutely guarantee the authenticity of the following adventure recounted by our traveler, whose hero is Sir Arthur Murray, a well-known squatter in Queensland (Australia).

The carnivorous tree is a compatriot of the platypus.

Sir Murray still operates a "station" today located south of the Gulf of Carpentaria, between Mount Corbett and the Leichhardt River, about fifty kilometers from the twentieth parallel.

The farmer was out hunting. The bullet from his small rifle had pierced a magnificent "blue macaw" cackling on the highest branch of a eucalyptus. The hunter watched the bird fall with the double satisfaction of a skilled marksman and a fine gourmet.

But, strangely enough, the game, which he had already seen on the spit, encountered in its fall a leaf of a beautiful dark green color, sixty centimeters wide, thick, fleshy, and cut up to half of the blade.

At this strange contact, the leaflets curled up, like the tentacles of an octopus, and imprisoned the bird, which disappeared, enclosed, grasped, and snatched away from under the nose of the dismayed hunter.

In vain, he waited for the plant thief to offer him his prey; the leaf remained tightly folded.

He then approached the tree, which he examined carefully.

It was no taller than ten meters. It had no, strictly speaking, a stem. Its branches, in whose axils bloomed enormous pink flowers, the size of cabbages, were arranged in regular tiers in concentric crowns and, when they joined together, formed a cone ending in a leafy bouquet like that of a palm tree.

The leaves were about six centimeters thick, and furnished at the top with an infinity of small, hollow, short, and dense tubes, on the opening of which sparkled a drop of a milky liquid, with opal reflections and the consistency of syrup.

Man-Eating Trees depicted in the comic strip "This Curious World,"
Nov. 13, 1935. Included here on a Fair Use, educational basis.

Wanting to see for himself what was preventing his quarry from falling, he bravely placed his closed fist in the middle of a leaf hanging at his height.

The phenomenon that had presided over the macaw's disappearance immediately recurred. The experimenter's hand and arm were forcefully compressed as if by a tight glove. He gradually felt a sort of painful numbness, then a burning, sharp, stabbing pain, as if hundreds of red-hot pins had been driven into his skin.

Judging that the experiment was sufficient, he cut the stem with a single stab of his knife.

The tentacles soon relaxed, and his hand appeared swollen and livid. Thin threads of reddish serosity, which flowed slowly, made him recognize that the liquid secreted by the leaf was capable of dissolving the animate tissues and probably making them assimilable to the vampire plant.

The Unnatural History of Man-Eating Plants

The leaf had resumed its original form the next day. The presence on the ground of a few bones stuck to feathers confirmed the truth of this supposition.

The macaw had been absorbed, digested, by the Australian colossus, like insects by the European Drosera.

Scientists, who have so long haggled over the platypus's name and place, have not yet given a name to the carnivorous tree.

We demand for it the right to be cited in botanical works and in the Jardin d'Acclimatation.

DEVIL'S TREE

Ellis Rowan, the renowned Australian artist who illustrated Alice Lounsberry's 1899 book, "A Guide to the Wild Flowers," and its 1900 follow-up, "A Guide to the Trees," was credited in the press as another source for a story about an Australian Man-Eating Tree.

As reported in the Apr. 22, 1900 Washington Post:

THE CANNIBAL TREE.

It Is a Strange Native of Australia and Eagerly Destroys Its Human Prey.

Mrs. Ellis Rowan, of Melbourne, Australia, who is at present in New York, and who has traveled more extensively in the cannibal country than any other European woman, has told recently of the existence in Australia of a forest tree which is perhaps one of the most wonderful plants of nature. It will hold in its center and devour the body of a man quite as readily as our insectivorous wild flowers trap the insects on which they partly subsist. The tree is called the cannibal tree.

As Mrs. Rowan describes it, its appearance may be imagined to resemble a mammoth pineapple, which often reaches to the height of eleven feet. Its foliage is composed of a series of broad, board-like leaves, growing in a fringe at its apex. Instead, however, of standing erect, as does the little green tuft at the top of a pineapple, these leaves droop over and hang to the ground. In the largest specimens they are often from fifteen to twenty feet long, and strong enough to bear the weight of a man. Hidden under these curious leaves is to be found a peculiar growth of spear-like formations, arranged in a circle, and which perform the same functions for the plant as do pistils for flowers. They cannot, however, abide to be touched.

Among the natives of Australia there is a tradition that in the old days of the antipodean wilds this tree was worshipped under the name of the "Devil's Tree." Its wrath was thought to be greatly dreaded. As soon as its huge green leaves began to rise restlessly up and down, its worshippers interpreted the sign as meaning that a sacrifice must be made to appease its anger. One among their number was therefore chosen, stripped of his raiment, and driven by shouting crowds up one of its leaves to the apex.

All went well with the victim until the instant that he stepped into the center of the plant and on the so-called pistils, when the board-like leaves would fly together and clutch and squeeze out the life of the intruder. By early travelers in Australia it is affirmed that the tree would then hold its prey until every particle of his flesh had fallen from his bones, after which the leaves would relax their hold and the gaunt skeleton fall heedlessly to the ground. In this way did its worshippers seek to avert disaster and to still the demon spirit among them.

The tree's present name and its uncanny actions remind us that the cannibals of Northern Australia have also a playful way of scattering about the bones of a victim after one of their feasts.

***

Now, it seems very likely that Rowan was simply retelling the oft-told story of the Man-Eating Tree that had by then become a newspaper staple. But Rowan's expertise in documenting the plant kingdom and her extensive travels around her home country cast a faint shadow of doubt on whether she was just spinning yarns. Sadly, the man-eater went undepicted in her and Lounsberry's tome on trees!

Ellis Rowan

SOURCES:

Bryan, William Jennings. *Speeches of William Jennings Bryan, Vol. 1.* Funk & Wagnalls Company, 1909.

"*Calamus australis.*" *Wikipedia,* https://en.wikipedia.org/wiki/Calamus_australis. Accessed 4 Sep. 2025.

"The Cannibal Tree." *Nashville Banner* [Nashville, TN], 29 Nov. 1889, p. 3.

"The Cannibal Tree." *Washington Post* [Washington, D.C.], 22 Apr. 1900, p. 29.

"Curious Trees." *St. Louis Post-Dispatch,* 15 May 1892, p. 26.

Australia

"*Dendrocnide moroides.*" *Wikipedia,* https://en.wikipedia.org/wiki/Dendrocnide_moroides. Accessed 4 Sep. 2025.

"Ellis Rowan." *Wikipedia,* https://en.wikipedia.org/wiki/Ellis_Rowan. Accessed 15 Jun. 2025.

"L'arbre Carnivore." *Le Petit Parisien* [Paris], 10 May 1879, p. 3.

Lounsberry, Alice and Ellis Rowan. *A Guide to the Trees.* Frederick A. Stokes Company, 1900.

"The Man-Eating Tree of Madagascar." *South Australian Register* [Adelaide, Australia], 27 Oct. 1874, p. 6.

McEwin, G. "A Description of the Adelaide Botanic Gardens—Part I." *South Australian Register* [Adelaide, Australia], 11 Mar. 1875, p. 6.

"McKinley Tariff." *Wikipedia,* https://en.wikipedia.org/wiki/McKinley_Tariff. Accessed 16 Jun. 2025.

"New Literature." *Illustrated Buffalo Express* [Buffalo, NY], 21 Jan. 1900, p. 19.

Saint-Hilaire, Geoffroy. *Philosophie Anatomique.* Paris, Méquignon-Marvis, 1818.

"Something in Trees." *Eyre's Peninsula Tribune* [Cowell, South Australia], 9 Jan. 1920. p. 4.

"Two Wonderful Trees." *Daily Transcript* [Holyoke, MA], 6 Dec. 1889, p. 2.

VampiricDemon. *Reddit,* 4 Sep. 2025, https://www.reddit.com/r/cryptobotany/comments/1n8fgxg/comment/ncemtqk/. Accessed 4 Sep. 2025.

"William Jennings Bryan." *Wikipedia,* https://en.wikipedia.org/wiki/William_Jennings_Bryan. Accessed 16 Jun. 2025.

"Wonderful Trees." *Cincinnati Enquirer,* 23 Nov. 1889, p. 15.

Wright, John W. "About Horned People." *Wichita Daily Eagle* [Wichita, KS], 23 Aug. 1889, p. 8.

Wright, John W. "The Bible's History." *Jackson Weekly Citizen* [Jackson, WI], 12 Aug. 1890, p. 3.

Wright, John W. "Celebrated Midgets." *Atchinson Daily Champion* [Atchinson, KS], 3 Apr. 1889, p. 5.

Wright, John W. "Marvelous Wells." *Bismarck Daily Tribune* [Bismarck, ND], 21 Feb. 1890, p. 4.

Wright, John W. "Moon Myths." *Jackson Daily Citizen* [Jackson, MI], 13 Feb. 1890, p. 8.

Wright, John W. "The Red Man's Warning." *Miner's Journal* [Pottsville, PA], 5 Sep. 1890, p. 2.

Wright, John W. "They Were Very Tall." *Muskegon Chronicle* [Muskegon, MI], 18 Feb. 1889, p. 4.

Wright, John W. "Two Wonderful Trees." *Wichita Daily Eagle* [Wichita, KS], 3 Jan. 1890, p. 8.

CARNIVOROUS PLANTS OF THE FUTURE.

A Man-Eating Venus Fly Trap.

From the column "Life in the Garden" by "Veronica," the "Official Organ of the New Zealand Sweet Pea Society and Auckland Horticultural Society." Published in the Feb. 23, 1910 issue of The Weekly Graphic and New Zealand Mail.

It is a fact recognised by botanists as beyond dispute that the carnivorous habit among plants is more widespread than it was formerly supposed to be. The specialized sundews (Droseras) are but the advance guard of a large army of species which depend for their existence more or less upon the absorption of animal salts through their foliage. There is no gainsaying the statement, recently put forward by more than one scientist, that the tendency to rely upon a carnivorous diet is on the increase.

Of course, this is only in a line with the simplest evolutionary principle. It is possible to trace the steps by which the highest types of species, which seize and hold their prey, such as the Venus fly trap (Dionaea), have been evolved from those which merely capture their

The Unnatural History of Man-Eating Plants

victims by the use of an adhesive fluid such as the fly catcher of Portugal (Drosophvllum). Still lower in the scale are the plants, such as the teasles (Dipsacus), which drown the injects in strange bucket-like contrivances located at the base of the leaves. Flies which may chance to fall into the water are of course drowned, and the plant absorbs the nitrogenous elements from their decaying bodies.

It is a startling conception that in ages to come the plant world as a whole may become so advanced in carnivorous tastes as to be a real menace to animal creation. Dreadful indeed must be the sundews and the Dionaeas to their insect victims at the present time. The unfortunate fly which is captured by the leaf of the sundew finds itself held down by strong arms which are able to resist its violent struggles. The largest Drosera on earth at the present time produces leaves which are perhaps nine inches in length. Magnify this plant until the leaves are ten feet in length, and we have an exceedingly formidable specimen. Many of the palms and other tropical species have foliage which is much in excess of this measurement, so that the idea of leaves as big as this is not altogether fantastic. To be in proportion, the tentacles could scarcely be less than ten inches in length, and these would be able to grapple with birds of considerable size. We may conceive that the giant sundew would be able to hold out some special inducement for its intended victims to visit the leaves. Probably the bait would be in the form of some sweet-tasting secretion. On alighting, the birds would probably not find the adhesive fluid which the leaves would produce more than slightly annoying. The movements which they would make, in an endeavour to free themselves, would be all-sufficient to give the stimulus to the sensitive tentacles. These would rapidly close in on their prey, and in a few moments escape would be out of the question. Finally, the unfortunate birds would perish miserably, the bodies in their decay yielding to the plant the nitrogenous matter desired.

Carnivorous Plants of the Future

A Goat-Eating Butterwort of the Future.

The Pinguiculas or butterworts are at the present time
innocent-looking plants rather attractive in appearance.
These species, as is well known, find their home in boggy
tracts, where they spread their foliage on the surface of
the ground in the form of a rosette. If the leaves of the
butterwort are closely examined, it will be seen that they
are thickly covered with two sets of glands, one set of
which is plainly visible to the naked eye. This visible

set resembles a miniature mushroom, while the other set is microscopic and is formed of eight cells grouped after the manner of a wart or a knob. It is the practice of these glands whenever they come into contact with any object to pour out copiously a mucilaginous fluid, which acts much in the same way as bird lime. Acid secretion is also produced, which aids the leaf in the digestion of the object—supposing that the capture should be an insect. In order to make assurance doubly sure, the edge of the leaf in certain species is seen to curl slowly inward. Now we can imagine that in the very far-away future with which we are dealing the Pinguicula will develop leaves which will hardly be less than five or six feet in length. These lying along the surface of the ground will make a special appeal to grazing animals. Perhaps as with the sundew the allurement will be in the form of some pleasant-tasting secretion which is peculiarly attractive to sheep and goats. We can imagine how these animals on first coming across the plants would start to regale themselves at the prepared feast. The strong sticky substances would take a firm hold of the hairs surrounding the mouth parts of the creatures, and in their endeavour to free themselves the animals would become more entangled. Gradually, too, the sides of the huge leaves would close inward, and the fate of the victim could not long be delayed. A pitiable spectacle indeed to see these animals done to death by a plant, but the same process on a smaller scale is repeated thousands of times during the summer in any place where the Pinguiculas abound.

We can hardly think in this advance of vegetable life that the many species of pitcher plants which catch their prey more by allurement than by force, would be behindhand in the forward movement. Even at the present time many of these species develop processes which are several feet in length, as exemplified in the case of the Sarracenias and Darlingtonias. In one of the accompanying illustrations is pictured one of the colossal pitchers which in the course of ages may be evolved from the comparatively small Cephalotus—a native of Australia. There is no knowing what

Carnivorous Plants of the Future

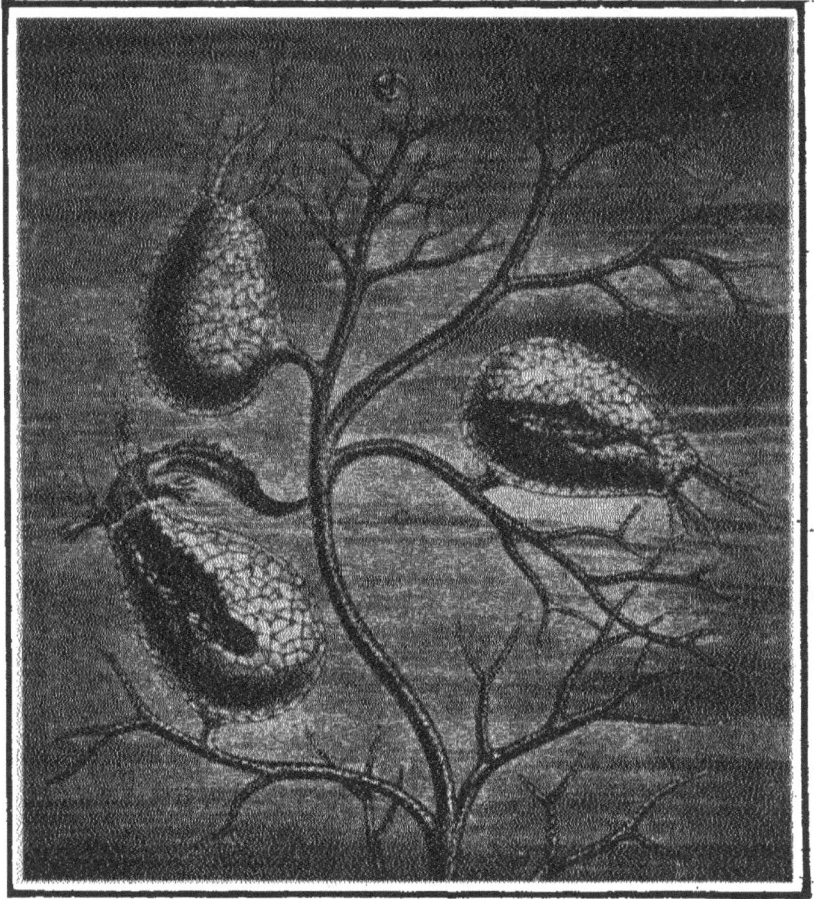

The Great Bladderwort Swallowing a Reptile.

inducements these plants might not be able to hold out for the capturing of even man himself. Perhaps the tissue inside the pitcher would be peculiarly succulent, and we know that where there is anything worth having there will always be found men daring enough to take the risk of getting it. Once inside the pitcher of the Cephalotus, escape would be possible only with a friendly assistant at hand. From the bottom of the pitcher three barriers would confront the prisoner anxious to get out. First of all there is a circular ridge projecting in such a way that it is most difficult to surmount. Secondly, a stretch of wall thickly covered with processes resembling the teeth of a comb and all pointing downward. Last of all, on the involute rim round the mouth of the pitcher is arranged a fringe of decurved spines which resemble a row of formidable bayonets. Indeed, it would be a far more simple matter to get out of the average well than to make one's escape from a giant Cephalotus pitcher.

Although the matter does not involve death, the giant Aristolochia flower brings about the imprisonment of flies for quite a long time. The system is in connection with the cross-fertilisation of the blossom. The insects are induced to enter the cavernous mouth of the great bloom by an odour strongly suggestive of carrion, which is peculiarly attractive to flies. Once inside, the flies are held captive by an ingenious arrangement whereby they are lost in the tortuous passages at the rear of the flower. After blundering around for some time, the winged creatures are able to emerge again, not, however, before they have become well dusted with pollen for transmission to another bloom.

It is possible that the Aristolochia of years to come will assume much larger proportions, and we may imagine that the flower will be able to hold out some allurement which will tempt large animals to enter its gloomy depths. It is more likely that escape from the colossal blossom would not be such a simple matter, and there might be a danger of a creature's coming unpleasantly near to starvation before seeing daylight again.

Far more dreadful than any of the plants described above would be the Venus fly trap of the future. This plant would be a vegetable terror. As is well known, the leaves of this plant are designed in the form of a trap. On the upper surface of each half of the leaf are three hairs. To touch any Of them is to cause the organ to shut up, inclosing the object which has given rise to the irritation. The bordering of the leaf is formed of sharp, fringed hairs, which, when the trap is closed, prevent escape. At the most the leaves of the Dionæa are not more than an inch in length, but we may get a little idea of

Carnivorous Plants of the Future

A Great Sundew, Millions of Years Hence, Catching a Stork.

what this plant may be in years to come, if we imagine the
foliage to be large enough to grapple with a man. It is
the habit of this plant to grow with its leaves half-
concealed beneath the sphagnum moss in which it thrives.
The leaves of the giant man-trap partly hidden by the
undergrowth would form the most terrible pitfall that the
world has ever seen. Any unfortunate man who should chance
to stumble into one of these leaves would be speedily

crushed to death by the steady pressure of the inclosing sides. One can imagine that a country in which the man trap abounded would be avoided as much as a district inhabited by man-eating savages.

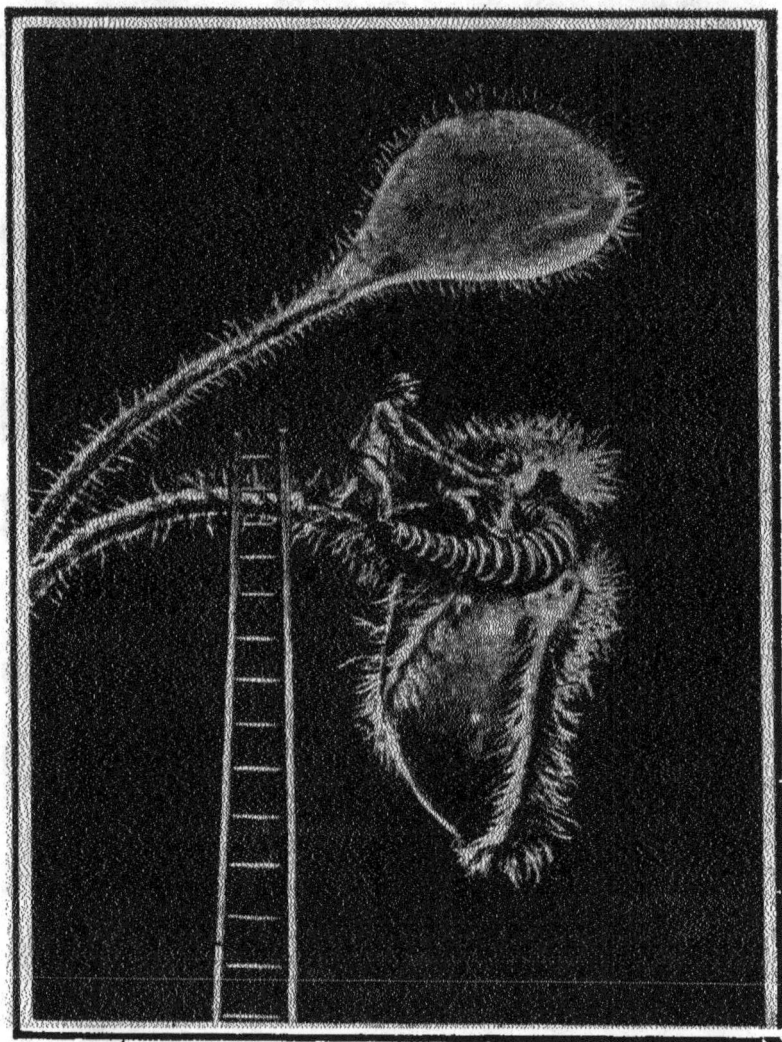

From a Giant Pitcher Plant a Man Could Escape Only with the Help of a Friend.

The aquatic plants such as the bladderworts (Utricularia) would scarcely be behindhand in this forward movement among the carnivorous species. These plants capture small

Carnivorous Plants of the Future

water creatures by means of little bladders which are attached to their stems. The entrance to these receptacles is guarded by a little door, which can be opened easily from the exterior, but may not be pushed aside from the interior. At the present time the bladders of the Utricularia are small, but there is no reason to suppose that they will always remain so. It is quite likely that they may increase in size so that they are able to grapple with good-sized fish and other water animals.

In these far-away days of which we have been speculating, plants will be divided into wild and tame sorts in the very real sense of the words. The botanical gardens of the time will be far more exciting than are the zoological collections of today. It is fortunate that all natural changes come about with great slowness, and it may be that the condition of man himself will have changed considerably by the time he is called upon to face these aggressive plants. It is to be hoped that they may be so, otherwise the outlook for the human race is distinctly disquieting.

SOUTH AMERICA

YATEVEO

American journalist James W. Buel described Yateveo, the Man-Eating Tree of South America, in his 1887 book "Sea and Land: An Illustrated History of the Wonderful and Curious Things of Nature Existing Before and Since the Deluge," a beautifully illustrated tome that vividly tours the Earth's natural world through a mix of science, history and legend. Buel was a prolific writer, penning more than 40 books, primarily travelogues and biographies, and contributing to popular U.S. magazines like Harper's Weekly and The Atlantic Monthly. Of the Yateveo, Buel wrote:

A MAN-EATING PLANT.

Travelers have told us of a plant, which they assert grows in Central Africa and also in South America, that is not contented with the myriad of large insects which it catches and consumes, but its voracity extends to making even humans its prey. This marvelous vegetable *Minotaur* is represented as having a short, thick trunk, from the top of which radiate giant spines, narrow and flexible, but of extraordinary tenaciousness, the edges of which are armed with barbs, or dagger-like teeth. Instead of growing upright, or at an inclined angle from the trunk, these spines lay their outer ends upon the ground, and so gracefully are they distributed that the trunk resembles an easy couch with green drapery around it. The unfortunate traveler, ignorant of the monstrous creation which lies in his way, and curious to examine the strange plant, or to rest himself upon its inviting stalk approaches without a suspicion of his certain doom. The moment his feet are set within the circle of the horrid spines, they rise up, like gigantic serpents, and entwine themselves about him until he is drawn upon the stump, when they speedily drive their daggers into his body and thus complete the massacre. The body is crushed until every drop of blood is squeezed out of it and becomes absorbed by the gore-loving plant, when the dry carcass is thrown out and the horrid trap set again.

A gentleman of my acquaintance, who, for a long time, resided in Central America, affirms the existence of such a plant as I have here briefly described, except that instead of the filaments, or spines, resting on the ground he says they move themselves constantly in the air, like so many huge serpents in an angry discussion, occasionally darting from side to side as if striking at an imaginary foe. When their prey comes within reach the spines reach out with wonderful sagacity (if I may be allowed to apply the expression to a vegetable creature), and grasp it in an unyielding embrace, from whence it issues only when all the substance of its body is yielded up. In its action of exerting pressure upon its prey, this dreadful plant resembles the instrument used in the dark ages for inflicting a torturous death. It was made of two long iron cylinders, on the inside of which were sharp, projecting pikes. The victim was placed inside, and the two cylinders then brought forcibly together, thus driving a hundred or more of the pointed pikes into all parts of his body and producing a frightful death. Generally this inquisitorial instrument was made, somewhat crudely, to represent a woman, hence the name applied to it was "The Maiden," by which it is still known.

Dr. Antonio Jose Marquez, a distinguished gentleman of the city of Barranguilla, in the United States of Colombia, in describing this wonderful plant to the author, affirms that when excited it violently agitates its long, tentacle-like stems, the edges of which, rasping upon each other, produced a hissing noise which resembles the Spanish expression, *ya-te-veo*, the literal translation of

THE YA-TE-VEO, OR CARNIVOROUS PLANT.

Illustration of Ya-Te-Veo by Armand Welcker, published in J. W. Buel's "Sea and Land," 1887.

which is *"I see you."* The plant is therefore known, in South America, by the name *Yateveo*. He further asserts that so poisonous are the stems that if the flesh of any animal be punctured by the sharp barbs, a rapidly-eating ulcer immediately forms, for which there is no known antidote, and death speedily ensues.

It is a singular thing, and much to be deplored, if such a voracious plant exists, that we can find no description of it in the most elaborate works on botany; and yet hundreds of responsible travelers declare they have frequently seen it, and not only watched it when in a normal condition, but one African explorer declares he once witnessed the destruction of a native who was accidentally caught by one. It has also been asserted that in the Fan country of Africa, criminals and those convicted of practicing witchcraft, are sometimes fed alive to this man-eating plant. All of which, however, I am inclined to doubt; not that there is no foundation for such statements as travelers sometimes make about this astonishing growth, but that the facts are greatly exaggerated.

***

Dr. Marquez, Buel's source for Yateveo, appears to have been Antonio José Márquez, a newspaperman and native of Barranquilla. He published many articles under the pseudonym Victor Heim in El Rocío, "The Literary Newspaper Dedicated to the Fair Sex and Youth," printed in Bogotá from 1872-1874. Márquez also published a 48-page pamphlet entitled "Leprosy and its Curability" in New York in 1881. Later, he owned and edited La Patria, the "Weekly Magazine of Politics, Science and Literature," circulated in Barranquilla between 1896 and 1899. Reflecting the editor's interest in medicine, the magazine provided updates on new cancer treatments and the like. It seems probable that Márquez could have written about Yateveo in El Rocio or elsewhere, but I have yet to locate this.

LAMPARAGUA

Writing for the religious-leaning Scottish magazine Good Words in 1901, J. Barnard James described an expedition he once made to

The Unnatural History of Man-Eating Plants

South America. "Some years ago I had occasion to penetrate a portion of the Virgin Forest that lies along the higher reaches of the Paraná River," wrote James, comparing the treetops to "the nave of a stately cathedral." (The Paraná River crosses through Brazil, Paraguay, and Argentina.) The author then set aside the inspirational tone and concluded his article with this unsettling gem of an anecdote:

Such are the features of the South American Virgin Forest that present themselves most strikingly to my mind. These things I have seen; much more I have heard about. But I am reluctant to mention here those weird and gruesome stories that our European civilisation proclaims to be merely unauthentic imaginings. Still, I have met men in the backwoods, men whose word I have found in all else to be reliable, who vow they have seen the Lamparagua, and have but narrowly escaped its encompassing toils. For this awesome tree has the reputation of subsisting, at least by preference, on animal diet; and in the damp atmosphere of night uncoils long tendrils which sway gropingly in the air and encircle any living creature that comes within their reach. Then, hugged in an invincible embrace, the victim dies a lingering death, as its vital fluids are sucked out to give nourishment to its captor. Men, even, are said to have met this terrible fate, and bleached skeletons have been found in piles about the roots or still suspended from the branches. Some there are who maintain that the Lamparagua is no tree, but a creature of the animal kind, possessing the power of locomotion. Of this, however, I have discovered but little evidence; while of the former assertion—well, without having seen it with one's own eyes, it is impossible to believe; and yet— I dare not say I entirely disbelieve. Surely there are more things in nature than have come within the ken of our philosophy.

Pre-dating James' article by a few years was "The Lamparagua," a short story by Irish author May Crommelin that appeared in the August 1897 issue of The Pall Mall Magazine. The story featured Crommelin's hero, Jock Ramsay, becoming deathly ill while traversing the pampas (extensive, desolate plains) of Chile, only to have a frightening run-in with the fearsome, hungry and ambulatory Lamparagua. The full short story is included later in this book, but here is a passage showing how Crommelin depicted the killer tree:

Then he started awake as a horrid cry roused his dulled ears. (It was the scream of a horse!)

What was this well-known valley? Where was he? For, raising himself weakly on one elbow, Ramsay saw a stream running past rocks which were strangely familiar,—and yet *when* had he seen them? The river emptied itself in marshy land. The dawn showed a dark grey surface beyond, like a sea—or lake.

With a cold terror the sick man recognised that he lay not two hundred yards from the marsh of the lamparagua: that headland; the water! All night they must have ridden in a circle.

The horrible scream was already fading from his sick memory like a dream, when a snorting and scuffling noise caused Ramsay to turn slowly his weak head. He saw his horse stamping, pulling back from its halter, and with distended eye-balls staring terrified at a tree, to a root of which it was fastened. What was wrong? The tree had two bare topmost branches like horns, and some lower ones also without leaves, yet this was summer-time; in December... It was withered! And, there above its onion-shaped bole was, surely, a dark scar, a crack! Oh, horror! the top of the tree was that of the lamparagua, in the marsh. And now, as Jock stared with fever-weakened eyes through the dim daybreak, the lower branches moved slowly downwards, clutching the horse's halter with claw-like twigs; the crack in the side of the *Thing* was widening. Again a fearful sound woke the sleeping glen: the horse's cry of terror. Jock tried instinctively to find his revolver, but his senses reeled as the tree aperture gaped, opening upwards. The horse was drawing towards it—nearer!— fighting, struggling. Then two shots rang out, and a man fainted, and knew no more.

The Unnatural History of Man-Eating Plants

Muddying the waters here is Crommelin's suggestion that her short story was based on actual accounts she heard of the Lamparagua. She included such a statement as the intro to her tale in The Pall Mall Magazine, and as a footnote in her 1900 novel, "The Luck of a Lowland Laddie," which continued the adventures of Jock Ramsay and reused "The Lamparagua" as one of its chapters. The footnote in the book reads:

The dread lamparagua is by no means a creature of pure fiction. When I was staying a few years ago in Chile, a well-known English landowner in the north gave me an account of this tree-beast. Mr. L— was assured by his laborers that one lamparagua, or more, infested the marshy edges of the lake on his own estate at [Culipran]. As to its size, and manner of movement, the details were not exact. But its appearance, diet, and means of seizing its victims are faithfully reproduced from the description unwillingly imparted by the peones to their master. These men dreaded it as a kind of wizard; they are very superstitious, but otherwise are declared by Europeans neither to feel pain or to know fear.

As noted by Crommelin, Lamparagua literally means "Lamp of the Water," "a kind of will-o'-the-wisp." Her sources never gave a reason for why a light is associated with the tree.

Crommelin was very well-traveled, and based many of her 42 novels on insights gleaned from her own adventures. She toured South America in 1894. Her biographical book about this trip, titled "Over the Andes from the Argentine to Chili and Peru," is an excellent travelogue containing Crommelin's detailed impressions of the people, culture, flora, fauna and landscapes she encountered. This adds an air of authenticity to "The Lamparagua," although it is unclear if the title character is truly based on an actual piece of Chilean folklore she heard during her South American trek, or whether it was mainly an artistic conceit.

Crommelin's Lamparagua appears to be a stew of legends from the areas she visited in Chile. It can hardly be coincidence that there is a "Lampalagua" within Chilean oral tradition, as documented by Julio Vicuña Cifuentes in his 1915 collection of the country's myths and superstitions. "El Lampalagua," according to Andes folklore [and translated from Spanish], "is a formidable reptile with strong claws that moves underground, not very deeply, along paths it opens itself, which resemble real tunnels. From distance to distance, it raises its head to the surface, in the middle of a pasture, at the entrance to a village, and if it is hungry, it devours everything around it, including people, animals, and crops, then continues its subterranean path, undaunted."

In Santiago, "The Lampalagua is a colossal reptile of extraordinary voracity. It indiscriminately devours everything in its path, either to satisfy its appetite or to remove obstacles that hinder its path. It has been seen drinking streams and rivers that blocked its path, and crossing over to the opposite bank on the dry riverbed, to continue its work of devastation with equal persistence."

May Crommelin

A parallel version of the Lampalagua story in Santiago describes it as a snake, and that gives us the clue as to what the creature might really be; for in neighboring Argentina, "Ampalagua" is a name for the *Boa constrictor occidentalis*. The reptile entered Chilean tradition, wrote Cifuentes, "exaggerating its proportions and appetites, [and was] given the mythical character by which it is only known in our country."

Argentine Boa Constrictor (Boa Constrictor occidentalis). Photo by Hugo Hulsberg, CC0, via Wikimedia Commons.

Another creature from Chilean myth, El Guirivilo or Nirivilo, might also be a main ingredient in this folkloric stew. The Mapuche, native to south-central Chile and southwestern Argentina, named this aquatic monster Guirivilo, a compound word of gurú (medium fox) and vilu (snake). (Notably, Crommelin depicted foxes living alongside the lagoon where dwelt the Lamparagua.) "Now the Mapuche imagination represents it as having a small, slender body, a cat's head, and an extremely long fox's tail," wrote Cifuentes. "It frequents the mouths and pools of rivers, and with its tail it entangles men and animals, drags them to the bottom, and drinks their blood." Other attributes of El Guirivilo, collected by Cifuentes, include a sharp claw on its tail; the ability to stretch like a snake to envelop and swallow man and animal whole; and in some versions it is "almost circular like a stretched cowhide."

Clearly, these pieces of Chilean folklore all worked their way into Crommelin's story. But it is unknown how or why Crommelin transformed the reptilian Lampalagua into the arboreal Lamparagua. Did she hear another version of the story in which the beast was a tree (or perhaps circular); was it a mistranslation or misunderstanding; or could it just have been creative license?

One possibility is that the Argentine Boa prefers wetlands and sometimes resides on and around trees, using them as shelter, perches for hunting, and sunbathing. They can at times be seen coiled in branches directly over water. The Argentine Boa, which can attain a length of 13 feet and a weight of 13 pounds, eats birds, rodents and other small animals. Cifuentes noted that, unlike the mythological version, it poses little danger to humans, although small children should be monitored in areas where the snake is present.

A brief passage from "Over the Andes" offers another possible moment of inspiration: As Crommelin and a female friend, hair streaming in the breeze, galloped on horseback over the hills south of Valparaíso, Chile, the author noted:

CHAJUAL PLANTS ; PEASANT RIDING.

The Unnatural History of Man-Eating Plants

"On the cliffs overhead grew strange-looking plants, like dead aloe-sticks, ten feet high, with mops'-heads outlined against the sky. These were *chajuals*, a kind of agave, among the rare flowers Miss Marianne North came to Chili to paint. A little later and their newly-sprouted sticks would blossom with spikes of yellow-greenish flowers. But I could not stay for the spring-time."

An illustration of the plants that Crommelin included with the passage shows *Puya chilensis,* known locally as Chagual (a slightly different spelling). Also dubbed the "Sheep-Eating Plant," this bromeliad native to central Chile is ironically thought to be protocarnivorous, absorbing the nutrients from decaying animals that get stuck on the hooked spines of its leaves and die.

Half a century later, the Lamparagua would receive an unexpected and confusing mention in Travel magazine in a letter from reader Andrea Razafkeriefo of Los Angeles. Razafkeriefo (whose father was a Malagasy nobleman who died fighting French invaders in 1895) complimented Raine Bennett's article, "Island Idyll: Madagascar," from the November 1953 issue. Razafkeriefo added, "The man-eating tree he mentions is called *Lamparagua* by the natives and is more legendary than real." Once again, all Man-Eating Tree tales trace their roots back to Madagascar!

DEATH FLOWER OF EL BANOOR

A short dispatch about the "Death Flower of El Banoor" appeared in numerous English-speaking newspapers in 1912:

The Death Flower.

The crew of the vessel which is setting out to solve the mystery of the mammoth statues of Easter Island must steer clear of El Banoor, another island of the Pacific. One of our early explorers, Hugh Arkwright, who sailed the Pacific in 1581, warns travelers against visiting El Banoor—the home of the death flower. This flower, we are told, is so large that a man can stand upright inside one of its blossoms. But if he does so he will surely fall asleep, lulled by the strange fragrance it distils. Then the flower folds its petals and suffocates him. "And so he passes into death through splendid dreams, and gives his body to the death flower for food."

The Death Flower, El Banoor and Captain Arkwright all appear to be the invention of William Wescott Fink, a poet from Des Moines, Iowa who was born in Ireland. They feature in "The Grotto Flower of Ell-Banoor," which closes out Fink's 1903 book of poetry, "Echoes from Erin." Published by G. P. Putnam's Sons, the volume received great praise from contemporary critics, especially Fink's selection of verses written in Irish brogue. The Los Angeles Times lauded Fink as a "prolific versifier" with a rich flow of language and a fresh and vigorous imagination.

Frink preceded his poem about the Gutter Flower with a passage said to be from the log-book of Captain Arkright (note no first name given, and the different surname spelling), A.D. 1581. Here is the full selection:

THE GROTTO FLOWER OF ELL-BANOOR

(". . . So, seeking an entrance through the coral reefs but finding none, we sailed slowly around the circular, green island to the point from which we had started. Finally the two natives, whom we had brought from a neighboring island, succeeded, by swimming and wading, in reaching the shore, where, finding the people friendly, and speaking their own tongue, they induced some of them to come out for us in their frail craft and take us ashore, which they did by winding in and out through many devious ways. . . . What was our surprise to find that what had seemed a great, circular island embowered in semitropical green, was, in very truth, an ancient coral reef, in the form of a vast ring, rising from the depths of the ocean, and enclosing a placid little sea dotted with scores of enchanting and luxurious islets. . . . The natives told us of a great, hooded flower, of weird and wondrous beauty, which grew in the depths of one of their isles called Ell-Banoor, meaning forbidden isle, or isle of death. This flower was of so great size that men might enter its mysterious depths: but woe to the one so daring! for the vast curving petals would close around him, and, overwhelming him with their sleep-laden perfume, hold him there till life went out in enchanting dreams, and his body was consumed by absorption as food for that great carnivorous plant. Only one of all the daring men who had sought to solve the mystery of that isle of death had ever returned. That one (the father of a beautiful maiden who, with her lover, had unwittingly landed on the isle) only lived to tell the story, and then, crazed by what he had seen, and by the overwhelming odors exhaled from the flower, sprang into the sea and perished."—From the log-book of Captain Arkright, A.D. 1581.)

Strange and beautiful the story,

Of a ring of emerald glory

Bending, like a green horizon,

'Round an Eden, ocean-born;

Many a league the ring enclosing

Held a hundred islands, dozing,

North of all Antarctic rigors.

South of burning Capricorn.

Forth from yonder's dainty harbor,

Where the vines have wrought an arbor

Climbing high, and intertwining

Through the arching boughs above,

Swept a bark, white sailed, and laden

With a dark-eyed youth and maiden,—

Faces of strange southern beauty,

All their glances soft with love.

South America

And the breeze, that gently bore them,

Swung love's glowing censer o'er them,

Till the swaying halo bound them

In its ambient folds secure,

Noting not the soft wind's shifting,

Till their boat, unguided, drifting,

Swept the swaying tendrils, pendent

From the banks of Ell-Banoor.

Ell-Banoor, or Isle Forbidden;

Death dwelt there, by beauty hidden,

For whoever dared to enter

Ne'er escaped its sylvan bowers.

E'en the birds, that shot like painted

Arrows through its fragrance, fainted

With the rapture of inhaling

Odors of lethean flowers.

Onward, through the deep'ning splendor,

Walked they under palms and slender

Waving boughs whose bells, translucent,

Tresses trailed of golden beams;

Down a path that still grew steeper,

Where the shimmering shades fell deeper,

To a drowsy brook that murmured

The Unnatural History of Man-Eating Plants

Mellow music in its dreams.

On the farther bank reclining,

Like a shell with golden lining,

Grew the hollow, purple-hooded

Grotto flower of Ell-Banoor.

From its vast and vaulted chamber

Issued, through its lips of amber,

Mellow beams, like those reflected

From a prostrate, jewelled ewer.

But one petal, lowly bending,

In a rainbow-curve extending,

Reached across the lazy water

Like a drawbridge o'er a moat.

Silent were its silken hinges,

But its pendent, purple fringes,

Swaying softly, smote together

With a dreamy, silver note.

"Roo Larmena! Preen sel moorma,"

Softly spoke the youth, "del oorma"—

"Dear Larmena! 'T is the portal

To the region of the blest."

O'er the arch, as in a vision,

South America

Passed they to its depths elysian;

But there blushed a crimson footprint

Where each shining sandal pressed.

There, upon a velvet anther,

Sesile, spotted as a panther,

Sat they, and in liquid language

Crooned the story, ever new,

While a cloud of incense bound them,

And the golden globe around them,

Swaying with slow convolutions,

Flushed and flamed a deeper hue!

Was it Nature's necromancy,

Or Larmena's timid fancy

That the airy, petal drawbridge

Slowly, silently arose?

Ah! it closed the amber crescent;

And they sat in opalescent

Splendor where lethean odors

Lulled to rapturous repose.

Round him fell her shining tresses,

Trembling to his last caresses;

And his voice went out in murmurs:

The Unnatural History of Man-Eating Plants

"Roo Larmena! Preen sel moor—"

Thus they passed Death's radiant portals

To the realm of the Immortals,—

While their boat swung idly waiting

By the banks of Ell-Banoor.

THE END

*Rafflesia in Bengkulu Province, Indonesia. Photo by
SofianRafflesia, CC BY-SA 4.0, via Wikimedia Commons.*

Roy P. Mackal, a biochemist and zoologist, researched the Death Flower of El-Banoor for his 1980 book, "Searching for Hidden Animals." Mackal wrote that the Death Flower "almost" has a match in *Rafflesia arnoldii*, the world's largest flower that grows to a monstrous size of three feet or more in diameter. *Rafflesia* is a parasitic plant that grows on the root of the vine *Tetrastigma* in the jungles of Sumatra. "This giant flower, much like a washtub, consists of thick petals, flesh-colored and speckled with cream-colored spots. At the center of the petals is a large bowl or nectary filled with 6 or 7 liters (6 quarts) of water. In the basin the true flowers, quite small, give the impression of torture devices. The plant, however, does not derive its nourishment from the bodies of dead humans, but from the root of the host," wrote Mackal. Dr. Joseph Arnold, accompanied by Sir Stamford and Lady Raffles of the Royal Society, discovered *Rafflesia* in 1818.

American Folklorist Charles M. Skinner dismissed the Death Flower story as a myth in his 1911 book, "Myths and Legends of Flowers, Trees, Fruits, and Plants." That didn't stop the tale from being picked up and printed without context as fact by British and North American newspapers in 1912.

MONKEY-TRAP TREE

A 1928 story of a carnivorous plant is attributed to one of Brazil's most celebrated heroes, Mashal Cândido Mariano da Silva Rondon. Once referred to as "Brazil's Daniel Boone," the army engineer led military efforts to lay telegraph lines and other infrastructure throughout the jungles of Mato Grosso and the western Amazon basin throughout the late 19th and early 20th centuries. This was also a mission of exploration, with the Rondon Commission surveying and mapping immense regions of the Amazon and establishing relationships with indigenous groups in remote areas.

Rondon discovered the headwaters of the River of Doubt in 1909 and was joined by former U.S. President Teddy Roosevelt for a scientific expedition to explore the river (later renamed Rio Roosevelt) in 1913-14. Rondon immediately impressed Roosevelt as "all, and more than all, that would be desired" as a companion on the expedition, having spent 24 years exploring the western highlands of Brazil, traveling "some 14,000 miles, on territory most of which had not previously been traversed by civilized man."

Rondon was known for his advocacy of indigenous Brazilians, establishing peaceful relations with an eye toward their integration into modern Brazilian society as it arrived at their doorstep. In 1910, Rondon was chosen as the first director of Brazil's Indian Protection Service. Roosevelt remarked in 1914 that Rondon "has an exceptional knowledge of the Indian tribes and has always zealously endeavored to serve them and indeed to serve the cause of humanity wherever and whenever he was able."

Teddy Roosevelt and Cândido Rondon, 1913-14 Brazil Expedition.

Roosevelt became severely ill and weakened on the expedition after he sustained a minor leg wound that progressed into tropical fever. The former U.S. president would suffer complications the rest of his life, which likely contributed to his death of a pulmonary embolism just five years later at age 60.

Between 1927 and 1930, Rondon was tasked with surveying all of Brazil's international borders. Aged 62 when this journey began,

Rondon crossed approximately 25,000 miles of territory on foot and via canoe.

The Rondon Commission set out by steamship in late July 1928, equipped with a seaplane and numerous animals, to survey Brazil's northern border with the Guianas. By the middle of October, they were approaching the border of Dutch Guyana (now Suriname) via the Trombetas River. It was during this time that the story of the carnivorous plant emerged, printed in a dispatch that appeared in German newspapers.

Here is a translation of an article that appeared in the Oct. 15, 1928 edition of Solinger Tageblatt:

TREES THAT EAT MONKEYS.

It is well known that there are people who would resent the idea of eating any kind of meat. They want to be happy as vegetarians, in their own way. Let them have their pleasure. But it may not be widely known that there are plants that aren't content to feed on dew and rain, and that require a distinctly meaty diet to thrive. And yet, there are carnivorous trees.

Mariano da Silva, a Brazilian explorer, recently returned from a long expedition that took him to certain areas of Brazilian Guiana. He also visited the Yatapu Indian settlement area and reported seeing a tree there that fed on animals.

Its trunk has a diameter of about three feet and is about twenty feet tall. At its base are leaves that are three to fifteen feet wide and about the thickness of a thumb. The tree exudes a peculiar, pungent scent. But woe betide those who are attracted by it!

It often happens that monkeys fall for this perfume. Then they're doomed. If they merely climb along the trunk, they can say goodbye to life. Very quickly, they are completely enclosed by the leaves. Nothing is heard or seen of these unfortunate animals again. About three days later, the leaves open again, releasing some completely gnawed bones onto the ground. One could safely say that these carnivorous trees are the terror of the jungle.

The Yatapú River (upper right corner), from "Adolf Stieler's Hand-Atlas," 1894.

It is unclear if Yatapu was the name of the tribe in this story, as references to these people appear to originate with this article about the "Monkey-Trap Tree" and its various retellings in German and English over the years. However, it is most certainly a reference to the area of the Jatapú aka Yatapú River, a major tributary of the Uatumã River. It is located roughly 175 direct miles northeast of the city of Manaus in the state of Amazonas, and about 250 direct miles southwest of the Suriname border. With a respected man like Rondon at the heart of this story, the Monkey-Trap Tree might bear further investigation.

OCTOPOD

As he told it, British Army Captain Thomas W. H. "Tiger" Sarll led a life that sounded like it was ripped from a pulp adventure novel. When Sarll was only five, famous American cowboy Buffalo Bill visited to see if the rumors he heard about the boy's skill with a revolver were true. Before departing, he gifted young Tiger a revolver that had once belonged to Kit Carson.

Florence Nightingale remarked to young Sarll that he was "a nice, upright boy" and "ought to be a soldier." Sarll agreed and in

1899, at age 17, he boarded a ship bound for South Africa to fight in the Second Boer War. While there, he fought alongside Winston Churchill and earned his nickname after fellow soldiers noticed that the towering (six-foot-four) Sarll emitted a noise between a purr and a growl as he entered battle. During the Battle of Colenso, a shell burst near Sarll's feet, driving sand and particles into his left eye; he never saw with it again, and ultimately adopted a distinctive monocle.

Sarll later fought in the Mexican Revolution and World War I, and served his homeland as a firefighter during World War II, saving people from bombed-out buildings during The Blitz. Throughout his remarkable 94 years, Sarll was a big game hunter (who rarely killed anything as an animal lover), a stage actor, a war correspondent, and an animal wrangler for zoos and private menageries who captured wild alligators and snakes with his bare hands, among many other accomplishments.

In the early 1930s, Sarll developed a sideshow act as an "animal hypnotist" with mastery over alligators and pythons. He dubbed himself "Rais Sarll," dressed in a turban, and claimed to have been trained by an Indian yogi. "There is no wild animal on the earth or under it that I couldn't tame," boasted Sarll. "Not one—except the shark. The shark is the most treacherous of all creatures. I once narrowly escaped falling into the jaws of one, so I know."

During this period, in November 1932, Sarll (who had resided in Buenos Aires in 1910 with his new wife, Sybil) declared his intent to return to South America to travel the Amazon and locate within the jungle a live specimen of the "Octopod." This "almost legendary" Man-Eating Tree was stated by London's People newspaper to be "the missing link between the animal and the vegetable kingdom."

"Just like the octopus, from which it takes its name, this uncanny tree stretches forth its limbs in the interior of the jungle and sets its traps for men and animal, whom it devours," said Sarll. Victims of the Octopod were tripped up by its giant limbs, huge as the arms of an octopus and dangerously concealed in the undergrowth. "I have heard of cases in which men have been caught in that vice-like embrace, slowly but surely drawn in towards the creature's body and held fast there until they died of starvation, wounds and fear," said Sarll. "Then they have been devoured by this hungry monster of the swamps."

Tiger "Rais" Sarll holding a 19-foot python at Bertram Mills' Circus in 1935. Included here on a Fair Use, educational basis.

Sarll said he hoped to set off for the Amazon within three months, declaring, "And I shall not come back until I have captured the Octopod!" This schedule appears to have been optimistic, as in July 1933 Sarll was testing 17-foot, all-rubber canoes in the English Channel, in view of using them to journey up the Amazon in January 1934 "to take films." The tests didn't go smoothly, with Sarll encountering a severe thunderstorm in which lighting

— L'arbre carnivore ! murmura-t-elle avec un accent d'inexprimable épouvante. Raô, à mon secours! Raô n'avait pas besoin de cet appel terrifié. Il avait compris ! Sans l'avoir jamais vu, il avait entendu parler de cet arbre qui, comme certaines fleurs le font pour les insectes, capturent les plus grosses proies et aspirent lentement leur chair à travers leurs fibres, dans une épouvantable agonie.
D'ailleurs, des témoignages le confirmaient : des cadavres momifiés de cerfs, de grands singes, pendaient çà et là, comme des mouches dans une toile d'araignée... C'est le même sort qui attendait Iaona !

"'The carnivorous tree!' she murmured with an accent of inexpressible terror. 'Rao, help me!' Rao didn't need this terrified cry. He understood! Without ever having seen it, he had heard of this tree which, like some flowers do for insects, captures the largest prey and slowly sucks their flesh through their fibers, in a terrible agony. Moreover, testimonies confirmed it: mummified corpses of deer and great apes hung here and there, like flies in a spider's web... The same fate awaited Iaona!" -A panel from "Futuropolis" by Martial Cendres and Pellos, published in the March 20, 1938 issue of French comic strip magazine, Junior. Included here on a Fair Use, educational basis.

struck and burned his mast. He obtained a new mast but met another storm that tossed all his money, food and kit overboard.

Further news of this particular globetrotting adventure did not materialize in the press. Godfrey Lias' 1961 biography of Sarll, "Adventurer Extraordinary," also makes no mention of the Octopod expedition. The book isn't shy about detailing weird episodes from Sarll's life, such as his sighting of a sea serpent with a back that looked "like the teeth of a huge saw." Sarll and fellow passengers saw the creature at a distance of less than a mile, two days out from Las Palmas in the Canary Islands. They were aboard the Garth Castle en route to Cape Town, South Africa in late 1899, Sarll headed to fight the Boers. "It is quite true that only bits of its back were visible... But I'm absolutely certain that each piece was part of one animal. We could see it quite plainly," said Sarll, dismissing the suggestion that he had witnessed a line of dolphins.

Sarll also described his bizarre residence at Morley House, a rambling Tudor structure in the village of Thorpe in northwest Surrey, England. He and his family insisted that the house was haunted, experiencing such phenomena as a strange man that smacked their three-year-old daughter, Daphne, in the night; the appearance of a man's shadow on the first landing and a ghostly black cat on the stairs; "a little, stooping dwarf" who stood opposite a walled-in corner of an upstairs room, wringing his hands; and an unseen force that on different occasions lifted a clock and a cup of tea, and pulled a mandolin from Sarll's hands as he was playing it, then continued strumming it invisibly as the instrument hovered in the air. It is doubtful that an Amazon expedition and an encounter with a Man-Eating Tree would have gone unmentioned had they come to fruition.

In reference to Sarll's Octopod, Harold T. Wilkins noted in his 1952 book, "Secret Cities of Old South America," that Brazil has its own Octopus Tree. Its location is signaled from a distance by a smell like rotting corpses, Wilkins wrote. The tree produces sweet berries which lure in birds, who the tree snatches with its tentacles. The birds are then pulled in to the trunk, where the feathered victims are immersed in thick, viscous suckers and pulverized. The blood of the avian prey is absorbed and the feathers cast away.

EL IUY-JUY

Wilkins also described El Iuy-Juy, a climbing plant known to natives of the Chaco Forest on the border of Bolivia and Argentina. Beautiful and seductive, El Iuy-Juy emits a perfume that acts as sleeping gas to any man or animal unfortunate enough to seek its shade as an escape from the afternoon sun. The floral canopy lowers beautiful flowers down onto its prone victims, each armed with a powerful sucker. These flowers drain the bodies of all their blood and juices, "leaving not even a fragment to tempt the vulture to shoot down from the skies to gorge on a bare skeleton," stated Wilkins.

Wilkins was a British journalist who wrote about treasure hunting. His books have been criticized as presenting pseudohistorical claims, namely that Atlanteans once occupied South America.

STICKY CANNIBAL TREE

In 1925, landscape painter and author Eric Sloane drove cross-country in a rickety Model T Ford, following the old Lincoln Highway from New York to Taos, New Mexico. It was an adventure he would recount in his illustrated 1960 autobiography, "Return to Taos" (along with his impressions of driving the same yet greatly changed route in a Model A 35 years later). During the earlier adventure, on a scorcher of a day, Sloane pulled his steaming Model T off a dusty road in Kansas in search of water. He met a neatly dressed old man with a carefully trimmed white beard who offered to lead him to a spring. As they passed through a finely wooded area, an uncommon sight in Kansas, the man cordially introduced the traveler to his "friends," the individual trees that towered above them. Amused, Sloane played along, greeting and complimenting the trees.

Sloane later sat and chatted with the old man, who expressed how important trees are to human life and that it should be a law to plant several trees when you purchase a carbon dioxide-polluting car. The older gentleman (whose name Sloane forgot in the following decades) then confided that he was the only white man who had encountered the "cannibal tree" during a trek in South America. His gun-bearers had suddenly grabbed him from the rear, pinning his arms behind him and yanking him backwards. The man had reached for his revolver, suspecting a mutiny. But then he realized that his companions had actually saved him.

"They were looking at a tree directly in his path. Its limbs were waving and reaching out toward them. The bark was covered with a sticky substance, and the whole tree was making loud sucking noises. Beneath the tree were scattered the bones of many animals," wrote Sloane.

The old man told the story so convincingly that the artist believed him, although he later decided it was just a tall tale dreamed up by an "insane imagination." But then a few years later, around 1930, Sloane read the same story, just as the old man had told it, on a two-page spread in the Sunday Journal-American. It included a sketch of the man he had met, the cannibal tree reaching out hungrily to snatch him. Sloane failed to find an old copy of the article when writing his book, although there are a few newspaper stories from the time period with drawings that fit the bill (particularly W. C. Bryant's tale). But he *was* left with an admiration for trees as silent, intelligent beings.

SOURCES:

Adolf Stieler's Hand-Atlas. Gotha, Germany, Justus Perthes, 1894.

Amaya, Isidoro Laverde. *Bibliografia Colombiana, Tomo I.* Bogotá, Columbia, Imprenta y Librería de Medardo Rivas, 1895.

"Bäume, die Affen fressen." *Solinger Tageblatt* [Solingen, Germany], 15 Oct. 1928, p. 3.

"*Boa constrictor occidentalis.*" *Wikipedia,* https://en.wikipedia.org/wiki/Boa_constrictor_occidentalis. Accessed 9 Sep. 2025.

South America

"*Boa constrictor occidentalis.*" Wikipedia (Spanish), https://es.wikipedia.org/wiki/Boa_constrictor_occidentalis. Accessed 9 Sep. 2025.

Brigham, Johnson. "Iowa in the World's Literature." *Quarterly of the Iowa Library Commission*, Jan. 1905, pp. 1-9.

Buel, J.W. *Sea and Land: An Illustrated History of the Wonderful and Curious Things of Nature Existing Before and Since the Deluge.* Philadelphia, Historical Publishing Company, 1887.

"Cândido Rondon." *Wikipedia*, https://en.wikipedia.org/wiki/C%C3%A2ndido_Rondon. Accessed 4 May 2025.

"Canoe Race from Oxford to Calais." *Western Daily Press and Bristol Mirror* [Bristol, England], 18 Jul. 1933, p. 8.

"Charles Montgomery Skinner." *Wikipedia*, https://en.wikipedia.org/wiki/Charles_Montgomery_Skinner. Accessed 15 Apr. 2025.

"A Comissão Rondon Na Guyana Hollandeza." *Diario Nacional* [Sao Paulo], 16 Oct. 1928, p. 4.

Crommelin, May. "The Lamparagua." *Pall Mall Magazine*, vol. 12, no. 52, Aug. 1897, pp. 502-509.

Crommelin, May. *The Luck of a Lowland Laddie.* New York, F. M. Buckles & Company, 1900.

Crommelin, May. *Over the Andes from the Argentine to Chili and Peru.* New York, The MacMillan Company, 1896.

"Cruel Octopod Faces Conquest by Hypnotism." *Victoria Daily Times* [Victoria, British Columbia, Canada], 11 Feb. 1933, Third Section, p. 1.

"The Death Flower." *Stalybridge Reporter* [Stalybridge, England], 29 Jun. 1912, p. 2.

"Death Flower of El Banoor." *Kook Science Research Hatch*, https://hatch.kookscience.com/wiki/Death_Flower_of_El_Banoor. Accessed 14 Apr. 2025.

Diacon, Todd A. *Stringing Together a Nation*. Duke University Press, 2004.

"Echoes from Erin." *Chicago Daily Tribune*, 2 Jun. 1903, p. 15.

Fink, William Wescott. *Echoes from Erin*. G. P. Putnam's Sons, 1903.

"Glimpses of America." *Google Books*, https://books.google.com/books/about/Glimpses_of_America.html?id=mM_WDwAAQBAJ&source=kp_author_description. Accessed 1 Jun. 2025.

Gow Smith, Francis. "Brazil's Daniel Boone." *Billings Gazette* [Billings, MT], 12 May 1929, pp. 10-11.

"Harold T. Wilkins." *Wikipedia*, https://en.wikipedia.org/wiki/Harold_T._Wilkins. Accessed 22 Jul. 2025.

"He Will Risk His Life to Capture the Tree of Death!" *People* [London], 27 Nov. 1932, p. 17.

"El Ideal de Juventud en la Prensa Literaria a Partir de los Periódicos: El Rocío (Bogotá 1872-1874), La Juventud (Cartagena 1870-1871), El Oásis (Medellín, 1873) y El Cachifo (Panamá, 1875)." *Universidad Santo Tomas Primer Claustro Universitario de Colombia*, https://repository.usta.edu.co/items/c9d4f02c-c17a-47c0-825e-a0e9ad873491. Accessed 1 Jun. 2025.

"It's Just a Craze!" *Evening Dispatch* [Birmingham, West Midlands, England], 19 Mar. 1934, p. 6.

James, J. Barnard. "The Virgin Forests of the Paraná." *Good Words: 1901*, edited by Donald MacLeod. London, Isbister and Company Limited, 1901.

"Jatapu River." *Wikipedia*, https://en.wikipedia.org/wiki/Jatapu_River. Accessed 4 May 2025.

Lias, Godfrey. *Adventurer Extraordinary*. London, Cassell, 1961.

"The Luck of a Lowland Laddie." *Arena* [Melbourne, Vitoria, Australia], 20 Apr. 1901, p. 9.

Mackal, Roy P. *Searching for Hidden Animals*. Doubleday & Company, Inc. 1980.

"May Crommelin." *Wikipedia*, https://en.wikipedia.org/wiki/May_Crommelin. Accessed 7 Sep. 2025.

McKernan, Luke. "'Tiger' Sarll." *Bioscope*, 7 Apr. 2007, https://thebioscope.net/2007/04/07/tiger-sarll/.

Moreira Pinto, Alfredo. *Apontamentos Para O Diccionario Geographico Do Brazil 'A-E.'* Rio de Janeiro Imprensa Nacional, 1894.

"La Patria: Revista Semanal de Política, Ciencias y Literatura." *Biblioteca Virtual del Banco de la República*, https://babel.banrepcultural.org/digital/collection/p17054coll26/id/5737. Accessed 1 Jun. 2025.

"Mapuche." *Wikipedia*, https://en.wikipedia.org/wiki/Mapuche. Accessed 9 Sep. 2025.

"Paraná River." *Wikipedia*, https://en.wikipedia.org/wiki/Paran%C3%A1_River. Accessed 8 Sep. 2025.

Prior, Sophia. Carnivorous Plants and "The Man-Eating Tree." *Botany Leaflet 23*, Field Museum of Natural History, 1939.

"*Puya chilensis*." *Wikipedia*, https://en.wikipedia.org/wiki/Puya_chilensis. Accessed 7 Sep. 2025.

"*Puya chilensis* Molina." *Chileflora*, https://www.chileflora.com/Florachilena/FloraSpanish/LowResPages/SH0416.htm. Accessed 8 Sep. 2025.

Razafkeriefo, Andrea. Letter. *Travel*, Apr. 1954, p. 50.

"El Rocío : Periódico Literario Dedicado al Bello Sexo y a la Juventud." *Descubridor*, https://descubridor.banrepcultural.org/discovery/fulldisplay?vid=57BDLRDC_INST:57BDLRDC_INST&docid=alma991003634529707486&context=L. Accessed 1 Jun. 2025.

Roosevelt, Theodore. "Through the Brazilian Wilderness." *Cincinnati Enquirer*, 26 Jul. 1914, Color Section, p. 2.

"Roosevelt–Rondon Scientific Expedition." *Wikipedia*, https://en.wikipedia.org/wiki/Roosevelt%E2%80%93Rondon_Scientific_Expedition. Accessed 4 May 2025.

"Serviço Radio-Telegraphico." *Republica* [Florianopolis, Brazil], 28 Jul. 1928, p. 3.

Skinner, Charles M. *Myths and Legends of Flowers, Trees, Fruits, and Plants*. J. B. Lippincott Company, 1911.

Sloane, Eric. *Return to Taos*, Funk & Wagnalls, 1960.

T.A.K. "Poetry." *Los Angeles Times*, 6 Jun. 1903, p. 4.

"Theodore Roosevelt." *Wikipedia*, https://en.wikipedia.org/wiki/Theodore_Roosevelt. Accessed 17 Aug. 2025.

"Tiger Sarll." *Wikipedia*, https://en.wikipedia.org/wiki/Tiger_Sarll. Accessed 17 May 2025.

"The Tree of Death." *Groper* [Perth, Australia], 26 Feb. 1933, p. 1.

Vicuña Cifuentes, Julio. *Mitos y Supersticiones Recogidos de la Tradición Oral Chilena con Referencias Comparativas a Los de Otros Paises Latinos*. Santiago, Chile, Imprenta Universitaria, 1915.

Wilkins, Harold T. *Secret Cities of Old South America*. Adventures Unlimited Press, 1952.

"Yateveo." *Kook Science*, https://hatch.kookscience.com/wiki/Yateveo. Accessed 1 Jun. 2025.

CENTRAL AMERICA

U.S. Department of Agriculture Chief Entomologist Charles V. Riley delivered a scientific, philosophical lecture exploring insectivorous plants, titled "The Inter Relation of Flowers and Insects," at the Brooklyn Institute on the evening of Feb. 2, 1892. "Have you ever stopped to think what the intricate adjustments between plants and animals, and especially between plants and insects, mean, when they have become so profoundly modified by each other that their present existences actually depend the one on the other?" Riley asked his audience.

The Brooklyn Daily Eagle dutifully reported the contents of Riley's presentation they next day. Then, two years later, other newspapers used this report as the jumping-off point for a widely syndicated article called "Man-Eating Plants." This attention-grabbing piece proclaimed, "Vampire vines, flesh and even man-eating plants are products of recent scientific discovery." Touching briefly on Riley's observation that the digestive glands of insectivorous plants parallel the stomachs of animals, the syndicated article continued, "Insect plants that feed on flies and wasps have been known long before the time of Darwin but a man-eating plant like some that have recently been studied in central Africa, Nicaragua or Tasmania is something new. About Lake Nicaragua the vampire vine, which seizes dogs, men and even cattle in its ample tendrils and sucks the life out of them, affords one of the chief obstacles to the exploration of the country."

DEVIL'S SNARE / VAMPIRE VINE

The Unnatural History of Man-Eating Plants

Just what was this "Vampire Vine" of Nicaragua that the news dispatch presented so alarmingly? It surely references the troubling tale of the Devil's Snare, which appears to have originated in the May 1890 edition of Frank Leslie's Popular Monthly. (An illustration of the plant later appeared in the May 1893 issue.) It then went on to be carried by newspapers far and wide, and across the world, over the next six years.

NICARAGUA SPECIMEN #1

Here is the original account as it was printed in Frank Leslie's Popular Monthly:

BLOOD-SUCKING PLANT.

LEROY DUNSTAN, a well-known naturalist of New Orleans, who has recently returned from Central America, where he had spent nearly two years in the study of the flora and fauna of the country, relates the finding of a singular growth in one of the swamps which surround the great lake of Nicaragua. He was engaged in hunting for botanical and entomological specimens in this swamp, which is known as San Sebastian's, when he heard his dog cry out as if in agony, from a distance. Running to the spot from which the animal's cries came, Mr. Dunstan found him enveloped in a perfect net-work of what seemed to be a fine, rope-like tissue of roots or fibres, the nature of which was unknown to him.

The plant or vine seemed composed entirely of bare, interlacing stems, resembling, more than anything else, the branches of the weeping-willow denuded of all foliage, but of a dark, nearly black hue, and covered with a thick, viscid gum that exuded from the pores. Drawing his knife, Mr. Dunstan endeavored to cut the animal free, but it was only with the greatest difficulty that he succeeded in severing the fleshy, muscular fibre. To his horror and amazement the naturalist then saw that the dog's body was covered with blood, while his hairless skin appeared to have been actually sucked or puckered in spots, and the animal staggered as if from weakness and exhaustion.

In cutting the vine the twigs curled like living, sinuous fingers about Mr. Dunstan's hand, and it required no slight force to free the member from its clinging clasp, which left the flesh red and blistered. The gum exuding from the vine was of a dark-grayish tinge, remarkably adhesive and of a disagreeable animal odor, very powerful and nauseating to inhale.

The native servants who accompanied Mr. Dunstan manifested the greatest horror of the vine, which they call *la sagenas de diable*, the devil's seine, or snare, and were full of stories of its death-dealing powers. One of these stories was of an Englishman residing in Managua, who, while hunting in the swamp a few years before, lay down beneath a tree where a large and powerful specimen of this singular plant was growing, and inadvertently falling asleep, awoke to find himself enveloped in its web, and, in spite of every effort made to extricate him, perished in its deadly embrace.

Another story was of an escaped convict, who had hidden in the swamp, and whose bones had been found in the folds of the sagenas only a short time before Mr. Dunstan's visit. These stories, remarkable as they may seem, are firmly believed in by the people, but the only three specimens which Mr. Dunstan was able to find were all small ones, though the meshes of the largest would probably, if extended in a straight line, measure nearly if not quite one hundred feet.

He was able to discover but very little about the nature of the plant, owing to the difficulty of handling it, for its grasp can only be torn away with loss of skin, and even of flesh; but, as near as Mr. Dunstan could ascertain, its power of suction is contained in a number of infinitesimal mouths, or little suckers, which, ordinarily closed, open for the reception of food.

The gum exuded seems to serve the twofold purpose of increasing its tenacity and of overcoming a victim by its sickening odor. The plant is found in low, wet places, and usually beneath a large tree, and, while dormant, seems only a network of dry, dead vines, covering the black earth for several feet, but, coming in contact with anything, will instantly begin to twist and twine upward in a horrible, life-like manner, breaking out with the gum-like substance spoke of before, and inwrap the object with a celerity that is almost incredible.

" VAMPIRE VINE " OF NICARAGUA.

"Vampire Vine" of Nicaragua. Illustration from Frank Leslie's Popular Monthly, May 1893.

If the substance is animal, the blood is drawn off and the carcass or refuse then dropped. A lump of raw meat being thrown it, in the short time of five minutes the blood will be thoroughly drunk off and the mass thrown aside. Its voracity is almost beyond belief, it devouring at one time over ten pounds of meat, though it may be deprived of all food for weeks without any apparent loss of vitality. Mr. Dunstan attempted to bring away a root of the sagenas, but it died during his return voyage, growing so foul with a strong odor of real animal corruption that he was obliged to get rid of it.

***

Central America

Leroy Dunstan, the well-known naturalist (who is otherwise elusive in the historical record), was most often said to be from New Orleans, although sometimes it was Philadelphia and even Limerick, Ireland.

Per Hathitrust, the illustrated Frank Leslie's Popular Monthly enjoyed a long life from 1876 to 1956, offering readers a variety of material that included "serialized stories, short stories, a little poetry, essays in science, art, literature, and anthropology, and plenty of jokes and anecdotes." The Devil's Snare story was presented as is, with no indication of whether it was news, fiction or a lark. But whatever the intent, it certainly struck a note with its audience.

NICARAGUA SPECIMEN #2

There was a "sequel" to the Devil's Snare story that appeared in dozens of American newspapers between 1892 and 1894. This new tale thrilled readers with testimony from an American railroad surveyor who accepted a temporary post managing a friend's coffee plantation in Nicaragua, quickly ran afoul of one of the employees, and was tricked by the aggrieved man into hunting along an isolated mountain pass strewn with the grasping tendrils of hungry plants. This oft-reprinted story first appeared in the Sep. 3, 1892 edition of the St. Louis Daily Globe-Democrat:

STORIES FOR NIMRODS.

A Man-Eating Tree in Central America.

Special Correspondence of the Globe-Democrat.

I have spent, in all, three years in Central America. I went there with a surveying party which was running the line of a projected railroad, one of those railroads which are built on paper alone. It has never yet materialized. While the line was being run I made the acquaintance of an American citizen who was the owner of a large coffee plantation, and he invited me to spend some time with him. I accepted, and in a little while a mutual friendship sprung up between us. The result was that before the time came for my departure he told me that it was necessary for him to pay a visit to his old home in Ohio with his wife, to settle up some legal business, and he had been trying to find some one who could take charge of his plantation during his absence. He urged me to take the position, and I accepted. Another week found me at the head of one of the finest coffee plantations in Nicaragua.

My duties were light enough. Bland had a competent general manager, and about all that I had to do was to act as the power behind the throne in the master's absence. I had but one difficulty during this time. The manager, a Cuban named Carlinos, was popular with the laborers, and all went smoothly until one day a Mexican, Michael Ferrara, positively refused to obey some order that Carlinos had given him, and Carlinos appealed to me. Upon investigation I calmly told the Mexican either to obey orders or to leave the place. With a sidelong scowl at Carlinos and myself, he did what the manager had commanded, and the storm seemed to have blown over, but I did not feel quite confident about it. The Mexican's look troubled me, and I mentioned it to Carlinos, but he treated the matter lightly and was inclined to be scornful in regard to Ferrara. "He is a coward," he said, shrugging his shoulders, and so dismissed the matter. I let the subject drop, ashamed of seeming afraid of a man whom this slender Cuban regarded with such disdain, and yet I could have sworn that when I waked that night, startled at some slight noise on the terrace outside my window, it was Ferrara's dark face I saw in the moonlight peering in at me. In an instant it was gone, and I was out of the room, running along the terrace, searching here and there. But no, though I gave the terrace a thorough search, and even went around to the end of the house, and the grove of banana trees beyond, I saw nothing moving anywhere save an owl that flitted out of the trees. I went back to my room concluding that I had dreamed the whole affair.

The next morning I felt quite sure of it. I met Ferrara several times in the course of the day, and he was especially pleasant. He was better educated than the majority of his class, and his position on the plantation gave him a kind of precedence over the others. I was near him several times before the day was over, and I noticed that on each occasion he took pains to speak pleasantly and greet me with his most courteous smile. I thought he was sorry for the bad temper he had shown the day before. I didn't know him as well then as I do now.

The next day Carlinos and I had decided upon a hunt in the mountains that made a jagged outline against the sky off to the south. While we were getting guns and cartridges into condition for use, Ferrara approached and said in his smoothest tones:

"If the senors went to the valley, down beyond the Contadino Pass, they would find where a great panther roams, and has been seen many times. I myself saw it but two days ago, but I was unarmed, so I put spurs to my horse and galloped away."

Carlinos turned to me with a look of interest. "That's a good idea," he said. "We'll look for the panther first, and if we fail to find him we can try the mountains."

We were about to turn away when Ferrara stopped us, with many apologies. "Beyond the Contadino Pass," he said, "you will find a narrow trail leading off eastward down the valley. Follow that trail half a mile, until you see a huge white cliff, a hundred yards to the right. At the foot of that cliff the panther has been seen again and again. Adios, senors!"

And so Carlinos and I went walking off, with swinging stride, toward the pass, glad of a day in the woods, and ready for any adventure that came along.

Except the one that actually did come. For within the next hour we passed through the most horrible experience that ever fell to the lot of mortals I am sure.

We found that pass—a mere gap in the mountains, not used for travel, as another pass, a few miles south, furnished the nearest road to the town. The pass was strewn with rough bowlders and jagged masses of rock, difficult to make one's way over, and for half an hour we had all the exercise we needed in climbing over and around these obstructions. At last, however, we were clear of them, and we shouldered our guns again after a brief rest, and went on until we found the trail among the bushes. It was such a path as would be made by cows or sheep, going to and from a watering place, and I was going along, paying very little attention to it, when Carlinos, who was in the lead, suddenly stopped and muttered: "That is very strange."

I looked over his shoulder, and there in the yellow sand was the barefoot track of a man. We easily traced it along, down the trail for several hundred yards, and then it suddenly disappeared, as though the owner of the track had turned off into the thick undergrowth. We both followed it up to that point, and then missing it, looked at one another and said again, "That is very strange!"

And then we both laughed, and Carlinos said, "But it might have been some herdsman looking for a stray cow or sheep."

But I noticed that Carlinos looked after his cartridges a little more closely, and held his gun in a position to use it, if necessary. And just then the cliff that Ferrara had described came into view, about a hundred yards away, and we turned off from the path toward this place in which the panther had been so often seen.

Scarcely had we started in that direction when we were startled by the long, fierce scream of the panther itself. As nearly as we could judge it was at that very moment at the base of the cliff. We stopped involuntarily at the sound, and then went stealing down the slope, with eyes watchful and nerves stretched to the utmost. Yet we went on and on, without seeing it, and suddenly found ourselves almost at the base of the cliff, which had been hidden by the thick and tangled brush through which we had passed.

Then we stopped and looked around, peering here and there through the bushes. It was easy to see that the spot of ground on which we stood had been the haunt of some wild animal, for all about us bones lay bleaching on the ground. But nothing was to be seen. The face of the cliff, up to a height of 12 or 15 feet, was covered with the matted tendrils of a dead vine, apparently. It suddenly occurred to me that the panther's den might be back under the cliff, hidden by the vine, and I was about to investigate when just behind us, not 10 feet away, sounded the horrible scream of the panther.

Both of us whirled, and Carlinos stepped back a little. In the moment of confusion I failed to notice him, but in an instant he gave a heart-rending cry: "Help! help! quick, the tree! The man-eating tree!"

"I BEGAN SLASHING AT THE HORRIBLE, WRITHING TENDRILS."

Never will I forget that cry, nor the sight that met my eyes. In stepping back he had stumbled against the dead vine, as I had thought it. And then in a moment every tendril had become instinct with life, and was twisting and writhing about him with the most horribly snake-like motions, matted around his body and legs, holding his arms tight and drawn across his face and clasped about his throat. Already when I looked around he was helpless. During the single moment while I stood there looking at him motionless with horror his face had begun to turn purple. And then all at once I recovered myself a little, and snatching my hunting knife from my belt began cutting and slashing at the horrible, writhing tendrils in the effort to cut their victim loose.

But before I had made three strokes something caught my arm and held it; then something crawled swiftly about my neck; and then there were others, around my hands, over my head, across my face—everywhere at once I was seized and held, while wherever the snaky monsters touched went fierce pains, as though my flesh was being torn from my body. I felt my consciousness slipping away, but as it was going suddenly the dark face of Ferrara peered out of the bushes in front of me, and he cried with mocking laughter:

"I hope you enjoy yourselves, senors. The panther is not far away, believe me! Only wait for him until he comes. Adios! Adios!"

The shock of anger roused me a little in the midst of my racking torture, and I saw Ferrara turn to go away; but all at once, amid a chorus of maledictions, a dozen hands seized him and pinioned him down, and we were surrounded by a crowd of the laborers from the plantation. With long knives they cut and hacked at the limbs that were sucking the blood from our veins, and in a few moments they had us free. How they got us home I never knew. It was not until the next day that I recovered consciousness, and I was unable to turn in my bed, even, for two weeks. The excoriations on my face and hands left painful wounds, which were a long time in healing, and which made dreadful scars. These have all gone, however, except the one on my neck, which resembles the scar left by a centipede.

As for Carlinos, he lay as if dead for several days, and there were times when he was pronounced really dead. Then he went off into fever and raving delirium, and it seemed that he could not possibly recover. After awhile, though, he did struggle back into life, but his health was wrecked, and he was never again able to walk as much as a hundred yards.

"HELP! HELP! QUICK!"

How did we happen to be rescued? Why, some of Ferrara's fellow-servants had heard his muttered imprecations against us, and when we had gone and they saw him sneak away after us, they held a consultation and decided to follow. I have always believed that Ferrara circled around us, got in ahead and imitated the cry of the panther himself to lure us on. I have never been able to find out, however. When I had regained strength enough to feel some little curiosity, and asked one of our rescuers what they had done with Ferrara, he answered, with the utmost unconcern:

"We gave him to the man-eating tree, Senor!"

***

Throughout the 1890s, the St. Louis Globe-Democrat published a regular page called "Stories for Nimrods," which is where the second Nicaragua Man-Eating Plant story debuted on Sep. 3, 1892. Each installment of the vividly illustrated page included man vs. animal tales (some sourced from other newspapers) such as "A Wedding Spoiled by an Alligator and a Quicksand," "Adventures of a Schoolmistress Imprisoned with a Bear" and "Struggle in a Cave with a Mexican Lion and Myriads of Bats."

Despite the lurid and perhaps somewhat unbelievable content in "Stories for Nimrods," the title isn't a pejorative. The modern American use of "nimrod" to mean "idiot" didn't emerge until the 1940s, in Looney Tunes of all places. In the 1948 cartoon short "What Makes Daffy Duck," the titular waterfowl taunts Elmer Fudd, calling him "my little nimrod." This actually refers to the original definition of nimrod, that being a hunter (named after the biblical king and mighty huntsman). However, hapless Elmer's perpetual foiling by Bugs Bunny and Daffy Duck seems to have altered the meaning of "nimrod." So, the Globe-Democrat section was more accurately "Stories for Hunters," not "Stories for Morons." Granted, not everyone at the time would have disagreed with Daffy Duck's take. "Just why a paper like the St. Louis Globe-Democrat should run such rot as 'Stories for Nimrods' is a hard matter to determine," complained the Austin Statesman.

NICARAGUA SPECIMEN #3

There is a third account of the Vampire Vine of Nicaragua from this era, albeit more obscure. One might think it just a regurgitation of details in the earlier stories. However, while the original tales provide little to no verifiable information about their protagonists, this latter story comes from sources well known within late 19th-Century U.S. and Nicaraguan politics.

William Newell served as U.S. consul to Nicaragua's capital of Managua during the late 1890s. In the years following his tenure, Newell wrote a number of articles for newspapers in his hometown of Buffalo, New York, detailing his adventures and observations of the Central American country. In a lengthy column published in the Buffalo Courier of June 4, 1899, Newell described his visit to Greytown, a community built to accommodate the by-then floundering effort to build the Nicaragua Canal. Greytown, per Newell, was located about three miles from San Juan del Norte, proper, on the seashore facing the ocean. We pick up Newell's account on the day he learned about a most unusual hazard encountered during the laying of infrastructure for the canal:

No preliminary feature of the canal was so difficult of accomplishment as the building of the railway through the Deseado Swamp. By previous appointment I met Mr. Davis, who had been my cicerone in the examination of the breakwater and dredges, at the railroad headquarters, the understanding being that a party would be taken over the twelve miles of the road then completed. The party was made up of United States Consul Von Braida, British Consul Mr. Bingham, Mr. Davis and the writer. After a wait of a few minutes' duration Mr. Davis came to the door of the office and said:

"We are ready, gentlemen."

A step, and we were outside, and, with one accord we began to look for the locomotive and car that was to convey us. There was nothing in sight. Then I began to wonder if we were to do the railway trip al pie or andar a' la mula. Our imaginings were ended by the appearance of a hand-car propelled by four Jamaica negroes in the usual way. On this Mr. Davis invited us to be seated and without the shout of "all aboard," and the usual accessories of a railway journey, we started on our tour. Soon we were bowling along at a lively speed. Not many minutes had passed before we found ourselves in a dense forest of grand, old cedars. A number of the trees showed great age, long strings of gray moss hung from their hoary tops. The parrot and the brilliant plumed jackdaw made the woods resound with their interminable chatter. Black monkeys grinned down at us from the branches, while strange pizate now and then crossed the track ahead of us. There was no evidence to indicate that there ever had been a swamp where the track was laid. There was nothing to indicate that great labor and great expense had been expended by the company to construct this road.

Count Von Braida, after we had traveled five miles of our journey, noticing the men dripping from their efforts in propelling the car in the heat of the midday sun, suggested that we call the rest of the trip off. This Mr. Davis agreed to with the proviso that we sample his larder that he had aboard.

Consul Bingham jocularly remarked, "I would never have taken this for a buffet car." Soon we dropped off the car, and seating ourselves in the shade, awaited the unfolding of the larder. Mr. Davis proved himself a picnic chef par excellence. While sipping our cognac and puffing our puros buenos y finos we drew from Mr. Davis the story of the building of the Deseado Swamp Railway, and, being a raconteur of no mean ability, I will let him tell it as he told it to us seated beneath the shade of a tropic jungle:

"The heaviest body of work to be accomplished on the whole line is concentrated within a distance of three miles, at what is designated the 'Eastern Divide,' and as the time that will be required to complete the canal is measured by the time spent in the opening of this deep cut, it was felt to be important to install a plant for this heavy rock cutting at the earliest date possible. The difficulties of transportation of heavy machinery from the harbor to the site of this heavy cutting were so great that it at once became apparent to us, that there was no alternative to be considered but the immediate construction of a railroad. This work we begun in the summer of 1890. Our surveys indicated that the most direct route was across what had always been considered an impassable swamp—the Deseado. Of the first ten miles of the way there were but four miles of hard ground; and this was covered with a dense mass of tangled vines and other vegetation so that nothing could be seen at a distance of fifty feet, every step being preceded by a blow of the machete to clear a way.

"Many a night did I go to bed with doubting heart, feeling that if the rest of the canal way was as difficult of accomplishment as this another 350 years must elapse ere the canal was a completed fact. The natives gave us frequent nods of misgiving and would say, 'Ustedes no pueden de hacer esta obra' (you cannot do that work). However, I felt that Yankee grit and ingenuity would pull us through—and it did. Hardly had we begun on the undertaking when the heavy rains set in, covering the swamp to a depth of from two to six feet. As no earth for filling could be had from along the track it was brought from a distance by train, which conditions necessitated a reversal of the ordinary proceeding, that is, laying the track first and making the embankment later.

"To accomplish this we were reduced to a novel plan. A heavy corduroy of logs, cut in the neighboring forest, was laid for many miles. These were rolled, floated or dragged by man power alone to the line of proposed track, and there arranged as compactly as possible. Upon them were laid longitudinal stringers, also consisting of native tree trunks—the straightest that could be found. When came the railroad ties, resting on the stringers, and lastly the steel rails, all spiked down.

"After this was done, we loaded the cars with sand and ran them out over the log embankment where they were dumped, the sand being packed into the interstices and under the ties, which were slowly raised by the laborers until the proper grade was gained. We had six miles of this kind of work, and many a strong amen resounded through the forest when the last car of sand was dumped and the last spike driven.

"Nearly all this work was done by man-power, in fact, the only labor not done by men, was the filling of the sand trains. You must bear in mind, too, that we worked in swamp water from knee deep, to often, waist and armpits deep. Notwithstanding that the men worked in the swamp, there was no material increase in the number admitted to the hospital.

"The material used in grading and ballasting the roadbed was taken from the canal prism, near the harbor, and delivered along the line by trains of cars, loaded by means of a steam shovel or 'navvy,' capable of delivering upon the cars 1,300 cubic yards per day.

NICARAGUA CANAL.   RAILROAD BUILDING THROUGH SWAMP.

"In some places we were compelled to put in pile bridges and frequently the piles were driven to a depth of ninety feet before striking a firm foundation. These piles were charged with sixteen pounds creosote oil to the cubic foot. The road is completed for a distance of eleven miles—the most difficult of the whole line, seven miles remaining to be finished in order to reach the divide."

Central America

When Mr. Davis had concluded his interesting story about the building of the Deseado Swamp Railway Mr. Bingham said that our host had left out one entertaining point, "the story of the man-eating plant, and the rescue of Mr. Davis' dog from this carnivorous plant." Our cicerone replied that he had related the story so often that he was apprehensive it would be placed among the Munchausen tales. "However, the story is true," said Mr. Davis, "and can be substantiated upon the testimony of many persons." As Count Von Braida stated positively that he had not heard it and as I had not been long enough in the country to know the fish and snake stories of that section, Mr. Davis consented to give us the tale.

"Our work for the day was about finished, the men had thrown their shovels onto the flat cars and were preparing to jump on the train, when all were startled by an indescribable cry of agony. I cannot tell you why, but immediately I thought of my dog, Don, and not seeing him, supposed that he and some wild animal were having an encounter. Grabbing up my gun, I started for the place whence came the cry. A walk of a half mile, and I came in sight of Don, who seemed enveloped in a perfect network of what appeared to be a fine, rope-like tissue of ropes and fibres. I whistled to him, but he did not stir. He trembled in every limb. Apparently he was on the point of sinking to the ground. Taking out a large knife I began cutting away the vines, and, after much trouble, succeeded in getting Don out of the net-work.

"When the dog was extricated from the plant I found on examination that his body was blood-stained, while the skin appeared to have been actually sucked or puckered in spots, and the poor old fellow staggered, as it from exhaustion.

"On returning to the train I explained the matter to the natives, who shouted out, 'El Gaslito del Diablo' (the Devil's snare). The natives also designate it as a flesh-eating or rather a man-eating plant. In form it is a kind of octopus or devilfish, and is able draw blood of any living thing which comes within its clutches. This plant is found only in swamps in Nicaragua.

"The next day after the occurrence of the incident mentioned I went to the spot to examine this singular species of carnivorous plant life. Owing to the difficulty in handling it, for its grasp can only be shaken off with the loss of skin and even flesh, one is not able to discover much about the plant. I ascertained, however, that its power of suction is contained in a number of infinitesimal mouths or little suckers which, ordinarily closed, open for the reception of food. If the substance is animal, the blood is drawn off and the carcass, or refuse, then dropped.

"I experimented on this carnivorous plant, and was astonished at its voracity. On one occasion I threw a lump of raw meat within reach of the plant. In the short space of five minutes the substance had been drained dry of blood and the mass thrown aside. After his experience on the occasion referred to, Don could never be induced to go into the tropic jungle and ever after avoided a vine-like plant."

At the conclusion of Mr. Davis' thrilling narrative we boarded the hand car for the return to Greytown. During the return ride I noticed that the rank grass of the tropics was insidiously spreading itself over the roadbed of the track and the morning glory vine was creeping along the rails. This indicated without argument that the road was not being kept in order for traffic. As work on the canal has been discontinued for a number of years, the road is now almost overgrown, necessitating the expenditure of a large sum of money before it could be utilized for its original purpose.

***

"Mr. Davis" was most likely George Whitefield Davis, who had a long and distinguished career in the U.S. Army, ultimately attaining the rank of major general. He fought with the Union during the Civil War, including the bloody battle of Antietam, and witnessed General Lee's surrender at Appomattox Court House. Serving as an engineer, he oversaw the construction of military posts across the western states and was instrumental in the completion of the long-unfinished Washington Monument.

George Whitefield Davis

Davis served in the Spanish-American War, including a post as acting military governor of Piner del Rio, Cuba. In May 1899, President McKinley assigned Davis as military governor of Puerto Rico.

Following a two-year command in the Philippines, Davis retired from the military in 1903. But he kept busy, accepting an appointment to the Isthmian Canal Commission and as governor of the Panama Canal Zone from 1904-05, playing an active part in early construction.

But Davis took a break from his extensive military career when, on Aug. 1, 1890, a special act of Congress granted him an indefinite leave of absence to serve as general manager and vice-president of the Nicaraguan Canal Company. It was part of the United States' ultimately abandoned efforts to build a canal through Nicaragua. The company shut down operations due to financial difficulties in 1893 and Davis soon returned to active duty. It was during this tenure that Davis claimed to have had a harrowing encounter with a most unusual species of flora.

Based at Greytown on the Atlantic coast, the Nicaraguan Canal Company had by late 1890 built a 700 break-water cut into the harbor and dug about 13-and-a-half miles inland to the Divide Cut, the highest point of elevation for the planned canal, at about 404 feet above sea level. Workers utilized eight huge Herculean dredges, four steam tugs, several barges, a diamond drill and various other machinery in their efforts to build the Nicaragua Canal through the interior of the country along Lake Nicaragua.

One of the company's most challenging projects was to construct the railroad running about 10 miles from Greytown, through the sprawling Deseado Swamp, and on to the Divide Cut, over which all material used in the construction would be transported.

Max Reber, one of the engineers working on the project, told his hometown newspaper, the St. Louis Post-Dispatch, that, "The country in the interior between Greytown and the Divide Cut is one vast swamp where the water lies about three feet deep. The growth of tropical vegetation and wild shrubbery is most dense, and the work of clearing the route ahead of the construction gangs is most arduous in consequence. With the completion of work through the Divide Cut, however, the Nicaraguan Company will have overcome the most difficult problem in the construction of the Nicaragua Canal, and will also have secured a supply of rock material of the utmost value in every phase of the work." It was during the construction of the Deseado Swamp Railway that

Davis and his men had their frightening encounter with a hungry plant.

Ex-U.S. Consul William Newell, 1900.

Newell later gave a speech at Odd Fellow's Hall in Rochester, New York on June 5, 1904 in which he argued Nicaragua's suitability for a canal over Panama. He did list some of Nicaragua's "minor disadvantages," including a minute description of the Devil's Snare, "a sort of vegetable octopus."

GUATEMALA SPECIMEN

On Jan. 22, 1901, the Los Angeles Record reported on yet another case of a Vampire Vine in Central America, but this time in Guatemala:

A CANNIBAL PLANT

The Unnatural History of Man-Eating Plants

Frank L. Howland, formerly of this city, has returned from Antigua, Guatemala, and will remain for a few days with his relatives on Thirty-first Street before leaving for Boston, where he is partner in the firm of Blake, Howland & Co., coffee raisers and importers. Mr. Howland has spent the past ten years in Guatemala and Costa Rica, engaged in raising coffee and sugar cane, and cutting mahogany. He has been through enough experiences to wear out a dozen average men in the wilds of Central America. One day he encountered a dark green [sort] of vine, which swayed toward him as he advanced. Just as he started to crush his way through the waving vines, he [saw] a startled animal like a small rabbit spring up from a crevice in the rock and start along the edge of the mesa. The long cup-shaped ends of the vines reached out and wrapped themselves around the animal and drew it struggling into their embrace. Fascinated, Mr. Howland watched the strange struggle, which only terminated with the death of the rabbit, which seemed to get smaller and smaller and the color of the stalks of the vines changed from green to blood red and in about half an hour unfolded again and let drop the skin and bones of the little animal, every drop of blood having been sucked and absorbed by the strange cannibal plant.

Mr. Howland did not venture into the waving arms, which were now reaching out toward him, but slashing at one of them with his knife, cut away a branch and beat a hasty retreat to the valley below. He says all along the vine were suckers like those on the arms of an octopus and on showing it to his guide was informed that it was known as the death plant and was feared and avoided by the natives. Mr. Howland had several large banana, coffee and sugar cane plantations and has accumulated a large fortune since leaving this city. He says capital can be invested there with large returns, but that nothing can be done without "standing in" with, or, in other words, bribing the officials, and owing to the frequent revolutions and changes of government, titles to properties frequently have to be bought several times to retain possession.

Cover art from "Un Mystérieux Message" by Jean Joseph-Renaud, illustrations by Raymond Pallier, 1924.

There was a Frank L. Howland who resided in Westdale/West Bridgewater, Massachusetts, about 30 miles south of Boston, in 1900 and successive years. However, he was the proprietor of a lovely inn and summer getaway called Walnut Lawn, with no indication of South American coffee importation or battles with carnivorous plants.

A possible analogue or even an inspiration for the Vampire Vine amongst scientifically accepted plants might be found in *Bauera rubioides*, a scrambling, tangled, flowering shrub with wiry branches, which can grow taller than six feet and is distributed through Australia and Tasmania. In fact, the 1894 articles that tie Riley's lecture to stories about Vampire Vines specifically describe the decidedly non-carnivorous yet hazardous properties of *Bauera rubioides*:

The following account of a "man-eating plant" is vouched for by an old resident in Tasmania (the scientific name is bauera rubioides; it is a native of Australia and Tasmania and the narrator and a friend have been entangled in its meshes and only escaped with great difficulty): "The bauera is not a creeper or climber but only a plant that is weak in the legs, having a thin, flexible stem, usually supporting itself on its neighbors. A bauera scrub at the outer edge of the patch may be only eighteen inches high but in the thick of it may reach ten to twenty feet; a man may be enveloped even before he is aware of it, and the tangled mass surround him till movement is impossible. You cannot cut it with an ax, because it offers no resistance, and if cut with a knife the rope-like stems only fall more closely round you. You cannot see where you are going and only struggle and flounder on to your exhaustion. It usually covers low-lying ground and throws up from the root a number of slender stems, tapering gradually, that become interlaced in all direction and to the solitary bushman or explorer it is formidable. He will perhaps try to wriggle along the damp ground under it and to tear the stems apart and struggle through. Then exhausted with this he perhaps climbs up some old stump and tries to flounder along on the top of the scrub but he soon sinks helpless into the yielding mass that quickly squeezes out his life."

The prevalence and consistency of Vampire Vine accounts beg the question of whether there could be a known, non-carnivorous species of vine in Nicaragua that forms a hazard via thorny brambles which could trap a person or animal. And there are indeed such species, whose range encompasses the vicinity of Greytown at the southeastern tip of Nicaragua, from which the arguably most plausible account originates. This includes *Desmoncus*, climbing palms with needle-like spines and grappling hook-like barbs that can tear clothing and inflict serious wounds; *Smilax*, aka Catbrier or Greenbrier, climbing and flowering plants that are lined with thorns and grow as shrubs in dense, impenetrable thickets; and *Uncaria tomentosa* (Uña de Gato, or Cat's Claw), a woody vine whose claw-shaped thorns explain its common name. Perhaps encounters with these thorny plants while traversing undeveloped, overgrown areas of Nicaragua inspired stories of the Vampire Vine.

As Man-Eating Vegetation goes, the Vampire Vine of Nicaragua (and possibly Guatemala) possesses the most consistent and greatest number of supposed first-hand accounts. It's enough to make one pause and ponder if there might truly be snaking, ravenous tendrils winding their way through the Central American hinterlands.

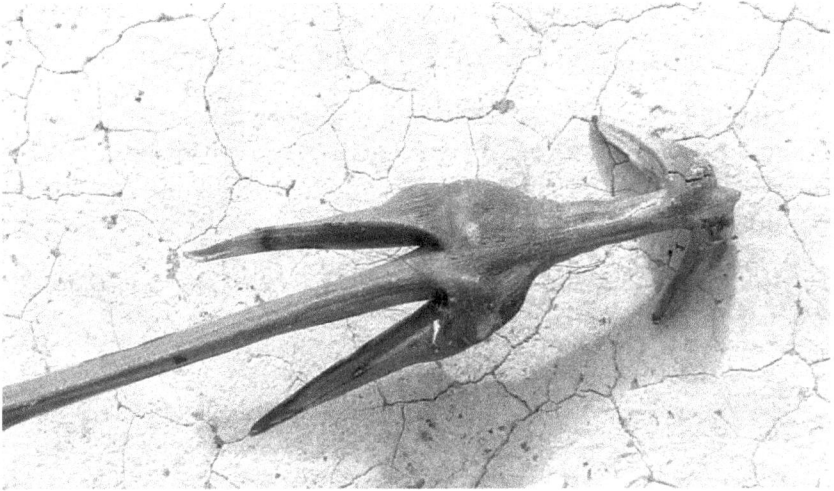

Acanthophylls of Desmoncus orthacanthos, the grappling hook-like structure common to most species of Desmoncus. Photo by Alex Popovkin, Bahia, Brazil from Brazil, CC BY 2.0, via Wikimedia Commons.

SOURCES:

"Attempts to Build a Canal Across Nicaragua." *Wikipedia,* https://en.wikipedia.org/wiki/Attempts_to_build_a_canal_across _Nicaragua. Accessed 30 Mar. 2025.

"*Bauera rubioides.*" *Wikipedia,* https://en.wikipedia.org/wiki/Bauera_rubioides. Accessed 19 Aug. 2025.

"Blair's Motion." *Joplin Sunday Herald* [Joplin, MO], 3 Aug. 1890, p. 2.

"A Blood-Sucking Plant." *Frank Leslie's Popular Monthly* [New York City], May 1890, pp. 542-543.

"A Blood-Sucking Plant." *Times* [Philadelphia], 9 Dec. 1889, p. 2.

"A Blood-Sucking Plant." *Yates Center Tribune* [Yates Center, KS], 4 Jan. 1890, p. 6.

"A Cannibal Plant." *Los Angeles Record*, 22 Jan. 1901, p. 2.

"*Ceraleurodicus keris* Martin, 2004." *TreatmentBank*, https://tb.plazi.org/GgServer/html/3D39810BFFDF9C1F7ADF9FECFD81ACA8/7. Accessed 1 Sep. 2025.

Coronado, Indiana M. "Estudio Etnobotánico y Ecológico de las Palmas Arecaceae y Cyclanthaceae en la Reserva Biológica Indio-Maiz Río San Juan, Nicaragua." *Encuentro*, vol. 32, no. 52, 2000, pp. 80-86.

Davis, Arthur, director. *Looney Tunes: What Makes Daffy Duck.* Warner Bros., 1948.

"*Desmoncus.*" *Wikipedia*, https://en.wikipedia.org/wiki/Desmoncus. Accessed 1 Sep. 2025.

"*Desmoncus moorei* AJ Hend." *Flora of Nicaragua*, http://legacy.tropicos.org/NamePage.aspx?nameId=100377012&projectId=7. Accessed 1 Sep. 2025.

"The Devil's Snare." *Bruce Herald* [Tokomairiro, New Zealand], 4 Sep. 1896, p. 3.

Essid, Joe. "Word of the Week! Nimrod." *Richmond Writing*, 19 Oct. 2018, https://blog.richmond.edu/writing/2018/10/19/word-of-the-week-nimrod/. Accessed 16 May 2025.

"For Recreation and Rest." *Boston Evening Transcript*, 27 May 1903, p. 25.

"Frank Leslie's Popular Monthly." *Hathitrust*, https://catalog.hathitrust.org/Record/100542085. Accessed 15 May 2025.

Central America

"From Ocean to Ocean." *Morning Call* [San Francisco], 23 Nov. 1890, p. 13.

Gates, Merrill E., editor. *Men of Mark in America, Vol. 1.* Men of Mark Publishing Company, 1905.

"Gen. George Davis Buried." *Fall River Evening News* [Fall River, MA], 15 Jul. 1918, p. 5.

"George Whitefield Davis." Wikipedia, https://en.wikipedia.org/wiki/George_Whitefield_Davis. Accessed 30 Mar. 2025.

"Indio Maíz Biological Reserve." *Wikipedia*, https://en.wikipedia.org/wiki/Indio_Ma%C3%ADz_Biological_Reserve. Accessed 1 Sep. 2025.

"Insect Help." *Brooklyn Daily Eagle* [Brooklyn, NY], 3 Feb. 1892, p. 2.

"Man-Eating Plants." *Alton Weekly Telegraph* [Alton, IL], 20 Sep. 1894, p. 10.

"Man-Eating Plants." *Mound City News* [Mound City, MO], 31 Aug. 1894, p. 7.

Marshall Weekly Messenger [Marshall, Texas], 5 Aug. 1892, p. 2.

Martin, Jon H. "Giant Whiteflies (Sternorrhyncha, Aleyrodidae): A Discussion of Their Taxonomic and Evolutionary Significance, with the Description of a New Species of *Udamoselis* Enderlein from Ecuador." *Tijdschrift voor Entomologie*, vol. 150, no. 1, 2007, pp. 13-29

Newell, William. "In the Land of the Canal." *Buffalo Sunday Morning News* [Buffalo, NY], 11 Feb. 1900, p. 12.

Newell, William. "The Land of the Canal." *Buffalo Courier* [Buffalo, NY], 4 Jun. 1899, pp. 8-9.

"Next Sunday's Courier." *Buffalo Enquirer* [Buffalo, NY], 5 Nov. 1898, p. 9.

"A Mexican's Revenge." *Mantorville Express* [Mantorville, MN], 4 Nov. 1892, p. 4.

"Panama Unfit for the Canal." *Rochester Democrat and Chronicle* [Rochester, NY], 6 Jun. 1904. p. 10.

Pike, Nicholas. "Plants with Carnivorous Proclivities." *Frank Leslie's Popular Monthly* [New York City], May 1893, pp. 605-608.

"A Remarkable Plant." *Sholhaven Telegraph* [Nowra, New South Wales, Australia], 7 Oct. 1891, p. 4.

Rueda, Ricardo M., et al. "Revisión Botánica del Benero *Smilax* (Smilacaceae) en Nicaragua." *Encuentro*, vol. 34, no. 61, 2002, pp. 59-72.

Schmidt, Richard J. "Palmae." *Botanical Dermatology Database*, Jul. 2024, https://www.botanical-dermatology-database.info/BotDermFolder/PALM.html. Accessed 1 Sep. 2025.

"*Smilax*." Wikipedia, https://en.wikipedia.org/wiki/Smilax. Accessed 1 Sep. 2025.

Stevens, W. D., et al. *Flora de Nicaragua*. Missouri Botanical Garden Press, 2001.

"Stories for Nimrods: Adventures of a Schoolmistress Imprisoned with a Bear." *St. Louis Daily Globe-Democrat*, 2 Feb. 1895, p. 16.

"Stories for Nimrods: A Man-Eating Tree in Central America." *St. Louis Daily Globe-Democrat*, 3 Sep. 1892, p. 16.

"Stories for Nimrods: Struggle in a Cave with a Mexican Lion and Myriads of Bats." *St. Louis Daily Globe-Democrat*, 17 Dec. 1892, p. 16.

"Stories for Nimrods: A Wedding Spoiled by an Alligator and a Quicksand." *St. Louis Daily Globe-Democrat*, 23 Jan. 1897, p. 12.

TLW. Comment on "The Nimrod Effect: How a Cartoon Bunny Changed the Meaning of a Word Forever." *Unremembered*, 1 Feb. 2022, 4:48 a.m., https://unrememberedhistory.com/2017/01/09/the-nimrod-effect-how-a-cartoon-bunny-changed-the-meaning-of-a-word-forever/.

"*Uncaria tomentosa.*" *Wikipedia*, https://en.wikipedia.org/wiki/Uncaria_tomentosa. Accessed 1 Sep. 2025.

"Where Summer May Be Enjoyed." *Boston Evening Transcript*, 27 Jun. 1900, p. 7.

Zurski, Ken. "The Nimrod Effect: How a Cartoon Bunny Changed the Meaning of a Word Forever." *Unremembered*, 9 Jan. 2017, https://unrememberedhistory.com/2017/01/09/the-nimrod-effect-how-a-cartoon-bunny-changed-the-meaning-of-a-word-forever/. Accessed 16 May 2025.

Aviatrix "Flyin' Jenny" stumbles across a Man-Eating Plant. Comic strip panel from 12/4/45 Muskegon Chronicle, by Russell Keaton and Glenn Chaffin. Included here on a Fair Use, educational basis.

NORTH AMERICA

POISIONOUS TOBACCO TREE

One of the oldest legends of a Man-Eating Plant covered in this book is from the New World, emanating from a time prior to the arrival of European settlers. The Shuswap (Secwepemc) from the Fraser River and North Thompson Divisions in British Columbia said that their country was once so full of evil beings and cannibals (creatures that eat the flesh of man) that it was hard to survive, let alone increase their population. As related to ethnographer James Teit and published in 1905, many of these cannibals were present-day animals who in ancient times were human beings with animal characteristics, and they used many methods to entrap and slay the unwary.

Guided by knowledge from his aunt, gifted with magic, and accompanied by his three brothers, a young man named TlEe'sa set out from his home near Kamloops to track down and rid the world of these evil beings. One of these cannibal monsters was not an animal at all but a poisonous tobacco tree that grew near Dead-Man's Creek, at Little Tobacco-Place (Pesma'menex). It was a large, very leafy tree, and all around it lay the bones of its victims; for anyone who touched its leaves, or rested in its shade, invariably died.

Upon locating the Cannibal Tree, TlEe'sa said, "I will smoke tobacco." His brothers tried to dissuade him, but he insisted. TlEe'sa bravely approached the tobacco tree and, using his arrow flaker as an axe, chopped it down. Taking the leaves, he smoked them himself, and gave his brothers the stalks to smoke. Then TlEe'sa said, "Tobacco shall never again kill people. It will be a

good plant, and people shall gather and smoke it without harm."
(TlEe'sa clearly didn't know about the effects of lung cancer, but
that is neither here nor there.)

This story mirrors tales from other Native American tribes of
brothers or twins embarking on a journey to slay the world's
monsters, such as Nayenezgani and Tobadzischini in Navajo lore
and Dore and Wahre'dua of the Iowa.

THE APPLE TREE THAT ATE ROGER WILLIAMS

Puritan Roger Williams, founder of Rhode Island, arrived from
England in the New World in 1631. He was a man ahead of his
time, bringing with him a fervent belief in the total separation of
church and state (i.e. the Church of England). This resulted in his
banishment from Massachusetts five years later. Williams and his
followers moved to a new site along Narragansett Bay,
establishing Providence in 1636 as a bastion for religious
dissidents. Williams was notable for his fair treatment of the
Narragansett Indians and protecting them from greedy European
settlers who wanted their land. He also founded the first Baptist
church in North America, although as a skeptic of organized
religion, he did not remain a member for long. This American
architect and icon of religious liberty has another groundbreaking
accolade to his name—he was completely devoured by an apple
tree.

OK, before you tell your friends that Roger Williams was the
victim of a Man-Eating Tree, perhaps I should explain. Williams
died in early 1683 (aged 79, presumably of natural causes). He
was buried in a family plot behind his Providence home and the
exact location was forgotten over ensuing generations.

There was renewed interest in Williams' legacy in the years
leading up to the Revolutionary War. In 1771, Providence
appointed a committee, including Deputy Governor of Rhode
Island Darius Sessions, to erect a monument over the pioneer's
grave. The burial plot was believed to be about 165 feet southeast
from the remaining foundation of Williams' former plantation
house (eventually being on the east side of North Main Street).
But the exact spot, a family plot with seven graves, wasn't
discovered and disinterred until March 22, 1860. Two months

later, Zachariah Allen presented his "Memorial of Roger Williams" to the Rhode Island Historical Society, revealing the strange state of Williams' final resting place.

"The utmost care was taken in scraping away the earth from the bottom of the grave of Roger Williams," wrote Allen. "Not a vestige of any bone was discoverable, nor even of the lime dust which usually remains after the gelatinous part of the bone is decomposed. So completely had disappeared all the earthly remains of the Founder of the State of Rhode Island, in the commingled mass of black, crumbled slate stone and shale, that they did not 'leave a wreck behind.'" The grave beside Williams, presumed to belong to his wife, Mary, was similarly vacant of human remains with the exception of a wonderfully preserved lock of braided hair.

Just what had happened to the bones of Rhode Island's founding father and his wife? According to Allen:

On looking down into the pit whilst the sextons were clearing it of earth, the root of an adjacent apple tree was discovered. This tree had pushed downwards one of its main roots in a sloping direction and nearly straight course towards the precise spot that had been occupied by the skull of Roger Williams. There making a turn conforming with its circumference, the root followed the direction of the back bone to the hips, and thence divided into two branches, each one following a leg bone to the heel, where they both turned upwards to the extremities of the toes of the skeleton. One of the roots formed a slight crook at the part occupied by the knee joint, thus producing an increased resemblance to the outlines of the skeleton of Roger Williams, as if, indeed, moulded thereto by the powers of vegetable life.

This singularly formed root has been carefully preserved, as constituting a very impressive exemplification of the mode in which the contents of the grave had been entirely absorbed. Apparently not sated with banqueting on the remains found in one grave, the same roots extended themselves into the next adjoining one, pervading every part of it with a net-work of voracious fibres in their thorough search for every particle of nutritious matter in the form of phosphate of lime and other organic elements constituting the bones.

Roger Williams statue, 1881 image from The Biographical Cyclopedia of Representative Men of Rhode Island.

At the time the apple tree was planted, all the fleshy parts of the body had doubtlessly been decomposed and dispersed in gaseous forms; and there was then left only enough of the principal bones to serve for the roots to follow along from one extremity of the skeleton to the other in a continuous course, to glean up the scanty remains. Had there been other organic matter present in quantity, there would have been found divergent branches of roots to envelope and absorb it. This may serve to explain the singular formation of the roots into the shape of the principal bones of the human skeleton.

In other words, the apple tree "ate" Roger Williams and one of its roots assumed the form of his corpse.

So thought the group conducting the exhumation, in any case. All present turned to the innocent-looking apple tree, viewing it as the thief that had stolen away the remains of Roger Williams. "There was no mistake, for it had been caught in the act of robbing a grave and of appropriating the contents to its own use, re-incorporating them into its living trunk and branches," said Allen. "The swollen buds showed that it was preparing to show off its spoils in a new suit of green leaves, with gay blossoms of many colors, as banners rejoicingly hung out. It was readily anticipated that it would soon incorporate a portion of these spoils into golden cheeked apples to tempt the owner of the orchard to participate in the fruits of this robbery."

One of the gentlemen assisting in the excavation turned to the owner of the orchard, who was present, and questioned if the partaker was not as bad as the thief. "It is sufficiently manifest why nothing is left of Roger Williams, for you have been eating him up in the shape of apples," accused the gravedigger.

The orchard proprietor admitted that appearances were against him but argued that, since his own father had planted the tree and consumed most of the fruit, might not he himself be considered among the offspring of Roger Williams?

Allen offered a more philosophical take on the apple tree's supposed absorption of Williams and his wife, emphasizing the transmutation of the human body into new plant life. "Under this view, the entire disappearance of every vestige of the mortal remains of Roger Williams, teaches after his death an impressive lesson of the actual physical resurrection of them, by ever-acting natural causes, into renewed states of existence constituting a physical victory over the grave, as his precepts and example, before his death, have taught the greater moral victory of the Christian faith over worldly oppression."

Williams finally got his memorial in 1939, just over three centuries after he first set foot in Providence. The 14-foot-tall granite statue rises between two pylons in Prospect Terrace. It depicts Williams standing at the bow of a ship, overlooking the city he founded. Despite Allen's assertion that nothing was left of the Williamses (but a braid of Mary's hair), some type of remains were moved to a family crypt in the Old North Burial Ground in 1860 following the dig. According to 1939 news reports about the memorial's unveiling, "the dust of Williams" was transferred from the vault of the Rhode Island Historical Society and interred in the base of the statue.

Roger Williams statue and final burial site at Prospect Terrace in Providence, Rhode Island. Photo by Rhododendrites, CC BY-SA 4.0, via Wikimedia Commons.

The Unnatural History of Man-Eating Plants

The apple tree root that was said to have taken on the shape of Williams' body, perhaps in the process of absorbing him, has been preserved and can be seen today at the Rhode Island Historical Society's John Brown House Museum. According to Director of Collections Kirsten Hammerstrom, "It's a popular item, and no matter how unlikely it is that an apple tree 'ate' Roger Williams, school children love to think of it that way and it is a story [worthy] of cable TV."

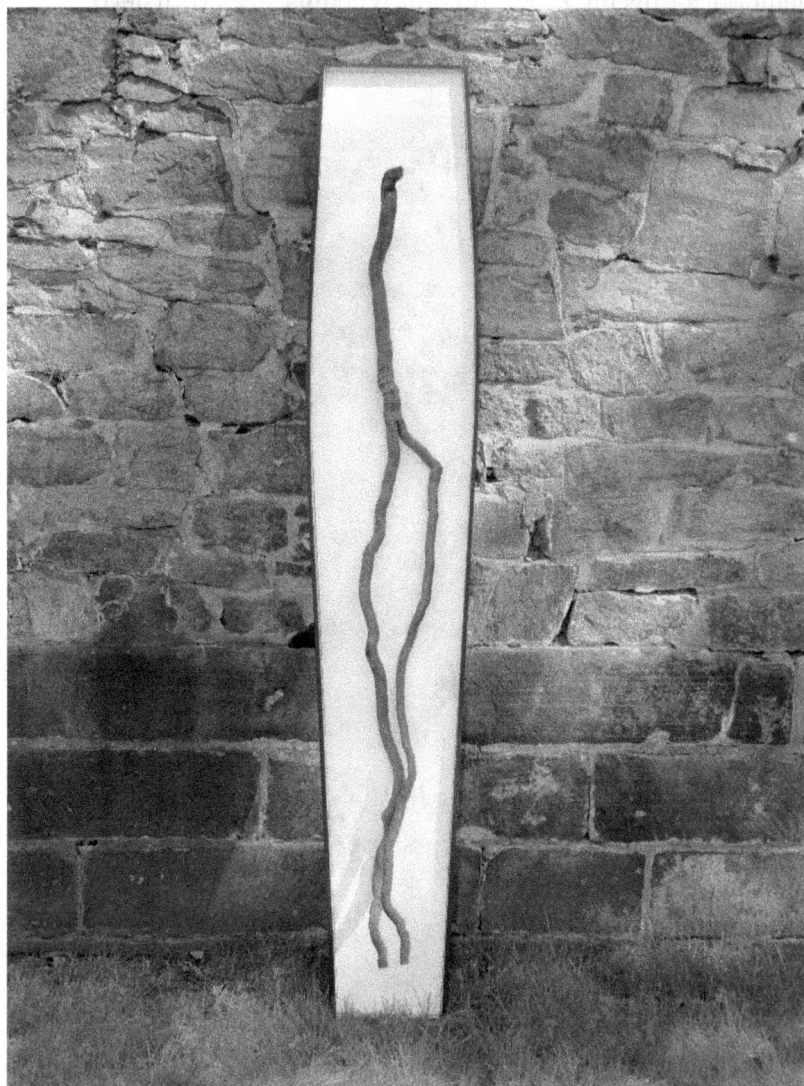

PREVIOUS PAGE: Roger Williams' Apple Tree Root: Section of apple tree root excavated in 1860 from the back portion of Roger Williams' home lot near the corner of Benefit and Bowen Streets, Providence. Image and caption courtesy of the Rhode Island Historical Society.

AUDREY MINUS ONE

On Aug. 16, 1885, the St. Paul Daily Globe recounted a wild saga it attributed to a well-known Chicago businessman (name withheld by the Globe) who sat among a group of conversationalists in the lobby of St. Paul's brand-new Hotel Ryan, discussing the topic of mysterious murders. The grave-faced man commanded the room with a tale befitting the Victorian Gothic style of the grand hotel, which once occupied seven stories on the northeast corner of 6th and Robert streets in downtown St. Paul. The unsolved murder he detailed occurred in Chicago sometime between 1850 and 1855:

NEW FOOD FOR PLANTS.

A Young Girl Relates to a Jury a Frightful Experience With a Carnivorous Plant.

A Mysterious Death Which Was Accounted For in a Highly Improbable Manner.

A Man-Eating Plant Alleged to Have Sucked the Life Blood of a Father.

A Chicago Man Spins a Yarn Which Knocks Out the Southern Snake Story.

I was sitting in the lobby of the Hotel Ryan the other day engaged in conversation with several St. Paul gentlemen, upon current topics, and our conversation had drifted to a discussion of several recent murders that had been surrounded with so much mystery that the efforts of police and detectives to apprehend the perpetrators were fruitless. Several peculiar cases were instanced and their recitation by the different individuals comprising the knot of gossipers was sufficiently interesting to attract the casual listener, and in a short time some ten or a dozen persons had gathered around the circle.

Among them was a Chicago gentleman, slightly past the prime of life, of grave demeanor and bearing a name which, were I to announce it, would be recognized by many readers of the GLOBE. This gentleman, who is a practical business man, not given to trifling, and bearing an unimpeachable reputation for sagacity, gave in the presence of the gathering the following strange, almost incredible account of a mysterious murder which occurred in Chicago some time between 1850 and 1855:

"I am satisfied, gentlemen, that you will give no credence to the story I am about to narrate unless you have perhaps thoroughly studied the nature and habits of insectivorous plants, as I have done, and therefore know of the possibility of their evolution in a carnivorous form.

THE LIE BEGUN.

"During the year 1852 or 1853, a man and a young woman came to Chicago from the East via the lake, and, purchasing a small tract of land about 200 feet south of what is now known as Hubbard court, erected a small frame building in which they took up their abode. The man, who was, I should judge, about 45 years of age, gave his name as Richard Bowse, and the girl, who was in her teens, was said to be his daughter. Bowse appeared to have some means, but the couple lived sparingly, he catching fish and doing odd jobs about town, and the girl officiating as his housekeeper. Those about the market places in proximity to the Bowse dwelling, and those who were his companions on the pier catching fish, often remarked the peculiar demeanor of the man; his singular reticence and his extraordinary fondness for his humble home. As time passed on, his peculiarities seemed to grow more notable until, through some idle remark, he was given the sobriquet of 'Crazy Dick.' Fishermen, laborers and idlers in the neighborhood quickly caught up the term, and within a year after the advent of Richard Bowse in the community he was known by no other name than 'Crazy Dick.'

"The girl, too, was strangely reserved, although she used to venture an acquaintance with a neighbor here and there, of whom she was wont to borrow books and other reading matter. She evinced considerable intelligence, and showed a taste for a quality of literature above the average grade perused by girls of her age. Whenever she conversed with any one, which was on rare occasions, she used good English and talked fluently. One morning she made her usual trip to the market, quickly made her purchases and retired in great haste, her face depicting a singular frightened expression often before noticed by the market people with whom she constantly traded. One half hour later little Chicago was gossiping over the mysterious murder of Richard Bowse.

THE INVESTIGATION.

"I was summoned as a member of the coroner's jury at the inquest of the murdered man. A police officer testified that at about the hour of 10:30 in the morning, as he was passing in the street in front of the dwelling, the girl ran screaming from the house, and informed him in terrified tones that her father was dead. The girl refused absolutely to return to the dwelling, and the policeman, leaving her, hurried forward. Entering the house he saw nothing unusual in the front room, but, on opening the door to a rear apartment, he saw, lying in the center of the room, the form of a man which he at once recognized as that of 'Crazy Dick.' Near the corpse was an axe and scattered in profusion about the room were the remnants of what appeared to have been a monstrous tropical plant. Its juices had saturated the floor all around the body and a nauseating odor arose from the moisture. Stooping over the body, he found it quite dead and there were marks of violence on the neck and arms. The tongue protruded from the mouth and the face was covered with red blotches as if it had received several heavy blows.

"Two doctors were called to the stand and testified that they had made an examination of the corpse and were convinced from the marks on the neck, the protruding tongue and evidence of internal disorder that the deceased came to his death from strangulation. As there was no instrument within his reach when found with which he could have strangled himself, they expressed their opinion as experts that he could not have committed suicide.

THE NEXT WITNESS

called was the daughter, or she who claimed to have been the daughter of the deceased. Her testimony, which was rapidly and nervously given, was interrupted by occasional bursts of tears, and, in the narration of the most exciting parts or her story, her face would become flushed, her eyes would dilate and a sensation of terror would appear to overtake her, followed by a nervous chill from which she would not recover for some moments. This is her story, substantially as she gave it:

"'I am Josephine Bowse, daughter of the deceased. I am 19 years of age and was born on board the sailing vessel Operto, of which my father was captain. My mother died in giving me birth, and my father, who was greatly attached to her, never fully recovered from the shock consequent to her loss. During all my life he has looked upon me as the destroyer of his wife, and I have never known [this said very bitterly] a father's affection or even consideration. Shortly after my mother's death my father gave up the sea and settled near New York. He established a fish mart and made money. One of the things he took from the vessel and which he appeared to regard as more valuable than myself, was

A SMALL PLANT

which had been presented to my mother by a sailor off the coast of Portugal. Because it had been my mother's he cared for it fondly, and watched its growth, which was very rapid, with exceeding interest. When I had grown to be 10 or 12 years of age I first noticed my father's peculiar regard for this plant, and also noticed that he was spending more and more of his time in the room where it was kept. One day I stepped suddenly into his presence and discovered him with a handful of live flies which he was apparently feeding to the plant. At first I couldn't believe my senses, but as he had not noticed my presence I stood and gazed with a strange fascination and surely enough he was tossing the helpless insects, one by one, into the palms of the leaves, which would quickly close and imprison them. Suddenly discovering me he showed great consternation, and having satisfied himself from my terror that I had seen and heard all he told me of a discovery he had made of the plant's strange proclivity for catching and imprisoning small insects, which seemed attracted to the leaves by some secretion on them. He said that he had followed up his discovery with experiments which proved the plant's capacity for absorbing animal matter, and that the process of daily feeding it was increasing that capacity until at that time it would accept and absorb all the flies he could catch and give to it. I was cautioned to tell no one of what I had seen and heard, and for over two years I held my peace, while my father continued to give the plant unnatural nourishment, under which it grew with greater rapidity than ever. One day he made an experiment with some fresh, bloody meat, which he minced up into very small particles. To his delight the plant accepted and devoured them, and from that day on the particles were increased in size until fully three ounces of meat would be absorbed by one single leaf, and nearly one-half pound of cartilage or other mucous animal matter. My father had long since ceased to water the earth around the plant, or pay any attention to it, and I noticed that its surface, which had become hard and dry, was cracking open as if there was a pressure underneath disturbing it.

THE REMARKABLE GROWTH

and development began to fascinate, and yet alarm me, while my father was nearly crazed with delight.

"'One day, while busying myself about the house, I released my pet canary from the cage and allowed it to flutter about the rooms. Suddenly I heard a strange noise in the room where the plant was standing, resembling the rustling of leaves in a breeze. Knowing there was scarcely a breath of air stirring, I stepped in to discover the cause of the sounds.

"'God in Heaven! what a sight met my gaze.

"'Poised directly over the monstrous vegetable was my beautiful bird, while below it was turbulence and confusion. The thick foliage seemed excited to destruction and the sound of the leaves as they swayed to and fro in their mad impatience resembled the hissing of a thousand snakes. Now and then a leaf would wrap itself around another and then slowly relax, while the ugly veins in its palm were swollen near to bursting with passion. Every leaf and stalk was stretched upward, yawning for its prey. Terrified, I sprang forward with uplifted arms. The bird, to avoid my grasp, swooped downward, and in an instant a monster leaf had wrapped itself around it. There was a smothered, shrill cry from the little throat, while the leaf slowly crushed it, as a serpent crushes a forest fowl.

"'Terrified to madness, I ran screaming from the house, and meeting a fisherman I tearfully told him that my father's plant had murdered my bird. He did not understand me and looked amused as I ran past him to meet my father coming from the quay. When I told him what had happened his face lit up with keenest pleasure and he hastened with me to the house.

IT ATE BIRDS.

"'For a long time he stood inspecting the plant and then, with a strange look in his eyes, he started for the rear of the house where an old hen was scratching with a broop of chickens. In an instant I divined his purpose and a new terror seized me.

"'Quickly stooping over the unsuspecting brood he grabbed up two of the beautiful downy things and hurried with them into the house.

"'You are going to commit a fiendish act,' said I, 'and I will not witness it.'

"'You will stay where you are,' said he, 'and let me warn you that if you ever dare to interfere with me, or harm this plant, you shall be its next victim.'

"'Paralyzed with fear, I sat motionless while he tossed first one and then the other of the helpless fowls into the foliage. The next morning the leaves slowly opened and there fell on the floor the three victims of the voracious plant. I picked them up. They were as bloodless as the remnants of a weasel's victim.

"'Upon learning of the remark I made to the fisherman, my father became alarmed lest his secret had been discovered and immediately decided to leave the community. We came to Chicago and it was here that I became convinced that my father's mind was impaired and that he was likely to become hopelessly insane over the plant. He often told me that he believed the thing would one day

BECOME A LIVING BEING,

and that it would tell him of his wife who had nourished it while young. He was continually muttering to it as though it could hear and understand him, and since the time of my canary's death he had continued to feed it upon live meat. Within a year after our arrival in Chicago it grew to fill nearly one-half of the room in which it was kept, and the roots had broken from the earth in the large tub and were rapidly growing over the floor. Their color turned quickly after exposure to a purple, and became soft and pulpy, like the trunk or body of the plant. When doves and pigeons were tossed into the foliage these roots, which were much like the tentacles of the devil-fish, would creep up to the foliage, as if to assist it in securing its prey.

"'One day, as my father and I were watching it, the house cat, a great pet of my father's, came purring through the room and rubbed its soft fur against the tub as if inviting a caress. Have you ever seen a snake allow an innocent dove, thrown in its cage by the keeper, to trip unsuspectingly over its coils while it lay biding its time to grasp and crush the poor thing? In just such a manner did poor tabby rub and purr among the deadly tentacles of the plant, until suddenly one of them fastened itself around her body, and, in spite of her desperate struggles, would soon have given her over to the foliage, which was now in a terrible commotion, the leaves bending downward until it seemed as if the stalks must snap in the frantic effort to reach the victim. But my father exhibited, for the first time in ten years, a sense of pity, for, grasping a large knife from the table, he severed the tentacle. The cat, freed from the deadly embrace, ran madly by with the coil of the root still clinging to it, while the injured stub lay quivering over the edge of the tub, and from its end oozed not blood, but a thick bluish substance in a considerable quantity.

THE HORROR OF THIS EXPERIENCE

brought me resolution, and I tremblingly told my father that he must destroy the entire plant, as he had just destroyed one of its members, or if he refused I would appeal to the authorities.

"'In an instant he became a maniac, and, springing upon me with all his force, he quickly overpowered me, and bound me hand and foot. I screamed. I implored, but all in vain. Raising me in his powerful hands high above his head he carried me into the presence of the loathsome plant. His demoniacal laugh was loud and long, but above it I could hear a sound which struck greater terror to my heart. It froze my blood and took from me the power to plead for my life. It was the sound of a thousand serpents struggling, hissing, gasping for their prey. It was but an instant that I was suspended in the air, and yet it seemed an hour when my father released me. I was numb; great, cold drops were on my face, and it seemed as if my heart had ceased to beat.

"'You know your fate, now go ahead and inform the authorities.'

"'That was all he said. I had not time for a reply before my father retired to the room of the plant and closed the door behind him.

"After I had regained the power of action I hurried from the place and made my morning purchases. Returning I busied myself about the room for several minutes. But I was nervous and excited; the quiet of the room intensified my mental condition until it seemed as if I must go mad if somebody did not speak to me. Impelled to recklessness by my increasing agony I moved toward the door of the fatal room and opened it. It needed but the spectacle before me to complete my madness. The plant was overturned. Beneath its foliage was the half-concealed form of my parent. A dozen tentacles had pinioned his arms and one huge one was around his throat. A hundred leaves were fastened on his body and a thousand more were struggling for his blood. I was seized with a fit of frenzy. An axe lay near the outer door, and grasping it

I RUSHED UPON THE MONSTER

with a maniac's strength. It struck into the lower part of the foliage. It was like disturbing the nest of a million hornets. A score of stalks bent toward me and their leaves fastened on my clothing. A tentacle wrapped itself around my ankle. I hued it off at a blow. A thousand furies possessed the monstrous thing, but in my madness I was possessed of as many more. Twice I was nearly taken from my feet by the slimy tentacles, but my ax severed one at every stroke. At last I had cut away to the heavy pulpy trunk and with a few well-directed blows I had severed it. This shattered the power of the plant and one by one the tentacles released or partly loosened their hold of my father, but I was in no mood to stop. Blow after blow fell until nothing was left but fragments. Then turning [I] looked for the first time, fully on the face of my prostrate father. The tongue hung from the gasping mouth and the eyes protruded from their sockets. The vision, as

The Unnatural History of Man-Eating Plants

I see it now, is like a horrible nightmare. My frenzy turned into fear and I ran screaming from the house. You all know the rest.'

"I see, gentlemen," said our narrator, "some incredulous smiles among you, which lead me to believe that you consider the girl to have been crazy or a very clever prevaricator. We members of the jury believed more than this. We believed her to be the murderess of Richard Bowse and her story to be a ruse to affect insanity or else really make the jury believe that the plant was the murderer. However the girl was seized with nervous prostration, from which she died before we had an opportunity of trying her, and the case was never cleared up.

"I am free to confess, though, that since I have thoroughly investigated the nature and the habits of insectivorous plants and have made a careful study of scientific authorities on the subject, I can believe the story to be not only possible but probably true.

"Darwin and other eminent scientists tell us of plants which catch and imprison insects. These plants have digestive organs, they are supplied with glands containing secretions of such a character and strength as will dissolve fibers of meat, the cartilage of a sheep, and any amount of insects. These plants have been known to exist entirely without the aid of the earth's nourishment when attention has been given to their insectivorous propensities. Why, then, if the disposition of a plant can be so changed as to enable it to exist, not as a vegetable, but an animal, cannot it be cultivated to show desire for that kind of nourishment in the same voracious ways that it exhibits when it draws its sustenance from the ground, spreading out its roots here and there, crowding out and killing its weaker neighbors and absorbing all the nutriment within its reach? The animal nature of this plant was cultivated by this lunatic sailor, and its natural nourishment was neglected until its rapid growth and the necessity of increasing

"The famous man-eating tree of Madagascar... which, you may be relieved to know, never really existed." Illustration from "Plants That Kill Animals and Devour Their Flesh" by Dr. Frank Thone. Published in the July 16, 1933 Evansville [Indiana] Press. Included here on a Fair Use, educational basis. Image partially restored by author.

nourishment rendered it greedy and rapacious, just like the rank weed, which, if allowed to plant its roots in the garden, will kill off all vegetation around it to gain the sustenance necessary to its own phenomenal growth."

I confess my incompetency to pass upon the gentleman's reasons for believing the girl's strange story, but the interest he has excited within me concerning these singular specimens of vegetation has been strong enough to attract me to the public library several times lately, and, strangely enough, I have run against several other gentlemen up there, whose faces are somehow associated, in my mind, with that gossiping afternoon at the Ryan.

C. M. O.

***

For such a salacious murder, the saga of Richard and Josephine Bowse does not appear to have been reported in contemporary Chicago newspapers. However, the Chicago businessman's story bears resemblance to a similar tale that was printed in the pages of the London Spectator on Oct. 24, 1891. Although published six years after C M. O.'s story, the article recalls (to the best of the author's ability) an earlier account brought to mind after reading the widely reported tale of the "Devil's Snare" plant in Nicaragua.

"Some years ago," wrote the Spectator, "a striking story was published in France describing a wonderful man-eating plant discovered by a great botanist. If we remember rightly, the story recounted how a certain collector discovered a plant of the fly-trap species of so gigantic a size that could consume huge masses of raw meat. Just as the fly-catching plant snaps up a fly, and draws nutriment from the fly's dead body, so this one fed itself on the legs of mutton and sirloins of beef which were thrown into its ravening maw. The botanist in the story, for some reason, possibly fear of having his plant destroyed as dangerous to public safety, keeps the existence of the plant a secret, and preserves it in a locked-up conservatory. His wife, however, who is made miserable by his absorption of mind—he thinks of nothing but how to feed and improve his wonderful and fascinating plant—determines to follow him. This she does, accompanied by an old school-friend of the husband. When the pair reach the inner conservatory, they see, to their horror, the infatuated botanist tossing bleeding joints of raw meat into the huge jaws of a giant fly-trap. They are at first petrified with horror. At last, however, the wife throws herself into the arms of her husband, and implores him to give up dwelling upon the horrible carnivorous monstrosity which he has discovered and reared. Unfortunately, however, the wife in appealing to her husband goes too close to the plant. Its huge tentacles surround her and then proceed to drag her in, and the two stupefied men see the plant begin to devour its victim. Fortunately, however, the friend catches sight of an axe lying near, and seizing this he strikes at the roots of the plant. A few frenzied blows do the necessary work, and the flesh-eating plant tumbles to the ground and releases from its clutches the terrified woman. The botanist, however, cannot survive his most cherished discovery, and with the exclamation, 'You have killed my plant!' he falls back dead."

Due to the obliqueness of the Spectator's reference to the French article, it was hard to know if that story influenced the Chicago-based account, vice versa, or if their similarities were coincidental. But this clue helped me solve the puzzle.

Searching historic French newspapers, I realized that the Spectator must have been referring to "Titane," a short story by French novelist and journalist Jules Lermina that was published in the literary supplement of the Le Figaro newspaper on April 25, 1885. The story was then translated into English as "The Titaness" and published in American newspapers throughout the spring and summer of 1885, such as a May 30 appearance in the St. Louis Post-Dispatch.

"Titane" or "The Titaness" tells the story of a woman named Paula who summons the narrator, her childhood friend, when she becomes afraid of Frederic, her scientist husband. Frederic had become withdrawn, obsessive and possibly insane over a secret project he kept locked in an enormous conservatory on his property. He carried several pounds of fresh meat into the large greenhouse nightly and would spend most of his time within. The narrator, a physician who had attended school with Frederic, attempted to appeal to his old friend and found him manic.

The Unnatural History of Man-Eating Plants

Nevertheless, Frederic didn't stop his old classmate when he insisted on accompanying him into the hothouse, but warned him of the danger. The narrator became unnerved when Frederic opened the door and a creeping, rustling sound resounded from within. Then he saw it:

In the centre of the hall, all tapestried with fantastic plants, towered a creature, a nightmare, a hideous thing....hydra, polyp, octopus....no man could have given it a name. It squatted there, enormous and horrible, upon the soil, in a sort of immense basin filled with spongy mosses and viscous growths. It had the form of a colossal wine-skin; and from the edges of it protruded huge and innumerable arms,—at the end of each of which was a ball, a rotundity, green like a monster-eye. The body was green; the arms had a purplish tint, but as they became thinner to end in those atrocious green eyes, a sanguinolent red mingled with the green,—a ghastly green as of corpses in putrefaction.

The strange noise the narrator had heard was the plant extending and contracting its tentacles. He realized it was a gigantic Drosera, the carnivorous sundew plant. Frederic began tossing raw meat to the grasping plant, yelling, "She eats! She eats! The Titaness gorges herself!" Frederic admitted his fear that the enormous, ravenous plant he had grown would, if unsated, burst free from the conservatory and "traverse the world like a monstrous octopus—devouring, destroying—threatening my wife, my child!" (Ever see the deleted ending of the 1986 "Little Shop of Horrors"?)

Just then, Paula stepped into the hothouse, having overcome her fear to see at last what force had so dominated her husband. Surprised, Frederic inadvertently placed a hand upon the tentacles of the Titaness—which promptly seized his wrist and sucked in his forearm. The narrator struggled fruitlessly to pull his friend free. Paula grabbed an axe from the ground and struck hard at the plant, severing it at the roots. As the plant collapsed, the narrator pulled Frederick free, only to see a bloody pulp where the man's hand and wrist used to be. The scientist fell into his wife's arms, only to utter, "Assassin—you have murdered the

Titaness!" And he fell back—dead. The narrator ended up caring for Paula like a brother and adopting her child. (See the short story section at the end of this book for the full version of "The Titaness.")

So, "The Titaness" appeared in print mere weeks, perhaps even days depending on the newspaper, before the St. Paul Daily Globe published its account of the Bowse family tragedy. It seems quite likely that Lermina's story inspired either the unnamed storyteller in the latter tale, or perhaps even the St. Paul journalist who penned "New Food for Plants."

[NOTE: While "*broop* of chickens" is likely a typo, it was too cute to fix.]

DEMON TREE OF HAWAII

E. Ellsworth Carey, whose interesting résumé we will explore shortly, wrote this titillating first-hand account for Honolulu's Daily Pacific Commercial Advertiser on March 10, 1892:

THE DEMON TREE

OF HAWAII.

A Strange Story of a Man-Eating Vegetable Told by an Eye Witness.

BY E. ELLSWORTH CAREY.

[Written for the P. C. ADVERTISER.]

In the latter part of the year 1867, I was commissioned by the Belgian government to find a certain rare wandering plant that was believed to grow on the higher slopes of Mauna Kea, a large extinct volcano situated on the northern part of Hawaii. I had a station built on one of the wooded slopes of the mountain far away from any other habitation. My only companion was a native who had lived all his life on this part of the island. About twice a month he would visit the sea coast to obtain needful supplies for our camp. This native, who said that his ancestors were "big chiefs," whose bones lay secretly buried in caves on the mountain side, was very old, although he could climb canyons and scale lava cliffs with wonderful agility.

During one of my botanizing excursions I passed by the mouth of a narrow canyon or gorge, and I asked *Pili, the old native, if he had ever explored the same. Pili suddenly became interested in his pipe, and didn't know anything about the gulch and did not understand what I said. This was rather strange in Pili, for natives generally know every rock and tree in the section where they live, and I knew Pili was lying when he said he did not understand me.

So, naturally, I determined to examine into the mysterious ravine. Some time after this, I was walking with Pili down a gentle slope, when I saw a number of bones. Pili stopped. He walked back a few rods and sat down on a stump. Not a word would he say. I began examining the bones, and for two hours or more puzzled my brain over a problem as I had never done before. What I found was this: a circular area of about 100 yards in diameter thickly covered with the bleached remains of birds, animals and human beings. These ghastly relics were scattered among the shrubs and grass. The larger bones were near the center; in fact I found that the bones became gradually smaller as I approached the periphery of this circular bone yard. In the center of the circle was a well like opening in the ground, from which emanated a sickening odor. No vegetation grew within fifty feet of this cavity. How came this hole with its horrible stench? How came these bones here? How came they to be arranged about the central opening? These questions continually presented themselves, but they remained unanswerable. A deep mystery seemed to hang over the spot. It was growing dark. I heard Pili calling, and hurried to him. He pointed in terror to the center of the bone covered area. A shadow was thrown on the scene by a rising bank of clouds. But I declare that I saw rising from the pit a visible vapor, a column of visible fog or smoke or gas that was luminous. Spell bound, I gazed at the spectral column. Near the ground it had the appearance of a phosphorescent flame, and gradually became fainter as it ascended. Your imagination will have to picture the unearthly phenomenon. Pili pulled at my arm, and in silence we left the spot, and we did not loiter by the way side.

As I was looking for a simple plant, and not blood curdling manifestations, I was inclined to break camp and leave. But by morning my nerves were in better order, and I went back to the scene of the evening adventure. I could find no clue to the mystery, and the matter gradually went out of mind as I prosecuted my labors.

But I had occasion after a time to visit a spot near where I had seen the canyon about which Pili was so apparently ignorant. One evening I made known my intention to Pili to return to the place, and to explore the gorge.

"When?" said Pili.

"In the morning," I replied.

Without a word, the old native arose from his mat on the floor, and departed. He was gone all night. He returned by sunrise, bearing on his shoulders a bundle. When we reached the canyon, he stopped and unpacked his load. I saw a stone idol, curious in shape; he placed it on the ground, and then took a small pig from his bundle. Making a fire, he sprinkled something in the flames, muttered strange sounds and made symbols in the air with his fingers. The animal offering was placed before the idol. After he completed his strange rites, he said that I might never come back, but he had done what he could to preserve my life. He would wait until the going down of the sun, and then, if I did not come back, he would wail for me as did his fathers long, long ago when a son fell in battle. Then he sat down, covered up his head, and was silent.

All this made me feel uncomfortable. The natives of the Hawaiian Islands are supposed to be Christianized, but in time of danger or trouble many often turn to the discarded gods of their fathers. I knew Pili believed that great danger awaited anyone who ascended the ravine. But I went.

The Unnatural History of Man-Eating Plants

I had gone about a mile, when over the tops of tree ferns I saw a waving mass of sea green foliage undulating in the wind. The object looked like a huge bunch of thick leaved sea weed, and the peculiar motion of the same arrested my attention. I was over 300 feet away from the curious object, and hurried to obtain a closer view. A wall of fern-covered lava about ten feet high stopped my course. Climbing up so that I just could see over the edge, I saw an object such as the eyes of civilized man never before beheld. Imagine a bunch of sea weed about twelve feet high; the edge of each piece lined with fine streamers which radiated in all directions and trembled like wire spirals; the whole object moving like the fringes of a sea anemone.

I was wearing a heavy felt hat with a wide brim, and I pushed it back from my forehead to get a better view. As I moved my arm the strange object ceased quivering, and every vibrating antennal or streamer pointed directly at me. Just then my foot slipped from a jutting rock on which I was standing and I fell, but not before something cleaved the air with a horrible hissing noise and struck on my hat crown. I felt the force of a blow as I fell, and knew no more for a time. I regained consciousness after a short time, and lay in a partial stupor. The wall above me was stripped of its verdure, and I saw a long sinewy, snake-like object writhing, twisting and curling on the rocks. It had missed its prey, and a low angry hum filled the air.

The thing I saw from the rocks was the Demon Tree; it is fixed to the ground, but can instantly locate any living object within a radius of 50 or 60 yards. It has several lasso-like arms over 100 feet long; these arms are about two inches in diameter, strong as steel cables, yet pliable and sensitive as an elephant's trunk. When in repose, they are coiled out of sight in the foliage; but when a victim approaches within the deadly circle they fly forth with unerring aim and terrible force. The victim feels a shock, falls, and the terrible coil tightens around the body, and it is slowly dragged to the tree.

When the flesh has been absorbed, the bones are cast out and fall about the tree.

I escaped only by falling out of reach of the deadly grasp. Possibly my escape was also due in some measure to the thickness of my old felt hat. This turned the blow, and also prevented me from receiving the full effect of the stupefying force, which appeared to be similar to the power displayed by certain electrical animals. The crown was cut from my hat, and there is a bald streak about an inch wide across the side of my head, which will always remind me of my horrible experience in the lonely ravines.

When I returned to Pili, somewhat to my wonder he exhibited no signs of astonishment or surprise. He said nothing, but packed up his god in a matter-of-fact way. This action is characteristic of the old time Hawaiians. He knew all about the cannibal plant up the ravine, but superstition would not let him speak of it. He told me it was the "Demon tree," and that bye-and-bye it would be struck by lightning and destroyed. In olden times the demon trees lived without this fate awaiting them; but since the introduction of cattle, sheep, goats, dogs, etc., the trees had more victims, and it appears that the absorption of so much animal substance generates a phosphorescent vapor which, in time, attracts a bolt from the sky. The bone-covered area before described once contained a cannibal tree, that had been recently destroyed.

I returned to the vicinity of the Demon Tree, and watched it with a field-glass, and gathered some of the facts given above. But my nervous system had received such a shock that I could not prosecute my hunt for the rare plant, and I soon left the island.

* *Pe-Ly.*

The Demon Tree of Hawaii article caused quite a stir as it made the rounds through the press over the next year. In February 1893, The Honolulu Daily Bulletin, a competitor of the Advertiser, complained, "Several American papers copied the story, giving our local contemporary due credit. The treated it, however, not as of 'the highly imaginative order,' but as a statement of fact, and hence Hawaii has been libeled as the possessor of a tree more noxious than the Upas with even its fabled lethal properties added. There are people here who have a recollection of reading in a San Francisco paper a very similar story years ago, of a tree in Mexico or somewhere in that direction. When the truth as to where the plagiarism began is divulged by some San Francisco paper, as it probably will on the head of the Advertiser's blatant indictment of the Examiner, our neighbor may find that the boot is on the other leg."

"Mauna Kea's Man-Eating Tree." Illustration from the Sep. 14, 1952 Honolulu Advertiser. Included here on a Fair Use, educational basis.

The "blatant indictment" referred to above was the Advertiser's accusation that the San Francisco Examiner plagiarized Carey's article, some passages word for word. The Advertiser insisted that the Examiner "pirated the story, interwoven with a love story, which was probably also a plagiarism." While the Advertiser wrote that the Examiner's version was called "A Moment of Horror," I have thus far been unable to find it to see if there is any merit in this claim. The Advertiser demurred on offering any direct hint of the "strange, weird" tale's veracity, only stating, "The story was of the highly imaginative order of the Rider Haggard school, and caused considerable comment."

North America

Elmer Ellsworth Carey was somewhat of an expert on the Pacific during the turn of the 19th to 20th centuries. He was in the service of the Hawaiian government under the monarchy "and was living in Honolulu during the stirring scenes which were enacted at the inauguration of the Provisional Government." This followed the January 17, 1893 overthrow of Queen Lili'uokalani by a committee composed mostly of Americans and Hawaiian subjects of American descent. Carey worked as a school teacher in Ookala, Hawaii, the Philippines, and California. He was also a journalist contributing articles to the Pacific Commercial Advertiser in Honolulu; managed the influential daily paper Freedom in Manila; and was chosen as editor of the Pacific Exporter in San Francisco, leveraging his trade knowledge as commerce expanded across the Pacific Ocean. Carey was a proponent of vegetarianism (perhaps owing to his encounter with the Demon Tree?) and beat the record for vegetarian fasting in 1909, completing his 45-day diet on Valentine's Day. He claimed to have lost half a pound each day.

Another of Carey's pieces for the Advertiser, titled "An Episode of 1902," eerily and somewhat accurately predicted the future. Published in August 1891, Carey presented the article as a news dispatch from 11 years onward. Though he placed the events decades earlier, Carey foretold World War I as the "Inter-European War" of 1894-1896. This future was followed by a 1902 incident in which a fleet of "airships" sunk a U.S. Navy warship off the coast of Oahu, uncomfortably foreshadowing Pearl Harbor. However, the conflict in this story was a trade war between the United States and the Kingdom of Hawaii itself, and unveiled a new age of warfare dominated by air power (with Hawaii having the early advantage). This was written, of course, in the days shortly before the Kingdom of Hawaii fell to a coup, leading to its eventual U.S. statehood in 1959.

The Demon Tree of Hawaii wasn't forgotten. In 1952, a reader wrote a letter to the editor of the Advertiser, saying the story had enthralled her for years and she wanted to know if there was any truth to the account. The editor replied, "Imaginative writers long have produced works of fiction concerning man-eating trees, but no botanist ever has seen one."

The Unnatural History of Man-Eating Plants

ARBOR DIABOLI

Perhaps a cousin of the Demon Tree, the "Devil's Tree," Arbor Diaboli, was reported by the St. Louis Globe-Democrat and received national coverage in 1889. As featured in the May 2 Osage County Enterprise in Chamois, Missouri:

THE DEVIL'S TREE

Discovery of a Third Specimen of the Carnivorous Arbor Diaboli

Special Correspondence of the Globe-Democrat,

CHIHUAHUA, MEX., April 22.—I, Mr. John H. Betterman, American and whilom resident of this city, beg to communicate to the Globe Democrat a most singular discovery which I have recently made.

I have taken much interest in the study of botany during my sojourn in this country, the flora of which presents one of the richest fields for the scientist in the world and have wandered some distance from town on several occasions in my search for specimens. On one of these expeditions I noticed a dark object on one of the outlying spurs of the Sierra Madre Mountains, which object excited my curiosity so much that I examined it carefully through my field glass. This revealed that the object was a tree or shrub of such an unusual appearance that I resolved to visit the spot. I rode to the mountain, the sides of which sloped sufficiently for me to make my way on horseback to within a few rods of the summit. But here I was stopped by an abrupt rise so steep that I despaired of reaching it even on foot. I went around it several times seeking for some way to climb up but the jagged, beetling rocks afforded not the slightest foothold. On the top of this knob stands the tree I had seen. From the spot on which I now stood I could see that it somewhat resembled in form the weeping willow, but the long, drooping whip-like limbs were of a dark and apparently slimy appearance, and seemed possessed of a horrible life-like power of coiling and uncoiling. Occasionally the whole tree would seem a writhing squirming mass. My desire to investigate this strange vegetable product increased on each of the many expeditions I made to the spot, and at last I saw a sight one day which made me believe I had certainly discovered an unheard-of-thing. A bird which I had watched circling about for some time, finally settled on the top of the tree, when the branches began to awaken, as it were, and to curl upwards. They twined and twisted like snakes about the bird, which began to scream, and drew it down in their fearful embrace until I lost sight of it. Horror stricken, I seized the nearest rock in an attempt to climb the knob. I had so often tried in vain to do this that I was not surprised when I fell back, but the rock was loosened and fell also. It narrowly missed me, but I sprang up unhurt, and saw that the fallen rock had left a considerable cavity. I put my face to it and looked in. Something like a cavern, the floor of which had an upward tendency met my sight, and I felt a current of fresh air blowing on me, with a dry, earthy smell. Evidently there was another opening somewhere, undoubtedly at the summit. Using my trowel, which I always carried on my botanizing expeditions, I enlarged the hole, and then pushed my way up through the passage. When I had nearly reached the top I looked out cautiously to see if I should emerge within reach of that diabolical tree. But I found it nowhere near the aperture, so I sprang out. I was just in time to see the flattened carcass of the bird drop to the ground, which was covered with bones and feathers. I approached as closely as I dared and examined the tree. It was low in size, not more than 20 feet high, but covering a great area. Its trunk was of prodigious thickness, knotted and scaly. From the top of this trunk, a few feet from the ground, its slimy branches curved upward and downward, nearly touching the ground with their tapering tips. Its appearance was that of a gigantic tarantula awaiting its prey. On my venturing to lightly touch one of the limbs, it closed upon my hand with such force that when I tore it loose the skin came with it. I descended then, and closing the passage went home. I went back next day carrying half a dozen chickens with which to feed the tree. The moment I tossed in the fowls, a violent agitation shook its branches, which swayed to and fro with a sinuous, snaky motion. After devouring the fowls, these branches, fully gorged, drooped to their former position, and the tree, giving no sign of animation, I dared approach it and take the limbs in my hand. They were covered with suckers, resembling the tentacles of an octopus. The blood of the fowls had been absorbed by these suckers, leaving crimson stains on the dark surface.

There was no foliage, of course, of any kind. Without speaking of my discovery to any one about, I wrote an account of it to the world-famous botanist, Prof. Wordenhaupt, of the University of Heinelberg [Heidelberg? -Ed.]. His reply stated that my tree is the Arbor Diaboli, only two specimens of which have ever been known—one on the peak of the Himalayas and the other on this Island of Sumatra. Mine is the third. Prof. Wordenhaupt says that the Arbor Diaboli and the plant known as Venus fly-trap are the only known specimen, growing on the land, of those forms of life which partakes of the nature of both the animals and vegetables kingdoms, although there are instances too numerous to mention found of this class in the sea. The Portuguese man-of-war may be mentioned, however, as one, and the spung is the best known specimen of this class.

MAGNETIC CACTUS

The Florence, Arizona Tribune announced on Feb. 4, 1899 that, "Joe Mulhatton was in Florence this week from the Ripsey country, where he has recently discovered a magnetic cactus, which from his account, must be a wonderful species of vegetation. Its attractive powers are so great that it draws birds and animals to it and impales them on its thorny spikes. Mr. Mulhatton approached no nearer than 100 feet to the cactus, which is of the saguaro variety, yet at that distance it was all he could do to resist its influence to draw him to it. While in town he purchased a long rope, which he will tie around his body, and four of his friends will take hold of it and allow him to approach near enough to minutely examine the wonder without danger. Mr.

Mulhatton, who is one of our most truthful citizens, promises an accurate description of his recent find for publication in the TRIBUNE."

The paper added, "Nobody supposes Joe Mulhatton would lie about a little thing like a cactus."

This news surely intrigued the readership of the Tribune, who received a follow-up in the Feb. 11 edition of the newspaper when Mulhatton was again in town from his mines:

The Magnetic Cactus.

The TRIBUNE is in receipt of additional particulars in regard to the wonderful Magnetic Cactus recently discovered in the Ripsey country. The following letter will fully explain itself:

DAGGER WELL,

Near Ripsey Mine,

Feb. 9th, 1899.

Editor FLORENCE TRIBUNE:

The magnetic cactus you wrote about in last week's TRIBUNE is a species of the Giant Sahuara [presumably Saguaro-Ed.]. It is found in many places between Casa Grande and Florence, between Florence and Mesa and between Florence and Riverside.

There is a belt of the earth within a radius of fifty miles of Florence that is very magnetic, no doubt caused by vast beds of copper or some other magnetic mineral that underlies it all, and this species of Cactus from its fibrous nature acts like a telegraph instrument to receive and discharge the earth's vast surplus of magnetism, not required by the moon's and sun's magnetic attraction.

All the Magnetic Cactii in this neighborhood are either positive or negative. One attracts; the other repels.

Two tramps passing along the road just above Donnelly's a few nights ago took refuge under a bunch of this cactus.

The Unnatural History of Man-Eating Plants

One of the men was at once drawn up to and impaled on the sharp blades of the cactus, while its octopus-like arms folded around him crushing him through and into the cactus, where his blood, flesh and bones turned into a pulp very much like ordinary mucilage, which trickled out slowly from the aperture made by the passing in of the man's body.

The cactus loses its magnetic power while it is digesting its victim. So we were enable to look at this wonderful yet gruesome sight and report these particulars.

Our party consisted of some of the best known and most responsible citizens of Pinal county—James Elder, a well-known mining man of Riverside, and Clay Hockett, now of Florence; A. F. Barker, W. Y. Price, ex-District Attorney Sniffen, Wm. Truman, John Keating, Geo. Truman, Tom Peyton, Pete Brady and Lem Drais.

The body of the other tramp was repelled by the negative cactus and thrown about one hundred feet distant against a positive magnetic cactus where it underwent a similar process to the one just described.

We left the sickening scene with sad hearts and with nothing to identify the victims. After and just before a great storm the attractive or repellant power of the cactus is indescribable. Calves, birds and young colts are attracted, impaled, drawn in and quickly converted by the digestive juices of the cactus into the thick mucilagenous substance just described.

There is very little travel through this wild section of Arizona, or this species of cactii would have been written about sooner.

Yours truly,

JOE MULHATTON.

***

Joseph Mulhatton, once dubbed "The Prince of Liars," was well-known and cherished in his day as a prolific purveyor of

American tall tales; so much so that he was profiled alongside names such as Mark Twain, Oscar Wilde, Thomas Edison, U.S. President Grover Cleveland and actress Sarah Bernhardt in the 1888 book "Prominent Men and Women of the Day." Mulhatton (sometimes spelled "Mulhattan") traveled widely throughout the southern and southwestern United States in his job as a hardware salesman. The aforementioned book described Mulhatton as "a remarkably bright and clever business man, [who] is genial and tender-hearted, sunny of disposition, truthful, excepting in joke, and a practical philanthropist."

Magnetic Cactus illustration, published in the Apr. 8, 1956 Arizona Republic Magazine. Included here on a Fair Use, education basis.

The Unnatural History of Man-Eating Plants

However, Mulhatton possessed a "harmless weakness" that grew out of the monotony of his work. He let his imagination run wild in penning clever and impossible yarns that he managed to place in newspapers throughout the country. These reports were often printed far and wide and sometimes without attribution or a tacit admission that they were fabrications.

As recalled in 1920 by the Arizona Republican, "Every reporter in the United States 25 years ago has heard of Joe Mulhatton. To most of them he was a myth, an unincarnated newspaper liar, the most famous in the United States. Telegraph and mail stores from all parts of the United States were received at the larger newspaper offices detailing the most incredible happenings. They were such vast products of the human imagination that they were readily printed. But Joe Mulhatton was a creature of flesh and blood. He was a hardware drummer of Louisville, Ky. The concoction of these marvelous tales was a sideline."

Mulhatton claimed he never made any money from his articles and wanted none. He was simply happy to entertain the public, recalled the writer of the Republican article, who personally knew Mulhatton.

Hoaxes from this "American Munchausen" that captured the public imagination included the 1878 discovery of "Grand Crystal Cave" in Glasgow, Kentucky, revealing approximately 40 miles of wide tunnels, three navigable underground rivers, and a room containing several Egyptian-style mummies in stone coffins; a giant meteorite that crashed onto a ranch in Fort Worth, Texas in 1883, and stood steaming 100 feet embedded in the earth and 70 feet towering above the surface (This news resulted in a team of scientists from Harvard going out to investigate!); and an 1888 report on California's Mono Lake, which contained the world's greatest deposit of natural hair dye, bestowing swimmers with blonde and eventually red hair the longer they bathed in its waters. Many of Mulhatton's hoaxes were admitted by him or connected to him by reporters in later years.

According to the Washington Post, expeditions costing hundreds of thousands of dollars set out (fruitlessly) to find the Arbor Diaboli, and then the story was traced back to Mulhatton. Much like how he fooled Harvard into investigating the giant meteorite that struck Forth Worth, Mulhatton suckered in eager botanists hoping to catalogue the Devil Tree. But the Prince of Liars must not have had his fill of Man-Eating Plants, for he followed up Arbor Diaboli with the Magnetic Cactus.

JOE MULHATTAN.

Joe Mulhatton's portrait from "Prominent Men and Women of the Day," 1888.

The New York Times wrote in 1891, "Joe Mulhattan is known in every city in the United States and has probably caused more trouble in newspaper offices than any other man in the country. His wild stories, written in the most plausible style, have more than once caused the special correspondents of the progressive journals of the United States to hurry from coast to coast to investigate some wonderful occurrence which only existed in the imagination of the great liar."

CHLOROFORM TREE

Once you know about Mulhatton and his prolific "journalism" career, it is hard not to suspect his hand in any strange story that appeared in newspapers at the turn of the 19th-20th centuries. However, I have yet to find any connection between Mulhatton and this article, which was published in the June 19, 1903 edition of the Daily Times-Index in San Bernardino, California:

PROSPECTORS' STRANGE FIND

Deadly Tree in the San Jacinto Mountains Whose Blossoms Exhale Chloroform

LOS ANGELES, June 18.—Two Mendocino County prospectors, John C. Hewett and Clarence N. Hotailing, were in the city this morning en route to their homes from a prospecting tour in the southern part of the state. While prospecting in a spur of the San Jacinto mountains, down near the Mexican line, they made a very remarkable discovery.

Their discovery is a new species of plant or tree, a branch of which, with its leaves and blossoms, they have with them. It was found in a little canyon which they visited in search of water.

The leaves of the tree resemble in size and shape those of a fig tree, but they are of a vivid purple color, and the under side of the leaf is thickly covered with stiff hairs, which stand out from the leaf fully half an inch. These hairs are thornlike and easily penetrate the flesh. One of the men who was pricked by the spines suffered great pain, and his flesh was much swollen, indicating that the plant is poisonous. The twigs and branches are mottled brown, and are covered with small scales, which give the branches a snaky appearance. The trees, of which they saw half a dozen specimens, attain a height of nearly 30 feet and a diameter of a foot or more.

The blossoms are as peculiar as are the branches and leaves. They are of a rusty red color and are about two inches in diameter. In shape they are a very good representation of the tarantula. There is a huge hairy bulb resembling in shape the abdomen of the poison spider, and there are several chives or stamens corresponding to the legs of that insect.

The most peculiar feature of the plant, however, remains to be told. Whenever one approaches the plant, or when the wind agitates the branches of the tree, the flowers give off an abundance of perfume, heavy, sickening and deadly. This perfume had the characteristic of chloroform, and a few inhalations of the odor produces unconsciousness. One of the men who made the discovery was rendered insensible upon approaching the tree for the purpose of examining it.

The plant has been shown to a number of persons well versed in plant lore, but no one has been able to classify it. As it seems to have no botanical name, it will probably be called by one of two names suggested by its characteristics. One name proposed is "the tarantula plant," the other is "the chloroform tree."

***

The strange and dangerous tree described in this story does not appear to match any known species. The Ficus Moreton Bay fig (*Ficus macrophylla*), a leafy evergreen banyan tree native to the subtropical rainforests of eastern Australia, was introduced throughout Southern California in the 1870s, thriving in the region's semiarid climate. California's Moreton Bay figs quickly grew to mammoth proportions, with branches that spread over 100 feet and shot down aerial roots that hardened into distinctive buttresses. While these trees were still fairly new and alien to the California landscape in 1903, they do not possess the strange attributes of the tree given in the prospectors' tale.

However, *Antiaris toxicaria*, the tree whose toxic sap led to exaggerated legends of the poison gas-emitting Upas Tree of Java, *is* a member of the fig family. (See the Asia chapter.) Perhaps an Upas Tree or relative made it to American shores...

BLACK VAULT TREES

W. H. Johnson of Worcester, Massachusetts was "an all-around man in gardening" who judged Worcester Horticultural Society exhibitions for five years, worked at the old Cook greenhouse on Lowden and Woodland streets in the city's south end, and was employed at the Charles D. Thayer florist shop on Ripley Street in February 1905 when interviewed by a reporter from the Worcester Telegram. "Since a boy of 10 years, he has been interested in plants and trees, and understands everything about them. He is considered an expert on horticulture," the reporter wrote.

"The United States government has some strange trees, and there are some remarkable specimens to be seen in the agricultural department," Johnson revealed. "The United States government sends agents into all parts of the world, and now varieties of plants and seeds are constantly coming in, as a result. The list of wonders is already large, but it increases every year, and the government spares neither money nor care in its search for useful and beautiful curiosities."

"There is the ancient dye plant used by Cleopatra, [the] beautiful lace tree of Jamaica," Johnson began his list of botanical marvels collected by the United States government, "and the cannibal tree that swallows a man in its horrible embrace. There is also another tree that will kill a man if he sleeps beneath it."

Wait, what? Johnson's testimony is enough to spark a brand-new conspiracy theory about a secret Black Ops arboretum on the grounds of Area 51, harboring a secret collection of man-killing vegetation. (It wouldn't be dissimilar to assertions that the Smithsonian collected and destroyed numerous bones of giants discovered on American soil during the late 1800s to maintain the historical order!)

"We also have three of the most dangerous and wonderful plants in the world among the many beneficent specimens," claimed

Johnson. "The first is called the cannibal tree, from Australia; the grapple plant, of South Africa; and the vegetable python of New Zealand.

"The cannibal tree grows in the shape of a huge pineapple, to a height of perhaps 11 feet. It has a series of broad, board-like leaves, growing in a fringe at the apex, something like a Central American agave. These leaves, from 10 to 12 feet long in the smaller ones, from 13 to 20 in the larger ones, hang down to the ground, and are easily strong enough to bear the weight of a man who weighs 150 pounds.

"In ancient time the tree was worshipped by the savages, under the name of devil tree, a part of the ceremony being the sacrifice of one of their number to its ready embrace. The victim was driven up the tree to the apex, and the instant he touches the pistils of the monstrous plant, the leaves would fly together like a trap, crushing the life out of the intruder.

"In that embrace it held its prey until every particle of life was extinct, and still later, until the flesh disappeared from the bones.

"The grapple plant grows in South Africa. It is a prostrate herb, with purple flowers, something like the English fox-glove. Its fruit has formidable hooks, which cling to any passing object, and thus moves from place to place. Sir John Lubbock says it has been known to clutch and strangle all kinds of animals.

"The vegetable python is another horror of nature. It is known to the botanist as the clusia, or fig, and is a strangler of trees. The seeds of the plant are held in a sweet pulp, enticing to the birds, who feed upon them, and thus convey them from tree to tree. Here germination begins, and it sucks its very life from the limbs of other plants.

"The leafy stem slowly rises upward, while the roots drop down until they reach the ground, and there take a fresh start and make new plants. The stems that go upward and outward wind themselves all over the side branches, which in their turn, twist and curl, until the poor tree, which first gave them a mere foothold is strangled to death.

The Unnatural History of Man-Eating Plants

"It withers and drops its leaves, soon decays, and is lost to sight beneath the green foliage of the vegetable python. It is a strange tragedy in the natural world."

***

It is unclear where Johnson obtained his clandestine knowledge of U.S. government operations, other than being a florist in the know. What is clear is that Johnson, or the reporter from the Telegram, cited the contents of an earlier, widely-published article almost word-for-word in describing the Australian Cannibal Tree and the fearsome-sounding, if not truly man-eating, South African Grapple Plant and New Zealand Vegetable Python.

Herb Roth illustration from "Fresh Tidings of Madagascar's Weird 'Man-Eating Tree,'" Springfield [Ohio] Daily News, Aug. 17, 1924.

North America

First appearing in the Feb. 28, 1897 Los Angeles Herald, "Three Interesting Plants" by John A. Morris recited details from earlier news accounts of the Australia Man-Eating Tree, which in turn were poached from stories of the Madagascar Man-Eating Tree. (See the Australia and Africa chapters for further details.)

The Grapple Plant, attributed to British scientist Sir John Lubbock, was described in the Los Angeles Herald article at greater length. Morris even recounted a tale in which the Grapple Plant took down a lion who was in the middle of hunting an antelope:

But along the plain came slowly rolling, propelled by the refreshing breezes, some purplish-colored flowers. Now they rounded themselves into balls, sometimes traveling faster, sometimes slower, sometimes stopping altogether, according to the varying strength of the breeze; and thus these treacherous, formidable-looking little hooks swept on until at last one lazily rolled under the hindquarters of the lion as he lay occupied with his victim. Unrolling itself the hooks slowly got hold of his tawny quarters, but the lion fed on unheeding. But as he sat still occupied with his supper the hooks began to creep and curl most cruelly into the flesh of the tawny beast until with a savage snarl he started and began to investigate. But investigation proved useless, and all his efforts to get rid of the annoyance by brushing it with his paw were also unavailing.

The hooks gradually tightening their hold were now giving the beast considerable pain, until maddened by desperation and agony, he seized the fruit in his mouth and tried to loose it from its lodging place. But the fruit remained firm. The lion now maddened beyond all self-control tore away with all his strength until the fruit gave way into the lion's mouth, winding its sharp prongs into the tongue, roof and throat of the poor distracted brute. Then began one of those tragedies of nature which are every day being acted in some way, shape or form—tragedies agonizing, awesome and horrible—a tragedy ending in the terrible death agony of the lion. Growling, moaning, rolling on the ground, standing up, rolling again, running round and round, standing still, lifting his head high in the air, then burying it in the sands, till becoming exhausted the convulsions and twitchings become less and less violent and finally ceased; and as the African moon reflected forth its light from a clear sky perfect stillness reigned over that habitation of strength and endurance. Luna and the stars shone down in splendor upon the mangled antelope, the choked lion and the buried seed.

The seed of this parable (as it were) about the harshness of nature can be found in Lubbock's article, "On Fruits and Seeds," in the July 1881 installment of Popular Science Monthly, as well as in his 1888 book, "Flowers, Fruits and Leaves." In discussing the role that animals play in the dispersal of seeds, Lubbock described the hooked fruit of *Harpagophytum procumbens*, which today is commonly known as Devil's Claw.

"Harpagophytum is a South African genus," wrote Lubbock. "The fruits are most formidable, and are said sometimes even to kill lions. They roll about over the dry plains, and, if they attach themselves to the skin, the wretched animal tries to tear them out, and sometimes getting them into his mouth perishes miserably."

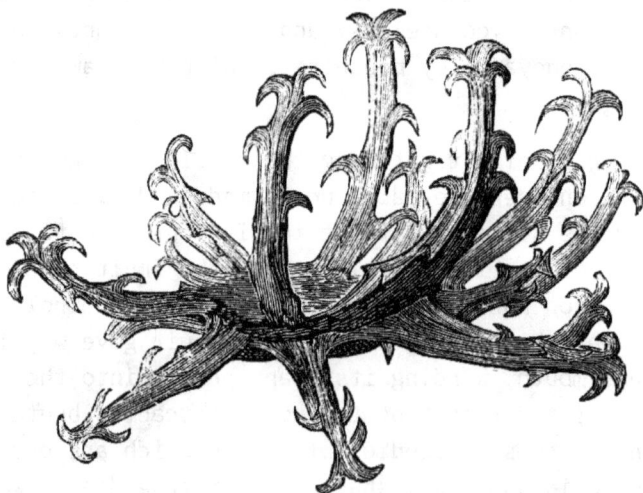

Harpagophytum procumbens (Devil's Claw), from Sir John Lubbock's "On Fruits and Seeds," Popular Science Monthly, 1881.

NEW ORLEANS PLANTIMAL

Man-Eating Plant stories most often depict horrors in faraway lands. That appears to be the case for this fantastic article about a "missing link" between the animal and vegetable kingdoms, titled "Horror in a Swamp." Although it took place in New Orleans, the news appears to have originated in the United Kingdom, running exclusively in British and Australian newspapers. As published in the Feb. 6, 1924 Daily Record and Mail in Glasgow, Scotland:

HORROR IN A SWAMP.

BOTANISTS' FIGHT FOR LIFE.

IN PLANT'S GRIP.

New Orleans, Tuesday.

A horrible, flesh-eating "plant-animal," rooted in the earth like a plant, but with the skin, muscles, and bony skeleton of an animal, is said to have been discovered in the depths of a great swamp 40 miles from New Orleans, by Joseph Villareux and George Gastron, two botanists, who were lost for over a week in the heart of the swamp.

The plant is said to be carnivorous and to devour small animals. The botanists believe, says a correspondent, that the plant is a "missing link" between the plant and animal kingdoms, since it possesses many of the characteristics of both.

They further say that every stem of this strange plant is built round a bone running through the centre.

Instead of vegetable structure the plant is formed of flesh like that of an animal. A wrinkled skin forms the outer surface of the plant's structure.

CRY FOR HELP.

The mysterious plant grew near the edge of the water on a small island, and resembled a palm tree to some extent, although its general colour was grey. Fragrant yellow flowers growing near the foot of the tree attracted Villareux, who attempted to pick them.

As he stooped he was suddenly seized by several of the large fronds of the freak plant and slowly drawn towards the main stem.

Calling loudly for help, Villareux at the same time seized the fronds that held him, but to his horror found that they were huge muscles like those of a giant.

When Gastron ran to the assistance of his companion, he, too, was seized by the creepers, and made prisoner, and it was not until the two men had used their sharp camp axes to cut through the "bone and sinew" that they were able to free themselves.

Their task occupied them a couple of hours, because, as they cut off some of the creepers, others seized them.

SNAKE-LIKE CREEPERS.

Several small animals, such as squirrels and rabbits, were caught by the plant during the time the men were held captive, and the sight of the snake-like, skin-covered creepers darting out to catch the terrified creatures was like a terrible nightmare.

When the small animals were captured the life was squeezed out of them, and they were lifted by the fronds to a big opening towards the top of the main stem which serves as the stomach of the plant.

The other man said that as the axe fell the plant writhed in apparent agony, and red sap, resembling blood, oozed from the wounds.

VAMPIRE PLANT

In "Mexico and The Poison Trail," Part III of his 1935 book, "In Quest of Lost Worlds," explorer Count Byron De Prorok recounted his 1932 visit to Mexico amidst political turmoil involving the Catholic Church, and his journey deep into the jungle to meet the isolated Lacandon people. Early on in the adventure, as the team cut through walls of vegetation with machetes in the humid heat, De Prorok encountered a fearsome (and puzzling) plant. He wrote:

Every now and then, the great bellow of Von Schmelling would shout a warning. "Achtung! Achtung!" or "Poison! Poison!" and we were taught to pass with hands raised high above our heads, so as not to touch the plants on either side. The poison trail had begun. Nor were the poisonous plants all we had to fear. We seemed at times to be fighting our way through a concentrated attack of every kind of thorn, which simply ripped our clothes. Every bush seemed armed with lances, daggers, fishhooks, bayonets, hayforks, and harpoons. The jungle fought our passage at every step.

Suddenly, Domingo came to a halt and called us over. Schmelling, too, thought it would be interesting. I had my first glimpse of the vampire plant which, two or three days earlier, had trapped a bright little bird on its treacherous leaf, and now was in the process of taking its meal.

De Prorok retold his Mexican adventure, in more lurid detail, across two parts in the July and August 1934 issues of Wide World: The Magazine for Men. This can be seen in his telling of the Vampire Vine incident, contained in the first part of "Midst Pygmies and Pyramids," in the July issue:

Suddenly I saw Domingo, the leader of the guides, standing before an enormous plant and making gestures for me to go to him. I wondered what could be the matter.

I soon saw; the plant had just captured a bird! The poor creature had alighted on one of the leaves, which had promptly closed, its thorns penetrating the body of the little victim, which endeavoured vainly to escape, screaming meanwhile in agony and terror.

"*Plante vampire!*" explained Domingo, a cruel smile spreading over his face.

Involuntarily I shuddered; the forest was casting its evil spell upon me. I thought of the venomous snakes we had already seen—horrible creatures the colour of dead tree-branches, hanging down from the boughs so that they resembled *lianas,* or else hiding in the herbage and the deep covering of dried leaves which lay everywhere over the soil.

Count Byron Khun De Prorok

Count Byron De Prorok had the credentials of an archaeologist. He was educated at the University of Geneva, spoke several languages, worked on excavations at Carthage from 1920 to 1925, and held the prestigious Norton Lectureship at the Archaeological Institute of America from 1922-1923.

"But instead of a distinguished career," wrote Mark Rose of Archaeology magazine, "he undertook a series of expeditions of dubious scientific value, pursuing ancient legends like so many wil-'o-the-wisps and becoming more and more a showman."

De Prorok (whose real name was Francis Victor Kuhn) allegedly held a dubious claim to a title, and was ultimately discredited as a tomb robber who was convinced that the Lost City of Atlantis was buried beneath the Sahara Desert, according to research by Michael Tarabulski.

Rose pointed out the archaeological nightmare that occurred when the floor of an Egyptian tomb De Prorok was investigating collapsed beneath his feet. Falling stones shattered beautifully painted sarcophagi in the catacomb below, and the count crashed straight though a wooden mummy case. Suffering a head injury and desperate to escape, De Prorok began stacking up the ancient coffins to climb out, each one collapsing as he clambered atop it. He passed out and was eventually rescued by his colleagues. It's like a destructive scene straight out of "Raiders of the Lost Ark."

De Prorok was a pioneer in capturing motion pictures of his explorations beginning in 1920 (including aerial photography to locate submerged ruins), but sadly those films appear to have been lost. In his day, though, De Prorok was an engaging lecturer who wowed audiences with his adventurous tales and films.

In the 2003 edition of De Prorok's "In Quest of Lost Worlds," Tarabulski noted, "Reader beware. Byron de Prorok was writing adventure stories, not ethnography." Tarabulski suggested that De Prorok had difficulties controlling his imagination when writing down his adventures. For example, De Prorok accurately described smaller details from his interactions with the Lacandon Maya during his 1932 expedition in Mexico, but didn't speak their language and mischaracterized much about them to the point of insult. He also amped up the adventure, in one case describing ancient ruins where only natural formations stood.

Anthropologist Jon McGee added that while De Prorok presented Jacques Soustelle, the respected ethnographer who worked for years among the Lacandon, in a comic tone, Soustelle in turn "wrote voluminously and in great detail on the Lacandon, but mentions nothing of de Prorok and doesn't tell lurid stories of poisonous plants, Lacandon booby traps set on trails, ambushes and the like."

ARIZONA FLY-CATCHER

A widely published newspaper feature called "And Some People Believe Them!" by Ronald L. Ives appeared in January 1938, recounting several American-born tall tales. One was the sad tale of Rot-Gut Pete, who disappeared one gloomy night while walking home, "three sheets in the wind and with no pilot," after celebrating at the Last Chance Saloon in Salome, Arizona.

After Pete failed to appear at his regular haunts for a few days, a search party tracked him into the desert. There, they found a pile of Pete's belongings—a watch, 42 boot nails, 11 buttons, a six-gun (identified by the number of notches), a belt buckle and two silver dollars—at the base of a large Fly-Catcher Plant.

The search party surmised that a drunken Pete had leaned against the plant in the darkness, and its hungry trap had closed upon him. Later, once the plant was gorged, it had opened up and dropped all the metallic debris from Pete's person to the ground.

Ives wrote that, "Guides in the wilder parts of the country still collect and tell wild tales of wilderness and mountain country to the 'dudes,' 'pale-faces,' and 'flatlanders' who each year leave their inhibitions and intellects in the city and spend two weeks collecting sunburn, poison ivy and mountain sickness."

Ives was a highly educated expert in many fields, holding bachelor's and master's degrees in geology and geomorphology, and master's and doctoral degrees in geography. He also held top secret clearance in the U.S. Army and specialized in electronics, working for a number of federal government contractors, including Cornell Aeronautical Laboratory.

But Ives' true passion was his lifelong, rugged explorations of the Pinacate Peaks in Mexico, a volcanic region along the Old Yuma Trail, and the surrounding desert borderlands of Arizona. "He traveled its ground, met its people, studied its riddles, and logged its answers," wrote biographer Bill Broyles. "He extolled the region's mysteries and vistas; he sketched its face and then probed its character."

Ives published more than 600 articles of a technical nature, a quarter of them pertaining to this region, as well as 230 popular articles. His variety of work focused on topics such as electronics; hiking; geological, meteorological, and historical research in arid lands; Spanish exploration in northern Mexico, Baja California, and Arizona; and American folklore. Ives wrote "You Don't Have to Believe It" (one of its slightly alternate titles) for Science Service, which sold the article to the Newspaper Enterprise Association for wide syndication in illustrated newspaper magazines. It is probable that Ives picked up the story of the giant Flycatcher Plant of Arizona and the other tall tales presented in his article from locals he met during his many travels.

Strange "unnatural history" tales of animals you never saw --and are not likely to see

"Pete leaned against one of the giant flycatcher plants, and the ferocious desert species closed on him." The tale of Rot-Gut Pete depicted in Ronald L. Ives' "And Some People Believe Them!" in the Jan. 16, 1938 Arizona Republic. Included here on a Fair Use, education basis.

However, the origin of the Rot-Gut Pete story might stem from an unexpected source—Sir Arthur Conan Doyle, the creator of Sherlock Holmes. Doyle published a short story called "The American's Tale" in the London Society magazine in 1880, and it appeared the following year in American newspapers. He then republished the story as "An Arizona Tragedy" in 1892, and it was again syndicated in American papers, that year and in 1893.

Doyle's short story takes place in Simpson's bar in Arizona, where a rowdy gunslinger named "Alabama" Joe Hawkins drunkenly picks a fight with a quiet British patron named Tom Scott. The normally reserved Brit startles Hawkins by quickly getting the drop on him by pulling out a Derringer. After a tense moment, Scott laughs and says he wouldn't shoot a half-drunk man, humiliating the cowboy. Silently fuming, Hawkins leaves the bar and decides to wait in ambush for Scott on his path home, hiding in a gloomy marsh called Flytrap Gulch.

As Doyle describes it (via the narrator, an American named Jefferson Adams who is telling the tale to his English pals in a "semi-literary society" smoking room), the gulch is home to the Arizona variety of Venus Flytraps, which stand as tall as trees and possess traps eight to 10 feet long, resembling "a brace of boats with a hinge between 'em and thorns at the bottom." The thorns were a foot long or more and looked like teeth.

When Hawkins fails to show in town the next morning and Scott appears unmolested, the gunslinger's friends assume the worst. They grab Scott and angrily drag him to Flytrap Gulch, where they intend to hang him from one of the giant plants. Arriving at the gulch, the lynch mob encounters an angry group of Scott's British friends. But before a violent melee can begin, the men discover a horrifying sight.

"One of the great leaves of the fly-trap, that had been shut and touching the ground as it lay, was slowly rolling back upon its hinges. There, laying like an oyster in its shell, was Alabama Joe in the hollow of the leaf. The great thorns had been slowly driven through his heart as it shut upon him. We could see as he'd tried to cut his way out, for there was a slit in the thick fleshly leaf, an' his bowie was in his hand, but it had smothered him first. He'd lain down on it likely to keep the damp off while he were awaitin' for Scott, and it had closed on him as you've seen your little hot-house ones do on a fly; and there he were as we found him, torn and mashed, and crushed into pulp by the great jagged teeth of the man-eatin' plant."

(The full version of Doyle's story is included in the short fiction section of this book.)

UNCLE HEBER'S FLYTRAP

The New Deal-era Writers' Program of the Work Projects Administration published a collection of North Carolina folklore in 1943, titled "Bundle of Troubles and Other Tarheel Tales." As stated in the book, "On Tidewater and swamp, back in remote mountain coves, even in urban and industrial centers, the telling of tales has never died out in North Carolina. Stories of witches, ghosts, and queer characters, tall tales, and hunting and fishing yarns are still told around the lingering country store, within the railed bar between court sessions, before family firesides, and around hunters' campfires. Old tales are passed along and new ones concocted."

"To collect and preserve some of these tales, workers of the North Carolina Writers' Project visited storytellers in their communities and recorded the tales. More than two hundred were collected and written down. The stories came from farmers, elderly porch-whittlers, housewives, [African-American] men and women, merchants, and many others. The tellers had one thing in common—they were not 'literary,'" the book explained.

Since the Venus Flytrap counts North Carolina among its small natural habitat, it should be of little surprise that local folklore developed around the carnivorous plant. "Uncle Heber's Flytrap" was told to James S. Beaman by William Wilson, a drawbridge tender in the Brice's Creek section of Craven County. "This tall tale is based upon the fertile land, the Venus's-flytrap, and a lazy character," explained the Writers' Program.

Here is the full (and amusing) tale, but be forewarned that it is presented in heavy, fairly distracting local dialect:

Uncle Heber's Flytrap

There ain't no question 'bout my ole Uncle Heber being the goldurnest laziest man in these parts, I reckon. Spent his full life trying to hatch up new ways of gitting outen work. Lots of folks 'cused him of shirking his dooties, and when he didn't make no comeback they said he didn't have no shame even, but I reckon the truth is he jes didn't have no energy to make argyment.

He never took no wife 'cause he was too lazy to go courting; and doing his own housekeeping like he done, he jes nacherly let his place go to rack and ruin. The shingles of his house all blowed off, and part of the roof caved in. Cracks come in the walls, and it rained in so hard that ever'thing in the house was wet. Uncle Heber stuck it out until the cracks got so big that the wind'd come in and blow the civers offen his bed. He caught cold and almost died 'cause he was too lazy to sneeze, even. At last the house sorta give up and caved in, and then Uncle Heber knowed he's got to move sommers else.

Feller told him 'bout a little island, eight mile up Brice's Crick, what nobody claimed, and Uncle Heber jes moved on up there. Was too lazy to explore it first, jes put his stuff together in a duffel bag, called his dog, and off he set.

The ground on that island was the richest, I reckon, anywhere could be found. No crops had ever been growed on it and it was made up of silt washed up from the crick. Uncle Heber was in the best piece of luck anybody ever heerd of, I reckon. All he had to do was push a stick in the ground, and goldurn if it didn't take root and grow. On the island was enormous trees of all kinds, some of 'em as thick in the trunk as a house. They was apple trees with apples as big as punkins, and persimmon trees with persimmons as big as your head and as sour as a old maid schoolteacher's mouth. The catfish in the crick was as big as alligators. Only trouble was that ever'thing else was in perportion. The good things was the bestest, but the bad things was the worstest anybody ever heerd tell of.

Uncle Heber sure was in clover. He found a big holler tree what he makes into a house, and there's plenty of fruit and fish and ever'thing he needs. He had brung along his old clay pipe and some fine-cut backer, and of course when he filled his pipe he spilt some backer and jes let it lay. Well, the backer took roots and growed up into the biggest and strongest backer leaves anybody ever heerd of.

He figgered out a good way to catch catfish and not tire hisself out. He'd balance his pole on a forked stick, and put a rock on the limb of a tree jes over the shore end of the pole. On the rock he tied a string. Then in the limb of the tree he rigged up a sharp knife atween two tater graters. He'd stretch hisself out on the crick bank, puffing on his pipe and cogerate hisself on how to cut down on his work. When he sees a nibble on the fishline, he pulls the string. The rock falls off on the end of the pole. This jerks the fish outen the water, 'crost the knife what guts it, and through the tater graters what takes off the scales. He didn't bother 'bout the heads and tails, jes cooked the fish thataway and left the rest for his dog.

Uncle Heber'd lost all his teeth when he was a young feller, jes 'cause he was too lazy to chew his food, I reckon, but he got 'round that all right. He traded a man outen a set of store teeth and then rigged up some clockwork to make the teeth champ up and down. Uncle Heber'd wind up the clockwork and put them in his mouth and let his jaw hang loose. Then he'd feed in his rations and the teeth'd chew it up for him. He used to keep the teeth in his hip pocket, but oncet they got started running in his pocket and bit a hunk outen Uncle Heber, and after that he kept 'em out on the table where he could see 'em.

Oncet he was laying on his back 'longside his fishpole on the crick bank, smoking his pipe and figgering how he was getting tired of catfish and wanted some fresh meat and how he could get some meat without trubble, when a big idee hit him. He 'membered 'bout a little plant he'd seen down near Wilmin'ton what folks call the Venus flytrap and this plant catches flies and little frogs. He figgered that in his fertile land mebbe one of them flytraps'd grow big enough to trap him some game.

The Unnatural History of Man-Eating Plants

After worrying 'bout it two or three months, he got up enough energy to push his raft acrost the crick, walk to the road, and pick up a ride to Wilmin'ton. He got a Venus plant and took it back to his island and planted it in a clear space.

In no time atall that plant begin to grow, and Uncle Heber see he had figgered proper and correct and the plant is going to be big as a live-oak tree. When the Venus plant was six foot high, it caught a rabbit one night. In the morning Uncle Heber see the jaws of the trap shet tight and a rabbit tail sticking out. He figgered and figgered how to git the rabbit out and fin'ly he hit on it. I be goldurn if he didn't light up his pipe with that strong backer and blow at the Venus trap. The plant got real white and began to shiver and opened up its trap and let the rabbit drop out.

Uncle Heber figgered this was the best luck of all. The Venus plant kept on catching him game, most every night, and in a few months it was big enough to catch a deer or a bear. Uncle Heber had so much game he didn't bother to fish no more, jes eat his fill on game. This went on for quite a spell, and Uncle Heber was sitting purty and the only thing he was worrying 'bout was how to find a easy way to dress his game.

Then late one night he was woke up by a awful yammering going on outside. He got up and crawled outen his holler tree, and it was bright moonlight, and he sees his dog chasing a big skunk 'round the Venus tree. The dog was right behind the skunk, but couldn't quite catch it. All a-sudden the tree reaches out one of its traps and grobs up the skunk and the dog in one gulp.

Now Uncle Heber thunk a lot of his dog. It was his onliest friend, and the only thing he could talk to, and he ruther have 'most anything happen to him 'cept lose his dog. So he runs back to his tree house to fetch his pipe so he can blow smoke on the trap and make it open up.

But I reckon that skunk was too goldurn potent for the
Venus trap. When Uncle Heber come up, the Venus tree is
shaking all over. It shake back and forth and dip up and
down. Big gobs of sticky sap, like 'lasses, come oozing
out and run down on the ground. First thing Uncle Heber
knowed one of the traps dip down and grob him up entire.

The Venus tree keeps on shaking like it's sick to its
stummick. Then it gives a powerful lunge and tore itself
up by the roots and landed smack in the middle of the
crick.

Iffen it hadn't been that Uncle Heber was smoking his pipe
when the trap grobbed him he'd a-been a goner, I reckon.
The Venus tree started down stream with him in one trap
and the dog and the skunk in 'nother, and he jes puffed up
a couple good puffs of that pipe and the Venus tree wilted

right down in the water and opened up its traps, wide open. Uncle Heber landed in the water, and the skunk and the dog landed in the water, and the three struck off for shore. Uncle Heber smelt the skunk, and the skunk smelt Uncle Heber, and the skunk jes turned 'round and jumped back in the Venus trap.

Uncle Heber was a changed man after that. He moved to town and got a job in a livery stable, and he give up smoking. Said he couldn't stand that sissy stuff they sold in town and called it backer.

VEGETABLE MAN

Like Audrey II or the more speculative background for the Venus Flytrap, some Man-Eating Plants have a cosmic origin...

Gray Barker, pioneering flying saucer investigator, publicized a bizarre close encounter with the "Vegetable Man" of West Virginia in the March 1976 issue of his newsletter. Barker was best known for his book about the Men in Black, "They Knew Too Much About Flying Saucers," and for his UFO 'zine, The Saucerian. The Vegetable Man brings to mind the flesh-eating "Plant-Animal" of New Orleans, only with an apparently otherworldly provenance.

Barker interviewed Jennings H. Frederick of Grant Town, who claimed to have encountered the Vegetable Man (as Frederick called it) in the middle of July 1968. The young man was returning to his father's property after an unsuccessful day bow-hunting for woodchuck when he stopped to rest under some maple trees. That is when he heard "a high-pitched jabbering" like a record playing at exaggerated speed. Frederick understood the words, perhaps through mental telepathy; they were telling him that the speaker came in peace and needed his medical assistance. Sweating, Frederick reached into his pocket for a handkerchief but felt a sudden pain as if his right arm had become entangled with a wild berry briar. Withdrawing his arm, Frederick saw attached to his wrist a thin and flexible right hand and arm, about the diameter of a quarter in size, and a plant-like green in color. There were three fingers grasping him, each about seven inches long with a needle-like tip and suction cups.

The being tightened its grip on Frederick's arm and punctured a vein. Frederick heard the suction and realized that the creature was drawing his blood. He swiveled around and looked straight into the human-like face of his assailant. It had yellow, slanted eyes and pointed ears. The body resembled "the stalk of a huge, ungainly plant" that masked remarkable strength. It held Frederick firm as it drained his blood, coupled with the hypnotic effect of the being's sing-song message.

Vegetable Man. By Robert Jacob Woodard

Frederick cried out in fright and pain. Suddenly, the creature's eyes turned red and appeared to rotate, with spinning orange circles emerging from them. The effect transfixed the young man, stopping him in his tracks as his pain and terror suddenly ceased.

The Unnatural History of Man-Eating Plants

The entire "transfusion" lasted maybe a minute before the Vegetable Man released its grip on Frederick. It then ran up the hill with massive leaps that covered 25 feet or more with each bound and cleared a five-foot fence with a few feet to spare. The "abominable green creature," per Barker, disappeared into the woods atop the hill, followed by a humming and whistling that Frederick suspected was its saucer taking off. The young man stumbled home and cleaned and bandaged his arm, the puncture wounds convincing him that the experience had not been just an hallucination.

Barker wrote that Frederick was an "amateur rocket expert lately turned UFO investigator," not by choice but to prove his own sanity after multiple extraterrestrial encounters. On the morning of April 23, 1965, his mother, Ivah, had witnessed from the front porch of the family home a landed saucer on a hillside pasture. The disc was about 10 feet in diameter and five-feet-tall, cream or silver in color, and rotated clockwise while emitting a loud buzz. There was a crystal dome that sparkled in the morning sun, with rows of windows underneath. The saucer hovered about five feet above the grass, although what appeared to be an elevator shaft with doorway projected downward from the ship to the ground. About 200 yards away, a small, "Satanic"-looking creature, more animal than human, was collecting grass and dirt and stuffing them into a small bag it carried. It was nude with black or dark green skin, had pointed ears and a tail, and displayed no facial features that Ivah could discern. A dark green umbilical cord-like cable connected the creature to its craft. This cable ran upward into the doorway.

After about 15 minutes, the creature retreated into the doorway on the "stem" of the craft. The saucer rotated faster, hummed louder, and then rose "like a feather" straight up into the sky. When Jennings, the oldest son, returned from school and heard his mother's account, he hurried to the landing site to investigate. There was a depression in the hillside from where the elevator had rested, which the boy estimated exceeded a ton. He also found the creature's footprints, each about six inches long and displaying four clawed toes; Jennings judged the being to have weighed about 45 pounds. He collected plaster casts of the footprints, along with hair samples found within, and sent them along with photographs of the site to the Air Force. The Air Force kept the samples and replied back with their explanation for the event—a weather balloon. Of course.

It is unclear if the being Ivah saw was the same or related in any way to the Vegetable Man her son would encounter three years later. Frederick told Barker that he had experienced additional UFO sightings, including one with a time distortion. He was nervous after reading books and articles by John Keel that described a pattern in which contactees were visited numerous times, causing great challenges in their personal lives.

Frederick did ultimately join the Air Force, and spent the final days of his enlistment with NASA. Though obtaining security clearance, Frederick explained in vague terms that there had been a major lapse in security that resulted in him learning of a secret project beyond his authorization, which Barker presumed to involve UFOs. Frederick received a dishonorable discharge and, four months later, the Men In Black came calling. He was awoken in the middle of the night by a red flash, and saw a small canister the size of an apple come bouncing into the room, emitting a red vapor. Before Frederick could pull his .38 pistol out from under his pillow, he felt a needle prick his left arm. (Poor Frederick had a penchant for getting poked and prodded.)

Three men—dressed in black turtleneck sweaters, pants, and ski masks—climbed through the windows, joining whomever had stuck Frederick with a needle. Frederick overheard them converse about having gassed the rest of his family and darted the dogs, and confirm that Frederick would be out shortly. As the shadow of unconsciousness enclosed him, Frederick saw the men put on gasmasks, pocket the canister, and open a briefcase containing a tape recorder. They covered his face and began to ask him about his UFO sightings, what he thought they were, the nature of time, and the future. When Frederick awoke the next morning, no one else in the house reported anything strange.

There is some ambivalence about Barker's reliability as a UFO investigator. The Clarksburg Harrison Public Library, which holds a collection of Barker's papers, cautions that the noted UFO author (a Clarksburg, Tenn. resident) was a "teller of tall tales, and hoaxer from the early 1950's until his death in 1984. Barker was noted for his dramatic style, blurring fact with fiction to capture the imagination."

Barker also succeeded in bringing Man-Eating Plant tales into the Space Age!

PINE BARRENS GIANT PITCHER

In 2017, Kai Russell, a viewer of the Truth Is Scarier Than Fiction YouTube channel, revealed their own encounter with a mysterious plant within the comments of a video called "Cryptobotany: Five Cryptid Plants." Russell, 26 at the time, said they lived within the New Jersey Pine Barrens and recounted a strange adventure that happened when they were about 12 and accompanied an older cousin on a hunting trip.

The duo walked over five miles into the wilderness in an area located about 15 to 20 miles from the Pygmy Forest. While it might sound like something out of Alice in Wonderland, the Pygmy Forest encompasses about 12,000 acres, primarily in the Warren Grove Recreation Area. It consists of mature pine and oak trees that average less than 11 feet in height, many waist high. These trees are believed to have developed genetic adaptations that allow them to thrive in soil poor in water and nutrients, as well as propagate despite frequent wildfires. Their serotinous cones only open when subjected to intense heat and they have an extraordinary ability to shoot up new growth from their roots, even when the rest of the tree has completely burned, according to the Pinelands Preservation Alliance.

"Midway through the day we come across a 4 or 5-foot high weird type of pitcher plant. My cousin, who was around 26 or 27 at that time, knew it wasn't the normal type of pitcher plant we see in the area. It was oozing a purple-ish white thick sap that look liked purple-ish marshmallow fluff and it smelled like a rotten corpse," wrote Russell. "The pitcher part of the plant was 80% of the plant while the known pitcher plants have these little tiny pitchers. The plant looked like it was from the rainforest or was CGI from the movie "Journey to the Center of the Earth." We didn't touch the thing but I wish we would have opened the pitcher. It could have been a deer in it rotting away; it was that big and wide, skinnier at the top and bottom."

Russell and their cousin researched this Giant Pitcher Plant when they got home but soon realized it was unrecognized by science. No one else they spoke with in the area had heard of it. Russell returned to the spot eight years later and couldn't find the plant, nor could they locate it on several return trips. The sighting remains a mystery.

The New Jersey Pinelands indeed has a native species of pitcher plant, the *Sarracenia purpurea* (Purple Pitcher Plant). This bog-dwelling carnivore is only a small monster, though, standing about a foot tall. It dines on any hapless insects who are attracted to its nectar and slide down to drown in the digestive fluid within its pitcher. The Pine Barrens are home to other small carnivorous plants, including three species of Sundew and at least 10 species of Bladderwort.

Zoologist Dr. Karl Shuker, who has conducted wide-sweeping research into the lore of Man-Eating Plants, examined the New Jersey case in 2018. He questioned the feasibility of the Giant Pitcher Plant as described. How could there have been only one individual? What would induce a deer to jump inside, and why wouldn't it simply be able to leap back out or kick its way through the walls of the pitcher? Shuker wrote that the largest pitcher on record belonged to a specimen of *N. rajah*, native to Borneo, which was measured at 16 inches tall in 2011—a far cry from the man-sized monster recalled by Russell. Shuker was unaware of any Pitcher Plant that drips vile sap. The eyewitness testimony did remind Shuker of a certain massive rainforest plant from the islands of Sumatra and Java that has a pitcher-like shape and a terrible smell, although it is non-carnivorous: *Amorphophallus titanum*, aka the Corpse Plant. Why anyone would place such an exotic specimen in a decidedly non-tropical, remote New Jersey forest is anyone's guess.

But I think everyone is missing a possible identity for the Pine Barrens mystery plant; perhaps it wasn't vegetation at all, but a Jersey Devil cocoon!

SOURCES:

Allen, Zacariah. *Memorial of Roger Williams*. Paper Read Before the Rhode Island Historical Society, May 18, 1860. Providence, RI, Cooke & Danielson, Printers, 1860.

"The American's Tale." *Arthur Conan Doyle Encyclopedia*, https://www.arthur-conan-doyle.com/index.php/The_American%27s_Tale. Accessed 15 May 2025.

"*Antiaris*." *Wikipedia*, https://en.wikipedia.org/wiki/Antiaris. Accessed 12 Aug. 2025.

Barker, Gray. "Vegetable Man -- A Semi-Abductee?" *Gray Barker's Newsletter*, No. 5, Mar. 1976, Cover, pp. 9-13 [2022 reprint edition, edited by Alfred Steber, Saucerian Publisher].

Berlitz, Charles. *Charles Berlitz's World of Strange Phenomenon, Vol. 2: Strange People and Amazing Stories*. Sphere Books Limited, 1990.

Broyles, Bill. "Loyal Loner: The Life of Ronald L. Ives, Southwest Geographer." *Journal of the Southwest*, vol. 61, no. 2, 2019, pp. 223-435.

"A Cannibal Plant." *Spectator* [London], 24 Oct. 1891, no. 3,304, pp. 557-559.

Carey, E. Ellsworth. "The Demon Tree of Hawaii." *Daily Pacific Commercial Advertiser* [Honolulu], 10 Mar. 1892, p. 5.

"Carey's Nom de Plume." *Hawaiian Gazette* [Honolulu], 25 Apr. 1893, p. 12.

C.M.O. "New Food for Plants." *St. Paul Daily Globe* [St. Paul, MN], 16 Aug. 1885, p. 13.

"Collection Catalog: Roger Williams' Apple Tree Root." *Rhode Island Historical Society*, https://rihs.minisisinc.com/rihs/scripts/mwimain.dll/144/RIHS_M3/LINK/SISN+63194?SESSIONSEARCH. Accessed 19 Jun. 2025.

"Cryptobotany: Five Cryptid Plants." *YouTube*, uploaded by Truth Is Scarier Than Fiction, 23 Apr. 2017, https://www.youtube.com/watch?v=AhSUzLFTK_Y.

Curtis, Edward S. *The North American Indian, Vol. 1.* Johnson Reprint Corporation, 1907.

Daily Bulletin [Honolulu], 4 Feb. 1893, p. 2.

"Darius Sessions." *Wikipedia*, https://en.wikipedia.org/wiki/Darius_Sessions. Accessed 11 Aug. 2025.

De Prorok, Byron. *In Quest of Lost Worlds.* Narrative Press, 2003.

De Prorok, Count Byron. *In Quest of Lost Worlds.* E. P. Dutton & Co., Inc., 1935.

DeProrok, Comte Byron Khun. "Midst Pygmies and Pyramids I." *Wide World*, Jul. 1934, pp. 294-303.

DeProrok, Comte Byron Khun. "Midst Pygmies and Pyramids II." *Wide World*, Aug. 1934, pp. 372-378.

"The Devil's Tree." *Osage County Enterprise* [Chamois, MO], 2 May, 1889, p. 2.

Doyle, A. Conan. "An Arizona Tragedy." *St. Louis Post-Dispatch*, 16 Oct. 1892, p. 37.

"An Episode of 1902." *Daily Pacific Commercial Advertiser* [Honolulu], 27 Aug. 1891, p. 2.

"Famous Western Liars." *Washington Post*, 17 Aug. 1913, p. 1.

"Fasted Forty-Five Days." *San Francisco Examiner*, 14 Feb. 1909, p. 1.

"*Ficus macrophylla*." *Wikipedia*, https://en.wikipedia.org/wiki/Ficus_macrophylla. Accessed 24 May 2025.

Florence Tribune [Florence, AZ], 4 Feb. 1899, pp. 2-3.

Gorski, Sam. "What is the Vegetable Man of West Virginia?" *12 WOY*, 3 Apr. 2023, https://www.wboy.com/only-on-wboy-com/paranormal-w-va/what-is-the-vegetable-man-of-west-virginia/. Accessed 23 Jul. 2025.

"Gray Barker UFO Collection." *Clarksburg Harrison Public Library*, https://www.clarksburglibrary.org/barker-collection. Accessed 13 Aug. 2025.

Hammerstrom, Kirsten. "The Root of the Matter." *Rhode Island Historical Society*, 22 Mar. 2012, https://www.rihs.org/the-root-of-the-matter/. Accessed 19 Jun. 2025.

"*Harpagophytum.*" *Wikipedia*, https://en.wikipedia.org/wiki/Harpagophytum. Accessed 12 Aug. 2025.

"Hawaiian Kingdom." *Wikipedia*, https://en.wikipedia.org/wiki/Hawaiian_Kingdom. Accessed 12 Aug. 2025.

Herringshaw, Thos. W. *The Biographical Review of Prominent Men and Women of the Day*. A. B. Gehman & Co., 1888.

"His First Visit After Six Years." *Arizona Republican* [Phoenix], 14 Dec. 1910, p. 11.

"Horrible and Gruesome Story." *Don Dorrigo Gazette* [Dorrigo, New South Wales, Australia], 21 Apr. 1926, p. 4.

"Horror in a Swamp." *Daily Record and Mail* [Glasgow, Scotland], 6 Feb. 1924, p. 12.

Ives Ronald L. "And Some People Believe Them!" *Arizona Republic* [Phoenix], 16 Jan. 1938, The Arizona Magazine of the Greater Sunday Republic supplement, p. 6.

Ives, Ronald L. "You Don't Have to Believe It." *Science News Letter*, vol. 33, no. 14, 2 April 1938, pp. 214-215, 222.

"Joseph Mulhatton." *Kook Science*, https://hatch.kookscience.com/wiki/Joseph_Mulhatton. Accessed 8 May 2025.

"Jules Lermina." *Wikipedia*, https://en.wikipedia.org/wiki/Jules_Lermina. Accessed 15 May 2025.

Kairussell7372. Comments on "Cryptobotany: Five Cryptid Plants." *YouTube*, uploaded by Truth Is Scarier Than Fiction, 23 Apr. 2017, https://www.youtube.com/watch?v=AhSUzLFTK_Y.

Kennedy, David. "Motion Picture Aerial Archaeology." *APAAME*, 3 Mar. 2017, http://www.apaame.org/2017/03/motion-picture-aerialarchaeology.html. Accessed 28 Jun. 2025.

Le Beau Lucchesi, Emile. "How Giant Skeletons Became the Ultimate Hoax." *Discover*, 7 Oct. 2024, https://www.discovermagazine.com/how-giant-skeletons-became-the-ultimate-hoax-46669. Accessed 12 Aug. 2025.

Lermina, Jules. "Titane (Histoires Incroyables)." *Le Figaro*. Supplément Littéraire du Dimanche, 25 Apr. 1885, p. 1.

Lermina, Jules. "The Titaness." *St. Louis Post-Dispatch*, 30 May 1885, p. 11.

"The Liar a Thief Also." *New York Times*, 12 Nov. 1891, p. 2.

The Literary Diary of Ezra Stiles, D.D., LL.D., President of Yale College, Vol. III: January 1, 1782—May 6, 1795. Edited by Franklin Bowditch Dexter, Charles Scribner's Sons, 1901.

Lubbock, Sir John. *Flowers, Fruits and Leaves*. London, MacMillan and Company, 1888.

Lubbock, Sir John. "On Fruits and Seeds." *Popular Science Monthly*, July 1881, pp. 354-368.

"The Magnetic Cactus." *Florence Tribune* [Florence, AZ], 11 Feb. 1899, p. 3.

Masters, Nathan. "Majestic Mammoths: A Brief History of L.A.'s Moreton Bay Fig Trees." *PBS SoCal*, 11 Apr. 2013, https://www.pbssocal.org/shows/lost-la/majestic-mammoths-a-brief-history-of-l-a-s-moreton-bay-fig-trees. Accessed 24 May 2025.

Matthews, Washington. *Navaho Legends*. Boston, Houghton, Mifflin and Company, 1897.

"Memorial Erected to Founder of State." *Newport Mercury and Weekly News* [Newport, RI], 30 Jun. 1939, p. 2.

"Memorial Unveiled to Roger Williams." *Springfield Daily Republican* [Springfield, MA], 30 Jun. 1939, p. 28.

Millett, Larry. "Lost Twin Cities: St. Paul's Ryan Hotel Was a Victorian Masterpiece." *Minnesota Star Tribune* [Minneapolis, MN], 4 Jan. 2019, https://www.startribune.com/lost-twin-cities-st-paul-s-ryan-hotel-was-a-victorian-masterpiece/503905672. Accessed 22 Mar. 2025.

"Monument for Roger Williams." *Waterbury Evening Democrat* [Waterbury, CT], 26 Feb. 1936, p. 8.

Morris, John A. "Three Interesting Plants." *Los Angeles Herald*, 28 Feb. 1897, p. 18.

"The Most Mysterious Plant in the World." *YouTube*, uploaded by Truth Is Scarier Than Fiction, 5 Jan. 2022, https://www.youtube.com/watch?v=HEr3vJEq2V0.

"Mr E Ellsworth Carey." *Pacific Commercial Advertiser* [Honolulu], 24 Nov. 1899, p. 7.

"New Jersey's Pygmy Forest is the Largest Tiny Forest on Earth." *Shore News Network*, 27 Nov. 2023, https://www.shorenewsnetwork.com/2023/11/27/new-jerseys-pygmy-forest-is-the-largest-tiny-forest-on-earth/. Accessed 9 May 2025.

"Of Plants and Trees." *Worcester Sunday Telegram* [Worcester, MA], 5 Feb. 1905, p. 22.

"One of Most Famous Reporters Made His Home in This City." *Arizona Republican* [Phoenix], 28 Dec. 1920, p. 31.

"Overthrow of the Hawaiian Kingdom." *Wikipedia*, https://en.wikipedia.org/wiki/Overthrow_of_the_Hawaiian_Kingdom. Accessed 11 Aug. 2025.

"Pacific Exporter." *San Francisco Call*, 17 Jan. 1901, p. 6.

"Pine Barrens Habitats." *Pinelands Preservation Alliance*, https://pinelandsalliance.org/learn-about-the-pinelands/ecosystem/habitats/. Accessed 9 May 2025.

"Prospect Terrace." *National Park Service,* https://www.nps.gov/places/prospect-terrace.htm. Accessed 11 Aug. 2025.

"Prospectors' Strange Find." *Daily Times-Index* [San Bernardino, CA], 19 Jun 1903, p.3.

"Provisional Government of Hawaii." *Wikipedia,* https://en.wikipedia.org/wiki/Provisional_Government_of_Hawaii . Accessed 11 Aug. 2025.

"Record Unit 7091: Science Service Records, 1902-1965 Collection Overview." *Smithsonian Institution Archives,* 17 Mar. 2022, https://siarchives.si.edu/collections/siris_arc_217249. Accessed 7 May 2025.

Reuters Fact Check. "Fact Check: Claims That the Smithsonian Destroyed 'Thousands of Giant Skeletons' Are Many Years Old and Satirical." *Reuters,* 4 Aug. 2022, https://www.reuters.com/article/fact-check/claims-that-the-smithsonian-destroyed-thousands-of-giant-skeletons-are-many-ye-idUSL1N2ZG1I0/. Accessed 12 Aug. 2025.

"Roger Williams." *Wikipedia,* https://en.wikipedia.org/wiki/Roger_Williams. Accessed 10 Aug. 2025.

"Ronald Ives Papers." *Arizona Historical Society-Tucson,* 1983.

Rosanova, Elisha. Letter. *Honolulu Advertiser,* 14 Sep. 1952, p. 4.

Rose, Mark. "Tales of the Count." *Archaeology,* vol. 5, no. 5, Sep./Oct. 2001.

"*Sarracenia purpurea.*" *Jersey-Friendly Yards,* https://www.jerseyyards.org/plant/sarracenia-purpurea/. Accessed 9 May 2025.

"*Sarracenia purpurea* (Purple Pitcher Plant)." *Gardenia,* https://www.gardenia.net/plant/sarracenia-purpurea. Accessed 9 May 2025.

Shuker, Dr. Karl. "Pitching in with News of a Giant Mystery Pitcher Plant." *Shuker Nature,* 21 Mar. 2018, https://karlshuker.blogspot.com/2018/03/pitching-in-with-news-of-giant-mystery.html. Accessed 9 May 2025.

Skinner, Alanson. "Traditions of the Iowa Indians." *Journal of American Folk-lore*, vol. 38, no. 150, Oct.-Dec. 1925, pp. 425-506.

"Student Information Sheet: Carnivorous Plants." *NJ.gov*, https://www.nj.gov/pinelands/infor/educational/curriculum/pinecur/scp78.htm. Accessed 9 May 2025.

Teit, James. "The Shuswap." *Jesup North Pacific Expedition: Memoir of the American Museum of Natural History*, edited by Franz Boaz, vol. 2, part 4, 1908, pp. 447-789.

"A Texas Yarn." *Chicago Tribune*, 17 Apr. 1883, p. 5.

"That 'Demon Tree.'" *Daily Pacific Commercial Advertiser* [Honolulu], 4 Feb. 1893, p. 3.

"Thinks Education Is Ruining Hawaii." *Pacific Commercial Advertiser* [Honolulu], 4 May 1909, p. 2.

"Today in History - February 5: Roger Williams, Rhode Island Founder." *Library of Congress*, https://www.loc.gov/item/today-in-history/february-05/. Accessed 10 Aug. 2025.

Vance, Arthur T. "Prince of Liars." *Evening Star* [Washington, D.C.], 5 Jan. 1901, p. 24.

"Why Eat Meat?" *Freeborn County Standard* [Albert Lea, MN], 17 Aug. 1904, p. 4.

"A Wonderful Cave." *St. Louis Evening Post*, 22 Jun. 1878, p. 5.

Workers of the Writers' Program of the Work Projects Administration in the State of North Carolina. *Bundle of Troubles and Other Tarheel Tales*. Edited by W. C. Hendricks, Duke University Press, 1943.

PART II: SHORT STORIES

INTRO TO MAN-EATING PLANT SHORT FICTION

The origin of Man-Eating Plants might stem from European Colonial-era literature, but I think it feeds upon something deeper and more base in our human nature -- the constant search for greater mystery. We don't run away from the fiercest monsters our minds can conjure; we rush toward them. There is no shortage of real horror in the world, but we remain, perhaps as a vestige of our primal survival instincts, completely obsessed with dinosaurs, and with mysterious Cryptids that evoke long-extinct megafauna (Bigfoot, lake monsters, Thunderbirds, etc.). Does humankind's love of Man-Eating Plant stories suggest that, in some distant epoch, we were the prey of our planetary flora and not solely the predator? The imagination reels, as can be attested by this curated collection of short fiction on the subject.

It's stunning to see just what a popular horror/adventure trope Man-Eating Plants were around the turn of the 19th to 20th centuries. The emergence of Man-Eating Vegetation in Fin de Siècle (end of century) Gothic fiction, per Elizabeth Chang in "Killer Plants of the Late Nineteenth Century," made it "clear that plants helped late Victorian readers think about themselves and their world, in all its political, economic, and scientific expanses." There were innumerable news articles, documented throughout the first half of this book, as well as many works of outright fiction of varying lengths. "The Devil-Tree of El Dorado" by Frank Aubrey was a popular 1897 novel on the subject, and these voracious vegetables were spotlighted in serialized fiction like "Lost in Africa" by C. L. Stoyle (Chapter IX, "The Vegetable Octopus"), published May-August 1897 in The Ludgate Monthly, and in newspaper comic strips such as "Tarzan and The Mayan Goddess" (appearing a bit later, in 1936).

I warned in the intro to this book's travelogue that the historical news articles about the world's Man-Eating Plants contained their fair share of racial and cultural insensitivities, and these short stories are no different. They are a product of their time, and are presented in their original form.

The earliest short story in this collection, 1883's **"The Balloon Tree,"** is included here because it follows the familiar patterns of Man-Eating Plant fiction established nine years earlier by the first report on "Crinoida Dajeeana," with a European exploring an exotic jungle—only to then subvert the genre with an unexpected twist. The author was Edward Page Mitchell, longtime editor and writer for the New York Sun, who alongside his accomplished and varied journalistic output wrote at least a score of short stories for the newspaper. Mitchell began his 51-year career with the Sun at age 23 under influential editor Charles Anderson Dana, who encouraged his reporters to also try their hand at fiction. Mitchell's short stories were described contemporaneously as possessing "ingenious form and delightful narrative."

French journalist and novelist Jules Lermina caused waves as a fervent anti-Bonapartist during the Second Empire and was a supporter of socialist ideas. He received a letter of support from "Les Misérables" author Victor Hugo after an 1867 arrest for participating in an anti-Imperial demonstration. In 1870, Lermina was given two years in prison after calling for the Emperor's impeachment, but he escaped and his sentence was overturned a few weeks later with the proclamation of the Republic. He joined the army to fight the Prussians, then enjoyed a successful career as a journalist. His fictional output included historical works, detective stories, adventure novels, sequels to Alexandre Dumas' "The Count of Monte Crisco," and several stories based around his love for the occult. Lermina's 1885 short story "Titane," published in Le Figaro and shortly afterward translated into English in American newspapers as **"The Titaness,"** is an early example of the trope of an obsessive, Dr. Frankenstein-like scientist who secretly nurtures a deadly plant in his lab. There are a few similar tales in this book!

The Unnatural History of Man-Eating Plants

Though born into great means as the daughter of a successful Philadelphia merchant, 19-year-old, newly-married Lucy Hamilton Hooper was compelled to employ her writing talents to earn a living after a commercial crisis ruined her husband's business in 1854. Hooper succeeded as a poet, journalist, author and playwright, and was both a contributor and associate editor for Lippincott's Monthly Magazine. Her work appeared in leading American periodicals for more than two decades. **"Carnivorine"** is very similar in plot structure and content to "The Titaness," and was perhaps even inspired by it, with Hooper residing in Paris later in life. Hooper's tale clearly demonstrates the influence that Darwin's Theory of Evolution and his studies on the animal-like attributes of carnivorous plants affected on popular culture.

Sir Arthur Conan Doyle would find eternal fame as the creator of Sherlock Holmes, but his darkly humorous tale about a giant Venus Flytrap found (incongruously) in the American Southwest represents his days as a young, struggling writer, being only his second published work, and anonymously at that. First printed under the name "The American's Tale" in December 1880, it marked the beginning of Doyle's fruitful association with London Society magazine, the first of 11 stories published over a five-year period. In 1892, the story was reissued in various publications as **"An Arizona Tragedy,"** this time under the now well-known author's name. "In 'The American's Tale,' Americanisms are abundant and Americanism unbridled," wrote Michael Adams in Scottish Literary Review. Doyle could hear American voices and imitate them effectively, and borrowed American words that he gleaned from the country's literature. "Early in his career, he lay American idiom thick on his fictional canvas, as with a painter's knife," wrote Adams. "Later, he applied Americanisms with the tip and edge of a restrained brush, proving his writerly assurance and incorporating his American material into a more sophisticated style."

Like with Doyle, a carnivorous plant story was among the early output of science fiction visionary H. G. Wells, published just one year before his first and seminal novel, "The Time Machine." The story plays on the burgeoning hobby of horticulture among the Victorian-Era British populace, with adventurers scouring the

ANOTHER TYPICAL DAY IN FLYTRAP GULCH -KJG

world for the bulbs of rare and exotic orchids. From his earliest student writing, Wells displayed a stoical perspective based in Darwinian evolution, with **"The Flowering of the Strange Orchid"** being one of many stories that displayed his interest in the unpredictable nature of man's environment, per J. R. Hammond.

"The Lamparagua" is an exceptionally well-written, pulse-pounding tale of man vs. nature in which the latter takes on a most unexpected and fearsome form. Author May Crommelin sets the action in South America and wonderfully weaves the local folklore of the indigenous characters into the main threat of the adventure. Crommelin, whose full name was Maria Henrietta de la Cherois Crommelin, was born in Ireland to a family considered "French gentry," descended from a Huguenot linen merchant. The family wasn't wealthy, though, and Crommelin began living independently in her own London flat in 1885, supporting herself as a writer. (Crommelin and her sisters were considered the heads of the family after the deaths of their father and brother.) She traveled extensively, and based many of her 42 novels on insights gleaned from her own adventures. (See more on Crommelin and the Lamparagua itself in our South America chapter.)

Whereas Wells' "The Flowering of the Strange Orchid" featured the perspective of the orchid *collector* back home in Britain, Fred M. White's **"The Purple Terror"** depicts the more adventurous experience of the orchid *hunter* seeking rare floral treasures in unexplored realms. The botanical "monster" in this story is well-realized. White was a prolific British writer with more than 100 novels and 400 short stories to his name. He worked in the science fiction genre, specialized in disaster fiction, and was a pioneer in the spy genre.

"The Wonderful Tiger Tree" is an adaptation of the Man-Eating Tree legend into the world of a whimsical, sprawling fairy tale. Walt McDougall wrote and illustrated this story for his regular "Good Stories for Children" feature that ran in New York Herald newspapers. Hired by the Herald in 1896, McDougall's editorial illustrations for humorist Bill Nye (not "The Science Guy") made him the first syndicated newspaper artist, and he produced some of the earliest political cartoons and full-color comic strips. MacDougall's political cartoons are, in fact, credited with contributing to James G. Blaine's narrow loss to Grover Cleveland in the 1884 U.S. presidential election. There is supposedly a real Tiger Tree in India, which you can read about in our Asia chapter.

THE TIGER TREE -KJG

"Professor Jonkin's Cannibal Plant" is a darkly comic take on what by 1905 had become an established trope, the mad scientist nurturing a carnivorous plant to gigantic and deadly proportions. The monster in this particular story is a Pitcher Plant, albeit one with traits of an active predator instead of just passive carnivore. Howard R. Garis was a well-known name in children's literature throughout the first half of the 20th Century, having created the popular Uncle Wiggily character.

"The Vampire Plant," short and sweet, presents the Man-Eating Plant in a new way—as metaphor. Author Edgar White was a regular contributor of fiction (including this tale) to the Daily

The Unnatural History of Man-Eating Plants

Story Publishing Company, launched in 1899. This syndicate offered short fiction to daily newspapers (as opposed to news or general material) at a time when newspapers commonly published such content, per Mark Seifert of Bleeding Cool.

"Spanish Revenge" appeared in numerous newspapers in 1906 and 1907 under different names, including "Jealous Mexican Beauty Consigns Texan to Death in Deadly Minotaur Tree" and the truncated "Jealous Beauty Planned Fearful Death for Youth." It appears to have first been published in the Chicago Tribune, although the author was uncredited. The Minotaur Tree is revealed to be one and the same as Yateveo, a rare appearance of this particular Man-Eating Tree outside of James W. Buel's 1887 book, "Sea and Land."

"Octopodousa Ferox" continues the plot device of a mad scientist cultivating carnivorous plants, but this time in the context of agriculture. The story questions the role of humans playing God in engineering plants for more productive farming, a debate that still rages today. Author Rowland Thomas raised fancy poultry and Airedale terriers on his farm in Duxbury, Massachusetts. After graduating from Harvard, Thomas spent two years in the Orient "in search of information and adventure." Upon returning to the U.S., he made a splash in the literary world with "Fagan," his first prize ($5,000) entry in Collier's Weekly's 1905 short story contest. Thomas drew from his travel experiences in writing "Fagan," about life in the Philippines, and in his book, "The Little Gods: A Masque of the Far East," about Eastern spiritual traditions. He worked as a staff correspondent and editorial writer for various magazines and newspapers.

English writer and poet Edith "E." Nesbit was an incredibly influential author credited with pioneering children's fantasy and adventure fiction. She provided her young readers with an honest perspective of the world that understood their point of view and acknowledged life's challenges and imperfections. Nesbit wrote more than 60 children's books, "The Railway Children" and "The Story of the Treasure Seekers" being among her most popular. Nesbit also penned several novels and short stories for adults. **"The Pavilion,"** published in the November 1915 edition of The

Intro to Short Stories

Strand Magazine, merges Victorian drawing room drama with the exotic tales of Vampire Vines that had permeated the press.

The launch of pulp fiction magazines like Weird Tales and Amazing Stories during the 1920s provided a new outlet for writers of horror, sci-fi and fantasy. And it established a new home for a wealth of stories centered on Man-Eating Plants! One fine example is **"The Plant-Thing"** by R. G. Macready, printed in the July 1925 issue of Weird Tales. This appears to be Macready's only published story, although he was a career journalist and taught English, history and journalism at the Oklahoma School for the Deaf (with Macready himself also being deaf).

"THERE IN THE MIDDLE OF THE POOL WAS THE GREAT GOLDEN-PURPLE FLOWER, ITS CENTER FLAMING GOLD..." -KJG

The Unnatural History of Man-Eating Plants

From 1911 to 1919, Oscar Cook worked as a government official in British North Borneo, during this time compiling a vocabulary of Bajau words. He frequently drew upon this experience in his writing, such as an autobiography that was considered an authority on Borneo, and several works of supernatural-themed fiction. **"Si Urag of the Tail"** is a truly weird and unsettling story about a vegetable predator, unique in its aquatic nature and the tattooed, be-tailed human servant who procures its meals. Like Cook's other works, it is flavored with his knowledge of Borneo.

In the early years of Amazing Stories, publisher Hugo Gernsback blended the magazine's science fiction with educational content. This is evident in **"The Malignant Flower"** by Anthos, a supremely trippy story whose gigantic vegetable predator is supported by information on a real-life carnivore, the Pitcher Plant, and real-world giant *Amorphophallus titanum*, aka the Corpse Flower. Anthos was most likely German writer, journalist and popular radio broadcaster Leonard Langheinrich, who used that synonym in his artistic endeavors. Langheinrich died following an air raid on Berlin in May 1944.

"The Devil-Plant" by John Murray Reynolds got the cover treatment for the September 1928 Weird Tales, featuring a gorgeous and now-iconic color painting by C. C. Senf of a woman caught in the plant monster's clutches. Terence E. Hanley, who researches the background of strange fiction's lesser-known authors for his Tellers of Weird Tales blog, wrote, "John Murray 'Jack' Reynolds is an example of a man who lived in the upper levels of society, yet wrote pulp fiction and was unashamed to do it." Among his many accomplishments, Reynolds graduated from Princeton University in 1922 with a geology degree, served as vice-president of the Sword Steamship Line, worked in intelligence and counter-intelligence for the U.S. Navy (including a role in the invasion of Normandy), and, after World War 2, resumed his role as a mover and shaker in the New York City maritime business, according to Hanley. During all this time, Reynolds managed to write and sell 150 short stories and seven books. Whew!

Seabury Quinn, whose name sounds like he was born to write detective fiction, did not disappoint. He became famous for his

Intro to Short Stories

tales of occult detective Jules de Grandin (Grandin being Quinn's own middle name), published in Weird Tales. Quinn also had, fittingly, a parallel career as a lawyer with a specialty in mortuary jurisprudence. (For 15 years he edited the trade journal Casket & Sunnyside.) Quinn wrote a whopping 500-plus short stories throughout his literary career. **"'The Kiss' of Madagascar"** features another of his detective characters, U.S. Secret Service "Ace," Major Sturdevant, who starred in a weekly series of stories called "Washington Nights' Entertainment" that Quinn wrote for the Washington Post in 1928. Quinn returned to the theme of Madagascar Man-Eating Plants with "The Black Orchid," a de Grandin adventure published in the August 1935 Weird Tales.

"Fruit of Their Tree" takes us back to Madagascar, serving as a semi-sequel to the original Karl Leche account. In today's eyes, it might be seen as an off-putting parable about the dangers of ignoring "God's plan" and societal expectations in favor of fame and earthly pursuits. But it is also a timeless reminder that it pays to discuss future goals with your partner before committing to marriage. Author Joseph Faus was a career writer, selling his first of many pulp stories at age 20 and working as a reporter in Miami. He penned a weekly column called "The Rock of God" from 1949-1954 for the Miami News, covering local churches and synagogues. He was also very active in his own church as a board member, youth counselor and usher, perhaps explaining the slight religious bent to his Man-Eating Tree tale.

Sophie Wenzel Ellis was a pioneering female writer of pulp science fiction, her stories appearing in Amazing Stories, Weird Tales and several other publications. Her tale, **"White Lady,"** presents a different sort of plant creature, one who consumes a man—not literally—but mentally, physically and spiritually. It continues the long tradition of "Mad Botanist Creates Man-Eating-Plant" stories, but with a—I suppose we could say—romantic twist.

As we close out this volume on "The Unnatural History of Man-Eating Plants," it's undeniable that the line between fact and fiction in this topic is a blurred one, perhaps meaningless. All of the tales in this book are fantastic, yet half were presented in their day with a hazy veneer of truth, while the other half made no secret that they were firmly grounded in the world of

THE WHITE LADY -KJG

imagination. Trying to weed out the veracity of these stories does, however, open up a portal to the past. It reveals an intersection of real-life adventure and unfathomable mystery in which a vegetable people-eater hiding in the humid darkness of untamed jungle seemed a slightly plausible possibility. Maybe we know better today... but it doesn't mean we don't *want* such stories to be true. Compared to all the man-made terrors of this world, a Man-Eating Tree in Madagascar seems almost a quaint and reassuring natural monstrosity.

—KJG

SOURCES:

Adams, Michael. "Arthur Conan Doyle's Americanisms." *Scottish Literary Review*, vol. 11, no. 2, 2019, pp. 143-156.

"Amazing Stories." *Wikipedia*, https://en.wikipedia.org/wiki/Amazing_Stories. Accessed 16 Sep. 2025.

"The American's Tale," *Arthur Conan Doyle Encyclopedia*, https://www.arthur-conan-doyle.com/index.php/The_American%27s_Tale. Accessed 6 Sep. 2025.

Chang, Elizabeth. "Killer Plants of the Late Nineteenth Century." *Strange Science: Investigating the Limits of Knowledge in the Victorian Age*, edited by Lara Karpenko and Shalyn Claggett, University of Michigan Press, 2017.

"E. Nesbit." *Wikipedia*, https://en.wikipedia.org/wiki/E._Nesbit. Accessed 17 Sep. 2025.

"Edward Page Mitchell, 74, For Years New York Sun Editor, Dies at Mohican." *Evening Day* [New London, CT], 24 Jan. 1927, p. 14.

"First Prize to Peabody Man." *Boston Globe*, 10 Feb. 1905, p. 4.

"Fred M. White." *Wikipedia*, https://en.wikipedia.org/wiki/Fred_M._White. Accessed 10 Sep. 2025.

Hammond, J. R. *H. G. Wells and the Short Story*. St. Martin's Press, 1992.

Hanley, Terence E. "John Murray Reynolds (1900-1993)." *Tellers of Weird Tales*, 7 Apr. 2016, https://tellersofweirdtales.blogspot.com/2016/04/john-murray-reynolds-1900-1993.html. Accessed 17 Sep. 2025.

Hanley, Terence E. "Joseph Faus (1898-1966)-The First Collaboration." *Tellers of Weird Tales*, 26 May 2023, https://tellersofweirdtales.blogspot.com/2023/05/joseph-faus-1898-1966-first.html. Accessed 12 Sep. 2025.

Hanley, Terence E. "R.G. Macready (1905-1977)-Part One." *Tellers of Weird Tales*, 20 Aug. 2025, https://tellersofweirdtales.blogspot.com/2025/08/rg-macready-1905-1977-part-one.html. Accessed 16 Sep. 2025.

Hanley, Terence E. "R.G. Macready (1905-1977)-Part Two." *Tellers of Weird Tales*, 23 Aug. 2025, https://tellersofweirdtales.blogspot.com/2025/08/rg-macready-1905-1977-part-two.html. Accessed 16 Sep. 2025.

"H. G. Wells Bibliography." *Wikipedia*, https://en.wikipedia.org/wiki/H._G._Wells_bibliography. Accessed 6 Sep. 2025.

"Howard R. Garis." *Wikipedia*, https://en.wikipedia.org/wiki/Howard_R._Garis. Accessed 10 Sep. 2025.

"Leonard Langheinrich." *Wikipedia* (German), https://de.wikipedia.org/wiki/Leonard_Langheinrich. Accessed 16 Sep. 2025.

"The Little Gods: A Masque of the Far East by Rowland Thomas." *Project Gutenberg*, https://www.gutenberg.org/ebooks/59920. Accessed 11 Sep. 2025.

"London Society." *Arthur Conan Doyle Encyclopedia*, https://www.arthur-conan-doyle.com/index.php/London_Society. Accessed 6 Sep. 2025.

Intro to Short Stories

"Lucy Hamilton Hooper." *Wikipedia,* https://en.wikipedia.org/wiki/Lucy_Hamilton_Hooper. Accessed 6 Sep. 2025.

"The Man from Maine Who Helped Dana Make the Sun." *Literary Digest,* 12 Feb. 1927, pp. 42-44.

"May Crommelin." *Wikipedia,* https://en.wikipedia.org/wiki/May_Crommelin. Accessed 7 Sep. 2025.

Musnik, Roger. "Jules Lermina (1839-1915)." *BnF Gallica,* 14 Jan. 2014, https://gallica.bnf.fr/accueil/fr/html/jules-lermina-1839-1915. Accessed 6 Sep. 2025.

O'Brien, Frank M. *The Story of The Sun.* George H. Doran Company, 1918.

"Oscar Cook." *Wikipedia,* https://en.wikipedia.org/wiki/Oscar_Cook. Accessed 11 Sep. 2025.

Quinn, Seabury. "The Black Orchid." *Weird Tales,* vol. 26, no. 2, pp. 180-196.

"Seabury Quinn." *Wikipedia,* https://en.wikipedia.org/wiki/Seabury_Quinn. Accessed 17 Sep. 2025.

Seifert, Mark. "The Chicago Newspaper Scene and the Origins of 10 Story Book." *Bleeding Cool,* 17 Nov. 2024, https://bleedingcool.com/comics/the-chicago-newspaper-scene-origins-of-10-story-book/. Accessed 16 Sep. 2025.

"Sir Arthur Conan Doyle: Complete Works." *Arthur Conan Doyle Encyclopedia,* https://www.arthur-conan-doyle.com/index.php/Sir_Arthur_Conan_Doyle:Complete_Works. Accessed 6 Sep. 2025.

"Sophie Wenzel Ellis." *Wikipedia,* https://en.wikipedia.org/wiki/Sophie_Wenzel_Ellis. Accessed 16 Sep. 2025.

"Summary Bibliography: Anthos." *ISFDB*, https://www.isfdb.org/cgi-bin/ea.cgi?13194. Accessed 16 Sep. 2025.

"Titan arum." *Wikipedia*, https://en.wikipedia.org/wiki/Titan_arum. Accessed 16 Sep. 2025.

"Walt McDougall." *Wikipedia*, https://en.wikipedia.org/wiki/Walt_McDougall. Accessed 10 Sep. 2025.

"Walter McDougall, 1858-1938." *Ohio State University Libraries*, https://library.osu.edu/site/newspaperartists/walter-mcdougall-1858-1938/. Accessed 10 Sep. 2025.

Washington Post, 19 Jan. 1928, p. 2.

"Wealth in Orchids." *Maryville Daily Democrat* [Maryville, MO], 2 Jan. 1892, p. 3.

"Weird Tales." *Wikipedia*, https://en.wikipedia.org/wiki/Weird_Tales. Accessed 16 Sep. 2025.

White, Edgar. "The Abdication of the Prince." *Buffalo Evening Times* [Buffalo, NY], 15 May, 1905. p.7.

"Writers of the Day." *Writer*, vol. 18, no. 8, Aug. 1906, pp. 122-125.

THE BALLOON TREE

By Edward Page Mitchell

(New York Sun, 1883)

The colonel said:

We rode for several hours straight from the shore toward the heart of the island. The sun was low in the western sky when we left the ship. Neither on the water nor on the land had we felt a breath of air stirring. The glare was upon everything. Over the low range of hills miles away in the interior hung a few copper-colored clouds. "Wind," said Briery. Kilooa shook his head.

Vegetation of all kinds showed the effects of the long continued drought. The eye wandered without relief from the sickly russet of the undergrowth, so dry in places that leaves and stems crackled under the horses' feet, to the yellowish-brown of the thirsty trees that skirted the bridle path. No growing thing was green except the bell-top cactus, fit to flourish in the crater of a living volcano.

Kilooa leaned over in the saddle and tore from one of these plants its top, as big as a California pear and bloated with juice. He crushed the bell in his fist, and, turning, flung into our hot faces a few grateful drops of water.

Then the guide began to talk rapidly in his language of vowels and liquids. Briery translated for my benefit.

The Unnatural History of Man-Eating Plants

The god Lalala loved a woman of the island. He came in the form of fire. She, accustomed to the ordinary temperature of the clime, only shivered before his approaches. Then he wooed her as a shower of rain and won her heart. Kakal was a divinity much more powerful than Lalala, but malicious to the last degree. He also coveted this woman, who was very beautiful. Kakal's importunities were in vain. In spite, he changed her to a cactus, and rooted her to the ground under the burning sun. The god Lalala was powerless to avert this vengeance; but he took up his abode with the cactus woman, still in the form of a rain shower, and never left her, even in the driest seasons. Thus it happens that the bell-top cactus is an unfailing reservoir of pure cool water.

Long after dark we reached the channel of a vanished stream, and Kilooa led us for several miles along its dry bed. We were exceedingly tired when the guide bade us dismount. He tethered the panting horses and then dashed into the dense thicket on the bank. A hundred yards of scrambling, and we came to a poor thatched hut. The savage raised both hands above his head and uttered a musical falsetto, not unlike the yodel peculiar to the Valais. This call brought out the occupant of the hut, upon whom Briery flashed the light of his lantern. It was an old woman, hideous beyond the imagination of a dyspeptic's dream.

"Omanana gelaãl!" exclaimed Kilooa.

"Hail, holy woman," translated Briery.

Between Kilooa and the holy hag there ensued a long colloquy, respectful on his part, sententious and impatient on hers. Briery listened with eager attention. Several times he clutched my arm, as if unable to repress his anxiety. The woman seemed to be persuaded by Kilooa's arguments, or won by his entreaties. At last she pointed toward the southeast, slowly pronouncing a few words that apparently satisfied my companions.

The Balloon Tree

The direction indicated by the holy woman was still toward the hills, but twenty or thirty degrees to the left of the general course which we had pursued since leaving the shore.

"Push on! Push on!" cried Briery. "We can afford to lose no time."

II.

We rode all night. At sunrise there was a pause of hardly ten minutes for the scanty breakfast supplied by our haversacks. Then we were again in the saddle, making our way through a thicket that grew more and more difficult, and under a sun that grew hotter.

"Perhaps," I remarked finally to my taciturn friend, "you have no objection to telling me now why two civilized beings and one amiable savage should be plunging through this infernal jungle, as if they were on an errand of life or death?"

"Yes," said he, "it is best you should know."

Briery produced from an inner breast pocket a letter which had been read and reread until it was worn in the creases. "This," he went on, "is from Professor Quakversuch of the University of Upsala. It reached me at Valparaiso."

Glancing cautiously around, as if he feared that every tree fern in that tropical wilderness was an eavesdropper, or that the hood-like spathes of the giant caladiums overhead were ears waiting to drink in some mighty secret of science, Briery read in a low voice from the letter of the great Swedish botanist:

"You will have in these islands," wrote the professor, "a rare opportunity to investigate certain extraordinary accounts given me years ago by the Jesuit missionary Buteaux concerning the Migratory Tree, the cereus ragrans of Jansenius and other speculative physiologists.

The Unnatural History of Man-Eating Plants

"The explorer Spohr claims to have beheld it; but there is reason, as you know, for accepting all of Spohr's statements with caution.

"That is not the case with the assertions of my late valued correspondent, the Jesuit missionary. Father Buteaux was a learned botanist, an accurate observer, and a most pious and conscientious man. He never saw the Migratory Tree; but during the long period of his labors in that part of the world he accumulated, from widely different sources, a mass of testimony as to its existence and habits.

"Is it quite inconceivable, my dear Briery, that somewhere in the range of nature there is a vegetable organization as far above the cabbage, let us say, in complexity and potentiality as the ape is above the polyp? Nature is continuous. In all her schemes we find no chasms, no gaps. There may be missing links in our books and classifications and cabinets, but there are none in the organic world. Is not all of lower nature struggling upward to arrive at the point of self-consciousness and volition? In the unceasing process of evolution, differentiation, improvement in special function, why may not a plant arrive at this point and feel, will, act—in short, possess and exercise the characteristics of the true animal?"

Briery's voice trembled with enthusiasm as he read this passage.

"I have no doubt," continued Prof. Quakversuch, "that if it shall be your great good fortune to encounter a specimen of the Migratory Tree described by Buteaux, you will find that it possesses a well-defined system of real nerves and ganglia, constituting, in fact, the seat of vegetable intelligence. I conjure you to be very thorough in your dissections.

"According to the indications furnished me by the Jesuit, this extraordinary tree should belong to the order of Cactaceæ. It should be developed only in conditions of extreme heat and dryness. Its roots should be hardly more than rudimentary, affording a precarious attachment to the earth. This attachment it should be able to sever at will, soaring up into the air and away to another place selected by itself, as a bird shifts its habitation. I infer that these migrations are accomplished by means of the property of secreting hydrogen gas, with which it inflates at pleasure a bladder-like organ of highly elastic tissue, thus lifting itself out of the ground and off to a new abode.

"Buteaux added that the Migratory Tree was invariably worshiped by the natives as a supernatural being, and that the mystery thrown by them around its cult was the greatest obstacle in the path of the investigator."

"There!" exclaimed Briery, folding up Professor Quakversuch's letter. "Is not that a quest worthy the risk or sacrifice of life itself? To add to the recorded facts of vegetable morphology the proved existence of a tree that wanders, a tree that wills, a tree, perhaps, that thinks—this is glory to be won at any cost! The lamented Decandolle of Geneva—"

"Confound the lamented Decandolle of Geneva!" shouted I, for it was excessively hot, and I felt that we had come on a fool's errand.

III.

It was near sunset on the second day of our journey, when Kilooa, who was riding several rods in advance of us, uttered a quick cry, leaped from his saddle, and stooped to the ground.

Briery was at his side in an instant. I followed with less agility; my joints were very stiff and I had no scientific enthusiasm to lubricate them. Briery was on his hands and knees, eagerly examining what seemed to be a recent disturbance of the soil. The savage was prostrate, rubbing his forehead in the dust, as if in a religious ecstasy,

and warbling the same falsetto notes that we had heard at
the holy woman's hut.

"What beast's trail have you struck?" I demanded.

"The trail of no beast," answered Briery, almost angrily.
"Do you see this broad round abrasion of the surface,
where a heavy weight has rested? Do you see these little
troughs in the fresh earth, radiating from the center like
the points of a star? They are the scars left by slender
roots torn up from their shallow beds. Do you see Kilooa's
hysterical performance? I tell you we are on the track of
the Sacred Tree. It has been here, and not long ago."

Acting under Briery's excited instructions we continued
the hunt on foot. Kilooa started toward the east, I toward
the west, and Briery took the southward course.

To cover the ground thoroughly, we agreed to advance in
gradually widening zigzags, communicating with each other
at intervals by pistol shots. There could have been no
more foolish arrangement. In a quarter of an hour I had
lost my head and my bearings in a thicket. For another
quarter of an hour I discharged my revolver repeatedly,
without getting a single response from east or south. I
spent the remainder of daylight in a blundering effort to
make my way back to the place where the horses were; and
then the sun went down, leaving me in sudden darkness,
alone in a wilderness of the extent and character of which
I had not the faintest idea.

I will spare you the history of my sufferings during the
whole of that night, and the next day, and the next night,
and another day. When it was dark I wandered about in
blind despair, longing for daylight, not daring to sleep
or even to stop, and in continual terror of the unknown
dangers that surrounded me. In the daytime I longed for
night, for the sun scorched its way through the thickest
roof that the luxuriant foliage afforded, and drove me
nearly mad. The provisions in my haversack were exhausted.
My canteen was on my saddle; I should have died of thirst
had it not been for the belltop cactus, which I found

twice. But in that horrible experience neither the torture of hunger and thirst, nor the torture of heat equalled the misery of the thought that my life was to be sacrificed to the delusion of a crazy botanist, who had dreamed of the impossible.

The impossible?

On the second afternoon, still staggering aimlessly on through the jungle, I lost my last strength and fell to the ground. Despair and indifference had long since given way to an eager desire for the end. I closed my eyes with indescribable relief; the hot sun seemed pleasant on my face as consciousness departed.

Did a beautiful and gentle woman come to me while I lay unconscious, and take my head in her lap, and put her arms around me? Did she press her face to mine, and in a whisper bid me have courage? That was the belief that filled my mind when it struggled back for a moment into consciousness; I clutched at the warm, soft arms, and swooned again.

Do not look at each other and smile, gentlemen; in that cruel wilderness, in my helpless condition, I found pity and benignant tenderness. The next time my senses returned I saw that Something was bending over me—something majestic if not beautiful, humane if not human, gracious if not woman. The arms that held me and drew me up were moist, and they throbbed with the pulsation of life. There was a faint, sweet odor, like the smell of a woman's perfumed hair. The touch was a caress, the clasp an embrace.

Can I describe its form? No, not with the definiteness that would satisfy the Quakversuches and the Brierys. I saw that the trunk was massive. The branches that lifted me from the ground and held me carefully and gently were flexible and symmetrically disposed. Above my head there was a wreath of strange foliage, and in the midst of it a dazzling sphere of scarlet. The scarlet globe grew while I watched it but the effort of watching was too much for me.

The Unnatural History of Man-Eating Plants

Remember, if you please, that at this time, physical exhaustion and mental torture had brought me to the point where I passed to and fro between consciousness and unconsciousness as easily and as frequently as one fluctuates between slumber and wakefulness during a night of fever. It seemed the most natural thing in the world that in my extreme weakness I should be beloved and cared for by a cactus. I did not seek an explanation of this good fortune, or try to analyze it; I simply accepted it as a matter of course, as a child accepts a benefit from an unexpected quarter. The one idea that possessed me was that I had found an unknown friend, instinct with womanly sympathy and immeasurably kind.

And as night came on it seemed to me that the scarlet bulb overhead became enormously distended, so that it almost filled the sky. Was I gently rocked by the supple arms that still held me? Were we floating off together into the air? I did not know, or care. Now I fancied that I was in my berth on board ship, cradled by the swell of the sea; now, that I was sharing the flight of some great bird; now, that I was borne on with prodigious speed through the darkness by my own volition. The sense of incessant motion affected all my dreams. Whenever I awoke I felt a cool breeze steadily beating against my face—the first breath of air since we had landed. I was vaguely happy, gentlemen. I had surrendered all responsibility for my own fate. I had gained the protection of a being of superior powers.

IV.

"The brandy flask, Kilooa!"

It was daylight. I lay upon the ground and Briery was supporting my shoulders. In his face was a look of bewilderment that I shall never forget.

"My God!" he cried, "and how did you get here? We gave up the search two days ago."

The Balloon Tree

The brandy pulled me together. I staggered to my feet and looked around. The cause of Briery's extreme amazement was apparent at a glance. We were not in the wilderness. We were at the shore. There was the bay, and the ship at anchor, half a mile off. They were already lowering a boat to send for us.

And there to the south was a bright red spot on the horizon, hardly larger than the morning star—the Balloon Tree returning to the wilderness. I saw it, Briery saw it, the savage Kilooa saw it. We watched it till it vanished. We watched it with very different emotions, Kilooa with superstitious reverence, Briery with scientific interest and intense disappointment, I with a heart full of wonder and gratitude.

I clasped my forehead with both hands. It was no dream, then. The Tree, the caress, the embrace, the scarlet bulb, the night journey through the air, were not creations and incidents of delirium. Call it tree, or call it plant-animal—there it was! Let men of science quarrel over the question of its existence in nature; this I know: It had found me dying and had brought me more than a hundred miles straight to the ship where I belonged. Under Providence, gentlemen, that sentient and intelligent vegetable organization had saved my life.

[At this point the colonel got up and left the Club. He was very much moved. Pretty soon Briery came in, briskly as usual. He picked up an uncut copy of Lord Bragmuch's Travels in Kerguellen's Land, and settled himself in an easy chair at the corner of the fireplace.

Young Traddles timidly approached the veteran globetrotter. "Excuse me, Mr. Briery," said he, "but I should like to ask you a question about the Balloon Tree. Were there scientific reasons for believing that its sex was—"

THE BALLOON TREE -KJG

"Ah," interrupted Briery, looking bored; "the Colonel has been favoring you with that extraordinary narrative? Has he honored me again with a share in the adventure? Yes? Well, did we bag the game this time?"

"Why, no," said young Traddles. "You last saw the Tree as a scarlet spot against the horizon."

The Balloon Tree

"By Jove, another miss!" said Briery, calmly beginning to cut the leaves of his book.]

THE TITANESS

By Jules Lermina

(Buffalo Commercial Advertiser, 1885)

From Le Figaro.

...—"I sent for you," said Paula, "because you are my best friend, the friend of my childhood.... I sent for you to help me. It is now just three years since I became Frederic's wife. To my girlish fancy, that man, already spoken of as a master in science, was also a master of men—one whose will none could resist. He took possession of me with a single word; his gaze subdued me, and I felt myself helpless in the grasp of his will. But still, my weakness was proud of being able to lean upon such strength; I felt anticipation of joy in proudly submitting my own individuality to such an all-dominating force of intellect. But today, things have changed. Frederic is kind; Frederic loves me: Frederic is the very best of husbands and fathers....Yet I live in fear—fear of everything—fear of him above all else. Could I only tell you why—were I even able to tell myself why....but this growing terror, that increases more every day and every night, is unbearable, especially just because I cannot explain...."

In spite of my endeavor to preserve at least an outward aspect of skepticism, I felt myself miserably ill at ease. And, lowering my voice to a whisper, I questioned her very gently, becoming more and more alarmed by the answers received, which seemed to lend substantial form to the mysterious horror that hovered about us.

Now, this is the substance of what she told me.

During the past six months,—that is to say, since the birth of her child,—Frederic, who had always borne himself as proudly as any wrestler who feels assured of an easy triumph, had suddenly become gloomy and depressed. "What could have happened to the learned Frederic Wertheim, whose labors were already celebrated by the world's scientific academies? Of what enigma was he seeking the solution? What combat had he dared to engage in? Taciturn, be held his peace, and answered his wife's questions only by haggard glances—as though silently requesting her not to excite some painful memory that he wished to forget.

For days and nights together he remained locked up in a great conservatory, which he had had built at immense expense, in the further end of the park. Sometimes weeks would pass in succession without his entering the chateau. Or, if he came at all, it would be late at night when he entered his wife's chamber stealthily, on tip-toe.

She used to watch him when he believed her to be asleep. She saw him, sitting there on a chair, with eyes fixed in a stare, as if fascinated by some frightful vision. An expression of unutterable horror contracted all his face. His whole frame shuddered; his hands, convulsively waving, seemed striving to push back some invisible enemy.

Then (Oh! she used to watch him well at such moments!) he would rise up suddenly at last with a gesture of iron determination, of triumphant will—and flee away. Going to the window, Paula would see him running to the great hot-house, whose never-extinguished furnace glowed through the night like a beacon fire.

Frankly, boldly she had questioned him. What was always going on there in that obscure portion of the park? Why was he so persistently obstinate in refusing to permit any one to enter the conservatory? With the old shudder of horror, be repelled her from him—roughly, harshly.

Then she sought to learn the truth for herself, by dint of a courageous hypocrisy. And she soon discovered one very strange thing. Every day Frederic ordered the steward to purchase several pounds of fresh meat for him; and this meat he carried into the hot-house every evening. But not the least remnant of any of this meat was ever found in the neighborhood of the hot-house.

What was he feeding? Was it some unknown and dangerous animal, which he made it a special duty to nourish daily—some strange creature with whom he had resigned himself to live all alone in the isolation of his scientific investigations? But, again, what was the great secret struggle going on—that struggle to which his mental revolt bore witness, above all in the hours of his nocturnal solitude?

Was he becoming insane?

This last thought pierced the tortured soul of Paula like the blade of a sword of ice.

She dared not interrogate him further;—the more deeply his face became furrowed by strange anxieties, the more he kept himself away from Paula. And he wholly ceased to seek repose at home, or to enjoy the relaxation of an affectionate conversation with her, during the intervals of his exhausting studies. Only at times she caught glimpses of him wandering all alone behind the high shrubbery of the parkwalks, bareheaded, gesticulating, as though talking to himself and shaking his fists at the sky.

***

These and other strange facts Paula told me, and as she confided to me the history of her fears, I felt myself slightly reassured at last. After all, I thought this change in Frederic is only a morbid condition—nervous overexcitement provoked by excessive mental labor. I had been his boy friend, his fellow-student; afterward I had often listened to his ardent discourses, when with a marvelous audacity, he plunged deeply into the abysses of hypothesis. I knew him well; I was now a physician, and I had learned how to combat with such troubles as his with success. Accordingly I reassured Paula as best I could, and feeling confident in my eloquence, and in my privileges, I went alone into the park, in search of Frederic.

Night was approaching. But my former sense of fear had entirely passed away. I strode forward with a feeling of inexpressible pride in my mission of protection and salvation. And with each step I took in those crepuscular alleys I felt the resolve of duty growing stronger within me.

Soon I perceived the hot-house of which Paula had spoken to me. It was an immense and admirably built conservatory— a series of inter-connected pavilions of glass and iron, surmounted by rounded domes huddled close together, like the cupolas of a Turkish bathhouse. Under the last faint gleams of daylight they glimmered like sheets of steel. The mystery was within. I was almost ready to laugh at my former fears. Ought I not to have remembered the exhausting, the torturing results, of excessive scientific study?

Even as the thought came to my mind I heard quick steps behind me, and turned hastily. In the deep penumbra of the shrubbery, I saw Frederic, or rather, I divined his presence, and I advanced boldly to meet him.

—"Friend," I exclaimed, "do you not recognize me?"

He halted brusquely.

—"Frederic," I continued, "don't you know me! I hold out my hand to you, and am astonished that I do not feel yours in it."

Then, as if guided rather by the sound of my voice than by the evidence of his eyes, he bent forward, looked at me, and in hoarse, broken tones, like the crackling of a great branch too roughly bent:

—"You!—What do you want here? Begone!"

—"Ah! is this the way you receive me after so long an absence? Have you quite forgotten our old friendship?"

He seemed to hesitate—moved uneasily to and fro. I then noticed he was carrying a basket which seemed to contain something heavy.

—"I can't stop now," he said. "Let me pass."

— "Certainly," I replied, "you can pass; but you won't surely prevent me from accompanying you, so that we can have a pleasant little chat—like we used to have in the old days."

He laughed a strange, sneering laugh:-

—"You want to follow me, you!—ridiculous!"

—"On my soul, you must be hiding something in that glass palace of yours—some treasure that you are dreadfully jealous of."

With his free hand he caught me by the arm. And while I remained silent, he bent forward as if listening. I thought I could discern a strange sound—a sound like the creeping of a reptile—

—"She is waiting for me?" he cried, in a tone of ill-disguised terror; —"I must go!"—

—"Hear me a moment," I prayed—"let us go together."

Yet another instant he hesitated. Then with a resolute gesture, he cried:—

—"Well, then, come! Perhaps, after all, you might be able to protect me if—"

He did not finish the sentence. But as his hand touched mine, I felt it was cold as hardened snow.

The Titaness

Now it was he who was drawing me along.

We reached the entrance of the hot-house. He took a key from his pocket and opened the glass door. And as I advanced, gropingly, unable to distinguish anything in the gloom, he suddenly pushed me back with violence.

—"As you value your life," he whispered, "do not move."

In spite of my former confidence I felt a strange terror creeping upon me. Again I heard the queer rustling noise which had fallen upon my ears a short while before. It was a sound of slow creeping—a sound as of paper moving over a marble surface.

And all of a sudden, without my having been able to perceive how it was done, a burst of blinding light filled the conservatory—and I shrunk back against the door, clinging to its iron framework, while every hair upon my head stood upright with horror.

***

In the centre of the hall, all tapestried with fantastic plants, towered a creature, a nightmare, a hideous thing....hydra, polyp, octopus....no man could have given it a name. It squatted there, enormous and horrible, upon the soil, in a sort of immense basin filled with spongy mosses and viscous growths. It had the form of a colossal wine-skin; and from the edges of it protruded huge and innumerable arms,—at the end of each of which was a ball, a rotundity, green like a monster-eye. The body was green; the arms had a purplish tint, but as they became thinner to end in those atrocious green eyes, a sanguinolent red mingled with the green,—a ghastly green as of corpses in putrefaction.

I shut my eyes, with a weird sickening at my heart....

But I still heard that creeping sound which I spoke before; and I knew that it was the sound of all those arms being extended or contracted. And at last, surprised that I had not been seized by that Thing,—so hideous, so mighty,—I opened my eyes with a superhuman effort, and looked about me.

Frederic, lividly pale, had taken, from the basket be brought with him, a great piece of meat; and, with infinite precautions, straining himself on tiptoe lest his hand might accidentally touch those hideous tentacles, be placed the flesh upon the extremity of those moving arms.

And suddenly, as if moved by a spring, the arms contracted, carrying the piece of meat backward to other and shorter arms which I then perceived for the first time, and which belonged to an inner circle of tentacles; —and these again, seizing the meat, handed it—(I cannot use any other expression)—to other arms, still further away, until it reached the centre. Then all those arms folded themselves over the central spot to which the meat had been conveyed; and I beheld the morsel no more.

Quivering with terror, I looked at Frederic.

His brow streamed with sweat; his teeth chattered...The demoniac beast was motionless, wholly absorbed in its monstrous work of deglutition.

—"She eats!—she eats!" he cried. "The Titaness gorges herself!"

"Titaness?" I repeated with a sense of stupor.

"Ah! you know nothing!-you understand nothing!" he cried. "What!—do you not recognize her! Look! look at her well!"— she is now tamed for the moment."

And in one sudden flash of comprehension, I perceived what that creature was.....

***

It was a gigantic Drosera—it was the carnivorous plant cultivated to fabulous dimensions—a vegetable colossus—an unutterable creation...and I shrieked aloud its name!

The Titaness

"She will remain thus for an hour," said Frederic. "Ah! I know why you came to see me! They think I am mad!—no; it is false!....I mad!—I, who by a masterwork of selection, have succeeded in developing the Drosera to this awful size! Behold her—the monster! Soon she will again hold out her hungry arms to me; and I must nourish her—I must gorge her... or else...."

And he gazed about him in terror.

—"Or else?" I queried.

"Listen," he said. "I will tell you my secret. You know with what ardor I studied the discoveries of Nitschke, of Warming, of Darwin, about those strange plants which are intermediary between the animal and the vegetable—which seize insects, entrap them, clutch them, beslime them, strangle them, and slowly digest them as food ...Oh! I fully comprehend the consequences of these fantastic studies—I never doubted the truth for one single instant. I felt assured that the Drosera, the Dionæa, the Drosohyllum were neither more nor less than degenerate forms—you hear me well!—than degenerate forms of monstrous animals, whose frightful shapes lingered as traditions in the memory of primitive man,—hydras, chimeras, dragons....All these forms have existed; human imagination never created anything; but partly by reason of climacteric adaptations, of geological upheavals, these abominably hideous beings were deprived of their accustomed nourishment; and by virtue of a retrogressive atavism fell back into the condition of vegetables,— immobilized, fettered to the soil by roots, because obliged to go back to earth for their nourishment, and thus become plants. But even as plants they still preserve that longing for carnivorous nourishment, that capacity for animal nutrition, which is the only vestige of their former life...."

"Well, it was my ambition to reconstitute atrophied being; I resolved that the plant should again be transformed into the beast. Oh! how many attempts I made in vain!...but chance at last placed me in possession of an exceptionally

373

huge Drosera, and I nourished it; I impregnated it with animal juices. Little by little it developed as I had hoped—a very triumph of deduction. The hydra, the dragon, lives again!

"Look at her now, my Titaness—enormous, sublime! Behold her ferocious with a hunger which I cannot satiate...."

And at this moment he flung a new meal to a couple of enormous tentacles which were stretching toward him......

"But you do not know at all," he continued in a lower voice. "If my Titaness were hungry (I guessed the fact long ago), at this stage of force and growth which she has reached, she would wrench herself free from the root which tethers her to the soil, below the mosses in that basin.

"And then, the execrable and victorious animal would escape from here;—the monster would wander through the land, trailing her viscous enormity over the plain;—and what is now the masterwork of my life would become my crime....And I should be accursed forever.

"She must never escape; I have resolved she shall remain in prison; and I am ever on the watch, fearful lest she might get hungry. Let me delay but a few seconds,—let me arrive only a few minutes too late; and I know that she would break forth and traverse the world tike a monstrous octopus—devouring, destroying—threatening my wife, my child!

"Let her eat!—let her eat! She *must* eat enormously in order that the desire to escape shall not come upon her."

And again I saw him drop whole quarters of meat. And through the fibres of the atrocious plant I could perceive the purple flow of blood digested in torrents.

***

Even at that instant, as I stood speechless, crushed by the intensity of my repulsion, the door of the conservatory, which I had imperfectly closed, suddenly opened.

The Titaness

And Paula appeared!

Her courage had proven stronger than her fear. Knowing that I was there, she had presumed to violate the secret of the hot-house.

—"Frederic!" she screamed.

But a horrible cry responded to her appeal.

In a thoughtless backward movement, totally unconscious of his danger, Frederick had inadvertently laid his hand upon the tentacles of the Titaness.

And with ghastly quickness, all the hideous trunks of the monster had flung themselves upon that hand—seizing the wrist, drawing in the forearm....

Horror!—I saw him caught by the irresistible suction;—I flung my arms around his body,—I strove with might and main to tear him from the frightful embrace of the Titaness....but the nameless creature was stronger than I...

My eyes fell upon an ax lying near me on the ground....

"Strike at the foot—at the root!" I screamed to Paula, "—strike!—hew!—cut it through!"

I never knew whether she understood my words, but she obeyed them. Weak woman though she was, she used the steel weapon well, and struck so true that she severed the root of the plant below the mosses. The horrible thing seemed to make a supreme effort to rise up—to fling itself upon us; and then, suddenly becoming powerless, it sank down heavily with a sound as of wet linen dropped on the ground. Simultaneously, the tenacles loosened their grip, and I tore my poor friend from them.

And I saw—(oh! hideous sight!)—that his hand and wrist were only a bloody pulp.

Paula had caught him in her arms.

The Unnatural History of Man-Eating Plants

He opened his eyes in a last spasm, fixed them upon me, and uttered only these words:

"Assassin!—you have murdered the Titaness!"

And be fell back—dead!

***

I cared for Paula like a brother, and I adopted the child.

THE TITANESS -KJG

CARNIVORINE

By Lucy H. Hooper

(Peterson's Magazine, 1889)

WHEN I, Ellis Graham, being a man of middle age, means, and leisure, determined upon starting, last autumn, for Rome, with a view to studying up the localities for my projected history of the Cenci family, I never expected assuredly that a momentous and important task, regarding other people's affairs and not my own, should be imposed upon me. Yet I could not well refuse the mission. I had known the Lambert family for many years, and had always cherished a warm friendship for Mr. and Mrs. Lambert—a friendship which, after the demise of the former, I had continued to his widow. And Julius, the elder son, had been quite a favorite of mine in his boyish days, though I could not altogether sympathize with his craze for scientific pursuits, and especially for botany. It must be confessed, however, that his researches into the formation and functions of the vegetable kingdom had led to some curious discoveries. But these discoveries had only served to arouse in his mind, as he grew to manhood, a wild ambition for further successes in the same line. I never exactly comprehended what course his investigations had taken, but I knew he was deeply interested in the Darwinian theories, and had set himself, in that connection, some inscrutable problem that he was trying to make out. He lived such a secluded life, shut up with his plants and his theories, that I had wholly lost sight of him for some years, though my visits to Mrs. Lambert were still continued.

I was a good deal surprised, however, on the eve of my departure for Europe, to receive from my old friend a few hurried lines, begging that I would call to see her before I left and fixing the very next evening for my visit. I responded to the appeal, and found the usually serene and dignified lady in a state of unwonted emotion.

"I have sent for you, dear Mr. Graham," she said, "to ask if you will undertake for me a very important mission. It is hardly right, I know, for me to make such a request of you, involving, as your consent will surely do, a good deal of trouble and the loss of a considerable portion of your time. But my peace of mind is at stake, and I do not know what else to do if you are not willing to help me."

"Anything that is in my power to execute, dear Mrs. Lambert, I will gladly undertake," I answered. And, indeed, I was so much moved by her distress and by noticing the traces left upon her still fair features by wearing anxiety, that I was ready to promise anything or to undertake anything in her behalf.

"I want you to find Julius for me."

"Julius? Is he absent from home? I did not even know that he had gone away."

"Yes; he sailed for Europe three years ago. You know, his uncle left him a handsome fortune a little before that time, and he went abroad—to pursue, as he stated, his scientific experiments. I know that he believed himself to be on the verge of a great discovery; but, of what nature that discovery was, he never would reveal, even to me. As you may remember, I have never sympathized with him in his studies, so I suppose he did not consider me worthy of his confidence. Perhaps I did wrong. Maybe, if I had interested myself more in his pursuits, he would not have left me as he has done. He told me, before he went away, that his experiments must be perfected in thorough seclusion, and that he never meant to relinquish them till he had arrived at some great result. We heard from him, afterward, at Paris, and, later on, at Milan; but he has not written to his brothers or to me for months."

"Have you no idea as to his whereabouts at present?"

"I have reason to think that he has taken up his abode somewhere in the neighborhood of Rome. He was seen there two winters ago, by Alan Spencer, the artist—who had quite a talk with him, but who could find out nothing from him respecting his residence or his pursuits."

"Did he seem well?"

"He looked tired and haggard, Mr. Spencer said, but was otherwise well. The reason for my anxiety is—is—well, I may as well confess it to you at once: I fear that there is some entanglement in the case—a passion for some woman, who may entrap Julius into matrimony."

"And have you any foundation for this dread?"

"Only this: he let fall something to Mr. Spencer about a personage called Carnivorine."

"What an extraordinary name! Did he give his friend any information concerning her?"

"No. He was singularly reticent on the subject, and seemed really distressed at having let even her name slip out unawares. He requested Mr. Spencer never to mention it; but Alan has always been on very intimate terms with Richard and Maude, and, seeing how uneasy we were at Julius's long silence, he did not hesitate, not having made any promise of secrecy, to tell us the little that he knew. So, when you reach Rome, if you will try to find our lost Julius for us, I shall be more indebted to you than I can well tell you."

I promised to do my best, and Mrs. Lambert, visibly relieved, added some details about her son's banker in Rome and also respecting the few persons that he knew in that city, and who might have learned something concerning him during the last few months. Also, she gave me the name and address of the herbalist before whose door—and, indeed, issuing from it—Alan Spencer had met Julius in such an unexpected fashion.

"You will write to me as soon as you have any news," she said, wistfully, to me, at parting. "And, above all, let me know everything you can find out about Carnivorine. Do not hesitate to tell me the worst—even if Julius has married this creature with the singular name."

"I must confess that, when I first arrived in Rome, so many personal interests claimed me that I did not at once begin my search for Julius Lambert, as I had intended to do. There were so many of my old friends and old haunts to revisit, and such numbers of new and interesting statues in the studios of the Roman sculptors, both native and foreign, to go to see, and my negotiations with the artists who were to execute the illustrations for my history of the Cenci family took up so much time, that the weeks insensibly slipped away before I had taken any steps in the matter. I had had the time to receive more than one letter from Mrs. Lambert on the subject before I commenced my investigations. I must acknowledge that I had come to the conclusion that the mystery, on investigation, would prove to be no mystery at all, and that Julius would be discovered in one of the minor hotels in Rome—too busy, or perhaps too much in love, to write. But, when I did finally set out in search of him, I found myself baffled at the very outset by an impenetrable wall of mystery. Nobody had seen him, and nobody knew anything about him. He had drawn all his funds from the banker's on his first arrival in the city. He had been in Rome some two years before, and had bought a collection of the curious insect-eating plants of South America from the old herbalist at whose door Alan Spencer had met him. That was all. If the earth had opened beneath his feet and had swallowed him up, he could not have vanished more utterly from human ken. I sought for him in every direction. I employed the services of a private detective. I offered a reward for any news of him. All was of no use. I succeeded in

Carnivorine

learning that he had not left Rome—and that was all I could find out.

Some months had elapsed, and I had pretty much abandoned the search in despair, when one day the fancy took me to go on a ride on horseback over the Campagna. I had long cherished the desire to explore the less frequented and scarcely known districts of that vast region, haunted by malaria and tenanted only by a few fever-stricken shepherds, that lies outside the beaten track of tourists and travelers beyond the city walls. As may be imagined, I found my excursion rather dreary. I rode on and on, passing now a flock of sheep watched over by a brigand-looking guardian and a fierce rough dog that looked ready, at a word or a sign from his master, to tear down my horse and throttle its rider, and then some huge arch of a ruined aqueduct that in the days of classic Rome had been musical with laughing water. Sometimes I came upon the shattered fragments of an abandoned hovel, or met with a herd of the gray-coated long-horned oxen of the region, beautiful placid-looking creatures, that gazed at me inquiringly out of their large soft eyes as I rode by, as though saying What is this stranger doing in this home of solitude and ruin? Still, I was interested by the very novelty of the dreary region, and I rode on and on, till the sun began to sink toward the western horizon. I have always considered myself fever-proof, but, all the same, a ride after sunset over the Campagna is not the healthiest experiment in the world, so I wheeled my horse round and started to return to the city. And, as I did so, I became aware of the existence of a house at a very short distance. I might very well have passed it without noticing it, as it was so embowered in a mass of vegetation, vines, and bushes, as well as trees, that its shape and architecture were barely discernible. As I rode nearer, I saw that it was a modern villa of imposing dimensions, which had been suffered to fall into almost total ruin. Whether the freak of a speculator or the wild idea of some Campagna proprietor had caused the erection, in this lonely unhealthy place, of a costly country residence, there was no evidence to reveal. The grounds, once spacious and well laid out, were overrun with a thick undergrowth of plants and grasses. Here and there, a statue in white marble, streaked with damp and green with mold, showed under the shadow of the trees, and one, a graceful figure of a nymph, overthrown from its pedestal, lay prostrate amongst the rank grass. The façade of the house itself was adorned with moss-grown sculptures, and one of the pillars supporting the doorway had been broken away and its place was supplied by the trunk of a cypress. One-half of the building showed deserted and ruinous with its broken windows and decaying roof. But there were traces elsewhere of human habitation. The roof of the right wing had been mended, the windows were in good condition, and a gleam of firelight from the lower rooms gave a cheery aspect to that part of the edifice. And, oddly enough, in spite of the universal decay and dilapidation, there were traces not only of comfort, but of luxury, in one portion of the premises, which I noticed as I drew near. This was a large conservatory adjoining the inhabited portion of the house. It was in perfect order. Not a pane was missing in its glazed walls, through which I could discern the red glare of the stove-fires within, as well as the dull green of the foliage of the plants.

Both I and my horse were weary, so I decided that I would halt for an hour or so at this singular habitation, and try for a feed of oats for my horse, as well as for a flask of Chianti and crust of bread for myself. I drew rein at the dilapidated doorway, and, just as I was about to announce my presence by a resounding knock from the butt-end of my riding-whip, the door was suddenly opened and a man came hurriedly forth. He started when he saw me, and was about to retreat into the house; but, by the red light of the waning sunset, I discerned his features and recognized him instantly. It was the man I had so long sought for and in vain—it was Julius Lambert.

Carnivorine

"Julius!" I cried, as he was about to vanish through the doorway. "Julius Lambert! Is it thus that you treat an old friend who has come so far to visit you?"

He turned back at the sound of my voice. "So it is really you, Mr. Graham," he said hesitatingly. "How in the world did you ever find me or the Villa Anzieri? Nobody has come near it or me either, for over two years past. But come in—my man shall take charge of your horse—and you can tell me something about home matters."

I willingly relinquished the charge of my wearied steed to the black-eyed, bronze-complexioned, picturesque-looking young fellow who came in answer to his master's call, and I followed Julius into the house. I could hardly believe my senses, or that I had found my missing friend at last. It had all happened so simply and yet so strangely. Meanwhile Julius, after he had gotten over the first shock of my intrusion, seemed really glad to see me. He piled fresh wood on the fire, and gave orders that dinner should be served as soon as possible, and plied me with questions respecting his mother and his brother and sisters. As for himself, I found him looking far from well. He was never very stout, but he had grown lean and emaciated, and the yellowish pallor of his face gave evidence of the effects that the malaria of the Campagna had on his system. Dinner was served at last—a very palatable stew flavored with red peppers and tomatoes, with the accompaniment of some fine oranges and grapes by way of dessert, and a flask or two of Chianti wine and one of the delicate Civita Lavinia. Throughout the repast, I noticed with pain that Julius talked in a feverish incoherent way, pressing me to eat or to drink, and hurrying questions and remarks about home matters, half the time without waiting for an answer.

At last, pushing my plate aside, I remarked:

"Now, Julius, I have told you everything that you wished to know. It is my turn now to ask for a little information. What have you been doing all this long time in this solitude?"

The Unnatural History of Man-Eating Plants

He moved uneasily in his chair, and his wandering glance avoided mine.

"Nothing," he muttered—"I have done—I am doing—nothing."

"Nonsense! You cannot persuade me of the truth of that assertion, so ardent and experimentalist as you have always been, and so interested in the cause of science. Confess, now—have you not made, or are you not on the verge of perfecting, some great discovery?"

I had touched the right chord. His eyes flashed, and his whole countenance grew bright with animation.

"Yes!" he cried. "I have succeeded at last in my researches. For years I have tried to perfect a demonstration of the link between the vegetable and the animal kingdom. If you have come to scoff at my discoveries, go—go at once! Otherwise, follow me—and be prepared for full conviction as to the truth of what I have said."

He rose as he spoke, and, taking me by the hand, he led me to a door at the extremity of the large room in which we had dined. This door he unlocked with a key which he took from his pocket. Night had closed in, and he completed his preparations by lighting a great torch of pine-branches.

"Wait on the threshold, as you value your life," he said to me impressively. Then he threw open the door.

It was the entrance to the conservatory. The first thing that struck me was a sort of faint rustling sound like that of a trailing garment or sweeping bird's-wing. Then, by the light of the torch with which Julius held on high, I discerned, in the centre of the room, a vast tub filled with masses of spongy moss, from which rose a strange plant—a hideous shapeless monster: a sort of vegetable hydra—or, rather, octopus—gigantic in size and repulsive in aspect and in coloring. So immense were its proportions, that it filled by itself the whole space of the conservatory. It consisted of a central bladder-shaped trunk or core, from which sprang countless branches—or, rather, arms—thick, leafless, of a livid green, and streaked with blotches of a dull-crimson. Each arm terminated in an oval protuberance, which had a resemblance to the human eye. Julius took, from a basket that stood near the door, a great slice of raw meat, and, fastening it to the end of a stick, he advanced it, taking infinite precautions to keep well out of reach within the circle of outstretched branches. Then I saw these great tentacle-like arms fold around their prey, which they transmitted to the central core; and then, closing around it, I saw it no more. It was the slow motion of the branches that had caused the rustling sound which had amazed me on my first entrance.

So repulsive was the aspect of this enormous creature, half plant and half animal, that I was glad to beat a retreat to the dining-room. Julius followed, flushed and elated at the healthful aspect of his monstrous creation.

"The plant you have just seen," he said, "is a Drosera, which, by dint of careful selection and persevering attention, I have developed into this unheard-of size. I have just studied the discoveries of Warming and of Darwin concerning those strange plants, the Drosera and the Dionœa—which, though still vegetables, feed on the insects that they kill. It has been my desire for years to perfect the missing link and to develop the animal side of these curious vegetable natures. It has always been my theory that the hydra, the dragon, and other monstrous forms of animal life really did exist, and that, in the evolution of ages and by reason of geological changes on the surface of the earth, these creatures, deprived of their accustomed forms of nourishment, degenerated into trees and plants and took root in the earth. Some of them still preserve their primitive forms, as witness the dragon-tree of Java. It has been my aim and endeavor to resuscitate the animal in the plant. Chance threw in my way a Drosera of great size. I have fed it on animal food for years, and developed it into something that is not yet a dragon or a hydra, but which is surely something more than a plant.

Had you ventured within reach of its branches, the grasp of a boa would not have been more swift or more deadly."

"And what further do you propose doing with your dreadful plant?"

"My aim now is to give it locomotion—to see it detach itself from the soil and go forth in search of prey."

"How can you contemplate the possibility of letting lose such a monster on the world?"

"For science, there is no such thing as a monster. Moreover, are there not crocodiles and anacondas and tigers upon earth, to say nothing of the shark and the octopus? Beside these, my creation—my Carnivorine—is a harmless creature."

I started as I heard the name. So this, then, was the object of my poor friend's affections—this ghastly shape, not yet wholly animal, yet scarcely vegetable, with the form of a plant and the appetites of a beast of prey?

Just then, Pietro, the man-servant, came in to announce that my horse was at the door. It was a beautiful moonlight night, promising a pleasant ride to the city. I took my leave of Julius, therefore, with something of the feeling of relief of a man who awakes from sleep after having been oppressed by a terrible nightmare. But I did not depart without leaving my address, and I begged Julius to let me know if his strange discovery took any new developments in the near future.

Weeks passed away, and I had nearly forgotten all about Julius and Carnivorine, when one day I received a letter from him, written in a strain of great exultation and excitement. "Come to me, dear friend," he wrote; "come at once! The hour of the perfecting of my experiment is at hand. Already, amid the masses that surround Carnivorine, I discern the stirring and striving of the roots, that are acquiring powers of independent locomotion. In a few days, the problem will be solved. I want you to be present as a witness of the phenomenon. My ambition is satisfied at

Carnivorine

CARNIVORINE -KJG

last—my name shall be inscribed on the list of the great discoverers of the world of science. Come to me, and be at my side in the moment of my triumph."

It was not without difficulty that I once more made my way to the Villa Anzieri. It was late in the afternoon when I drew rein at the dilapidated doorway that I remembered so well. I knocked loudly at the door, but there was no response to my call. Looking around, I saw that the whole place wore an inexplicable air of desertion. No firelight was visible at the windows, and the red glare of the stove-fire no longer shone behind the dim panes of the hot-house. Finally, in vague alarm, finding that my shouts and knocking produced no response, I tied my horse to one of the door-posts, and, singling out a window of the large room in which we had dined on the occasion of my former visit, I swung myself up to it by the help of a thick stem of ivy, and peered into the room. The sight that I beheld within froze my soul with horror.

At the end of the room, near the entrance to the conservatory, rose the hideous form of Carnivorine, no longer planted in a tub, but supported on what seemed, to me, a pair of paddle-like feet or paws like those of some misshapen and antediluvian animal. The powerful branches—or, rather, tentacles—were upraised and closely folded around some central object. And at the summit of these livid green, closely-pressed, serpent-like stems appeared a ghastly object: it was a livid human head—the head of a corpse—and the pallid features were those of Julius Lambert!

With one stroke of my arm, I burst open the casement. I sprang into the room and hastened toward the dreadful object. The long arms quivered and began to unfold themselves. But, before the creature could put itself in motion, a shot from the revolver that I always carried during my Campagna wanderings pierced its central core. The tentacles fell apart, and the hideous plant sank prone upon the ground, bearing with it, in its fall, the crushed and lifeless form of Julius Lambert. A stream of reddish

Carnivorine

sap that looked like blood flowed from the shattered stem and mingled with the branches, stained as they were with a ruddier crimson—the life-blood of my unhappy friend.

I never discovered how or when the catastrophe took place. From the condition of the body, death must have taken place at least twentyfour hours before my arrival. The servants, brought face to face with such a shocking—and, to them, inexplicable—catastrophe, had fled from the house, taking with them whatever money or valuables they could lay their hands upon. I tried to trace them out, but in vain. As to the rest, it was all mere conjecture on my part. The uptorn earth and mosses in the tub in which Carnivorine had originally found an abode seemed to prove that a sudden development of the long-sought-for powers of locomotion in the creature had unexpectedly taken place, and that Julius had been seized either in the act of inspecting its condition or at the moment of offering it food. At all events, the vegetable-animal or animal-vegetable had made a solitary trial of its newly-formed powers, and had found a solitary prey when the bullet from my pistol put an end to its existence.

Among the papers left behind by Julius was a series of memoranda, respecting the experiments he had tried and the processes he had used to bring his dread creation to full perfection. These I destroyed without hesitation. It would not have been well to have suffered the race of the vegetable octopus to be extended and propagated by curious scientists in the future. Then, lest a new growth should spring from the stem or branches of the accursed tree, I hewed them to pieces with my own hand and burned the fragments to ashes. The annihilation of my friend's discovery may be a loss to science, but humanity will only have cause to rejoice in the total destruction of CARNVORINE.

AN ARIZONA TRAGEDY

By Arthur Conan Doyle

(St. Louis Post-Dispatch, 1893)

Illustrations from March 28, 1926 Dimanche-Illustre.

STRANGE DEATH OF JOE HAWKINS, FOR WHICH SCOTT NARROWLY
ESCAPED LYNCHING.

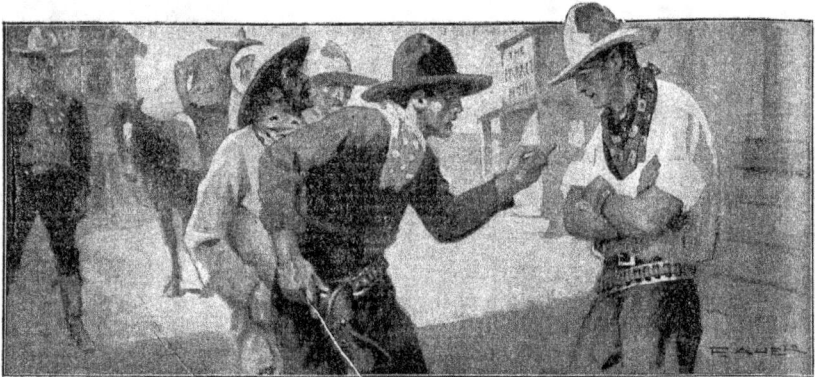

"It air strange, it air," he was saying as I opened the
door of the room where our social little semi-literary
society met; "but I could tell you queerer things than
that 'ere—almighty queer things. You can't learn
everything out of books, sir, nohow. You see it ain't the
men as can string English together and as has had good
eddications as finds themselves in the queer places I've
been in. They're mostly rough men, sirs, as can scarce
speak aright, far less tell with pen and ink the things
they've seen; but if they could they'd make some of your

An Arizona Tragedy

European's har riz with astonishment. They would sirs, you bet!"

His name was Jefferson Adams, I believe; I know his initials were J. A., for you may see them yet deeply whittled on the right hand upper panel of our smoking-room door. He left us this legacy, and also some artistic patterns done in tobacco juice upon our Turkey carpet; but beyond these reminiscences our American story-teller has vanished from our ken. He gleamed across our ordinary quiet conviviality like some brilliant meteor, and then was lost in the outer darkness. That night, however, our New Mexican friend was in full swing, and I quietly lit my pipe and dropped into the nearest chair, anxious not to interrupt his story.

"Mind you," he continued, "I hain't got no grudge against your men of science. I likes and respects a chap as can match every beast and plant, from a huckleberry to a grizzly with a jaw-breakin' name; but if you wants real interestin' facts, something a bit juicy, you go to your whalers and your frontiersmen, and your scouts and Hudson Bay men, chaps who mostly can scarce sign their names."

There was a pause here, as Mr. Jefferson Adams produced a long cheroot and lit it. We preserved a strict silence in the room, for we had already learned that on the slightest interruption our Yankee drew himself into his shell again. He glanced round with a self-satisfied smile as he remarked our expectant looks, and continued through a halo of smoke.

"Now, which of you, gentlemen, has even been in Arizona? None, I'll warrant. And of all English or Americans as can put pen to paper, how many have been to Arizona? Precious few, I calc'late. I've been there, sirs, lived there for years, and when I think what I've seen there, why, I can scarce get myself to believe it now.

"Ah, there's the country! I was one of Walker's filibusters, as they chose to call us, and after we'd busted up and the chief was shot, some on us made tracks and located down there. A reg'lar English and American colony, we was with our wives and children, and all complete. I reckon there's some of the old folk there yet, and that they hain't forgotten what I'm agoin' to tell you. No. I warrant they hain't, never on this side of the grave, sirs.

"I was talking about the country, though, and I guess I could astonish you considerable if I spoke of nothing else. To think of such a land being built for a few 'Greasers' and half-breeds! It's a misusing of the gifts of Providence, that's what I calls it. Grass as hung over a chap's head as he rode through it, and trees so thick that you couldn't catch a glimpse of blue sky for leagues and leagues, and orchids like umbrellas! Maybe some on you has seen a plant as they calls the 'fly-catcher' in some parts of the States?"

"Diancea muscipula," murmured Dawson, our scientific man par excellence.

"Ah, 'Die near a municipal,' that's him! You'll see a fly stand on that 'ere plant, and then you'll see the two sides of a leaf snap up together and catch it between them, and grind it up and mash it to bits, for all the world like some great sea squid with its beak; and hours after, if you open the leaf, you'll see the body lying half digested, and in bits. Well, I've seen those fly-traps in Arizona with leaves eight and ten feet long, and thorns or teeth a foot or more; why, they could—But darn it, I'm going too fast!

"It's about the death of Joe Hawkins I was going to tell you; 'bout as queer a thing, I reckon, as ever you heard tell on. There wasn't nobody in Arizona or New Mexico as didn't know of Joe Hawkins—'Alabama' Joe, as he was called there. A reg'lar out and outer, he was, 'bout the hardest case as ever man clapt eyes on. He was good chap enough, mind ye, as long as you stroked him the right way; but rile him anyhow, and he were worse nor a blizzard. I've seen him empty his six-shooter into a crowd as chanced to jostle him agoing into Simpson's bar when there was a dance on; and he bowied Tom Hooper 'cause he spilt his liquor over his weskit by mistake. No, he didn't stick at murder, Joe didn't; and he weren't a man to be trusted when he had the devil's drops in him.

"Now at the time I tell on, when Joe Hawkins was swaggerin' about the town and layin' down bye laws with his shootin'-irons, there was an Englishman there of the name of Scott—Tom Scott, if I rec'lects aright. This chap Scott was a Britisher to his boot heels, and yet he didn't freeze much to the British set there, or they didn't freeze much to him. He was a quiet simple man, Scott was— rather too quiet for a rough lot like that; sneakin', they called him, but he weren't that. He kept hisself mostly apart, an' didn't interfere with nobody so long as he were left alone. Some said as how he'd been kinder ill-treated at home—been a Chartist, or something combustible, and had to up and git; but he never spoke of it hisself, an' never complained. Bad luck or good, that man kept a stiff lip on him.

"This Scott was a sort o'butt among the men about Arizona, for he was so quiet an' simple-like. There was no party either to take up his grievances, for, as I've been saying, the Britishers hardly counted him one of them, and many a rough joke they played on him. He never cut up rough, but was civil to all hisself. I think the boys got to think he hadn't much grit in him till he showed 'em their mistake.

"It was in Simpson's bar as the row got up, an' that led to the queer thing I was going to tell you of. Alabama Joe and one or two other rowdies were dead on the Britishers in those days, and they spoke their opinions pretty free, though I warned them as there'd be an almighty muss. That partic'lar night Joe was fighting-drunk, and he swaggered about the town with his six-shooter, lookin' for a chance. Then he turned into the bar where he know'd he'd find some o' the English as ready as he was hisself. Sure enough, there was half a dozen lounging about, an' Tom Scott standin' alone before the stove. Joe sat down by the table, and put his revolver and bowie down in front of him. 'Them's my argiments, Jeff,' he says to me, 'if any white-livered Britisher dares give me the lie.' I tried to stop him, sirs; but he weren't a man as you could easily turn, an' he began to speak in a way as no chap could stand. Why, even a 'Greaser' would flare up if you said as much of Greaserland! There was a commotion at the bar, an' every man laid his hands on his wepins; but afore they could draw we heard a quiet voice from the stove: 'Say your prayers, Joe Hawkins, for you're a dead man!' Joe turned round, and looked like grabbin' at his iron; but it waren't no manner of use. Tom Scott was standing up, covering him with his derringer; a smile on his white face, but the very devil shining in his eye. 'It ain't that the old country has used me over-well,' he says, 'but no man shall insult it afore me, and live.' For a second his finger tightened round the trigger, an' then he gave a laugh an' threw the pistol on the floor. 'No,' he says, 'I can't shoot a half-drunk man. Take your dirty life, Joe, and use it better nor you have done.' He swung contemptuously around, and relit his half-smoked pipe from the stove; while Alabama slunk out o' the bar, with the laughs of the Britishers ringing in his ears. I saw his face as he passed me, and on it I saw murder, sirs—murder, as plain as ever I seed anything in my life.

"I stayed in the bar after the row and watched Tom Scott as he shook hands with the men about. It seemed kinder queer to me to see him smilin' and cheerful-like, for I knew Joe's bloodthirsty mind, and that the Englishman had small chance of ever seeing the morning. He lived in an out-of-the-way sort of place, you see, clean off the trail, and had to pass through the Flytrap Gulch to get to it. This here gulch was a marshy, gloomy place, lonely enough during the day even; for it were always a creepy sort o' thing to see the great eight and ten-foot leaves snapping up if aught touched them; but at night there was never a soul near. Some parts of the marsh, too, were soft and deep, and a body thrown in would be gone by morning. I could see Alabama Joe crouchin' under the leaves of the great Flytrap in the darkest part of the gulch, with a scowl on his face and a revolver in his hand; I could see it, sirs, as plain as with my two eyes.

"'Bout midnight Simpson shuts up his bar, so out we had to go. Tom Scott started off for his three-mile walk at a slashing pace. I just dropped him a hint as he passed me, for I kinder liked the chap. 'Keep your derringer there or about it,' I says, 'for you might chance to need it.' He looked around at me with his quiet smile, and then I lost sight of him in the gloom. I never thought to see him again. He'd hardly gone afore Simpson comes up to me and says, 'There'll be old hell in the Flytrap Gulch to-night, Jeff; the boys say that Hawkins started half an hour ago to wait for Scott and shoot him on sight. I calc'late the coroner 'll be wanted to-morrow.'

"What passed in the gulch that night? It were a question as were asked pretty free next morning. A half-breed was in Ferguson's store after daybreak, and he said as he'd chanced to be near the gulch 'bout 1 in the morning. It warn't easy to get at his story, he seemed so uncommon scared, but he told us at last, as he'd heard the fearfulest screams in the stillness of the night. There weren't no shots, he said, but screams after screams, kinder muffled, like a man with a serape over his head, an' in immortal pain. Abner Brandon and me, and a few more, was in the store at the time; so we mounted and rode out to Scott's house, passing through the gulch on the way. There weren't nothing partic'lar to be seen there—no blood nor marks of a fight, nor nothing; and when we gets up to Scott's house, out he comes to meet us as fresh as a lark. 'Hullo, Jeff!' says he, 'no need for the pistols, after all. Come in an' have a cocktail, boys.' 'Did ye see or hear nothing as ye come home last night?' says I. 'No,' says he; 'all was quiet enough. An owl kinder moaning in the Flytrap Gulch—that was all. Come, jump off and have a glass.' 'Thank ye,' says Abner. So off we gets, and Tom Scott rode into the settlement with us when we went back.

"An allfired commotion was on in Main street as we rode
into it. The 'Merican party seemed to have gone clean
crazed. Alabama Joe was gone, not a darned particle of him
left. Since he went out to the gulch nary eye had seen
him. As we got off our horses there was a considerable
crowd in front of Simpson's, and some ugly looks at Tom
Scott, I can tell you. There was a clinkin' of pistols,
and I saw as Scott had his hand in his bosom too. There
weren't a single English face about.' 'Stand aside, Jeff
Adams,' says Zebb Humphrey, as great a scoundrel as ever
lived, 'you ain't got no hand in this game. Say, boys, are
we, free Americans, to be murdered by this sort o' scum?'
It was the quickest thing as ever I seed. There was a rush
an' a crack; Zebb was down, with Scott's ball in his
thigh, and Scott himself was on the ground with a dozen
men holding him. It weren't no use struggling, so he lay
quiet. They seemed a bit uncertain what to do with him at
first, but then one of Alabama's special chums put them up
to it. 'Joe's gone,' he said; 'nothing ain't surer nor
that, an' there lies the man as killed him. Some on you
knows as Joe went on business to the gulch last night; he
never came back. That 'ere Britisher passed through after
he'd gone; they'd a row, screams is heard 'mong the great
flytraps. I say agin he has played poor Joe some o' his
sneakin' tricks, an thrown him into the swamp. It ain't no
wonder as the body is gone. But air we to stan' by and see
English murderin' our own chums? I guess not. Let Jedge
Lynch try him, that's what I say.' 'Lynch him!' shouted a
hundred angry voices—for all the rag-tag an' bobtail o'
the settlement was 'round us by this time. Here, boys,
fetch a rope and swing him up. Up with him over Simpson's
door!" 'See here, though,' says another, coming forrards;
'let's hang him by the great flytrap in the gulch. Let Joe
see as he's revenged, if so be as he's buried 'bout
theer.' There was a shout for this, an' away they went,
with Scott tied on his mustang in the middle, and a
mounted guard, with cocked revolvers round him; for we
knew as there was a score or so Britishers about, as did't
seem to know any Jedge of that partic'lar name.

An Arizona Tragedy

"I went out with them, my heart bleedin' for Scott, though he didn't seem a cent put out, he didn't. He were game to the backbone. Seems kinder queer, sirs, hangin' a man to a flytrap, but our'n were a reg'lar tree, and the leaves like a brace of boats with a hinge between 'em and thorns at the bottom.

"We passed down the gulch to the place where the great one grows, and there we seed it with the leaves, some open, some shut. But we seed something worse nor that. Standin' round the tree was some twenty men, Britishers all, an' armed to the teeth. They were waiting for us evidently, an' had a business-like look about 'em, as if they'd come for something and meant to have it. There was the raw material there for about as warm a scrimmage as ever I seed.

"As we rode up, a great red-bearded Scotchman—Cameron were his name—stood out afore the rest, his revolver cocked in his hand. 'See here, boys,' he says, 'you've got no call to hurt a hair of that man's head. You hain't proved as Joe is dead yet; and if you had, you hain't proved as Scott killed him. Anyhow, it were in self-defense; for you all know as he was lying in wait for Scott, to shoot him on sight; so I say agin, you hain't got no call to hurt that man; and what's more, I've got twenty six-barreled arguments against your doin' it.' 'It's an interesting pint, and worth arguin' out,' said the man as was Alabamas Joe's special chum. There was a clickin' of pistols, and a loosenin' of knives, and the two parties began to draw up to one another, an' it looked like a rise in the mortality of Arizona. Scott was standing behind with a pistol at his ear if he stirred, lookin' quiet and composed as having no money on the table, when sudden he gives a start an' a shout as rang in our ears like a trumpet. 'Joe!' he cried, 'Joe! Look at him. In the fly-trap!' We all turned an' looked where he was pointin'. Jerusalem! I think we won't get that picter out of our minds ag'in. One of the great leaves of the fly-trap, that had been shut and touching the ground as it lay, was slowly rolling back upon its hinges. There, laying like an oyster in its shell, was

Alabama Joe in the hollow of the leaf. The great thorns
had been slowly driven through his heart as it shut upon
him. We could see as he'd tried to cut his way out, for
there was a slit in the thick fleshy leaf, an' his bowie
was in his hand, but it had smothered him first. He'd lain
down on it likely to keep the damp off while he were
awaitin' for Scott, and it had closed on him as you've
seen your little hot-house ones do on a fly; and there he
were as we found him, torn and mashed, and crushed into
pulp by the great jagged teeth of the man-eatin' plant.
There, sirs, I think you'll own that as a curious story."

An Arizona Tragedy

"And what became of Scott?" asked Jack Sinclair.

"Why we carried him back on our shoulders, we did, to Simpson's bar, and he stood us liquors round. Made a speech too—a darned fine speech—from the counter. Somethin' about the British lion an' the 'Merican eagle walkin' arm in arm for ever an' a day. And now, sirs, that yarn was long, and my cheroot's out, so I reckon I'll make tracks afore it's later;" and with a "Good-night!" he left the room.

"A most extraordinary narrative!" said Dawson. "Who would have thought a Diancea had such power!"

"Deuced rum yarn!" said young Sinclair.

"Evidently a matter-of-fact, truthful man," said the doctor.

"Or the most original liar that ever lived," said I.

I wonder which he was.

THE FLOWERING OF THE STRANGE ORCHID

By H. G. Wells

(The Stolen Bacillus, 1894)

The buying of orchids always has in it a certain speculative flavour. You have before you the brown shrivelled lump of tissue, and for the rest you must trust your judgment, or the auctioneer, or your good-luck, as your taste may incline. The plant may be moribund or dead, or it may be just a respectable purchase, fair value for your money, or perhaps—for the thing has happened again and again—there slowly unfolds before the delighted eyes of the happy purchaser, day after day, some new variety, some novel richness, a strange twist of the labellum, or some subtler colouration or unexpected mimicry. Pride, beauty, and profit blossom together on one delicate green spike, and, it may be, even immortality. For the new miracle of Nature may stand in need of a new specific name, and what so convenient as that of its discoverer? "Johnsmithia"! There have been worse names.

It was perhaps the hope of some such happy discovery that made Winter Wedderburn such a frequent attendant at these sales—that hope, and also, maybe, the fact that he had nothing else of the slightest interest to do in the world. He was a shy, lonely, rather ineffectual man, provided with just enough income to keep off the spur of necessity, and not enough nervous energy to make him seek any exacting employments. He might have collected stamps or coins, or translated Horace, or bound books, or invented new species of diatoms. But, as it happened, he grew orchids, and had one ambitious little hothouse.

"I have a fancy," he said over his coffee, "that something is going to happen to me to-day." He spoke—as he moved and thought—slowly.

"Oh, don't say *that!*" said his housekeeper—who was also his remote cousin. For "something happening" was a euphemism that meant only one thing to her.

"You misunderstand me. I mean nothing unpleasant...though what I do mean I scarcely know.

"To-day," he continued, after a pause, "Peters' are going to sell a batch of plants from the Andamans and the Indies. I shall go up and see what they have. It may be I shall buy something good, unawares. That may be it."

He passed his cup for his second cupful of coffee.

"Are these the things collected by that poor young fellow you told me of the other day?" asked his cousin as she filled his cup.

"Yes," he said, and became meditative over a piece of toast.

"Nothing ever does happen to me," he remarked presently, beginning to think aloud. "I wonder why? Things enough happen to other people. There is Harvey. Only the other week; on Monday he picked up sixpence, on Wednesday his chicks all had the staggers, on Friday his cousin came home from Australia, and on Saturday he broke his ankle. What a whirl of excitement!—compared to me."

"I think I would rather be without so much excitement," said his housekeeper. "It can't be good for you."

"I suppose it's troublesome. Still... you see, nothing ever happens to me. When I was a little boy I never had accidents. I never fell in love as I grew up. Never married.... I wonder how it feels to have something happen to you, something really remarkable.

The Unnatural History of Man-Eating Plants

"That orchid-collector was only thirty-six—twenty years younger than myself—when he died. And he had been married twice and divorced once; he had had malarial fever four times, and once he broke his thigh. He killed a Malay once, and once he was wounded by a poisoned dart. And in the end he was killed by jungle-leeches. It must have all been very troublesome, but then it must have been very interesting, you know—except, perhaps, the leeches."

"I am sure it was not good for him," said the lady, with conviction.

"Perhaps not." And then Wedderburn looked at his watch. "Twenty-three minutes past eight. I am going up by the quarter to twelve train, so that there is plenty of time. I think I shall wear my alpaca jacket—it is quite warm enough—and my grey felt hat and brown shoes. I suppose—"

He glanced out of the window at the serene sky and sunlit garden, and then nervously at his cousin's face.

"I think you had better take an umbrella if you are going to London," she said in a voice that admitted of no denial. "There's all between here and the station coming back."

When he returned he was in a state of mild excitement. He had made a purchase. It was rare that he could make up his mind quickly enough to buy, but this time he had done so.

"There are Vandas," he said, "and a Dendrobe and some Palæonophis." He surveyed his purchases lovingly as he consumed his soup. They were laid out on the spotless tablecloth before him, and he was telling his cousin all about them as he slowly meandered through his dinner. It was his custom to live all his visits to London over again in the evening for her and his own entertainment.

"I knew something would happen to-day. And I have bought all these. Some of them—some of them—I feel sure, do you know, that some of them will be remarkable. I don't know how it is, but I feel just as sure as if someone had told me that some of these will turn out remarkable.

The Flowering of the Strange Orchid

"That one"—he pointed to a shrivelled rhizome—"was not identified. It may be a Palæonophis—or it may not. It may be a new species, or even a new genus. And it was the last that poor Batten ever collected."

"I don't like the look of it," said his housekeeper. "It's such an ugly shape."

"To me it scarcely seems to have a shape."

"I don't like those things that stick out," said his housekeeper.

"It shall be put away in a pot to-morrow."

"It looks," said the housekeeper, "like a spider shamming dead."

Wedderburn smiled and surveyed the root with his head on one side. "It is certainly not a pretty lump of stuff. But you can never judge of these things from their dry appearance. It may turn out to be a very beautiful orchid indeed. How busy I shall be to-morrow! I must see to-night just exactly what to do with these things, and to-morrow I shall set to work."

"They found poor Batten lying dead, or dying, in a mangrove swamp—I forget which," he began again presently, "with one of these very orchids crushed up under his body. He had been unwell for some days with some kind of native fever, and I suppose he fainted. These mangrove swamps are very unwholesome. Every drop of blood, they say, was taken out of him by the jungle-leeches. It may be that very plant that cost him his life to obtain."

"I think none the better of it for that."

"Men must work though women may weep," said Wedderburn with profound gravity.

"Fancy dying away from every comfort in a nasty swamp! Fancy being ill of fever with nothing to take but chlorodyne and quinine—if men were left to themselves they would live on chlorodyne and quinine—and no one round you but horrible natives! They say the Andaman islanders are most disgusting wretches—and, anyhow, they can scarcely make good nurses, not having the necessary training. And just for people in England to have orchids!"

"I don't suppose it was comfortable, but some men seem to enjoy that kind of thing," said Wedderburn. "Anyhow, the natives of his party were sufficiently civilised to take care of all his collection until his colleague, who was an ornithologist, came back again from the interior; though they could not tell the species of the orchid, and had let it wither. And it makes these things more interesting."

"It makes them disgusting. I should be afraid of some of the malaria clinging to them. And just think, there has been a dead body lying across that ugly thing! I never thought of that before. There! I declare I cannot eat another mouthful of dinner."

"I will take them off the table if you like, and put them in the window-seat. I can see them just as well there."

The next few days he was indeed singularly busy in his steamy little hothouse, fussing about with charcoal, lumps of teak, moss, and all the other mysteries of the orchid cultivator. He considered he was having a wonderfully eventful time. In the evening he would talk about these new orchids to his friends, and over and over again he reverted to his expectation of something strange.

Several of the Vandas and the Dendrobium died under his care, but presently the strange orchid began to show signs of life. He was delighted and took his housekeeper right away from jam-making to see it at once, directly he made the discovery.

"That is a bud," he said, "and presently there will be a lot of leaves there, and those little things coming out here are aërial rootlets."

"They look to me like little white fingers poking out of the brown," said his housekeeper. "I don't like them."

The Flowering of the Strange Orchid

"Why not?"

"I don't know. They look like fingers trying to get at you. I can't help my likes and dislikes."

"I don't know for certain, but I don't *think* there are any orchids I know that have aërial rootlets quite like that. It may be my fancy, of course. You see they are a little flattened at the ends."

"I don't like 'em," said his housekeeper, suddenly shivering and turning away. "I know it's very silly of me—and I'm very sorry, particularly as you like the thing so much. But I can't help thinking of that corpse."

"But it may not be that particular plant. That was merely a guess of mine."

His housekeeper shrugged her shoulders. "Anyhow I don't like it," she said.

Wedderburn felt a little hurt at her dislike to the plant. But that did not prevent his talking to her about orchids generally, and this orchid in particular, whenever he felt inclined.

"There are such queer things about orchids," he said one day; "such possibilities of surprises. You know, Darwin studied their fertilisation, and showed that the whole structure of an ordinary orchid-flower was contrived in order that moths might carry the pollen from plant to plant. Well, it seems that there are lots of orchids known the flower of which cannot possibly be used for fertilisation in that way. Some of the Cypripediums, for instance; there are no insects known that can possibly fertilise them, and some of them have never been found with seed."

"But how do they form new plants?"

"By runners and tubers, and that kind of outgrowth. That is easily explained. The puzzle is, what are the flowers for?

The Unnatural History of Man-Eating Plants

"Very likely," he added, *"my* orchid may be something extraordinary in that way. If so I shall study it. I have often thought of making researches as Darwin did. But hitherto I have not found the time, or something else has happened to prevent it. The leaves are beginning to unfold now. I do wish you would come and see them!"

But she said that the orchid-house was so hot it gave her the headache. She had seen the plant once again, and the aërial rootlets, which were now some of them more than a foot long, had unfortunately reminded her of tentacles reaching out after something; and they got into her dreams, growing after her with incredible rapidity. So that she had settled to her entire satisfaction that she would not see that plant again, and Wedderburn had to admire its leaves alone. They were of the ordinary broad form, and a deep glossy green, with splashes and dots of deep red towards the base. He knew of no other leaves quite like them. The plant was placed on a low bench near the thermometer, and close by was a simple arrangement by which a tap dripped on the hot-water pipes and kept the air steamy. And he spent his afternoons now with some regularity meditating on the approaching flowering of this strange plant.

And at last the great thing happened. Directly he entered the little glass house he knew that the spike had burst out, although his great *Palæonophis Lowii* hid the corner where his new darling stood. There was a new odour in the air, a rich, intensely sweet scent, that overpowered every other in that crowded, steaming little greenhouse.

Directly he noticed this he hurried down to the strange orchid. And, behold! the trailing green spikes bore now three great splashes of blossom, from which this overpowering sweetness proceeded. He stopped before them in an ecstasy of admiration.

The flowers were white, with streaks of golden orange upon the petals; the heavy labellum was coiled into an intricate projection, and a wonderful bluish purple mingled there with the gold. He could see at once that the genus was altogether a new one. And the insufferable scent! How hot the place was! The blossoms swam before his eyes.

He would see if the temperature was right. He made a step towards the thermometer. Suddenly everything appeared unsteady. The bricks on the floor were dancing up and down. Then the white blossoms, the green leaves behind them, the whole greenhouse, seemed to sweep sideways, and then in a curve upward.

*   *   *   *   *

At half-past four his cousin made the tea, according to their invariable custom. But Wedderburn did not come in for his tea.

"He is worshipping that horrid orchid," she told herself, and waited ten minutes. "His watch must have stopped. I will go and call him."

She went straight to the hothouse, and, opening the door, called his name. There was no reply. She noticed that the air was very close, and loaded with an intense perfume. Then she saw something lying on the bricks between the hot-water pipes.

For a minute, perhaps, she stood motionless.

He was lying, face upward, at the foot of the strange orchid. The tentacle-like aërial rootlets no longer swayed freely in the air, but were crowded together, a tangle of grey ropes, and stretched tight, with their ends closely applied to his chin and neck and hands.

She did not understand. Then she saw from under one of the exultant tentacles upon his cheek there trickled a little thread of blood.

With an inarticulate cry she ran towards him, and tried to pull him away from the leech-like suckers. She snapped two of these tentacles, and their sap dripped red.

THE STRANGE ORCHID -KJG

Then the overpowering scent of the blossom began to make her head reel. How they clung to him! She tore at the tough ropes, and he and the white inflorescence swam about her. She felt she was fainting, knew she must not. She left him and hastily opened the nearest door, and, after she had panted for a moment in the fresh air, she had a brilliant inspiration. She caught up a flower-pot and smashed in the windows at the end of the green-house. Then she re-entered. She tugged now with renewed strength at Wedderburn's motionless body, and brought the strange orchid crashing to the floor. It still clung with the grimmest tenacity to its victim. In a frenzy, she lugged it and him into the open air.

Then she thought of tearing through the sucker rootlets one by one, and in another minute she had released him and was dragging him away from the horror.

He was white and bleeding from a dozen circular patches.

The odd-job man was coming up the garden, amazed at the smashing of glass, and saw her emerge, hauling the inanimate body with red-stained hands. For a moment he thought impossible things.

"Bring some water!" she cried, and her voice dispelled his fancies. When, with unnatural alacrity, he returned with the water, he found her weeping with excitement, and with Wedderburn's head upon her knee, wiping the blood from his face.

"What's the matter?" said Wedderburn, opening his eyes feebly, and closing them again at once.

"Go and tell Annie to come out here to me, and then go for Doctor Haddon at once," she said to the odd-job man so soon as he brought the water; and added, seeing he hesitated, "I will tell you all about it when you come back."

Presently Wedderburn opened his eyes again, and, seeing that he was troubled by the puzzle of his position, she explained to him, "You fainted in the hothouse."

"And the orchid?"

"I will see to that," she said.

The Unnatural History of Man-Eating Plants

Wedderburn had lost a good deal of blood, but beyond that he had suffered no very great injury. They gave him brandy mixed with some pink extract of meat, and carried him upstairs to bed. His house-keeper told her incredible story in fragments to Dr. Haddon. "Come to the orchid-house and see," she said.

The cold outer air was blowing in through the open door, and the sickly perfume was almost dispelled. Most of the torn aërial rootlets lay already withered amidst a number of dark stains upon the bricks. The stem of the inflorescence was broken by the fall of the plant, and the flowers were growing limp and brown at the edges of the petals. The doctor stooped towards it, then saw that one of the aërial rootlets still stirred feebly, and hesitated.

The next morning the strange orchid still lay there, black now and putrescent. The door banged intermittently in the morning breeze, and all the array of Wedderburn's orchids was shrivelled and prostrate. But Wedderburn himself was bright and garrulous upstairs in the glory of his strange adventure.

THE LAMPARAGUA

By May Crommelin

(The Pall Mall Magazine, 1897)

[When staying lately in Chile, being interested in the superstitions of the lower caste, which is mainly of Indian origin, I heard, among other curious legends, darkly of one which seemed peculiar to this country. Next, chance acquainted me with a gentleman, one of the principal English residents in Chile, who kindly gave me details of the dread lamparagua. This wizard-like creature, of which many persons in the country have never even heard, is strangely enough supposed to inhabit fertile and cultivated districts. And Mr. L— was assured by his labourers that one lamparagua or more infested the marshy edges of a lake, as is its favourite haunt, on his own estate, Culipran.

In the following tale I may have overstated the height of the Thing, concerning which and its mode of progression the details were not exact. Otherwise, its appearance, diet, and the means it employs to secure its victims, are faithfully reproduced, according to the description unwillingly confided to Mr. L— by some of his own peones. And these are men who are declared by Europeans neither to feel pain nor to know fear.]

THE two men had held on steadily riding since two hours before dawn, going all day without stopping, save for a brief noontide halt. During the afternoon of yesterday their track had lain across an utterly desolate pampa, therefore they had pushed on to reach cultivated country again, and water before nightfall. Now, towards evening, they found themselves near a long lake, bordered with reeds, the haunt of numberless wildfowl.

A small rocky valley, down which the active Chilian ponies weariedly scrambled, grew greener towards the lake shore, where a stream which the travellers had followed for some time widened into a V-shaped marsh.

"It is near sunset, Pedro. Let us camp here for the night," said Ramsay, shivering slightly; for the fever had taken him two days ago. "Own the truth, man! You have lost your bearings, and don't know whether we are nine miles or nine leagues from the silver mine. Besides, the horses, poor beasts, will be dead beat."

"Of what good is a horse that cannot do his sixty miles when asked?" returned the Chilian guide. "But, truly, the devil seems to have been driving round on these hills, changing their shapes since last I came this way."

He gazed with discontent deepening on his swarthy features at the hills behind, hiding the sandy desert, far beyond which rose the mighty range of the Andes, still veiled in rosy haze this hot December evening. Then, in sudden recollection,—

"There is a rich Englishman who lives near a lake in this neighbourhood. He has smelting works and a large estate. The house may be close at hand."

"Or it may be on the opposite shore," said Ramsay, wearily dismounting. "Hobble the horses, and let us go up to yonder hilly ground jutting into the lake.

"Then if you can see signs of a *hacienda*, we'll make a last push for it. If not, I rest."

"Why not, patron?" said the *huaso*, using the almost invariable courteous Chilian assent to assertions or requests.

The Lamparagua

Up among rocks and brushwood master and man climbed, till, advancing to the far crest of the hillock, they scanned the lake shores attentively. Northwards, at a mile's distance, a wooded headland arrested their vision; south and west there was no human habitation in sight, though the ground here and there showed signs of cultivation and the pasture was good.

Right across the lake the sun was sinking gloriously red, against a background of the pale olive green and lilac hues seen so often in a Southern Pacific sky. Soothed by the spectacle, Ramsay sat down on a rock to rest and smoke; and with Indian impassibility Pedro did the same. All *gringos* were mad, he knew; if this one liked staring at nothing, he was more easily pleased than some of the foreign lunatics. But presently Pedro became aware that there was something to be seen among the rocks below. Signing to Ramsay, both men peered stealthily past screening myrtle bushes and witnessed an evening domestic scene in animal life.

The ground rose in two broken ledges from the marsh, and on the upper one a dog-fox and vixen were playing with their cubs near some crannies where was doubtless their home. Presently the mother left the rest, and stretched herself sleepily in the evening sunlight midway on the grass ledge. One cub followed to bite her neck, but, on being repulsed, returned to gambol with his brothers. As he watched them, Ramsay also noticed vaguely a low withered tree, standing in the marsh twenty yards below, alone, and partly submerged, with a hollow cleft in its side.

All at once the peon touched his master's arm and pointed open-mouthed towards the vixen. She had risen as if in terror, both her head and brush curved towards the ledge. Then, while her four paws seemed firmly planted gripping the turf, she was drawn broadside some yards towards the edge by invisible means. The other foxes, old and young, meantime disappeared in the twinkling of an eye into the rock crevices.

The Unnatural History of Man-Eating Plants

As both men eagerly gazed, the vixen's tension relaxed. On the brink she recovered herself and standing still for three or four seconds, as if dazed after deadly effort, she turned tail and darted towards her lair. Two springs only,—on the third she paused in mid-flight! Once more she resisted, but was dragged back towards the edge, this time *tail foremost*. At the same time a rush of wind sounded like a *sh-h* in the stillness. Ramsay knew now he had heard the same sound two minutes before, but had fancied it a light breeze among the leaves. Craning his neck forward, Jock believed he could see an agonised expression in the creature's eyes, as against her will she slid inch by inch—*over!*

The fall was not great. A lower grassy terrace surmounted the marsh. Even as they whispered, the watchers saw the victim rise. A second time—but feebly, like a mouse released from the deadly grip of a cat—the poor she-fox crawled away with drooping brush towards the sheltering rocks. Ramsay searched the marsh with a sportsman's keen glance, to discover whether the creature had been lassoed by some invisible means, and where was the native hunter. Then he bounded to his feet and pointing towards the withered tree, his arm stiffened with amazement, exclaimed, "Look!"

The cleft in the tree-trunk was visibly widening and gaping, till it looked like a hideous bark-lipped mouth that was drawing a long inspiration. Again there came the same sound in the air, and the vixen, curled in a helpless quivering ball, was borne five yards, as on a wind-blast, disappearing right into the hollow of the tree. The withered wooden lips contracted over the creature's living head; two dead branches above stirred slightly, like antennæ, the cleft closed, leaving a jagged scar in the tree-trunk. That was all.

The scene was still and peaceful as before. A flight of wild duck circled twice over the lake and then alighted on the surface with distant quacks. Behind in a fuchsia

The Lamparagua

thicket a native thrush was singing. The tree was immovable.

Wondering if he could be dreaming, Ramsay turned to the peon. Pedro's copper skin had taken a pale yellow hue, and he was shivering, though a Chilian peasant is brave to savagery.

"The *Lamparagua!* Fly!" he gasped, with a cry of horror, and plunged downwards among the rocks. Jock overtook him just as the *huaso* leaped barebacked on his horse.

"Stay for me, my lad, at the valley head in safety. I'll not leave the saddles and blankets," said the Scotchman coolly. But his own breath fluttered in his throat more than from the run, and while his hands tugged at strap and buckle, his head turned to glance at the tree that remained motionless in the distance.

Rejoining Pedro, who waited half a mile away, the master found the peon on his knees, crossing himself and gabbling over and over every scrap of the Latin prayers he could remember, which the *padres* had taught him in boyhood. They were few, and he mixed them so ludicrously that his listener almost laughed.

"Holy Santa Rosa—miserable sinner!" ended Pedro, rising and saddling up with remarkable haste while throwing off some last ejaculations of this rare access of piety. "It was a witch, *señor*; the country is full of spirits. Holy Saint Peter, I ducked your image last autumn in the sea. Forgive!—but those fishermen are such blasphemers, and rail against you at the first bad weather. I abjure all evil-livers, holy—" An awful oath followed as the pony swerved. Pedro stuck his huge rowels in the beast's flanks and cantered furiously away, his *poncho* filling with air as he worked his arms like a windmill's sails, shouting, "Ride ride, patron! Leave this God-forsaken country, quick!"

"Aye, if only our horses can travel," muttered the Scotchman.

The Unnatural History of Man-Eating Plants

True enough, the tired beasts soon showed that they could not be roused long beyond an ambling motion, not unlike the gait of a Peruvian pacer; but which, when unbroken all day, may cover a great distance before nightfall. Not till they had gone some miles could Ramsay persuade his terror-stricken guide to talk sensibly.

"What is this beast-tree? *Lamparagua,** you called it. Does it exist elsewhere in Chili?"

"Who knows, *señor*? I only heard of such rare trees as northern witches from a rough *roto* who came from this country. I remember it was one evening in July, ten years ago, as we sat in a circle on the ground round the brasier. We thought he was improvising a tale, as we had in turn improvised or recited songs and legends—telling lies for fun, as the patron may know is our custom. There was naught more I can call to mind, save that they swallowed animals and lived near marshy places. Saints preserve us! Ride on—on to the mines. *Stop here?* Never!"

Ramsay dared not lose sight of the man. At least Pedro knew something of the country. He might strike their right track soon. So the soft twilight of the south drew round them, as they rode wearily. And the night came, black and moonless, as they bent in their saddles, more weary yet. The reins lay loose on the horses' necks now, Pedro trusting to the animals' instinct; for "the good land" could not be far where men lived, and there were homesteads and supper and provender.

When midnight was past, Ramsay felt his strength going from him. By the faint starlight they had just plashed through a gravelly stream, in which the horses stopped to drink before reluctantly stumbling up the far bank where their hoofs struck muffled on grass.

"Pedro, I can hold up no longer," called the engineer feebly, reeling in his saddle, as an ague fit shook him like a rigor. "Leave me—if you will. I—must—lie down."

The Lamparagua

Guessing by his master's voice that the latter must be very ill, the peon hastily came to Ramsay's help in dismounting, then guided him to the shelter of some bushes that were faintly discernible. Here he placed a saddle under the sufferer's head, and laid a blanket over him.

Not far off there was a small grove of shrubs, darker than the surrounding twilight, beside which rose a big tree with a huge bulbous base and exposed roots like those of a cotton tree. Near this Ramsay's horse strayed, cropping the grass; so Pedro, following, tethered him to one of these roots, which he had discovered by stumbling against them in the blackness.

"*Caramba!*" he muttered. "Stay there; animal not to be trusted." His own beast knew him, and never went far from its owner's side.

Then the guide sat down beside his exhausted patron, who slept for fevered snatches, or woke to ramble in delirious talk. So the time passed till the faint light strengthened.

All at once Ramsay fancied he heard Pedro's voice crying out in a tone of desperation—or was it terror?—"*Me voy!* I'm off to bring you help!"

The sick man did not heed, though vaguely conscious he was left alone. It seemed to him that he was in a hospital. The doctor would come round presently; if not, it was peaceful to lie still. Was that his mother, lifting the hair on his fevered brow?

Then he started awake as a horrid cry roused his dulled ears. (It was the scream of a horse!)

What was this well-known valley? Where was he? For, raising himself weakly on one elbow, Ramsay saw a stream running past rocks which were strangely familiar,—and yet *when* had he seen them? The river emptied itself in marshy land. The dawn showed a dark grey surface beyond, like a sea—or lake.

The Unnatural History of Man-Eating Plants

With a cold terror the sick man recognised that he lay not two hundred yards from the marsh of the lamparagua: that headland; the water! All night they must have ridden in a circle.

The horrible scream was already fading from his sick memory like a dream, when a snorting and scuffling noise caused Ramsay to turn slowly his weak head. He saw his horse stamping, pulling back from its halter, and with distended eye-balls staring terrified at a tree, to a root of which it was fastened. What was wrong? The tree had two bare topmost branches like horns, and some lower ones also without leaves, yet this was summer-time; in December... It was withered! And, there above its onion-shaped bole was, surely, a dark scar, a crack! Oh, horror! the top of the tree was that of the lamparagua, in the marsh. And now, as Jock stared with fever-weakened eyes through the dim daybreak, the lower branches moved slowly downwards, clutching the horse's halter with claw-like twigs; the crack in the side of the *Thing* was widening. Again a fearful sound woke the sleeping glen: the horse's cry of terror. Jock tried instinctively to find his revolver, but his senses reeled as the tree aperture gaped, opening upwards. The horse was drawing towards it—nearer!— fighting, struggling. Then two shots rang out, and a man fainted, and knew no more.

When Jock Ramsay came to himself, the sun was high in the heavens. He was sheltered by wild myrtle from its heat, and though very weak, his senses had come back. Memory was slower. Ah—he *remembered!* Opening his eyes in a wide stare of apprehension, Ramsay saw himself lying alone. There was a thicket near, but not the awful tree. Pedro was gone; so were the horses. But perhaps—perhaps—that last vision of the Thing engulfing the poor roan cob had been a nightmare, a fevered frenzy. Feebly reconnoitring the ground, the sick man noticed that he lay on a grassy slope between the stream and the rocks where the foxes lived: a small cape. Behind his head the ground must be open up the valley. There lay safety, away from the horrible marsh and the lamparagua—if there were such a tree indeed. Surely it had all been a hideous dream.

THE LAMPARAGUA -KJG

Drawing the myrtle leaves aside, as one might a curtain, Jock feebly turned himself to examine the glen. Then his fingers clenched, his breath stopped, and a thrill of horror froze his spine. *The Tree was there!* Out in the open, on the grass, with not a bush near it, right between himself and safety.

Take it quietly! For manhood's sake, think out this business, and don't turn faint like a schoolgirl seeing a snake. First, was the whole affair a dream? Was that withered tree out yonder on the sward the very lamparagua? For if so, there were several, or it could change its situation. It was neither in the marsh, nor by the fuchsia thicket. It.... O God!

For, as he peered, Ramsay believed that the tree was moving. It was horribly near, and it was surely creeping forward by inches. He held his breath, and marked a grass tuft at its bulbous base.

Now—now it had passed beyond the tall silvery grass plumes and spear-leaves, and was close by a stone—was stealthily rounding it. Yes, the Thing was approaching him; doubtless it had stayed quiet till now, gorged with its morning meal, but it was slowly nearing its next victim. With eyes fascinated by fear, Ramsay saw its roots moving forward like giant knotty suckers that gripped and held fast in the herbage, noiselessly moving with the motion of a tortoise.

The hair of the young man's flesh stood up, an icy coldness numbed his blood. Then with a strong effort he gathered his senses to think out escape. The rocks ahead were his only chance. There among the crannies, where the foxes had their dens and hid in safety, he could hide. But he could not rise! His head was dizzy with fever; his strength was as running water; his legs and feet seemed not his own, mere useless weights to be dragged on by sheer pluck. For he had already started—

Grasping the myrtle stems to give himself an impetus, Ramsay was crawling away towards the rocks, foot by foot. He lay outspread like a lizard, for his only strength remained in his arms and chest. Inch by inch, he crept onward as fast as he could go, clutching at the grass tufts, at the sage-bushes, drops of perspiration running down his face.

Faster, faster, if it could only be done! The man had covered some yards; surely the tree moved more slowly. *Ah!*

A blast blew backwards over Ramsay's head, raising his hair. By instinct he dug his nails into the ground, flattening his body as much as he possibly could. The

The Lamparagua

indraught was as if air had rushed by into a deep cavity, while a sound like that of an escape pipe hissed in the air. Then it was over.

As drowning men are said to see a thousand past scenes in a few moments, so in an agonisingly lucid flash, Jock Ramsay reviewed his life. Then he recalled yester-evening, how the wretched fox had gotten breathing-time twice, as once he had now. How long would this horrible game last? The beast-tree was paralysing the human being: he thought of a snake fascinating a rabbit.

Slowly, more feebly, the victim still crawled. Why did that second blast not follow? Could the lamparagua be so near, it needed no aid beyond that of its cruel hooked branches? *He must see!*

Turning his head, as he still dragged himself onward, the fever-stricken wretch beheld a strange sight. He had left his blanket behind upon the ground when first making his escape, and it was now wrapped round the tree-bole, as if the lamparagua had failed to suck it in, and was wrestling with this unknown prey, both branches holding it fast outspread on claw-like twigs. It was a respite! A few seconds more of air, light, life!

Yes, the beast-tree was standing still; yet it had covered more ground than its hunted prey, during the time both had moved. Ramsay felt for the revolver in his pocket. There was one bullet left, he knew, and if escape were hopeless, then—

At last! The rocks were near. The man began scrambling painfully up a steep incline of loose earth and rounded stones which resembled a moraine, and that gave no hold to his desperate grasp. Looking up, he saw with hopeless eyes that there had been a slight landslip lately, which had left the bank projecting overhead, so that he could not reach the top; looking down, that the lamparagua was slowly but steadily approaching once more over the grass, foot-root following foot-root. There was a torn piece of crimson blanket hanging on one bough.

The Unnatural History of Man-Eating Plants

He must struggle across the face of this treacherous slide to where a clump of yuccas were smouldering, their stems blackened as one often sees them, whether from spontaneous combustion or sun-fired in some inexplicable manner, no man knows.

Fire! The smoking plants suggested a thought to the man. He stayed still, holding on half-way up the scree. He felt for his matchbox; there were two matches left.

Then Ramsay, instead of longer seeking escape upwards, flung himself in still more desperate eagerness down the steep slope again towards his enemy. He was at bay.

Where the grass began, the man stopped and stooped, plucking dry blades and twigs with the haste of one who has but a few moments to live should this plan fail of success. Not a drop of rain had fallen since last October; the scorching summer heat had burnt the grass to tinder. There came the spurt of a match.

Two moments: five--!

The fire-spark, kindling, seemed about to spread, when a roaring wind-gust through the valley's stillness blew it out, and the man felt himself sucked irresistibly towards a clump of prickly pear, to which he clung palpitating, with his face pressed against the thorny broad discs that tore the skin to bleeding. Ah!—*that was over!*

For the last time one chance was left,—one match! Again Ramsay snatched what dry fuel lay within his grasp, as he sheltered beneath the bushes. His papers, cheque-book, all were in a small valise he had instinctively thrust overnight under his saddle-pillow. There was one letter left in his breast pocket, which he had carried there two years—the last one ever written by his mother. He tore it out.

With shaking fingers, and blinded by blood-drops he dared not wait to wipe from his eyes—knowing the while that the lamparagua was stalking a yard nearer at each motion—its victim carefully struck the match. Sheltering the tiny flame with one hand, he turned the wax-stem gently till it lit. Next the letter; and the fire licked the words "My dearest Son," then blazed and crackled in the funeral pyre of broken bramble and dried myrtle leaves that burnt a dead woman's last token of love to her youngest born. Gladly would she have known it sacrificed on the slight chance to save his life! Ramsay thrust both hands deep into the burning mass, and recovering strength in the excitement of hope, he staggered towards some clumps of tall grass of the pampas a few feet away. The sparks fell, making a trail as he went that caught the dry herbage. Hurrah! How the giant grass-stems took fire, blazing high in a glorious bonfire!

A hasty glance over his shoulder. The lamparagua was not twelve yards distant; its jaws were widening. But the fire-wall was between them.

There came a rush of wind ending in a sound more fierce than a wounded lion's roar. The man was caught by the blast as he stood upright, weak yet defiant, matching his puny being against the strength of the brute-tree with the help of the mind within him controlling the fiery element as a weapon. Sucked forward, blinded by smoke, scorched, Ramsay fell on his face and lay still with a last conscious effort to save his life. Beyond his body the myrtles and fuchsias were crackling, the tall *chajual* blossoms blazed like high torches, the fire was spreading, leaping up to the *boldo* branches in yonder thicket, running over the open ground in a low sheet that burnt the lamparagua roots.

For half a minute the Thing stayed, trying to stand its ground. Now it was in full flight! The great sucker-feet were travelling over the burning herbage, dragging its tree-trunk with agonised efforts, yard upon yard, towards the stream.

Five minutes later, there came a galloping of horses down the valley; men's shouts. But Ramsay did not hear them. He seemed to lie prone at death's door, too weak to enter unless spirit hands lifted him over its threshold and brought him within to be at peace and rest.

But they were earthly hands that were now trying to pour some brandy down Ramsay's throat. When his eyes opened, Pedro was supporting his master's head, while a group of men around were watching the stranger curiously, foremost among whom was an English gentleman.

"Coming to all right?" said the latter. "A near shave that. You began to smoke, I take it, finding yourself pretty nearly lost and famished, so the valley got fired. We have been out searching for you since morning, when your man rode up to my *hacienda*, worn out and demented. We passed the head of the valley at ten o'clock, but could see no sign of your horse, which Pedro said he had tied to a tree. What's the matter?"

For Ramsay struggled up, and was staring round.

"*The tree!* It was out there before the fire: Pedro, you know—where is it gone?"

Pedro only shivered and stared. Some of the other peones, muttering, and giving sidelong glances at each other, crossed the burnt ground looking about them. One saw a partly submerged tree at some distance down stream, floating slowly into the marsh. His attention was caught by a gleam of something scarlet tangled in the topmost withered bough.

* * * * * *

A few days later, Ramsay was stretched at ease in a cane deck-chair, with a tall glass of iced drink in the wicker socket by his arm. Overhead a verandah was shaded with masses of roses, stephanotis and bignonia. Sunshine flooded the garden stretching beyond like a dream of enchantment, where tall palms shot above high flowering trees, and oranges and lemons were mingled lower with gardenias and poinsettias.

The Lamparagua

Jock had just finished after talking during some twenty minutes, so felt thirsty, exhausted, and excited.

"That's the whole story," he ended. "Now, do you believe me, Mr. Campbell? Till now, I fancy you thought me mad."

"No, but possibly a bit delirious in your fever, so that you imagined some tale Pedro told you of the lamparagua had really happened to yourself. That was all," said the kindly host.

"Man alive! There is Pedro to witness also. And where is my horse? And your own lad saw the torn red blanket in the marsh!" cried Ramsay.

"True, quite true," nodded Campbell, coolly reflecting. "Well, my dear fellow, if it is any satisfaction to you, I do believe you are one of the few living human beings who have seen the lamparagua. What is more, for some years back I have heard rumours of such a thing, and that it haunted this lake and another adjoining it, both on my estate. But, to confess the truth, I fancied the story was a convenient legend of my cattle-herds to account for missing beasts. Yes, I believe. But hardly any one else will, even in Chile, among our own wise educated class. Of course the peones know. They are nearer Nature than we."

MAY CROMMELIN.

* Literally, "Lamp of the Water": a kind of will-o'-the-wisp. Though why a light is associated with the tree was not apparent in the account of it given to the writer.

THE PURPLE TERROR

By Fred M. White

(The Strand, 1899)

I.

LIEUTENANT WILL SCARLETT'S instructions were devoid of problems, physical or otherwise. To convey a letter from Captain Driver of the *Yankee Doodle*, in Porto Rico Bay, to Admiral Lake on the other side of the isthmus, was an apparently simple matter.

"All you have to do," the captain remarked, "is to take three or four men with you in case of accidents, cross the isthmus on foot, and simply give this letter into the hands of Admiral Lake. By so doing we shall save at least four days, and the aborigines are presumedly friendly."

The aborigines aforesaid were Cuban insurgents. Little or no strife had taken place along the neck lying between Porto Rico and the north bay where Lake's flagship lay, though the belt was known to be given over to the disaffected Cubans.

"It is a matter of fifty miles through practically unexplored country," Scarlett replied; "and there's a good deal of the family quarrel in this business, sir. If the Spaniards hate us, the Cubans are not exactly enamoured of our flag."

Captain Driver roundly denounced the whole pack of them.

The Purple Terror

"Treacherous thieves to a man," he said. "I don't suppose your progress will have any brass bands and floral arches to it. And they tell me the forest is pretty thick. But you'll get there all the same. There is the letter, and you can start as soon as you like."

"I may pick my own men, sir?"

"My dear fellow, take whom you please. Take the mastiff, if you like."

"I'd like the mastiff," Scarlett replied; "as he is practically my own, I thought you would not object."

Will Scarlett began to glow as the prospect of adventure stimulated his imagination. He was rather a good specimen of West Point naval dandyism. He had brains at the back of his smartness, and his geological and botanical knowledge were going to prove of considerable service to a grateful country when said grateful country should have passed beyond the rudimentary stages of colonization. And there was some disposition to envy Scarlett on the part of others floating for the past month on the liquid prison of the sapphire sea.

A warrant officer, Tarrer by name, *plus* two A.B.'s of thews and sinews, to say nothing of the dog, completed the exploring party. By the time that the sun kissed the tip of the feathery hills they had covered some six miles of their journey. From the first Scarlett had been struck by the absolute absence of the desolation and horror of civil strife. Evidently the fiery cross had not been carried here; huts and houses were intact; the villagers stood under sloping eaves, and regarded the Americans with a certain sullen curiosity.

"We'd better stop for the night here," said Scarlett.

They had come at length to a village that boasted some pretensions. An adobe chapel at one end of the straggling street was faced by a wine-house at the other. A padre, with hands folded over a bulbous, greasy gabardine, bowed gravely to Scarlett's salutation. The latter had what Tarrer called "considerable Spanish."

"We seek quarters for the night," said Scarlett. "Of course, we are prepared to pay for them."

The sleepy padre nodded towards the wine-house.

"You will find fair accommodation there," he said. "We are friends of the Americanos."

Scarlett doubted the fact, and passed on with florid thanks. So far, little signs of friendliness had been encountered on the march. Coldness, suspicion, a suggestion of fear, but no friendliness to be embarrassing.

The keeper of the wine-shop had his doubts. He feared his poor accommodation for guests so distinguished. A score or more of picturesque, cut-throat-looking rascals with cigarettes in their mouths lounged sullenly in the bar. The display of a brace of gold dollars enlarged mine host's opinion of his household capacity.

"I will do my best, señors," he said. "Come this way."

So it came to pass that an hour after twilight Tarrer and Scarlett were seated in the open amongst the oleanders and the trailing gleam of the fire-flies, discussing cigars of average merit and a native wine that was not without virtues. The long bar of the wine-house was brilliantly illuminated; from within came shouts of laughter mingled with the ting, tang of the guitar and the rollicking clack of the castanets.

"They seem to be happy in there," Tarrer remarked. "It isn't all daggers and ball in this distressful country."

A certain curiosity came over Scarlett.

"It is the duty of a good officer," he said, "to lose no opportunity of acquiring useful information. Let us join the giddy throng, Tarrer."

The Purple Terror

Tarrer expressed himself with enthusiasm in favour of any amusement that might be going. A month's idleness on shipboard increases the appetite for that kind of thing wonderfully. The long bar was comfortable, and filled with Cubans who took absolutely no notice of the intruders. Their eyes were turned towards a rude stage at the far end of the bar, whereon a girl was gyrating in a dance with a celerity and grace that caused the wreath of flowers around her shoulders to resemble a trembling zone of purple flame.

"A wonderfully pretty girl and a wonderfully pretty dance," Scarlett murmured, when the motions ceased and the girl leapt gracefully to the ground. "Largesse, I expect. I thought so. Well, I'm good for a quarter."

The girl came forward, extending a shell prettily. She curtsied before Scarlett and fixed her dark, liquid eyes on his. As he smiled and dropped his quarter-dollar into the shell a coquettish gleam came into the velvety eyes. An ominous growl came from the lips of a bearded ruffian close by.

"Othello's jealous," said Tarrer. "Look at his face."

"I am better employed," Scarlett laughed. "That was a graceful dance, pretty one. I hope you are going to give us another one presently—"

Scarlett paused suddenly. His eyes had fallen on the purple band of flowers the girl had twined round her shoulder. Scarlett was an enthusiastic botanist; he knew most of the gems in Flora's crown, but he had never looked upon such a vivid wealth of blossom before.

The flowers were orchids, and orchids of a kind unknown to collectors anywhere. On this point Scarlett felt certain. And yet this part of the world was by no means a difficult one to explore in comparison with New Guinea and Sumatra, where the rarer varieties had their homes.

The blooms were immensely large, far larger than any flower of the kind known to Europe or America, of a deep pure purple, with a blood-red centre. As Scarlett gazed upon them he noticed a certain cruel expression on the flower. Most orchids have a kind of face of their own; the purple blooms had a positive expression of ferocity and cunning. They exhumed, too, a queer, sickly fragrance. Scarlett had smelt something like it before, after the Battle of Manila. The perfume was the perfume of a corpse.

"And yet they are magnificent flowers," said Scarlett. "Won't you tell me where you got them from, pretty one?"

"THE GIRL CAME FORWARD, EXTENDING A SHELL PRETTILY."

The girl was evidently flattered by the attention bestowed upon her by the smart young American. The bearded Othello alluded to edged up to her side.

"The señor had best leave the girl alone," he said, insolently.

Scarlett's fist clenched as he measured the Cuban with his eyes. The Admiral's letter crackled in his breast-pocket, and discretion got the best of valour.

"You are paying yourself a poor compliment, my good fellow," he said, "though I certainly admire your good taste. Those flowers interested me."

The Purple Terror

The man appeared to be mollified. His features corrugated in a smile.

"The señor would like some of those blooms?" he asked. "It was I who procured them for little Zara here. I can show you where they grow."

Every eye in the room was turned in Scarlett's direction. It seemed to him that a kind of diabolical malice glistened on every dark face there, save that of the girl, whose features paled under her healthy tan.

"If the señor is wise," she began, "he will not—"

"Listen to the tales of a silly girl," Othello put in, menacingly. He grasped the girl by the arm, and she winced in positive pain. "Pshaw, there is no harm where the flowers grow, if one is only careful. I will take you there, and I will be your guide to Port Anna, where you are going, for a gold dollar."

All Scarlett's scientific enthusiasm was aroused. It is not given to every man to present a new orchid to the horticultural world. And this one would dwarf the finest plant hitherto discovered.

"Done with you," he said; "we start at daybreak. I shall look to you to be ready. Your name is Tito? Well, good-night, Tito."

As Scarlett and Tarrer withdrew the girl suddenly darted forward. A wild word or two fluttered from her lips. Then there was a sound as of a blow, followed by a little, stifled cry of pain.

"No, no," Tarrer urged, as Scarlett half turned. "Better not. They are ten to one, and they are no friends of ours. It never pays to interfere in these family quarrels. I daresay, if you interfered, the girl would be just as ready to knife you as her jealous lover."

"But a blow like that, Tarrer!"

"It's a pity, but I don't see how we can help it. Your business is the quick dispatch of the Admiral's letter, not the squiring of dames."

Scarlett owned with a sigh that Tarrer was right.

II.

IT was quite a different Tito who presented himself at daybreak the following morning. His insolent manner had disappeared. He was cheerful, alert, and he had a manner full of the most winning politeness.

"You quite understand what we want," Scarlett said. "My desire is to reach Port Anna as soon as possible. You know the way?"

"Every inch of it, señor. I have made the journey scores of times. And I shall have the felicity of getting you there early on the third day from now."

"Is it so far as that?"

"The distance is not great, señor. It is the passage through the woods. There are parts where no white man has been before."

"And you will not forget the purple orchids?"

A queer gleam trembled like summer lightning in Tito's eyes. The next instant it had gone. A time was to come when Scarlett was to recall that look, but for the moment it was allowed to pass.

"The señor shall see the purple orchid," he said; "thousands of them. They have a bad name amongst our people, but that is all nonsense. They grow in the high trees, and their blossoms cling to long, green tendrils. These tendrils are poisonous to the flesh, and great care should be taken in handling them. And the flowers are quite harmless, though we call them the devil's poppies."

To all of this Scarlett listened eagerly. He was all-impatient to see and handle the mysterious flower for himself. The whole excursion was going to prove a wonderful piece of luck. At the same time he had to curb his impatience. There would be no chance of seeing the purple orchid to-day.

For hours they fought their way along through the dense tangle. A heat seemed to lie over all the land like a curse—a blistering, sweltering, moist heat with no puff of wind to temper its breathlessness. By the time that the sun was sliding down, most of the party had had enough of it.

They passed out of the underwood at length, and, striking upwards, approached a clump of huge forest trees on the brow of a ridge. All kinds of parasites hung from the branches; there were ropes and bands of green, and high up a fringe of purple glory that caused Scarlett's pulses to leap a little faster.

"Surely that is the purple orchid?" he cried.

Tito shrugged his shoulders contemptuously.

"A mere straggler or two," he said, "and out of our reach in any case. The señor will have all he wants and more to-morrow."

"But it seems to me," said Scarlett, "that I could—"

Then he paused. The sun like a great glowing shield was shining full behind the tree with its crown of purple, and showing up every green rope and thread clinging to the branches with the clearness of liquid crystal. Scarlett saw a network of green cords like a huge spider's web, and in the centre of it was not a fly, but a human skeleton!

The arms and legs were stretched apart as if the victim had been crucified. The wrists and ankles were bound in the cruel web. Fragments of tattered clothing fluttered in the faint breath of the evening breeze.

"Horrible," Scarlett cried, "absolutely horrible!"

"IN THE CENTRE WAS NOT A FLY, BUT A HUMAN SKELETON."

The Purple Terror

"You may well say that," Tarrer exclaimed, with a shudder. "Like the fly in the amber or the apple in the dumpling, the mystery is how he got there."

"Perhaps Tito can explain the mystery," Scarlett suggested.

Tito appeared to be uneasy and disturbed. He looked furtively from one to the other of his employers as a culprit might who feels he has been found out. But his courage returned as he noted the absence of suspicion in the faces turned upon him.

"I can explain," he exclaimed, with teeth that chattered from some unknown terror or guilt. "It is not the first time that I have seen the skeleton. Some plant-hunter doubtless who came here alone. He climbed into the tree without a knife, and those green ropes got twisted round his limbs, as a swimmer gets entangled in the weeds. The more he struggled, the more the cords bound him. He would call in vain for anyone to assist him here. And so he must have died."

The explanation was a plausible one, but by no means detracted from the horror of the discovery. For some time the party pushed their way on in the twilight, till the darkness descended suddenly like a curtain.

"We will camp here," Tito said; "it is high, dry ground, and we have this belt of trees above us. There is no better place than this for miles around. In the valley the miasma is dangerous."

As Tito spoke he struck a match, and soon a torch flamed up. The little party were on a small plateau, fringed by trees. The ground was dry and hard, and, as Scarlett and his party saw to their astonishment, littered with bones. There were skulls of animals and skulls of human beings, the skeletons of birds, the frames of beasts both great and small. It was a weird, shuddering sight.

"We can't possibly stay here," Scarlett exclaimed.

The Unnatural History of Man-Eating Plants

Tito shrugged his shoulders.

"There is nowhere else," he replied. "Down in the valley there are many dangers. Further in the woods are the snakes and jaguars. Bones are nothing. Peuf, they can be easily cleared away."

They had to be cleared away, and there was an end of the matter. For the most part the skeletons were white and dry as air and sun could make them. Over the dry, calcined mass the huge fringe of trees nodded mournfully. With the rest, Scarlett was busy scattering the mocking frames aside. A perfect human skeleton lay at his feet. On one finger something glittered—a signet ring. As Scarlett took it in his hand he started.

"I know this ring!" he exclaimed; "it belonged to Pierre Anton, perhaps the most skilled and intrepid plant-hunter the *Jardin des Plantes* ever employed. The poor fellow was by way of being a friend of mine. He met the fate that he always anticipated."

"There must have been a rare holocaust here," said Tarrer.

"It beats me," Scarlett responded. By this time a large circle had been shifted clear of human and other remains. By the light of the fire loathsome insects could be seen scudding and straddling away. "It beats me entirely. Tito, can you offer any explanation? If the bones were all human I could get some grip of the problem. But when one comes to birds and animals as well! Do you see that the skeletons lie in a perfect circle, starting from the centre of the clump of trees above us? What does it mean?"

Tito professed utter ignorance of the subject. Some years before a small tribe of natives invaded the peninsula for religious rites. They came from a long way off in canoes, and wild stories were told concerning them. They burnt sacrifices, no doubt.

Scarlett turned his back contemptuously on this transparent tale. His curiosity was aroused. There must be some explanation, for Pierre Anton had been seen of men within the last ten years.

"There's something uncanny about this," he said, to Tarrer. "I mean to get to the bottom of it, or know why."

"As for me," said Tarrer, with a cavernous yawn, "I have but one ambition, and that is my supper, followed by my bed."

III.

SCARLETT lay in the light of the fire looking about him. He felt restless and uneasy, though he would have found it difficult to explain the reason. For one thing, the air trembled to strange noises. There seemed to be something moving, writhing in the forest trees above his head. More than once it seemed to his distorted fancy that he could see a squirming knot of green snakes in motion.

Outside the circle, in a grotto of bones, Tito lay sleeping. A few moments before his dark, sleek head had been furtively raised, and his eyes seemed to gleam in the flickering firelight with malignant cunning. As he met Scarlett's glance he gave a deprecatory gesture and subsided.

The big mastiff growled and then whined uneasily. Even the dog seemed to be conscious of some unseen danger. He lay down again, cowed by the stern command, but he still whimpered in his dreams.

"What the deuce does it all mean?" Scarlett muttered. "I feel certain yonder rascal is up to some mischief. Jealous still because I paid his girl a little attention. But he can't do us any real harm. Quiet, there!"

"I fancy I'll keep awake for a spell," Scarlett told himself.

For a time he did so. Presently he began to slide away into the land of poppies. He was walking amongst a garden of bones which bore masses of purple blossoms. Then Pierre Anton came on the scene, pale and resolute as Scarlett had

always known him; then the big mastiff seemed in some way
to be mixed up with the phantasm of the dream, barking as
if in pain, and Scarlett came to his senses.

"A RARE HOLOCAUST."

He was breathing short, a beady perspiration stood on his
forehead, his heart hammered in quick thuds—all the
horrors of nightmare were still upon him. In a vague way
as yet he heard the mastiff howl, a real howl of real
terror, and Scarlett knew that he was awake.

The Purple Terror

Then a strange thing happened. In the none too certain light of the fire, Scarlett saw the mastiff snatched up by some invisible hand, carried far on high towards the trees, and finally flung to the earth with a crash. The big dog lay still as a log.

A sense of fear born of the knowledge of impotence came over Scarlett; what in the name of evil did it all mean? The smart scientist had no faith in the occult, and yet what *did* it all mean?

Nobody stirred. Scarlett's companions were soaked and soddened with fatigue; the rolling thunder of artillery would have scarce disturbed them. With teeth set and limbs that trembled, Scarlett crawled over to the dog.

The great, black-muzzled creature was quite dead. The full chest was stained and soaked in blood; the throat had been cut apparently with some jagged, saw-like instrument away to the bone. And, strangest thing of all, scattered all about the body was a score or more of the great purple orchid flowers broken off close to the head. A hot, pricking sensation travelled slowly up Scarlett's spine and seemed to pass out at the tip of his skull. He felt his hair rising.

He was frightened. As a matter of honest fact, he had never been so horribly scared in his life before. The whole thing was so mysterious, so cruel, so bloodthirsty.

Still, there must be some rational explanation. In some way the matter had to do with the purple orchid. The flower had an evil reputation. Was it not known to these Cubans as the devil's poppy?

Scarlett recollected vividly now Zara's white, scared face when Tito had volunteered to show the way to the resplendent bloom; he remembered the cry of the girl and the blow that followed. He could see it all now. The girl had meant to warn him against some nameless horror to which Tito was leading the small party. This was the jealous Cuban's revenge.

The Unnatural History of Man-Eating Plants

A wild desire to pay this debt to the uttermost fraction filled Scarlett, and shook him with a trembling passion. He crept along in the drenching dew to where Tito lay, and touched his forehead with the chill blue rim of a revolver barrel. Tito stirred slightly.

"You dog!" Scarlett cried. "I am going to shoot you."

Tito did not move again. His breathing was soft and regular. Beyond a doubt the man was sleeping peacefully. After all he might be innocent; and yet, on the other hand, he might be so sure of his quarry that he could afford to slumber without anxiety as to his vengeance.

In favour of the latter theory was the fact that the Cuban lay beyond the limit of what had previously been the circle of dry bones. It was just possible that there was no danger outside that pale. In that case it would be easy to arouse the rest, and so save them from the horrible death which had befallen the mastiff. No doubt these were a form of upas tree, but that would not account for the ghastly spectacle in mid-air.

"I'll let this chap sleep for the present," Scarlett muttered.

He crawled back, not without misgivings, into the ring of death. He meant to wake the others and then wait for further developments. By now his senses were more alert and vigorous than they had ever been before. A preternatural clearness of brain and vision possessed him. As he advanced he saw suddenly falling a green bunch of cord that straightened into a long, emerald line. It was triangular in shape, fine at the apex, and furnished with hooked spines. The rope appeared to dangle from the tree overhead; the broad, sucker-like termination was evidently soaking up moisture.

A natural phenomenon evidently, Scarlett thought. This was some plant new to him, a parasite living amongst the tree-tops and drawing life and vigour by means of these green, rope-like antennæ designed by Nature to soak and absorb the heavy dews of night.

For a moment the logic of this theory was soothing to Scarlett's distracted nerves, but only for a moment, for then he saw at regular intervals along the green rope the big purple blossoms of the devil's poppy.

He stood gasping there, utterly taken aback for the moment. There must be some infernal juggling behind all this business. He saw the rope slacken and quiver, he saw it swing forward like a pendulum, and the next minute it had passed across the shoulders of a sleeping seaman.

Then the green root became as the arm of an octopus. The line shook from end to end like the web of an angry spider when invaded by a wasp. It seemed to grip the sailor and tighten, and then, before Scarlett's affrighted eyes, the sleeping man was raised gently from the ground.

Scarlett jumped forward with a desire to scream hysterically. Now that a comrade was in danger he was no longer afraid. He whipped a jack-knife from his pocket and slashed at the cruel cord. He half expected to meet with the stoutness of a steel strand, but to his surprise the feeler snapped like a carrot, bumping the sailor heavily on the ground.

He sat up, rubbing his eyes vigorously.

"That you, sir?" he asked. "What is the matter?"

"For the love of God, get up at once and help me to arouse the others," Scarlett said, hoarsely. "We have come across the devil's workshop. All the horrors of the inferno are invented here."

The bluejacket struggled to his feet. As he did so, the clothing from his waist downwards slipped about his feet, clean cut through by the teeth of the green parasite. All around the body of the sailor blood oozed from a zone of teeth-marks.

The Unnatural History of Man-Eating Plants

Two-o'clock-in-the-morning courage is a virtue vouchsafed to few. The tar, who would have faced an ironclad cheerfully, fairly shivered with fright and dismay.

"What does it mean, sir?" he cried. "I've been——"

"Wake the others," Scarlett screamed; "wake the others."

Two or three more green tangles of rope came tumbling to the ground, straightening and quivering instantly. The purple blossoms stood out like a frill upon them. Like a madman Scarlett shouted, kicking his companions without mercy.

They were all awake at last, grumbling and moaning for their lost slumbers. All this time Tito had never stirred.

"I don't understand it at all," said Tarrer.

"Come from under those trees," said Scarlett, "and I will endeavour to explain. Not that you will believe me for a moment. No man can be expected to believe the awful nightmare I am going to tell you."

Scarlett proceeded to explain. As he expected, his story was followed with marked incredulity, save by the wounded sailor, who had strong evidence to stimulate his otherwise defective imagination.

"I can't believe it," Tarrer said, at length. They were whispering together beyond earshot of Tito, whom they had no desire to arouse for obvious reasons. "This is some diabolical juggling of yonder rascally Cuban. It seems impossible that those slender green cords could——"

Scarlett pointed to the centre of the circle.

"Call the dog," he said, grimly, "and see if he will come."

"I admit the point as far as the poor old mastiff is concerned. But at the same time I don't—however, I'll see for myself."

The Purple Terror

By this time a dozen or more of the slender cords were hanging pendent from the trees. They moved from spot to spot as if jerked up by some unseen hand and deposited a foot or two farther. With the great purple bloom fringing the stem, the effect was not unlovely save to Scarlett, who could see only the dark side of it. As Tarrer spoke he advanced in the direction of the trees.

"What are you going to do?" Scarlett asked.

"Exactly what I told you. I am going to investigate this business for myself."

Without wasting further words Scarlett sprang forward. It was no time for the niceties of an effete civilization. Force was the only logical argument to be used in a case like this, and Scarlett was the more powerful man of the two.

Tarrer saw and appreciated the situation.

"No, no," he cried; "none of that. Anyway, you're too late."

He darted forward and threaded his way between the slender emerald columns. As they moved slowly and with a certain stately deliberation there was no great danger to an alert and vigorous individual. As Scarlett entered the avenue he could hear the soak and suck as the dew was absorbed.

"For Heaven's sake, come out of it," he cried.

The warning came too late. A whip-like trail of green touched Tarrer from behind, and in a lightning flash he was in the toils. The tendency to draw up anything and everything gave the cords a terrible power. Tarrer evidently felt it, for his breath came in great gasps.

"Cut me free," he said, hoarsely; "cut me free. I am being carried off my feet."

He seemed to be doomed for a moment, for all the cords there were apparently converging in his direction. This, as a matter of fact, was a solution of the whole

"THE SLEEPING MAN WAS RAISED GENTLY FROM THE GROUND."

sickening, horrible sensation. Pulled here and there, thrust in one direction and another, Tarrer contrived to keep his feet.

Heedless of possible danger to himself Scarlett darted forward, calling to his companions to come to the rescue. In less time than it takes to tell, four knives were at work ripping and slashing in all directions.

"Not all of you," Scarlett whispered. So tense was the situation that no voice was raised above a murmur. "You two keep your eyes open for fresh cords, and cut them as they fall, instantly. Now then."

The horrible green spines were round Tarrer's body like snakes. His face was white, his breath came painfully, for the pressure was terrible. It seemed to Scarlett to be one horrible dissolving view of green, slimy cords and great weltering, purple blossoms. The whole of the circle was strewn with them. They were wet and slimy underfoot.

Tarrer had fallen forward half unconscious. He was supported now by but two cords above his head. The cruel pressure had been relieved. With one savage sweep of his knife Scarlett cut the last of the lines, and Tarrer fell like a log unconscious to the ground. A feeling of nausea, a yellow dizziness, came over Scarlett as he staggered beyond the dread circle. He saw Tarrer carried to a place of safety, and then the world seemed to wither and leave him in the dark.

"I feel a bit groggy and weak," said Tarrer an hour or so later; "but beyond that this idiot of a Richard is himself again. So far as I am concerned, I should like to get even with our friend Tito for this."

"Something with boiling oil in it," Scarlett suggested, grimly. "The callous scoundrel has slept soundly through the whole of this business. I suppose he felt absolutely certain that he had finished with us."

"Upon my word, we ought to shoot the beggar!" Tarrer exclaimed.

"I have a little plan of my own," said Scarlett, "which I am going to put in force later on. Meanwhile we had better get on with breakfast. When Tito wakes a pleasant little surprise will await him."

Tito roused from his slumbers in due course and looked around him. His glance was curious, disappointed, then full of a white and yellow fear. A thousand conflicting emotions streamed across his dark face. Scarlett read them at a glance as he called the Cuban over to him.

"I am not going into any unnecessary details with you," he said. "It has come to my knowledge that you are playing traitor to us. Therefore we prefer to complete our journey alone. We can easily find the way now."

"The señor may do as he pleases," he replied. "Give me my dollar and let me go."

Scarlett replied grimly that he had no intention of doing anything of the kind. He did not propose to place the lives of himself and his comrades in the power of a rascally Cuban who had played false.

"We are going to leave you here till we return," he said. "You will have plenty of food, you will be perfectly safe under the shelter of these trees, and there is no chance of anybody disturbing you. We are going to tie you up to one of these trees for the next four-and-twenty hours."

All the insolence died out of Tito's face. His knees bowed, a cold dew came out over the ghastly green of his features. From the shaking of his limbs he might have fared disastrously with ague.

"The trees," he stammered, "the trees, señor! There is danger from snakes, and—and from many things. There are other places—"

"If this place was safe last night it is safe to-day," Scarlett said, grimly. "I have quite made up my mind."

The Purple Terror

Tito fought no longer. He fell forward on his knees, he howled for mercy, till Scarlett fairly kicked him up again.

"Make a clean breast of it," he said, "or take the consequences. You know perfectly well that we have found you out, scoundrel."

Tito's story came in gasps. He wanted to get rid of the Americans. He was jealous. Besides, under the Americanos would Cuba be any better off? By no means and assuredly not. Therefore it was the duty of every good Cuban to destroy the Americanos where possible.

"A nice lot to fight for," Scarlett muttered. "Get to the point."

Hastened to the point by a liberal application of stout shoe-leather, Tito made plenary confession. The señor himself had suggested death by medium of the devil's poppies. More than one predatory plant-hunter had been lured to his destruction in the same way. The skeleton hung on the tree was a Dutchman who had walked into the clutch of the purple terror innocently. And Pierre Anton had done the same. The suckers of the devil's poppy only came down at night to gather moisture; in the day they were coiled up like a spring. And anything that they touched they killed. Tito had watched more than one bird or small beast crushed and mauled by these cruel spines with their fringe of purple blossoms.

"How do you get the blooms?" Scarlett asked.

"That is easy," Tito replied. "In the daytime I moisten the ground under the trees. Then the suckers unfold, drawn by the water. Once the suckers unfold one cuts several of them off with long knives. There is danger, of course, but not if one is careful."

"I'll not trouble the devil's poppy any further at present," said Scarlett, "but I shall trouble you to accompany me to my destination as a prisoner."

"HE HOWLED FOR MERCY."

Tito's eyes dilated.

"They will not shoot me?" he asked, hoarsely.

"I don't know," Scarlett replied. "They may hang you instead. At any rate, I shall be bitterly disappointed if they don't end you one way or the other. Whichever operation it is, I can look forward to it with perfect equanimity."

THE WONDERFUL TIGER TREE

By Walt MacDougall

(Salt Lake Herald, 1905)

The Wonderful Tiger Tree and How a Royal Youth Saved a Neighboring Kingdom and Won a Beautiful Bride

The Story of a Little Prince Who Was Tired of His Mode of Life and Wonderful Experiences He Had When He Ran Away

EVERY prince that I ever met has told me that he wished he had been born something else, and most of them wished they were artists. When they grow up and become kings they generally change their minds and begin to like their jobs better. But little Prince Otto, of the Kingdom Of Wissol, even when he was but ten years old, had grown so tired of his splendid position that he had determined to run away at the very first chance and become a fisher-boy or a shepherd on the dim blue mountains that could be seen from the palace windows looming up in the distance.

When you realize what it means to be a prince you will readily see what had driven him to this determination. He had to learn Latin and Greek, astronomy, algebra, geometry, French, German, Turkish, Yiddish, Italian, Russian and Spanish; also horse-shoeing, medicine, painting, music, dancing and navigation, as well as a host of other things. Of course, horseback-riding, shooting and automobiling were pleasant tasks, but as so many hours in the day had to be devoted to the others he had little time to give to these, and as he was especially fond of chemistry, of course he had to sit up nights to study that, for there was no time for it during the day.

The Tiger Tree With the Dreadful Fruit Just Ready to Fall

Many a time the whole palace was aroused at midnight by some tremendous report, only to find that Prince Otto had been experimenting with some new chemicals and had blown up his bedroom, so fond was he of this study, which was finally very useful in the adventure that befell him.

One day he found that he had discovered a mixture that made the most wonderful sticky fly-paper in the world; a mess that not only held every fly securely, no matter how lightly it touched it, but also drew the pesky things to

The Wonderful Tiger Tree

it with an attraction they couldn't resist for a moment. He was very much delighted, for he now knew that his name would be forever famous, for it is far greater to have invented something useful than to be a prince.

*****

He had spread the stuff upon a great sheet of paper and left it upon his table, and when he awoke in the morning he heard a small, squeaky voice in his room. He sat up in bed and looked around, but saw no-one, yet it was still audible. Somebody was crying, and tiny as was the voice it seemed to be right in the room. Then he heard words plainly, saying:

"Shame upon you, false, fleeting friends! My fate will be on your heads!"

"What is the matter!" cried Otto, jumping out of bed.

A silence followed, but when Otto asked "Who is here and in trouble?" the tiny voice replied:

"Help! Help! I am stuck in this awful stuff and can't get out."

Otto saw nothing on the fly-paper, yet it was from that the voice came. He passed his hand over it, however, and was amazed to find it touch something that was invisible. It moved beneath his fingers as if trembling as he asked:

"What is it? Who are you?"

"I am the elf Kaskara," replied the voice. "I am caught here, else you would not have me at your mercy."

"But you are not at my mercy," cried the Prince. "I would never hurt an elf, I am sure. The idea! Nothing is farther from my mind."

"Then why did you set this trap?" asked the elf, invisible still.

"I set a trap? Why, that's for flies. Who ever expected to catch an elf? Ha, ha!" laughed Otto.

"That's right, laugh at me. You've caught me and you may laugh," grumbled Kaskara.

"But why can't I see you?" asked Otto. "Just show yourself, and I'll get you out of that in a jiffy!"

He suddenly saw the elf, standing over his ankles in the sticky stuff. He was dressed in red leather and his beard came to his knees. His face was very anxious as he looked up at the Prince, but the boy was so kindly and so smiling that he soon seemed easier in his mind, and as Otto removed the stickiness from about his feet, he smiled himself. Then the Prince carefully lifted him. After which he took turpentine and extract of Alzamosoline, and in a very short time had effaced even the traces of the sticky fluid from his tiny low shoes and wool stockings.

*****

The elf sat down upon a pill box and said:

"You are very good," said Kaskara, "and now as a sort of a fine for trespassing I will give you three wishes; or, rather, two now and one later, after you see how the others work. What do you most wish for?"

"Oh," replied the boy, "I would wish to be loved by everybody, for a prince is so very lonely and so lofty that he is never really loved."

"That's easy enough," said the elf, smiling, "but I am afraid so much affection will bother you. What's the next wish?"

"What! Have I wished once?" cried Otto, in surprise.

"Certainly. That was a wish, and it's all accomplished. Next!"

"Well I certainly wish that I could be invisible like you when I want to," added Otto thoughtfully.

"All you have to do is put your thumbs together and say 'Zobasto' and it's done. To become visible, say 'Pastik.'

The Wonderful Tiger Tree

Now, in a week or two I'll see you again and we will talk over the third wish. I can stay no longer, for I must be off to punish my comrades for running away and leaving me in the lurch, although, after all, I am not sorry now, as I have learned that human beings are not to be feared. So I will be off. Good morning."

Otto was left alone, and the first thing he did was to put his thumbs together and say "Zobasto," after which he went downstairs and was delighted to find that nobody could see him at all.

"Oh, my! Now I'll have fun!" he cried. "This is splendid. Now to find out how my first wish works." He said "Pastik" and walked out into the great palace garden where all the courtiers spent their time.

As soon as he appeared every one ran to him and showed the greatest pleasure at seeing him, and it was very evident that he was loved by all. Even the Regent, who ruled the kingdom for him, as he was an orphan, showed real feeling, although the day before he hated him, for he wished himself to be king, but had not dared to seize the throne for fear of the people. Wherever the Prince appeared he was greeted with cheers, flowers were thrown over him, presents given to him and all the ladies wanted to fondle and kiss him every minute. The change was most wonderful, as before that nobody thought much of him, because, kept indoors by his many studies, he had been rarely seen abroad.

But in a few days all this excessive loving began to be somewhat of a nuisance to the boy, as he now couldn't take a step without being bothered; for, of course, both great and small wished to express the feeling they had for their prince. Many a time he was compelled to put together his thumbs and say "Zebasto" just to avoid a loving crowd of his subjects; and soon the mysterious absences, for that's what they were considered, of course, began to be gossiped about all over the land, and the place of his sudden retreats was sought for everywhere.

The Unnatural History of Man-Eating Plants

It amused him to walk in the midst of a crowd and hear them guessing as to where he had hidden himself, as well as telling of their great affection for him; but after a time, when they all began to discuss the project of sending the much-hated Regent away and making Otto king, although still so young, he became alarmed, for he did not wish to be king for ever so long yet.

When at last he overheard in the garden several of the principal nobles arranging the plot he determined to go away and stay for a time, for, of course, without him they would not act. So packing up his diamond-studded gold hair-brushes, his crown, his ruby-mounted toothbrush, his box of paints and a bag of gold in a small valise, and after putting on the plainest suit of clothes he could find among the hundreds hanging in his closets and girding on his jeweled sword, he softly said "Zobasto" and stole forth early in the morning.

Past the guards of the castle he walked stealthily, and out upon the great highway that led across his kingdom toward the blue mountains on the border. On the road were many wagons moving into town filled with potatoes, cabbages, apples and other farm produce, although the sun was hardly up yet, and he wondered when these people who drove them got out of bed.

Quail came running out of the woods at the roadside and rabbits scampered across the highway, while overhead so many birds were making music that it seemed as if the very air was a river of melody flowing along with him.

Every animal that he passed or met acted in the same way, all flocking to him lovingly and many followed him for a long distance, which caused a panic among a crowd of gypsies traveling townwards when they came upon him and his followers at a turn in the road. As soon as they saw him they shouted "Wizard!" "Magician!" and began to get out their guns, for they were strangers and did not know the Prince of Wissol.

The Wonderful Tiger Tree

The animals crowding about Otto seemed uncertain what to do, but when the first gun went off the Prince quickly uttered the magic word, and no longer seeing him they fled in a hurry, I tell you. They were frightened, but their fright was as nothing to the terror of the gypsies when Otto vanished like smoke before their eyes and nothing was to be seen but the bare road winding among the trees. So alarmed were they that they turned their wagons and in a hurry whipped up their horses to leave a place too full of mystery, but Otto, who had grown somewhat tired, ran to a wagon and climbed in.

Here he found a woman and a child lying on cushions who had not seen the cause of the alarm, and they were trying to discover what it was by peering out through a hole in the canvas covering of the wagon. Otto, when he had made himself comfortable, said "Pastik," and when they turned they saw him sitting there. Although greatly surprised, they of course loved him at once and began to ask questions, whereupon he explained what had happened, although he did not tell them that he had been invisible.

The woman was the gypsy queen, Berlina, and she soon called for her husband who came on a run, still filled with wonder and alarm.

*****

Otto was not sorry to be able to ride with them, for he had never thought of taking a horse from the royal stables and making his journey on horseback. Anyway, it would have looked very funny, he reflected, to see a horse going along alone if he happened to wish to become invisible, so it was perhaps best as it was.

He found the gypsies very entertaining, telling most wonderful stores of the lands they had seen and the things they had done, so the time passed very pleasantly. They journeyed slowly; it took them four days to make the nine leagues to Umpallan, for it was toilsome work climbing the tall mountains, as the road wound around and around beside yawning chasms and deep valleys, yet never seeming to bring them nearer to the top, until suddenly they came out between two great cliffs, and lo! they saw the vast plain on the other side stretching out before them in the bright sunshine like a great green carpet.

Away off on the extreme horizon Otto saw what seemed to be an immensely tall palm tree against the blue sky, and as he turned to ask the gypsy king what sort of tree it was, he saw that the king turned pale and trembled.

"What is the matter?" asked the Prince.

"Luck is against us," answered Moribundo, the gypsy. "We must turn back at once. I dare not go on, but I do wish that somebody had told us about this before we started to climb the mountains."

"But what is it? Why must we return?"

"Yonder is the reason," replied Moribundo. "That tree which you see in the distance is the Tiger Palm! It has bloomed again!"

*****

"What of it? Is it unlucky?" asked the boy.

"Worse than unlucky! It means death itself! That tree grows but once in a century, but when it blooms it sheds death and destruction!"

"Is it a poisonous tree?" asked Otto.

"Have you never heard of the dread Tiger Palm?" cried Moribundo. "It is not really a tree, for instead of a crown of leaves, it bears at its top an enormous tiger's head, around which a hundred legs armed with sharp claws hang down. Look! Even from here you can see it raise its head! In a short time it will fall to the ground, and then what sorrow and woe will be upon this land, for it will devour many people. Nothing can escape the terrible beast once it is loosened from the tall stalk upon which it grows now.

The Wonderful Tiger Tree

"Yes, we must turn and get as far away from this place as possible, for well I know what will happen, as my grandfather told me what his father told him about the last time the Tiger Palm bloomed in this ill-fated land."

"Well, I will go on," said Otto, "for I wish to learn more about this wonder. We have no such in Wissol."

"For which you should be truly thankful," added the gypsy, and then he tried to induce Otto to return with him, but the Prince was true to his determination; and so saying farewell to them all he started down the winding road to Umpallan. On the way he thought over the wonderful Tiger Palm, and came to the conclusion that the people of the land must be exceedingly simple not to have destroyed it long before it grew up. He decided to make the attempt himself, for he thought that it would be rather easy to accomplish. After a while, when he had reached the level land, he came to a small house beside the road, and stopping he knocked at the door. An old woman of so hideous an appearance that she startled him opened it, and was about to tell him to begone, but in a moment the elf's spell was working and she fell in love with him, as everybody else had done, and she invited him to enter.

"What do you here, my lad with the pleasant face?" she asked. "What seek you with the witch of Umpallan? Do you need charms?"

"I wish to buy some food," responded Otto, "for I have eaten but little since last night." Then he told her how the gypsies had been frightened away before they had breakfast. She hastened to set food before him, smiling as she did so a smile that made her awful face more hideous. He ate what she gave him and offered her some gold from his bag, but she said:

"No, I will take no pay. I know not how it is, but you must have some magic power, for you are precious in my eyes. From another I would have taken not only all his gold, but his wits as well. Wither go you?"

"I am the Prince of Wissol, and I journey to see the world. What shall I find beyond?" asked Otto.

"Two things to dread and avoid," she replied. "One is the Tiger Tree that in a few days, perhaps, will be ripe and drop its dire fruit, when all the land will weep; the other is old Quintessence, the uncle of Princess Azoline, a man of blood and villainy. I tell you this, I who have been his partner in crime. Why I tell you I know not, for it is a strange thing to me, but it is the truth. He will slay you for your gold, or imprison you to toss you to the tiger when he gets loose."

"I will probably slay him first if he tries to play any pranks on me," said Otto.

"Avoid him! Keep far from the palace, where he now rules until the Princess comes of age"

"She seems as unlucky as myself," said Otto. "Is she, too, an orphan?"

"Yes. Her parents have been dead seven years, and it will be some years still before she is old enough to be queen; but that will never happen, for Quintessence has been teaching the people that if she is sacrificed to the tiger just before he drops to the ground the beast will be satisfied and depart from the land. Thus he hopes to rid himself of her, and afterward destroy the tiger by a magic spell that I sold him, but I will tell you that the spell is all tommy rot and foolishness, for it won't work. So old Quintessence, as well as all of us, perhaps, will be eaten up finally, and that's what I want. I hate everybody here, except you, of course."

"You are a bitter old creature," said Otto, "but I will not let you harm any more people with your spells and enchantments."

"Why, bless your heart," she cried, "you don't suppose I can really do harm! Why, all my spells are rubbish. Don't you know there's no such thing? I just let them believe in them, but, dear me, they're all harmless. Indeed, I wish I was a witch, but there are none really. But so long as the fools believe in me and pay me, why not take their money?"

He soon came in sight of the city over which, high in the air, hung the terrible Tiger with his hundred legs suspended limply, his glaring eyes shining with the light of hungry impatience, for he was nearly ripe and ready to drop. Many of the houses were empty, deserted by their occupants from fear of the Tiger, but since old Quintessence had announced that the sacrifice of the young princess would avert all danger, the rest of the inhabitants of Umpallan remained in the city, but with fear and trembling.

He went close to the tree at last, closer than anyone had ever dared to go, and the Tiger glared down at him, showing his teeth and growling, but Otto grinned at him carelessly and the beast felt a thrill of fear go through him as this was the first time anyone had dared to meet his eye. Something told him that here was his destroyer below him, and he trembled so that the tree trunk wobbled.

Then Otto went to the palace and asked for admission but as he was dusty and travel-stained the pompous doorkeeper refused to admit him, telling him to go around to the kitchen door, as befits all tramps. Otto was about to strike him with his sword, but recollected in time that he had no right to cut off the heads of any but his own subjects, so he went around to the kitchen and asked the cook for lodging.

*****

You see he had not given the doorkeeper time to fall in love with him, as he asked so suddenly for admission but on this occasion he waited until the fat cook had taken a good look at him and the charm worked. She said that he could stay there and he could share her bed, but he promptly declined, saying that he wouldn't trouble her for the world. Then she told him that he could sleep in the hay in the stable over the horses. After supper he went to sleep there, tired and yet happy, for he had solved the problem of destroying the Tiger.

Early in the morning the Princess Azoline, looking out of her window, spied Otto asleep on the hay, and she, of course, promptly fell in love with him. Running down, she tiptoed lightly into the stable and bent over him. She saw that he was very handsome, although so dusty, but when she looked into his valise and saw the gold crown, the brushes and the bag of gold she knew at once that he was a prince in disguise.

Then she told the cook to bring him to breakfast, but when the cook went to awake him he had disappeared. There lay his leather bag, and she saw the place where he had slept in the hay, but no prince was visible, because as soon as he awoke Otto said "Zobasto," for he wished to watch the old Prime Minister Quintessence without being visible, as, once seen, the old man would love him and he could not properly punish him for his wickedness.

He softly stole through the many rooms of the palace, up and up, until at last, on the very top floor, he found him in a very small room where he mixed the nasty-smelling potions and compounds for which he paid the so-called witch for instruction, thinking them very potent and deadly to his foes. He also had many chemicals around him of which he knew almost nothing, but which he bought to give his room the appearance of a laboratory or chemist's workshop, so that people would consider him an alchemist and astrologer.

When Otto stole in the curtains were drawn tight and the room was very dark, but he saw the old man bending over a small lamp, the blue flame of which dimly lighted the hard old face and wicked eyes. Then Otto, seeing the chemicals, with all of which he was so familiar, resolved to frighten the pretend astrologer, and taking some phosphorous he mixed it with sulphur and then wrote on the wall with his finger dipped in the mixture. This is what he wrote:

"SAMOLIO DUPLEXUS BISMALLAH SWAX ORAPROMISKUS!"

The Wonderful Tiger Tree

The words shone in fire as bright as sunlight. Then he spoke in a hollow tone and said:

"Quintessence thou old villain, turn!"

The Prime Minister, astounded that anybody should so address him, turned in great wrath, but when he saw nothing but the mysterious flaming words upon the wall he fell back in a fright. After a moment he managed to ask, weakly:

"Who and what are you? What means these dread words on the wall?"

*****

Of course he thought that at last some spook had answered to his incantations, or some mighty demon of the dark had responded to his frequent summons and yet he was terrified. Otto answered:

"I am the genie of the cave, Abuzzeram the Shining One! I am come to demand an accounting of your trust! What have you done with all the gold and jewels of the kingdom which the late king left with you? What are you about to do with the Princess Azoline?"

Quintessence fell on his knees, shaking with terror.

"I have the gold, O lord Genie! I have concealed it in the cellar as well as all the jewels of the late king and queen, in the cellar of an old house which I own in the city. You shall have them all, all!"

"Where is this house?" asked Otto.

"At the corner of Doldrum and Bitumen streets," replied the old thief. "I was about to sacrifice the Princess to the Tiger, oh Shining One, but if you wish I will give her to you!"

"You will do nothing of the sort!" replied Otto. "This is what you will do: In less than half an hour you will be in your carriage and moving out of the kingdom quickly, never to return, and dare not go near your old house for the gold, for that I have guarded with flaming demons, ten in number, who will eat you alive if you approach. If you are here a half-hour hence I will sick them on you at once. So get!"

Otto couldn't think of any more to say, therefore he drew a great skull and crossbones in fire on the wall, as the old man knelt there paralyzed with terror and wrote under the picture the words:

"THIS FOR YOU!"

That settled him. Quintessence sprang up and flew howling down the stairs and shrilly yelled for his carriage and the fastest horses he had. In less than ten minutes the people were amazed to see the Prime Minister leap into his carriage, and, pale with fright, order his driver to hurry. He was never seen again in Umpallan, but it was a long time before he was forgotten and the people ceased to dread his return.

Then Otto went to the Princess and told her that he had come to destroy the Tiger Palm.

*****

Then he called the towns-people together and informed them that he had come to rescue them after which he led them out to the Tiger Palm and commanded them to cut down all the small trees for yards and yards, while he measured the height of the palm by trigonometry, thanking his stars, after all, that he had been forced to study that science so well. Then he ordered all the blacksmiths to build a huge cage, a cage so strong that a dozen tigers couldn't even jar it, just seventy-five feet from the foot of the tree.

It took a week to build the great cage, which was constructed with a door on top, all of steel as thick as your arm, and when it was ready Otto called for all the wood-choppers to assemble. He took a ladder, and, much to the alarm of the people, climbed far up the tree-trunk,

The Wonderful Tiger Tree

after which he fastened rope to it, giving the end to a
man at a distance. Then he bade the wood-choppers cut down
the tree. At it they went, and in less than an hour it
began to totter, while the enraged and terrified tiger on
top struggled, roared, scratched, wriggled, twisted,
clawed, squirmed and panted.

Then, as the great tree began to fall, the men at the
ropes pulled and hauled in different directions, guiding
it in its descent as Otto ordered, until at last down it
came with a bang, landing the enraged Tiger upside down in
the steel cage. They sawed the tree trunk off just
outside, after shutting down the door and fastening it,
and while the Tiger clawed around inside they stood there
and laughed at him for nobody feared him a bit now.

They got him just in time, for he was very ripe, and that
very day he came off the stalk, so to speak, and went
rampaging up and down his cage like anything but the fruit
of a tree. It was of no use, however. They pulled away the
fragment of the tree trunk and ran in some steel bars, and
he was as harmless as a mouse. Then they mounted the cage
on wheels and hauled him to the city museum, where now you
may see him yourself if you ever happen to go to Umpallan,
which is, as I've said, nine leagues from Wissol in a
straight line over the mountains.

Otto married the Princess, and now is king of both
countries. He is famous as the only king who knows more
than Emperor William does, and that's fame enough for
anybody. Later on I will tell you about his third wish and
what came of it, and that's a very strange story, also.

PROFESSOR JONKIN'S CANNIBAL PLANT

By Howard R. Garis

(The Argosy, 1905)

A triumph of cultivation which threatened a tragedy in mastication.

AFTER Professor Jeptha Jonkin had, by skilful grafting and care, succeeded in raising a single tree that produced, at different seasons, apples, oranges, pineapples, figs, cocoanuts, and peaches, it might have been supposed he would rest from his scientific labors. But Professor Jonkin was not that kind of a man.

He was continually striving to grow something new in the plant world. So it was no surprise to Bradley Adams, when calling on his friend the professor one afternoon, to find that scientist busy in his large conservatory.

"What are you up to now?" asked Adams. "Trying to make a rose-bush produce violets, or a honeysuckle vine bring forth pumpkins?"

"Neither," replied Professor Jonkin a little stiffly, for he resented Adams' playful tone. "Not that either of those things would be difficult. But look at that."

He pointed to a small plant with bright, glossy green leaves mottled with red spots. The thing was growing in a large earthen pot.

Professor Jonkin's Cannibal Plant

It bore three flowers, about the size of morning glories, and not unlike that blossom in shape, save, near the top, there was a sort of lid, similar to the flap observed on a jack-in-the-pulpit plant.

"Look down one of those flowers," went on the professor, and Adams, wondering what was to come, did so.

He saw within a small tube, lined with fine, hair-like filaments, which seemed to be in motion. And the shaft or tube went down to the bottom of the morning-glory-shaped part of the flower. At the lower extremity was a little clear liquid.

"Kind of a queer blossom. What is it?" asked Adams.

"That," said the professor with a note of pride in his voice, "is a specimen of the Sarracenia Nepenthis."

"What's that? French for sunflower, or Latin for sweet pea?" asked Adams irreverently.

"It is Latin for pitcher plant," responded the professor, drawing himself up to his full height of five feet three. "One of the most interesting of the South American flora."

"The name fits it pretty well," observed Adams. "I see there's water at the bottom. I suppose this isn't the pitcher that went to the well too often."

"The Sarracenia Nepenthis is a most wonderful plant," went on the professor in his lecture voice, not heeding Adams' joking remarks. "It belongs to what Darwin calls the carnivorous family of flowers, and other varieties of the same species are the Dionaea Muscipula, or Venus Fly-trap, the Darlingtonia, the Pinguicula and Aldrovandra, as well as—"

"Hold on, professor," pleaded Adams. "I'll take the rest on faith. Just tell me about this pitcher plant. It seems interesting."

"It *is* interesting," said Professor Jonkin. "It eats insects."

The Unnatural History of Man-Eating Plants

"Eats insects?"

"Certainly. Watch."

The professor opened a small wire cage lying on a shelf and took from it several flies. These he liberated close to the queer plant.

The insects buzzed about a few seconds, dazed with their sudden liberty.

Then they began slowly to circle in the vicinity of the strange flowers. Nearer and nearer the blossoms they came, attracted by some subtle perfume, as well as by a sweet syrup that was on the edge of the petals, put there by nature for the very purpose of drawing hapless insects into the trap.

The flies settled down, some on the petals of all three blooms. Then a curious thing happened.

The little hair-like filaments in the tube within the petals suddenly reached out and wound themselves about the insects feeding on the sweet stuff, and which seemed to intoxicate them. In an instant the flies were pulled to the top of the flower shaft by a contraction of the hairs, and then they went tumbling down the tube into the miniature pond below, where they were drowned after a brief struggle. Their crawling back was prevented by spines growing with points down, as the wires in some rat-traps are fastened.

Meanwhile the cover of the plant closed down.

"Why, it's a regular fly-trap, isn't it?" remarked Adams, much surprised.

"It is," replied the professor. "The plant lives off the insects it captures. It absorbs them, digests them, and, when it is hungry again, catches more."

"Where'd you get such an uncanny thing?" asked Adams, moving away from the plant as if he feared it might take a sample bite out of him.

Professor Jonkin's Cannibal Plant

"A friend sent it to me from Brazil."

"But you're not going to keep it, I hope."

"I certainly am," rejoined Professor Jonkin.

"Maybe you're going to train it to come to the table and eat like a human being," suggested Adams, with a laugh that nettled the professor.

"I wouldn't have to train it much to induce it to be polite," snapped back the owner of the pitcher plant.

And then, seeing that his jokes were not relished, Adams assumed an interest he did not feel, and listened to a long dissertation on botany in general and carnivorous plants in particular.

He would much rather have been eating some of the queer hybrid fruits the professor raised. He pleaded an engagement when he saw an opening in the talk, and went away.

It was some months after that before he saw the professor again. The botanist was busy in his conservatory in the mean time, and the gardener he hired to do rough work noticed that his master spent much time in that part of the glass house where the pitcher plant was growing.

For Professor Jonkin had become so much interested in his latest acquisition that he seemed to think of nothing else. His plan for increasing strawberries to the size of peaches was abandoned for a time, as was his pet scheme of raising apples without any core.

The gardener wondered what there was about the South American blossoms to require such close attention.

One day he thought he would find out, and he started to enter that part of the conservatory where the pitcher plant was growing. Professor Jonkin halted him before he had stepped inside and sternly bade him never to appear there again.

As the gardener, crestfallen, moved away after a glimpse into the forbidden region he muttered:

"My, that plant has certainly grown! And I wonder what the professor was doing so close to it. Looked as if he was feeding the thing."

As the days went by the conduct of Professor Jonkin became more and more curious. He scarcely left the southern end of the conservatory, save at night, when he entered his house to sleep.

He was a bachelor, and had no family cares to trouble him, so he could spend all his time among his plants. But hitherto he had divided his attention among his many experiments in the floral kingdom.

Now he was always with his mysterious pitcher plant. He even had his meals sent into the green-house.

"Be you keepin' boarders?" asked the butcher boy of the gardener one day, pausing on his return to the store, his empty basket on his arm.

"No. Why?"

"The professor is orderin' so much meat lately. I thought you had company."

"No, there's only us two. Mr. Adams used to come to dinner once in a while, but not lately."

"Then you an' the professor must have big appetites."

"What makes you think so?"

"The number of beefsteaks you eat."

"Number of beefsteaks? Why, my lad, the professor and I are both vegetarians."

"What's them?"

"We neither of us eat a bit of meat. We don't believe it's healthy."

Professor Jonkin's Cannibal Plant

"Then what becomes of the three big porterhouse steaks I deliver to the professor in the green-house every day?"

"Porterhouse steaks?" questioned the gardener, amazed.

"Do you feed 'em to the dog?"

"We don't keep a dog."

But the butcher boy questioned no further, for he saw a chum and hastened off to join him.

"Three porterhouse steaks a day!" mused the gardener, shaking his head. "I do hope the professor has not ceased to be a vegetarian. Yet it looks mighty suspicious. And he's doing it on the sly, too, for there's been no meat cooked in the house, of that I'm sure."

And the gardener, sorely puzzled over the mystery, went off, shaking his head more solemnly than before.

He resolved to have a look in the place the professor guarded so carefully. He tried the door when he was sure his master was in another part of the conservatory, but it was locked, and no key the gardener had would unfasten it.

A month after the gardener had heard of the porterhouse steaks, Adams happened to drop in to see his friend the professor again.

"He's in with the Sarracenia Nepenthis," said the gardener in answer to the visitor's inquiry. "But I doubt if he will let you enter."

"Why won't he?"

"Because he's become mighty close-mouthed of late over that pitcher plant."

"Oh, I guess he'll see me," remarked Adams confidently, and he knocked on the door that shut off the locked section of the green-house from the main portion.

"Who's there?" called the professor.

"Adams."

"Oh," in a more conciliatory tone, "I was just wishing you'd come along. I have something to show you."

Professor Jonkin opened the door, and the sight that met Adams' gaze startled him.

The only plant in that part of the conservatory was a single specimen of the Sarracenia Nepenthis. Yet it had attained such enormous proportions that at first Adams thought he must be dreaming.

"What do you think of that for an achievement in science?" asked the professor proudly.

"Do you mean to say that is the small, fly-catching plant your friend sent you from Brazil?"

"The same."

"But—but—"

"But how it's grown, that's what you want to say isn't it?"

"It is. How did you do it?"

"By dieting the blossoms."

"You mean—?"

"I mean feeding them. Listen. I reasoned that if a small blossom of the plant would thrive on a few insects, by giving it larger meals I might get a bigger plant. So I made my plans.

"First I cut off all but one blossom, so that the strength of the plant would nourish that alone. Then I made out a bill of fare. I began feeding it on chopped beef. The plant took to it like a puppy. It seemed to beg for more. From chopped meat I went to small pieces, cut up. I could fairly see the blossom increase in size. From that I went to choice mutton chops, and, after a week of them, with the plant becoming more gigantic all the while, I increased its meals to a porterhouse steak a day. And now—
—"

Professor Jonkin's Cannibal Plant

The professor paused to contemplate his botanical work.

"Well, now?" questioned Adams.

"Now," went on the professor proudly, "my pitcher plant takes three big beefsteaks every day—one for breakfast, one for dinner, and one for supper. And see the result."

Adams gazed at the immense plant. From a growth about as big as an Easter lily it had increased until the top was near the roof of the green-house, twenty-five feet above.

About fifteen feet up, or ten feet from the top, there branched out a great flower, about eight feet long and three feet across the bell-shaped mouth, which, except for the cap or cover, was not unlike the opening of an immense morning glory.

The flower was heavy, and the stalk on which it grew was not strong enough to support it upright. So a rude scaffolding had been constructed of wood and boards, and on a frame the flower was held upright.

In order to see it to better advantage, and also that he might feed it, the professor had a ladder by which he could ascend to a small platform in front of the bell-shaped mouth of the blossom.

"It is time to give my pet its meal," he announced, as if he were speaking of some favorite horse. "Want to come up and watch it eat?"

"No, thank you," responded Adams. "It's too uncanny."

The professor took a large steak, one of the three which the butcher boy had left that day. Holding it in his hand, he climbed up the ladder and was soon on the platform in front of the plant.

Adams watched him curiously. The professor leaned over to toss the steak into the yawning mouth of the flower.

Suddenly Adams saw him totter, throw his arms wildly in the air, and then, as if drawn by some overpowering force, he fell forward, lost his balance, and toppled into the maw of the pitcher plant!

Professor Jonkin's Cannibal Plant -KJG

Professor Jonkin's Cannibal Plant

There was a jar to the stalk and blossom as the professor fell within. He went head first into the tube, or eating apparatus of the strange plant, his legs sticking out for an instant, kicking wildly. Then he disappeared entirely.

Adams didn't know whether to laugh or be alarmed.

He mounted the ladder, and stood in amazement before the result of the professor's work as he looked down into the depth of the gigantic flower, increased a hundred times in size.

He was aware of a strange, sickish-sweet odor that seemed to steal over his senses. It was lulling him to sleep, and he fought against it. Then he looked down and saw that the huge hairs or filaments with which the tube was lined were in violent motion.

He could just discern the professor's feet about three feet below the rim of the flower. They were kicking, but with a force growing less every second. The filaments seemed to be winding about the professor's legs, holding him in a deadly embrace.

Then the top cover, or flap of the plant, closed down suddenly. The professor was a prisoner inside.

The plant had turned cannibal and eaten the man who had grown it!

For an instant, fear deprived Adams of reason. He did not know what to do. Then the awful plight of his friend brought back his senses.

"Professor!" he shouted. "Are you alive? Can you hear me?"

"Yes," came back in faint and muffled tones. "This beast has me, all right."

Then followed a series of violent struggles that shook the plant.

"I'll get you out! Where's an ax? I'll chop the cursed plant to pieces!" cried Adams.

"Don't! Don't!" came in almost pleading tones from the imprisoned professor.

"Don't what?"

"Don't hurt my pet!"

"Your pet!" snorted Adams angrily. "Nice kind of a pet you have! One that tries to eat you alive! But I've got to do something if I want to save you. Where's the ax?"

"No! No!" begged the professor, his voice becoming more and more muffled. "Use chloroform."

"Use what?"

"Chloroform! You'll find some in the closet."

Then Adams saw what the professor's idea was. The plant could be made insensible, and the imprisoned man released with no harm to the blossom.

He raced down the ladder, ran to a closet where he had seen the professor's stock of drugs and chemicals stowed away on the occasion of former visits, and grabbed a big bottle of chloroform. He caught up a towel and ran back up the ladder.

Not a sign of the professor could be seen. The plant had swallowed him up, but by the motion and swaying of the flower Adams knew his friend was yet alive.

He was in some doubt as to the success of this method, and would rather have taken an ax and chopped a hole in the side of the blossom, thus releasing the captive. But he decided to obey the professor.

Saturating the towel well with the chloroform, and holding his nose away from it, he pressed the wet cloth over the top of the blossom where the lid touched the edge of the bloom.

There was a slight opening at one point, and Adams poured some of the chloroform down this. He feared lest the fumes of the anesthetic might overpower the professor also, but he knew they would soon pass away if this happened.

For several minutes he waited anxiously. Would the plan succeed? Would the plant be overcome before it had killed the professor inside?

Adams was in a fever of terror. Again and again he saturated the towel with the powerful drug. Then he had the satisfaction of seeing the lid of the pitcher plant relax.

It slowly lifted and fell over to one side, making a good-sized opening. The strong filaments, not unlike the arms of a devil fish, Adam thought, were no longer in uneasy motion. They had released their grip on the professor's legs and body.

The spines which had pointed downward, holding the plant's prey, now became limber.

Adams leaned over. He reached down, grasped the professor by the feet, and, being a strong man, while his friend was small and light, he pulled him from the tube of the flower, a little dazed from the fumes of the chloroform the plant had breathed in, but otherwise not much the worse for his adventure.

He had not reached the water at the bottom of the tube, which fact saved him from drowning.

"Well, you certainly had a narrow squeak," observed Adams as he helped the professor down the ladder.

"I did," admitted the botanist. "If you had not been on hand I don't know what would have happened. I suppose I would have been eaten alive."

"Unless you could have cut yourself out of the side of the flower with your knife," observed Adams.

"What! And killed the plant I raised with such pains?" ejaculated the professor. "Spoil the largest Sarracenia

Nepenthis in the world? I guess not. I would rather have let it eat me."

"I think you ought to call it the cannibal plant instead of the pitcher plant," suggested Adams.

"Oh, no," responded the professor dreamily, examining the flower from a distance to see if any harm had come to it. "But to punish it, I will not give it any supper or breakfast. That's what it gets for being naughty," he added as if the plant were a child.

"And I suggest that when you feed it hereafter," said Adams, "you pass the beefsteaks in on a pitch-fork. You won't run so much danger then."

"That's a good idea. I'll do it," answered the professor heartily.

And he has followed that plan ever since.

SPANISH REVENGE

Author Unknown

(Hamilton Advocate, 1906)

*Along the Rio Grande a thousand tales of Mexico are told,
but no romance can equal the adventures of a Texas youth
who had been brought back to his home from the hospital at
Monterey. During his visit to the southern republic he
fell under the spell of a fair senorita, and afterwards
became the victim of her fury. That he escaped with his
life was due largely to the devotion of Cherry Mellnote,
said to be one of the most beautiful girls in the world.
She rescued him from the deadly clutches of the minotaur
tree and nursed him back to life and love.*

*When Arno T. Savry, a handsome Texas youth of ample means,
found himself ready to accept an invitation of a friend to
visit Mexico, he recalled the stories of other gallant
young Texans who had gone down into the land of the
beautiful to find sweethearts—and return no more forever.*

"But I am not so soft as others," he said. This confident
young man had a sweetheart and a cottage under the Lone
Star, and he vowed over and over that there was not a girl
in Mexico with eyes so bright or face so fair as his Texas
beauty, nor one who could make him forget for a moment
little Fanny Frayne. He had known Fanny all his life and
loved her when they were schoolmates, and if there was a
girl in all the world who could blot her name from his
heart she would have to possess supernatural powers.

The Unnatural History of Man-Eating Plants

CHERRY MELLNOTE

That was about the way this self-reliant youth talked when he had his foot in the stirrup and set out to visit Don Diego Montamoran at his hacienda near Sabinas, in the state of Nueva Leon, Republica de Mexico.

During unhappy days for his country Diego had suffered exile. He had spent five years in Texas. It was at this period that Arno and the banished Mexican became comrades and the warmest of friends. After a long period of waiting the edict of banishment was annulled through the influence of Diego's father—a rich and powerful senator—and the happy young man was invited to return to his home. Aided by his friend Arno, Diego had prospered in exile and he returned to his father's house not a prodigal son, but one upon whom fortune had showered favors.

Near the hacienda of Montemoran, the youthful traveler recalled that his old comrade had several sisters. He wondered whether they were pretty and hoped some of them could speak English. But one of his reasons for making the long journey was that the trip would bring him in daily contact with a people whose language he was anxious to learn. He reflected that if the ladies whose hospitality he was about to enjoy could not understand him he would be forced to learn their language and perhaps have the pleasure of being instructed by a fair teacher.

Senator Montemoran had anticipated the coming of his son's friend and he stood at the great front gate of the hacienda to welcome him. Arno was delighted with the warm reception extended by the fine looking old man. In another matter he was disappointed, for he soon learned that his friend was away from home. He had been summoned in an affair of law as far away as Chihuahua.

"O, how he raved," said the senator, "for he was expecting you. He will soon return, however. We have written to him."

Everything amazed and entranced the young Texan. The hacienda was a grand old castle, looking as if it had been constructed and furnished by an opulent knight of medieval Spain. As Arno entered one of the spacious apartments the fragrance of tropical flowers, the song of birds, the laughter of maidens, the music of playing fountains greeted him. He began to fear that he was dreaming. He soon felt that he was in the presence of one destined to exert some strange influence over his career.

The daughters of the senator came hurrying to meet the young man, of whom their brother had told them so much. Selma, Leona, and Mercedes entered together with extended hands. "Three Graces" were the words uppermost in the mind of the astounded visitor. Never before had he looked upon such charming young girls.

"Brother has told us about you, over and over," they said. "We know how kind you were to him when he was in exile, and we are eager to do any service. You must feel at home and all of us will try to make you enjoy yourself until Diego returns."

The Unnatural History of Man-Eating Plants

At that moment Arno felt that nothing could be added to the environment that would increase his felicity. In the presence of these beautiful girls mere existence became bliss. The trials and sufferings of the past were buried deep and the future glowed with sunshine.

The evening was spent walking about the ground of the hacienda. The young Texan found something to admire and excite his curiosity at every step. For the first time he looked upon golden pheasants, birds of paradise strutting in magnificent plumage of every color, and the Quezel—the sacred bird of the old Aztecs—said to be the most beautiful living thing on earth.

When night came Savry was left alone in his room. He found his nerves shattered. Trembling, he threw himself into a great chair and buried his face in his hands. He was violently in love with Leona Montemoran and his heart smote him. He had lied and his solemn vows to Fanny Frayne no longer held him. The pleasures of the next day and the next added increased fervor to the passion of the recreant lover. He was not only rapidly forgetting his little sweetheart far away in Texas, but at the rate he was traveling he confessed himself that home and native land would soon become no more than a dream.

It was no ordinary passion that possessed this unfortunate young man. Every hour was devoted to the dark eyed beauty of the sun lands. He lived for her and acted as if it might give him pleasure to die for her. He followed her with his eyes during all the long hours of daylight, and it seemed to give him pain for other people to look at her.

At last an evening came when he went to his room so happy that he could not sleep. Leona had told him that he might hope.

"I think I love you a little," she said. Then she gazed fixedly at him and pointed towards Texas. He promptly placed his hand over his heart and shook his head. The little pantomime was full of meaning. She accused him of having a sweetheart at home and he lied with alacrity and without shame.

The next day Selma said to him, "You are too rapid; you should have waited until Cherry comes."

"Who is Cherry?" said Arno.

"The most beautiful girl in the world!" was the reply.

"Impossible! There can be no other like Leona."

Selma laughed. "Leona could not hold a candle by the side of Cherry Mellnote," she said.

"No matter, I shall not fall in love with her."

"Before she is here a week you will be rolling in the dust at her feet."

One evening as Arno walked alone through a little grove he met an old Aztec woman who was regarded as a witch. She hissed a string of words at him that he could not understand, but he caught enough to startle him.

"Americano, Americano," she shrieked, "beware, beware, a Mexican girl never forgives a false lover. The little stiletto at her throat flashes and the sting finds the heart of the betrayer."

How often had he seen Leona toying with a little dagger, the jeweled handle of which peeped from her bosom.

"Cherry Mellnote will arrive today," exclaimed Mercedes, clapping her hands. "I have a letter." This was at breakfast one morning.

"Pardon us," said the senator, turning to his guest. "You are in the dark, but be assured we have a pleasing surprise in store for you."

"Tell him about Cherry, papa," said one of the girls.

"That I will with pleasure," said the old gentleman. "You must know Senor Savry that Senorita Mellnote, who is the most beautiful young lady in all the world, is an old friend of ours. She attended school with my girls. She is a living romance. She has just returned from Madrid whence Her great beauty was recognized and her great beauty was recognized and she enjoyed the admiration of nobility and royalty without a rival. It is said that she refused dozens of counts, dukes, and lords, and even one prince of royal blood. Gen. Herara was her grandfather. He was the finest looking man in Santa Ana's army. An imitator of Murat, he always wore a uniform glittering with gold lace, and a plume that swept back over the tail of his horse. His coat buttons were gold and the hilt of his sword was decorated with diamonds. It was this dashing warrior with his big carbineers who turned back your Indiana regiment at Buena Vista. He was slain in battle. His daughter, a woman of great beauty, married Col. Mellnote of Maximilian's army. Cherry, an only daughter, inherited his fortune. There is no other like her. She has yet to see the first man who did not instantly fall in love with her. You will see her today.

When Cherry Mellnote swept into the great hall of the hacienda glittering with jewels, compelling adoration in all eyes and scattering sunshine and joy in all hearts, the lover of Leona found himself rooted to one position and gasping for breath. He felt that they had hardly half described the beauty and charms of the young lady who was passing before him. He saw more of her during the day and every moment increased his admiration. Every glance at the young Texan and every word that dropped from her lips served to draw him nearer to hopeless slavery.

Scarcely a week had passed before Arno found himself devoting all his time to Cherry to the utter neglect of Leona. It was patent to all that Leona had lost her lover. As time passed the passions of the Texan verged upon madness.

He was treading upon dangerous ground, and one of the girls found an opportunity to warn him. Blinded by his infatuation he failed to see the look of burning hatred and thirst for revenge in Leona's sparkling eyes.

Spanish Revenge

The devoted Mexican girl had loved and trusted him. Now she thirsted for his blood. Arno had no moments for the poor girl into whose pure heart he had thrust so much sorrow. From dawn until the stars twinkled he worshipped at the feet of one who had had a thousand lovers, not one of whom had ever quickened the beating of her heart.

Leona planned to be revenged. One bright morning there was a new look in the dark eyes of the girl whose sorrow all had noticed. Her pretty face sparkled with animation and she danced and sang as one who had always lived amidst scenes of pleasure.

"Senor Arno," she said, "I have planned to make this a memorable day, one that we can never forget. I have sent some peons to Ave Silvestre springs bearing baskets of good things to eat and drink. It is not far. We will have a day long to be remembered."

Cherry appeared to be puzzled, for the first time. She looked grave and she had little to say. She tried to induce Arno to ride with Leona. "Mind, it is good advice I give you," she said. "Leona's joy is too pronounced. You don't know (these) hot blooded Mexican girls, Senor Arno," she added seriously. The Texan was too madly under the spell of the beauty to realize fear. He rode by her side to the springs, and kept close to her every moment. Leona's animation did not abate.

When the lunch had been spread under the shade of the trees, Leona said, "There is one thing lacking, but it is within easy reach. If Arno will come with me we will add flavor to the occasion."

Cherry signaled the Texan to sit still, but either he did not see or he thought to make reparation for his ingratitude by at least one little act of magnanimity.

The girl led the way, singing a love song, and Arno followed, almost by her side. Cherry Mellnote sat choking, and her pretty face was almost as white as her dress. Five minutes had passed when the party at the springs heard a shriek that caused them to spring to their feet.

This is what had happened. Approaching a peculiar looking plant resembling a large cactus with many long thorny arms, Leona said:

"There, cut a leaf of that. It has a delicious fragrance." The youth was standing by the terrible minotaur tree, a carnivorous plant that lives upon the flesh of birds and animals.

He had no sooner touched one of the stems than a long arm, like the horrible tentacle of the octopus, hissed through the air and wrapped about his body. He had only time to see the smile on Leona's face when other long thorny arms grasped him. They wrapped about his arms and around his legs.

Powerless and screaming for help he felt himself being drawn into the awful tangle of crushing leaves. Cherry Mellnote was first to answer the cries for help. Others quickly followed, and fortunately a company of vaqueros who were passing galloped upon the scene.

Spanish Revenge

"Yateveo, yateveo," they shouted, firing their guns at the main trunk of the plant, hoping to make it release its victim. Some slashed the leaves and others threw ropes to the struggling man. Arno managed to get a noose under his arms, and when a Mexican had caught one of his legs they all united their strength and the mangled youth was drawn from the embrace of the terrible plant.

The Mexicans declare that in its anger its swaying arms hiss the word "Yateveo," which means "I see you." The clothing of the unfortunate young man was torn to shreds and his body was covered with blood. At first it was thought that he was dying, but after some moments he breathed easier, and when Cherry raised his head he drank a little wine from her hands.

The vaqueros made a litter and Arno was hurriedly carried to the hacienda, where a physician was summoned. From the doctor Cherry learned that though the young man was badly hurt and poisoned with the juice of the minotaur it would be possible to save his life if he could be moved to the hospital at Monterey. She did not hesitate a moment. A carriage was ordered and only a few moments passed before the sufferer was on his way to the station. Leona's smile had passed. She looked on in silence. No one knew her feelings.

The unfortunate Texan lay for many weeks unconscious in the hospital. At last one of the doctors said: "He will open his eyes today and probably know you." Later in the day Cherry saw a look of intelligence in his face, and when Arno tried to sit up he saw someone disappearing from the room. Finding a note pinned to his bosom he read:

"The doctors say that you can get well. Profit by your awful experience and be true to your first love. From one who—well, it might have been—Cherry."

When the young Texan again opened his eyes after a long rest he looked into a sweet smiling face, and he heard the whispered words, "Arno, are you not glad to see me?" He struggled to hold out his arms, saying: "If you can forgive me I will love you forever." His eyes had filled with tears, but through them he recognized his first love— little Fanny Frayne.

THE VAMPIRE PLANT

By Edgar White

(Buffalo Evening Times, 1907)

She was good company and it was nice to have a congenial comrade with whom to while away the spare hours, or to escort to the theater and elsewhere. He had been introduced to her by a friend, who assured him she was an excellent young woman. Closer investigation had thoroughly borne out the statement. In the early days of their acquaintance he had been in the habit of sending her notes when he should call, and from this they tacitly adopted two evenings a week on which he should call without announcement.

As the years went by he found himself in a somewhat peculiar position because of the way the world had unanimously linked his fate with hers. He could not with decency, it seemed, take the initiative in terminating the platonic relationship. It never occurred to him that she would care, and yet he knew, unless another friend appeared to take his place, those who reason from the looks of things—the majority of mankind—would say she had been jilted.

There had been none of the little bickerings and poutings that accompany the genuine article of love. She had always pleasantly yielded to his wishes whenever he suggested attending any entertainment or social event with him, or taking a drive along the river front, or visiting in any part of the city. Even when business or something else caused him to break engagements with her she refused to become offended and never chided him. Of course there couldn't be any sentiment under such prosaic circumstances. She was a nice girl and belonged to one of the very first families of the place—had been born with a silver spoon in her mouth, as they say—but the courtship—if such it might be called—lacked the zest of opposition.

The feeling that his well-bred and refined comrade who lacked the germs of inspiration was an incubus had never presented itself until he met Mercedes. Ah! there was a girl. Tall, slender, of tawny locks, bright black eyes—"a goddess of the tropics," he called her not long after they met. Her Mexican costumes were as dazzling as her eyes, and the scent of the lotus hovered around them. Impulsive, warm-blooded, daring, magnetic beyond all powers or describing—what a contrast with demure little Nellie, the patrician who never crossed the dead line of perfect propriety. Pending the arrival of her halo the "goddess" kept books for a fruit importing firm. But what of it? Wasn't work honorable, and especially in a girl who had no recourse for her daily bread and butter save the exertions of her own white arms? With fine generosity his heart went out to the poor creature and he would gladly have saved her from drudgery were it not for—

The weekly calls to the woman who did not work became less frequent and he invented all sorts of excuses to explain them. He sent her books and flowers galore, along with prettily worded notes about the distressing demands of commerce. Nellie never asked for details; never showed pique. He wondered if she knew, and what she would do if she did. Not a hint of Mercedes had he ever given her; as far as in his power he resolutely kept up the mask, telling his conscience it were better so. He was even kinder and more considerate during his shortening visits. One night as he was leaving her she placed a little hand on his arm and said, just a trifle tremulously:

"My friend, I will not expect you next Sunday evening, unless—unless you care to call."

The Vampire Plant

His heart gave a great bound. They were the words he been longing to hear for nearly a year. Yet it would look vulgar in him to tear the mask off all at once. So he played the hand.

"Why—why, Nellie! What does that mean?" he asked with what he fancied was well-feigned surprise; "are you angry at me?"

She looked steadily beyond him as she calmly replied:

"Not at all, Robert; but I do not think it necessary to tell you what I mean."

Her face was pale but she addressed him in the same gentle tone that was characteristic of her. He mumbled something in the way of puzzlement, at which she smiled sadly and bade him good night.

When he told the maid of tawny hair he was free she threw her arms around his neck and turned a warm face to his.

"Did it knock her all in a heap, Bob?" she, asked, unpityingly.

"She acted very nice about it, dear," he said, as he walked with the goddess to a sofa and sat down; "I was afraid she would make a scene, but she didn't."

"Those proud aristocrats!" exclaimed the girl, fiercely; "how I hate them!"

"Why, Mercedes?" he asked, amazed at the outbreak; "what has she ever done to you?"

"Everything! She rides in her fine carriages, with a coachman, while I have to walk, or be crowded with cattle in a street car. She lolls on soft cushions, reading novels all day long, while I have to toil over dirty old ledgers to keep body and soul together! Why shouldn't she soil her dainty hands as well as I?"

The man with gloomy brow saw his gilded house of clay topple and lay a crumbling mass of ruins at his feet.

The Unnatural History of Man-Eating Plants

Hoping his ears had deceived him as to her true meaning, he said, gently:

"You should not misjudge her, Mercedes; I am sure you will find her very kind should you ever meet her."

"Kind as the king is to the slave," she said, bitterly. "She would toss a few pennies to me, along with words of compassion. It were better for her that we never meet." Then the strange girl's mood changed. "But, come, Bob; kiss me and forgive me, for I have you and I love you and only you!"

In the days that followed the man and the "goddess" were seen everywhere together, and it was no secret that they were to be married soon. Friends at the club smiled queerly when he entered, and some pretended to think it all a joke.

"He'll never do it," said Farnham, who had been associated with him in a number of business ventures, and was a warm personal friend. "I hope to the Lord he won't," he added, less confidently.

"But he will," said another man of 'the street;' "he's blind now and don't know where he's going. Wonder how he could be such a fool?"

The subject of discussion came into the room and threw himself heavily in a chair. He was nervously smoking a cigar and his eyes, unnaturally bright, seemed to dance in their sockets. Farnham drew his chair up to him.

"Ever hear the story of Count Lacroix?" he asked, in an easy matter-of-fact tone.

"Never; it must be new."

"No; it's as old as humanity. Lacroix was a French botanist. Having plenty of means to indulge his tastes, he went to Africa in search of some rare plants. At the edge of a large woodland swamp he encountered a number of the beautiful white lilies which have since been transplanted in Europe and christened 'The Imperial.' Their color is a

"HER MEXICAN COSTUMES WERE AS DAZZLING AS HER EYES, AND THE SCENT OF THE LOTUS HOVERED AROUND THEM." - KJG

peculiar blending of pearly white and rose tint and in the center is a tiny spear crowned with something like a princess's coronet. In all the world, it is said, there has never been found a purer or more beautiful plant.

"While admiring them, Lacroix observed far across the swamp something which fascinated his student's eyes. It seemed like a ball of fire, with a background of leaves and sprouts representing vividly every color of the rainbow. As he looked the coloring appeared to change, growing more intense under the glow of the central sun. It lacked all the artistic elements of beauty and harmony that characterized the 'Imperial,' but it had the greater power of mystery and the botanist determined to secure it.

"Crushing the delicate lilies under his feet he plunged into the murky water and made his way step by step, his longing eyes fixed on the plant of wondrous brilliancy. Careless of all danger he kept steadily on till his feet slipped and he stumbled at the foot of the plant he sought, grasping its waxen tendrils in an effort to right himself.

"Then a curious thing happened. Like coiling snakes the roots of the plant rose out of the marsh and wrapped themselves around his arm, body and legs. He struggled and shouted but no one heard. Weeks afterwards an exploring party came across his shrunken body. His arms were entwined around the plant, but the roots were resubmerged in the dark waters.

"That dazzling specimen of the marsh now has a name. They call it the 'Vampire plant,' and wherever he discovers it the white man tears it up and burns it."

The three men sat in silence. Farnham looked steadily into the face of the man whom he had told the story. Robert threw his cigar away and arose unsteadily.

"Thank you, Farnham," he said; "I see."

***

The Vampire Plant

That night, in a voice vibrating with the emotion of a new light the man told all to the woman, and then as she listened quietly and did not chide, he told her something else born of the clearer vision that had come to him out of the darkness. He knew now he was not worthy of her, but the story had risen from his very soul and he had to tell her that he loved her and always had loved her, although he knew that his conduct only merited her scorn and contempt. He dared ask nothing but her forgiveness, and if, in time, she ever thought of him would she try to remember him as one who had been awakened to his better self by her gentle powers, and who would guide his future life so that for her sake it might be above reproach.

She heard him through without comment, the expressive blue eyes now unfathomable. He did not look at her until he had finished, and then it was only a wistful glance as if in anticipation of the blow. Then came the thought of her wounded patrician pride, and he shuddered at the opening his statement had left for assault. With head bowed like the condemned on the block he awaited her judgement. At last she arose and took a step toward him.

"Robert," she said, and the cadence of evening bells was in the voice; "I am glad you have come back to me. I should have died without you."

OCTOPODOUSA FEROX

By Rowland Thomas

(Everybody's Magazine, 1909)

Illustrations by Peter Newell

To while away a drizzly afternoon a few travelers, gathered in the smoking-room of the Overland, had agreed each to relate the most gruesome experience in which he himself had had some part. The tales climbed on from climax to climax of horror, till finally the word came to a person of middle age and sober dress, who sat half facing a window. His quiet, detached manner, his keen yet delicate features, his clear eye, and the warm brown of his cheek, all marked him as one of those happy gentlemen who spend a perpetually busy leisure in the half-scholarly, half-active, and thoroughly wholesome pursuits of country life. His speech was remarkable for a tone of grave authority which lent weight to every word, a characteristic I must beg you to remember as you read my transcription of his narrative, for he spoke of uncommon, almost incredible things.

It is five years now since Roberts gave up business and settled down in Oncoast once for all. He came in what is still remembered as the Hessian-bug year, and the sprightly pests were a stinger to his dreams of an agricultural old age. His place lies next to ours, and on June evenings Roberts and I used to meet at the boundary with our pipes, and compare notes. He was a thorough

Octopodousa Ferox

believer in Paris green, while I inclined to arsenate of
lead, and many a hot argument we had. But the bugs took my
leaded deutzias and Roberts's be-arsenicked beans on the
same day. Corn, melons, peaches, plums, peas, cherries,
spinach, carrots, beets, potatoes, tomatoes—all came in
their way; and when mid-July saw the last of them, Roberts
and I condoled over acres of skeleton leaves and drooping
trees and shrubbery.

Roberts recovered his courage first. "Hang it all!" he said. "There *must* be some way of fooling 'em, if you can't *kill* 'em. I didn't sell out the shops for twice as many bonds as they were worth to come down here and die young to please a lot of little striped bugs. The trouble with you professional country gentlemen is that you've lost your initiative. You wait to see what the bugs will do next. Now I'm going to find a way to get them *worried*. It may not be according to Hoyle, but it'll be a *way*."

He attacked the problem with characteristic energy, and long before we had gathered our mutilated harvest his plan was mature. "I've got 'em," he said to me as we sat in a ducking-stand under a September moon, waiting for the tide. "Bet you a hundred shells the Hessians don't get one decent feed out of me next summer."

"How are you going to kill 'em?" I asked.

"Kill 'em!" he snorted. "Who's thinking of killing them? I'm simply going to fool 'em. Drop the market under 'em like a lame elevator. They're sold short now, and when they try to cover—"

"Talk English. You know you can't fool 'em," I objected. "You can't catch 'em; they'll eat anything; they get fat on arsenate—"

"Eat anything?" Roberts repeated scornfully. "How many of the Brassicaceæ did you ever see 'em eating?"

"Brassicaceæ!" I echoed, for I had never heard Roberts speak botanists' Latin before.

"Cabbages!" he interrupted impatiently. "Ever see 'em getting very busy with the Cucurbitaceæ?"

"Cucurbit—"

"Squashes," he explained briefly. "Seen 'em crowding up to buy Allium preferred? That's onions. And there's where I put the squeeze on little Mr. Hessian-bug. Not a beastly thing in the whole garden that he'll eat."

Octopodousa Ferox

"But you'll get awfully tired of eating nothing but cabbages and squashes and—"

"Hoyle again!" he retorted. "How many kinds of cabbages do you think there are, anyway?" He did not wait for an answer. "There's cabbage and broccoli and Brussels sprouts and cauliflower, and kale, and sea kale and—I'd plant skunk cabbage, only that's Symplocarpus—and kohl-rabi and—turnips! Didn't know turnips were cabbages, did you? Well, they *are*. And squashes are squashes, and so are pumpkins and crook-necks and cucumbers and watermelons and marrows and muskmelons and gourds. And onions—there's onion sets and onion seeds, and chives, and shallots—Lady of Shallot—and leeks—"

"Did you ever eat a leek?" I asked. "Or ever know any one that had?"

"And leeks and garlic and—"

"Mrs. Roberts wouldn't have garlic in the house—"

"Well, I can *raise* it," he shouted, and just then the 'coys called outside and we closed our mouths and opened the peepholes.

The next spring Roberts's garden was a novel sight. Long rows of all the various cabbages and squashes and onions he could discover stretched away as flat and peaceful and monotonous as a Dutch landscape. A few of his choicest trees were ghostly in tents of muslin, and he looked with serene pity on my doomed plats "according to Hoyle." And then—it turned out to be a cutworm year.

Morning after morning I saw Roberts standing in impotent rage above his prostrate plants. His trim rows of onion sets grew ragged, his January-sown cauliflower fell before the unseen destroyer, his blossoming squashes and melons wilted in an hour. And evening after evening I listened to him with sympathy.

"They're the larvæ of some Lepidoptera," he said. "One species at least is known to climb trees and gnaw off young fruit for the fun of hearing it drop. And all of them are specially partial to cabbages, squashes, and melons. Good Lord! And there ain't a Hessian in sight."

"The books say—"

"Yes," Roberts broke in scornfully, "one book says they'll all commit suicide if you sow pills of bran and arsenic. Huh! Even a June-bug would know more than *that*. And another book wants me to put little paper collars round all the plants. I'd like to have the joker who wrote that for my gardener. No, I'm all in. The bugs are playing me for a sucker going and coming, and realizing every trip. I'm through. It's a knockabout for me, and vegetables down from the city—though where the market-gardeners get any is a mystery to me."

"It's a bad year," I began. " Don't get discouraged—"

"It's always a bad year," said Roberts glumly. "I'm done. I'm not afraid to take a reasonable chance. I'm game for a flyer in copper prospects or cotton futures or anything *tangible* any time, but when it comes to gambling on weather and bugs—I take off my hat to the hardy farmer. That's all."

But it wasn't all. Roberts's active brain could not be diverted long by the mild excitement of yachting in the bay. He came over to me in August, full of a new idea. "Bank on a farmer to tackle any problem the wrong way to every time," he began with characteristic abruptness.

"Meaning?" I asked.

"Meaning bugs," said Roberts, and laughed good-naturedly. He set his feet wide apart, rolled his cigar into the corner of his mouth, and gradually, as he warmed to his theme, took on what I called his prospectus manner. "Bugs," said he, "are the greatest problem of the ages. Where does the food of man and every useful beast come from?" he asked oratorically. "Primarily from the fields, the cultivated fields. The fabled home of aboriginal man was a garden, and every unspoiled heart burns to pass its old age next the soil, so strong is the voice of Nature still. And why should not the whole world be once again a garden of Eden? Because of bugs. Bugs alone. For fifty centuries man has gone on earning his bread in the sweat of his face, because for every mouthful he raises for himself he raises three for the bugs. Eliminate bugs and you quadruple the food supply of the world, and vastly lessen the labor.

"And what have we done in all these thousands of years?" Rhetoric had him in its grip. "Nothing. Nothing at all. *Absolut Nichts*. Worse than nothing. Even our simian relatives are wiser than we, for they at least consume plant and bug together. But we have gone on perversely improving, inventing new plants, new and choicer food for bugs, and against the real evil we have devised only two miserable subterfuges that couldn't deceive an intelligent bug for a minute. We either try to poison the bug, or we set one bug to catch another, in either case expecting the victim to step aside from the plain path of natural eating to invite his fate. The abnormal bug, the over-curious and flighty bug, may step aside and perish, but the great normal bug! And all the time Nature has held the solution before our eyes!"

Under the turgid current of Roberts's words I began to see a rock bottom of truth, one of those ideas so great—and so simple—that we call the men who first perceive them geniuses. "I see," said I. "You would—"

"I would set the plant to catch the bug and feed on him," said Roberts simply. "Develop the latent protective powers of the plant, add new ones to it by breeding. Nature has our material ready. I've been reading about them for a week. In the swamps of Carolina grows a plant, Venus's flytrap, which captures insects and feeds on them. Dozens of plants move very perceptibly—Sicyos, Echinocystis, and the rest. Desmodium gyrans of the Indies waggles its leaves impatiently all day long. The tendrils of the grape and other vines have enormous prehensile strength. Combine these powers, develop them to the utmost, give them meaning, graft such a plant on each and every useful vegetable, and you have what? A self-protected garden which is self-nourishing as well. No more spraying, no more fertilizing, no more grubbing—"

"Roberts, I congratulate you!" I cried, as I dug a fat white grub from the roots of a drooping strawberry. "The greatest opportunity of history lies before you. Think of the fame, and the wealth—"

"Think of the good," said the good-hearted fellow quietly, but his eyes shone. A procession of heavily-loaded wagons swung into his drive at that moment. "Greenhouses," he explained. "The old ones were too small. And I go to the agricultural college to-day to study the latest methods of propagation. When I do a thing, I do it. Wish me luck, old fellow."

"I *do* wish you luck," I assured him. "And I know you will succeed."

Roberts gripped my hand and swung down the Oak Path with his vigorous strides, and that was the last I saw of my old friend and neighbor for many months. He did not visit me nor write, and I kept away, for I knew he was busy heart and soul. Alchemist seeking touchstone could go no deeper in a quest than Roberts went. But along in the spring, four years ago, his old gardener, Higgins, brought me a note.

"Can you come over?" it read. "I've been waiting till I could report progress. It has been a long hunt, but I believe I'm on the way to results. Come and see for yourself."

"Let me get a cap, Higgins," I cried joyfully. "I knew Mr. Roberts would succeed."

"Call it success if you like, sir," said Higgins so dolefully that I looked at him in surprise. His face was pale and drawn, his eyes were furtive. As I inspected him, the breeze whipped the corner of a curtain softly against his sleeve, and he leaped forward jerkily, with all the horror of a victim of delirium tremens in his face. He caught my eye, and stared sullenly at the floor. "Beg your pardon, sir," he muttered. "I'm a bit nervous."

"What's wrong, Higgins?" I asked.

"Nowt, perhaps," he grunted. Then suddenly he broke into speech. "I make bold to beg you not to go, sir. Let them as pries into devils' secrets go their gait alone. There's un-Christian doings yon, sir, that make an honest body's flesh creep. Have no part in 'em, sir."

"Nonsense," I said sharply, but I was far from calm. Higgins's manner was disquieting in its semblance to madness, and for the first time certain unpleasant possibilities occurred to me. We went down by the Oak Path in silence, and up to a great range of glass houses. Higgins stopped at the door. "There's them that has business inside, I suppose," he said stolidly. "I bide in God's air."

I was greeted by a lean, bespectacled young man, who was clad in white linen, and who had the impassive bearing and noiseless movements common to men bred in hospitals and laboratories. The matter-of-fact scientist was stamped on every line of him, and yet his first words gave me a shock of surprise. "We shall find Mr. Roberts in the diet-kitchen," he said. His tone was so grave that I hid the smile his phrase provoked, and he led me away to a high, white-tiled room.

Roberts was bent over a test tube that bubbled on a table, so intent on its contents that he did not note our arrival, and I had a moment to note the changes in him. His figure, once burly, had lost its erectness and its rotundity, and his motions were catlike in their delicacy. But when he turned I saw a greater alteration. His ruddy cheeks were smooth and pallid, his eyes grave and searching, and his whole face bore the mask of passionless alertness which I had noted in my conductor and in another young man who had joined us in the corridor.

The Unnatural History of Man-Eating Plants

His voice, too, had lost its boisterous heartiness; but he greeted me warmly nevertheless, and after we had chatted a moment the strangeness wore off, and I began to see the humor of the situation.

"And so this is the 'diet-kitchen,'" I said with a laugh. "Even plants eat nowadays?"

Roberts looked at me gravely. "Plants have always eaten," he said, and the lean assistants smiled a trifle superciliously. I laughed again. "But not all have been fortunate enough to get cooked food," I said.

"You forget that we are dealing with carnivorous plants," said Roberts, still without the shadow of a smile. My amusement faded, as once more an unpleasant sense of the possibilities of his experiments came to me. I believe that even then I had a dim foreboding of the evil that was to come.

But the long aisles of the growing houses into which we passed were commonplace enough. By the variations in heat and moisture I could tell that the plants which crowded about me had been gathered from many climates, but otherwise there was nothing out of the ordinary in what I saw. Nothing, certainly, to justify Higgins's preference for "God's air."

At last we stepped into a little internal court, where stood a small house with roof and walls of whitened glass. As we approached it, the assistants dropped their low-toned chatter, and an additional shade of solemnity came into Roberts's face. He lowered his voice as he opened the door. "You have seen what we had to work with," he said. "Now see the result."

My first sensation was one of disappointment, my next of pity for my friend. Ranged along a bench on the western wall stood perhaps a dozen stout, fleshy plants, much resembling the common century plant with the central cone of leaves removed. Trailing along the opposite wall and festooned to the roof were some uncommonly heavy creepers.

Octopodousa Ferox

And that was all. But as I stood and strove for some unmeaning word to break the embarrassing silence, I became aware of a gentle murmur, a soft rustling of leaves, and looking closer I saw that all was in motion about me. The thick stems of the creepers swayed slowly with a writhing motion, their leaves fanned gently in the still, hot air, the fleshy bayonets of the century plants slowly coiled and uncoiled their finger-like tips. "Good heavens!" I cried. "They're alive!"

"All plants are alive," said Roberts dryly, and again his assistants' lips curled. "But these are alive enough to strike even the careless eye," he went on. "Dr. Judd, suppose you give Saprogens a drink."

The lean assistant filled a small beaker with some reddish liquid, and set it beside one of the century plants. For some time there was no change, and we all grew impatient. *"He doesn't smell it!"* muttered Roberts suddenly, and sprinkled a drop or two of the liquid on the plant. Instantly a leaf contracted violently.

Then slowly it bent outward and downward, and the fleshy finger at its tip closed firmly about the beaker. "Come closer," cried Roberts eagerly. Reluctantly I approached and—believe it who can—the center of that plant, where the spike of leaf buds should have been, was a hole, lined with some dull leathery substance, which palpitated as I watched. Fascinated by the very repulsiveness of the thing, I saw that leathery throat gape wider and wider as the beaker approached, and then I started back with a nervous shudder. For all along the bench other plants were tossing and writhing their fat arms with helpless appetite!

"It is unpleasant," said Roberts kindly. "I feel it myself, and Saprogens will never be my pet. But it is indispensable for our work. Its carnivorous instincts are very highly developed."

He showed me the other products of his toil: the huge creepers armed with the modified and strengthened clamps of the Venus's flytrap at every tip; the Convolvulus agilis, as he called it, a tiny plant which shot out its little tendrils at passing insects with the speed and precision of a lasso; and, most curious of all, a wonderful grubbing thing which sent its roots burrowing under ground, each one armed with the deadly trap, and engulfed a worm from the surface as we watched it. As I

I SAW THAT LEATHERY THROAT GAPE WIDER AND WIDER AS THE BEAKER APPROACHED.

saw these marvels at work, my horror was forgotten and my enthusiasm returned. Standing with my back to Saprogens, I congratulated Roberts warmly, and in response to my words the old boyish sparkle came into his eyes. "I feel I shall succeed," he said. "All my material is ready at last. Give me another year of solitude, and then—a plant with the rapid growth and wonderful strength of those climbers, with the agility of Agilis, the root action of that Panicum, the digestive powers and unquenchable appetite of Saprogens! Think of it! Plant one a sentinel every thirty feet, and—"

I cried out with uncontrollable horror. A cool firm touch had fallen on my neck. Jerking my head about, I saw the armed end of a second creeper swinging toward me through the air. I had learned the secret of Higgins's nervousness, and I shrank away.

"There was a ladybug on your coat," Roberts explained. "It startled you? One gets used to it soon."

But the quiet, murmuring room had become unbearable to me, and I took my leave of it and Roberts as soon as possible. "Give me a year more," were his last words, "and then we'll have time for the boating and shooting again. I'm going to win."

He waved me a cheery farewell, but I hurried away with the foreboding of evil things to come strong upon me. I could not forget the hungry, writhing leaves of Saprogens, nor the devilish precision of Agilis. Above all I could not forget those words of Roberts's, *"He doesn't smell it!"* It was all very well for him to say that all plants are alive, but he treated these as sentient animals. He was meddling with the boundaries of Nature.

For a long time I was nervous and troubled, and after the least excitement would have dreams of cold, green, writhing, gripping, hungry things; but long before a year was up Roberts and his world ceased to play any active part in my life.

The Unnatural History of Man-Eating Plants

Coming back from the South this last spring, however, I remembered that the period set by Roberts was long over, and soon after reaching Oncoast I went across to visit him. Dr. Judd met me in the lobby of the glass houses, and I fancied I saw a shade of embarrassment in his greeting. "Mr. Roberts is out of town for a day or two," he said.

"Away!" I cried. "That means that he's succeeded. Roberts is not the man for jaunting when his work is waiting. He *has* succeeded?"

A slight film seemed to cross Dr. Judd's eyes. "Yes," he said hesitatingly, "I may say—that the experiments—have been successful. More successful, in a way, than we had hoped or perhaps wis—successful beyond all expectation," he amended. "Come in and see the result. I am sure Mr. Roberts would wish it. The fact is, he's away."

Puzzled by the distrait manner of young Dr. Judd, I followed him without a word, and presently we emerged into the little central court. The walls and roof of the small house had been covered with a heavy lattice-work of iron rods, and the door was secured with a heavy padlock. To my surprise, also, a freshly painted placard announced in large letters,

"DANGEROUS. KEEP OUT."

Unheeding this warning, young Dr. Judd unlocked and opened the door, with no sign of emotion beyond a certain doggedness of look and movement, and after a moment of hesitation I followed him within. The room was almost dark, and the air was hot and close and heavy with an acrid, pungent odor which I did not recognize at once. The light from the open door penetrated but a few feet, enabling me to see only a heavy screen of woven wire.

"Don't be alarmed," said Dr. Judd in a whisper. "I will close the door and your eyes will adjust themselves in a moment. It is supersensitive to-day, and we've darkened the house to calm it."

Octopodousa Ferox

The weird suggestion of his words was lost on me, for in the gloom beyond the screen the reality was beginning to take shape. The interior of the house had been stripped of benches and plants, and in its center, on a mound of grayish earth, squatted a huge Saprogens. A Saprogens, and yet unlike any others I had seen, for from the circle of fleshy leaves rose a crown of creepers—I suppose I must call them that—of round corded arms thick as a man's wrist, incredibly long, and armed at the ends with huge traps; and the gray dust about the—plant—rose in little clouds as the roots wormed about beneath. Wormed about—for all the deadly thing was quivering with life, its broad leaves writhing and coiling and licking the air greedily with their fleshy fingers, its arms drawing in and lashing out with aimless fury, its traps opening and shutting with lightning rapidity, and all in silence. No, silence would not have been so horrible. There was the soft thud of the falling dust, and a thin, whistling murmur, crescendo and decrescendo in regular gradations. When the meaning of that sound burst on me my heart seemed to stand still.

"My God, man," I cried, "it is alive! It—breathes!"

At the sound of my voice a convulsion seized the thing. Writhing and lashing, it seemed struggling to tear itself from the ground, and the quivering roots creaked with the strain, while Dr. Judd's voice whispered: "All plants breathe. In Octopodousa ferox, as might be expected, the transpirational processes are exaggerated and accelerated till they become perceptible. It is very—"

A lashing arm struck the grating just before my face and my nerves gave way. I flung open the door and fled the court, followed by the remainder of Dr. Judd's sentence, "—interesting in its present excitability. I must call Mr. Roberts at once."

"Call Roberts," I echoed, as Dr. Judd came out. "Then he's here?"

Dr. Judd flushed slightly. "I regret the deception," he said. "I indulged in it only because a layman is apt to overemphasize the risks which are concomitants of all research. Mr. Roberts is in his room, slightly injured."

"By— by *That?*"

"By Octopodousa," said the doctor. "He incautiously ventured too close while it was feeding, it lashed out with a tendril, and his arm was torn by the modified leaves."

"The infernal thing must be killed at once," I cried.

A LASHING ARM STRUCK THE GRATING JUST BEFORE MY FACE.

Octopodousa Ferox

Dr. Judd smiled slightly. "Mr. Roberts would hardly consent," he said, "for it is the only adult male plant of the sort in existence. Any botanist would gladly be torn in pieces by it. Besides," he added thoughtfully, "it's rather doubtful if it could be killed by any means we know."

To my surprise Roberts, when I saw him a day or two later, seemed to share Dr. Judd's feelings and made light of my disgust and terror. "My dear fellow," he said, "the plant was in a hyperirritated state, and I simply paid the penalty of carelessness. To bring it to the reproductive stage we planted it in ground bone and fed it—with blood, and those two substances, furnishing almost all the elements which make up animal flesh, developed its carnivorous instincts to their utmost degree. By simply regulating its diet we can hold it at any degree of ferocity which seems desirable."

"How do you know that?" I demanded.

"By analogy," said Roberts.

"And you'll trust to analogy and sow Oncoast with those devilish things," I cried. "You should be locked up."

A gleam of the old business keenness shot across his face. "Thank you for reminding me," he said. "We have enough young plants to protect an acre, and they must be set out at once. Don't be alarmed; all the insects in the county could hardly rouse them to real activity. We shall have to stimulate by feeding."

To be brief, Roberts did actually set a garden of two acres with sentinels of Octopodousa ferox, as he had named it, and for several months the results were all that could be desired. It was a year of abundant insects, and the plants kept the vegetables free from their attacks. The only difficulty arose with the gardeners. Higgins quit at the very start, and his successor, one Patrick Mulvaney, left just at the beginning of July. "Get ye a man that don't drink at ahl," he advised. "I do be havin' bad dreams at night. An' weedin's the sorry work anny-way, with them plants clinging round yer legs, an' runnin' their fingers down yer neck, an' stickin' their greasy hands in yer paw-w-kets."

You smile, gentlemen. So did I at the time, for I was lulled in a sense of false security. But now— To get on, Roberts and Dr. Judd took care of the garden between them, and the vegetables throve, and Roberts throve as well. With success the shroud of detachment which his search had wrapped around him fell away, his figure regained its stoutness, his cheeks their red, his voice became hearty once more, and his humor had the old boisterousness. I used often to stroll over of a morning to watch the Octopodousæ at work, and many an evening we whiled away smoking and talking of the future and watching them catch browntail moths.

"Show me the Hessian that can outwit that!" Roberts would say." It's too good to be true. Only wait, now, till we decide on the way to turn this over to the Department of Agriculture, and we'll go away and fish in comfort."

"Then you will give it—"

"Yes, it's my contribution to the world," he said. "It's a lot of easy money to throw away," he murmured wistfully, "but—here's where your Uncle Robert gets even with the lambs he's fleeced." And he smiled kindly at his busy plants.

All might have gone well, I still believe, but for a coincidence which no man could foresee. I refer to the coming of the seventeen-year locusts. Early in August the advance swarms arrived, and the Octopodousæ showed the effect of their increased nutriment at once. On the morning of the third, while Roberts and I stood beside the fields, a long arm suddenly shot up and grasped a robin which was flying over. "Strange!" Roberts muttered. "That tendril must have developed over night."

Octopodousa Ferox

DR. JUDD HAD BEEN GRASPED BY TWO PLANTS AND WAS UNABLE TO
FREE HIMSELF.

The Unnatural History of Man-Eating Plants

Before our eyes the field was stirred to a feverish activity, and the ruddiness left Roberts's cheek as he gazed. Suddenly a faint call for help rose from the upper corner of the field. It was Dr. Judd, who had been grasped by two plants as he was hilling up potatoes, and was unable to free himself. With some difficulty Roberts and I reached him and released him, and we all three regained the edge of the field a trifle upset by this misadventure. "If this goes on," said Roberts, the scientific mask slipping back over his face, "we shall have to adopt repressive measures."

That afternoon the main body of the locusts descended on us, the largest cloud I have ever seen, and the Octopodousæ were very busy up to the time I went to bed. On the morning of the fourth I went over early, full of anxiety, but to my relief the situation seemed unchanged. The locusts poured in all that day.

On the morning of the fifth, Roberts was accompanied to the field by his Airedale bitch, Floss, and four puppies which were just beginning to run about. As they stood some twenty feet from the edge, three arms suddenly lashed out, seized the puppies, and whisked them into the growth of Octopodousa, which now overshadowed all else. Floss, with the silent gaminess of her breed, dashed to the rescue, but had hardly reached the edge when she gave one shriek of deadly terror. An enormous arm had seized her and swept her away. She was never seen again.

Roberts was sick, all of us were sick, with the shock of that, but worse was to come.

The field by this time was in a state of the wildest excitement, the breathing of the plants was distinctly audible, and their arms were lashing continually thirty feet in the air. But on the evening of the ninth there was a temporary lull in their activity, and deceived by that, the nurse of little Miss Maysie, Roberts's orphan niece, was tempted too close to the edge of the field with her charge, and all at once an arm caught both child and woman. Roberts and Judd, who were strolling near,

Octopodousa Ferox

fortunately heard their cries, and after a tremendous struggle released them. But the shock was too great for little Miss Maysie's nerves, and two nights later she died in convulsions of mortal terror.

I had been with Roberts from the time of her accident, and Dr. Judd and I now took him in charge, one of us being constantly with him, for his mental condition was alarming. He seemed to regard the field with a personal hatred, and once had been detected stealing toward it with an eight-bore gun, muttering incoherent threats. We watched him unobtrusively, striving to soothe him in every way, but his reason was too far gone, and at last—

I shall never forget that night of the fifteenth. Roberts had seemed far more rational than usual, and at ten I went to bed, leaving Judd with him. Suddenly I was roused by the sound of running feet on the roof of the veranda and a muffled cry from Judd. As quickly as possible we ran down and out through the orchard, calling loudly. But we got no answer, and when we reached the edge of the fatal fields all was silent. Only the Octopodousæ were awake, tossing and breathing with excitement and appetite, their glaucous arms glistening gray and snaky in the moonlight. That, I am sure, as I stood there beside the living grave of my friend who had suffered the bitterest of all fates, to be eaten by a plant he had himself created, was the most gruesome moment of my life.

The climax of the grave gentleman's tale held his audience in breathless silence for a moment. Then suddenly the porter, who had been an eager though unobtrusive listener, gave way to a mellow and irresistible chuckle. "Sold again!" ejaculated a person in a plaided waistcoat and laughed somewhat sheepishly, and one by one the others joined him. But their mirth was quickly hushed.

"Not R. D. Roberts, sir?" said a young man brokenly, putting a trembling hand on the narrator's arm. "You don't mean HIM?"

"Robert Dale Roberts was the name of my unfortunate friend," said the grave gentleman. "You seem shocked. I hope—"

"He had offices in Broad Street," said the young man, controlling himself with difficulty; "he had a small wart on his nose."

For the first time the grave gentleman showed some excitement. "It is the same," he muttered with twitching lips. "Speak; he was your—"

"Good heavens, sir," cried the young man. "He was my—"

A cry of horror drowned his words. The porter's face was pallid, his eyeballs rolled up, his jaw hung loose, and his teeth chattered. "My Gawd, gen'l'm'n," he moaned. "Oh, my Gawd! AH DONE THOUGHT ALL DAT WAS DES A STORY!"

THE PAVILION

By E. Nesbit

(The Strand Magazine, 1915)

Illustrated by James Durden.

THERE was never a moment's doubt in her own mind. So she said afterwards. And everyone agreed that she had concealed her feelings with true womanly discretion. Her friend and confidante, Amelia Davenant, was at any rate completely deceived. Amelia was one of those featureless blondes who seem born to be overlooked. She adored her beautiful friend, and never, from first to last, could see any fault in her, except, perhaps, on the evening when the real things of the story happened. And even in this matter she owned at the time that it was only that her darling Ernestine did not understand.

Ernestine was a prettyish girl with the airs, so irresistible and misleading, of a beauty; most people said that she was beautiful, and she certainly managed, with extraordinary success, to produce the illusion of beauty. Quite a number of plainish girls achieve that effect nowadays. The freedom of modern dress and coiffure and the increasing confidence in herself which the modern girl experiences aid her in fostering the illusion; but in the 'sixties, when everyone wore much the same sort of bonnet, when your choice in coiffure was limited to bandeaux or ringlets, and the crinoline was your only wear, something very like genius was needed to deceive the world in the matter of your personal charms. Ernestine had that genius;

hers was the smiling, ringletted, dark-haired, dark-eyed,
sparkling type. Amelia had the blond bandeau and the
appealing blue eyes, rather too small and rather too dull;
her hands and ears were beautiful, and she kept them out
of sight as much as possible. It was she who, at the age
of fourteen, composed the remarkable poem beginning:—

> I know that I am ugly: did I make
> The face that is the laugh and jest of all?

and went on, after disclaiming any personal responsibility
for the face, to entreat the kind earth to "cover it away
from mocking eyes," and to "let the daisies blossom where
it lies."

Amelia did not want to die, and her face was not the laugh
and jest, or indeed the special interest, of anyone.
Really life was a very good thing to Amelia, specially
when she had a new dress and someone paid her a
compliment. But she went on writing verses extolling the
advantages of the Tomb, and grovelling metrically at the
feet of One who was Another's. Until that summer when she
was nineteen and went to stay with Ernestine at Doricourt.
Then her muse took flight, scared, perhaps, by the
possibility, suddenly and threateningly presented, of
being asked to inspire verse about the real things of
life.

At any rate, Amelia ceased to write poetry about the time
when she and Ernestine and Ernestine's aunt went on a
visit to Doricourt, where Frederick Doricourt lived with
his aunt. It was not one of those hurried motor-fed
excursions which we have now and call week ends, but a
long, leisurely visit, when all the friends of the static
aunt called on the dynamic aunt, who returned the calls
with much ceremony, a big barouche, and a pair of fat
horses. There were croquet parties and archery parties and
little dances, all pleasant informal gaieties arranged
without ceremony among people who lived within driving
distance of each other and knew each other's tastes and
incomes and family history as well as they knew their own.

The Pavilion

And at Doricourt life was delightful even on the days when there was no party. It was perhaps more delightful to Ernestine than to her friend, but even so, the one least pleased was Ernestine's aunt.

"I do think," she said to the other aunt whose name was Julia—"I dare say it is not so to you, being accustomed to Mr. Frederick, of course from his childhood, but I always find gentlemen in the house so unsettling. Especially young gentlemen. And when there are young ladies also. One is always on the *qui vive* for excitement."

"Of course," said Aunt Julia, with the air of a woman of the world; "living as you and dear Ernestine do, with only females in the house—"

"We hang up an old coat and hat of my brother's on the hatstand in the hall," Aunt Emmeline protested.

"—the presence of gentlemen in the house must be a little unsettling. For myself, I am inured to it. Frederick has so many friends. Mr. Thesiger perhaps the greatest. I believe him to be a most worthy young man, but peculiar." She leaned forward across her bright-tinted Berlin woolwork and spoke impressively, the needle with its trailing red poised in air. "You know, I hope you will not think it indelicate of me to mention such a thing—but dear Frederick—your dear Ernestine would have been in every way so suitable."

"Would have been?" Aunt Emmeline's tortoiseshell shuttle ceased its swift movement among the white loops and knots of her tatting.

"Well, my dear," said the other aunt, a little shortly, "you surely must have noticed—"

"You don't mean to suggest that Amelia—I thought Mr. Thesiger and Amelia—"

"Amelia! I really must say! No, I was alluding to Mr. Thesiger's attentions to dear Ernestine. Most marked. In dear Frederick's place I should have found some excuse for shortening Mr. Thesiger's visit. But of course I cannot interfere. Gentlemen must manage these things for themselves. I only hope that there will be none of that trifling with the most holy affections of others which—"

The less voluble aunt cut in hotly with "Ernestine's incapable of anything so unladylike."

"Just what I was saying," the other rejoined blandly, got up, and drew the blind a little lower, for the afternoon sun was glowing on the rosy wreaths of the drawing-room carpet.

Outside in the sunshine Frederick was doing his best to arrange his own affairs. He had managed to place himself beside Miss Ernestine Meutys on the stone steps of the pavilion, but then Eugene Thesiger lay along the lower step at her feet, a good position for looking up into her eyes. Amelia was beside him, but then it never seemed to matter whom Amelia was beside.

They were talking about the pavilion on whose steps they sat, and Amelia, who often asked uninteresting questions, had wondered how old it was. It was Frederick's pavilion after all, and he felt this when his friend took the words out of his mouth and used them on his own account, even though he did give the answer the form of an appeal.

"The foundations are Tudor, aren't they?" he said. "Wasn't it an observatory or laboratory or something of that sort in Fat Henry's time?"

"Yes," said Frederick; "there was some story about a wizard or an alchemist or something, and it was burned down, and then they rebuilt it in its present style."

"The Italian style, isn't it?" said Thesiger; "but you can hardly see what it is now, for the creeper."

"Virginia creeper, isn't it?" Amelia asked, and Frederick said, "Yes, Virginia creeper." Thesiger said it looked more like a South American plant, and Ernestine said Virginia was in South America, and that was why. "I know, because of the war," she said modestly, and nobody smiled or answered. There were manners in those days.

"There's a ghost story about it, surely?" Thesiger began again, looking up at the dark closed doors of the pavilion.

"Not that I ever heard of," said the pavilion's owner. "I think the country people invented the tale because there have always been so many rabbits and weasels and things round dead near it. And once a dog, my uncle's favourite spaniel. But, of course, that's simply because they get entangled in the Virginia creeper—you see how fine and big it is—and can't get out, and die as they do in traps. But the villagers prefer to think it's ghosts."

"I thought there was a real ghost story," Thesiger persisted.

Ernestine said, "A ghost story. How delicious! Do tell it, Mr. Doricourt. This is just the place for a ghost story. Out of doors and the sun shining, so that we can't *really* be frightened."

Doricourt protested again that he knew no story.

"That's because you never read, dear boy," said Eugene Thesiger. "That library of yours—there's a delightful book—did you never notice it?—brown tree-calf with your arms on it; the head of the house writes the history of the house as far as he knows it. There's a lot in that book. It began in Tudor times—1515, to be exact."

"Queen Elizabeth's time." Ernestine thought that made it so much more interesting. "And was the ghost story in that?"

"It isn't exactly a ghost story," said Thesiger. "It's only that the pavilion seems to be an unlucky place to sleep in."

"Haunted?" Frederick asked, and added that he must look up that book.

"Not haunted exactly. Only several people who have slept the night there went on sleeping."

"Dead, he means," said Ernestine, and it was left for Amelia to ask:—

"Does the book tell anything particular about how the people died, what killed them, or anything?"

"There are suggestions," said Thesiger; "but there, it *is* a gloomy subject. I don't know why I started it. Should we have time for a game of croquet before tea, Doricourt?"

"I wish *you'd* read the book and tell me the stories," Ernestine said to Frederick, apart, over the croquet balls.

"I will," he answered, fervently; "you've only to tell me what you want."

"Or perhaps Mr. Thesiger will tell us another time—in the twilight. Since people like twilight for ghosts. Will you, Mr. Thesiger?" She spoke over her blue muslin shoulder.

Frederick certainly meant to look up the book, but he delayed till after supper, when he went alone to the library, found the brown book, and took it to the circle of light made by the colza lamp.

"I can skim through it in half an hour," he said, and wound up the lamp and lighted his cigar.

The earlier part of the book was written in the beautiful script of the early sixteenth century, that looks so plain and is so impossible to read, and the later pages, though the handwriting was clear and Italian enough, left Frederick helpless, for the language was Latin, and Frederick's Latin was limited to the particular passages he had "been through" at his private school. He recognized a word here and there—*mors*, for instance, and *pallidus* and *sanguinis* and *pavor* and *arcanum*, just as you or I might; but to read the complicated stuff and make sense of it! Frederick replaced the book on the shelf,

closed the shutters, and turned out the lamp. He thought
he would ask Thesiger to translate the thing, but then
again he thought he wouldn't. So he went to bed wishing
that he had happened to remember more of the Latin so
painfully beaten into the best years of his boyhood.

And the story of the pavilion was, after all, told by
Thesiger.

There was a little dance at Doricourt next evening, a
carpet dance they called it. The furniture was pushed back
against the walls, and the tightly-stretched Axminster
carpet was not so bad to dance on as you might suppose.
And even in those far-off days there were conservatories.

It was on the steps of the conservatory, not the steps
leading from the dancing-room, but the steps leading to
the garden, that the story was told. The four young people
were sitting together, the girls' crinolined flounces
spreading round them like huge pale roses, the young men
correct in their high-shouldered coats and white cravats.
Ernestine had been very kind to both the men, a little too
kind perhaps—who can tell? At any rate, there was in their
eyes exactly that light which you may imagine in the eyes
of rival stags in the mating season. It was Ernestine who
asked Frederick for the story, and Thesiger who, at
Amelia's suggestion, told it.

"It's quite a number of stories," he said, "and yet it's
really all the same story. The first man to sleep in the
pavilion slept there ten years after it was built. He was
a friend of the alchemist or astrologer who built it. He
was found dead in the morning. There seemed to have been a
struggle. His arms bore the marks of cords. No; they never
found any cords. He died from loss of blood. There were
curious wounds. That was all the rude leeches of the day
could report to the bereaved survivors of the deceased."

"How funny you are, Mr. Thesiger!" said Ernestine, with
that celebrated soft, low laugh of hers.

"And the next?" asked Amelia.

"The next was sixty years later. It was a visitor that time, too. And he was found dead, just the same marks, and the doctors said the same thing. And so it went on. There have been eight deaths altogether—unexplained deaths. Nobody has slept in it now for over a hundred years. People seem to have a prejudice against the place as a sleeping apartment. I can't think why."

"Isn't he simply killing?" Ernestine asked Amelia, who said:—

"IT WAS ON THE STEPS OF THE CONSERVATORY THAT THE STORY WAS TOLD."

The Pavilion

"And doesn't anyone know how it happened?"

No one answered till Ernestine repeated the question in the form of "I suppose it was just accident?"

"It was a curiously recurrent accident," said Thesiger, and Frederick, who throughout the conversation had said the right things at the right moment, remarked that it did not do to believe all these old legends. Most old families had them, he believed. Frederick had inherited Doricourt from an unknown great uncle of whom in life he had not so much as heard, but he was very strong on the family tradition. "I don't attach any importance to these tales myself."

"Of course not. All the same," said Thesiger, deliberately, "you wouldn't care to pass a night in that pavilion."

"No more would you," was all Frederick found on his lips.

"I admit that I shouldn't enjoy it," said Eugene; "but I'll bet you a hundred you don't *do* it."

"Done," said Frederick.

"Oh, Mr. Doricourt!" breathed Ernestine, a little shocked at betting "before ladies."

"Don't!" said Amelia, to whom, of course, no one paid any attention; "don't do it!"

You know how, in the midst of flower and leafage, a snake sometimes will suddenly, surprisingly rear a head that threatens? So, amid friendly talk and laughter, a sudden fierce antagonism sometimes looks out and vanishes again, surprising most of all the antagonists. This antagonism spoke in the tones of both men, and after Amelia had said "Don't!" there was a curiously breathless little silence. Ernestine broke it. "Oh," she said, "I do wonder which of you will win! I should like them both to win, wouldn't you, Amelia? Only I suppose that's not always possible, is it?"

Both gentlemen assured her that in the case of bets it was very rarely possible.

"Then I wish you wouldn't," said Ernestine. "You could *both* pass the night there, couldn't you, and be company for each other? I don't think betting for such large sums is quite the thing, do you, Amelia?"

Amelia said no, she didn't, but Eugene had already begun to say:—

"Let the bet be off, then, if Miss Meutys doesn't like it. That suggestion is invaluable. But the thing itself needn't be off. Look here, Doricourt. I'll stay in the pavilion from one to three and you from three to five. Then honour will be satisfied. How will that do?"

The snake had disappeared.

"Agreed," said Frederick, "and we can compare impressions afterwards. That will be quite interesting."

Then someone came and asked where they had all got to, and they went in and danced some more dances. Ernestine danced twice with Frederick and drank iced sherry and water, and they said good night and lighted their bedroom candles at the table in the hall.

"I do hope they won't," Amelia said, as the girls sat brushing their hair at the two large white muslin-frilled dressing-tables in the room they shared.

"Won't what?" said Ernestine, vigorous with the brush.

"Sleep in that hateful pavilion. I wish you'd ask them not to, Ernestine. They'd mind, if *you* asked them."

"Of course I will if you like, dear," said Ernestine, cordially. She was always the soul of good-nature. "But I don't think you ought to believe in ghost stories, not really."

"Why not?"

"Oh, because of the Bible and going to church and all that," said Ernestine.

"What was that?" said Amelia.

"That" was a sound coming from the little dressing-room. There was no light in that room. Amelia went into the little room, though Ernestine said, "Oh, don't! How can you? It might be a ghost or a rat or something," and as she went she whispered, "Hush!"

The window of the little room was open and she leaned out of it. The stone sill was cold to her elbows through her print dressing jacket.

Ernestine went on brushing her hair. Amelia heard a movement below the window and listened. "To-night will do," someone said.

"It's too late," said someone else.

"If you're afraid it will always be too late or too early," said someone. And it was Thesiger.

"You know I'm not afraid," the other one, who was Doricourt, answered hotly.

"An hour for each of us will satisfy honour," said Thesiger, carelessly. "The girls will expect it. I couldn't sleep. Let's do it now and get it over. Let's see. Oh, hang it!"

A faint click had sounded.

"Dropped my watch. I forgot the chain was loose. It's all right, though; glass not broken even. Well, are you game?"

"Oh, yes, if you insist. Shall I go first, or you?"

"I will," said Thesiger. "That's only fair, because I suggested it. I'll stay till half-past one, or a quarter to two, and then you come on. See?"

"Oh, all right. I think it's silly, though," said Frederick.

Then the voices ceased. Amelia went back to the other girl.

"They're going to do it to-night."

"Are they, dear?" Ernestine was as placid as ever. "Do what?"

"Sleep in that horrible pavilion."

"How do you know?"

Amelia explained how she knew.

"Whatever can we do?" she added.

"Well, dear, suppose we go to bed?" suggested Ernestine, helpfully. "We shall hear all about it in the morning."

"But suppose anything happens?"

"What could happen?"

"Oh, *anything!*" said Amelia. "Oh, I do wish they wouldn't! I shall go down and ask them not to."

"*Amelia!*" The other girl was at last aroused. "You *couldn't!* I shouldn't *let* you dream of doing anything so unladylike. What would the gentlemen think of you?"

The question silenced Amelia, but she began to put on her so lately discarded bodice.

"I won't go if you think I oughtn't," she said.

"Forward and fast, auntie would call it," said the other. "I am almost sure she would."

"But I'll keep dressed. I sha'n't disturb you. I'll sit in the dressing-room. I *can't* go to sleep while he's running into this awful danger."

"Which he?" Ernestine's voice was very sharp. "And there isn't any danger."

"Yes, there is," said Amelia, sullenly, "and I mean *them.* Both of them."

The Pavilion

Ernestine said her prayers and got into bed. She had put her hair in curl-papers, which became her like a wreath of white roses.

"I don't think auntie will be pleased," she said, "when she hears that you sat up all night watching young gentlemen. Good night, dear!"

"Good night, darling," said Amelia. "I know you don't understand. It's all right."

She sat in the dark by the dressing-room window. There was no sound to break the stillness, except the little cracklings of twigs and rustlings of leaves as birds or little night wandering beasts moved in the shadows of the garden, and the sudden creakings that furniture makes if you sit alone with it and listen in the night's silence.

Amelia sat on and listened, listened. The pavilion showed in broken streaks of pale grey against the wood, that seemed to be clinging to it in dark patches. But that, she reminded herself, was only the creeper. She sat there for a very long time, not knowing how long a time it was. For anxiety is a poor chronometer, and the first ten minutes had seemed an hour. She had no watch. Ernestine had, and slept with it under her pillow. There was nothing to measure time's flight by, and she sat there rigid, straining her ears for a foot-fall on the grass, straining her eyes to see a figure come out of the dark pavilion and cross the dew-grey grass towards the house. And she heard nothing, saw nothing.

Slowly, imperceptibly, the grey of the dewy grass lightened, lightened; the grey of the sleeping trees took on faint dreams of colour. The sky turned faint above the trees, the moon perhaps was coming out. The pavilion grew more clearly visible. It seemed to Amelia that something moved among the leaves that surrounded it, and she looked to see him come out. But he did not come.

"I wish the moon would really shine," she told herself. And suddenly she knew that the sky was clear and that this growing light was not the moon's dead cold silver, but the growing light of dawn.

She went quickly into the other room, put her hand under the pillow of Ernestine, and drew out the little watch with the diamond "E" on it.

"A quarter to three," she said, aloud. Ernestine moved and grunted.

There was no hesitation about Amelia now. Without another thought for the ladylike and the really suitable, she lighted her candle and went quickly down the stairs, still dark, paused a moment in the hall, and so out through the front door into the grey of the new day. She passed along the terrace. The feet of Frederick protruded from the open French window of the smoking-room. She set down her candle on the terrace—it burned clearly enough in that clear air—went up to Frederick as he slept, his head between his shoulders and his hands loosely hanging, and shook him.

"Wake up!" she said. "Wake up! Something's happened! It's a quarter to three and he's not come back."

"Who's not what?" Frederick asked, sleepily.

"Mr. Thesiger. The pavilion."

"Thesiger?—the—*You*, Miss Davenant? I beg your pardon. I must have dropped off."

He got up unsteadily, gazing dully at this white apparition still in evening dress with pale hair now no longer wreathed.

"What is it?" he said; "is anybody ill?"

Briefly and very urgently Amelia told him what it was, imploring him to go at once and see what had happened. If he had been fully awake, her voice and her eyes would have told him many things.

"HE TOOK IT, LAUGHING KINDLY. 'HOW ROMANTIC YOU ARE!' HE SAID, ADMIRINGLY."

"HE TOOK IT, LAUGHING KINDLY. 'HOW ROMANTIC YOU ARE!' HE SAID, ADMIRINGLY."

"He said he'd come back," he said. "Hadn't I better wait? You go back to bed, Miss Davenant. If he doesn't come in half an hour—"

"If you don't go this minute," said Amelia, tensely, "I shall."

"Oh, well, if you insist," Frederick said. "He has simply fallen asleep as I did. Dear Miss Davenant, return to your room, I beg. In the morning, when we are all laughing at this false alarm, you will be glad to remember that Mr. Thesiger does not know of your anxiety."

"I hate you," said Amelia, gently; "and I am going to see what has happened. Come or not, as you like."

She caught up the silver candlestick, and he followed its steady gleam down the terrace steps and across the grey dewy grass.

Half-way she paused, lifted the hand that had been hidden among her muslin flounces, and held it out to him with a big Indian dagger in it.

"I got it out of the hall," she said. "If there's any *real* danger—anything living, I mean. I thought—but I know I couldn't use it. Will you take it?"

He took it, laughing kindly.

"How romantic you are!" he said, admiringly, and looked at her standing there in the mingled gold and grey of dawn and candle-light. It was as though he had never seen her before.

They reached the steps of the pavilion and stumbled up them. The door was closed, but not locked. And Amelia noticed that the trails of creeper had not been disturbed; they grew across the doorway as thick as a man's finger, some of them.

"He must have got in by one of the windows," Frederick said. "Your dagger comes in handy, Miss Davenant."

The Pavilion

He slashed at the wet, sticky green stuff and put his shoulder to the door. It yielded at a touch and they went in.

The one candle lighted the pavilion hardly at all, and the dusky light that oozed in through the door and windows helped very little. And the silence was thick and heavy.

"Thesiger!" said Frederick, clearing his throat. "Thesiger! Halloa! Where are you?"

Thesiger did not say where he was. And then they saw.

There were low stone seats to the windows, and between the windows low stone benches ran. On one of these something dark, something dark and in places white, confused the outline of the carved stone.

"Thesiger!" said Frederick again, in the tone a man uses to a room that he is almost sure is empty. "Thesiger!"

But Amelia was bending over the bench. She was holding the candle crookedly, so that it flared and guttered.

"Is he there?" Frederick asked, following her; "is that him? Is he asleep?"

"Take the candle," said Amelia, and he took it obediently. Amelia was touching what lay on the bench. Suddenly she screamed. Just one scream, not very loud. But Frederick remembers just how it sounded. Sometimes he hears it in dreams and wakes moaning, though he is an old man now, and his old wife says, "What is it, dear?" and he says, "Nothing, my Ernestine, nothing."

Directly she had screamed she said, "He's dead," and fell on her knees by the bench. Frederick saw that she held something in her arms.

"Perhaps he isn't," she said. "Fetch someone from the house—brandy—send for a doctor. Oh, go, go, go!"

"I can't leave you here," said Frederick. "Suppose he revives?"

"He will not revive," said Amelia, dully; "go, go, go! Do as I tell you. Go! If you don't go," she added, suddenly and amazingly, "I believe I shall kill you. It's all your doing."

The astounding sharp injustice of this stung Frederick into action.

"I believe he's only fainted or something," he said. "When I've roused the house and everyone has witnessed your emotion you will regret—"

She sprang to her feet and caught the knife from him and raised it, awkwardly, clumsily, but with keen threatening, not to be mistaken or disregarded. Frederick went.

When Frederick came back with the groom and the gardener—he hadn't thought it well to disturb the ladies—the pavilion was filled full of white revealing daylight. On the bench lay a dead man, and kneeling by him a living woman on whose warm breast his cold and heavy head lay pillowed. The dead man's hands were full of green crushed leaves, and thick twining tendrils were about his wrists and throat. A wave of green seemed to have swept from the open window to the bench where he lay.

The groom and the gardener and the dead man's friend looked and looked.

"Looks like as if he'd got himself entangled in the creeper and lost 'is 'ead," said the groom, scratching his own.

"How'd the creeper get in, though? That's what I says." It was the gardener who said it.

"Through the window," said Doricourt, moistening his lips with his tongue.

"The window was shut, though, when I come by at five last night," said the gardener, stubbornly. "'Ow did it get all that way since five?"

The Pavilion

They looked at each other voicing, silently, impossible things.

The woman never spoke. She sat there in the white ring of her crinolined dress like a broken white rose. But her arms were round Thesiger, and she would not move them.

When the doctor came he sent for Ernestine, who came flushed and sleepy-eyed and very frightened and shocked.

"You're upset, dear," she said to her friend, "and no wonder. How brave of you to come out with Mr. Doricourt to see what had happened! But you can't do anything now, dear. Come in and I'll tell them to get you some tea."

Amelia laughed, looked down at the face on her shoulder, laid the head back on the bench among the drooping green of the creeper, stooped over it, kissed it, and said to it quite quietly and gently, "Good-bye, dear; good-bye!" took Ernestine's arm, and went away with her.

The doctor made an examination and gave a death-certificate. "Heart-failure" was his original and brilliant diagnosis. The certificate said nothing, and Frederick said nothing of the creeper that was wound about the dead man's neck, nor of the little white wounds, like little bloodless lips half-open, that they found about the dead man's neck.

"An imaginative or uneducated person," said the doctor, "might suppose that the creeper had something to do with his death. But we mustn't encourage superstition. I will assist my man to prepare the body for its last sleep. Then we need not have any chattering women."

"Can you read Latin?" Frederick asked. The doctor could. And, later, did.

It was the Latin of that brown book with the Doricourt arms on it that Frederick wanted read. And when he and the doctor had been together with the book between them for three hours, they closed it and looked at each other with shy and doubtful eyes.

The Unnatural History of Man-Eating Plants

"It can't be true," said Frederick.

"If it is," said the more cautious doctor, "you don't want it talked about. I should destroy that book if I were you. And I should cut down the creeper and burn it and dig up the roots. It is quite evident, from what you tell me, that your friend believed that this creeper was a man-eater; that it fed, just before its flowering time, as the book tells us, at dawn; and that he fully meant that the thing, when it crawled into the pavilion seeking its prey, should find *you* and not him. It would have been so, I understand, if his watch had not stopped at one o'clock."

"He dropped it, you know," said Doricourt, like a man in a dream.

"All the cases in this book are the same," said the doctor; "the strangling, the white wounds. I have heard of such plants; I never believed." He shuddered. "Had your friend any spite against you? Any reason for wanting to get you out of the way?"

Frederick thought of Ernestine, of Thesiger's eyes on Ernestine, of her smile at him over her blue muslin shoulder.

"No," he said, "none. None whatever. It must have been accident. I am sure he did not know. He could not read Latin." He lied, being, after all, a gentleman; and Ernestine's name being sacred.

"The creeper seems to have been brought here and planted in Henry the Eighth's time. And then the thing began. It seems to have been at its flowering season that it needed the—that, in short, it was dangerous. The little animals and birds found dead near the pavilion. But to move itself all that way, across the floor! The thing must have been almost conscient," he said, with a sincere shudder. "One would think," he corrected himself at once, "that it knew what it was doing, if such a thing were not plainly contrary to the laws of Nature."

THE WOMAN NEVER SPOKE. SHE SAT THERE IN THE WHITE RING OF HER CRINOLINED DRESS LIKE A

"THE WOMAN NEVER SPOKE. SHE SAT THERE IN THE WHITE RING OF
HER CRINOLINED DRESS LIKE A—

BROKEN WHITE ROSE. BUT HER ARMS WERE ROUND THESIGER, AND SHE WOULD NOT MOVE THEM."

—BROKEN WHITE ROSE. BUT HER ARMS WERE ROUND THESIGER, AND SHE WOULD NOT MOVE THEM."

"Yes," said Frederick, "one would. I think if I can't do anything more I'll go and rest. Somehow all this has given me a turn. Poor Thesiger!"

His last thought before he went to sleep was one of pity.

"Poor Thesiger," he said; "how violent and wicked! And what an escape for me! I must never tell Ernestine. And all the time there was Amelia. Ernestine would never have done *that* for *me!*" And on a little pang of regret for the impossible he fell asleep.

Amelia went on living. She was not the sort that dies even of such a thing as happened to her on that night, when for the first and last time she held her love in her arms and knew him for the murderer he was. It was only the other day that she died, a very old woman. Ernestine, who, beloved and surrounded by children and grandchildren, survived her, spoke her epitaph. "Poor Amelia," she said; "nobody ever looked the same side of the road where she was. There was an indiscretion when she was young. Oh, nothing disgraceful, of course. She was a lady. But people talked. It was the sort of thing that stamps a girl, you know."

THE PLANT-THING

By R. G. Macready

(Weird Tales, 1925)

A Frightful Tale of a Carnivorous Tree

"THIS morning, Dick, I have something special for you," said Norris, city editor of the *Clarion*, as I approached his desk. "Interview with Professor Carter. You've heard of him, of course?"

"Certainly," I replied. "There are some rather weird stories concerning him."

"Exactly. And the latest of these stories is that Carter is conducting wanton vivisection on a prodigious scale. Holder, of the local Society for the Prevention of Cruelty to Animals, went over yesterday to investigate but was turned away at the gate. He laid the matter before me and I promised to try for an interview."

"Who started the vivisection story?"

"Several farmers, according to Holder. During the past four months they've sold Carter more than a hundred and fifty pigs, sheep and calves. It is well known that the professor is a scientist and not a stock-raiser; ergo he dissects the animals....Can you start now?"

EN ROUTE to the Carter home I stopped at a hardware store and bought a thirty-foot length of rope. I foresaw

538

The Plant-Thing

difficulty in securing admittance to the professor's domain.

While driving, I brought to mind everything I knew about him. Four years ago he had bought the old Wells place, ten miles west of town. No sooner had it passed into his hands than he commenced the construction of a high board wall about the five acres, in the center of which the house was situated. The wall completed, he had moved in with a young lady, apparently his daughter, and eight Malay retainers. From that time on he and his household might have been dead for all the town saw of them. Our tradesmen made frequent trips to the place, but all their business was transacted with a Malay at the gate.

I drove rapidly and soon came in sight of my destination, which stood on a hill a half mile back from the road. Five minutes later I drew up before the gate, and in response to my hail the Malay appeared. He was a nice-looking young chap, dressed irreproachably, and spoke excellent English. I gave him my card and after a perfunctory glance at it he shook his head.

"I am sorry, sir, but it is the master's order that no one be admitted; and if you will pardon my saying so, least of all, representatives of the press."

"But my business is urgent. Serious charges have been laid against him, and it is possible that I may be the medium by which these charges are refuted."

The Malay's ivory teeth flashed in a smile.

"Thank you, sir, but I do not doubt that the master is able to take care of himself. Good day." This last was spoken in a tone of polite finality as he turned on his heel and walked away.

I entered my car and drove back to the highway. However, I was determined to get that interview by crook if not by hook; if I may say it, this policy of mine had made me star reporter of the *Clarion's* staff. So I continued on down the road a few hundred yards and parked the car in the grove, where it was hidden well. I then took the coil of rope and made my way through the grove, which swung in a huge, narrowing semicircle up the hillside to the northwest corner of the Carter grounds. Arrived there under the fifteen-foot wall, I looked cautiously about me. So far as I could see, I was unobserved.

Just within the wall grew a great oak, one of whose major branches extended well outside. Quietly I flung one end of my rope over this limb, fashioned a running noose and drew the rope tight. Then slowly I wormed up the barrier.

From the top I gazed down upon a glory of wonderful, luxuriant flora. Stately ferns waved gently in the stirring air, beautiful flowering shrubs were interspersed here and there, while everywhere in the emerald grass, still wet with dew, nodded strange, exotic plants. Ever a lover of flowers, I forgot my mission as I looked. There came to my nostrils odors more fragrant and elusive than any I had heretofore known.

Suddenly I crouched low. On noiseless feet there passed beneath me a Malay, who had emerged without warning from a clump of ferns. He paused for a moment to brush an insect from a shrub, then disappeared from view in a thicket of high, green bushes.

Stealthily I slid to the ground and started toward the house, guiding myself by the observations I had made while on the wall. It was very likely, indeed, that the professor would kick me forth the instant he discovered my presence, but at any odds I should have something to tell the readers of the *Clarion*. Too, my audacity might count in my favor.

I HAD not gone far before I became conscious of an odor utterly different from the others. It was vague, but none the less disquieting. A feeling of loathing and dread pervaded me, a desire to clamber back over the wall and return to the city. The scent came again, much stronger,

The Plant-Thing

and I stood irresolute for several minutes, fighting down a sense of faintness as well as the longing to take flight. Then I advanced. In thirty seconds I came to the edge of a small, open space. At what I beheld, I put out a hand to a large fern to steady myself.

In the middle of that tiny clearing grew a thing which, even now, I shudder to describe. In form it was a gigantic tree, unspeakably stunted, fully twelve feet in diameter at the base and twenty-five feet high, tapering to a thickness of two feet at the top, from which depended *things*—I cannot call them leaves—for all the world resembling human ears. The whole was of a dead, drab color.

Dreadful as was the appearance of the thing, it was not that which made me reel as I looked. It was writhing and contorting, twisting itself into all manner of grotesque shapes. And *eyes* were boring into me, freezing the current of my blood.

Something rustled in the grass. I looked down and saw an immense creeper snaking toward me. For the first time I observed that it was joined to the trunk of that frightful thing, and so near the ground that I had not seen it for the tall grass. With a cry of horror I turned to run.

The creeper leapt at me and fastened around my middle with horrible force. I felt something in me give way. Frantically, I struck and tore at the ghastly, sinuous girdle that encircled me, undulating like the tentacle of an octopus. Fruitless, fruitless! I was drawn relentlessly forward.

I screamed. In the trunk of the thing there had appeared a mighty, red-lipped orifice. The tentacle tightened and I was lifted off my feet toward that orifice.

A BEAUTIFUL girl was bending over me when I opened my eyes. She spoke, in a musical voice: "Please do not move. One of your ribs is broken."

The Unnatural History of Man-Eating Plants

A tall, gray-haired man who had been standing in the background now came to my bedside.

"I am glad that I came in time, my boy. Otherwise..."

THE PLANT-THING -KJG

The Plant-Thing

He was Professor Carter. He presented the girl as his daughter Isobel.

Here one of the dark-skinned servants entered with some articles, which he deposited upon the center table.

"I am going to set your rib," announced the professor. And forthwith he took off his coat and rolled up his sleeves. When the job was finished to his satisfaction, I besought him to telephone to town for a taxicab.

"I shall certainly do no such thing," he said. "I insist that you remain our guest until you are recovered."

ISOBEL CARTER proved a wonderful nurse during the three days that followed. Indeed, the moment I had first looked into her deep black eyes, I knew that I loved her. I should have liked to remain in bed indefinitely with her to care for me, but was ashamed to do so. On the third morning I was moving cautiously about the house, she supporting my steps, although there was no need of it. The professor joined us.

No mention had been made of my weird adventure in the grounds, but at my request he now told me how I had been saved from the hideous creature.

"Your first cry reached my ears as I was walking toward the house and I immediately dashed in its direction. You were about to be swallowed when I arrived. I gave a sharp command, and my travesty released you."

"It obeyed your command?" I exclaimed incredulously.

"Precisely. It acknowledges me as its master. For six months, its period of life so far, I have superintended its growth and ministered to its needs."

"But what is it?"

A dreamy look came into Carter's eyes.

The Unnatural History of Man-Eating Plants

"For many years my brother scientists have sought for the so-called 'missing link' between man and ape. For my part, I dare to believe that I have discovered the 'link' between the vegetable and animal kingdoms. The creature out there, however, has, to my mind, not as yet passed the initial stage of its development. Whether it will attain the power of locomotion remains to be seen."

He paused, gazing out of the window, then continued.

"Twenty years ago, in Rhodesia, I chanced upon a carnivorous plant that gave me my clue. Since then I have labored unremittingly, crossing and recrossing my specimens, and you have seen the result. It has cost me three-fourths of my fortune, and countless trips to Asia and Africa."

He indicated a vast pile of manuscript on the table.

"The life history, precedents included, of my travesty. It will form the basis of a work which, I do not doubt, will revolutionize science."

Glancing at the clock, he rose to his feet.

"It is feeding time. Do you care to accompany me?"

I assented, and we went out.

THE thing remembered me, for the huge tentacle swept out in my direction, curling impotently in the empty air. I shuddered, and kept my distance.

A Malay appeared leading a calf. It was lowing piteously, for it had sensed danger.

The tentacle thrashed about, endeavoring to clutch the animal, which lunged back, wild with terror. The man wrapped his arms about it and hurled it forward. It was seized. A loud cracking of bones broke the momentary silence, and was followed by an agonized cry. Six feet from the ground the great orifice gaped wide. The calf disappeared. A fleeting second and the mouth closed. There was no sign of its location; the trunk was smooth and unbroken.

A nausea had gripped me during the scene. The professor and the Malay were apparently indifferent. They conversed briefly. Then, linking his arm in mine, Carter led the way back to the house. As we walked thither, I broached the subject of departure. He would not hear of it, insisting that I stay until Saturday.

While in his study I had noticed an elephant-gun in a corner. I asked him whether he had done any big-game hunting.

"That gun? Tala had me get it. He asserted that he could foretell tragedy in connection with the creature; that a day would come when I should lose control of it. I scouted the idea, but to humor him purchased the weapon, which stands there loaded in the event need of it arises. Still, it would assuredly break my heart if anything necessitated the slaying of my travesty."

At the door of his study he excused himself and went in. Isobel carried me off to the veranda hammock. As we talked, it was inevitable that the subject of the plant-thing should come up, and a shadow crossed her face as we discussed it.

"Tala says that Father does not know how dangerous it is. He is right. But Father will not listen."

THE next morning I again went with Professor Carter to the little clearing.

It was a sheep this time. The poor beast was paralyzed with fright, and stood passive, waiting for death.

The tentacle shot forth, wavered a second, then encircled, not the sheep, but Professor Carter, who seemed stricken by surprise.

The Unnatural History of Man-Eating Plants

He ripped out an order: "Off!"

The tentacle only tightened. Agony settled upon Carter's face. I sprang forward to drag him back. The tentacle released its hold for one lightning flash, then seized us both. We strove in vain against the viselike cable. The Malay, with a wild cry, turned and rushed down the path, shouting as he ran.

The thing was playing with us as a cat plays with mice it has caught. It could have crushed us effortlessly, but the tentacle tightened by degrees. In spite of all we could do, we felt that we were being dragged forward to where the frightful red mouth yawned. Our eyes bulged, and I could see that Carter's face was taking on a greenish tinge. I extended my free arm and our hands clasped. Then there was the roar of a gun at close quarters and the tentacle gave a spasmodic jerk that flung us twenty feet. We rose, staggering.

Tala stood by, the smoking elephant-gun in his hands, staring at the thing. Following his eyes we discerned a large, ragged hole in its trunk, from which a stream of *blood* was flowing and forming a great pool on the ground.

Even as we looked, the travesty went into the death-agonies. And as it writhed it emitted a sound that forever haunts me. Presently its struggles ceased. The professor buried his face in his hands.

I had not noticed Isobel's presence. Now I turned and saw her beside me, gazing with horror-filled eyes at the terrible drooping form. I took her away from that tragic spot, for I knew that Professor Carter wished to be alone.

SI URAG OF THE TAIL

By Oscar Cook

(Weird Tales, 1926)

*"Slowly the pistil of the great orchid curved inward. Over
the golden bell-shaped center it poised. Then it bent its
head; its silver rim distended and then closed."*

DENNIS sat on the veranda of his bungalow, and gazed
meditatively around him. He could not look at the view

because there was none to speak of, since the house was built on an island in the middle of the Luago River. On all sides of the island grew the tall rank elephant grass and nipa-palm. Here and there a stunted, beetle-ridden coconut tree just topped the dense vegetation, a relic of some clearing and plantation commenced by some native, then left to desolation and the ever-encroaching jungle.

Dennis was bored. He was two years overdue for leave; also the day was unusually hot. The hour was about 4, but though the sun was beginning to slant there was no abatement in the fierceness of its rays. After lunch he had followed the immemorial custom and undressed for a short siesta, but sleep was denied him. The mechanical action of undressing had quickened his brain. The room seemed stifling; the bed felt warm. He bathed, dressed and betook himself to the veranda. Here he smoked and thought.

And his thoughts were none too pleasant, for there was much that was troubling him. Throughout the morning he had been listening to the endless intricacies of a native land case—a dispute over boundaries and ownership. He had reserved his judgment till the morrow, for the evidence had been involved and contradictory. He had meant to go over the salient points during the afternoon, and instead, here he was seated on his veranda, smoking and thinking of an entirely different matter. Try as he would, his mind would not keep on the subject of the land, but roamed ever and ever over the mystery that was fast setting its seal of terror and fear on the district.

From a village in the *ulu* (source) of the river strange rumors had come floating downstream. At first they were as light and airy as thistledown —just a passing whisper—a fairy story over which to smile;—then they passed, but came again, more substantial and insistent, stronger and sterner and not to be denied. Their very number compelled a hearing; their very sameness breathed a truth. Inhabitants from the village had gone forth and never returned; never a trace of them had been found. First a young girl, then her father. She had been absent six days and he had gone to look for her. But he looked in vain and in his turn disappeared. Then a young boy, and next an aged woman. Then, after a longer period, a tame ape and finally the headman's favorite wife.

Fear settled on the village; its inhabitants scarce dared leave their houses, save in batches to collect water and food. But Fear travels fast and the rumors reached Klagan and came to Dennis' ears. In the end the mystery caught him in its toils, weaved itself into his every waking moment and excited his interest beyond control.

An idle native story: the tale of a neighboring village with an ax of its own to grind. He was a fool to worry over it. Such mare's nests were of almost daily occurrence, thus Dennis argued; and then from two other villages came similar tales. Two little girls had gone to bathe in the height of the noonday sun. At moonrise they had not returned. Nor in the days that passed were they ever seen again. Two lovers met one moonlight night and waded to a boulder in midstream of the river. Here they sat oblivious of the world around them. They were seen by a couple of natives passing downstream in their boat and then—never again.

Down the river crept the cold, insidious Fear like a plague, taking toll of every village in its path. In their houses huddled the natives, while crops were unsown and pigs uprooted the plantations; while crocodiles devoured untended buffaloes, and squirrels and monkeys rifled the fruit trees. From source to mouth the Fear crept down and in the end forced Dennis' hand, compelling him to action.

Thus as he sat on his veranda and cursed the heat of the sun and the humidity of the tropics, unbidden and unsought the mystery filled his thoughts; and he began to wonder as to if and when his native sergeant and three police would return. For he had sent them to the *ulu* to probe and solve the meaning of the rumors. They had been gone three weeks, and throughout this time no word had been heard of or come from them.

The Unnatural History of Man-Eating Plants

In the office a clock struck 5. Its notes came booming across to Dennis. Then silence—not complete and utter stillness: such is never possible in the tropics, but the silence of that hour when the toilers—man and animal—by day realize that night is approaching; when the toilers by night have not yet awakened.

Lower and lower sank the sun. In the sky a moon was faintly visible. Dennis rose, about to call for tea, then checked the desire. From afar upstream came the chug, chug, chug of a motorboat. Its beat just reached his ears. He looked at his wrist watch. In ten minutes he would go down to the floating wharf. That would give him plenty of time to watch the boat round the last bend of the river. In the meanwhile—

But he went at once to the wharf after all, for the mystery gripped him, causing him feverishly to pace up and down the tiny floating square.

Chug, chug, chug, louder and louder came the noise; then fainter and fainter and then was lost altogether as the dense jungle cut off the sound as the boat traversed another bend of the river. Chug, chug, chug, faintly, then louder and stronger. A long-drawn note from the horn of a buffalo smote the air and the boat swung round the final bend. Only a quarter of a mile separated it now from Dennis.

As the boat drew nearer he saw that she was empty save for the serang (helmsman) and boatmen. Then the Fear gripped him, too, and he quickly returned to the house. With shaking hand he poured out a whisky and soda, flung himself into a chair and shouted for his "boy."

"Tuan!" The word, though quietly spoken, made him flinch, for the "boy" had approached him silently, as all well-trained servants do. Quickly, too, he had obeyed the summons, but in that brief space of time Dennis' mind had escaped his body and immediate wants to roam the vast untrodden fields of speculation and fear.

Si Urag of the Tail

With an effort he pulled himself together.

"The motorboat is returning. Tell the serang to come to me as soon as he has tied her up. See that no one is within earshot."

"*Tuan.*" And the boy departed.

SCARCELY had the boy left than the serang stood in front of Dennis. His story was brief, though harrowing, but it threw no light upon the mystery. For two days, till they reached the rapids, they had used the motorboat. Then they trans-shipped into a native dugout, leaving the motor in charge of a village headman. For three days they had paddled and poled upstream till they came to the mouth of the Buis River. Here the sergeant and police left them, telling them to wait for their return, and struck inland along a native track.

For sixteen days they waited, though their food had given out and they had taken turns to search the jungle for edible roots. Then on the sixteenth day it happened—the horrible coming of Nuin.

The boatmen had gone to look for roots. The serang was dozing in a dugout. Suddenly it shook and rocked. Something clutched the serang's arm. It was Nuin's hands. Startled into wakefulness, the serang sat up; then he screamed and covered his eyes with his hands. When he dared look again Nuin was lying on the river bank. His clothes were in rags. Round his chest and back ran a livid weal four inches wide. His left leg hung broken and twisted. His right arm was entirely missing. His face was caked in congealed blood.

As the serang looked, Nuin opened his lips to speak, but his voice was only a whisper. Tremblingly, haltingly, the serang went to him, and put his ear to his mouth. "Sergeant—others—dead—three days—west—man—with—big—big—others." The whisper faded away; Nuin gave a shudder and was dead.

The Unnatural History of Man-Eating Plants

They buried him near the river and then left, paddling night and day till they reached the rapids. A night they spent in the village, for they were racked with sleeplessness, and they left the next morning, reaching Klagan the same day.

Such was the serang's report.

The Fear spread farther down the river till it reached the sea and spread along the coast.

In the barracks that night were two women who would never see their men again; was born a baby, who would never know his father; wept a maiden for the lover whose lips she would never kiss again.

AS THE earliest streaks of dawn came stealing across the sky, the chugging of a motorboat broke the stillness of the night. Dennis himself was at the wheel, for the serang was suffering with fever. With him were nine police and a corporal. They carried stores for twenty days.

The journey was a replica of the serang's, save that at the village by the rapids no friendly headman or villagers took charge of the motorboat. The village had fled before the Fear. On the fifth day Buis was reached as the setting sun shot the sky with blood-red streamers.

On the banks of the river the earth was uprooted; among the loosened earth were human bones and the marks of pigs' feet. Among the bones was a broken tusk, sure sign of some fierce conflict that had raged over Nuin's remains.

Dennis shuddered as he saw the scene: his Murut police, pagans from the interior of North Borneo, fingered their charms of monkeys' teeth and dried snake-skins that hung around their necks or were attached to the rotan belts around their waists, that carried their heavy *parangs* (swords).

Occasionally throughout the night the droning noise of myriad insects was broken by the shrill bark of deer or kijang. Sometimes the sentry, gazing into the vast blackness of the jungle, saw the beady eyes of a pig, lit up for a moment by the flames of the campfire. Sometimes a snake, attracted by the glare, glided through the undergrowth, then passed on. Once or twice a nightjar cried and an owl hooted—eery sounds in the pitch-black night. Otherwise a heavy brooding stillness, like an autumn mist, crept over the jungle and enveloped the camp. Hardly a policeman slept; but dozed and waked and dozed and waked again, only to wake once more and feel the Fear grow ever stronger. Dennis, on his camp-bed under a *kajang* awning, tossed and tossed the long night through.

Dawn broke to a clap of thunder. Rain heralded in the new day.

"Three days—west." This was all Dennis knew; all he had to guide him. For this and the next two days the party followed a track that led steadily in a westerly direction. On the evening of the third day it came out into a glade. Here Dennis pitched his camp. The tiny space of open sky and glittering stars breathed a cooler air and purer fragrance than the camps roofed in by the canopy of mighty trees. Thus the tired and haunted police slept and Dennis ceased his tossing. Only the sentry was awake—or should have been. Perhaps he, too, dozed or fell fast asleep, for a few unconscious moments. If so he paid a heavy penalty.

DENNIS awoke the next morning at a quarter to 6 to see only the smoldering remains of the campfire.

"Sentry!" he called. But no answer was vouchsafed. "Sentry!" he cried again, but no one came. Aroused by his voice the sleeping camp stirred to wide and startled awakeness.

The corporal came across to Dennis, saluted, then stood at attention waiting.

"The fire's nearly out; where's the sentry?" Dennis queried.

The corporal looked around him, gazed at the smoldering fire, counted his men, then looked at Dennis with fear-stricken eyes.

"*Tuan!*" he gasped; "he is not—there are only eight men!"

"Is not? What d'you mean? Where's he gone?" As Dennis snapped his question cold fear gripped his heart. He knew; some inner sense told him that the man had disappeared in the same mysterious fashion as those early victims. Here, in the midst of his camp, the terrible, unseen thing had power!

"Where's he gone?" Dennis repeated his question fiercely to quench his rising fear. "What d'you mean?"

For answer the corporal only stood and trembled. His open twitching mouth produced no sound.

With an oath Dennis flung himself from his bed. "Search the glade, you fool," he cried, "and find his tracks! He can't be far away. No, stay," he added as the corporal was departing. "Who is it?"

"Bensaian, *Tuan*," gasped the terrified man.

Dennis' eyes narrowed and a frown spread over his face.

"Bensaian!" he repeated. "He was Number 3. His watch was from 12 till 2."

"Then he's never been relieved. From 2 o'clock at least, he's been missing!"

"*Tuan!* I must have slept. I saw Auraner relieve Si Tuah, but I was tired and—"

"Search for his tracks," Dennis cried, breaking in on his protestations, "but see no man enters the jungle."

In that tiny glade the search was no prolonged affair, but no traces of the missing man were found—save one. A brass button, torn from his tunic, lay at the foot of a mighty billian tree. But where and how he had gone remained a mystery. Only the regular footprints as he had walked to and fro on his beat were just discernible and these crossed and recrossed each other in hopeless confusion.

Over the tops of the trees the sun came stealing, bathing the glade in its warming light, but Dennis heeded it not.

"Three days—west." The words kept hammering in his brain, as he sat on the edge of his bed and smoked cigarette after cigarette. Up and down the glade a sentry walked. Round the fire the police were crouched cooking their rice; over another Dennis' boy prepared his *tuan's* breakfast.

At length, when ready, he brought it over to him, poured out his coffee and departed to join the whispering police. But though the coffee grew cold and flies settled on the food, Dennis sat on, unmoved, deep in his distraction.

This was the fourth day! For three days they had journeyed west, following Nuin's almost last conscious words. The glade was hemmed in by the impenetrable jungle; no path led out of it save that along which they had come. It formed a cul-de-sac indeed! And Bensaian was missing!

As Dennis sat and pondered, this one great fact became predominant. Bensaian was missing. Then what did it mean? Only that here the thing had happened, lived or breathed or moved about. Here, then, would be found the answer to the riddle! In this little glade of sunlight must they watch and wait. Into the trackless jungle he dared not enter, even if his men could hack a path. To return the way they had come would make his errand worse than fruitless. Watching and waiting only remained.

So they waited. Day turned to evening and evening into night; the dawn of another day displaced the night; the sun again rode over the tops of the jungle. But nothing happened. Only the policemen grew more frightened; only

The Unnatural History of Man-Eating Plants

Dennis' nerves grew more frayed. Then once again the night descended, but no one in the camp dared really sleep.

UP AND down walked the sentry, resting every now and then, as he turned, against the billian tree. A gentle breeze stirred the branches of the encircling trees, bearing on the air a faint aromatic smell, that soothed the nervous senses of the resting camp, as a narcotic dispels pain. One by one the police ceased whispering and gently dozed, calmed by the sweet fragrance. Dennis ceased his endless smoking; stretched himself at ease upon his bed. The sense of mystery seemed forgotten by all; a sense of peace seemed brooding over them.

Midnight came and the wakeful sentry was relieved. His relief, but half awake, railed at his fate—the half-unconscious dozing was so pleasant, and this marching up and down the glade, while others rested, so utterly to his distaste.

As for the fortieth time he turned about at the base of the great billian tree, he lowered his rifle, rested for a few seconds with his hands upon its barrel, then leaned against the dark ridged stem; just for a moment he would rest, his rifle in his hands—just for a moment only, then once again take up his beat.

The wind in the trees was gradually increasing; the fragrance on the air became more pronounced. The camp was almost wrapt in slumber. On his bed Dennis sleepily wondered whence came the pleasing, soothing odor, that seemed to breathe so wondrous a peace. Against the billian tree the sentry still was leaning; his rifle slipped from the faint grasp of his hands, but he heeded not the rattle as it struck the ground.

Peace in the glade from whence came so much mystery! Peace while the dread, though unknown, agent drew near apace!

Down from the top of the billian tree It slowly descended, branch by branch; slowly, carefully, silently, till it rested on the lowest branch still thirty feet above the sentry.

The bark of a deer broke the stillness of the night. From afar came an answering note. Somehow the sound awakened the sentry. He looked around him, saw the fire was burning bright, picked up his fallen rifle and commenced to walk about.

Down the far side of the tree a bark rope descended till its weighted end just rested on the ground. Down the rope, a man, naked save for a bark-made loin-cloth, descended till he, too, reached the earth. Then, pressed flatly to the great tree's trunk, he waited.

Across the glade the sentry turned about. With listless, heavy steps he was returning. Nearer and nearer he approached. At the foot of the billian tree he halted, turned and leaned against its trunk. The tension of his limbs relaxed. The rifle slipped from his grasp, but hung suspended by the strap that had become entangled over his arm. A light unconsciousness, hardly to be designated sleep, stole over him. From the camp there was no sign of wakefulness.

Slowly a figure crept noiselessly round the tree and stood gazing at the policeman. Naked indeed he was, save for the *chawat* (loin-cloth) of bark; his thick black hair hung over his neck and reached beyond his shoulders, framing a face out of which gleamed two fanatical shining eyes. His body to the waist was covered with tattoo. From each of his breasts the designs started, spreading to waist-line and round to the back. The nipple of each breast gleamed a fiery burnished gold, while from their fringe spread outward, like a full-blown flower, five oval petals of wondrous purple hue. From the golden center of each flower ten long pistils spread, curving downward and round his body. At their source they too were of a purple hue, but as they reached the petals their color turned to gleaming gold which slowly changed to glistening silver as their ridged ends were reached. These ridged ends were circular and their silver rims framed brilliant scarlet mouths, shaped like the sucking orifice with which the huge and slimy horse-leech gluts its loathsome thirst for blood.

The man's arms were unusually long; his finger-nails had never been clipped; the splay of his toes, especially between the big and the next one, uncommonly wide.

One hand still clutched the bark rope; the other hung loosely at his side. Though he was tall, standing five feet ten inches, and heavily built, he moved as lightly as a cat.

Lightly he let go the rope and extended his two long arms toward his unconscious prey. The cry of a nightjar sounded close at hand. The somnolent sentry stirred as the sound just reached his brain. With a spring the man was upon him. One hand upon his mouth; one arm around his chest pinioning his arms to his side. With a swiftness incredible he reached the far side of the tree, let go his grasp upon the sentry's mouth, and using the rope as a rail commenced to climb step over step with an amazing agility.

"*Tolong!*"(help). The cry laden with overwhelming fear rent the stillness of the night, "*Tol —*"

All further sound ended in a gurgle as the relentless pressure round the sentry's chest squeezed out all breath from his body. The camp at that sudden cry of human agony and fear awoke to life. Instinctively the police seized their rifles: the corporal blew fiercely on his whistle; Dennis hurriedly pulled on his mosquito boots and picked up his revolver from under his pillow.

"Corporal!"

"*Tuan!*"

"*Siapa itu?*" (who's that?)

The cries rent the air simultaneously. Then came silence for the fraction of a second, as everyone stared hopelessly at one another as they realized the glade was empty of the sentry.

Si Urag of the Tail

"Si Tuah! Tuah!" Dennis' voice rose in a long cry, breaking the sudden silence that followed the camp's awakening. "Tu-ah," he called again.

Somewhere from among the trees came a sound—a kind of muffled sob—a choking, gurgling cry of fear. To the edge of the jungle close to the billian tree Dennis and the corporal darted.

"Look, *Tuan*! a rope!" the latter gasped.

"My God!" Dennis whispered. "What does it mean?"

"It's made of bark and—" began the corporal, but the rest of his words were drowned by a loud report.

"*Jaga! Tuan, Jaga!*" (look out!) he cried as a jumbled shape came hurtling down from the branches of the tree and the frayed ends of the rope came writhing about them. The snapping of a twig overhead, and a smoking rifle fell at their feet.

As the shape reached the ground with a sickening bump, two figures fell apart and then lay still.

"Seize that man and bind him!" Dennis cried, pointing to the naked form as he bent over the prostrate figure of Si Tuah. "Gently, men, gently," he added as four police picked him up and carried him over to their *kajang* shelter.

His left arm hung loosely by his side, two ribs were also broken, but his heart still faintly beat. Dennis poured a little brandy down his throat. Slowly Si Tuah came to. He tried to rise to sitting posture, but fell back with a groan of pain.

"He came upon me from behind the tree—I must have dozed," he muttered. "He picked me up—the pressure of his grasp was awful—and then commenced to climb the tree, holding the rope as a rail and walking up step by step. I struggled—just as we neared the branches his grip slackened—I could not cry—I had no breath—I only groaned, I struggled once again—my foot kicked the butt of my

rifle—my toe found the trigger and I pressed and pressed—
there came a report—we fell—and—"

Si Tuah had fainted again. Dennis' eyes met those of the
corporal. "The shot must have severed the rope," he
whispered.

"*Tuan*, his *nasib* (fate) was good," the corporal answered,
and they crossed to where the human vulture lay, one leg
twisted under him. his *chawat* all awry. As the policemen
rolled him over on his face to knot the ropes—they showed
but little pity for his unconscious state—the *chawat* came
undone and slipped from his waist.

"Look. *Tuan*, look!" the corporal gasped, and pointed with
shaking finger. "Look, he has a tail—it's not a man—it has
a tail!" And feverishly he fingered the charms that hung
around his neck.

Dennis looked, following the pointing finger, then bending
down, looked long and closely. It was as the corporal
said. The man possessed a tail—a long hard protuberance
that projected from his spine for about four inches.

"Bring him to the camp," he ordered. "Place two sentries:
one over him, one on the camp. He is only stunned; there
are no bones broken. In the morning when Tuah's better
we'll learn some more."

DENNIS walked across to his bed. The Fear was gone, but
the mystery was still unexplained. The campfire burnt
brightly, giving out a smell of pungent wood smoke. The
soothing aromatic scent of an hour ago was no more. From
the police came intermittent whisperings; from the man
with the tail nought but heavy breathing. On his bed
Dennis tossed and wondered.

As the early dawn first faintly flooded the sky, shriek
upon shriek rent the air. Si Tuah had become delirious.
The man with the tail awoke and listened. From a group of
police squatting over a fire their voices reached him. His

eyes blinked in perplexity. Quietly as he lay, he dug with his nails a small round hole in the earth about five inches deep. Then gingerly he moved and in spite of his bonds sat up. From his bed Dennis watched him. Into the hole he fitted his tail, then looked at his bonds and the group of police. He opened his mouth, but no sound came forth. His tied hands he stretched out to them. His face expressed a yearning. It was as if their voices brought a comfort or recalled a past. Then tear after tear rolled down his cheeks.

Calling the corporal, Dennis crossed to the weeping man. At Dennis' approach he looked up, then with a cry buried his face in his bound hands and rocked his body to and fro. He was afraid—afraid of a white man, the like of which he had never seen before.

"Peace, fool!" the corporal said roughly, speaking unconsciously in Murut, "stop your wailing, the *tuan* is no ghost but a man, albeit all-powerful."

Slowly the tailed being ceased his weeping and looked up. "A man!" he muttered. "A man and the color of the gods!" He spoke a bastard Murut and Malay that caused Dennis to start and the corporal to frown in perplexity, for his meaning was clear, though many of the words, though akin to either language, were yet unlike either. But they understood him.

"And your name?" Dennis asked, in Malay, but the being only shook his head in fear, extending his hands in supplication.

"Loosen his bonds," Dennis commanded. "Ask him his name and tribe and village."

The corporal obeyed, and then translated.

The man's name was Si Urag. He came of a Murut race that years ago had captured some Malay traders. All had been killed except the women. These had been made to marry the headmen. Then came a plague and nearly all died. The remnants, according to custom, moved their village. For days and days they walked in the trackless jungle. Then from the trees they were attacked by a race of dwarfs who lived in houses in the branches. All save him were killed. He lay stunned; when he recovered consciousness he saw that the dwarfs had tails and that they were disemboweling the dead and dying and hanging their entrails round their necks. Fear seized him. He tried to rise and run away. He staggered to his feet, tottered a yard or two and then collapsed. Terrified, face downward, he waited for his foes. With a rush of feet they came. He waited for the blow. It never fell. Suddenly he felt a gentle pull upon his tail—the tail over which all his life he had been ridiculed; then came a muttering of voices. From the face of the moon a cloud passed by. He was in a glade and lying near a pool. Over the air a heavy scent was hanging. Suddenly the waters stirred. Out of their depths a flaming gold and purple flower arose. Ten tentacles spread out with gaping, wide-open, blood-red mouths. Shriek upon shriek of utter agony rent the air. Into the flaming golden center each tentacle, curving inward, dropped a dwarf. Into the depths of the pool the flower sank down. All was still. Si Urag was alone.

That night he slept in a house among the branches of a tree. The surviving dwarfs had fled.

In the morning he collected the corpses of his friends and placed them near the lake. That night from his tree-house he watched. The moon was one day off the full. When at its highest point in the sky, the waters of the pool became disturbed. Again the golden-purple flower arose from its depths and the soothing scent spread over the jungle. Again the red-mouthed tentacles spread over the shore and sucked up the corpses, curved themselves in toward the golden center, dropped in its bell-shaped mouth the stiffened bodies. Once again the human-feeding flower sank beneath the waters. Once again all was still. Gradually the narcotic smell grew less; slowly the moon sank in the west. All was dark and silent.

Si Urag of the Tail

On the next and two following nights the flower appeared.
Each night the hungry tentacles sought for food—human or
animal. Then with the waning of the moon the flower rose
up no more. Still in his treehouse Si Urag watched and
lived. Where else was he to go? His tribe was killed; the
dwarfs had fled and of them he was afraid. On account of
his tail he was shy to intermingle with other humans, even
if he knew where to find them. Here was his house, safe
from wild beasts that roamed at night; in the pool were
many fish, in the jungle many roots and fruit. Here was
the wondrous flower that fed on men, that spread its
wondrous scent, to whom he felt he owed his life. Here,
then, he would live and consecrate his life in a kind of
priesthood to the flaming gold and purple orchid.

The corporal ceased and his eyes met those of Dennis.
There was no need to answer the unspoken question in them.
The mystery of those disappearances was explained.

"And that?" Dennis pointed to the tattooing on the
prisoner's body.

Si Urag understood the gesture, if not the words.

"Is the picture of the Flower I serve," he answered,
looking at the corporal. "Two nights ago I fed it with a
man clothed like that"—and he pointed to the police. "A
night ago I caught a pig and deer; last night I caught a
man"—he pointed to where Si Tuah lay in his delirium—"but
a magic spoke from out a tube that flashed fire and the
rope was severed and—" He shrugged his shoulders with a
world of meaning, then, "I am hungry; give me some rice,"
he begged.

For a while he ate his fill. Then when the sun rose high
over the little glade Dennis questioned him further, and
from his answers formed a great resolve.

The glade of the golden-purple flower was but a few miles
away. A little cutting of the jungle, and a hidden path—Si
Urag's path—would be found. That night the moon would be
but two days past its zenith, the wondrous flower would

rise for the last time for a month—or rise never to rise again, hoped Dennis.

Si Urag was complacent. Was it fear or cunning? Who could tell? His face was like a mask as he agreed to lead the little party to the pool where dwelt the sacred flower.

THE hour was after midnight. In the camp three police watched the delirious Si Tuah. Along a narrow track that led from the jungle to a pool, silently stole eight men. In the west a clipped moon was slowly sinking. Out of the jungle crept the men, into a glade silvered by the light of the moon.

"To the right ten paces ex—" Dennis' whispered orders faded away, giving place to a breathless gasp of surprize. There in the middle of the pool was the great golden-purple flower, its center flaming gold, its petals deepest purple, its ten pistils curling and waving about—curling and waving toward the little group of men as they emerged from the track; the blood-red, silver-rimmed mouths opening and shutting in hungry expectation. Over the glade lay the heavy aromatic scent.

Speechless, spellbound, the little party looked at the wondrous, beautiful sight. The deadening spell of that narcotic scent was spreading through their veins. Lower and lower slowly sank the moon.

Si Urag fell upon his knees, covered his face with his hands and commenced to mumble a prayer. His action jerked the rope with which he was attached to Dennis and the corporal. "With a start the former awoke as from a trance. All the waving pistils were pointing and stretching toward the huddled group. The moon was nearly touching the farther edge of the sky. Soon—soon—

"To the right ten paces extend!" Like pistol shots Dennis' words broke in upon the night. Unconsciously, automatically, the police obeyed. Si Urag remained in prayer. "Load!" The one word cut the stillness like a knife. The waving pistils changed their curves—followed the extending men, stretched and strained their blood-red mouths.

"At point-blank—fire!" Six tongues of flame; one loud and slightly jagged report. Four pistils writhed and twisted in an agony of death. In the flaming golden center, a jagged hole. The heavy aromatic scent came stealing stronger and stronger from the maimed and riddled center. The moon just touched the far horizon. Slowly the wondrous flower began to sink, the waters became disturbed, the pistils seemed to shrink.

Si Urag rose from his knees and prayers; uncovered his ears, over which he had placed his hand at the sound of the report. From Dennis to the corporal he looked in mute and utter supplication. From head to foot he trembled.

Slowly the moon and flower were sinking. One pistil, bigger, stronger, fuller-mouthed than the rest, seemed reluctant to retreat, but pointed and waved at the silent three.

Into his *chawat* Si Urag dived his hand. Quick as lightning he withdrew it. A slash to the right, another to the left, and he was free. A mighty spring, a piercing cry and he hurled himself, as a devotee, into the great ravenous blood-red mouth. Slowly the pistil curved inward. Over the golden bell-shaped center it poised. Then it bent its head; its silver rim distended and then closed. Si Urag was no more.

The moon sank down out of sight; the wondrous flower with its maddened, fanatical victim slipped beneath the waters of the pool. The stillness of the jungle remained; the scent of dew-laden earth arose. Darkness—and a memory—surrounded the group of seven.

THE tropic sleepiness of 3 p. m. hung over Klagan. Suddenly the chugging of a motorboat was heard coming from afar upstream. Down to the tiny floating wharf the populace descended, headed by the serang. Round the last bend swung the motorboat, drew alongside the wharf and came to rest. Out of it silently stepped Dennis and the weary police. One of them carried two rifles, which told the wondering people of a death. Two of them supported Si Tuah, which told them a struggle had taken place. Over his features spread a smile as his hands met those of his wife. "'Twas a near thing, Miang," he murmured, "and it happened at the dead of night. A man with a tail and a golden-purple orchid which he worshiped."

From the people rose a gasp of wonder and cries of disbelief. Then Dennis raised his hand.

"Si Tuah speaks the truth," he said, "but Si Urag of the Tail no longer lives, and the flower no more can blossom. The Fear is dead."

Then unsteadily he walked to his house.

THE MALIGNANT FLOWER

By Anthos

(Amazing Stories, 1927)

THIS story, which has just come to us from Germany, is not only a little literary masterpiece, but is a scientific gem as well. Of course, stories of man-eating plants are nothing new in literature, but we believe that this one is so unusual, and so excellent, that it deserves your particular attention. And lest you think that a man-eating plant is an impossibility, your attention is called to the illustrations which we are printing elsewhere, being actual photographs of flowers as tall as, and taller than, human beings. The story of man-eating plants has persisted for many years and there is no good reason why such a plant should not, or could not, exist. Flesh-eating plants are well known to science. There are many flowers and plants that catch not only flies and other insects, but small mammals as well. There is, therefore, no reason to doubt the existence of such plants. It is quite possible that even if no such plants are in existence today—which is a possibility—there might have been many of them in the remote ages.

LALA Daulat Ras had finished his story. For a while he stood there, stiff and straight as a statue in front of the Englishman who was immersed in deep thought. He measured him with a glance in which the mysticism of ancient wisdom of his native home and enigmatic cruelty were mingled. Then he left slowly with measured steps.

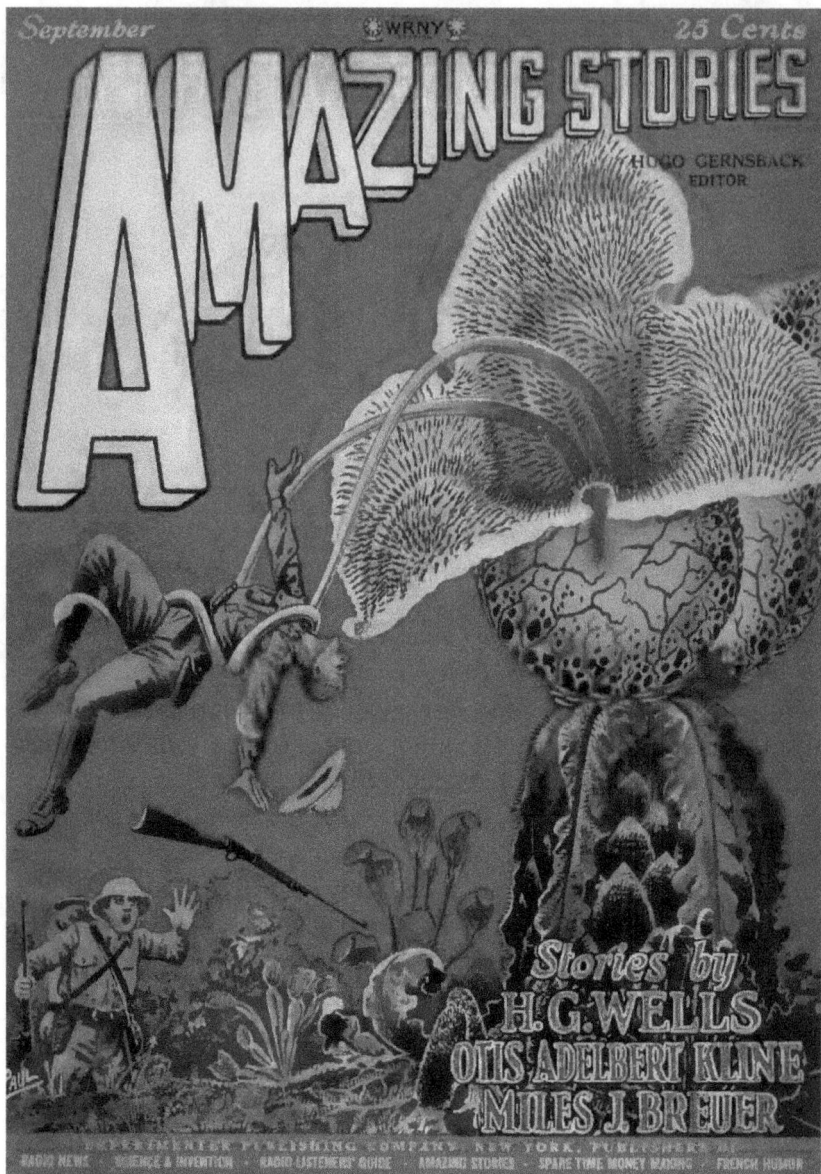

Cover of Amazing Stories - Sept. 1927.

Sir George William Armstrong started up from his dreaming and gulped down a glass of whiskey. It was perfect lunacy what the Hindoo had told him, and yet, and yet one had to believe him word for word, for Baulat Ras was a Yoghi, and a Yoghi never lies. But he wanted to, and had to settle

for himself whether occult powers abided in these strange
men, who hate the European and very seldom bring to light
the "nature secrets" of their land. Sir George was well
off and without any ties. No sport was strange to him. He
could certainly start the undertaking, but he needed a
reliable as well as taciturn companion. The native servant
familiar with the ways of the land, to whom he disclosed
his plan, said he would sooner be thrown alive to a tiger
or be buried in an ant-hill. So he had to turn to his
faithful old John Bannister.

In the long full years of their connection, he had become
more than a mere valet. Indeed, he was a sort of
confidential friend. True and watchful as a dog, tenacious
and indefatigable in hardships, courageous in danger. His
skin was like parchment, no red blood seemed to flow
beneath it, but in spite of his 65 years he was muscular
and had a constitution like iron and steel. And Sir George
took him into his confidence. But this it was which Daulat
Ras had related:

Some ten days journey from here, in an accurately-
indicated little valley of the Himalayas, which is about
200 yards long, there is a curious little bit of earth, a
ravine hedged in by three high perpendicular walls. The
only access is on one of the four sides, over a sort of
quagmire or pond, out of which poisonous vapors rise. You
had to row closely along the edge of it in a boat in order
to avoid the poisonous gases. The ravine itself,
completely overgrown with flowers, is the home for demons,
mischievous satanic forms, mixtures of man and woman,
against whom all the weapons of civilization are useless.
In spring and in fall they reveal their mysterious power.
Woe to him who treads upon their reservation. Death and
insanity is his fate. If he escapes the destruction alive,
he remains dead,—as far as earthly love is concerned. Mark
this,—death for all earthly love.

John Bannister smiled sneeringly. His master stood
immersed in deep thought. He thought of the blonde
fiancée, whom in this very month he was to take to her

....John Bannister hastened to the flower with giant paces...and tried to destroy the tough tentacles of the plant, closely clinging to each other. ...He seized the axe and accurately and carefully delivered blow after blow, which swelled up to a sort of clangor, as if a bell were cracking.

future home. Near Calcutta, in a picturesque suburb, is a charming bungalow, which was even then being erected in feverish haste according to his directions. Then he would

be at an end, once for all, as a restless globe-trotter
and adventurer. But till then, Harriet Richards was to
suspect nothing of the goal of the journey, was not to be
given one second of worry or of anxiety. He would pretend
a business trip. And he laid out his plan. The railroad
went part of the way. He would buy reliable maps of the
country, would get provisions and a little row-boat, would
use porters until he would get to the entrance of the
ravine. In the bright mid-day he would enter it, while
this last bit of the journey, he and his valued John
Bannister should conquer alone. John rubbed his hands in
satisfaction. He was satisfied with the party........

THE Hindoo had spoken the truth. The ravine was there.
Behind dusky black marshlands was a bright tropical carpet
of flowers in the most gorgeous colors of the young
autumn. The goal was reached. The porters pushed the boat
into the swamp and lay down trembling in a little hollow.
Three hours of waiting was assigned them, enough time for
the adventurers to go all over the little valley which was
to be explored.

Countless little bubbles rose. The air was filled with
strong biting vapors as the two discoverers glided along
the edge of the turbid and scum-covered river. On each
side the bare cliffs were in curious contrast to the
blooming flora which awaited them in the valley. A
quantity of withered thorn bushes, with dried and crooked
branches, rose on the edge of the stream, which thickened
steadily. The sun poured down obliquely. No wind stirred
in this silent afternoon siesta of nature. As they got out
of the boat, a heavy veil of vapor stretched over the
upper valley. The atmosphere seemed to brew sultry over
all and purple lightning jerked over the landscape. A
hedgehog sprang up before them. Fearless and confident, he
sized up the unusual visitors, trotted alongside of them
for a while, then sat upon his hind legs and nibbled at an
artichoke. Their shadows fell before them, dumb, trembling
companions, while the adventurers, between bare cliffs,

dropped down into the valley of the flowers, which stood in their second most exquisite bloom. Sir George forged ahead, carefully watching every step. Directly behind him came his companion, and both were armed to the teeth.

A wonder garden spread before their enraptured gaze. Flower after flower, each of inimitable brilliancy of color, pictures of never glimpsed dimensions, ever thicker, ever higher, rather trees than flowers. A whole forest through which it was only with difficulty that one could make his way. Orchids of the most varied kinds were here on the frontier of the highest giant cliffs of the world! Wary, dreamlike, gigantic flowers, with heat-trembling calyxes, covered the whole ravine, cutting off all vision beyond it. Brusquely and undeterred, Sir George forced his way forward and onward, and his companion had more than once to warn him to look out for unknown dangers. What would rise up from behind or between this colored scenery? What kind of beings lurked behind it all, waiting for them?

There was nothing to be seen but flowers and more flowers. In feverish excitement they observed the size of the strange forest with its great plant growths as high as men, whose flowers in silent and majestic quiet were throned upon their stems. Nothing moved. Once only a Himalayan fox moved past them like a streak of lightning, and again there was the silence of a graveyard. Only the overcoming perfume of these myriads of blooms increased, and further progress seemed to oppress the very senses, and the two wanderers were overcome by a fantastic dreamlike mood. These flowers, these giant butterflies, or magnificent dazzling color, fluttering around them—were they not all satanically beautiful beings, which resembled reasoning creatures, benumbing the senses with a whirl, while they simulated the human organs—ear, eyes, lips, and tongue? Sir George gave free reign to his imagination. These ruthless beings which emitted this perfume out of their great languishing calyxes, at once seeming to have unsatisfied longing and dreaming, were they not half-flower, half-animal? Like slender white giant candelabra, their bodies rose upward. What kind of a secret did they hide?

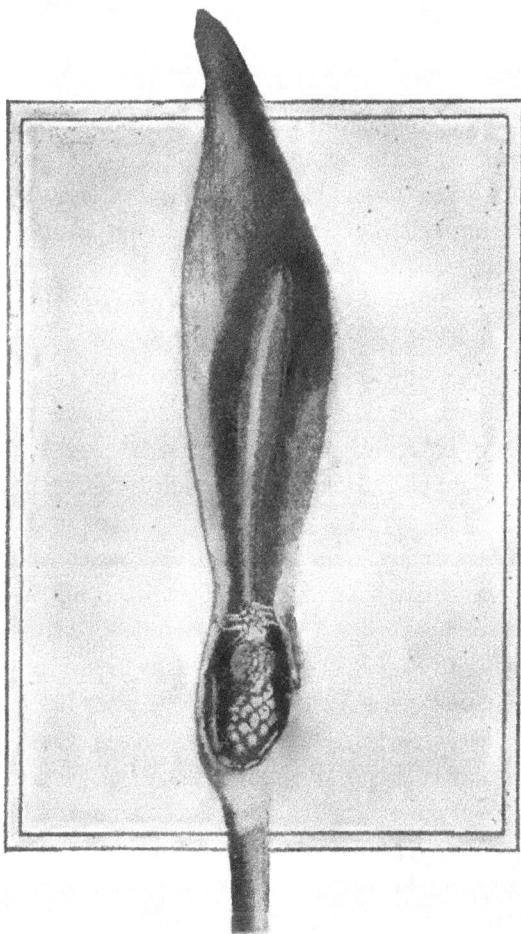

Here is an unusual photograph of an insect-eating or insectivorous flower in cross section. The small spider is caught at the constriction in the plant. The claim is made that the plant itself derives nourishment from feeding upon all sorts of insects and arachnids which are unfortunate enough to travel down to imbibe of the sweet nectar.

And he began energetically and impatiently to forge ahead. Already he was easily ten yards ahead of his companion, half of the length of the valley through which they were walking was well behind him. The black, bare, steeply-rising cliff, which might have been poured from sealing wax, and which closed the valley, seemed to vibrate far in the distance. John Bannister started to run in order to catch up with his master, but his progress was ever retarded by creeping plants or round rock boulders, and now a sudden thicket rising from the ground cut off his steps and his view ahead. He forced his way through laboriously and found himself in an open glade nearly at the end of the ravine. And the sight that met his gaze.......... "But such a thing is impossible!" thought John Bannister to himself, as he rubbed his hand over his eyes. The unheard-of wonder did not vanish, but stood in a monumental quiet. In the middle of the glade a colossal flower rose up to a height of nearly 10 feet, the stem nearly a foot thick, looking like an immense hemlock cone. From the top five or six great leaves, resembling leather, reached down to the ground. From the blooms there dropped a fluid of overcoming strength of scent. And he saw Sir George William Armstrong, sunk in wonder, standing close by this queen of the valley. John Bannister involuntarily stood still. Something had moved. The pair of blooms of this great flower which hitherto had hung down, stiffened themselves visibly,—the piercing sweet perfume streamed out of them overpoweringly, and the three-fold thorny lips with their colored pattern trembled in the atmosphere back and forth, while the Doric column of the stem, dark yellow and sprinkled with black spots, seemed to curve upwards, showing a labyrinthian net of blood red veins. What was this frightful spotted viperlike body, whose spots swelled up to thick berrylike eruptions?

Whatever it was, it meant danger. And John Bannister screamed out with the full strength of his lungs, "Sir George, take care, for Heaven's sake!"

But even then the awful thing came to pass. The flower slowly opened, and something bright and flesh-colored shot out of it. What darted so suddenly? Was it the sucking arms of an octopus? Was it the soft arms of a woman? From

The Malignant Flower

Sir George there came a scream that cut to the very marrow, and John Bannister, frozen stiff with fright, saw his master lifted by his shoulders, up, higher and higher, saw him hanging for a couple of seconds in uncertain balance, and finally disappearing slowly into the calyx of the atrocious, malignant flower, whose petals once more drew themselves together with a start. In this way Sir George celebrated a symbolic marriage with nature, a festival more overcoming, but also more horrible than that for which he had prepared himself. Over the whole scene horror seemed to sweep on dark bat's wings.

There was the fraction of a second only, and John Bannister had regained his senses. He hastened to the flower with giant paces, drew his knife and tried to destroy the tough tentacles of the plant, closely clinging to each other. The knife went to pieces like glass in his grip, then he seized the axe, and accurately and carefully delivered blow after blow, which swelled up to a sort of clangor, as if a bell were cracking. After ten minutes of strenuous work, he had freed his master from his dangerous position, literally peeled out of a sheath.

Pale as death he lay before him on the grass, a grim and frozen smile as if half of supernatural pleasure, half of the fear of death was on his rigid features. But he breathed, lived, appeared uninjured, and allowed himself to be dragged away as if lifeless.

The return journey was silent and oppressive, first going back to the waiting porters, then the whole party returned to civilization. Nothing could induce Sir Armstrong to open his lips. He stared before him as if his mind had completely left him.

Later when Harriet Richards came to his bed in the hospital, he at first failed to recognize her. Then, while foam appeared at the corners of his lips, he rose up in his bed and with a frightful, piercing yell, he pushed her away....

The Unnatural History of Man-Eating Plants

And Sir George has not led Harriet Richards to the altar.
Fourteen days after the catastrophe his hair became white
as snow. A broken man for the rest of his life, he was
taken to the City Insane Asylum, lingered there a year and
a half until death set him free.

RETURNING from the burial, John Bannister suddenly saw
Daulat Ras, the Yoghi, who seemed to have risen from the
ground as by magic. "You had your warning," said he, and
an undefinable expression played about his lips. "But how
was it," cried out the other, "that Sir George rushed to
his fate and to destruction, while I was spared?" On the
features of the Asiatic lay the impenetrable mask of the
Sphynx. With his forefinger he touched the parchment white
face of the old servant. "Blood," said he, meaningly,—then
he glided back and disappeared in the crowd of mourners.

THREE years passed. Harriet Richards moved to Liverpool,
and managed the household for her brother Jack, the ship-
owner. Life resumed its usual way and even in her memory,
the frightfulness of the events gradually paled. One
evening, as Harriet sat in the comfortably-heated sitting
room opposite her brother, the winter storm howling over
the Atlantic, her glance rested on a column in the "Daily
Telegraph."

Instinctively she took it up and read: "The Life Memoirs
of the recently deceased Professor Dr. de Palfi, known as
a botanist and explorer will soon appear. The professor's
greenhouses, with their orchid cultures, situated in
Vienna, his adopted home city, have enjoyed great European
fame for the last ten years. In his memoirs, the professor
tells in an impressive way of his extended explorations
which took him into the most distant regions of all the
continents. With the permission of the publisher we can
quote from its contents today the sensational information
that de Palfi on his last journey in which he reached the
interior of Madagascar, actually came upon the much-

The Malignant Flower

debated 'Man Eating Plant.' It is supposed to be a very rare variety of *Cypripedia gigantea* belonging to the class of the giant orchids, and is the largest flower on earth. These plants, growing in certain remote valleys, have ascribed to them the power to seize small and also larger animals, and even men, who come within their reach. In the spring and fall, always according to de Palfi's observation, the pericarp, or seed-container, forms a sort of natural trap. It thrusts out a quantity of sharp claw-like points, which, as they sink into the flesh, are strong enough to hold the large animals prisoners. Within, the plant is covered all over with suction caps, containing a sort of resinous gum that acts like birdlime in a bird trap. By virtue of a certain plant stimulus, a reflex motion back and forth sets up, enabling the enormous orchid to draw into itself even the body of a full-grown man. The plant, it is understood, is a pure flesh-eater. It feeds itself principally on large animals and men. Sometimes the victims can be freed from the embraces of the flower after the murderous attack of the plant. Otherwise the captured individual is completely absorbed and fourteen days later the bare skeleton is cast out."

THE END

***

The Largest Flower in the World

We reprint this article and pictures from SCIENCE & INVENTION, to prove once more the possibility of seemingly impossible things. Here and on the previous page are photographs of actual flowers which exist today. Who knows but that some bold explorer might venture into still unknown lands and discover a flower even more nearly approximating the description of "The Malignant Flower?"

ON the Island of Sumatra, in the Dutch East Indies, some of the most exotic and curious plants are to be found growing wild. It is here that we must look for the largest flower in the world. On the 19th of March, 1925, a scientist planted a large bud of the Giant Amorphophalle. Twenty-two days later it was 22 inches high. It continued to grow and in June 24th at midday, the point of the spathe began to unroll itself, and four hours later the flower, which then had a height about 6 feet 6 inches, appeared in all its beauty. M. Dakkus, the scientist conducting the experiment, fortunately took the trouble to photograph the Amorphophalle in its whole expansive bloom, so as to preserve for us the fragile beauty of this rare and transient flower.

In March, 1926, the Amorphophalle presented the appearance of a small tree about 10 feet tall. The plant blooms but once in its life-time.

The Malignant Flower

The Giant Amorphophalle blooming in a Java garden, June 24, 1925. The stick is 2 meters long and the flower 6 feet 6 inches in height.

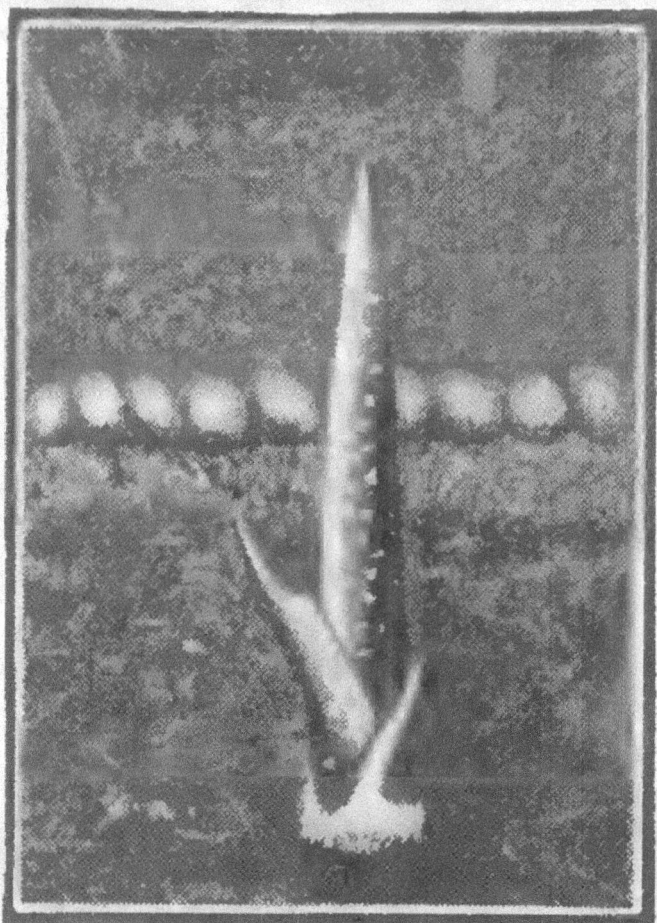

Thirty-two days after planting, the Giant Amorphophalle presented the appearance of a spire 34 inches in height, as in the photograph above.

THE DEVIL-PLANT

By John Murray Reynolds

(Weird Tales, 1928)

THE public will recall the disappearance of Jonathan Darrowby, about four years ago. A noted explorer, he went alone into the jungles of Brazil and never returned. Nothing was known of him until the so-called "Darrowby Manuscript" was found, a little less than a year ago.

At first that strange document, "The Darrowby Manuscript," was believed to be a hoax. What it related was so weird, so horribly unbelievable, that it was thought to be a practical joke or the product of a diseased imagination. But now that the handwriting has been definitely established as that of Jonathan Darrowby, and Professor Briggs has located the site of Palaos, there is no longer any doubt of the authenticity of the papers.

The manuscript, or rather diary, is written in a small, leather-covered note-book. It was found on a shelf in a junk store in Para, still wrapped in the oiled silk that had protected it when found floating down the river three years before, tied to a piece of wood. The first part contained valuable but technical and rather dull notes on the author's explorations, but the last few pages are here reproduced exactly as written.

J. M. R.

Weird Tales Sept. 1928 Cover Art by C. C. Senf.

FEBRUARY 18. Arrived at Palaos today. Came here just after noon, a little mud flat at the junction of the Orinoco with a smaller stream. Desolate little place. Dark jungle walls crowding close on each hand, the muddy river flowing by, and then the delta—with half a dozen miserable hovels

The Devil-Plant

raised on shaky piles above the mud and a larger house (this one) standing alone behind. One of these inexplicable little settlements, fungus growths that spring up in out-of-the-way places and drag out monotonous existences. It's damp and unhealthful and fever-ridden, but it is like heaven after weeks of the jungle alone.

Natives had told me that a white man lived here, but I hadn't really believed it till I saw this house. Then I knew it was true; you could tell at first glance no native had built it. I wanted to shout aloud at the prospect of someone to talk to after weeks of lonely silence.

As I stood there on the river bank a moment, just before splashing through the shallows of the smaller stream and crossing to the village, there came a faint breeze. It was blowing *from* Palaos, and it brought a mixed odor of garbage and wet bamboo and unclean humanity. Then a new smell came down on the strengthening breeze. The odor was faint and undefinable, but it was definitely unclean—evil. A phrase once used by an old river boatman recurred to mind: "The Devil breathes behind Palaos, *Senhor!*" The Devil's Breath! The thing is well named, whatever it is. Then the breeze died and the smell was no longer perceptible. With a shrug I waded through the shallows and came to Palaos.

When near enough to this house I shouted, and the owner walked out on the porch and waved his hand.

"Hello, friend," he called cheerfully in English. "Come on in. Glad to see you."

He is a queer little man, my host, this dweller in the heart of the jungle. He is fat and rotund, but he can not be over five feet two or three inches in height and his frame is so small that his actual bulk is not great in spite of his stoutness. The lower half of his face is hidden by a bushy and unkempt black beard, and he wears the thickest spectacles I have ever seen. The heavy lenses give his eyes a distorted look. At least, I think it's the lenses. Sometimes I'm inclined to believe there is something a little queer about the eyeballs themselves.

In such far-flung sentry posts as this there is little that is artificial. The man with the beard did not even invite me to stay; it was a foregone conclusion that I would share his house. As I slipped the pack from my shoulders he took it from me. He carried it in here and laid it on the floor beside one of the two cots in the bedroom.

The little room has a floor of rough boards covered with a coarse matting, and the walls are of smooth poles. Beyond the netting-filled window this afternoon was a world of sunlight with the river a brown smear across the green of the jungle; now it is a patch of warm blackness with insects buzzing ineffectually against the netting.

"Make yourself comfortable, friend," my host told me. "There is water, and you will find a towel hanging on the nail. You will wish to change your clothes, no? Somewhere I have a suit that is for me a little big; perhaps you can wear it. I will search."

WHAT a relief to wash up and shed my travel-stained clothing! The white duck provided by my host is tight across the shoulders and very short in the arms and legs, but it can be worn. When finished, I found him out on the wide porch, sitting in a long chair with a palm-leaf fan in one hand and a long-stemmed amber and meerschaum pipe in the other. He was reading a French scientific book.

"Well, friend," he said when I appeared, "how do you feel now?"

I started to thank him, but he only made spluttering noises and refused to let me. Seems to be one of those people who are embarrassed by gratitude. Incidentally, I can 't quite place his accent. It seems predominantly German, but at times it holds certain peculiar undertones I have noticed in the speech of Russians. He has not told me his origin and I have not asked. It is always better not to.

"Well, friend"—he inevitably addresses me that way—"my name is Wanless. You have not heard of me, no?"

I had to admit that I hadn't, and he laid down his pipe and slapped his plump thigh and laughed uproariously. Seemed to consider it a huge joke. At last he subsided into quiet chuckles, then added:

"No, friend, not yet. But you will. A time will come when the whole world will know the name of Wanless. I have patience. I can wait, and it will not be long now."

We sat talking all afternoon. Not for many dragging weeks have I seen a white man, and it must be years since the last one visited Palaos. Wanless tells me he has not been over a hundred miles down the river in more than ten years.

A girl came at his call and brought us drinks—necessarily warm and without ice, but refreshing for all that. I was rather surprized to see the girl. Wanless hadn't struck me as a man who would go in for that sort of thing. She is some kind of a mixed breed, part Portuguese and part Indian. Tall and slender and rather good-looking. She wore a shapeless dress of very dirty white cotton and had a square of scarlet silk tied over her head and knotted at the side. Her hair is black and straight, quite fine and silky, evidently a heritage from her Portuguese blood. Wanless calls her Lucia.

The relationship between the two is rather puzzling. Wanless tells me he bought the girl from a passing trader, a man who abducted her from some down-river settlement and then tired of her unsubdued hatred. He also says he keeps her because she seems contented and is useful around the house, but the instinctive and unthinking consideration he shows the girl convinces me that his feeling really goes deeper. As for Lucia, it is evident that she worships him.

The Unnatural History of Man-Eating Plants

Wanless has gone to bed and is snoring loudly; I stayed up to get these notes in shape. God! What a relief it will be to sleep in a bed again, even a little iron cot, after weeks of the jungle!

FEBRUARY 19. Loafed around and rested up most of the day. It is pleasant to sit in a chair on the porch and do nothing at all. In a day or so, after a little rest, I will move on.

Wanless and the girl puzzle me more all the time. There is another factor in their relationship, one more difficult to understand. It is fear. That Wanless is unaffected by the fear is evident; that he is not the immediate cause of it is equally so. But I hadn't seen Lucia half a dozen times before I was convinced that the girl lives in mortal terror of—what? Something. It shows in her eyes; there is a latent horror in their depths that is never entirely absent.

In the middle of the afternoon Wanless joined me on the porch and we yarned till twilight began to dim the outlines of the mud flats before us and the jungle behind. We spoke of the jungle and its ways, of the million unanswered mysteries of South America's dark interior, and of the fascination and repugnance of this Orinoco country. But mostly we talked of the varied life that teems in these muddy waters and throughout the fever-ridden thickets behind. I know a good deal about them myself, but Wanless' knowledge is extraordinary. He has a keen faculty of observation, and an immense fund of scientific knowledge. It was just before sunset that he showed me his garden.

That man *is* a botanist! I firmly believe he knows more about flowers and plants and their ways than any man who has ever lived. And his garden is superb. He has a wonderful assortment of growing things, ranging all the way from giant orchids that would set any flower show crazy to miniature nyctoginaceæ that are marvels of delicacy. I begin to realize that the man is a genius.

The Devil-Plant

Such of his chubby face as showed above the black beard beamed with delight at my enthusiasm.

Not all the plants in that garden are beautiful, however. Some are a little too queer for that. They are crosses. There is a whole section full of new varieties which Wanless has obtained by crossing and recrossing existing species. It is evidently the branch of his work in which he is most keenly interested, but I can't share his enthusiasm. It might be different with someone else, but I have never liked the idea of trying to set aside nature's laws in that manner. It is dangerous.

Somehow I don't think I shall ever forget that moment—the two of us standing there in that misplaced garden, with a red sun setting behind the jungle and the old Orinoco slipping muddily by. On one side the beautiful flowers with the giant orchids above them, and on the other those queer, perverted plants.

Then there came the faint stirring of a breeze. The underbrush swayed slightly, a few ripples ran across the stagnant ponds in the hollows of the mud flats, and an occasional palm frond rustled softly. Then the breeze quickened, and with it came the smell. Vile, unclean, revolting, it was the same that had greeted me when first I looked on Palaos.

The words of the old river-man again came back to me: "The Devil breathes behind Palaos, *Senhor*!" Hastily I turned to Wanless.

"What is that?" I asked.

"What is what, friend?"

"The breeze, that unholy smell!" I said impatiently.

Wanless looked at me for a long moment. Almost he spoke, then he seemed to change his mind and it was as though the shutters of his brain had closed. He shrugged.

"Who knows? The jungle has many smells, none of them pleasant!"

"Isn't that what they call 'The Devil's Breath'?" I persisted.

"Who knows?" he repeated. "I listen to no legends. Shall we go into the house?"

Whatever he knows, and I am certain he knows something, he is evidently determined to say no more at the time.

FEBRUARY 22. There is something strangely vivid about this place. The raw colors, the varied smells, the steaming noonday, the chill mists of dawn, all leave strong and not too pleasant impressions.

Nothing particular has happened, but Palaos is getting on my nerves very badly. I just get comfortable in a chair on the porch, when all at once the palms along the jungle edge begin to quiver with moving airs and the Devil's Breath comes down on the wind. Then I jump to my feet and restlessly pace the long porch, sucking on an empty pipe, till the breeze dies.

Today Wanless showed me his laboratory. I don't know the source of his income, but it must be quite substantial. That laboratory is a marvel of completeness—all the more remarkable because it is way up the Orinoco and back of nowhere. Everything in it has been transported for thousands of miles. My eye happened to be caught by half a dozen glass domes that stood against one wall. They were about the shape of the old helmets policemen used to wear, but two or three times the size.

"What are those used for?" I asked.

Wanless smiled. "Well, friend, I do not use them at all in my work any more. Some day I will show you what I did with them, but not now."

FEBRUARY 23. Have definitely determined to leave and move on in a day or so. Wanless can spare enough supplies to fit me out again. I may even turn down river. The decision to go is a great relief, lifts a great weight from my mind. Yet I don't quite know why.

The Devil-Plant

Wanless is busy in his lab or garden most of the day, but several times I noticed him walk back and disappear into the jungle behind the house. On these occasions Lucia always stands by the window without moving till he returns, stands staring at the dark wall of vegetation with the fear strong in her eyes and her face pale. Once I asked her:

"What do you fear, Lucia?"

"I fear the *thing*, Senhor."

"What thing?"

"The *thing* in the hut, *Senhor*," she replied, and refused to say more.

"The Devil's Breath?" I hazarded.

She threw me a frightened glance, but did not reply.

FEBRUARY 24. Wanless took me into his confidence tonight. He had been on the verge of telling me that first evening in the garden. Whether he held back because he was afraid I might be spying on him, or just what his reason was, I don't know. Probably it was only natural caution. At any rate, he told me all about it tonight as we sat in his laboratory. It was stifling hot, but the hordes of insects had driven us inside and we sat there in the little room with a single oil lamp for light and the long rows of bottles and jars looking down at us from the shadowy shelves.

Lucia sat unobtrusively on the floor in the corner. Now that I'm no longer a novelty she has abandoned the dress donned in my honor and reverted to her favorite household costume—a red waist-cloth and several strings of beads.

"Friend," Wanless started off with his usual form of address, "did you ever hear of the *Zoophyte giganticus wanlessi?*"

Lucia started suddenly and I heard her beads rattle, then she bent her head and began to play with an anklet.

The Unnatural History of Man-Eating Plants

"No," I replied, "I never did."

Wanless chuckled as at a huge joke.

"No, friend, not yet. The world does not yet know of my great work. You are the first I have told, and I only tell you because my work is almost completed. Tomorrow I will show you."

That is what he calls the thing: *Zoophyte giganticus*. Almost anyone scholarly enough to understand the implications of the name could understand from that what Wanless has been doing. For myself I became distinctly uncomfortable. Never have I liked taking liberties with nature. There was a long moment of silence, while Wanless leaned across the table with his eyes seeming to bulge more than ever behind his glasses. It was so still that I could hear Lucia's quick, nervous breathing, and a cougar crying somewhere far off in the jungle, and a rustling under the floor of the house where a pig was rooting in the refuse. After a minute Wanless went on:

"You are not a botanist, friend, but you know much of such matters and can understand what I am about to tell you. As you know, the animal kingdom is one form of life and that of the plants is another. Along different lines have they developed, but their basic principles are the same. And in the lower forms it is often difficult to tell them apart. There are plants which move about, and there are animals which are fixed in one place. There are plants which feed on bugs and insects, and there is an animal which contains chlorophyl. It is simply that these are two divergent lines of development. Do you see what I mean, friend?"

Of course I saw what he meant. I had not forgotten those perverted plants growing in the garden. Also, I began to understand something of Lucia's fear. But I only nodded.

"For years I have been doing this thing," Wanless continued, "doing it experimentally, here in my laboratory. Trying to cross an animal with a plant. Under those glass domes against the wall did I see my first zoophytes survive and grow. That was five years ago. Since then I have experimented with generation after generation of my plants. And I have succeeded, friend, I have succeeded! Out there, in a hut on the edge of the jungle, is a full-grown specimen of my giant animal-plant. Tomorrow I will show you."

When he finished I glanced at Lucia: the girl's face was positively haggard. She did not know much English, but she had understood enough to know what we were talking about. I have now this explanation of the latent terror that never leaves her eyes. Not that I feel any too comfortable myself. Somehow I don't think I shall sleep very well tonight.

FEBRUARY 25. Wanless was true to his word. This morning early we started off to a little clearing that lies about a quarter-mile back in the jungle. He explained that he had been afraid the natives might idly interfere with his experiments, but has found they never go near the place. I am not surprized. We perceived the odor known as the Devil's Breath before we had left the mud flats, and by the time we were within a hundred yards of the clearing the air was poisoned by the vilest, most horrible smell I have ever known.

In the center of the open space stood a hut about ten feet square. It is an ordinary thatch and mud cabin, but windowless and with a door supported on leathern hinges. Wanless tells me he built it alone and unassisted.

As we neared the place the stench became almost overpowering. God, that odor! Will I ever forget the taint of it? I can't compare it with any other; it beggars description. Primarily it's a stench of rottenness and decay, of putrefaction and death. The odor of long-dead carrion, the smell of a slaughter-house, the vile gasses of stagnant marshes, all are mild compared to what emanates from *that* unholy place. It was almost more than I could bear. Made the senses reel, and I think it could easily drive a man mad.

The Unnatural History of Man-Eating Plants

"Ah yes, the odor!" said Wanless with a chuckle when he saw me gasping. "It is unpleasant, no? But I have become used to it. Not that I enjoy, but I no longer notice."

"But what in God's name does it come from?" I asked him.

"From within the hut, friend. The zoophyte feeds entirely on carrion. Come."

He opened the door and we entered. Only half the hut was roofed over, the rest being open to the sun. The shadows in the covered part were deep and disturbing, but the other half was light enough.

Growing in the hut was—well, a plant. It can be called that for lack of a better name. The central mass was about eight feet high, grotesque, shapeless, and evil. It seemed tortured, distorted, and the many short, thick branches were twisted as though in pain. The thing looked as if its first ancestor had been a Venus flytrap, one of those carnivorous flowers that feed on insects, but it was greatly changed. There was one central cavity, lined with stiff hairs to entrap anything within reach—a cavity of death with a ghastly, dead-white, silky lining, like the skin of a corpse. I can see it yet! Crimson and white and brown, with that silky cavity yawning below and the yellow pollen sticks above, it was like a figment of madness.

As I said, we entered the hut. And I swear to God that the damnable plant turned and *looked* at us! Looked isn't quite the word, for of course it has no eyes. Perceived is better. In some way it indefinably sensed our entrance and seemed to inspect us, and I felt the hair bristling all across my scalp.

I have heard before of giant plants of the fly-catcher species, but this is far worse. The thing has—well, it has personality. It is menacing. There was no breeze within the walls of that hut, yet the misshapen branches were continually in motion. The opening of the central cavity suddenly closed; it was like a huge, malevolent mouth.

The Devil-Plant

On the floor of the hut was the vilest imaginable collection of rotting, loathsome carrion. Portions of the torn carcasses of various small animals lay about in all stages of decay. Around the foot of the *thing* these fragments formed a solid carpet of filth. The air was rank and foul, and a faint miasmatic mist seemed to be rising from that revolting mass of rotting flesh. The very sunlight that came through the hole in the roof was different and somehow unhealthy. This was the thing that for years had poisoned the wind behind Palaos, and had given rise to the legend of the Devil's Breath.

We stood there a while, Wanless beaming with a childlike pride and I simply staring. The thing has a ghastly fascination. Then one of the lower branches reached down, seized on half a young pig, and tossed it into the suddenly opened cavity. The jaws closed again with a snap, and I had seen enough. I turned and charged out of the hut, and Wanless followed more slowly.

Not till I was back on the river bank did I pause. The fever-filled air of this Orinoco jungle is like the breath of heaven after what I had just been breathing.

"What was it?" I asked when Wanless had caught up with me.

"My zoophyte, friend, my giant animal-plant. Born of my years of experiment, developed from a Venus fly-trap, and sired by half the animal kingdom!"

"But good God, man," I almost shouted at him, "why did you have to choose a plant of *that* sort to start with?"

"Because I wanted one as nearly animal at the beginning as I could get it. By that much did I make my task easier."

After we came back to the house Wanless gave me the details of his experiments. Some of them are pretty horrible. Most things sprout almost at once in this climate, and by intensive fertilization he has speeded up growth so that he has raised as many plant generations in the last five years as would normally grow in thirty or forty. Gradually he has trained the *thing* to feed on carrion. The rest of his methods are better forgotten; they are not pleasant.

As we came back I noticed that Lucia had, as usual, been keeping her vigil at the window.

FEBRUARY 26. By now I am thoroughly convinced that, like so many geniuses, Wanless is slightly mad. No ordinary man could have done what he has done. The most normal thing about him is his treatment of Lucia. It seems remarkable that the cold-blooded sponsor of the zoophyte could be so kind and considerate toward a mixed-blood native girl. I believe that in his own queer way he really loves her.

Tomorrow I move on. Thank God for that!

MARCH 3. Move on? Not for a week yet—if then. The fever has me. An hour after I wrote the last entry above I was flat on my back with the local variety of malaria. And have been ever since.

Somehow I think the foul air I breathed in the hut of the zoophyte may have something to do with this. That may not be medically possible; I'm not much of a medico. Whatever the cause, here I am, and almost too weak even to write.

MARCH 5. A little better now. Lucia takes care of me, administering suitable doses of quinine and keeping me supplied with water from the big canvas cooler that always hangs from the porch roof. I 've grown quite fond of the girl. She is a primitive creature in many ways, but she's kind-hearted and means well. She sits cross-legged on the floor beside my cot for hours, with a water jug between her knees and her eyes fixed on vacancy. Perhaps she thinks; perhaps not. One never knows.

MARCH 7. Am convalescing now. Wanless is seldom in evidence, but he did have a talk with me today and I learned the reason for his absence. He is quite jubilant.

"Progress, friend, progress!" he said, and beamed till his beard quivered. "I have again tried feeding my zoophyte on living flesh instead of on carrion. This time it is greatly a success—the plant becomes almost human. Now I range the jungle and trap small game for it. Soon it may hunt for itself—who knows? The roots are shallow, and it moves them. What do you think?"

I guess the fever must have soured me, for I snarled at him: "Since you ask me, I think you ought to let the damn thing starve to death."

"No, no, friend," he laughed; "to science it would be too great a loss. But you speak of hunger. Always is it hungry now; since it has tasted living flesh it will not touch carrion. And I can not seem to trap food fast enough. You should see how it snatches at anything I bring it! And it is strong, too; today I held out a stout stick I was carrying, and it snapped it like kindling. When you are well I will show you."

"Like hell you will!" I answered, and turned over to try to sleep. It seemed impossible to make the man angry.

MARCH 9. God! What a day of horror this has been! But to go back to the beginning:

I was quite a bit better this morning and sat propped up in a chair on the porch. Wanless had disappeared before I awoke, but Lucia was busy about the house. It struck me that she was even more silent than usual, and when she looked out the door for a minute I received a distinct shock. The girl was terrified! If ever I saw stark, primitive fear on a face it was then. I called to her, but she turned away without answering. The sense of menace that has been with me ever since I arrived in Palaos increased, and I grew restless and irritable.

It was sometime after noon that Lucia finally came out on the porch, walking with a slow, mechanical tread. There was an air of fatality about her, of resignation. In one hand she carried a chicken, its legs tied together with a cord.

"What is the trouble, Lucia?" I asked her in the bastard Portuguese she used.

"It is that I must go to the *thing* in the hut, *Senhor*," she told me, and I noticed that little beads of perspiration were standing out all over her tawny hide. "The Master is hunting, and he told me to feed this chicken to the *thing* at noon."

I tried to dissuade her, but she shook her head. She was terribly afraid, but Wanless had said something must be done and there was no stopping her. Finally I let her go. God forgive me for it! At that I don 't know just what I could have done to stop her, for the fever hasn't left me much strength. Down the path she went, winding back across the mud flats toward the jungle, walking with a slow and lagging tread. Then the first bushes swallowed her, and she was gone.

For perhaps twenty minutes I was not particularly worried. I did not exactly forget about the girl, but I did manage to dismiss her from my mind. And then suddenly came the realization that half an hour had passed without her return. I felt cold all over, and my hands began to shake. I remembered what I had seen in the hut, and I remembered what Wanless had told me of the new hunger of the *thing*. At the end of forty-five minutes I could no longer sit still.

Throwing aside the thin robe that covered me, I swung to my feet and started to cross the wide porch to the open door of the house. The fever has weakened me even more than I realized, for my knees were unsteady and tremulous and I fell prone on the floor before I had taken half a dozen steps. Slowly and laboriously I pulled myself to my feet and tried again. The result was the same. I was still lying full length on the splintery boards of the porch floor when Wanless appeared, making his way back between the native huts. When he saw me he threw down the small game he had been carrying, and came running up to the house.

Wanless was strong, for all his small frame. With scarcely an effort he gathered me up in his arms and dumped me back on the chair where I had been sitting. In my haste I choked on the words, but finally I gasped out what had happened. His face darkened, and without a word he turned on his heel and hurried away down the path to the jungle. As he went there came a faint puff of wind that bore with it a trace of that never-to-be-forgotten stench. It was almost as though the *thing* knew of his coming, and mocked him.

For a while nothing happened. It seemed that the sun paused, that the earth ceased its movement, and that time slumbered; and then at last Wanless came running back. He ran at full speed, looking at nothing, his face set in grim and terrible lines. Most of his clothing was ripped from his body; strange red welts covered his arms and shoulders; and one side of his head was crimson with blood where his ear had been nearly torn off and hung dangling from a single flap of skin.

I called to him, but Wanless never noticed me. He was past all thought or reason, and intent on only one idea. Across the porch and into the house he charged like a maddened boar, and I heard him throwing things around in the store-room. An instant later he reappeared, ran out with a long-bladed machete gleaming in each hand. Leaping down the steps in one bound, he ran back toward the jungle. His torn clothes fluttered behind him and the blood from his wound left a scarlet trail across the bushes.

This time he did not return. Time passed, with nothing disturbing the sultry calm, and when I could bear it no longer I again tried to stand up. This time I seemed a little stronger. Holding to the chairs and then to the walls themselves for support, I managed to enter the house. From a bottle on the table I poured out half a tumbler of brandy. The fiery spirits seemed to give new strength to my weakened legs.

With an energy born of desperation I commenced to dress. I slipped on my trousers, and a pair of high boots. My Colt lay on a chair, but I did not even take it—how can one shoot at a thing without vitals? Instead I went to the store-room and found another machete. With this, and a heavy staff to keep me upright, I started toward that ill-omened jungle clearing.

IT TOOK a long time to make that journey of about a third of a mile. God knows it seemed like ages! It was as though I struggled against unseen currents, and every movement was sluggish. Fever is a weakening thing, and I fell frequently in spite of my staff. When this happened I would lie still for a moment, fighting for breath, then once again stagger to my feet and start forward. At last there came that ghastly stench of decay, and I knew I was approaching the clearing.

The place was silent and still under the glare of the afternoon sun. An ominous silence. The grass seemed to undulate and quiver in the heat, and even the trees around the edge of the clearing drooped listlessly. The door of the hut was open and a severed branch lay athwart the entrance. It had been cut off by a stroke of a machete and was covered by a slimy yellow liquid, a sort of blood. And then I looked inside the hut....

I will not attempt to write what lay therein. God knows it will be long before I sleep well at night, for the memory of it. The girl had nursed me, and Wanless had been my friend. Yet the culminating horror was not their fate but the fact that the *thing* was gone. Even now, right at this minute, it must be somewhere at large.

For minutes on end I stood staring, unable to move my eyes. At last I uttered a strangled cry and staggered out into the clearing. Many dry bushes and shrubs lay nearby, and I piled them high around the walls of the hut and set the whole thing afire. I think I was slightly mad just then—and I am none too sure of my sanity even now. A great column of greasy black smoke mounted up into the air as I began my painful journey back here to the house.

It is now evening, with the last light fading, and I am feverishly working to finish up these notes. I have ready

The
DEVIL-
PLANT
JOHN·MURRAY·
REYNOLDS·

"He turned and charged out of the hut."

"He turned and charged out of the hut."

a large square of oiled silk and a block of wood, and if anything happens I will wrap the book in the silk and throw the whole thing out the window into the river.

Later. Something is coming! I can hear a slow splashing in the puddles out on the mud flats. A moment ago a dog was howling furiously; he ended with one ghastly scream and has since been silent.

I have a machete, and the door *may* hold. If not—? The porch is creaking as though under a weight, I think I will...

[*The manuscript ends abruptly at this point, and the above may be regarded as Jonathan Darrowby's last words. Professor Briggs located the site of Palaos after some difficulty, and found that the few natives had moved away and the jungle had reclaimed the place. The big house had evidently been destroyed by fire, perhaps from an overturned lamp. There was nothing to be gained by staying, and Professor Briggs left that same night.]*

"THE KISS" OF MADAGASCAR

By Seabury Quinn

(The Washington Post, 1928)

Mysterious Vampire, Draining Life Blood of French Official, Vanquished by Great Detective.

STRANGE stories of the fragrant goddess, the man-eating tree, came from the jungles of Madagascar. And when La Peruse, French Colonial official, falls strangely ill in Washington, Maj. Sturdevant remembers his Madagascar enemies—and, remembering, fathoms a fascinating mystery.

"HEY, somebody lend me twenty-five bucks?"

Bailey, who represented the Post-Intelligencer at Washington, peered through the Record's office door, glancing hopefully from Williams, the Record's correspondent, to Loomis, of the Clarion-Call.

"Kind o' original in your needs, ain't you?" Loomis asked. "Most of us don't need more than ten or fifteen bucks, anyhow."

"Aw, fellers," Balley pleaded, "don't throw me down; I need this dough, I tell you. Gotta get my sweetie some flowers. She's goin' to a doings up at the Highlands tomorrow, and I want to knock her dead with an orchid corsage. I'll pay you back when my check comes next week, honest—"

"Orchid," Loomis cut in again. "Gosh, he'd actually give her orchids."

"Hey, what's biting on you?" Bailey asked angrily. "You talk as if I was fixin' to present the dame with a lovers' knot of rattlesnakes, or something."

"You might as well, according to my way of thinking," Loomis returned. "Listen: Do you remember when the French Madagascar Commercial Mission was over here last year?"

"Yes," Bailey agreed sulkily, "I remember, all right. But what's that got to do with your disliking orchids?"

"Everything," Loomis answered. "When that aggregation hit Washington last year they looked like a constellation of bright stars of hope to me. I'd slipped up on important matters three times hand-running, and it looked as if I'd soon be hunting a Government clerkship when the Frenchmen came along.

"'Here's where I get in solid,' I told myself. 'I'll just run up and cop off a red-hot story and square myself with the old man.'

"Did I? I did not. The Frenchies were occupying the Bushnell residence, in Sheridan Circle, and they'd had time to dig in by the time I rang the front doorbell. A tenth-assistant secretary, who smelled like a ladies' hairdressing emporium, gave me a supercilious look and a sheet of mimeographed legal cap. 'Zat ees all ze Commeesion haff for pooblication,' he said, and nodded to the doorkeeper to give me the gate.

"I started down Massachusetts avenue toward Dupont Circle, when some one hit me a crack on the shoulder.

"'Hello, Frank,' my assailant said, 'what's the trouble? You look as if you were taking a guilty conscience out for an airing.'

"It was Maj. Sturdevant, of the Secret Service, and he'd been responsible for my scoring more beats than all the luck I'd had since coming to Washington.

"'No; it's the job,' I said. 'Those Frenchmen back there gave me a raw deal.'

****

"'WELL, well,' he commented, 'I reckon I can give you a lift. I know La Peruse, the director of the commission, slightly—was on my way to see him when I bumped into you. I'll take you back with me.'

"'Next time you want ten or a dozen guys murdered, call on me, Major,' I asked as we mounted the Bushnell steps and Sturdevant rang the bell.

"'Ze Commeessionaire, he air not to see de journaleests,' the overgrown porter announced.

"Sturdevant thrust his card forward, adding the oral explanation, 'Service de Surete.'

"'Oh, mais oui, M'sieur, certainment,' the porter agreed, his hostility evaporating before Sturdevant's announcement.

"We rode up two floors in the automatic electric elevator, and entered a large parlor on the third floor which seemed to combine the duties of lounging room and office.

"'Ah, Monsieur Sturdevant,' a big, blond man greeted as we followed the porter through the tapestry lambrequins at the door.

"The Major shook hands cordially and presented me to the Frenchman. He was well over 6 feet tall and proportionately broad, with the prominent nose and cheekbones that bespoke Basque ancestry and the fair skin and light eyes that told of descent from the Northmen who overran Brittany in the days before Hastings.

"'Mister Loomis,' he acknowledged Sturdevant's introduction in excellent English, 'I had not thought to give anything but a formal statement to the press at this time; but I make an exception of you. Here are some memoranda you may find of interest. Copy what you wish and announce your dispatches as coming from the commission.'

"I thanked him and dug into the papers, getting enough live stuff to fill two columns comfortably.

****

"STURDEVANT and La Peruse talked of adventures in far places as I worked, and it was not till the library clock struck midnight that I realized how long we had been there.

"'But, gentlemen, you will surely remain the night, certainly.' La Peruse insisted as we rose to go. 'It is past twelve, and the snow is deep. I can make you most comfortable.'

"I looked out the window and saw he was correct. Both Sturdevant and I hastened to accept the invitation.

"'Queer chap, La Peruse,' the Major told me as he snapped off the light. 'He could have retired twenty years ago, if he'd wished, but colonial administration seems a sort of passion with him. Africa, Polynesia, Madagascar—wherever the French have possessions, he's given the best years of his life and a lot of his own money to carrying on their work. This commissionership he holds now is only an honorary position; he doesn't get a cent out of it. Why— Good Lord! What's that?'

"We leaped out of bed and rushed into the darkened hall as a second blood-chilling cry echoed through the house.

"'Down there!' Sturdevant shouted, running headlong toward a room at the turn of the corridor. In a moment we were at the door.

"'La Peruse!' he called. 'La Peruse, what's wrong; are you ill?'

"We pressed our ears to the wood, waiting a reply, but no word came from the bedroom. Only a gurgling noise, like water escaping through a drain, or a man fighting desperately for breath. Then we burst open the door.

****

"FEELING his way along the wall, Sturdevant located the electric switch and snapped on the light. La Peruse lay on his bed, the covers kicked to the floor, his hands flexed in a rigidity like that of death, fingers digging into the yielding mattress. His pajama jacket was open at the neck, and on the white skin of his throat, below the line of tan, was a ruby disc where warm blood welled up from a tiny wound. His eyes were wide open, staring, and on his sunburned face, was such a look of mortal terror as is seldom seen outside the phantasies of nightmare.

"'La Peruse,' the Major called, hurrying to the bedside and laying a hand over the Frenchman's heart.

"His warm touch seemed to revive the stricken man. He rose unsteadily on his elbow, staring at us in pathetic bewilderment. 'Where is it?' he asked in a shaking voice. 'Did you see it, Sturdevant, mon ami?'

"'See what?' Sturdevant asked. 'What hurt you, La Peruse?'

"The other passed a trembling hand across his forehead. 'The vampire,' he answered with a shudder. 'The demon un-dead, Major. It was here, I tell you, sitting on my breast, sucking the life-blood from my veins—' he crossed himself awkwardly. 'I saw it, flickering like a flame of hell-fire over me—'

"'Rats!' Sturdevant interrupted. 'My dear fellow, you've had a bad dream. A vampire! You'll be seeing old Mother Hubbard and her dog, next!'

"The Frenchman smiled wanly. 'So?' he said. 'Look,' he touched the wound at his throat and held his blood-stained fingertips up for inspection. 'Is this blood or not blood, my friend? And if it be blood, how comes it there? You, yourself can testify my door was locked; there is no other entrance to the room. Yet when you broke in what did you find, hein? If it was no vampire, then, pour l'amour de Dieu, what was it?'

****

"SERVANTS and varying attaches of the Commission, in varying stages of dishabille, were crowding into the room. La Peruse waved them away and turned to Sturdevant.

"'My friend,' he said, 'I am afraid. And my fear is the greater because I know not what it is I fear. How long I slept before It came I can not tell, but I remember waking with a feeling of suffocation—no pain, but weakness and utter impotence—to see a red, fiery thing waving like a flame above me and to smell the odor of a charnel house. At first I knew not where I was, but realization came slowly. The thing that seemed to burn above me I can not describe, for the darkness of the room and its very nearness obscured my vision. How long I lay wondering I have no idea; but suddenly I became aware of a feeling like a pulling at my throat. Then I knew: The thing was sucking my blood.'

"'Rubbish!' Sturdevant replied. 'I don't doubt you think you saw this thing, but you couldn't have. No one ever saw a vampire, or anything like one, outside a book or a bad dream.'

"'You do not know the things I have seen, my friend,' the other returned. 'Here in what we call civilization we have forgotten the ancient things of nature, so we say they do not exist. But the people who live in the silent places have not forgotten; they remember, and they know. Listen, my friend:

"'The revolt of the Hova in 1898, which led ultimately to the exile of Queen Ranavalona, was not particularly anti-European. The Malagasy government had long employed English and French army officers and engineers, and found Europeans quite tolerable. But there is no question the Hova were violently opposed to Christianity. Travelers say the Hova had no definite religion of their own. That is not so. They worshiped a goddess known as "The Fragrant One," whose manifestation was said to be a man-eating tree.

"'I was in Gallieni's army of pacification when we put down the rebellion. One day word come by a convert, Andevo, that Hova insurrectionists had captured a missionary priest. We hurried inland to the rescue, and arrived to find the mission a smoldering ruin. Two days forced marching brought us to the Hova camp fires' ashes, still warm. Another day our scouts surprised the war party dancing about something white on the ground. One volley of musketry sent them into the jungle, and when we charged their camp we found a skull and several bones in the center of their dancing circle.'

"'Cannibalism?' Sturdevant asked.

"'Non, non,' La Peruse denied. 'The skull and bones were clean, clean as though scraped with sandpaper; there was no evidence of fire upon them, but something more we found; their surfaces had been eaten away—how do you say?— eroded? —as though by acid.'

****

"'H'M,' Sturdevant commented. 'Whose skull was it?'

"'The skull was that of a white man, and in the front of the mouth was a gold tooth—what you call a crown—the priest had set in by an American dentist in Paris. Our guide, the convert, recognized it at once, for that golden tooth had been the marvel of the mission settlement.'

"'Still, I don't see any evidence of your man-eating tree,' Sturdevant objected. 'The Hova might have used an acid substance to pickle their victim's skeleton. Such things are not uncommon among barbarous peoples.'

"'Yes, yes, you are right to be skeptical,' the Frenchman admitted, 'but wait. The guide told us the Hova made sacrifices to "The Fragrant One" by placing the victim (preferably a Christian) in the tree's branches. It is supposed to be a sort of vegetable octopus, with tentacles to catch and hold its prey. When the tree had eaten the offering, the bones were collected and kept as souvenirs by the devotees.

"'Now I, myself, had always scouted these stories; but when I saw the murdered priest's skeleton I reconsidered. Do you know the Venus' flytrap?'

"'You mean the insect-catching plant of Carolina?' Sturdevant asked.

"'Yes,' La Peruse answered, 'the same. That plant, as you know, has a flower so delicately sensitive that the slightest touch by an insect closes the petals like the leaves of a book. Once imprisoned, the unfortunate insect is slowly dissolved by a powerful acidulous liquid excreted by the plant. As you would say, he is digested.

"'Now consider: In tropical lands the flora of the temperate zone attains much greater size. If America and south Europe produce "flytrap" plants large enough to digest the humble bee, why should not a tropic island like Madagascar develop a tree large enough and fierce enough to devour a man? Eh?'

"'H'm, possibly,' Sturdevant tugged at his beard, 'you may be right. At any rate, we're still in the dark regarding the cause of your wound. It's nearly morning; lie down and try to sleep. I'll stay with you the rest of the night.'

"I left them together and crawled back in my own bed, but did precious little sleeping. The echo of the Frenchman's ghastly cry and the sight of his still, horror-drawn face stayed with me till daylight.

****

"WE had a continental breakfast—coffee and rolls—in our bedroom, and I turned my overcoat collar up against the storm as I plunged my way toward Connecticut avenue. La Peruse begged Sturdevant to stay with him so piteously that the Major consented to remain an hour or so.

"The Kiss" of Madagascar

"I knocked the information I'd gotten into shape and sent it off to the home office. The job was moderately safe for awhile longer, anyhow.

"I hadn't been in the office fifteen minutes next morning when a call came from Sturdevant. 'Hello, Loomis,' he said, 'there's something dam' queer going on up here.'

"'What's the trouble?'

"'I don't know; that's where the difficulty comes in. La Peruse is worse. I stayed here again last night, and ran in to see how he was getting on about every half hour till 5 o'clock this morning. Everything seemed O.K., and I'd turned in for a couple of hours' sleep when he gave another one of those war whoops, and when I got to his room he was lying just as we found him yesterday morning. I had more trouble in bringing him to this time, and he's so weak from loss of blood we've had a physician up to look him over.'

****

"I REPORTED at the Bushnell house about seven that evening, and Sturdevant took me to La Peruse's room at once. The Frenchman was like a wraith of his former self. Violet half-moons under his eyes, a waxen pallor beneath his sunburn and a queer, pinched look about the nostrils testified eloquently to sudden and overwhelming weakness. The hand he extended unsteadily in greeting was as thin and bloodless as a fever patient's.

"'Now, Frank,' the Major said, 'I want you to act as relief guard tonight. I'll sit with La Peruse while you sleep; then you take your turn at sentry-go.'

"We sat talking till I began to feel drowsy, and the Major took up his vigil by the sick man's bed.

"He shook me awake shortly after 2 o'clock, and I slumped down in an easy chair beside the night light, a copy of the Clarion-Call in my hand.

"'Do you wish coffee, sir?' some one asked in a strong English accent. I looked up and saw a small and exceedingly black man with regular features and wire-straight hair, standing in the doorway, a tray containing a coffee pot and cup in his hands.

"'Yes, thank you,' I answered. 'Pour it black, please.'

"'Very good, sir,' he replied, filling my cup. I swallowed a mouthful of the steaming black beverage and turned back to my paper.

"'The old man had a riproaring editorial in that issue, lambasting the tar out of the administration about the coal strike, but, somehow, the words seemed to have lost their punch as I sipped my coffee. Presently the lines of type began to run together before my eyes. I nodded, shook my head to clear my vision, and—

****

"'LOOMIS, Loomis, wake up. Give me a hand here!'

"'Eh, wha -what?' I asked stupidly, half rising from my chair, then sinking down again as the room commenced whirling like a Coney Island carrousel.

"Gradually I began to see things. Sturdevant, his white hair and beard bristling with anger and excitement, bent above La Peruse. La Peruse lay half out of the bed, head downward, eyes staring glassily, the bandage on his throat displaced, and a thin trickle of blood oozing from his reopened wound.

"'Good Lord!' I exclaimed, bracing myself against the arms of my chair. 'What's happened, Major?'

"'La Peruse has been murdered while you sat there snoring.'

"'But I wasn't asleep,' I protested. 'I felt a little queer after I drank that coffee, but—'

"'Eh? What's that?' he asked sharply. 'You drank coffee? Where? When? Who gave it to you?'

"'Why, the boy!' I answered.

"'H'm,' the Major lifted La Peruse to the bed, and glared at me. 'Go find that servant and have some one phone the doctor. There's still a flutter in this poor chap's pulse. No thanks to you, though.'

"I roused a secretary and asked him to call a physician, then inquired my way to the servants' quarters. Three minutes' search sufficed to find the man who served me, peacefully sleeping,

"I brought him, still in his pajamas, to Sturdevant.

"'Did you serve coffee to this gentleman?' the Major asked, eyeing him sternly.

"'Yes, sir,' the black man answered. 'I thought some black coffee might help him stay awake.'

"'H'm,' Sturdevant looked him over from head to feet. 'Pretty bold, doping him right under my eyes, aren't you?'

"'Doping him?' the man's assumption of horrified incredulity was masterly. 'You surely don't think that, sir.'

"He turned to me. 'How much coffee did you drink, sir?' he asked.

"'Not more than half a cup,' I answered.

"'Ah,' his insolence was superb as he stretched out his hand, lifted the cup, and drained it at a single gulp.

"He looked at Sturdevant. 'If the coffee is drugged, sir,' he announced, 'it surely should act on me.'

"'H'm, all right; you may go.'

"'Thank you, very much, sir,' the other replied, as he bowed his way from the room.

I brought him, still in his pajamas, to Sturdevant.

"The physician came bustling in. 'What's all this?' he asked testily, making a hasty examination of the patient.

"'Why the man's almost dead from exhaustion. Every indication of severe hemorrhage. Where's the blood?'

"Sturdevant shrugged in annoyance. 'We know no more about it than you do, doctor,' he replied.

"'Then you're dam' ignorant,' the physician blurted. 'There'll have to be an immediate transfusion of blood if we're going to save this man's life.'

"Hurried telephone calls to the doctor's office for paraphernalia, an examination of half a dozen of the commission's personnel for a suitable blood count, and the big porter was chosen to supply the vital fluid.

"When morning came La Peruse was resting easily, his body refreshed with new blood.

"'We saved him this time,' the doctor said as he struggled into his ulster, 'but I'll not answer for the consequences if he has another hemorrhage. See that he's watched every moment.'

"'He'll be watched, all right, doctor, you may depend on it,' Sturdevant assured him.

"As I was leaving he whispered, 'Come up again tonight, Loomis. We'll find out what's what this evening, or know the reason why.'

****

"LA PERUSE was slightly improved, though still very weak, when I arrived at the Bushnell house about 11 o'clock that evening.

"'Hello, Frank,' Sturdevant greeted as I was divesting myself of hat, muffler and overcoat.

"He led me to the room assigned us, shut the door carefully and lighted one of his long, black cheroots. 'Been doing some visiting and exploring today,' he announced. 'Had quite a conference with Prof. Stockton, of the Smithsonian Institution. He's the foremost authority on tropical flora in the country.'

"'What's the idea?' I asked. 'Did you want to check up on La Peruse's theory of the man-eating tree?'

"'Partly,' he replied. 'Stockton says La Peruse may not be far wrong. He gave me a lot of interesting data on Madagascar, too.'

"'Shall I take the first trick?' I asked as we walked toward La Peruse's room.

"'Not much; we'll handle this business together,' he answered. 'I can't risk having you sleep at the switch a second time.'

"'We tiptoed across the room, and I was about to take a chair when the Major put out his hand, giving me a slight push. 'Under the day bed, Loomis,' he ordered.

"'What?' I whispered incredulously.

"'Get under that day bed there,' he repeated. 'You're going to be the silent partner in our little game tonight, and the invisible one, too. Crawl under that couch and keep your mouth shut and your eyes open. Go on.'

"I slipped to the floor beneath the couch.

"THE Major pressed the bell communicating with the servants' rooms. In a few moments the little black man who had waited on me the previous night entered. 'You rang. sir?' he asked.

"'Yes,' Sturdevant replied without looking up from his book. 'Bring me some coffee at midnight, please.'

"'Very good, sir.'

"The time crawled by like a frost-bitten snake. The servant entered with the coffee, set the tray on the table and stood waiting Sturdevant's orders.

"'That's all, thank you,' the Major said as he resumed his chair and picked up the cup. He took a swallow of the drink, then resumed his reading. Five, ten, fifteen minutes ticked off on my wrist watch, nothing happened. Then the room's quiet was disturbed by a low guttural sound. I looked at Sturdevant in fascinated horror. His head had fallen forward on his chest, the book had dropped from his hand. He was asleep—snoring.

****

"I WRIGGLED a few inches on the floor, intent on crawling from under the couch and waking him, then froze where I lay.

"Stepping softly as a panther, the colored servant came into the room, followed by another. The second one carried a tray with coffee pot and cups, the first bore a bundle of some sort carefully between his outstretched hands.

"Pausing beside the Major a moment, they smiled at each other, then placed another cup exactly like that from which Sturdevant had drunk on the table, pouring an amount of coffee equal to that he had left into the substituted cup. Quietly the fellow with the coffee turned and walked quickly down the hall.

"The trick by which I'd been drugged the night before, and which had enabled the suspected black to demonstrate his innocence and my dereliction of duty, was so simple as to be childish, yet Sturdevant and I had been fooled by it.

"I lay where I was, watching the man's movements.

"Quickly he leaned over the sleeping Frenchman, unfastening the bandage at his throat with a deftness the most experienced pickpocket might envy. A moment more and he produced a jar of oil, touched the sleeping man's wound with the unguent, then, with a tiny scalpel, removed the softened scab.

"I saw a spot of blood form and grow larger as the wound was opened, and fixed my muscles for a spring when his next move struck me stone-still with mystification.

"Something like a ball of coarse moss, doubled upon itself like a giant sleeping spider, dangled from a thread as the man drew his hand from the bundle he carried. I saw him swing the thing through the air several times, slowly at first, then faster and faster, till it whirled round his head like a wheel of light. Carefully he slackened the swinging thing's speed, finally dangling it at arm's length from him above La Peruse. The rapid motion through the air had opened the thing he held till its parts were fully displayed.

"Leaning forward, he dropped the knot of moss upon the Frenchman's open wound.

"My eyes almost started from my head in horror. While I watched the thing upon the sleeper's throat began to live, putting out tiny tendrils like the fronds of an asparagus fern, but red as rust iron in color. Like a living animal, the thing's leaves waved and swayed in the air. Gradually like a toy balloon slowly inflated, a great, tri-petaled, blood-red flower began unfolding.

"La Peruse moaned and stirred uneasily in his sleep.

****

"'AT him, Loomis!' With a bound Sturdevant was out of his chair. He leaped across the room, hands outstretched to seize the black.

"With a snarl of bestial ferocity, the little man dodged, hurling himself toward the door.

"I squirmed from my hiding place and leaped in his path, driving my fist at the point of his jaw.

"He fought like a wildcat. Shorter than I by almost a foot, and underweighing me by at least 40 pounds, he was all I could handle, and more.

"'Ah! Got him!' Sturdevant dropped on the fellow's shoulders, seized his elbows in an iron grip and pressed them into his sides.

"'Now, you little hellion,' he rasped, 'take that accursed thing off La Peruse and see you don't leave any roots in his wound.'

"'Ha! You think to make me?' the other answered with a snarl. 'You can not. Your friend will die. You may kill me, cut me in pieces, if you like, but the cursed Frenchman dies. I'll make no move to save him from his judgment.'

"'No?' Studevant replied, seizing the man's left wrist in his right hand and slowly forcing it upward in a hammer-lock. 'No? We'll see about that.'

"Perspiration glistened on the fellow's forehead, his eyes started in their sockets like a frog's, his mouth drew taut with agony as Sturdevant slowly increased his pressure.

"Step by step the Major forced his captive toward the bed. At last the other dropped to his knees beside La Peruse.

"The Kiss" of Madagascar

'Let me go,' he begged. 'Let me go, you white beast, and I'll take "the Kiss" from him.'

"The captive reached out, seized the waving, red thing at the Frenchman's throat, and lifted it carefully from his wound. Like an inflated bladder pricked with a pin, the infernal plant began wilting as its terrible nourishment was cut off.

"'Now we'll gather in the other one,' Sturdevant announced as he snapped a pair of handcuffs over the prisoner's wrists.

"The other black was lying in bed, apparently sound asleep, when we reached his room, but it required our combined efforts to subdue and shackle him when he leaped up as we entered the door.

"'HOW'D you dope it all out, Major?' I asked, when La Peruse, rebandaged and soothed with a strong sedative, had fallen asleep once more.

"He bit the end from a cigar as he replied: 'Just adding a few facts together, Loomis. A knowledge of Madagascar, plus a knowledge of the West Indies, plus a little thought—and there you are.

"'Take Madagascar, for instance. We know the difficulties the French had subduing the place and every effort the natives made to get back autonomy.

"'When Gallieni and his forces defeated the Hova in 1896 they overthrew one of the most corrupt governments in the world. Ranavalona III had come to the throne by the simple expedient of murdering her predecessor with slow poison. The island's inhabitants consisted of three classes, Andriana, or nobility; the Hova freemen, and the Andevo, or slaves. But actually there were no freemen but the Andriana. They had a custom called fanampoona, which meant simply forced labor. The government would notify a man he was "honored" by being selected to work for it, and work he had to, without compensation.

The Unnatural History of Man-Eating Plants

"'The natural result was the impoverishment of the people and the enrichment of the nobility. The French changed all this. They freed the slaves, forbade fanampoona and made the nobles go to work. You can imagine how popular such a policy was with the ruling classes.

"'La Peruse was one of the leaders in perfecting the new order of things, and he's had more attempts made on his life than any man in the island, I suppose.

"'A little conference with our historical experts and a talk with the French embassy revealed the existence of a well-developed, though unsuccessful, organization among descendants of the Malagasy nobility to assassinate the directors of the colonial administration and restore the old regime.

****

"'NOW, when I talked with Prof. Stockton yesterday he not only agreed La Peruse's theory concerning the man-eating tree might be correct; but he told me something that furnished a definite working hypothesis for the cause of La Peruse's illness. It seems there is a beautiful orchid of the epiphyte variety known as Angraecum, which grows on the west coast of Madagascar. But the natives whisper strange stories of a vampire plant, a sort of vegetable leech, which infests the interior. Stockton searched for the thing for months, but never found anything like it. Everywhere he heard of "the Kiss," as they call it—a red, terrible plant that fastened on travelers as they slept and sucked their lives away, but no specimens could be found. He finally abandoned the hunt and decided the strange orchid was only a native myth. However, when he mentioned it, I saw where such a thing—provided it actually existed—could easily account for La Peruse's strange sickness.

"'The next question was: "Who is the logical suspect?" The natives of Madagascar aren't negroes in the generally accepted sense, though their skins are black when they happen to be pure-bloods, unmixed with Malay, Chinese or

"The Kiss" of Madagascar

Hindu stock. These small, straight-haired, regular featured black boys we captured tonight didn't look like them.

"'The fact that you went to sleep after drinking his coffee was even a stronger clue, and the insolent manner in which he alibied himself only served to make my suspicions stronger.

"'I took the precaution to search his room today, and got into every box he had, except one. That was of iron and fastened with two Yale locks. If it hadn't been for two things I'd have thought he had ordinary valuables in it; but I found a box of gold coin in his bureau drawer secured by an ordinary lock, and in another drawer I found a dagger about ten inches long with a waved, razor-edged blade—a Malay kris.

****

"'NOW what would a servant have more valuable than a box of gold? If the man were an ordinary servant, as he assumed to be, there was no explanation for his possession of so much gold; but if he were the agent of a conspiracy, well supplied with ready cash from the conspiracy's war chest, it was simple enough. Also, if he were a West Indian, as he claimed, why should he have a Malay kris concealed among his clothes?

"'That's the way I figured it, and I staged our little party last night on those assumptions. I knew he'd hardly try the drugged coffee again unless I gave him an opening, so I pretended to trust him, and everything worked out exactly as I'd figured. Pretending to drink his coffee was one of the hardest things. My shirt front is still sticky where I poured the villainous stuff down my collar.'

"'What are you going to, do with "the Kiss?"'" I asked.

"'Give it to Stockton,' Sturdevant answered with a grin. 'He spent six months looking for a specimen in its native habitat, and now I've got him one right here in Washington.'"

The Unnatural History of Man-Eating Plants

****

LOOMIS drew a deep breath and stared hard at Bailey. "Now you see why I can't abide the sight or thought of an orchid," he explained. "Do you wonder I was horrified when you said you wanted to give your girl some of the awful things? Why, they're all first cousins to 'The Kiss of Madagascar.'"

"Gosh," Bailey commented, "lend me $10 will you? That'll just pay for the violets."

FRUIT OF THEIR TREE

By Joseph Faus

(Evansville Press, 1929)

Illustrations by Paul Kroesen

The Stern Law Of Nature's Justice Metes Out Primitive Punishment To a Husband Who Denied His Wife The Sacred Happiness Of Motherhood

GLADYS CRANDON was born and brought up in a little city in Illinois. The town's sole claim to fame was the dignified old university there. In this staid institute of learning, her father, a kindly and very understanding man, was an instructor in mathematics. Her mother was a frail little woman, intensely devoted to Gladys, her only child, and as passionately wrapped up in her husband as she had been the day of their marriage.

In the loving and sympathetic atmosphere of this home the girl was reared. After graduating from the local high school she entered the university, receiving her degree from it when she was 22 years of age.

It was a month before this exciting event that she met Eric Thorhansen, the man who was to be her husband.

As a professor of natural history in a great eastern college and as a botanist of considerable note, Eric created a flutter among the admiring faculty and students of the humble university. He also engendered a commotion in the hearts of many fair co-eds, of which Gladys was one of the prettiest.

GLADYS CRANDON

"You have," he romantically whispered in her ear one night, "the grace of the willow, the beauty of the magnolia, the delicacy of the orchid, the fragrance of the rose."

"You are," she dimpled back, "characteristically the naturalist. And—may I prefix an adjective?—a complimentary naturalist."

Fruit of Their Tree

"I am," he promptly responded, "when I am with you, characteristically the *man*! And—may I prefix an adjective? —a truthful man."

Gradually, she fell in love with the distinguished, handsome and young professor. She would have liked to think that he fell in love with her, too. Later he told her he did; but, eventually, she found herself doubting, for Eric was a strange man: first, indeed, the cold-blooded and analytical naturalist—second, the lover.

GLADYS trembled at the inadvertent meeting, at a football game, between Eric and George Lamont. For George, till the advent of the former, was the only boy she had ever "gone with." He was also a student—of medicine—at the university. Her parents, as she, liked George for his sturdy, dependable looks, his honesty, his blunt truthfulness, and for the courageous and ambitious gaze of his steady gray eyes. George, wasn't "mushy" like most boys; he was, she thought, as a brother to her.

Eric, after introduction, calmly appropriated the happy girl, and George faded unobtrusively into the noisy background. Gladys never missed him, though, as time went on, for more passionate grew her love for Eric. Supreme ecstasy was hers the moonlit night he took her in his arms, gently kissed her responsive lips and said that he wanted to marry her.

"Mother! Daddy!" The parents looked up from their books. Gladys stood before them, exultation and joy writ on her beautiful countenance. "Mother! Daddy! You're going to lose your little girl!"

"No, dear," disagreed her father, as he lovingly patted her shoulder and his wife's arms went about her daughter, "we aren't going to lose you. Instead, we gain Eric. And," a sweet reverence crossed his face, "in time, we hope and pray, a little tike in rompers, a little sweetheart in dresses."

The Unnatural History of Man-Eating Plants

Crimson swept to Gladys' temples and she hugged her father in fond embrace. "Why," she half-cried, half-laughed, "who could want a better grand-daddy than my daddy!"

The marriage was a month later; and to the New England city wherein was the famous college that Eric graced, they went to live. The husband bought a comfortable home; they had a maid. Eric was the soul of generosity and goodness, solicitous of her physical welfare, ardent in his constant passion for her; and in return she gave him the full love of her being.

BUT two years brought grave dissension. Like every normal young wife, Gladys wanted a child; and Eric, to her astonishment and dismay, vetoed the wish. His arguments against this natural wifely desire varied from selfish, practical reasons to ridiculous ones.

"First," he said with bleak mathematical precision, "we have planned to go on exploring trips that are liable to start any time, and so it would be rash, foolhardy, to have a baby—it would suffer, be in the way."

"But, darling!" she intervened. "I will gladly forego any trip or all trips." To this, however, her husband sulked and refused to listen.

"Secondly," he proclaimed, "you might lose your figure. Dearest, you know I love you for your grace and beauty. Would you thus seek deliberately to kill my love?"

"Eric! Oh, Eric!" she wailed, in humorous exasperation.

"Thirdly," he continued firmly, "I don't like 'kids,' anyway. They 'bawl' too much. They are ruinous to good dispositions. They would interrupt my well-organized existence. And," as he saw tears come to her eyes, his voice rose perilously close to a shout, "come right down to it, I refuse to give you one." Angrily he slammed himself out of the house.

Fruit of Their Tree

A verse by the Psalmist David came to the mind of the distraught wife, and clung tenaciously: "And he shall be like a tree planted by the rivers of water, that bringeth forth his fruit in his season; his leaf also shall not wither; and whatsoever he doeth shall prosper."

And equally applicable—in sudden fear, she ruminated—these words were to the man or woman who goes against the wishes of his Creator; if he does not bring forth his fruit in his season his leaf shall wither and nothing that he does shall prosper.

Well? Their season—hers and Eric's—was at hand, and their tree bore no fruit!

She recalled how, as a child, she mothered her dolls; how, as a grown girl, she cuddled friends' babies yearningly to her breast. She was, she brooded, meant to be a mother, and now her husband sought to kill the maternal instincts with which a wise God had endowed her!

Guiltily, she evaded the disappointed eyes of her parents whenever they visited her. She sensed, as the years went by, a Damoclean sword hovering over Eric's head; she herself had the qualms of a sinner.

Ostensibly she was a happy and contented young wife, but because of her suppressed desire her heart was eating itself away. And Eric was truly happy in his manner: he was making a success; he had progressed amazingly at the college; he had written a book on certain trees and plants in South America—as a result of an expedition of theirs to that country—and his name in educational circles evoked due admiration from all.

THEN, one afternoon in the sixth year of marriage, Eric, waving a letter, excitedly burst into the house.

"Darling!" he ejaculated joyously, "I'm on Olympus, the golden fleece in sight!"

The Unnatural History of Man-Eating Plants

"What!" she laughed. "Don't tell me you've turned a toadstool into a mushroom!"

An association of American naturalists, it eventuated from the letter Eric insisted she reread to him, was planning an expedition to the island of Madagascar to study the unusual plant life there, but chiefly to investigate the purported authenticity of a "carnivorous" tree—a tree that devoured animals and men and lived thus on its strange diet. And he, Eric, was invited to go along as the representative of his institution.

"Are you going?" she queried.

"Am I!" he repeated indignantly and with eloquent inadequacy.

And then, to his wife's horror and to his own evident relish, Eric read to her from the letters of Liche, pioneer explorer of Madagascar, the only known eye witness' account of this monster tree:

"If you can imagine a pineapple eight feet high and thick in proportion, resting upon its base denuded of leaves, you will have a good idea of the trunk of this tree. Its color was a dark, dingy brown; it was apparently as hard as iron.

"From the apex of this trunk—at least two feet in diameter—eight gigantic leaves hung sheer to the ground, like trap-doors swung back on their hinges. These leaves were about 12 feet long; they were about two feet through at the thickest point, and three feet wide, tapering to a sharp point that looked like a cow's horn. The outer face was very convex, the inner slightly concave. This concave face was thickly set with long, thorny hooks.

"The apex of the cone was a round, white concave figure like a small plate set within a larger one. This was not a flower but a receptacle, and there exuded into it a clear treacly liquid which I discovered later to be honeysweet and possessed of violent intoxicating and soporific qualities.

Fruit of Their Tree

"From underneath the rim of the undermost plate a series of long, hairy, green tendrils stretched out in every direction. These were seven or eight feet long, and tapered from four inches in diameter, but they seemed as iron rods.

"Above these, from between the upper and under cups, six white transparent palpi reared themselves toward the sky, twirling and twisting with a marvelous incessant motion, yet constantly reaching upward. They made me shudder in spite of myself, with their suggestion of flayed serpents dancing upright on their tails."

PERFORCE, Gladys philosophically resigned herself to another six months of loneliness, though it was not the first time her husband had run off on trips that would increase his knowledge of botany and zoology and thus, incidentally, broaden his fame—a fame of which he rather egotistically vaunted.

Once, timorously, she said that as long as she wasn't to go on this extended trip, she—they—that is, he might at last consent...

"No!" he actually snarled. "Can't you ever forget that obsession of yours? I don't want a brat underfoot when I return! For the sake of our happiness, I advise you never to mention that subject again!" And, anguished, she determined not to.

The day of sailing came. A wildly enthusiastic Eric was off on another of his scientific crusades.

She had letters from him, from Liverpool, Cape Town in Africa, and Masikoro in Madagascar—short, pithy epistles that gave a sentence each in endearments for her, the rest regarding the trip, his hopes, his plans. Oh, she mused, Eric was first of all the naturalist!...After Masikoro a long silence—long and dreadful.

The Unnatural History of Man-Eating Plants

Almost a year later the party of exploring scientists returned, and her husband was not with it.

A van-dyked member came to her home the day of that arrival.

"My husband!" she cried, after his introduction. "Tell me! Where is he?"

"Your husband," he replied, and his voice was strangely curt and quasi-cruel, "did not come back with us."

"Tell me!" White stole to her face, slow-born terror to her eyes. In her lap her hands twisted convulsively. "Go on—please! please!"

HER husband, the scientist began—and his voice turned sympathetic—one day mysteriously disappeared from the camp in the jungle; an old Madagascarian guide was also discovered to be missing. Of Eric, despite utmost search, the party could find no trace. Neither did their explorations reveal any trace of the man-eating tree. Finally, bitterly disappointed, they returned to Masikoro, the seaport, to embark for home.

In that dirty, cosmopolite town, however, to their great surprise they ran across the old native guide, and he, after much bribery and begging, finally told them the account of his and Eric's disappearance from the party.

Thorhansen, while in camp, found that the old guide knew the whereabouts of a "sacred tree" of Madagascar, which, it was rumored, could devour a human or animal. Day after day Eric besought the fellow to guide him to it, offering him much gold and geegaws, and saying frankly that he wished to be the first American to see the famous tree—also, that he, in plain parlance, would like to steal a march on his confreres.

However, the Madagascarian was seemingly obdurate, declaring that knowledge of the tree voluntarily or otherwise given the white man was considered a crime against it, and as such punishable with the extreme penalty—death at its "hands."

But stubbornly, day after day, Eric continued to dangle gold before the greedy eyes of the old man; and at last he consented to the request.

In the dead of the tropical night they cautiously slipped away from the camp.

The afternoon of the second day, after winding over torturous trails, through lagoons and swamps, they came upon a specimen of the frightful tree of Madagascar.

There was even then (went on the informant) before the huge plant a group of worshiping natives. Eric and his guide cleverly bribed their way to the innermost circle. Their anger and greed allayed, the blacks—who are called Mkodos, and are very primitive, go naked, and possess no religion save that regarding the "sacred" tree—allowed the curious Eric to go to the foot of the tree-god and examine it; and a few minutes later he was also permitted to share in one of their periodical sacrificial rites—the offering of a propitiatory gift to the monster-plant. The "gift" was a tiny little girl child.

The blacks, in a frenzy of revolting idol worship, danced a mad measure around the trembling body of the little jungle maid, whining and shrieking the weird minor noises that keyed them to the horrible climax of the brutal rite.

Now and again the mob raised its glistening arms toward the gruesome tree with its snake-like branches, calling upon the seemingly waiting brute of the vegetable kingdom to accept its homage of tender human flesh.

ERIC, rapt, watched every preliminary detail of the awesome ceremony. And suddenly, so the old guide said, he begged the native leader to allow him to hoist the child into the leafy jaws of the plant.

The Unnatural History of Man-Eating Plants

Grinning diabolically, the wicked fellow acquiesced; and with the wailing sing-song chorus of the worshiping horde ringing in his ears, the white man deposited the terrified baby in the branches.

Glancing back at the prostrate and unseeing natives, an impulsive thought must have entered his brain; for, with his usual bold disregard for all consequences, he did an incomprehensible thing—he himself quickly crawled into the tree!

He did it, confident in the knowledge it was for a moment only. He wanted to get the "sensation." No other white man had been in like situation—why, he could portray it in a book! Those, evidently, were his selfish and ambitious thoughts.

But the seemingly harmless tree, with the weight of Eric and the child, came abruptly to ferocious life. The long sinuous palpi swooped ravenously, like a dozen cowboys' ropes, about the man's shoulders—tightening cruelly, suffocating him.

When, a few seconds later at a dreadful cry, the kneeling natives looked up, they saw Eric, white of face, trying with all his splendid young strength to extricate himself from the snake-like tentacles of the tree. Beside him was the child, mercifully in a dead faint.

With the victims secure in the folds of the rapacious palpi, the giant green leaves began simultaneously to rise, met together, after a few terrible seconds, and with the inexorable force of a machinist's vice closed over the struggling man and child, obliterating them from view.

As the frightened Madagascarians, chattering in consternation, arose and fled from the gruesome scene, down the trunk of the Gorgonian tree trickled the blood of humans.

Ten days later, according to the guide, he went back to the tree—a tree that gave up its fruit in due season!

Fruit of Their Tree

On the ground at its base lay the bare white bones of the man and child!

And the great leaves, with their appetites satisfied, had unfolded and reverted to their usual position, the palpi had unrolled themselves and once more stood twirling in ghastly fashion toward the sky—awaiting another victim!

Eric, rapt through every detail of the awesome ceremony of sacrifice, deposited the terrified baby into the leafy jaws of the plant...and, to the consternation of the wailing natives, started to crawl into the thing himself.

The Unnatural History of Man-Eating Plants

"IT—it was too horrible to write," concluded the man, "and so we just had to wait till our return to explain."

"Horrible? Horrible?" The wife of the dead Eric Thorhansen numbly caught up the word. "Horrible! Horrible!" she screamed, and then fell to the floor unconscious.

For days and nights awful nightmares rode her down: The man-eating tree of Madagascar had borne its fruit in due season—and that fruit was Eric! It—it was his own ironic punishment for not bearing *his* fruit of the tree of life!

When she came out of her delirium, weeks later, she found herself in a room in a hospital. A solicitous nurse hovered nearby; a physician was at her bed-side, and it was George Lamont, friend and companion of her school days. Even in her weakness, in her dull, comatose condition, she recognized him.

He pressed her lax hand, gently, sympathetically. "Gladys," he said softly, "I think I know and understand it all. Remember, I am here to help you—always will be here as long as you need me." And tenderly he smiled.

She felt her lips forming, actually, into a real smile. Bright hope, somehow, penetrated dark terror, and Life wooed her back.

That night she slept soundly, peacefully—a sleep fraught with a dream of a tree, but not the terrible one of Madagascar. Instead, she saw herself running eagerly toward an apple tree, radiant and beautiful with the blossoms of spring, with their promise of precious fall fruit; and clasped in her hand, as she ran, she felt another hand—warm, sympathetic and yearning.

She looked suddenly, in her dream, up into the face of the owner of the hand, and then laughed happily.

For it was George Lamont.

WHITE LADY

By Sophie Wenzel Ellis

(Strange Tales, 1933)

*In purest love André served his weirdly beautiful flower —
his White Lady of passion, of jealousy, of hate.*

BRYNHILD knew that something had waked her, something
pleasant and exhilarating, which was to be expected on
this strange island in the most remote corner of the warm
Caribbean sea, where André Fournier, her fiancé,
experimented fantastically with tropical plant life.

Presently she heard it again, music so wild and delicate
that she felt its rapturous vibrations in her nerves,
rather than heard them.

Below her, from the house to the placid sea in the
distance, spread an unnatural panorama, lighted by the
sun's gaudy hood just coming out of the water.

She looked, and was glad that she had accepted the
invitation of Madame Fournier, André's gracious mother, to
visit their lonely Ile-de-Fleur.

In a few minutes she was dressed and on the trail of the
puzzling music. When she closed the back door behind her,
she was immediately in a curious maze of floral wonders,
unreal as a painting by Doré. The jungles of the sun-
warmed lands had given to André their rarest treasures,
which now sucked a richer life from the black soil of the
Ile-de-Fleur. Nature, in her most whimsical mood, had not

633

been permitted to rule here; everywhere, among frond and spray and giant runner, bloomed hybrid blossoms whose weird forms and colors suggested André's tampering with Nature.

Brynhild heard the music clearer now, long notes that had an eery, half-human sound, like the tuneless music of a demented savage. It baffled her, teased her into wilder plunges through the flower thickets, all jeweled with liquid beads.

WHEN she mounted a hillock and saw, just beyond, a tiny cage built of copper screen, she knew that she had reached her goal. The music seemed to come from this little bower, which was puzzling, for the sole occupant was a blooming plant.

A golden gauze seemed to drop suddenly from the sky, which was the tropical sun's first rays shooting from the sea. The stronger light brought a gasp from Brynhild, for now she could see that even in this land of queer vegetation, the imprisoned plant was a monstrous alien.

From a mass of thick frondage, white and fleshy as her own bare arms, reared a flower whose round, pallid petals formed a face like the caricature of a woman. Draped around this eldritch flower-face and flowing down to meet the colorless foliage, was a mass of gauzy matter that had the startling appearance of a bridal veil.

But what brought a cry from Brynhild was not the human look of this fantastic plant, but what it was doing. Just below the head, almost as large as her own, protruded two slender, dagger-pointed white spines, set in sockets in such a manner that they could be moved like arms. These two spines, rubbing together, produced the music that had captivated her.

After the first frightful moment of comprehension, she longed to see the spectacle closer. She pressed her forehead against the copper screen.

White Lady

Instantly the spines ceased their serenade, the white flower-face turned and fronted her, and she felt eyes watching her, eyes she could not see. For a moment, flower and foliage remained rigid; then a spasm passed through the entire plant, the arms came together again, and hideous discord shrieked out.

Brynhild, sensing that her presence had caused the change from elfin music to the blood-freezing dissonance, dropped behind a concealing thicket and watched.

WHILE she waited, footsteps approached. André was coming. Like a tall young pagan priest he came forward, arms and shoulders naked, sunshine splashing his bronze curls. He had a beautiful, poetic face and a luminous smile that was now turned on the strange plant.

Instantly the flower music commenced again, louder and more seductive than ever, the queer blossom reeling on its stem as though animal excitement quivered through its pallid flesh.

André called out in his soft French:

"*Bon jour*, White Lady. Are you happy this morning, eh?"

The woman-face swayed toward him; the dagger arms caressed each other rapturously.

Brynhild crouched lower behind her hiding-place, each moment more astonished and horrified. André lifted the latch on the door and went inside.

The music sank to a low, plaintive throbbing, tender as a bird's love-song. André came closer to the flower and touched the white foliage with gentle fingers. Down drooped the flower head until the fleshy cheeks brushed his face.

"Ah, *ma petite!*" André whispered. "My own White Lady! If I could but bridge the gap!"

Brynhild could endure no more. "André!" she shrieked, leaping from her hiding-place.

"My own White Lady!"

Instantly the flower-head stiffened, and turned toward her with a gesture so human that the girl sickened. As André called out an impulsive greeting and came toward her, the unnatural foliage quivered violently and the daggers came together with a piercing din.

ANDRÉ laughed. "She's jealous, the White Lady!" His English had the barest accent. "Did you ever imagine such a flower, Brynhild? Should you have believed if someone had told you of this?"

White Lady

"It is a nightmare!" She covered her eyes with soft, beautifully formed hands.

"No, Brynhild. She is my dream materialized."

"Stop! I can't bear to hear you speak of it as though it were a woman." Her face had blanched until it was as pale as the flower before her.

In the cage, a terrific noise was going on, shocking in its metallic harshness.

André turned around and looked at the flower. "I'd better go to it for a moment, dear. Come! White Lady is like a dog: if you are good to her, she'll respond with love that is almost human."

Hesitant, as though she feared something evil, Brynhild entered the cage behind André. André caressed the leaves and put his face against the humanlike head. The daggers, rubbing together, gave forth a feline purr.

"Come, Brynhild," said André, with his lucent smile, "pet her."

Brynhild shrank back. How could she touch those leprous, fleshy leaves, that flower-face as unnatural as a vampire's? Trembling, she reached out her little hand to the bleached foliage.

Quick as a streak of lightning, the daggers struck at her, viciously, inflicting a long, bleeding scratch on her hand. The girl screamed and fell into André's arms.

"Darling!" groaned the young man, bending over her solicitously. "I never thought—"

Brynhild buried her golden curls against his shoulder.

"André!" she sobbed. "I can't endure it. That monster—it hates me." Her voice rose hysterically. "Why did you create it?"

"Hush!" He spoke sternly. "She never would have scratched you if she hadn't sensed that you are an enemy."

The Unnatural History of Man-Eating Plants

"You're mad!" She broke from his arms and raised her beautiful face angrily. "This vile monster has gone to your head. Now, as always, you prefer your unnatural flowers to me."

HER white skirt flashed through the open door and on out between the flowery tangle beyond. He followed her, calling a contrite apology. When he caught her and again held her fast in his arms, they were both breathless.

"*Pardonne-moi!*" he pleaded, his thin, spiritual face full of penitence. "But, Brynhild, I'd give half my life if you'd love plants as I do."

And with his hand pressing hers, he told her, in his peculiarly quiet voice, of the supreme joy that can be had from a sympathetic understanding of Nature's strange ways.

"Man has a connection with plant life," he said, "which all scientists will some day concede. Naturalists already agree that there is no real dividing line between the lowest forms of plant and animal life. And what is man but the highest animal?"

He had grown excited, as he always did when discussing plants. His sensitive face glowed with earnestness.

"Who can say," he continued, "how close is the kinship between animals and the carnivorous plants that devour meat? White Lady is not the only plant that has voluntary motion; nor is she the only one that senses instantly the presence of the destroyer." He looked at her intently. "Some of our commonest garden plants have eye-cells in the epidermis of leaves and stalks—eyes that have lenses and are sensitive to light. White Lady is the result of careful cross-breedings that have developed the most humanlike traits found throughout plant life. Oh, Brynhild!" He held her hand against his cheek. "If you could only understand, dear! You would not be shocked that my White Lady is more than an animal plant; that the exquisite, lovely thing has intelligence!"

White Lady

A LONG shiver ran through the girl's slender body.

"It is wrong to bring such a monstrosity into existence, André!"

"No!" His eyes filmed with tears. "My only sin is that I developed just one. Had I developed two, White Lady would not now be the loneliest living thing in existence." He flushed as he spoke.

Sudden horrible understanding gripped Brynhild, understanding so overwhelming that she swayed dizzily.

"That monster—it loves you, André! It loves you as a dog loves its master."

He stroked the gleaming gold of her hair, all alive under the sunlight.

"Don't go near it again, dear one," he soothed. "There might be real danger for you. Now there! Mother is calling us to breakfast. Be happy and smiling, won't you?" He tilted up her chin and kissed her gently.

At the breakfast table, Madame Fournier was very much disturbed; André took nothing except milk, into which he dissolved a pinkish pellet.

"No coffee this morning, son?" asked the mother, anxiously.

André flushed. "No, mother; just milk."

"Why, André!" protested Brynhild. "You scarcely eat enough to live. I watched you last night. You actually shivered over the lettuce mother made you eat. Don't you feel well?"

"Excellent. Remember that I drink quantities of milk."

After breakfast, Madame Fournier drew Brynhild aside.

"I'm uneasy," she said. "André's is becoming fanatical in his love for growing things. Think of it! He says he can hear his lettuce cry out when he cuts into it."

The Unnatural History of Man-Eating Plants

"A year ago," shivered Brynhild, "I'd have called that nerves; but now that I've seen that monstrous White Lady thing—" She put her hands over her eyes.

NO more that day did Brynhild go near White Lady. That night, while the island slept, she sat by her window and enjoyed the splendor of the moon-bathed panorama. Dimly, from the enchanted flowery reaches, came stealing the wild music of White Lady. With the first note, Brynhild stiffened, but, as the seductive sounds sent their sorcery through her, she listened with increasing delight, forgetful of her horror of the morning. Within a few moments, she was reaching for her dressing gown.

Following where White Lady's music pulled her, Brynhild stepped lightly through the thick leafage, exalted as though she were blown along by a jubilant wind.

André's strange world of flowers was like the inside of a giant pearl, for the Caribbean moon, riding full and low, had bleached the island to a luminous whiteness. From the pale hypnosis above and from the honeyed breaths that trembled over the flowers, she drew a new kinship with Nature. There was solemn joy in knowing that the same mysterious force called life which animated her own young body also sent the sap flowing through the plants about her.

Every growing thing on the island seemed to respond to the beauty of the night as happily as she. On all sides, flower-faces that seemed delirious with the joy of living lifted to the white radiance above.

The beauty of the world, then, did not exist for man's sole enjoyment.

Perhaps there was truth in André's contention that plants, with their partially developed consciousness, respond with more delicate delight than cultivated man to such elemental joys as the beauty of moonlight and the soft kisses of the night wind.

White Lady

She was sure of this when she saw White Lady. The mysterious woman-flower was moon-mad. The roof of the bower, built to shade partially, cut off the moon which was directly above, but White Lady had curved her stem so that her face reached the light.

THE music that throbbed from the rubbing arms was so rapturous that Brynhild felt her senses reel. She threw herself upon the grassy ground directly in front of the cage.

Instantly the music ceased, and the monstrous blossom withdrew to the shadows, where it stood tall and straight on its rigid stem, spectral in its veil and cadaverous foliage. Brynhild was prepared for the hideous discord that she had heard in the morning, but from the shadows came such low, enticing harmonies, sweet as the breathings of a wind harp, that she drew closer. The nearer she approached, the dimmer came the music, until the horrible thought came to her that White Lady was enticing her within the cage.

Pressing her hands over her ears, she fled, frightened with the paralyzing fear of the unknown.

The next morning, when she told André, he caught her in his arms and cried out:

"Keep away from her! As you value your life, keep away. She has intelligence, but no conscience—no pity for what she hates."

"But, André!" She searched his ascetic face closely. "Will you let such a thing live? Shan't you cut it down?"

"Cut down my White Lady, the supreme achievement of my life?" He looked as though he thought her insane.

"Not even though it hates me, André? Not even though it is trying to destroy me?"

641

"But I warned you to keep away. Wouldn't you—wouldn't any human being have a right to fight an enemy? You are her enemy, and she knows it."

The dispute ended with Brynhild in tears, but with André as firm as ever about not cutting down his unnatural creation.

BRYNHILD was jealous, jealous of a flower, and her jealousy increased with the passing of time. Whenever she heard the seductive song of White Lady, elemental hate surged in her heart. She wanted to destroy it, to tear apart those thick, white leaves, to crush that singular woman-face under her heel.

She was afraid to go too close to the screen cage, but sometimes she stole near enough for a good glimpse of the flower. Always she was delighted to see the rage of the horrible thing, and, at a safe distance, laughed at the shrieking dissonance that the flower's striking daggers made. At times, when she approached the cage, White Lady merely stiffened, and then Brynhild knew that it watched her as a cat watches a mouse. André had told her that the invisible eyes in the leaves and stem were very highly developed.

It gave Brynhild unholy delight to know that her very presence was torment to this human flower that seemed to adore André. As though the thing could understand, she would stand at a safe distance and tell how André loved her, and of the wedding which was only three weeks distant. Once, after a scene like this, White Lady lunged at her so viciously with her daggers that Brynhild was barely able to escape.

And the girl knew that, sooner or later, one would succumb to the other.

"It shall be that *bête blanche*," vowed Brynhild, quoting the name that Madame Fournier had given the plant.

White Lady

AS the days passed, André grew thinner, whiter, more spiritual. He was absolutely unlike the brown young athlete with whom Brynhild had fallen in love, two years ago, in Bermuda.

"It's the way he eats," moaned his mother. "How can a strong man who works live on little else than milk? What are we to do, Brynhild? He is killing himself. Sometimes I even wonder if his mind is not going." She began to cry softly. "Did you notice him in the rain yesterday?"

"No. Tell me."

"He walked around as in a dream, with his white face held up toward the dripping sky. When I went to him and asked him to come in, he refused. He told me to leave him alone, because he had found the mood in which he could react to the cool rain just as a plant. He's doing something mysterious to make himself as much as possible like things that grow in the ground."

"It's that White Lady!" said Brynhild bitterly. "Constant brooding over a monster like that will unhinge anyone's mind. The horrible freak is getting on my nerves, too. I do silly things." She blushed, thinking of her own scenes with the strange plant.

"We'll have to watch him, Brynhild."

Brynhild did watch, and thereby brought greater suffering to herself, for her surveillance revealed that he not only spent much of the day with White Lady, but that he often went to the plant at night.

Much of his passion for herself had died. His love seemed to have ascended to a spiritual plane which was ethereal in its purity and tenderness. He spoke no more of their approaching marriage, seemed almost to have forgotten it.

When the two were alone, he frequently turned the conversation to morbid subjects.

"Death is beautiful in a land of flowers like this," he told her. "Isn't it a happy thought, Brynhild, to know that when you are put into the warm, sweet earth, your body resolves into its chemical elements and again reaches up to the light in leaf and stalk and fragrant bloom?"

ONE night, when the forgotten wedding was only a week off, André fainted. After he had responded to the frantic ministrations of his mother and Brynhild, he turned his great, dark eyes pleadingly to them and gasped:

"I want you both to make me a promise."

"What, son?" asked the mother.

"That when I'm dead, you'll bury me, not too deep, under my White Lady." His tired lids fluttered down. "Oh, mother! To think of the roots of that sweet creature reaching down, down for me and resurrecting my atoms to a newer and sweeter life."

"André, darling! Don't! You're breaking our hearts!"

"But will you promise?"

"Yes! Oh, God—help me!"

With André restored and quiet in his room, Brynhild and Madame Fournier sought a secluded corner for their frantic grief.

"It can't go on another day, daughter," said the mother. "André will die before the wedding. We must destroy that *bête blanche*."

"But, mother, wouldn't that grieve him too much at this time?"

"Rather a few days' grief than a grave under that monster." Madame Fournier shuddered.

"Where is the ax, mother?" Brynhild's face was as pale as her dress.

"I'll do it, my dear. I'm an old woman and his mother. Perhaps it might be something like murder to kill that human thing, but I have a mother's right."

"No!" Brynhild's voice was almost fierce. "I want to do it. White Lady hates me, and I hate her. Where is the ax?"

"Wait a little. It is early. One of the Negroes might see you."

AND Brynhild waited until the night grew older and blacker, when she crept from the house with an ax and a flash-light. There was no moon to-night to guide her through the flowery mazes. A strong wind, coming from the sea, followed behind her like an animal sniffing her footprints. It pulled her skirts and her long, flowing sleeves and whipped her hair across her face.

She had the furtive feeling of one who plans a deed of blood and violence. In her mind she outlined what she must do. She would place the flash-light so that its light could fall upon White Lady. Then she would quickly unlatch the door and chop.

Never had White Lady been so beautiful. In the glow of the flashlight, she stood straight and silent in her waxy foliage, with the gossamer veil whipping around her airily and her dagger arms folded like a demure bride waiting for her bridegroom. Brynhild never knew what to expect from this unnatural creature, and its silence frightened her more than the wildest noise it had ever produced.

Before lifting the latch, Brynhild stood regarding it, horrified, trembling, pitying. White Lady was watching, too, and waiting.

The moment Brynhild opened the door and went inside, a scream like the piercing voice of a woman tore through the night. Again and again the awful shriek wailed from the scraping dagger arms, and Brynhild knew that it rode on the wind to the ears of listeners in the house beyond.

The Unnatural History of Man-Eating Plants

Her nerveless hands almost dropped the ax. How could she wield her weapon against that fleshy, human face—against a thing that could cry out like a woman?

But André's burning eyes haunted her. She must, for his sake.

GRASPING and raising the ax, she went forward, with the wind pushing at her body and snatching her hair over her eyes. The ax fell, with poor aim. It merely crashed through part of the foliage, which cracked with a sickening snap as of crushed bones.

One more dreadful shriek rent the night, a shriek of murder and of rapine; but before its shrill echoes died, another and less hideous woman-voice gave an agony cry.

It was Brynhild.

The wind, tampering with her clothes, had blown her long, loose sleeve against White Lady, where it caught or was grasped by one of the dagger arms. The other dagger arm lifted and plunged, lifted and plunged.

The girl was wild with pain and fright. Held fast as she was, she could scarcely use the ax to an advantage, especially as she was forced to avoid the stabbing dagger.

The white veil fell from the thing's head. Before Brynhild could again wield the ax, another dagger thrust found her body. Through the flesh of her left shoulder it cut this time, and she crumpled, half fainting.

Even as she fell, she heard running feet. André's voice called out:

"Brynhild!"

Instantly White Lady paused in her stabbing and sent forth another shriek of triumph. Then again the dagger plunged, and Brynhild felt the warm blood flow from her arm.

White Lady

She never completely lost consciousness, and dimly she was aware of chopping blows made by another, and of her left arm coming away from its horrible mooring. She felt herself lifted and carried for several yards. She felt André's rough, unshaved cheek against her own, and heard soft love words fall from the lips that bent to hers.

André laid her down carefully and shouted for help. Poor fellow! There had been a time when he could have carried her all around the island.

With a supreme effort, Brynhild opened her eyes. The flashlight was still where she had placed it, so that its round eye fell upon White Lady, or what was left of her. Now the plant was only a mass of crushed leaves and petals.

"Yes, I did it," came André's stern voice. "The *bête blanche* would have killed you, darling!" He kissed her hungrily. "I've been a beast, myself—and a fool. Forgive me!"

And later after Brynhild's gaping wounds were dressed, she heard André say four simple words that filled her with delight.

"I am hungry, mother."

Excerpt from "Lost in Africa, Chapter IX: The Vegetable Octopus" by C. L. Stoyle, 1897

Prayers and sacrifices were offered up as peace offerings for a safe and speedy passage through the dreaded Valley of Death, or Desolation, as it is called, that we were about to enter; for there the Vegetable God, or Octopus, reigns supreme, which is more dreaded by the natives than the fiercest wild animals, because of its mysterious and deadly powers. At my very urgent request I was taken to see one, and never wish to repeat my experience.

About a dozen of us ascended a grassy slope, and there, in the centre of a hollow we saw, at first, nothing more formidable than a smooth green stump of a tree. It stood alone in a bare, dank-looking spot. From its lower stem dark brown fibrous roots held it firmly to the ground, also supplying it with the requisite amount of moisture. It then appeared harmless and inoffensive enough, though the bleached remains of birds, animals and even human beings that lay scattered around its base bore ample testimony to satisfy the most skeptical of its evil and ghastly power. I had often heard of it with doubts of its existence when in Ettuawa's country, rather fancying it purely imaginary on the natives' part; though I had heard that many tribes drive cattle, and often their fellow creatures, into the valley, as sacrifices in cases of plague or sickness, as they believe that when this strange vegetable is hungry it has the power of sending forth its deadly vapours and so destroying them.

As we stood watching the gruesome thing, we noticed it visibly swell until its outer edges gradually uncurled, opening like a huge sea anemone does at the incoming tide, until it represented a monster fern with waving, palm-like fronds, tipped with pale green, more resembling in color the foam of the sea when in mid ocean than anything else, causing by their movement a violent wind to spring up in their immediate vicinity—where till then a dead calm had prevailed—increasing in proportion to the velocity of the fronds until they seemed in a violent rage, beating the air as it whirled around with a hissing sound of fury; then suddenly, out from its very centre, shot a mighty tongue, dividing into countless whip-like thongs, twirling and whirling madly in every direction.

I felt thrilled with a fascinated excitement and utterly powerless to move, and should undoubtedly have been its next victim had not somebody pulled me from behind, bringing me forcibly in contact with mother earth.

Also by Kevin J. Guhl:

Thunderbirds, Lost Temples and
Skeleton Ghosts
An Anthology of
American Strangeness,
Vol. 1

Wild West Dragons, Flaming
Space Fossils and Phantom
Automobiles
An Anthology of
American Strangeness,
Vol. 2

www.ingramcontent.com/pod-product-compliance
Lightning Source LLC
Chambersburg PA
CBHW050447270326
41927CB00009B/1638